THE EVOLUTION OF THE TROUBLES 1970–72

Thomas Hennessey
Canterbury Christ Church University

IRISH ACADEMIC PRESS
DUBLIN • PORTLAND, OR

First published in 2007 by Irish Academic Press
44, Northumberland Road,   920 NE 58th Avenue Suite 300
Ballsbridge,   Portland, Oregon,
Dublin 4, Ireland   97213-3786

www.iap.ie

copyright © 2007 by Thomas Hennessey

British Library Cataloguing in Publication Data
An entry can be found on request

ISBN 978 0 7165 2884 5 (cloth)
ISBN 978 0 7165 2885 2 (paper)

Library of Congress Cataloging-in-Publication Data
An entry can be found on request

All rights reserved. Without limiting the rights under copyright reserved alone,
no part of this publication may be reproduced, stored in or introduced into
a retrieval system, or transmitted, in any form or by any means (electronic, mechanical,
photocopying, recording or otherwise), without the prior written permission of both the
copyright owner and the above publisher of this book.

Typeset in 10.5/12pt Times NR by FiSH Books, Enfield, Middx.
Printed by Biddles Ltd., King's Lynn, Norfolk

Contents

Acknowledgements iv

Chronology and Background v

Introduction x

Bomb

1 End of the Honeymoon — 6
2 The Phoney War Ends – the IRA Campaign Intensifies: August 1970–March 1971 — 52
3 The Road to Internment: March–August 1971 — 85
4 Internment without Trial — 120
5 The Real War: Intelligence, Interrogation and Propaganda — 152
6 British Disillusionment and Reassessment: August 1971–January 1972 — 169
7 The War on the Ground: August 1971–January 1972 — 206
8 The Road to Bloody Sunday: Derry, July 1971–January 1972 — 229
9 Operation FORECAST – Bloody Sunday, 30 January 1972 — 274
10 Judgement Day – The End of Stormont — 312

Conclusion — 342

Bibliography — 350

Index — 363

Acknowledgements

In writing this book I have a number of people I would like to thank: in particular the staff of The National Archives of the United Kingdom, the National Archives of Ireland, the Public Record Office of Northern Ireland, the Belfast Central Library; and the Political Collection of the Linen Hall Library, Belfast. Thanks too to the readers who commented on the manuscript and proposal, and to Professor Geoffrey Warner, whose comments were always honest and wise. I would like to thank Lisa Hyde at Irish Academic Press for her faith, patience and counsel. Finally, I would single out Linda Herviel, Elizabeth Cantello, Janet Allen and Brenda Didmon for their invaluable help in typing up material for me – thank you for everything.

This book is dedicated to the memory of the woman who used to threaten me with a green plastic hurley when I was a naughty child – my grandmother. She never believed they ever landed on the Moon ('they look like those Muppets from the telly') because beyond the clouds were 'where God lives'. To the end she was a loyal 'Dev' supporter. The book is also dedicated to her daughter Mary.

Catherine Coffey
(12 October 1904–9 October 2006)

Mary Lackey *nee* Coffey
(19 May 1930–10 October 2006)

Chronology and Background

1920	Government of Ireland Act partitions Ireland Asserts Westminster's Sovereignty over Ireland
1922	Irish Free State secedes from the United Kingdom Northern Ireland remains within the United Kingdom
Northern Ireland	c.2/3 Protestant (Unionist) c.1/3 Roman Catholic (Nationalist)
Politics	Unionists – Union with Great Britain Nationalists – United Ireland
System of Government	Devolved Northern Ireland Parliament (Stormont from 1932) Northern Ireland Government
Governing Party	Ulster Unionist Party 1921–72
State Security	Royal Ulster Constabulary (RUC) Ulster Special Constabulary (B Specials) Civil Authority (Special Powers) Acts
Threats to State	Irish Republican Army (IRA)

Birth of Northern Ireland: Communal Violence 1920–22

July 1920–July 1922	557 killed: 303 Catholics 172 Protestants 82 Police & British Army
December 1921– May 1922	8,700–11,000 Catholics driven from jobs 23,000 Catholics fled homes 500 Catholic businesses destroyed
The IRA Border **Campaign 1956–1962**	8 IRA men and 6 RUC constables killed
Catholic Claims **of Discrimination**	Special Powers Acts – Emergency Powers including Internment Job/Housing Discrimination in Local Government Gerrymandered Boundaries: Londonderry Corporation Majority of Population – Catholic Majority of Councillors – Unionist
Protestant Fears	Catholics Disloyal Refuse to Recognise Legitimacy of Northern Ireland Nationalists Seek Destruction of State Power of Roman Catholic Church in Republic of Ireland Republic Seeks to Absorb Northern Ireland & Claims Sovereignty Over
1963	Captain Terence O'Neill becomes the Prime Minister of the Northern Ireland Government.

1965	Sean Lemass, Taoiseach (Irish Prime Minister), travels to Belfast to meet O'Neill.
1966	Rioting brakes out in Belfast as Loyalists held counter demonstrations to oppose commemorations of the Easter Rising in 1916. Reverend Ian Paisley helps establishes the Ulster Protestant Volunteers (UPV). Ulster Volunteer Force (UVF) re-formed
27 May	UVF shoot and mortally wound John Scullion (28), a Catholic civilian, in the Clonard area of west Belfast. Scullion died from his injuries on 11 June.
26 June	UVF shoot three Catholic civilians in Malvern Street in the Shankill area of Belfast. Peter Ward (18), dies at the scene.
28 June	UVF declared illegal. Jack Lynch succeeds Sean Lemass as Taoiseach.
1967 **29 January**	Northern Ireland Civil Rights Association (NICRA) formed. Call for reforms to end discrimination against Catholics: only rate-payers were entitled to votes in local government elections; additional votes for companies should be abolished; The association also pressed for the end to gerrymandering of electoral boundaries and an end to discrimination in the allocation of public sector housing and appointments Also: repeal of the Special Powers Acts; disbandment of the 'B-Specials'.
1968 **20 June**	Austin Currie, Nationalist MP, illegally occupies a house in Caledon, County Tyrone. House allocated by Dungannon Rural District Council (Unionist) to 19 year-old unmarried Protestant woman, Emily Beatty, who was the secretary of a local Unionist politician. Emily Beatty given the house ahead of older married Catholic families with children.
24 August	First Civil Rights march from Coalisland to Dungannon.
3 October	Proposed Civil Rights march in Derry banned by William Craig, NI Home Affairs Minister.
5 October	RUC break-up banned Civil Rights march by baton-charging crowd. Two days of rioting between Derry Catholic and the RUC result. This marks the start of the 'Troubles'.
4 November	O'Neill, William Craig and Brian Faulkner, Minister of Commerce, meet in Downing Street, London, with Harold Wilson, UK Prime Minister and James Callaghan, UK Home Secretary
22 November	Terence O'Neill, under pressure from Wilson and Callaghan, introduces reform package: • a nine member 'Development Commission' to take over the powers of the Londonderry Corporation; • an ombudsman to investigate complaints against government departments; • the allocation of houses by local authorities to be based on need; • the Special Powers Act to be abolished as soon as it was safe to do so; and • some reform of the local government franchise (the end of the company votes).

CHRONOLOGY AND BACKGROUND

11 December	Terence O'Neill, sacks William Craig
20 December	Peoples' Democracy (PD), a radical student group from Queen's university, Belfast, announce a protest march from Belfast to Derry.

1969

4 January	PD march ambushed and attacked by a loyalist mob at Burntollet Bridge. March attacked in Irish Street, Derry a mainly Protestant area of the city. RUC entry into the Catholic Bogside leads to serious rioting.
15 January	O'Neill, announces the setting up of an official inquiry into the disturbances in Derry and elsewhere.
24 January	Brian Faulkner, Deputy Prime Minister and Minister of Commerce, resigns from the Northern Ireland cabinet in protest at the lack of 'strong government'.
26 January	William Morgan, Minister of Health and Social Services, resigns from the Northern Ireland government.
3 February	O'Neill, announces dissolution of Stormont parliament
24 February	Of 39 unionist candidates returned in NI election 27 were in support of the policies of O'Neill, while 12 were against or undecided. Ian Paisley comes within 2,000 votes of unseating O'Neill.
25 March	Paisley and Major Ronald Bunting jailed for organising illegal demonstration in Armagh
30 March	UVF explosions at electricity substation Castlereagh, east Belfast to discredit O'Neill. Blamed on IRA. Members of Paisley's Ulster Protestant Volunteers involved.
4 April	UVF/UPV bomb explodes at a water installation at Dunadry, County Antrim.
19 April	Rioting in the Bogside following clashes between NICRA marchers, Protestants and the RUC. Samuel Devenny, beaten, in his home, with batons by the RUC; this causes internal injuries and induces a heart attack. Devenny dies on 17 July as a result of his injuries.
20 April	UVF explosion at Silent Valley reservoir in County Down cuts off water supplies to Belfast. Second explosion at an electricity pylon at Kilmore, County Armagh.
23 April	Unionist Parliamentary Party votes by 28 to 22 to introduce universal adult suffrage in local government elections in Northern Ireland. James Chichester-Clark, Minister of Agriculture, resigns in protest at the timing of the reform.
24 April	UVF explosion a water pipeline between Lough Neagh and Belfast.
26 April	UVF bomb explosion at water pipeline carrying supplies to Belfast.
28 April	O'Neill resigns as Prime Minister of Northern Ireland.
1 May	Major James Chichester-Clark is next Prime Minister. Brian Faulkner appointed Minister of Development. Chichester-Clark announces reforms will continue.
24 June	Parliamentary Commissioner Act (NI) becomes law. The Act provides for a Commissioner to investigate complaints of maladministration against government departments.

12 July	Rioting in Derry, Belfast and Dungiven.
14 July	Francis McCloskey (aged 67), a Catholic, dies one day after being hit on the head with a baton by an officer of the RUC during street disturbances in Dungiven, County Derry.
15 July	Chichester-Clark mobilises the 'B-Specials'.
8 August	Chichester-Clark meets with James Callaghan in London. Annual Apprentice Boys of Derry march allowed to proceed.
12 August	**The Battle of the Bogside** Apprentice Boys parade passes close to the Bogside in Derry. Serious rioting erupts. RUC use armoured cars and water cannons, to enter Bogside. Catholics repel RUC. Police use CS Gas to re-enter Bogside. Rioting continues for two more days.
13 August	Serious rioting spreads across Northern Ireland. Protestants and Catholics confront each other in Belfast. RUC overstretched. Taoiseach Jack Lynch announces that 'field hospitals' would be set up in border areas. Irish troops moved to the Border. Many Protestants & Catholics expect an invasion of the North.
14 August	British troops deployed in Derry.
15 August	Troops deployed in Belfast.
19 August	UK–NI Government meeting declares: 'The Border is not an issue' and: NI Consent needed for Constitutional change NI affairs a UK domestic issue Troops withdrawn when Law & Order restored Reforms to Continue Equality for all citizens General Officer Commanding NI to be Director of Security
26 August	2 Senior UK Civil Servants as Liaison Officers in NI. Oliver Wright: UK Govt Representative (UKREP) in NI
26 August	Hunt Committee appointed to consider the structure of the RUC and the 'B-Specials'.
10 September	A 'peace line' completed by the British Army in areas of Belfast. 'No-go' areas for the Security Forces, in Derry and Belfast, are recognised.
9 October	James Callaghan, visits Northern Ireland. Callaghan and the Stormont Government issue Joint Communique: central housing authority to established; reforms of the RUC in the Hunt Report accepted; reforms to the legal system accepted; issue of fair employment discussed.
10 October	Hunt Report: RUC should become an unarmed force; Ulster Special Constabulary should be disbanded; new RUC Reserve should be set up; new locally recruited part-time force should be established under the control of the British Army – becomes the Ulster Defence Regiment (UDR). Sir Arthur Young, an Englishman, appointed Inspector-General of RUC
11 October	Victor Arbuckle (aged 29), RUC, shot dead by Protestants during street disturbances on the Shankill Road in Belfast.
11 November	Ministry for Community Relations established

CHRONOLOGY AND BACKGROUND

25 November	Electoral Law Act (Northern Ireland) makes the franchise in local government elections in Northern Ireland the same as that in Britain.
27 November	Commissioner for Complaints appointed to deal with matters related to local government and public bodies.
18 December	Act to establish Ulster Defence Regiment passed.
28 December	The Irish Republican Army (IRA) splits. The breakaway group became known as the Provisional IRA and the remaining group became known as the Official IRA.
1970	
Official IRA	Cathal Goulding Chief of Staff 1969–72
Provisional IRA	Sean Mac Stiofain (John Stephenson) Chief of Staff 1970–72
	Joe Cahill Belfast O/C PIRA
	Ruairi O Bradaigh (Rory O'Brady) President of Provisional Sinn Fein 1970–83
	Daithi O Conaill (David O'Connell)
PIRA Strength	Mid-1970 c.1500
	800 in Northern Ireland
	600 Belfast
	100 Derry
	100 Other
26 March	Police Act (NI): NI Govt accepts principle of unarmed Police. Police Authority established: representative of community. RUC Reserve established.
1 April	Ulster Defence Regiment replaces B-Specials. To assist Regular Army & guard key installations/patrols/check points/road blocks. Not to be used for crowd/riot situations
3 April	Ballymurphy Riots: 1st major clash of Catholics & Army. Protestants Expelled from New Barnsley estate. 500 Troops flown into NI (6500 in total)

The Irish Government & Northern Ireland

15 August 1969:	Irish Cabinet Meeting. Charles J Haughey, Minister of Finance, to fund Relief Committee for Refuges.
	Secret Govt Plan Doomsday Plan: incursions into North in event of pogrom against Catholics
Arms Crisis 1970	Captain John Kelly (Military Intelligence) establishes contact with Defence Committees (IRA dominated) in Catholic area. Arms to be imported; money through Relief Committee Haughey & Neil Blaney, fellow Cabinet Minister implicated; acquitted in court

Introduction

The late John Whyte wrote: 'It is quite possible that, in proportion to its size, Northern Ireland is the most heavily researched area on earth.[1] Since that was written, in 1989–90, even more research has been conducted on Northern Ireland and the Troubles. So why another book? The answer is that it is now possible to change the nature of that research. When I was in my teens, long before I had any dreams of becoming a historian, I remember reading about the 1971 tripartite meeting between the Prime Ministers of the United Kingdom, Ireland and Northern Ireland. I remember seeing, for the first time, the often reproduced photograph of Edward Heath, Jack Lynch and Brian Faulkner at Chequers. And I remember, with some awe, wondering what was said there among those three men who were trying to map out the destiny of a divided Ireland. Now I know. The Government archives, in London, Dublin and Belfast are being opened for historians to delve into Ireland's recent, and troubled, past. Of course, when one undertakes such a survey, immediately one has to think about how the ghosts of the past haunt any attempt at historical and academic assessment of that past. Such has been the individual and communal suffering experienced in Northern Ireland that suggesting how an event, or events, are remembered is not, perhaps, what actually may have happened, is itself to challenge long-held myths. And Ireland is an island of myths, some new ones being created in the early 1970s – the formative years of the northern Troubles. And, often, when one reads a book or article on Northern Ireland, by an academic, there appears to be a fear of offending couched in impartiality or understanding. But decisions were taken, by participants, both rational and irrational, that had tremendous consequences for a generation of men, women and children. Now it is possible to establish a better understanding of how and why those decisions were made.

There have, of course, been many pioneering academic works, from Paul Bew and Henry Patterson,[2] and from Michael Cunningham.[3] But all these works have had to rely on public, rather than archival, sources. Other works have been journalistic in origin: Henry Kelly[4] and Peter Taylor;[5] in particular, Taylor's later work is an outstanding demonstration of the power of oral history and an ability to win the trust of many of the participants in the conflict. It has proved difficult for others to live up to this. The problem with many of the accounts that have not had the access to archival sources is that they often speak with an authority on the subject only to be plain wrong: Tim Pat Coogan is a case in point. He refers to the Cabinet Committee on Northern Ireland, set up by the Tories, as GEN 42: it was, in fact, GEN 47. Coogan claims, with confidence, that Brian Faulkner, in his first meeting with Edward Heath, as Prime Minister of Northern

Ireland, pressed for internment: the record shows he did not. By 25 May 1971 it is claimed that Faulkner felt confident to signal a new hard-line policy on the part of the Army, stating that anyone seen by a soldier, carrying a weapon or acting suspiciously might fire to warn or with effect without waiting for orders. 'It was the implementation of this policy which caused the shooting of Cusack and Beattie and the consequent withdrawal of the SDLP from Stormont.'[6] Faulkner was in no position to dictate to the British military or Government. Westminster and the Ministry of Defence decided security policy. Most other accounts that mention the first years of the Troubles follow the traditional interpretation as put forward by political scientists such as Brendan O'Leary and John McGarry. While impressive on the deeper, underlying causes of the conflict, they argue that the Tory Government of Edward Heath 'opted to support centrists in the UUP [Ulster Unionist Party] by attempting to balance reforms with repression in Catholic urban areas'. Internment, in 1971, proved to be a military disaster.[7] But did it?

More recently, what one might call the Queen's school of historians and political scientists have led the way in ploughing through the archival material. Graham Walker has produced an archival-based history of the Ulster Unionist Party;[8] Alvin Jackson's most recent work considers the hundred-plus years that home rule has been a factor in Irish politics;[9] and Richard English has produced an archival-based history of the Provisional IRA[10] that compliments Patterson's earlier work in this field. Jackson acknowledges Northern Ireland's last but one Prime Minister, James Chichester-Clark, as 'honourable and decent' and is sympathetic to the position Brian Faulkner inherited in 1971. Faulkner's premiership 'provides some evidence of both a high-voltage political imagination and a willingness to tackle the central structural weaknesses of the devolution settlement'. But the reforms offered by Faulkner were in fact initiated, in a civil service review, under Chichester-Clark. Jackson credits Faulkner with the 'revelation' in recognizing that 'the British democratic system was a profoundly inadequate model for a society with the cultural and political divisions of Northern Ireland, and it looked forward to cross-community participation in the Stormont executive' in the Green Paper of October 1971. Yet as the internal discussions between Heath and Faulkner reveal, at no stage was the Prime Minister of Northern Ireland prepared to let 'Republicans' – by which he meant the Social Democratic and Labour Party – into Government; only Catholics who accepted the constitutional status of Northern Ireland within the United Kingdom and did not seek unification (such as G.B. Newe, appointed by Faulkner to the Cabinet in 1971 and the only Catholic ever to hold executive office at Stormont under majority rule) were acceptable.[11]

English points out that the Northern Irish conflict was about the failure of two national and state traditions to deal adequately with their respective minorities: the UK had not satisfactorily accommodated or absorbed Catholics in the north of Ireland; and the Irish Nationalist tradition and its southern Irish state had never made significant progress in attracting or appealing to northern Protestant opinion. His 'key point to recognize is this: that both the Provisional IRA and the northern troubles arose out of an interwoven, complex sequence of events, none of which is singly responsible for what followed'. Each of these actions made internal sense to their practitioners; each contributed to the emergent war; 'and between them led to the birth of the Provisional IRA'.[12] English focuses upon 'a *definite* IRA politics: defence, defiance, retaliation and anti-imperialism were interwoven in their thinking'.[13] The reaction of day-to-day events as they unfolded – loyalist attacks, friction with the British Army, the experience of a hostile Northern state, all injected life and energy into Provisional republicanism. 'What happened at the end of the 1960s and the beginning of the 1970s was that urgent contemporary circumstances in the north seemed to validate certain traditional republican assumptions.'[14] English adds that state repression – and the role of the British Army – was important or even decisive (as might be sectarian hostility to Protestants).[15]

Both these studies, alongside that of Walker, cover a considerable period of time. This is where this study differs: to date only Geoffrey Warner has looked at one of the controversial events in these years in considerable depth – in an outstanding reappraisal of the Falls Road Curfew.[16] What this book studies is but two years – the crucial years of 1970–72 and, as such, follows on from an earlier volume looking at the 1960s.[17] In doing so the book attempts to shed new light on this period and challenges many of the myths that have grown up concerning the evolution of the Troubles from a communal conflict to an insurgency against the state.

Notes

1. John Whyte, *Interpreting Northern Ireland* (Oxford: 1990), p.xviii.
2. Paul Bew and Henry Patterson, *The British State and the Ulster Crisis. From Wilson to Thatcher* (London: 1985).
3. Michael J. Cunningham, *British Government Policy in Northern Ireland 1969–89: Its Nature and Execution* (Manchester: 1991).
4. Henry Kelly, *How Stormont Fell* (Dublin: 1972).
5. Peter Taylor, *Provos. The IRA and Sinn Féin* (London: 1997)); *Loyalists* (London: 1999); *Brits. The War Against the IRA* (London: 2001).
6. Tim Pat Coogan, *The Troubles. Ireland's Ordeal 1966–1995 and the Search for Peace* (London: Hutchinson, 1995), pp.122–3.
7. Brendan O'Leary and John McGarry, *The Politics of Antagonism. Understanding Northern Ireland* (London: Athlone, 1992), p.176.
8. Graham Walker, *A History of the Ulster Unionist Party: Protest, Pragmatism and Pessimism* (Manchester: Manchester University Press, 2004).
9. Alvin Jackson, *Home Rule. An Irish History* (London: 2003).
10. Richard English, *Armed Struggle. A History of the IRA* (Basingstoke: 2003).
11. Jackson, *Home Rule*, pp.250–1.
12. English, *Armed Struggle*, pp.146–7.
13. Ibid., p.133.
14. Ibid., p.128.
15. Ibid., p.123.
16. Geoffrey Warner, 'The Falls Road Curfew Revisitied', Irish Studies Review, 14, 3, pp.325–42.
17. Thomas Hennessey, *The Origins of the Troubles* (Dublin: 2005).

Bomb

On Saturday 4 March 1972, Belfast was thronged with shoppers. Among them were Rosaleen McNern and her sister Jennifer. Rosaleen, 22, was a secretary. Jennifer, 21, was a school meals supervisor. Rosaleen was to be married on 5 August to Brendan Murrin, a young man from Donegal who was working with an insurance firm in London. The sisters were in town to shop for clothes for her wedding. On the way to a boutique they passed the Abercorn Restaurant, a favourite for shoppers. Rosaleen decided to have a cup of coffee and the sisters went inside. They joined a queue for a table, found one and sat down. The last thing they both remembered was Jennifer asking for the bill as an explosion ripped through the Abercorn. Sitting near the girls was Jimmy Stewart, aged 36. After lunch, near his home in the Shankill, he had gone to the city centre to pick up a tape recorder that he had left in for repair and to buy sweaters for going on holiday to Scotland. Jimmy was a deeply committed evangelical Christian and a Sunday school teacher. Shortly before 4.30 p.m. he picked up his bill from the table in the Abercorn, collected his parcels from the floor and moved towards the cash desk at the front. He never reached it. He glimpsed the explosion – a bright green glow from the inside of his eye as the bomb went off. The bomb went off at 4.29 p.m. One minute earlier a man had telephoned a warning to the Post Office exchange. He said that a bomb would go off in Castle Lane in five minutes. No exact location was given.[1] A witness had seen two young girls walk from the restaurant, leaving a bag, shortly before the explosion. She remarked to a companion that the girls must have forgotten their bag and would be back for it. The phone call warning of the bomb was traced to a Falls Road pub.[2]

The bomb had been left under a table near the back of the restaurant, on the left-hand side. It was electrically detonated with the help of a small clock. At a pre-selected time the alarm rang, the winder-key rotated and completed an electrical contact through a battery to a detonator in the charge. A detonation wave travelled through the explosive and disrupted the molecules. These recombined to form other products, usually gaseous. This in turn had two main effects. There was a rapid shock wave travelling at some 13,000 miles per hour. This pulverised the floor and caused the ground to shudder. But the shock wave slowed down quickly. It did not do the greatest damage though skin and bone close to the bomb could be severely affected. The major damage was caused by a blast wave which followed at some 600 miles per hour. It had the pressure of the pent-up gases behind it and the blast wave had a tearing, heaving, wrecking motion. It was the blast wave that ripped off arms and legs and tore away the soft tissue of the body. Associated with the blast wave was a fireball which lasted only for micro-seconds. It was a blinding white or yellow flash which caused heat damage. The fireball singed hair, eyelashes and eyebrows. The combination of shock wave, blast and fireball was devastating in the confined space of the restaurant. In the Abercorn there was heavy blasting along part of the left-hand wall. The blast wave bounced back to reinforce the original explosion. Tables on the left-hand side were wrenched from the floor, chairs were hurled in all directions and the roof collapsed. Personal belongings were scattered across the restaurant. Shopping bags, toys, shoes, scraps of paper and beads lay grotesquely beside cups, plates and scraps of food. One policeman noticed scraps of flesh plastered to a wall. The explosion had hurled Jimmy Stewart to the floor. He was lying on his back. He felt shock waves go through him. His body was tingling. Then he heard a voice say: 'Everyone keep steady. We are in a bomb blast.' He tried to get up but his legs would not function. He felt helpless. He lay where he was. Then the pain started. Two ambulance-men clawed through the dust towards him. 'Get this man away,' said one of them. 'He's badly hurt.' They placed Jimmy Stewart on a stretcher and kept asking his name.

Earlier, and elsewhere in the city, Dr Bereen, who worked at the Royal Victoria Hospital, had left his home on the south side of Belfast to pick up his wife in the city centre. Mrs Ada Bereen had actually walked past the Abercorn minutes before the bomb had gone off. She was standing on a pavement one hundred yards away when she heard the bang. Her husband was on the other side of the street; he saw the puff of smoke and thought that a pub beside the Abercorn had been blown up. Dr Bereen wanted to help but his instruments were in his car several streets away. He decided, reluctantly, that there was nothing he could do. They later heard, on a radio bulletin, that two women had died and at least 136 people had been injured. At home Dr Bereen was telephoned by a senior doctor from the Royal who asked him to come in because the hospital was crowded with casualties and the staff were under pressure. He decided immediately to help. Bereen specialised in neuro-surgery and dealt with injuries to the head and spine. He and his colleagues dealt with three patients including a boy of four who had shrapnel in his head. Shortly after 11 p.m. they had finished. He rejoined his wife who was hosting a dinner party. Bereen was not hungry: 'I don't want anything,' he said. 'It's been a bad night. I have seen many a dirty few hours with casualties but tonight was as bad as I have seen.' He had served with the Royal Army Medical Corps in the Middle East during the War. His first reaction on seeing the casualties in the Royal was: 'My God, its El Alamein all over again.' Only this time people had been wounded by domestic objects not bullets and bomb shrapnel. Cups and saucers and knives and forks had imbedded themselves in civilian bodies. The leg of a table protruded through one patient's thigh. Now, as he settled for a cup of coffee, the phone rang just on midnight. It was a colleague. He told Bereen that the police had been trying to contact him. Immediately he thought: 'It's a car accident. Jan's been hurt.' The Bereen's had given their daughter, Janet, a new Mini as a 21st birthday present. Dr Bereen's friend told him to stay by the phone. The police would ring him back and it would be better if he were alone. At that moment Dr Bereen knew that something terrible had happened. A police officer phoned and began to talk to him quietly. He asked him if he would go to the 'Laganbank'. To a layman it would not have been significant. But to a doctor it could mean only one thing. The 'Laganbank' was a polite term for the city mortuary. Janet Bereen was dead. She had been in the Abercorn.[3] The other girl killed was Ann Owens who had survived an earlier bomb at the Electricity Board. She was with her friend, Janet Bereen, in the Abercorn when the bomb had exploded. Both girls had been waiting to be served when the explosion occurred.[4]

Jennifer McNern regained consciousness in the Royal several days after the Abercorn explosion. She opened her eyes and began looking around. She did not talk as she tried to find her bearings, but she began to realise she was in a hospital. Her arm was in plaster. She was heavily drugged and she felt content. She thought she had broken her arm but she did not worry about anything else. Then one day her mother and a friend were visiting her. They prepared to leave her after the visit. When they left the room Jennifer began to curl up and to go to sleep again. She had done this many times before but on this occasion, by sheer accident, she glanced down at her right side. She felt a surge of horror. Part of her right leg was missing. She began to scream.

Her sister, Rosaleen, meanwhile, lay seriously ill in intensive care. Doctors thought at first that she might not live. But she did. She could not remember when she became conscious. But she remembered exactly how she was told of her injuries. One day a sister in the intensive care unit talked to her. She guided the conversation round and explained to Rosaleen exactly what had happened. 'I know,' said Rosaleen simply. She felt she had been told by the staff previously. Subconsciously she had been prepared for the reality. Rosaleen had lost two legs and an arm. Jennifer had lost both legs; but she still suffered from terrible 'phantom pains' in parts of her body that were no longer there. The pain was worse because she could not rub her limbs to ease them even though she thought she could still wiggle her toes. Rosaleen suffered from 'cold feet'. Even though her legs were no longer there the hospital staff piled blanket upon blanket on top of the bed in the already warm ward to bring her some relief.

When Jimmy Stewart regained consciousness he lay for more than 48 hours without knowing about his injuries. Then, when chatting casually one morning to a doctor taking his temperature, he mentioned his right leg. There was a pause. 'Mr Stewart, I'm sorry,' said the doctor, 'but we could not save it'. 'That's alright,' replied Stewart, barely pausing to think. 'How's the other one?' There was another pause. 'I'm sorry, Jimmy,' said the doctor, 'we had to take it off as well.' Jimmy Stewart felt like crying but the tears would not come. He was utterly miserable. He lay and thought for a while. Then, in his own words, he 'committed himself to the Lord'. There was only one occasion when he was reduced to tears. He was lying alone in the ward. He began to think of his injuries. 'Why did it happen to me?', he asked. 'I did no one any harm.' The self-pity welled over him and the tears began to come. He felt everything was against him; he thought he would never walk again. But the staff encouraged him. A girl who had lost a limb in another explosion came to see him. She encouraged him and he began to take heart.

On 5 October 1974, Jimmy Stewart married Florrie Orr at the Welcome Evangelical Church in Cambrai Street, Belfast. He walked down the aisle, on artificial limbs, with his bride. He became philosophical about the past: 'When you come so close to death, you see just how great life is. I am glad to be alive, and my disabilities don't get me down. I only feel sorry for the people who put me in this condition. They just don't know how great life can be.' Two years earlier, on 5 August 1972, Rosaleen McNern was married to Brendan Murrin in the tiny Donegal village of Killybegs. Jennifer McNern was one of the bridesmaids. Jennifer and Rosaleen were taken up the aisle in wheelchairs. Jennifer recalled how:

> What helped to ease my mind after the explosion was the ward in Musgrave Park Hospital. I felt that I had been very lucky. Although I had lost my own legs, I could at least stand up straight with the help of artificial limbs. There were people in the ward who would never do that again. I saw what could happen and what did happen to men in their teens. Some of them were paralysed from the neck down. They would never walk again. I found that so shocking. I never thought in my life that you would see a war in Northern Ireland. I still can't believe it.

Rosaleen said:

> You don't get past your luck. There is an old saying 'If you are going to drown you will never be hung'. If it's for you, it's for you. It is one of those things you have to go through. If we were not sitting in that restaurant, it would have happened to someone else. At the beginning you did ask yourself 'Why should this happen to me? I never did any harm to anyone.' You feel sorry for yourself, but you overcome that. I look back on the days when we had our own limbs. You did not say, 'Aren't we lucky'... I don't feel cynical, and I don't feel bitter about the people who caused the explosion. It is more of a curiosity. I would like to know why they did it. I sometimes wonder if they thought they were right. Somehow I think that the people who did it will feel worse than us in the end.

Jimmy Stewart echoed similar views:

> If I was not a Christian I might grow to hate the people responsible. Now in the spirit of Christ I can forgive. I would still like to know their motive. Why did they do it? What were they trying to achieve? The terrifying thing is that the explosion could have happened to anyone.[5]

Notes

1. Alf McCreary, *Survivors* (Belfast: 1976), pp.19–20.
2. David McKittrick, Seamus Keltars, Brian Feeny and Chris Thornton, *Lost Lives: The*

Stories of the Many Women and Children Who Died as a Result of the Northern Ireland Troubles (Edinburgh: 1999), p.161.
3. McGeary, *Survivors*, pp.21–30.
4. McKittrick *et al.*, Lost Lives, p.161.
5. McGeary, *Survivors*, pp.40–46.

1

End of the Honeymoon

A Private in the 1 Battalion of The Parachute Regiment (1 PARA) recalled how, when British troops were deployed on the streets of Belfast, in 1969:

> The civilians weren't too sure of us. We did have some trouble in the Shank[ill], but on the Catholic side it was open arms. We couldn't go wrong there. These were early days. The Protestants were upset, because they were stopped doing what they wanted... We used to do observations from the top of Divis Flats – always tea and coffee from the Catholics. We had a position down on the peace line, and every morning at 6.30 this little old lady used to travel across with a fully cooked breakfast for two of us, every morning – we used to fight to get that one. At Christmas we were invited out for dinners and on every step there was a bottle of whiskey to take back to the boys. It was brilliant. We felt like knights in shining armour, like Sir Galahad. We were the do-gooders: Her Majesty's Government had sent us there to put things right. At that stage I had no fear. Things were good.[1]

Or as a member of The Gloucestershire Regiment put it: 'We were treated as saviours.'[2] The complexities of Northern Irish politics could be mysterious, even for Irishmen in the British Army; one Corporal in 1 PARA was from Southern Ireland:

> Being Irish cost me sore ears, mostly from the Protestant side. A funny thing was said to me one night. I decided that I wasn't going to masquerade as an Englishman any more... We stood around and they [the Protestants] were going on about Fenians... these people were saying 'Fenians this, Fenians that', and all the rest of it. I turned round and I said, 'Well, I'm a Fenian.' They replied, 'But English Fenians are different to Irish Fenians'... I started to realise then what it was all about.[3]

A Corporal in 2 PARA reminisced:

> We used to just wander around in pairs like policemen. You'd go out for a two-hour patrol and in two hours you drank twenty cups of tea because everybody wanted to give you a cup of tea and a sandwich. We called it the honeymoon tour. We had a disco every night and the girls used to come in, all the girls used to come in. That's where a lot of lads met their wives.

A Private in the same battalion noted how: 'The women liked the soldiers because they had more to offer than football and motorbikes. Girls come and go, and obviously a lot of us soldiers did marry Irish girls.'[4] When 1 PARA left for home, its first tour of duty completed, it was, as one soldier remembered,

> a day of great sadness. I was leaving friends, people we knew. Leaving the girls behind was probably the saddest thing of all. They all lined up to wave goodbye. It was like the Wailing Wall of Jerusalem. I remember a hit at the time – 'Leaving on a Jet Plane'. You know, the lines about 'packing my bags and hating to go and don't know when I'll be back again'. We were singing our heads off and the girls were waving and throwing their knickers at us. God bless 'em! And they were all shouting 'We'll wait for you!'[5]

THE PROVISIONALS' CAMPAIGN BEGINS

In January 1970 a defining moment occurred in the history of the Troubles: the Army Council of the Provisional Irish Republican Army met to decide military policy. With the summer marching season of 1970 as the most likely flashpoint, the Provisional IRA determined that the most urgent priority would be area defence from loyalists and the British Army. All energies would be devoted to providing material, financial and training assistance for Northern units. As soon as it became feasible and practical, the Provisionals would move from a purely defensive position into a phase of 'combined defence and retaliation'. After a sufficient period of preparation, when the movement was considered strong enough and the circumstances ripe, it would go into the third phase, launching an all-out offensive action against the 'British occupation system'.[6] By the end of January 1970 the Provisionals had a Belfast Brigade that was structured into battalion and company levels. The Belfast Staff had McKee as OC with Seamus Twomey as his Adjutant. Leo Martin became Intelligence Officer; Sean McNally, Quartermaster; Tom O'Donnell, Finance Officer; Sean Murphy, Training Officer; Albert Price controlled the Auxiliaries. They divided the city into three battalion areas. The 1st Battalion area stretched from the Upper Falls and extended north to cover the Ballymurphy estate and west Andersonstown. The 2nd Battalion operated in the Lower Falls, Clonard and the Divis Flats. The 3rd Battalion covered Ardyone and The Bone to the north, the New Lodge and Unity Flats and the Short Strand/Ballymacarrett just over the bridges on the fringe of Protestant east Belfast.

McKee was regarded as a disciplinarian by his men; single, and a devout Catholic, he attended Mass daily. Twomey, like McKee, was from the Pound Loney, having been born in Marchioness Street in 1919. He joined the Movement's youth wing, Fianna Éireann, in 1936 and the IRA in 1937. Twomey had been interned during the Second World War.[7] Jimmy Steele was in charge of publicity. Born in 1907, Steele joined Na Fianna Éireann at a very early age. After the Treaty split he was first arrested in 1923; his first term of penal servitude came in 1936; more prison terms followed in 1940 and 1943.[8] Steele

– at the time of his death in August 1970 he had risen to the rank of Lieutenant General within the Provisional IRA – set up *Republican News*, the Provisionals' mouthpiece. Tom O'Donnell was a '50s man from the Short Strand. Born in July 1932 he joined the Republican Movement in 1950 at the age of 18. He was interned in 1957. In 1969, when a Defence Association was set up in the Short Strand, he and another local man, Jimmy George, were arrested in England for attempting to procure arms. After six months in Brixton Prison the charges were dropped and they returned to Belfast where O'Donnell joined the new Provisional Staff. Another leading figure at this time who played a key role in the reorganization of the Movement was Frank Card – Proinsias MacAirt. Another internee of the 1940s, he assisted Steele in the foundation of *Republican News*, later becoming editor.[9]

For the Provisionals the responsibility for the impending military conflict lay with Britain's illegal partition of Ireland. In the view of their first Chief of Staff Sean MacStiofain, 'England could not hold any part of Ireland except by military force.' As an individual, MacStiofain 'was sorry for anyone's death, whether Irishman or Englishman'. But this did not prevent British soldiers from 'volunteering to harass and kill the people of another country which they knew next to nothing about'. There was no conscription in the British Army. Every man in it was a professional taking his military chances for money and promotion.[10] With a return to traditional values, Republicans who had dropped out rejoined. Martin Meehan, before long a future senior IRA commander in Belfast, had been disgusted by the failure of August 1969; now he was assured by Billy McKee that the first priority would be the protection of nationalist areas. While there was not going to be an immediate offensive against the British Army, the intention was there: McKee said 'these things take time. People have to be trained. People have to be motivated. People have to be equipped. All this won't happen overnight.' Meehan rejoined.[11] Another Volunteer, Brendan Hughes, recalled that the

> only objective I ever heard in the early days was to get the Brits out of Ireland. I remember sitting in Proinsias McAirt's house which was the hub of Republican activity at the time, and I recall Billy McKee saying that this is our opportunity now with the Brits on the streets, this is what we wanted, open confrontation with the army. Get the Brits out through armed resistance, engage them in armed conflict and send back across the water with their tanks and guns. That was the Republican objective.[12]

Recruitment for the Provisionals began in earnest. Hughes, born in 1948 in the Grosvenor Road area of west Belfast, joined the Movement in 1969:

> My whole family had a history of militant Republicanism...I was always reminded by people in the streets who told me my father was a good IRA man, as was his grandfather, and they went to jail and that sort of thing. In 1969 though I was caught in a political conflict because I lived in a Protestant area and Catholics were getting burned out, and Catholics (not Republicans)

sometimes came down the Grosvenor Road to burn the Protestants out in revenge, so I was caught in a dilemma. My feelings were with the Catholic people who were after revenge and it was a sectarian thing... It was only then that I began to look at the nature of the state, to analyse what my father had been through, working on building sites all his life. It was then that I looked at my background, my family history and Republicanism... I think I was... a militant Republican but with little or no direction, no political content at that period, no ideology. But that dormant Republicanism was always there.

Hughes joined the Movement after a specific incident: when Orangemen were marching up the Grovsvenor Road. He was approached by an IRA man and asked to go to a meeting. He went with six other people where they were addressed by Joe Cahill; he warned them that if they joined they would probably get killed and, at the very least, end up in jail.[13] Hughes recalled that:

Everybody wanted to be involved with guns and there were gun lectures going on almost every night. People were being trained on whatever weapons were there and being trained at particular houses. It was done largely in the kitchen or the bedroom or whatever room was available at that particular time. A group of people would assemble and the Training Officer would come and strip the weapon down and put it back together again. He'd explain what sort of ammunition it took and so forth. All the basic training on the weapon itself would be done in that sort of way. The weapons would be transported about in prams or a woman would carry it in some way. British soldiers were very reluctant to stop and search a woman. The houses were pretty well known to the British army. I remember one particular night sitting in a house in the Lower Falls with six or seven others and a well-known British army officer opened the door and walked in and said, 'what weapons are you training on tonight lads?' That sort of thing happened during the honeymoon period. The army was basically gathering intelligence and we weren't as yet on a war footing. I think the army looked upon it as a sort of a joke – as if we were only a wee bunch of lads and weren't any danger to the British army at that time.

So tension-free was the relationship between the Provisionals and the British Army that soldiers would go into pubs and leave their weapons lying around. Hughes recalled:

There's a wee pub just down Leeson Street and the troops used to walk in and sit down and we used to sit down beside them. We used to ask them about their weapons and how they worked and very often they would give you a whole run-down on the weapon... a lot of my training came from pubs, you know, from the British army, British troops, young lads of eighteen and nineteen. We weren't much older than that ourselves though.[14]

It was not long before Hughes and his fellow Volunteers would try and shoot those same soldiers.

That was to come. For now the Provisionals were ready to make their presence felt in other ways. Although in theory there were three stages leading to an all out offensive against the British, in practice the Provisionals rapidly moved into a limited offensive mode by initiating a bombing campaign.[15] A small unit had been selected in early 1970 to take part in sanctioned operations against commercial targets. The main body of Volunteers were unaware of this.[16] For example, on 19 February 1970, the eighth explosion in Belfast since the beginning of the year damaged two parked cars and blew out windows in about twenty homes in University Avenue.[17] This was followed by a bomb on the Antrim Road, composed of gelignite to which an 18-inch length of fuse had been taped, which ripped off the door of a public house.[18] Five men were slightly injured when a bomb wrecked the Belfast Corporation Electricity Club in Donegall Street. These were the first injuries since bombings had begun at the beginning of the year. Following news of the explosion there were Catholic–Protestant confrontations – eventually dispersed by the Security Forces – in North Queen Street, Unity Flats, Millfield and at Peter's Hill.[19] The next attack occurred only 300 yards away from the Electricity Department's Social Club, on 1 March, when a bomb destroyed a statue of Reverend Hugh Hanna. The bomb had been made from a polythene bag filled with gelignite attached by wires to a package about the size of a cigarette box.[20] On 3 March a target was attacked with more than one explosive device for the first time. For some reason the target was an unoccupied garage in Andersonstown. One of three devices failed to explode.[21]

While the suspicion was that these explosions were from Republican sources it was clear that Protestant extremists were also active: on 8 March, Austin Currie, the Nationalist Party MP, and his family had a narrow escape when a bomb exploded against the wall of their home in Dungannon, County Tyrone. It was the second serious attack on the Currie home: shots had been fired at the house in August 1969.[22] But the main thrust was emanating from the Provisionals. Sometimes it ended in tragedy. Thomas McCool, aged 40, died with his young daughters, Carol, aged 4, and Bernadette, aged 9, alongside two other Provisional IRA members, Joseph Coyle, aged 40, and Thomas Carlin when a bomb exploded as it was being assembled at the McCool home in Derry on 26 June 1970. The Republicans were among the most senior Provisionals in Derry at the time and were the first to be killed by their own bomb.[23] On 4 September, Michael Kane, aged 35, was killed when the bomb he was handling exploded prematurely at Newforge Lane off the Malone Road, where he was attempting to destroy an electricity transformer. He came from Ballymurphy and belonged to a traditional Republican family. The Provisionals were using clothes pegs with tin tacks pushed through the end as contacts. The spring in the peg would gradually overcome the strength of the rubber on the wire and close the end where the tin tacks would meet, completing the circuit. These proved to be dangerous devices for the bomb-maker because he could not estimate accurately when the bomb would explode. The Army's bomb disposal team reckoned this was what happened to Kane. It was only with Kane's death that many Volunteers became aware of the fact that it was their organization which was behind the bombing campaign in the Province.[24]

What played into the Provos' hands was the continuing disorder on the streets. In the early hours of 2 May, the Springfield Road Police Station was besieged for half an hour by a 200 strong mob that smashed almost every window in the building. The station was the HQ of The Royal Scots, which had come in for criticism from locals following riots in Ballymurphy.[25] This was the prelude to the fiercest rioting in Belfast since August: on the weekend of 9/10 May violence broke out on the New Lodge Road and continued for several hours. Twenty-seven soldiers, six policemen and four civilians were injured during the disturbances.[26] But the significance of these disturbances was how local Catholics perceived them. The St Patrick's Parish Defence Committee protested at allegations that weekend disturbances was merely hooliganism. It claimed that there were a deliberately engineered series of events throughout the day which culminated on the Saturday night with a Protestant mob storming down Lepper Street from Tigers Bay. The men of the New Lodge Road repelled the attack and the Protestant mob took refuge behind a cordon of Royal Ulster Constabulary (RUC) – who had watched impassively. The arrival of the Army was greeted with relief but this turned to dismay when the Army proceeded to drive the Catholics back into their homes and immediately used tear gas. This created considerable ill-feeling among the residents towards the Army.[27] Thus, for many Catholic residents the troops had overreacted; the RUC, in containing the Protestants, had demonstrated their bias, while the Catholics were unjustly treated. However, from the point of view of the authorities the police had dealt with the Protestant faction, who soon faded away, while it was the Catholic faction that continued to harass the military throughout the night with considerable violence, including the use of petrol bombs. This was why the military used CS grenades to quell the disturbances.[28]

Writing after the dramatic events of the Arms Crisis in the Republic, on 12 May, Ronnie Burroughs, the United Kingdom Representative in Northern Ireland (UKREP), drew the attention of the Foreign and Commonwealth Office (FCO) and the British Embassy in Dublin to a definite deviation in the pattern of the new disturbances from the normal pattern. Prior intelligence had indicated that Republican elements were deliberately planning disturbances. And 'if a few Catholics were pushed around...this would help [Neil] Blaney's cause. (A Catholic martyr would have been a major bonus).' Tension had been generated during the afternoon by several incidents, including the beating up of a policeman by six masked men. A temporary lull followed but an explosion outside Protestant properties bore the appearance of having been a pre-arranged signal. New and more dangerous techniques were used in this explosion and IRA expertise was suspected. The RUC confirmed that they came under Republican gunfire. Burroughs noted that the following night was calm but warned that a recrudescence of the political crisis in Dublin might be the signal for further engineered disturbances in Belfast.[29] In London the Foreign Secretary, Michael Stewart, duly told John Peck, Her Majesty's new Ambassador to Dublin, that he might want to tell the Irish that there was some evidence to suggest that the disturbances were deliberately provoked by the Republicans, although the evidence was not yet sufficiently strong for London to say with complete confidence that this was the whole explanation.[30]

More violence followed. After a quiet Saturday night violence broke out again in Belfast at about midnight on Sunday, 17 May. The disturbances again took place in the New Lodge Road area and also in the Ardoyne area. One bomb explosion and three fires coincided with the disturbances; the Home Office thought they were probably linked. There was also some looting in the New Lodge Road. Crowds of Catholic rioters, never numbering more than about 100, continued to harass the military throughout the night, and thirty CS gas grenades and thirty-three CS cartridges were used. Some twenty to thirty petrol bombs were thrown at the troops, together with other missiles. Seven arrests were made and six soldiers were slightly injured. A statement purporting to come from the Official IRA subsequently condemned the disturbances and claimed that no member of the organization had taken part in them. On the night of 18/19 May there was another confrontation between crowds of Catholics and Protestants in the Ardoyne and New Lodge Road areas of Belfast, but the RUC contained both disturbances; three petrol bombs were thrown at military vehicles in the Ardoyne. Overall, the continuing weekend violence had kept the situation tense.[31]

Increasingly, the disturbances in Belfast on 17 May appeared, to the authorities, to have been pre-planned and organized, as did the disturbance on the previous weekend, and in both cases the confrontation was between exclusively Catholic mobs and the military. The Security Forces mounted a number of patrols, road blocks and searches, paying special attention to the Ardoyne and New Lodge Road areas. The most significant discovery was of what appeared to have been an illicit explosives factory in the Ardoyne area.[32] In Jamaica Street a joint patrol of the RUC and The King's Own Scottish Borderers found eighteen uncharged grenades, two large sweet jars, one of which was filled with a white substance and one with brown crystals, and two small jars, one labelled potassium chloride and the other potassium nitrate. A container of sulphuric acid was also found.[33] Preparations were being made for more sophisticated and organized attacks on the Security Forces. And it was not just the Security Forces who took this view. The Rector of Holy Cross, Father O'Donnell, who had been out all night appealing for peace, believed that it was a small section of people who were bent on causing trouble against the wishes of a great majority of the local people. He observed that:

> The majority of the residents of Ardoyne to whom I spoke are seriously worried about this fresh outbreak of violence and fear that it could escalate into another bloody confrontation between Catholics and Protestants that had the people living in sheer terror last August... Some people are convinced that the disturbances on Sunday and yesterday morning were organised by a small group of militant people who are determined to get rid of the military.
>
> Allegations have been made that members of the Army have been behaving in a provocative manner, similar to that in Ballymurphy some time ago, but I could find no prof [sic] of this allegation. One man told me that as far as he was concerned the soldiers were a well-disciplined force and he could find nothing wrong with them. There are people in this area who apparently do not want normal conditions to prevail and are out to create trouble at all costs.[34]

The Roman Catholic hierarchy immediately recognized the consequences that might arise from organized violence when it warned that if the 'many deep-seated wrongs' were to be undone then violence would only delay the day when they could be removed. Cardinal Conway, the Primate of All-Ireland, and the Bishops of Derry, Dromore, Kilmore, Down and Connor, and Clogher, warned that it would be a 'stab in the back' to the Catholic community for any individual or group to take it upon themselves to deliberately provoke violent incidents. Moreover, if such acts could be pointed to as the beginning of serious trouble 'it is not the handful of self-appointed activists who will be blamed, but the whole Catholic community'. Already, they warned, people were not above suggesting that the trouble of recent days convicted the Catholic community for what had happened in August.[35] The Provisionals denied that any of their units were engaged in the Ardoyne during the disturbances or that any member of their organization had been responsible for the incident which sparked off the trouble,[36] but the burden of suspicion fell on them.

It was in this manner that Republicans began the transformation in Catholic–Army relations. The upsurge in violence was the last thing the military had wanted. For the Army it was frustrating that, for the foreseeable future, they would continue to be tied down in Northern Ireland. The reason for this was the continuing inability of the RUC to take over from the military. This led to strains between the Army and RUC leaderships – particularly between the General Officer Commanding Northern Ireland (GOC NI), Sir Ian Freeland, and Sir Arthur Young, the Chief Constable. In the beginning the relationship was cordial. But the determination of Young to turn the RUC into a civilized, unarmed force at all costs – even to the extreme of virtually no involvement in any riot control – led to the antagonism with the GOC. From the moment he took over as Inspector-General (the post was subsequently redesignated Chief Constable), Young was a man on a mission. He was a formidable character: a constable at 18; a detective at 24; an inspector at 29; a chief constable at 39; he became Commissioner of the City of London Police at 43, the first man from the ranks to do so. Young had helped to establish a police force in Italy after the Allies were victorious in the Second World War; he was 'borrowed' three times to advise on the organization and training of police in the Gold Coast, Malaya and Kenya, earning the journalistic cliché of 'Commonwealth trouble-shooter'. He was also the longest serving UK member of Interpol. It was at the age of 62 that Colonel Sir Arthur Edwin Young inherited his current job. Young had a profound impact on those who worked with him. Jim Page, the Acting Commissioner in London, described him as 'an outstanding police officer – and outstanding for his personal charm and consideration. Everyone here misses him.' Bob Boyes, Deputy Chief Constable of Mid-Anglia, said simply: 'I have thirty years' police service in England and I regard Arthur Young as the number one policeman.' In Belfast he was variously described by RUC colleagues as 'charming'; 'considerate'; and 'very hard working'. Added to this were 'integrity' and 'sincerity' – again and again. One man called him a 'human dynamo'. Another spoke of his resilience: 'He is like a rubber ball. Thump him and he comes back for more.' He had tremendous self-confidence and could inspire people at all levels. But he could also be very demanding: 'He doesn't suffer fools gladly,' said a colleague. 'You have to perform.' In 1952, at the height of the Emergency, Young had been sent to Malaya by London. The Governor had been assassinated; hundreds of policemen had been murdered; and there was a crisis of public confidence in the Security Forces. Paddy Jackson, then in command of the police in Jahore but now retired in County Wicklow, recalled: 'His attitude was not to tell us what to do but rather for us to tell him our problems and he would try to solve them. The police force were crying out for leadership, a big man who could get things done. We got that from Sir Arthur.'[37]

Under his guidance the Hunt Committee's recommendations were being implemented in Northern Ireland. A further report, published in February 1970, restructured the RUC along the lines of forces in Great Britain.[38] Young's goal was to turn the RUC from a police force with paramilitary trappings into a police service based on the British model. In his own words Young lived literally 'over the shop' at RUC HQ and used half his room as an office, half as a sitting room, with a bedroom and kitchen close by. He liked cooking – bacon, eggs, stew, curries, hams – partly as a kind of therapy. He had a deep love of music – Beethoven and Mozart – 'And Nat King Cole is a chap with great charm.' He was widely read, particularly attracted to biographies and the classics. If he watched television for more than an hour he considered it a waste of time. He also possessed a strong sense of spirituality – at one stage he considered taking Holy Orders, when he was a young policeman. Yet he did not consider himself a religious man: 'I am not a religious but I have a deep and abiding faith. I have always had it. I have a profound sense of my relationship with God and a profound faith in the life to come and that eternity is now and that the purpose of living is to improve one's character.' He was a member of the Church of England 'whatever that may mean'.

Young continually made the point that the real criterion of police efficiency was public confidence – that the police needed the support of every law-abiding citizen and that the maintenance of law and order was a two-way contract between police and people: 'Perhaps people who think I am a softie too long might get a surprise. One has to be firm on the right grounds for the right reasons... The "Softly, Softly" slogan has served its purpose. My latest slogan is "Keep the peace".' Young had no doubt that if, following the disorders of 1969, the police had gone back into the Falls Road by force there would have been more bloodshed. All that force would do would be to set up a reaction: 'If you subdue by force, it will take force to subdue it the next week.'

When the disturbances broke out in August 1969, Young was verging on 63 with retirement only two years away; he was enjoying enormous satisfaction in his job. So, it was 'like a bombshell exploding' when James Callaghan, the Home Secretary, asked him to come to Northern Ireland: 'I said that I did not want to go. He said I was the most qualified man for the job and when he said that I regarded it as a matter of duty to make myself available.' Having come to Northern Ireland, Young found himself 'completely enthusiastic... The thing that I still want more than anything else is responsibility. It is almost like a drug.

I cannot resist it.' However, he was adamant that he wanted to return to his old job before retirement and, considering that he thought his current job at the RUC was really 'a ten-year stint', Young hoped he could 'set the pattern and aim for the target' so that his successor would have an easier job than he had. When asked for a postscript to describe himself, Young selected Tennyson's *Ulysses*, where Ulysses was rallying his weary comrades:

> 'Tis not too late to seek a newer world...
> It may be that the gulfs will wash us down;
> It may be that we shall touch the Happy Isles,
> And see the great Achilles whom we knew.
>
> Tho' much is taken, much abides; and tho'
> We are not now that strength which in old days
> Moved earth and heaven; That which we are, we are;
> One equal temper of heroic hearts,
> Made weak by time and fate, but strong in will
> To strive, to seek, to find, and not to yield.[39]

His military counterpart, Ian Freeland, was a completely different egg altogether – but he matched Young for determination. At school, Freeland had started near the bottom. The Reverend C.W. Trevelyan, who taught him at Wellington College, remembered him well: 'He was a delightful person. I knew him when he was 13 and I may say he was in the bottom form but that was no disgrace. I found the boys in that form were good brains coming on slowly.' Freeland took the advice of his teacher and worked. After a term he moved up. J.L. Hislop, a racehorse breeder and businessman in Newbury, was in the same dormitory: 'I always said he would go a long way,' he said. 'He had a very good brain and was a nice chap – a good athlete and cricketer.' Hislop remembered one conversation they had together: 'We were talking about girls and he said: "I am never going to marry one of those flash chorus girl types because they are the sort that go off. I am going to marry a nice girl." He was 12 years old and it really was a most remarkable thing to say.' And he was true to his word, marrying Mary, the daughter of a general, whom he met in India in 1938. During the War, Freeland won the Distinguished Service Order for his handling of the 7 Battalion The Royal Norfolks in the fighting for the Brieux bridgehead over the Orne. Now, as the GOC NI, Freeland admitted he had felt rather despairing lately: 'I had hoped that things were improving about Christmas, but the week before last had been a bit of a set-back. There are enough trouble-makers and simple people to follow them. One realises the difficulty. I cannot solve it. My job is to try and keep the peace while the politicians and economists try to solve it.' It was an exasperating situation for the Army in Northern Ireland. 'We have to take a middle of the road line. We try to see everybody's point of view but a lot of people do not seem to see how difficult it is for us.' The Army had a lot of experience of doing 'this sort of thing' in other parts of the world but no one had done it in the United Kingdom. It was difficult for the Army because of the divided nature of Northern Irish society: 'And as time goes on the Army becomes the scape-goat.'[40]

These were the two personalities who shaped security policy as the Province began its slide into insurgency in 1970. One of Young's first moves as Inspector-General had been to secure Freeland's agreement to give up control of the deployment and tasks of the RUC which had been invested in his role as Director of Operations for security in the Province. Freeland was persuaded to be content with the power of coordinating the deployment and tasks of the RUC. This modification was approved at ministerial level but was never made public. At the same time there was some discussion as to whether the Army's control of Internal Security (IS) could be further restricted. For example, some consideration was given within the Home Office as to whether or not the Army's control within Northern Ireland should be restricted to those areas that on past experience had given rise to Internal Security problems. On 18 November 1969, the Prime Minister of Northern Ireland, Major James Chichester-Clark, had seen James Callaghan, the Home Secretary, and indicated that the position of the GOC in relation to the RUC should be further reviewed. He was not sure that it was still necessary for the GOC to retain a coordinating function. It was agreed at this meeting that the Joint Security Committee (JSC) would be asked to consider the extent to which troops could be withdrawn and when the withdrawals could take place. Terms of reference and guidelines were drawn up for their appreciation. On 8 December, Young sent to Freeland a letter setting out his views on how the RUC should act in the future and how the Army should act during the continuation of the present emergency. He based his views on the principle that the RUC should only undertake such duties as were of a similar nature to those considered appropriate to any other force in the United Kingdom. He did not want the unarmed RUC to be seen in an aggressive role and decided that the RUC Special Patrol Group (SPG) would no longer make an aggressive use of batons or carry shields or protective gear. The RUC would rely entirely on passive measures with the proviso that active and positive action might be necessary to arrest individual offenders and to avoid the commission of serious crime. Young hoped that the Army would reinforce the police and if necessary use CS gas or open fire where circumstances demanded it. He indicated that the Police Commander on the spot should be consulted by the Military Commander. This letter was, for Freeland, inflammatory. He immediately wrote to the Chief of the General Staff (CGS), Sir Geoffrey Baker, pointing out that the Army could not possibly be put under the control of the police, giving his personal view that the size of the police force would have to be increased very substantially and SPGs equipped with every modern type of equipment to deal with the tough Irish rioters 'who do not hesitate to use any weapon at hand'.[41]

It was over this issue of crowd/riot control that a fundamental disagreement arose. The GOC's position was that the Army had no police function except to aid the civil power when the civil power needed the kind of aid that the Army – and only the Army – could provide, or when the situation reached the stage when it was beyond the ability of the police to control crowds unaided. The Chief Constable's position was that the police should be 'non-aggressive' and 'non-retaliatory'; he appeared, from the perspective of the senior officer in the British Army, Baker, to think that in the field of dealing with disorder there was a fixed boundary between police and military functions. The Army's view was that, in dealing with disorder, there was no point at which in principle a situation passed beyond the duty of the police to deal with. In practice there was obviously a point at which the civil power was entitled to call on military assistance, but the involvement of the military at this point did not remove any duty from the police. Refusal to accept this principle seemed to get close in practice to entailing acceptance of the view that there should be a third force like the French riot police, for it had to be accepted that it was not one of the permanent functions of the Army to maintain internal order. If it was correct that there was in principle no point at which the duty of the police to maintain public order ceased, whether or not the military had become involved, the CGS argued that two main consequences followed:

a. The police may have to use more force than is consistent with maintaining popularity. It is sad that the police should have to use force, but for the population at large it is of little consequence whether it is the Army or the police who use force if force is to be used at all. The combination of a gentle police and a rigorous Army is no better than a rigorous police.
b. The police will have to be prepared to use weapons such as CS and possibly also batons and water, to the extent that these may be judged effective. These are not exclusively military weapons.

Sir Geoffrey Baker argued that none of this was intended to suggest that the police should use more force than was necessary, or revert to the heavily armed methods which they formerly employed. Nor was it inconsistent with the aim to restyle the RUC on the lines of Great Britain's police forces. The latter already had on occasion to use force, including the use of truncheons. The CGS supported his GOC and believed that the approach here was that the RUC should be prepared to pursue measures of the kind that the British police would adopt if they were faced with the kind of disorders that existed in Northern Ireland.

The problem was that Young was clearly not happy with his position vis-à-vis the GOC, with the latter being overall Director of Operations. He wanted to see a situation in which overall military control of operations ceased and reverted to a situation in which the military were called out in aid of the civil power only when the police advised the civil power that this was necessary. But the Army pointed out that, from a legal point of view, the troops were now acting in aid of the civil power. The civil power was not synonymous with the police, but connoted an authority wider than that of the police. In England the civil power was a pretty intangible entity because there was no central control of the police; in Northern Ireland it was more tangible in that the Minister of Home Affairs was much more clearly responsible. But to speak as the Chief Constable did, of reverting to a situation in which the Army were acting in aid of the civil power, was not in truth to suggest any change in the legal position.

There was no inconsistency in the police being subordinate to the military in a situation in which the military were acting in aid of the civil power. What was really being discussed was practical control: for example, if there was to be a difficult demonstration in Armagh who decided what measures were to be taken? If one looked at it from this point of view, it was not possible to contemplate any change in the existing arrangements so long as the military were deployed in Internal Security operations in aid of the civil power. Unless the principle that the police had a full law enforcement duty was accepted, and a start was made to put this into practice, no change in the command and control arrangement could be contemplated.[42]

The confusion as to the role of the police was highlighted in June 1970. On 21 June the RUC made a baton charge at Strabane which Young thought unjustified. He did not regard a baton charge as the right way to deal with an unruly crowd. On 23 June he issued a Force Order forbidding baton charges or any other form of direct force to subdue an unruly crowd. He pointed out that direct use of force was inimical to a relationship with the public in which a police service could flourish. It was perhaps not surprising that although this particular force order also said that force was justified to prevent serious crime, the RUC were uncertain what to do during the weekend 26 to 28 June when there was gunfire across the Crumlin Road between the Ardoyne and the Shankill and in the Ballymacarratt area as well as considerable trouble at Ballymurphy and other parts of Belfast. Both the Army and the police were severely criticized for their respective parts in this weekend's events. It was immediately clear that closer liaison was necessary and on 29 June, Young published a force order indicating that each military unit commander down to company level would have a member of the police attached to him to provide local knowledge and experience and to help in liaison with the police. At the same time the SPG were again given permission to use riot shields.[43] The events of June and July 1970 signalled the beginning of the end of Young's noble attempt to de-paramilitarize the police.

UNIONISM: STRESSES AND STRAINS

The last thing Major James Chichester-Clark, the Prime Minister of Northern Ireland, probably needed right now, in the summer of 1970, was an electoral contest that would expose the tensions within Unionism. Unfortunately a UK General Election was on the cards: Harold Wilson, according to legend, hoped England's successful defence of the World Cup in Mexico would provide the background for a return to power. He called a General Election for June 1970. Regrettably, Gordon 'Banks of England' ate an ice cream he shouldn't have done; Peter 'the Cat' Bonetti ran out of goalkeeping lives; Gerd Müller delivered the eliminating goal; and England lost. Wilson did so too. Chichester-Clark didn't have a great summer either. It wasn't long before any façade of Unionist unity crumbled. This time his headache originated from his supporters. Three Stormont MPs on the 'progressive' wing of his Ulster Unionist Party (UUP) – Robin Ballie,

Basil McIvor and Anne Dickson – sent a letter to the acting secretary of the South Antrim Imperial Unionist Association asking that, before the selection of a candidate for South Antrim, those seeking the nomination should be asked to give general support to the leader of the Party, the Prime Minister, and the Northern Ireland Government and its declared programme and policies. In fact no such assurances were asked for or given and in the event James Molyneaux was chosen as the Unionist candidate.[44] In order to prevent more bloodletting, Chichester-Clark stepped into the row in South Antrim and gave his endorsement to all the twelve official Unionist candidates in the General Election – without stipulating that they should declare their support for all the policies of his Government. Molyneaux had long been associated with the former MP for the constituency, Sir Knox Cunningham – whose anti-Wilson and anti-O'Neill rants had received prominent coverage in the Reverend Ian Paisley's *Protestant Telegraph* – and there existed a certain amount of ambiguity on whether or not the new candidate fully supported all the Stormont reforms. The Prime Minister's endorsement meant that, in effect, the candidates did not have to say whether or not they were in favour of the Government's reform programme or whether or not they took a similar line to those Unionist MPs who had already lost the Party Whip – 'big beasts' such as Bill Craig and Harry West – for their criticism of the Government's policy.[45] Given the unity debacle during the Crossroads election of 1969 this was a shrewd move on Chichester-Clark's part.

Despite the fact that a record forty candidates were in the field for the twelve Westminster seats,[46] once again the main focus was on the intra-Unionist battle. This meant Paisley versus Chichester-Clark's Ulster Unionist Party. The former's Protestant Unionists decided against putting up a candidate against the UUP candidate in Armagh, Jack Maginnis, because, according to Paisley: 'If we went in for the Armagh seat we would put it in jeopardy to a rebel and that we will never do.' The situation in Armagh was very serious because the Protestant majority was almost gone – this was put down to the inroads made by Newry Catholics into Armagh by reason of the houses being built there by Newry Urban Council: 'We are united against the common foe and in the county of the Diamond on election day let your answer be Derry, Aughrim, Enniskillen and the Boyne.' Paisley's theme was clear when he warned:

> We are living in serious days and in the midst of a tremendous battle. I am making a call tonight, lets have the B-Specials back again. When the country is in danger, fellow Protestants, what do you do? You strengthen its defences. What did this Government do? They tore down our defences, the first line of which was the RUC and armed RUC. They took the guns away from the police and to please Bernadette Devlin gave them cloth belts instead. The very name of the 'B' Specials put a cold shiver up the IRA men's backs. They did away with them.[47]

One sitting Unionist MP, Henry Clark, was angered by Paisley's comment that he – Clark – was 'delighted' with the Hunt Report. Clark described this as typical of Paisley's use of the 'half-truth'. He accepted that the Specials were 'undoubtedly the most effective deterrent against armed IRA attacks with their local knowledge and ability to turn out at short notice' but 'the policy was dictated from Westminster' and Clark had worked hard with his brother, the Ulster Special Constabulary (USC) District Commandant in South Derry, during the Hunt Commission trying to convince Callaghan of the necessity of adequate protection against IRA attacks. He was proud that his grandfather had raised the original Ulster Volunteer Force (UVF) and, latter, the Specials in South Derry.[48] One notable absentee was Major Ronald Bunting who bowed out of Ulster politics, lamenting that he had been 'outmanoeuvred' in his efforts to be nominated for Mid-Ulster. He now decided to 'take a rest from politics'; but not before making a parting shot at his former colleague, Paisley: 'If he wins North Antrim then Northern Ireland will be on the road to no-where.'[49]

After the debacle during recent by-elections, it was made clear that Orangemen would not be given any 'advice' on how to vote.[50] Instead, the announcement of the Orange day resolutions revealed that all reference to the Government of Northern Ireland were deleted from the Twelfth resolutions put to the eighteen Orange demonstrations; instead Orangemen were asked to pass a resolution which quoted one that was first put at demonstrations 'in the dark and hard days of 1922', calling on the 'authorities' to give full, proper and immediate protection to law-abiding citizens and restore the proper enforcement of law and order throughout Northern Ireland.[51] How much things had changed was evident in South Down where Captain Orr, who had represented the constituency for exactly twenty years, declared: 'I am a Protestant Unionist. But I am [an] official Unionist. Here in South Down I am glad to say that we are united and my nomination papers have been signed by members of Paisley's Free Presbyterian Church and by Unionists.' Orr gave support to the reform package in 'broad' terms.[52] In South Antrim, Tom Caldwell, the 48-year-old Stormont MP for Willowfield, entered the fray as an Independent Unionist against Molyneaux, who he described as a duplicate Sir Knox Cunningham pursuing 'unimaginative, hard-line and extremist policies'. Molyneaux, a 49-year-old bachelor, denied this, pointing out that he supported the reform programme – apart from the Central Housing Authority seeing it as an attack on local government.[53] Stratton Mills, standing against Paisley's colleague William Beattie in North Belfast, believed that the difference between 'Official Unionists' and the Protestant Unionists was that the logic of the latter's policies and attitudes was an independent Ulster which, 'abandoned by Westminster would be defenceless and broke'.[54]

But it really hit the fan as Paisley generated a storm – nothing unusual there – when he alleged that after talks 'at the highest level' he had reached a pact with the Unionist Party not to put up Protestant Unionist candidates in South Down, Armagh and Londonderry. Approaches had been made to the Protestant Unionist Party by 'top men' in Unionist constituency associations and by the secretary of the UUP, Jim Ballie, as well as other prominent Unionists. Paisley claimed that Chichester-Clark had been aware of this. The Prime Minister denied this, stating emphatically that he had 'not approved or countenanced any kind of pact or deal' with the Protestant Unionists. Paisley, in turn, called the

Prime Minister's denials an 'absolute falsehood', adding: 'Who does the Prime Minister think he is kidding?'[55] Chichester-Clark repeated his denial that he had not been a party to any deals with Paisleyites – but he did not deal with the allegation that other senior Unionists negotiated an election pact. The Prime Minister acknowledged that there had been 'chance meetings' between Ballie and Paisley at which the former had made it clear that unofficial candidates could hand seats to 'anti-Constitution' candidates. The Prime Minister insisted that these 'chance encounters' were not arranged meetings nor negotiations, for Ballie could not have negotiated without specific authority from him as leader of the Party 'which I would not give'.[56] But Paisley was on the march again: when the results came through he had won in North Antrim. Dr Paisley was on his way to Westminster and had struck another blow into the solar plexus of the Ulster Unionists.

If 1970 was a traumatic year in Unionist politics it was certainly a significant one in Nationalist politics. Following the meltdown of the Nationalist Party – echoing that of the old Home Rule Party in 1918 – a new generation of Catholic politicians had come to prominence. Their rise, on the back of the success of the Civil Rights Movement, signalled the end of that organization as a significant political force. Now a new political force would come to dominate Catholic politics for the next thirty plus years – until history repeated itself and a new generation of (often literally) foot soldiers replaced it. The new force in Northern Catholic politics was the Social Democratic and Labour Party (SDLP). The origins of the SDLP, as stated, lay in the break-up of the Civil Rights Movement. It had served its purpose. It was also becoming increasingly unrepresentative of Northern Catholic society in general with an increasing influence in its upper councils of people with sympathies towards the People's Democracy (PD) and left leaning segments of the Republican Movement. In January 1970, Austin Currie – of the Nationalist Party – urged Southerners not to make the mistake of thinking that any significant section of Northern opinion was represented by the political philosophy of the People's Democracy: there were those in the North who believed in a workers' republic but who would not touch PD with a barge pole. While they had played an important part in the Civil Rights campaign the PD was now just another political party and had had to be judged as such. On this basis it was difficult to find anywhere in Irish history a 'bunch of political opportunists to compare with PD'. Currie gave one example: a 'workers' republican' who was at the same time a member of the Northern Ireland Labour Party (NILP) – a 'partitionist body' – which was pledged to unity with Britain and which preferred the Red Flag and the Internationale to the Tricolour and the 'Soldier's Song'. There were a number of these people in the PD. A united Ireland would come but not on the basis of an ideology which 99 per cent of the Irish people found repugnant.[57]

In the event, PD members decided not to stand in the upcoming election to the Northern Ireland Civil Rights Association (NICRA) Committee on the grounds that Northern Ireland's problems would not be solved by 'obtaining equal shares of poverty and misery'. They could only be solved by regaining control over the land, factories and the workshops – 'Socialism in short'. NICRA was not a

Socialist organization and by its nature could not extend its fight from the immediate injustices of Unionist rule to the stranglehold of British imperialism which underlay them. PD wanted to devote all their energy to the struggle against imperialism, North and South of the Border, and the achievement of a Workers' and Farmers' Republic. PD members, however, would continue to be individual members of NICRA and would be in the forefront of the militant campaign for Civil Rights. Finally, it was noted that for some time there had been hysterical yelpings from the 'lunatic right-wing' of NICRA about infiltration by the PD. This had gone together with almost total inactivity by the yelpers. Now 'we hope they will finally shut up and we will watch with interest to see what action will be proposed by this group'.[58]

This, however, was not the end of the argument. The tensions and divisions within NICRA came to a head during a two-day gathering at its annual general meeting in mid-February. Three former members of the executive, and eight others, withdrew their names for re-election. Prominent NICRA members, such as Con McCluskey, John Donaghy and Brid Rodgers, announced that it was 'with sadness in their hearts' that they had decided not to stand again. They accused the Civil Rights Movement of having ceased to be what it originally was: 'a broad based movement commanding widespread respect and mass support'. The trio claimed that it had become increasingly apparent in recent months that dedicated and seasoned Civil Rights workers had been coming under attack from 'certain politically-motivated people' within the Movement because they refused to go along with a particular political ideology. The strength of the Movement had rested in the 'unity of people with many shades of political opinion' and the 'mass support of the people for reasonable, simple, and clearly defined aims'. The new executive included a number of those associated with Cathal Goulding's brand of Republicanism.[59] One of them, Frank Gogarty, lashed out at those who had opted out of NICRA in order to devote their energies and time to its destruction: 'They should be ashamed of themselves,' he said. At least NICRA could now apply itself more vigorously and more representatively to the continuing struggle for civil rights for all, whatever their religion or politics. Gogarty lamented how it was a pity that the Protestant men and women of the Shankill and the Fountain were still suspicious and frightened of NICRA.[60] The truth, however, was that NICRA was a spent force. It was time for new elements to march onto Northern Ireland's political landscape. Some drew their mandate from the living, vibrant, energies released by the desire for reform. Others drew their mandate from the dead. And would add to their number in due course.

In Stormont the disparate elements that constituted the 'Opposition' found more common ground in criticizing the Unionist Government. In February the major talking point was Chichester-Clark's appointment of Captain John Brooke as the head of the Government's Information Service. Predictably, the sight of someone detested by the Civil Rights Movement – not least because of his background in Fermanagh's local politics – in the Government produced the usual calm reaction: John Hume spoke of the appointment as a 'clear indication of a right-wing takeover'; while Ivan Cooper saw the appointment as 'sheer lunacy' and indicative of what was to come. It proved, said Cooper, what Opposition spokesmen had been saying for months regarding a Unionist right-wing Cabinet: 'The speed at which they are eating into the Government can only be compared to the way cancer devours the body.' This was another 'kick in the teeth' to moderate opinion and put Northern Ireland back to the 1920s.[61] Hume then went further, and in warning that the Government Information Service could become a party political propaganda machine, pointed out that such an appointment was unprecedented with the last occasion having been in Nazi Germany during the 1930s.[62] Gerry Fitt tried to restore some perspective. He asked that the Prime Minister take a firm stand with recalcitrant members of his party. He pledged the cooperation of the Opposition, provided the Government was sincere and realistic in its intent to govern in the interests of all the people. The minority was afraid that attempts would be made to cut down their numbers and drive them from the state in which they were born. He acknowledged Protestant fears of the Catholic birth-rate and the political implications this might have.[63] One of Chichester-Clark's problems was that if he could not please his own supporters – who, if they supported the reforms, did so reluctantly – then he certainly could not please the Opposition either. Paddy Kennedy, the Republican Labour MP, claimed that there was evidence of a determined move by B Specials to join the RUC Reserve as a body to take it over: it was their intention to place themselves in a position to get into police stations and obtain information about the activities of ordinary members of the public (i.e. Catholics).

Hume, at least, welcomed the Police Bill and the fact that the police would be disarmed: a gun was a psychological insult to the community as a whole in that it indicated that a gun was necessary to maintain law and order. However, he was disappointed at the rejection of the Hunt recommendation that members of secret societies should not be allowed to join the RUC. His target was, of course, the Orange Order. Such membership was not in keeping with an impartial police force. These organizations were clearly sectarian in their whole attitude to society in the North of Ireland. Furthermore, unless there was a change in the RUC uniform it would be difficult to accept that there had been a change in heart.[64] To counter this argument, Robert Porter, the Minister of Home Affairs, quoted a letter from Sir Arthur Young in which he said that the expression or manifestation of political or sectarian opinions on the part of any member of the force was strictly forbidden. No member of the force was permitted to attend, organize or assist in organizing any procession or parade except with the Inspector-General's sanction. Nor was he allowed to attend, organize or assist in organizing any meeting or gathering at which political sectarian speeches or discussion might take place. Young explained that members of the force were not debarred from belonging to any society which was not prohibited by the Oath which they had taken. They could attend in plain clothes the private meetings of these societies provided they did not conflict with their position as policemen.[65] The Opposition were not appeased by these reassurances. Nor were they pleased by the hold up in other areas. Robert Simpson, the Minister for Community Relations, told Hume at Stormont that he had been advised that there were great difficulties in framing legislation prohibiting incitement to religious hatred that would be enforceable – when passed into law the relevant Act did, indeed, prove unenforceable – without inhibiting the expression of legitimate opinion. Fitt described Simpson's comment as a confession of failure while Currie highlighted how most of the incitement to hatred came from the written word, including certain periodicals and newspapers. It appeared to him to be a problem which could be easily dealt with.[66]

The Opposition also had concerns over the number of firearms in 'unionist' hands. John Taylor, a hardliner and now a junior minister in Home Affairs, explained that anyone who held a firearm at any time had to be in possession of a certificate or permit issued by the County Inspector of Police if the officer was satisfied that the applicant was a responsible and fit person for having such a weapon. A detailed record was held at police stations of the description of every weapon in the RUC district and the addresses of those authorized to possess such weapons. Opposition members, however, attacked such practices as discriminatory. Currie claimed that it was extremely difficult for an ordinary member of the community to obtain a permit for a revolver, whereas a large number of USC members obtained permits because they were members of a so-called police force. Paddy Kennedy believed Taylor's figure of 87,000 permitted weapons to be a gross underestimation as a certificate allowed the holder to possess more than one weapon. Paddy Devlin of the NILP wanted to know why revolvers were required by anyone when they had been withdrawn from the RUC. Taylor admitted that it was correct that more than one firearm could be approved under one certificate. In all there were in the region of 51,000 such certificates. But he also pointed out that of the 50,000 weapons in the possession of the USC over the past fifty years only twenty had been mislaid.[67]

Once again this did not satisfy the concerns of the Opposition. But common concerns and the need for a coherent approach to problems led, ultimately, to the formation of the SDLP. The Social Democratic Labour Party was a coalition of Nationalist groups and individuals. It absorbed supporters from Independents, the old Nationalist Party, the National Democratic Party, the NILP and the Republican Labour Party. The party was launched at Stormont in August 1970: Gerry Fitt became its leader – he was from Republican Labour; John Hume, Ivan Cooper and Paddy O'Hanlon were three Independents prominent in the Civil Rights campaign; Austin Currie defected from the Nationalist Party; Paddy Devlin joined from the NILP; and Paddy Wilson was a Republican Labour Senator.[68] The SDLP's aim was to 'organise and maintain in Northern Ireland a socialist party' and to 'promote the cause of Irish unity based on the consent of a majority of people in Northern Ireland'.[69] While the party was new, its interpretation of Unionism and the Northern Ireland problem was not.

Those politicians who emerged from the Civil Rights Movement may have seen themselves as a vibrant and new element within Northern Irish politics; the truth was that they possessed a common – and long standing – ideological interpretation of the Northern Ireland problem. Therefore, Ivan Cooper could quite genuinely point out that the Opposition understood the fears on the part of the Protestant community. Those who talked about ending partition in the morning were only adding fuel to the fire. The Opposition were only looking for equality.[70] True, but the Opposition also believed that once equality was achieved Unionism's *raison d'être* would disappear and, with it, obstacles to Irish unity. Currie, for example, reassured Southerners that a reunited Ireland was inevitable, whether it be as a republic, a federation or within a united Europe. He recalled that Lord Craigavon had recognized this inevitability and today more and more Unionists agreed with him – in private of course. Currie believed that:

> The spirit of Nationality has never been higher in the North as it has been since the eruption of last August. At the beginning of the Civil Rights campaign with its emphasis on 'British rights for British subjects' some people had been concerned lest the desire for national unity would be diminished. They need not have worried – the fire burns brighter and stronger than ever.

Currie pointed out that unity could only be achieved by peaceful means. Not only was this desirable but there was no alternative. What was needed, to use a phrase that had become a cliché, was a union of hearts and minds. A forced unity in the aftermath of a bloody civil war, against the wishes of the majority of Unionists, was not worth having. Anyway, on the practical side, argued Currie, sufficient force to overrun and hold the North was just not available. Unity was also inevitable because:

> The loyalist of the North suffers from a lack of identity. He no longer knows what he is loyal to. If he is loyal to Her Majesty, why has he shot at her troops? If he is loyal to the British Government why does he hate it so much? If he is loyal to the British people why does he resist the introduction of their standards? Sooner or later he will come to the conclusion that his future lies with his fellow-Irishmen.[71]

Likewise, Gerry Fitt believed that the Protestant working class had been 'deluded' into the belief that they were superior to the Catholic working class, and the Catholic working class had been made to believe that they were inferior. There were signs that both the Protestant and Catholic working class were now coming together so that Northern Ireland could have a 'real "polarisation" of the right and left divisions'. Fitt predicted that if the 'anti-Unionists' got increasing Protestant support it would 'spell the death-knell for the Unionists in Northern Ireland', and that 'This will eventually lead to a united Ireland Republic where the working class interests will be paramount... a process of education and enlightenment will bring home to the Unionists that we are all Irish; that this is our own country and our future is tied up in a 32-county Ireland.'[72] Such views were common among the Opposition – even the most thoughtful of them.

The most original thinker was John Hume. He asked: 'How do we recognise the Constitution? Do we walk up and sign something[?].' Hume stressed that the

Opposition had no wish to change the constitution of Northern Ireland without the consent of the majority of people in Northern Ireland. He asked what exceptions could anyone take to that position? As citizens they had played their full part and were seeking to have public bodies and boards made more representative so that they could play a fuller part. 'Yet we are met with this continuous refusal.' As for those who sought a united Ireland, Hume thought it was a perfectly acceptable political viewpoint provided it was put forward in a democratic manner.[73] Hume warned that they were now faced with what amounted to 'amazing negligence' on the part of those who governed them. The negligence was found in the fact that while efforts were made by the British Government to produce a package of reforms to meet immediate grievances, no attempt had been made to examine the Northern Ireland problem in depth to find and deal with the underlying causes of all the unrest. In short it appeared that the heart of the problem was to be left untouched for another generation and another Government to solve. The symptoms were being dealt with but not the causes. This, as Callaghan had said, had brought peace. But the fundamental question that required close scrutiny and change was what had come to be known as 'the Constitution'. This had been the sacred cow of Northern Ireland politics, the question that could never be touched or even discussed, although the constitutions of other countries changed and evolved continuously, as they had to, in order to meet the needs of an ever changing world.

Hume pointed out that there were weaknesses in the Acts of Parliament that made up Northern Ireland's constitution which were as fundamental to it as the link with Britain itself; weaknesses which affected the whole Northern community. In the first place no one in Northern Ireland had any say over what type of society they had. The people of the North could not decide whether they wanted a Socialist or Conservative society for they were totally dependent on the type of Government in power in Britain. If Britain passed Socialist legislation so did Northern Ireland. If Britain had a Conservative Government, Northern Ireland got Conservative legislation. Hume considered Northern Ireland to be unique in Western Europe in that they had one and a quarter million people in a so-called democracy who had no power to decide what sort of society they wished to live in. Such a situation would be a fundamental cause of unrest in any society because the desire and right to self-determination was fundamental in any democracy. And, indeed, the unrest evident among the Unionist population had its roots in the same problem as instanced by the 'UDI mentality'. The last few months had established all too clearly where the power lay. But since 15 August 1969 'we have had no Government in Northern Ireland. For a Government that cannot control law and order is not a government. The troops are still in the streets – a reminder of our failure to rule ourselves.' A second and equally important weakness in the Government of Ireland Act was the one that had directly contributed to the present disturbances: there were almost no guarantees in the 'constitution' to ensure the rights of all citizens. One would have thought that such guarantees were essential in a community with a clear minority problem. Section 5 of the Government of Ireland Act 1920 required immediate amendment to guarantee civil rights in all fields that had been in question for the past year. This would involve incorporating the European Convention on Human Rights into this section and extending it to include discrimination in local Government electoral law and public and semi-public sectors – as the Council of Europe was at that time discussing as an option. But while the constitutional question was allowed to remain the party political issue in Northern Ireland, the hopes of moving away from fixed political positions into normal politics was dim. For there was no chance of the Unionist Party casting aside sectarianism as a political weapon. Their whole past was built upon it. Their whole future depended upon it. Many Unionists, believed Hume, seemed to feel that those who held that the Border needed to be removed should be outlawed and that they were automatically disloyal citizens. It was time, declared Hume, that loyalty should be defined. For loyalty meant loyalty to the state, loyalty to its people and anyone who believed that the people's best interests were served by an alternative constitution were being absolutely loyal. The Government of Ireland Act, therefore, had to be brought out of cold storage and openly discussed. There was now an opportunity to challenge those Unionists who claimed that they wanted a society in the North that would be free from sectarian bitterness and strife. If they did they would support Hume's call for the roots of the problem to be examined. Therefore, in the coming months Hume called for a concentration on the causes, not the symptoms, of the problem.[74]

Hume argued that one of the failures of those who advocated the removal of the Border by peaceful means was to analyse the meaning of the Border and to spell out detailed policies for it. Irish unity did not mean the unity of a piece of earth but unity of the people. Therefore all policies should be geared to removing sectarian barriers. Perhaps one of the reasons for the failure to spell out detailed policies in the past was that it would necessarily mean accepting ideas and structures which were emotionally unpopular but which were necessary if they were to build the understanding required to produce a united people. Sectarianism was the real curse of society in the North. Hume found that most people in politics would not come out clearly as to whether they wanted Northern Ireland to govern itself or whether there should be Direct Rule from London. Those who wanted Direct Rule were opening up the prospect of evils which might be worse than at present. Northern Ireland could become an outpost of London. In the North there were a large group of people who believed that the country should be reunited. Their feeling went beyond the bounds of logic and could not be eradicated. There was also a large group who had no identity, such as the Prime Minister, who was afraid to say whether he was Irish or British. That confusion ran through the whole community.[75] He was referring to Chichester-Clark's statement, in an interview, that he did not know whether he was British or Irish. It did not occur to Hume that Chichester-Clark did not know because he was so comfortable with being *both* British and Irish. Instead, Hume argued that the Prime Minister's confusion ran through the whole Unionist community.[76] Hume compared the Unionist ruling classes and their supporters in Northern Ireland to the white ruling elites in Rhodesia and South Africa. He pointed out what he considered the basic contradictions within Unionism, scrutinizing the link between Britain and the Unionists, and asking why many parts of the North were 'culturally dead today, and are dull uninteresting places'. There was little evidence of any real traditional culture amongst Unionists. Their 'hysterical outpourings on garble walls, or the red, white and blue kerbstones' were 'pathetic evidence of all to which they have to cling. It is really little wonder that there should be such confusion amongst them about their identity.'[77] Whether the SDLP's colour scheme should be more Green or Red was a problem to be decided at another time. For now Catholics had a dynamic and articulate new political party to represent them.

A NEW GOVERNMENT IN LONDON

There were other changes afoot as well in, and outside, Northern Ireland. It was in late June that the Army almost lost control of Belfast as the city came close to open communal warfare. It allowed the Provisional IRA to redeem themselves and demonstrate that they could be the protectors of the Catholic community. The political personnel in London confronted with this situation were no longer the Labour principals – Wilson, Callaghan or Healy. In June 1970, Edward Heath became the new Prime Minister of the United Kingdom: he appointed Reginald Maudling as Home Secretary; Sir Alec Douglas-Home as Foreign Secretary; and Lord Carrington as Defence Secretary. As the son of a skilled carpenter and former maid in Broadstairs, Kent, Heath's achievement in becoming Conservative leader has rightly been described as exceptional. From grammar school to Oxford and then on to wartime service in the artillery, he passed equal top into the Civil Service in 1946 but a year later became a Conservative candidate. Elected MP for Bexley, in 1950, he was a founder-member of the One Nation group and a confirmed Europhile. Heath rose rapidly within the Tory Party: a Whip in 1951; Chief Whip in 1955 playing a key role in preserving party unity in the aftermath of Suez; he entered the Cabinet as Labour Minister in 1959; and he became deputy to Lord Home at the Foreign Office as Lord Privy Seal with special responsibility for Britain's negotiations to join the European Common Market in 1961. After supporting Douglas-Home as Harold Macmillan's successor, Heath became President of the Board of Trade. After the Tory defeat of 1964, he made his reputation when he replaced Reginald Maudling as Shadow Chancellor and savaged Callaghan's Budget of 1965. His combative style won him the first ever Tory leadership contest in July 1965, beating Maudling and Enoch Powell. Heath personified a new, less class-bound Toryism but his managerial approach always lacked inspiration. On television he looked wooden. He was also a bachelor, with interests in classical music and sailing. Despite the Tories' heavy defeat in the 1966 Election, Heath appeared vindicated, soon afterwards, following his warnings over Labour's running of the economy. His main priority upon his surprise election victory was securing British entry into the EEC.[78]

It was to Reggie Maudling, as the new Home Secretary, that the onerous responsibility for Northern Ireland was to fall. Educated at Merchant Taylors' School and Oxford, Maudling spent the War in RAF Intelligence and the Air Secretary's private office. After the War he worked on *The Industrial Charter*, often seen as the first step in Conservative acquiescence in the post-war Attlee consensus. Elected to Parliament for Barnet in 1950, he joined Heath in the One Nation group in 1951 and was promoted to the Front Bench in 1952 as a Civil Aviation Minister. The following December he was appointed Economic Secretary to the Treasury and in 1955 to Supply Minister. As Paymaster General, Maudling joined the Cabinet in 1957. Instrumental in establishing the European Free Trade Association, he served at the Board of Trade, before proving a radical Colonial Secretary, pushing through a constitution for Northern Rhodesia (Zambia) and devising a land settlement scheme for Kenya. The peak of his career came in 1962 when he was appointed Chancellor of the Exchequer. His Chancellorship was controversial due to the reflationary 'dash for growth' policies he employed. Having lost out to Heath in the leadership contest of 1965, Maudling became Deputy Leader but never quite regained his old confidence.[79] Alexander Frederick Home, the 14th Earl of Home, was the last aristocrat to hold the highest office. From the Scottish Borders, he was educated at Eton and Oxford and elected MP, under the courtesy title of Lord Dunglass, for Lanark in 1931. Appointed Private Secretary to Neville Chamberlain, who was Chancellor of the Exchequer, he accompanied him in the same capacity as Prime Minister to Munich in 1938 (and was a firm supporter of Appeasement). After a brief spell in Churchill's Caretaker Government, in 1945, he lost his seat in the Labour landslide of the same year before being re-elected in 1950. He succeeded to his father's title in 1951, becoming Minister Resident in Scotland following the Tories' election victory that year. His political breakthrough came with his appointment as Foreign Secretary in 1960. His calm assurance was evident during the Cuban Missile Crisis as he was present when President Kennedy phoned Macmillan with the latter acting as a trusted sounding board. Following the Prime Minister's resignation in 1963, Douglas-Home 'emerged' as an unlikely Premier following Macmillan's determination to prevent Rab Butler succeeding him and reported American unease at the prospect of Lord Hailsham as Premier. Having renounced his peerage he became Sir Alec Douglas-Home and was elected MP for Kinross and West Perthshire. This confirmed the 'grouse-moor' image of the Tories which Harold Wilson used so effectively in the run-up to the 1964 General Election. The expected Conservative defeat, however, was much smaller than many had predicted.[80] Finally, Peter Carrington, the 6th Lord Carrington, was appointed Secretary of State for Defence; he had first reached the Cabinet under Douglas-Home in 1963. He claimed descent from an 'honest Nottingham grocer with whom people often lent their money till he became a banker'.[81]

The election of the new Government did witness a shift in Westminster–Stormont relations. The most obvious difference between the approaches of the Conservative and Labour Governments was in their attitude to the status of the Northern Ireland Government. As Heath explained to the

Taoiseach, Jack Lynch, during an ad hoc meeting in New York in October 1970, the policy of his Government was to demonstrate its support of Chichester-Clark and to make clear that Stormont was not a puppet of the British Government. For this reason, unlike the pattern that had developed under Labour, there was no question of summoning Chichester-Clark to London when the Tories took office after the Election; instead the Home Secretary had gone to Stormont to consult with Chichester-Clark.[82] This involved a new mindset in London the outcome of which was avoiding Direct Rule at almost any cost. This was the crucial change. Callaghan later claimed that, had Chichester-Clark moved to the right or been forced to resign, he had decided that he would 'not hesitate to introduce direct rule and I was not bluffing about it'. Callaghan's intention had been to revive his old Round Table Conference idea of 1969 to try to devise some new constitutional settlement on the basis that, despite the civil unrest, 'we were still operating against a background of relative peace and quiet and a constitutional conference in that atmosphere would have stood a much better chance of success than one called after hundreds of murders and shootings and explosions'. Callaghan knew that 'we could not sit back and rely on the reform programme to solve all our problems'. That, in Callaghan's view, 'was to be Maudling's mistake when he became Home Secretary'.[83] As far as Callaghan was concerned, the result of the General Election 'was a disaster for Northern Ireland'. Not only were the initiatives Labour intended not followed up but the break in continuity 'came at the very worst time for the success of the struggle to prevent the Provisional IRA from capturing the sympathy of the minority'.[84] Callaghan's attitude to Stormont and the use of troops was, as he put it years later:

> Look here, they can be used in aid of the civil power of course, but if a riot of the kind of proportions that you envisage took place in Durham it would be the British government that would take charge and not the Durham County Council. And frankly on this basis I regarded them [Stormont] as much like the London County Council.

The population of Northern Ireland was a million-and-a-half. 'We weren't going to hand over to a government – especially of that complexion.' And he was unsure as to how long the existing settlement could have continued:

> The honeymoon was getting a little dated by the time the election came along. And I don't know how long we could have kept it up. It would have been necessary to have a Northern Ireland Office... One of the problems was, I think, that Quintin Hailsham [Shadow Home Secretary] wasn't appointed [Home Secretary] but that Reggie Maudling was... and on the night the election was over, Quintin... rang me up and said, 'Look what are we going to do and how do I handle this? I'm going to become Home Secretary.' I went in some detail with him and we arranged to meet and I said I'd have a long talk with him about it and I told him what I thought were the things that were going to happen. The next thing that happened was that he wasn't appointed.

Reggie Maudling was... But Reggie Maudling was too laid back. He simply didn't believe in this kind of day-to-day supervision.[85]

In fact, Callaghan had the Home Office draw up a draft memorandum, in May 1970, to consider the appointment of a resident minister in Belfast following the suspension of Stormont. But, the memorandum also stated that this was for discussion only.[86]

A key Home Office official, however, presents the case for the defence in regard to Maudling:

> Indeed I think Reggie Maudling is much criticised for not being active in dealing with the situation. He was in fact prescient about what was possible and what was not possible. He said privately that, whatever happens in the meantime, they will have to try internment, and it won't work and we shan't like it. Then there will be Direct Rule, and that won't work either, if what you mean by work is solve the security problem and bring all the disorders to an end.[87]

Ironically, a psychological clue as to why, perhaps, the Tories were so reluctant to introduce Direct Rule is provided by Callaghan:

> There was common ground between all parties, including the Liberal Party, that it would be very stupid indeed for the British to get themselves involved in Northern Ireland as long as there was a government there that was carrying on. We'd all had our fingers burned before. The memories of 1921 were still alive.[88]

Here it was a case of the British having long memories – something the Irish often accused them of not having with regard to Ireland.

A key question we must ask is: was there any change in security policy by the new Government? This has long been a key belief among many Catholics in Northern Ireland. Certainly, it was not long before the new Government faced its first – of many – Northern Ireland decisions. This was whether reinforcements were to be sent to Ulster in response to the GOC's advice that 'we may run into serious trouble in mid-July during the Orange Day period'. Heath was informed, on 21 June, that to add some five more military units – as was being requested by the Army – to the nine already in Ulster was a major step; but all the intelligence reports were pessimistic. The Prime Minister was also advised by the Cabinet Secretary, Sir Burke Trend, that his first Ministerial meeting on Northern Ireland should perhaps devote a few moments to considering the longer-term prospects in Ulster. Trend believed there were perhaps three ways in which the situation could develop:

(a) It could improve of its own accord. But this would be so nearly a miracle that we can perhaps disregard it.
(b) It could remain much as it is – stabilised only by the presence of British

troops and trembling on the edge of disaster but never quite tipping over. The resultant burden on ourselves, in terms of both men and money, would be so intolerable if it were maintained indefinitely that we ought not to contemplate it if it can be avoided.

(c) It could get worse and finally tip over the edge – the Northern Ireland Government proving incapable of holding the position, civil war breaking out within the Province and Dublin being compelled to intervene. This would present us with a political and constitutional crisis of the first order; and certain very secret contingency plans have already been prepared against this possibility.[89]

With this unsettling series of scenarios before him, Heath met with his Ministers the next day. Attending were Maudling, Douglas-Home, Carrington and Quintin Hogg the Lord Chancellor. Sir Geoffrey Baker reported that Freeland envisaged reinforcements being required for about a fortnight, although this question and the related question of whether additional forces would be required in connection with the Protestant celebrations in Londonderry in August would depend on the course of events in the Belfast area. The CGS said that Freeland had considered, in consultation with the Northern Ireland Government, the possibility of banning the Belfast demonstrations but had reached the conclusion that this would make the security situation more, rather than less, explosive. He had also considered the desirability of diverting the processions from their traditional – and provocative – routes but had rejected this for similar reasons and also because no such restriction had been imposed on the Catholic and Nationalist demonstrations at Easter. The Ministers agreed that the present situation, in which one faction was allowed to carry out provocative marches and demonstrations in the territory of the other, was an invitation to disorder and should not be allowed to continue indefinitely. If, as seemed likely, marches and demonstrations could not be banned altogether, efforts should be made to route them in such a way as to prevent the Protestants trailing their coats in Catholic areas and vice versa. It was noted that the military had already had this point under consideration. But they agreed that to attempt at this stage to divert marches from their traditional routes, and a fortiori to ban them altogether, would create a situation which could be contained, if at all, only by the use of forces even larger than those currently contemplated. In particular, a high degree of tension would be generated if the Security Forces barred the traditional routes and the marchers tried to force their way back on to them. It was thought possible, however, in the light of the studies being undertaken, to secure the adoption of less provocative routes in 1971.

So, the Conservative Ministers agreed to the despatch of military reinforcements. More generally, they concluded that the advent of a new British Government afforded an opportunity of placing relations between the United Kingdom and Northern Ireland on a fresh footing. The Protestants could not doubt the strength of the British Government's commitment to the integrity of Northern Ireland. If their apprehensions on this score could be allayed, Catholic apprehensions also should decrease and there should be a general lowering of tension. At the same time, it was important that 'we should not only do all we could to maintain the momentum of reform but should also take every opportunity of building up the authority and position of the Northern Ireland Government'. There was general approval of a suggestion that Maudling should take an early opportunity of visiting Northern Ireland both for this purpose and in order to acquaint himself with the situation at first hand.[90] These policy decisions are important to note, for, in the aftermath of subsequent events, Catholics were to claim that the advent of a new Conservative Government heralded a shift to a concentration on a repressive security policy at the expense of the reform programme. This was incorrect. Perhaps, as Callaghan suggested, there should have been a change in political strategy; but there was no change in British security policy. What changed was the deterioration in the security situation – Ulster not Westminster was the source.

Violence first broke out in Derry. On 22 June, Bernadette Devlin's appeal against her six month sentence for her part in the Battle of the Bogside was dismissed. On 26 June she was arrested at a road block on her way to a meeting and taken to Armagh women's prison. Supporters claimed that she had intended to give herself up later. Following the arrest there was severe rioting in Derry where a crowd pelted troops with stones and petrol bombs before the soldiers used CS gas to break up the riot.[91] In Belfast rioting erupted as Orangemen paraded down the Crumlin Road passing the Catholic Ardoyne. Insults from Protestants were answered with bottles and stones from Catholics. The next day – 27 June – was the scene for a much bigger parade. Orange Lodges from the Shankill, the Bone, Cliftonville and Oldpark all joined forces. The route they were to follow passed the Catholic areas of the Clonard and Springfield Road. Rioting broke out. It spread across the city. Martin Meehan of the Provisional IRA claimed that Protestants fired first. Three Protestants were shot dead by the Provisionals who saw themselves acting in a defensive role against Protestant aggression. More importantly, many Catholics saw them acting in a similar fashion. Meehan recalled:

> The IRA had proved what they said they were going to do, they had done. The date – 27th of June 1970 – is more significant for that than anything else. As a result, the whole broad spectrum of the nationalist people actually supported what the IRA was doing. Everybody, man, woman and child came out and supported us in any way possible. I never saw support like that in my life. It was unbelievable.[92]

Across in east Belfast tension was also high in the Catholic area of Ballymacarrett, the Short Strand. Its 6,000 population constituted a Catholic island in a Protestant sea dominated by the shipyards of Harland and Wolff and the Shorts aircraft factory. On that Saturday evening, as the Gertrude Street Orange Band returned home, stones were thrown as a Tricolour was waved from the Catholic Seaford Street. Shots were exchanged. Tom O'Donnell of the Provisional Brigade Staff began to issue orders for weapons to be lifted from dumps concealed in homes and yards within the district. A company of

Provisionals, numbering twelve in total, were mustered together in Lowry Street, close to an adjoining school and church grounds. Alongside them the local Citizen's Defence Committee (CDC) men were deployed in small sections to various points across the district. Jim Gibney recalled:

> I saw neighbours, people I knew, coming down the street carrying rifles. I was just dumbstruck by this experience. I'd never seen such a thing before. They were much older than me, of course. I watched them take up position on the corner and fire up the street that I lived in. I was fifteen going on sixteen and it was incredible to witness this at first hand. On one level it was exciting of course, because of what you were witnessing. It was something that you only see on the television or in films. The gun battle lasted right through into the early hours of the following morning.

Across the city, Billy McKee was attending evening Mass at Clonard. Afterwards he called at the home of Proinsias MacAirt who told his OC that trouble was still on-going over in Ballymacarrett. McKee decided to go and assess the situation himself. Arriving around 10 p.m., McKee and some comrades found Tom O'Donnell who reported, amid periodic shooting around St Matthew's Roman Catholic Church in the Short Strand, that the situation was going to deteriorate further. A car was despatched back to the Falls to return with six M1 Carbines each to be accompanied by five full magazines. McKee remained in the area and was joined by Bill Kelly, the 3rd Battalion OC. As petrol bombs landed close to the church, setting a sexton's house on fire, the defenders' first action was to clear the petrol bombers from the roofs of the buildings opposite the church. This was done by gunfire from a defensive position which swept across the tops of the buildings. The Protestant attackers retreated and a hail of gunfire was sent down the Protestant streets facing the church.

After midnight McKee asked Paddy Kennedy MP to approach Mountpottinger Barracks to find out if troops could be deployed into the district. The reply was that troops would be deployed at 1.05 a.m. McKee instructed O'Donnell to have weapons off the street and back in their dumps as soon as possible. After this was done McKee remained in the grounds of the church. But the troops who arrived were only of platoon strength and as soon as they came under petrol bomb attack they withdrew. There was now nothing between McKee and a hostile mob. The first person to arrive alongside McKee was Henry McIlhone, from Sheriff Street, a 33-year-old scaffold rigger. He was not a member of either IRA faction. McKee instructed him to position himself behind a tree looking toward the burning sexton's house and the Newtownards Road and to open fire at anyone coming toward him through the grounds. Shortly afterwards two men were challenged approaching through the grounds from the Newtownards Road; McKee told McIlhone to open fire with his revolver, which he did. He missed the targets. McKee then turned back to speak to McIlhone; as he did so there was a thud in his back causing him to spin and reach toward the wall for support. McKee had been shot in the back with the bullet going up through his neck. Holding himself against the wall for support he heard a loud thump beside him. It was McIlhone hitting the ground, shot in the throat. Two men approached and, looking at the amount of blood on McKee's white shirt, thought he was dead; one man fired another shot anyway, hitting him in the arm. As he lay there, still conscious, a Volunteer rushed over to him. McKee told him McIlhone was shot and to retrieve his revolver. It was just after 2 a.m. when both men were moved into a nearby school and into the hands of the Knights of Malta first aid team. They were taken to the Mater Hospital. Around St Matthew's the battle continued with the defenders gaining the upper hand. Alongside the Provisionals were two Officials from the Falls along with the Short Strand's own Official unit. Across the Albertbridge, in the Markets area, other IRA men assembled, less than 10 minutes from the Short Strand, to reinforce the district should a full-scale attack be mounted. By 5 a.m. the gunfire had ceased. As British troops moved along Bryson Street they found St Matthew's intact. The Provisionals had emerged from their first major engagement victorious,[93] defending Catholics from Protestant mobs.

Protestants, of course, saw these incidents differently: they were the victims of attacks by IRA gunmen. Protestants remained angry at what they saw as Republican propaganda, insisting that they were defending themselves from Nationalist attacks. The journalist Peter Taylor found that, thirty years after the event, Protestants were still enraged that commentators such as him had fallen for what they believed was 'Republican propaganda'.[94] According to Protestant accounts, in the Short Strand it was they who were attacked by a Catholic mob. They claimed that in forcing the Catholics back into the Short Strand they were lured into a carefully prepared trap. The confrontation quickly escalated into an exchange of gunfire. Robert Neill, aged 38, was shot around 2 a.m.. He was hit while standing at the corner of his own street, Central Street off the Newtownards Road. James McCurrie was shot by an IRA sniper during the same clashes. Elsewhere in the city, Protestants again saw themselves as the victims of Republican violence. In north Belfast a crowd had poured out of Hooker Street on the Catholic side. A similar crowd emerged from Herbert Street, throwing bottles and stones. In the ensuing riot up to 200 shots were fired. Alexander Gould, aged 18, was one of three Protestants shot by Republicans during rioting in the Crumlin Road area. William Kincaid, aged 28, was shot at Disraeli Street. A man came out of Hooker Street and knelt on one knee and fired into a crowd in Disraeli Street. Kincaid was killed by a single gunshot wound to the chest. Daniel Loughlins, aged 32, was shot by two men who came out of Herbert Street. John Reid, aged 46, died in hospital six days after being hit on the head by a missile thrown from a Catholic crowd. He was injured at the corner of Mayo Street and Springfield Road, apparently as he watched the rioting.[95]

On Sunday morning, 28 June, the Joint Security Committee (JSC) met to consider the situation. The sense of crisis was palpable. Chichester-Clark, acting in his capacity as Minister of Home Affairs – Robert Porter had resigned for health reasons in March and the Prime Minister had taken up the portfolio – informed the JSC that he had met with representatives of the Orange Order who had said that it would be a practical impossibility to call off or restrict that afternoon's parade at such short notice. Efforts were being made to limit, as much as possible in the short time available, the parading of bands to assembly points and afterwards away from dispersal points. Sir Ian Freeland warned that his troops would be fully committed in other directions in the afternoon and could not possibly protect this parade. It would have to be covered by the police to the limit of their unarmed role. The JSC then approved Freeland's decision that 'all civilians seen carrying firearms or using firearms in any way whatsoever are liable to be shot without warning'. Considerable military reinforcements were earmarked to arrive from Britain within twenty-four hours. The JSC agreed that it would be impossible to impose an absolute curfew. Martial law was not to be considered 'at this stage'. Freeland reported that east Belfast was experiencing an uneasy calm but the situation was serious. 'Troublesome' areas would be 'flushed out' as soon as possible. The Ardoyne was being searched while Ballymurphy and New Barnsley were also experiencing an uneasy calm. In Belfast there had been forty-four arrests. Three soldiers had gunshot wounds; five soldiers had other injuries. Some 264 CS grenades and 1,331 CS cartridges had been used. Five civilians were dead while fifty-eight civilians had gunshot wounds and a further fifty-four other injuries. Most of the gunshot wounds had been sustained in east Belfast and the Crumlin Road. Incendiarism in Belfast had been 'sophisticated and nasty'. In Londonderry there had been no shooting but two soldiers had been seriously injured. Forty-two people had been arrested while seven CS grenades and 365 CS cartridges had been used. Chichester-Clark raised the possibility of granting official status to vigilante – that was Protestant – activities: he suggested that they might be brought under some authority such as the RUC Reserve. A comment scribbled on the JSC minutes in London considered this 'very dangerous'.[96] The next day Freeland was able to report that the situation in Belfast was now quieter. Army resources were still stretched but things were under better control. But the GOC emphasized that it was physically impossible, with the resources at his disposal, to protect a whole city against widespread attack as had been experienced over the weekend. Without prior intelligence about subversive activities it was unreasonable to expect an immediate military response to all attacks.[97]

Following on from the JSC decision as to when troops could open fire, HQNI had signalled all Army Brigades and major units that soldiers were to be instructed to open fire against anyone seen carrying a weapon in an area in which there was or had been firing taking place; and against anyone carrying a weapon 'in quiet areas' who refused to halt when called upon to do so. As for petrol bombs, these were considered 'lethal weapons'. While every effort was to be made to deal with petrol bombers short of opening fire, if this was not successful and if petrol bomb attacks continued against troops and property, fire might be opened after a deliberate warning had been given in the areas concerned. Once this warning had been given, anyone throwing a petrol bomb in that immediate area 'may be treated in the same way as a sniper'.[98] This signal was clarified on 30 June to include opening fire on anyone seen carrying a weapon where there was a 'reasonable suspicion' that he was about to use his weapon for offensive purposes.[99] This marked a considerable relaxation of the rules of engagement but reflected the crisis facing the Army in holding the line. Fortunately, by the evening there had been a significant reduction in trouble. New tactics were being employed by the Army to prevent crowd assembly: air reconnaissance was being used to spot assemblies and 'striking forces' were on call to 'sort them out'.[100] Nevertheless, it had been a bad weekend. The following day, 500 Catholics were expelled from the shipyards by their Protestant co-workers.[101]

In his report to London, Ronnie Burroughs recorded that 'there is no doubt whatsoever that the Catholics started the rioting'. Catholic leaders could not deny this after the first night's rioting. The Orange procession had been allowed along what was regarded as Catholic territory as a compromise. In return the Orange Order surrendered a number of minor parades in return for one large procession along a route which they regarded as traditional. The assessment of the security authorities had been that the dangers of rerouting were greater than those attendant on pushing the Orange parade through. This, however, was only the 'primer to the subsequent explosion' in which both sects took part. But, concluded Burroughs, if the Scarman Tribunal – now sitting and investigating the disorders of 1969 – was demonstrating that in the previous year the Protestants were the main aggressors, on this occasion there was convincing evidence that the Catholic side was initially to blame and probably still was. Guns had been fired on both sides. But, disputing Republican accounts, Burroughs was clear that the first shots were fired from the Catholic side. The IRA was often considered a bogey invented by Protestants, he noted, but the activities of the last two nights so closely approximated to advance intelligence that 'we must assume that the Brady [Provisional] group of the IRA had a large hand in fomenting and exploiting the recent troubles... The sophisticated techniques practised last night in burning down large English-based business premises fit into the pattern.' During talks with Catholic leaders on the eve of the troubles 'they told me they were losing control of the situation. The fact that they have temporarily ceased to bombard me with accusations or pleas, convinces me that they acknowledge where the principal fault lies. They are ashamed of republican activities and in a state of shock.'[103] The casualty totals are revealing: six people were killed (five Protestants and one Catholic) and 113 wounded, including fifty-four Protestants, four Catholics, fifty-two soldiers and three members of the RUC.[104] While the Provisionals have portrayed this as a defensive action – and in part it was – the events of June 1970, when one steps back and looks at all the evidence clearly became offensive in nature. The discrepancy in the numbers of Protestants and members of the Security Forces wounded is quite staggering when compared to that of Catholics.

THE FALLS ROAD CURFEW

The Protestants were angry – as Reggie Maudling had found out when he made his first visit to Northern Ireland as Home Secretary. Chichester-Clark began by pointing out that 'law and order was the issue fundamental to the credibility of the Northern Ireland Government which was now at a low ebb'. Robert Porter, the soon-to-resign Minister of Home Affairs, spoke of 'an incident in which, it was alleged, five gunmen stepped out of a crowd and not only fired across the road into a Protestant crowd but were seen to reload in the presence of the military before firing again without any action being taken against them'. The Minister of Development, Brian Faulkner, said that he had personally visited the disturbed areas and had encountered demands by Catholics and Protestants alike that 'the police and army should deal toughly with hooligans'. Maudling had the same hostile reception when he met UUP backbenchers. The GOC later explained to him how, in view of the RUC's low morale, only the Army was in a position to 'be tough' and there were two options open to him: 'He could either open fire on rioters or ask for sufficient soldiers to enable him to keep order by a massive military presence.' He rejected the first alternative, as it would only lead to IRA retaliation and a worsening of both the Army's morale and image. He therefore appealed to the Government 'to face up to the necessity of sending as many men as were required to Northern Ireland in order to enable the peace to be kept'. His task, he went on, would be made easier if the use of new weapons, such as rubber baton rounds, could be authorised. Turning to the upcoming Orange marches, Freeland said that 'the three Bs...bands, by-standers, and booze' were at the root of the problem.[104] It was understandable that Maudling, as he left what he might have thought was still the seventeenth century for the late twentieth century and 'normal' politics, remarked that Northern Ireland was 'a bloody awful country'[105] and asked for a large Scotch.

The violent sequel to the June rioting came only a few days later. The Falls Road Curfew has been seen as one of the defining moments in relations between the Army and the Catholic community, particularly in Belfast. The operation started at 4.30 p.m. on Friday 3 July as a single search for arms, of the kind, in the GOC's description, 'constantly and impartially' carried out by the Security Forces in all parts of Northern Ireland. A 'large cache of arms' was discovered and removed by 5.30 p.m. by a small party of the RUC and two platoons of troops. Six minutes later, 'heavy organised rioting' erupted.[106] However, the account, relayed by the journalist, Simon Winchester, of *The Guardian*, told a different story: the cache was only fifteen pistols, a rifle, a Schmeisser sub-machine gun and some ammunition – 'It was, by IRA standards, a small arsenal.' By 5.30 p.m. the soldiers were ready to go. Three Land Rovers made it away but the lorry loads of Royal Scots were not so fortunate. Catholic crowds jostled with the infantrymen as they tried to get back to their lorries and one-ton Humbers (Armoured Personnel Carriers [APCs] and nicknamed Pigs). The soldiers used their batons. The crowd began to throw stones. A Pig reversed suddenly into the mob and one man was crushed on some cast-iron railing stakes. He died later in hospital.[107] As the Central Citizen's Defence Committee (CCDC) subsequently pointed out, since the barricades had come down in September, the Lower Falls had been the only sensitive area in Belfast that had been completely free of serious street disturbances. The CCDC complained that it was only after the last Army vehicle in the initial search was driving away that 'some stones' were hurled. Instead of driving on, the vehicle stopped and immediately CS gas was fired. On several occasions stewards and priests again had the situation under control; but on each occasion the 'small silent groups of people', stewards and priests, were showered with CS gas. The CCDC found it 'difficult not to reach the conclusion that the British Army had no interest in allowing the Lower Falls to remain peaceful'. The situation then rapidly deteriorated toward tragedy as 'both sides' overreacted.[108]

But from the Army's point of view, what had started as a riot quickly escalated into something more sinister. After the events of the previous few days there was no question that Army searches for arms should cease. The 2 Battalion The Queen's Regiment, which had been deployed to the Falls Road along Albert Street at approximately 5.30 p.m., found a large hostile crowd rioting at the junction of Raglan Street and Albert Street. Armour was sent in at about 6 p.m. to disperse the crowd. The crowd was pushed down Raglan Street and side streets. The crowd at this stage was throwing rocks, bottles and metal grating and firing catapults at the troops. The troops were forced to withdraw from Raglan Street and took up a position on Albert Street. At this point about six hand grenades were thrown at the troops. They dismounted from their armoured vehicle and took over positions at the junction of Raglan Street and Albert Street. At least two more hand grenades were thrown. A bus was driven across the mouth of Raglan Street and was set on fire. After two baton charges the Officer Commanding withdrew the company to the Falls Road in an attempt to take the heat off the situation. The crowd followed the troops up Albert Street shouting 'Easy-Easy' throwing bricks and missiles. After securing the Albert Street/Falls Road junction the troops remained there until 22.00 hours. The troops were then told to get into their armoured vehicles and drive down to the junction of Albert Street and Raglan Street to secure the area for the night. On deployment at Raglan Street the troops came under fire from Servia Street. They returned fire. The Sergeant in charge of the sub-section returning fire had two of his men hit by gunfire. Shots were then fired at the troops from the side streets of Raglan Street. Fire was returned. Shots were directed at the Officer Commanding and his troops from the chimney stack of a house approximately 100 yards further down Raglan Street. The troops engaged this sniper for some time. The sniper moved his position in the darkness. Ferrets – light armoured vehicles – were used to spotlight him. After returning fire the firing from the sniper ceased. Sporadic firing continued from the Raglan Street area. Heavy automatic fire in Servia Street was directed at the troops. At this stage a sniper – discharging what appeared to be a .45 revolver or a large calibre weapon – opened fire from the chimney stack of a house at the junction of Ross Place/Albert Street. After a game of cat and mouse with the sniper, who was moving around, a Corporal shouted that a Private thought he had hit him. This was about 2.30 or 3 a.m. About an hour and half later an investigation troop went with a section and carried out a search for a body. The body of an unidentified male was recovered.[109]

The Provisionals had taken the initiative but had then withdrawn, leaving the Officials to engage with the Army.[110] Billy McKee had previously telephoned the

Official IRA commander in the Lower Falls and offered assistance but the offer had been declined. 'We're going to take on the British army,' McKee had been told. Some Provisionals ignored the Officials' rejection of help and decided to engage the Army. The initiative came from Charlie Hughes, commander of D Company, the Provisional unit on the Lower Falls. The Provisionals later claimed that most of the fifteen British soldiers wounded in the subsequent engagement were shot by Volunteers of D Company. Brendan Hughes, soon to emerge as a key Provisional commander himself, and a cousin of Charlie Hughes, recalled:

> Word went around that the British army were coming in to take the IRA's weapons and they were going to leave the Catholic people, the nationalist people, undefended. Charlie said the curfew was going to be broken and that he was going to do it. That night a group of people left his house and there was a major gun battle in Cyprus Street. It didn't last very long because the people [the Provisionals] had only a couple of rifles, one Thompson submachine gun, and a couple of short arms. I think the ammunition ran out and there wasn't any more. So people had to get away but there wasn't anywhere to go. They ran over yard walls and into houses to take cover. I ended up in someone's house and that's where I was over the period of the curfew, sitting there and not knowing when we're going to get out or what was going to happen.[111]

During the confrontation the Army imposed movement controls which were described as a 'curfew'. It lasted for thirty-four hours, except for a two hour break to allow shopping, over an area of the Catholic Lower Falls, covering around fifty streets. MPs Paddy Devlin and Paddy Kennedy and Fathers Padraig Murphy, Teggert, O'Donnell and McCabe complained that every time they got a bad situation cooled down more gas had been plunged in – in some cases into streets where there was no one. People who were friendly to the military were becoming incensed with the way the latter reacted to a situation, said Devlin:

> I think the whole operation has been brought about to try and help Chichester-Clark in his present critical position in Government...Chichester-Clark thinks the whole thing is running away with him. Now that he has a Government in Britain favourable to him he had now got a more favourable response to try and engage the Catholic population with the military and so hold the Protestant backlash that everybody knows is coming.

Devlin attacked Freeland for refusing to stop the use of gas, after being asked repeatedly to do so, and for refusing to withdraw his troops when it was obvious that had they been withdrawn the whole situation would have cooled down. 'He has curfewed...many streets in my constituency and says that any person found on the street will be arrested...The people are panicking. How can they come out for fresh air after gas has saturated their homes [?]. If they show their faces they will be arrested.' Kennedy described the use of gas as 'totally indiscriminate'. No such measures had been taken on the Shankill Road and Newtownards Road after 'worse trouble' by hostile Protestant crowds.[112] Devlin traced the origin of the military operation to the aftermath of a Stormont debate, in mid-week, when 'extremist Unionist MPs made "call to arms" speeches to their extremist supporters'.[113] He had been put against a wall in Plevna Street and told by soldiers of The Devon and Dorset Regiment: 'You will be shot if you turn round.' After being arrested he was also told: 'We will beat your brains out if you don't shut up.' Later an officer from the regiment apologised to Devlin and explained to him that the troops had had a 'trying time' and appealed to him to 'let bygones be bygones'.[114]

HQNI presented a different perspective. They informed London that the Army operation was not an elaborately pre-planned cordon/curfew/search exercise: 'It was a battle.' The Army acknowledged that it was 'quite inevitable that hardships were caused to thousands of innocent people' but told the MOD that 'the responsibility lies squarely upon the gunmen and their hooligan accomplices'. Complaints that in a battle of this kind soldiers were rough and ready, abusive, threatened to shoot, and caused minor damage in homes in the course of searches, 'are simply unacceptable'.[115] Furthermore, twelve soldiers were wounded by gunshots and six by grenades. As Freeland explained, a street battle of this nature inevitably and regrettably involved many innocent people; but gunmen had to be evicted from houses they had occupied. Once the Army were attacked the military considered it necessary to conduct a thorough search for arms in the course of and immediately after the battle. Therefore, from Freeland's perspective, people had to be kept off the streets partly for their own safety and partly to allow for searches for arms to proceed unimpeded and without risk of renewed rioting. Restrictions were therefore imposed in order that the Army could discharge its responsibility to maintain the peace. Thus arms searches and searching continued well into the following day and the restrictions were accordingly maintained until the afternoon of Saturday 4 July when people where allowed to leave their houses to buy food. Restrictions were then re-imposed for the evening to ensure that renewed rioting did not break out, and were finally lifted at 9 a.m. on Sunday 5 July. As a result of these searches a large quantity of arms and ammunition, including fifty pistols, twenty-eight rifles, five sub-machine guns and 25,000 rounds of ammunition were seized. Freeland pointed out that a pistol, a stolen radio, and a large quantity of ammunition were found in the house in Leeson Street where the CCDC regularly met.[116] The Curfew was not a decision that originated in Westminster, from the election of a new administration: it was the product of London's 'man on the spot' – Freeland.

There were human costs as well as political ones. By the end of the curfew several people were dead. William Burns was shot by the Army as he stood with a neighbour at the doorstep of his shop. A burst of gunfire came from soldiers positioned at the nearby derelict Clonard cinema. A former member of the RAF, Charles O'Neill, aged 36, was killed when he was struck by an APC. He was apparently trying to communicate with troops at the time. The CCDC later claimed that a Saracen armoured car deliberately accelerated towards him. A bizarre state of affairs surrounded the next victim, Zbigniew Uglik, aged 24, a postman and a freelance journalist of Polish extraction living in London, who was shot by an Army sniper. Described as a 'Walter Mitty'-type character, he posed as a *Daily Telegraph* photographer. He was probably mistaken for a gunman by a soldier who fired at a figure walking along the top of a yard wall at the back of a house. Later the body of a man wearing a black polo-neck and dark trousers with a face apparently camouflaged with dark marks was found. The last fatality was Patrick Elliman, aged 62, who died on 11 July from injuries on 3 July.[117]

Not only were the deaths an immediate issue – there was also the question as to whether or not the curfew was legal. Nationalists, and Gerry Fitt in particular, led the cry that it was not. The truth was that London did not know whether Freeland had acted legally. In an attempt to find out, the Director of Law Reform in London was reduced to consulting a few statutes and text books and talking to the Attorney General and Ministry of Home Affairs on the telephone. The Director believed that the Army did possess power to impose restrictions of the kind that it did. *Stephen's History of the Criminal Law* (1883) defined Martial Law as the assumption by officers of the Crown of absolute power, exercised by military force, for the suppression of an insurrection, and the restoration of order and authority. The officers of the Crown were justified in any exertion of physical force, extending to the destruction of life and property to any extent, and in any manner, that might be required for the purpose. They were not justified in the case of cruel and excessive means, but were liable civilly or criminally for such excess. They were not justified in inflicting punishment after resistance was suppressed, and after the ordinary courts of justice could be opened. This interpretation was backed up by several other sources. It was pointed out that, should this opinion prove wrong, there was precedent for an Act of Indemnity[118] which would make the curfew retrospectively legal. Armed with this, Reggie Maudling defended the Army's actions on the basis that it had a Common Law right and duty to maintain public order and in the circumstances the arrest of anyone disobeying instructions to keep indoors was quite justified under the Common Law. Maudling pointed out that it would have been difficult to have explained the exact legal niceties in the circumstances. Entry into the Falls – Fitt had been prevented from entering – was in general not permitted until the curfew had been raised because safety could not be guaranteed, and the presence of people on the streets conflicted with the requirements of the military situation. Doctors and relief workers were allowed in only because they had a particular job that had to be done at the time. The press were taken on a conducted tour for a similar reason.[119] But this remained a fragile defence: it was only later, when a Northern Irish court ruled that the curfew was legal, that a thin veil of legality was draped over the actions taken by Freeland, unless one accepts that a state of martial law had been in force, albeit undeclared.

Of more immediate effect was the impact the actions of the troops had on the Catholics who experienced first hand the imposition of the curfew. In the aftermath there were many accusations of misbehaviour by the troops. Fitt and Devlin left for London to protest to Maudling about the alleged brutality – particularly that of Scottish troops from The Black Watch (which was believed to contain many Scots Protestants). Fitt claimed that the looting of food shops by the soldiers had left most of the side streets of the Falls without food. In an attempt to remedy this a food centre was set up in Sultan Street and within minutes of the door of the centre being opened there was a long queue of women and children (the service was provided by the Legion of Mary and the Knights of Malta). In the aftermath of battle the streets were littered with boulders and broken bottles. Children played in the streets as troops, in full battle dress, crouched behind sandbags. Heavy Army vehicles were in every street. A helicopter circled above all day. A centre was set up to record the allegations of brutality.

Mrs Mary McCann, of Pelvna Street, told of Scottish soldiers using obscene language, dashing into her house and ripping up the linoleum on the kitchen floor. They pulled out all the clothes from the wardrobe and flung them on the floor. They smashed the windows, wrenched the locks off the doors and then pulled the staircase down. William Elliott, of Leeson Street, alleged that the soldiers stole £33, two watches and a number of valuable coins. They tore the floor coverings up and damaged the furniture. Mrs Francis Carson claimed the Army broke every lock in her house and smashed the glass in the vestibule. There was no one in the house at the time. Seamus Kennedy, of Granville Street, claimed that twin sisters were ordered out of their beds by the Army and pushed out into the street. In another case a woman who was just out of hospital after a kidney operation was refused permission to go to the toilet by soldiers. After the Hallier family of Albert Street vacated their home, troops occupied it. Neighbours watched as the troops put their rifle butts through all the windows looking onto Albert Place. They also smashed the windows of Murphy's Bar next door and handed out drink to soldiers in the street. The Halliers returned to their house during the relaxation of the curfew and found that the soldiers had been sleeping in the house and tins of food had been opened and sandwiches made and a bottle of whiskey had been drunk. The front door had been kicked in. The Halliers left their home again; when they returned they found even more damage had been done. The contents of drawers had been thrown onto the floor. Locked cabinets had been forced open and some of their contents looted. £35 had been stolen and coins which Mr Hallier's son had been collecting had also been taken. Mr Hallier, a watchmaker all his life, had a workshop in the house and found his equipment was scattered all over the floor; watches and travelling clocks had been stolen. Mr Hallier's son found that his wedding ring had been taken.[120] Nor did it help when Captain John Brooke toured the area with the press in an open lorry[121] confirming an impression of Unionist triumphalism.

On 6 July Fitt, Paddy Devlin and Frank McManus, the Unity MP for Fermanagh–South Tyrone, held a crisis meeting with the Minister for Defence, in London, to voice their concerns. Fitt considered that the situation in Northern Ireland was now very dangerous, partly because whereas the Army had originally been welcomed by both sides, and it was recognized that they managed to save lives, they had now lost the support of the Catholic community. He conceded that many of those in the Falls Road would like to see the unification of Ireland and many of them possessed weapons but these were for self protection. As a supporter of the Labour Government he had expected to get more cooperation from them than from the Conservatives and this was the view shared by many of his constituents who said to him after the General Election: 'We have lost everything, but thank God we have got you.' He believed that the election of a Conservative Government had given Orangemen more courage and in particular more resolution to continue their marches. Fitt regarded the timing of the searches as inept, and complained that the military had made a show of arresting a woman in the house in which arms had been found and cited an instance in which two Scots soldiers had molested two girls. Devlin complained that the troops, by their very presence, had deliberately created a riotous situation while Fitt felt that the arms searches were biased against the Catholic sector of the community and that the Catholics were afraid of being left defenceless.[122]

As Devlin later recalled, the military, 'cock-a-hoop with their illegal takeover of the Falls', had proceeded to put the 'boot in with a vengeance'. Overnight the population turned from neutral or even sympathetic support for the military to outright hatred of everything related to the Security Forces. As the 'self-styled generals and godfathers took over in the face of this regime, Gerry Fitt and I witnessed voters and workers... turn against us to join the Provisionals. Even some of our most dedicated workers and supporters... turned against us.'[123] The mother of a future Provisional IRA Volunteer and martyr, Mairead Farrell, recalled the impact the Curfew had on her daughter, already brought up in a Republican family:

> We'd heard over the radio and TV that the shops were going to be allowed open between four and five and that all shopkeepers had to be at their premises by 2pm. I was worried because one person had arranged to come in and collect some baby clothes from our draper's shop and I thought she might need them urgently. So we decided to go down and to take some bread and milk for our relatives at the same time. When we got to Springfield Road corner, a soldier stopped us and asked us where we were going. He said we couldn't go any further... In the end he let us through but insisted on coming in the car with us. When we reached the shop he put us in and closed the door. Everyone was peering through the windows. One girl put her head right out to see what was going on. The soldier turned and shouted, 'If you don't take your head in, I'll blow it off.' And she was even a married woman with children. Mairead was horrified. She always talked about that – how horrible it was the way they spoke to the people.[124]

Simon Winchester, of *The Guardian*, assessed the aftermath: 'The mood in the streets was angry. The rhetoric flowed ceaselessly. Yet somehow it seemed that the residents were strangely enjoying the new martyred role in which they had been cast – beaten by the English, the old enemy, in an unfair fight. An elderly woman combing her hair said: "They'll never beat the Irish. They'll never beat us like that."'[125] The impact of the Curfew was felt beyond Belfast, as demonstrated by the comments of a Catholic from Downpatrick: 'As a Catholic I cannot but feel bitter that for the second time in less than a year an immeasurable amount of suffering has been visited on my co-religionists – only this time by the very forces which initially were called in to protect them! Is this the deliberate policy to be pursued in other Catholic areas?'[126]

The events on the Falls had diplomatic repercussions as well. Paddy Devlin had attacked the performance of the Taoiseach, Jack Lynch who, he said, 'should be doing something more positive and I am not talking about words'. The British Embassy took this to be an implicit demand for Irish intervention in the North. In an interview on Radio Telefís Éireann (RTE), Patrick Hillery, the Minister for External Affairs, was forced to defend the Taoiseach's policy towards the North, adding that it should be made very clear to the Catholic minority that they were going to be protected. The Minister said he would have no objection to visiting Belfast for a first-hand view: 'I would not consider it undiplomatic.' Hillery believed that what the Catholic minority needed were 'vast and full guarantees' and felt that the British would give these. He had no evidence that the British had reneged on their previous commitments although he recognized that the man in the street in the North could be forgiven for not seeing what was done. Legislation was a process which took time and before reforms became visible there had to be patience.[127] Later that day – 6 July – Hillery secretly drove from Dublin to Belfast and toured the Falls. Hillery made the trip, at the Taoiseach's request, to reassure the people of the Falls and to seek the facts.[128] His purpose was to 'relax tension'. He'd earlier described the guns found in the arms search as 'out-dated guns' collected by people to protect themselves after a savage attack; they now found themselves unprotected.[129] Lynch observed that Protestants possessed a large quantity of weapons but that the British had so far made no attempt to search for them. There was fear in the Falls Road and a danger that because of that fear many would turn to extremists. Hillery's trip was to counter this fear: although it ignored 'diplomatic niceties' it was a move for peace.[130]

The visit did not lead to the crisis in Anglo-Irish relations that it appeared to be from outside: far from it. When the British Ambassador, John Peck, saw Hillery later that evening, he was made aware of the real concerns and pressures which had pushed the Irish into such a dramatic intervention. Hillery had, at that moment, just arrived back from Belfast. At this stage no news had leaked out to the press, although the Minister told them immediately after the interview with Peck. Hillery asked the Ambassador to convey to Sir Alec Douglas-Home his grave anxiety about the situation in the North. He said that the weekend's events had put his Government in serious hazard and his visit to the Falls was aimed at relieving the pressure on Lynch against whom accusations were growing that he was abandoning defenceless Catholics to their fate. A more serious development had been Brian Faulkner's public praise, the day before, of the Taoiseach's statesmanship.[131] Peck, explaining that he was speaking without instructions, reiterated Her Majesty's Government (HMG's) support for the Taoiseach's avowed policy towards the North. But on the matter of the Falls search – Hillery 'barely mentioned any complaints about [the] troops['] behaviour' – Peck pointed out that it was vital, in the interests of communal peace, that the two

Governments had a 'community of interest' to root out extremists who were hell bent on the destruction of all law and order. Hillery did not contest this. Peck's strongest impression from his contacts was that Lynch and Hillery were terrified that any worsening situation in the North, caused by the imminent Orange parades, would topple the Dublin Government through the pressure of Southern public opinion and that civil war would inevitably follow. Hillery's aim in seeing him was thus to persuade HMG to take every available measure to demonstrate that the Conservative administration was willing and able to reinforce the guarantees already made of equality of treatment for the Catholic minority.[132] So, while at Westminster Sir Alec told the House of Commons that the visit was a 'diplomatic discourtesy',[133] in Dublin relations between the Ambassador and Hillery reflected the more relaxed relationship which continued to exist between the British and Irish Governments. When Peck saw Hillery to deliver the text of the Foreign Secretary's statement, the Minister said it was 'fair enough'; he later observed that a dressing down from London would, in fact, be the reverse of harmful for him in Dublin. Hillery confirmed that the great fear of the Irish Government was that the mass of moderate opinion in the North would feel that it had no voice or outlet – except the extremists and subversives – if it lost all contact with the South. Recent events, through coincidences and bad public relations, had conspired to convince Catholics that Stormont, London and the Army were all in league against them and it was essential that 'we should rapidly and visibly dispel this belief'.[134] The British were well aware of the damage done. Reflecting some months later, Ronnie Burroughs recognized the Curfew as being of especial significance: it had not only changed the image of the British soldier from a beneficent protector to an oppressor, but gave new life to traditional Irish Nationalism and created an atmosphere in which the resurgent militancy of the IRA could flourish.[135]

However, it would be a mistake to adopt the impression, given by many writers on the impact of the Curfew, that Catholic alienation was complete. For many Catholics it was a watershed: the end of the Army's honeymoon. For others, like Mairead Farrell, it was the beginning of a process. But there remained a large body of Catholics who were also angered by the activities of the rioters and the paramilitaries. As one Catholic letter writer declared: 'I am tired of listening to people talking about the "Army of Occupation" in Belfast and calling for their withdrawal. These same people have very short memories. They seem to forget it was the Catholic people of the Falls and Ardoyne who begged for the British Army's protection, last August; and it is because of us the soldiers are here.' The writer pointed out that it was only the soldiers that had recently kept Protestant mobs from the Shankill. 'I would add that the soldiers in this district, both English and Scots, have behaved like gentlemen at all times. It is terrible to think that a few teenage louts and layabouts can dictate to older people what they can or cannot do and make us feel that to bid a soldier the time of day is being a traitor to Ireland. It seems now that we are being ruled by a lot of teenage generals. A little bit of power seems to have gone to their heads.'[136] A 'lifelong Republican' warned that, after the attack on the non-Unionist population the previous August:

... the shooting, burning and pillaging of our houses, brought worldwide sympathy and help to us... We are daily losing more and more sympathy, not only around the world but in our own country... We believe the British Army should not be here, but let us face the facts, can we do without them at this juncture? The answer is obvious. We cannot. No doubt if the British Army withdraws the democrats would triumph over the Unionists in the course of time but the cost in destruction and loss of innocent lives, men, women and children on both sides would be terrible. We have achieved so much over the last two years, thanks to the non-violent activities of our young people. By reverting to the tactics of violence, street fighting etc we are playing the game to suit the Paisley element.[137]

That Catholic opinion was more complex than a simple blanket, Province-wide, alienation was also demonstrated by the re-entry of the RUC into the Bogside, later in July. By this stage Chichester-Clark felt that the policy followed over the past year of gradually infiltrating the RUC back into all areas of Northern Ireland, while the reform programme gradually improved the atmosphere, was 'obviously not working'. He pointed out to London that there were two areas in Belfast (the Falls) and Londonderry (the Bogside), where the writ of the RUC did not run. The problem in the Bogside, although the area was smaller, was more severe. If normality could be restored in the two areas concerned, argued Chichester-Clark, this would enormously strengthen the hand of the Northern Ireland Government against Protestant extremists. It would also be possible to argue that the Security Forces were so fully committed on these tasks that they should not be subjected to the strains of further Orange parades. As a result it would become politically possible to cancel both the Apprentice Boys' Parade on 12 August in Londonderry and larger Orange parades on the last Saturday of August in several centres in Northern Ireland.[138]

Chichester-Clark won the day and it was decided that the level of RUC activity in the Falls Road was acceptable, and that it was only the Bogside that worried Stormont. Given what had just happened in the Falls, any operation was a calculated risk. The final decision was that an operation in Londonderry should go ahead, and that once entry into the Bogside had been successfully accomplished there should be an announcement on the banning of the 12 August marches. As part of the operation it was essential to establish an RUC police post in Creggan, on the fringe of Bogside. No prior warning was to be given of the operation, and it would be conducted by a large number of RUC entering the Bogside at the time of the operation. The Northern Ireland Government were concerned that, should the operation go badly, and the RUC get into difficulties, the Army should go to the aid of the RUC and insisted that such a guarantee should be given before the operation started. Freeland, although perfectly prepared to give this guarantee, felt that such a decision must be made by Ministers in London: he did not consider that the odd stoning of the odd policeman would justify calling in the Army.[139] From 21 July, mixed RUC and Royal Military Police (RMP) patrols pushed into the Bogside. On 24 July a detachment of seven RUC entered the area and set up a permanent police post. There was no hostile reaction from the Bogsiders:

Burroughs had taken a chance on John Hume's discretion and prepared the ground with him the night before. Hume agreed to issue a statement welcoming the announcement and saying that the Bogsiders would support any law-keeping force which was seen to be impartial.[140]

With the successful deployment of the RUC, the Government felt confident enough to announce a ban on all processions throughout Northern Ireland up to and including 31 January 1971, with the exception of customary processions to and from churches or war memorials on Remembrance Day.[141] But, instead of making things easier for Chichester-Clark this balanced operation actually made things more difficult for him! Burroughs warned that the Protestant reaction to the blanket prohibition of marches was mounting rapidly. He then gave an insight into the extraordinary balancing act that the British were faced with in regard to Northern Ireland. The UKREP explained to the Home Office how the political acumen of minority leaders in accepting without fuss the reintroduction of normal policing in the Bogside and Falls had contributed to the political reaction on the Protestant right, inasmuch as the balance of the decisions on policing and marching had been disturbed. Because Catholics had not complained, Protestants saw themselves alone as victims of the Government's action. In the meantime, Burroughs suggested that the Stormont Government could not but be helped politically by any productive searches for arms in Catholic areas, particularly in the Bogside, and by a period of silence on the problems of the Province on the part of the Irish Government.[142] But one consequence of the Falls operation was a politically imposed restriction on arms searches. The British Government was anxious to avoid a repeat performance. The GOC was now obliged to seek Ministerial authority from London before an operation to search houses for arms could be mounted, although it was conceivable that an immediate operational requirement might arise which might, in exceptional circumstances, render reference to London impracticable. The Ministerial Committee on Northern Ireland decided, on 13 July, that 'The political implications of searches or other security operations in the Bogside, or in any Roman Catholic area, were potentially so serious that no action of this kind should be taken without previous reference to Ministers in London.'[143]

Notes

1. Max Arthur, *Northern Ireland Soldiers Talking* (London:1987), pp.14–15.
2. Peter Taylor, *Brits. The War Against the IRA* (London: 2001), p.32.
3. Arthur, *Northern Ireland*, p.14.
4. Ibid. p.19.
5. Taylor, *Brits*, p.38.
6. Sean MacStiofain, *Revolutionary in Ireland* (Farnborough: 1974), pp.145–6.
7. Raymond J. Quinn, *A Rebel Voice. A History of Belfast Republicanism 1925–1972* (Belfast: 1999), pp.155–7.
8. *Irish News*, 12 August 1970.
9. Quinn, *A Rebel Voice*, p.157.
10. MacStiofan, *Revolutionary*, p.167.
11. Ibid., pp.63–4.
12. Kevin Bean and Mark Hayes (eds), *Republican Voices* (Monaghan: nd), p.50.

13. Ibid.
14. Peter Taylor, *Provos: The IRA and Sinn Féin* (London: 1997), pp.71–2.
15. Ibid., p.70.
16. Brenda Anderson, *Joe Cahill: A Life in the IRA* (Dublin: 2002), pp.190–1.
17. *Irish News*, 20 February 1970.
18. Ibid., 23 February 1970.
19. Ibid., 26 February 1970.
20. Ibid., 1 March 1970.
21. Ibid., 3 March 1970.
22. Ibid., 9 March 1970.
23. McKittrick et al., *Voices*, pp.48–9.
24. Ibid. p.58.
25. *Irish News*, 2 May 1970.
26. Ibid., 11 May 1970.
27. Ibid., 12 May 1970.
28. NAUK PRO FCO 33/1075 Northern Ireland: Political Summary of Events 8–14 May 1970. Memorandum by the Home Office, 15 May 1970.
29. NAUK PRO FCO 33/1075 UK Rep to FCO, 12 May 1970.
30. NAUK PRO FCO 33/1075 Dublin Telegram No.84; 13 May 1970.
31. NAUK PRO FCO 33/1075 Northern Ireland: Political Summary for the Period 15–20 May 1970. Memorandum by the Home Office, 21 May 1970.
32. Ibid.
33. *Irish News*, 20 May 1970.
34. Ibid., 19 May 1970.
35. Ibid., 22 May 1970.
36. Ibid., 20 May 1970.
37. *Belfast Telegraph*, 20 February 1970.
38. Ibid., 12 February 1970.
39. Ibid., 20 February 1970.
40. Ibid., 9 February 1970.
41. NAUK PRO DEFE 24/980 Relations Between the Army and the RUC, 29 July 1970.
42. NAUK PRO DEFE 25/274 Functions of the Army and the Police Note by CGS, 30 June 1970.
43. NAUK PRO DEFE 24/980 Relations Between the Army and the RUC, 29 July 1970.
44. *Belfast Telegraph*, 4 June 1970.
45. Ibid., 5 June 1970.
46. Ibid., 8 June 1970.
47. Ibid.
48. Ibid., 11 June 1970.
49. Ibid., 10 June 1970.
50. Ibid., 26 May 1970.
51. Ibid., 12 June 1970.
52. Ibid., 10 June 1970.
53. Ibid.
54. Ibid., 11 June 1970.
55. Ibid., 12 June 1970.
56. Ibid., 13 June 1970.
57. *Irish News*, 23 January 1970.
58. Ibid., 14 February 1970.
59. Ibid., 16 February 1970.
60. Ibid., 17 February 1970.
61. Ibid., 31 January 1970.
62. Ibid., 13 February 1970.
63. Ibid., 2 February 1970.
64. Ibid., 20 February 1970.

65. Ibid., 27 February 1970.
66. Ibid., 25 February 1970.
67. Ibid., 5 March 1970.
68. W.D. Flackes and Sydney Elliott, *Northern Ireland: A Political Directory 1968–88* (Belfast: 1989), p.254.
69. Ian McAllister, *The Northern Ireland Social Democratic and Labour Party: Political Opposition in a Divided Society* (London: 1977), pp.39–40.
70. *Irish Times*, 1 October 1969.
71. *Irish News*, 23 January 1970.
72. *Sunday Press*, 30 August 1970.
73. *Irish Times*, 2 October 1969.
74. *Irish News*, 24 January 1970.
75. Ibid., 2 March 1970.
76. Ibid.
77. *Sunday Press*, 11 October 1970.
78. John Ramsden (ed.), *The Oxford Companion to Twentieth Century British Politics* (Oxford: 2002), p.294.
79. Ibid., p.427.
80. Ibid., pp.204–5.
81. Ibid., p.100.
82. NAUK PRO PREM 15/476 Meeting between PM and Taoiseach in New York, 21 October 1970.
83. James Callaghan, *A House Divided. The Dilemma of Northern Ireland* (London: 1973), pp.136–7.
84. Ibid., p.142.
85. Centre for Contemporary British History, 'British Policy in Northern Ireland 1964–1970', Witness Seminar, 14 January 1992.
86. NAUK PRO CJ 3/46 Memorandum by the Secretary of State for the Home Department, May 1970.
87. CCBH, British Policy in Northern Ireland 1970–1974 Witness Seminar, 11 January 1993.
88. CCBH British Policy in Northern Ireland 1964–1970 Witness Seminar, 14 January 1992.
89. NAUK PRO PREM 15/100 Northern Ireland Note for Prime Minister, 21 June 1970.
90. NAUK PRO PREM 15/100 Cabinet: Northern Ireland. Minutes of a Meeting on 22 June 1970.
91. Paul Bew and Gordon Gillespie, *Northern Ireland: A Chronology of the Troubles 1968–93* (Dublin: 1993).
92. Taylor, *Provos*, pp.74–7.
93. Quinn, *A Rebel Voice*, pp.160–5.
94. Peter Taylor, *Loyalists* (London: 1999), p.80.
95. McKittrick et al., *Lost Lives*, pp.49–52.
96. NAUK PRO DEFE 13/730 Joint Security Committee Conclusions, 28 June 1970.
97. NAUK PRO DEFE 13/730 Joint Security Committee Conclusions, 29 June 1970.
98. NAUK PRO DEFE 24/980 HQ Northern Ireland, 29 June 1970.
99. NAUK PRO DEFE 24/980 HQ Northern Ireland, 30 June 1970.
100. NAUK PRO DEFE 13/730 Joint Security Committee Conclusions, 30 June 1970.
101. Taylor, *Provos*, p.77.
102. NAUK PRO FCO 33/1076 Telegram No.183 UK Representative to FCO, June 1970.
103. Warner, *Falls Road*, p.329.
104. Ibid., pp.329–30.
105. Ibid., p.238.
106. NAUK PRO FCO 33/1077 Press Release by HQNI: Booklet by CCDC.
107. Simon Winchester, *In Holy Terror* (London: 1974), pp.68–9.
108. *Irish News*, 6 July 1970.

109. NAUK PRO DEFE 24/980 Statement of Sergeant A... 'A' Company 2nd Queen's Regiment, 8 July 1970.
110. Patrick Bishop and Eamonn Mallie, *The Provisional IRA* (Aylesbury: 1987), p.159.
111. Peter Taylor, *Provos. The IRA and Sinn Féin* (London: 1997), pp.79–80.
112. *Irish News*, 4 July 1970.
113. Ibid., 6 July 1970.
114. Ibid., 6 July 1970.
115. NAUK PRO DEFE 25/273 HQNI to MOD, 6 July 1970.
116. NAUK PRO FCO 33/1077 Press Release by HQNI: Booklet by CCDC.
117. McKittrick, *Lost Lives*, pp.52–5.
118. NAUK PRO DEFE 24/980 Opinion from the Director of Law Reform, 5 July 1970.
119. NAUK PRO DEFE 24/980 Maudling to Fitt. Entry into Lower Falls.
120. *Irish News*, 6 July 1970.
121. Desmond Hamill, *Pig in the Middle. The Army in Northern Ireland 1969–1984* (London: 1985), p.37.
122. NAUK PRO DEFE 24/980 Meeting between the Minister for Defence, Mr Gerard Fitt MP, Mr Frank McManus MP and Mr Paddy Devlin, 6 July 1970.
123. Paddy Devlin, *Straight Left: An Autobiography* (Belfast: 1993), p.134.
124. Peter Taylor, *Families at War* (London: 1989), pp.34–6.
125. Winchester, *In Holy Terror*, p.74.
126. Catholic Ex-Moderate letter, *Irish News*, 9 July 1970.
127. NAUK PRO DEFE 25/273 Telegram No.200 British Embassy to FCO, 6 July 1970.
128. NAUK PRO DEFE 25/273 Telegram No. 207 Peck to FCO, 7 July 1970.
129. *Irish News*, 7 July 1970.
130. NAUK PRO DEFE 25/273 Telegram No.207 Peck to FCO, 7 July 1970.
131. NAUK PRO DEFE 25/273 Telegram No.204 Peck to Douglas-Home, 6 July 1970.
132. Ibid.
133. Bew and Gillespie, *Chronology*, p.29.
134. NAUK PRO DEFE 25/273 Telegram No.211 Peck to FCO, 7 July 1970.
135. NAUK PRO DEFE 25/304 Valedictory Despatch from Mr R.A. Burroughs, 14 April 1971.
136. Veronica letter, *Irish News*, 16 July 1970.
137. Ever Hopeful letter, *Irish News*, 5 August 1970.
138. NAUK PRO DEFE 25/273 Note of the Prime Minister's Meeting with the Prime Minister of Northern Ireland, 17 July 1970.
139. NAUK PRO DEFE 25/273 Meeting of Northern Ireland Security Committee, 21 July 1970.
140. NAUK PRO FCO 33/1076 Telegram No.4 Burroughs to Home Office, 23 July 1970.
141. NAUK PRO FCO 33/1076 Telegram No.5 Burroughs to Home Office, 23 July 1970.
142. NAUK PRO FCO 33/1076 Telegram No.6 Burroughs to Home Office, 29 July 1970.
143. NAUK PRO DEFE 24/980 Hockaday to Woodfield, 9 November 1970.

2

The Phoney War Ends – the IRA Campaign Intensifies: August 1970–March 1971

ESCALATION

Ironically, and mercifully, the expected trouble over the 12th didn't materialize: it was as if all sides in the Province had been taken aback by the level of the disorder in June and July – and paused for thought. Another factor was that both factions of the IRA had been surprised by the military's response; for now Republicans in Belfast were disinclined to take on the Army in such a forthright manner. Within the Security Forces the violence of June and July forced Sir Arthur Young to accept that the police would have to adopt a more robust attitude towards policing. On 4 July, Young issued Force Order No.105/70 in which he said inter alia that the police were 'obliged to use such force as may be necessary' to protect the public from those whose actions were intended to cause injury to persons or damage to property. This included 'the use of batons and in such extreme circumstances as imminent danger to life the use of firearms when all other efforts have failed'.[1] There had been no change in security policy independent of, or preceding, the violence of June/July. From the Army's point of view the change in the security situation was not driven by it but by the IRA – it was certainly not at the behest of the new Tory administration. Freeland saw the rioting of 26/27 June in Belfast as a watershed: it was the first clear evidence of a new IRA campaign and radically altered the picture in that firearms were used against the Security Forces. Intelligence indicated that the IRA threat could be Province-wide. The GOC identified the main security threats as coming from continuing sectarian animosity and Republicans. Some of the known IRA plans had been executed and the following were known to have been discussed within the IRA and potentially posed a major threat to the security of the Province:

   a. Deliberate escalation of any sectarian confrontation leading to the overstretching and discrediting of the Security Forces.
   b. Sabotage on British business properties, public buildings and shipyards.
   c. Attacks on border Police Stations.
   d. Attacks on individual members of the Security Forces.

All the above intelligence predictions came to pass. More immediately, intelligence on IRA reaction to the events in the Falls on 3/4 July was still scanty. Freeland believed that what happened on 3/4 July was presumably a factor in their decision not to intervene on the 12th. But there was no indication that they were prepared to abandon the initiative. The renewed IRA threat, the wide area of potential operations and the number of troops deployed were no longer an acceptable task for two Brigade HQs. Belfast alone, bearing in mind the number of areas in which trouble could be quickly and simultaneously fomented, was too large a task for one HQ. There was thus a requirement for a third Brigade HQ in Northern Ireland[2] to cover the southern frontier of the Province. As the Army's commitment to Northern Ireland increasingly became bedded in, further changes became necessary. To lighten the workload on the GOC a new post – Commander Land Forces Northern Ireland (CLF NI) – was created. The CLF was the second most senior officer in Northern Ireland after the GOC. Major General Anthony Farrar-Hockley, a veteran of the Korean War, was the first, in 1970. Sir Michael Carver, a future CGS and one of the Army's most intelligent soldiers, described Farrar-Hockley as 'the sort you needed to restrain'. The decision to appoint a CLF made it difficult to find a role for a deputy, particularly in Northern Ireland: 'You either give commands directly to the brigadiers or to the chief of staff and this created difficulty for the brigadiers.'[3] Farrar-Hockley's successor (in 1971), Major General Robert Ford, described the role of CLF as being responsible for the day-to-day conduct of Army operations in the Province and directly reporting to the GOC whose responsibilities were wider – 'i.e. politico-military issues at Government level' – hence the need for a deputy.[4] The situation in Northern Ireland also required changes back at the MOD with the creation of a Military Operations Branch 4 (MO4). Colonel Dalzell-Payne was to head the branch. He worked for the Director of Military Operations who worked for the Chief of the General Staff and the Vice CGS. Dalzell-Payne had no strategic role; he reacted to orders and disseminated information: for example, the terms of the Yellow Card, laying out soldiers' rules of engagement, were drafted by the School of Infantry and sent to him. He sent it on to the MOD Legal Department and it was then sent to the CGS for final approval. MO4 was also the coordinating branch in MOD for the introduction of internment in 1971.[5]

On the ground the violence of the summer crystallized the potential of what might happen with so many firearms floating about. And those with the most arms were the British Army. The use of lethal force by soldiers in Northern Ireland was governed by the Yellow Card, which was issued to all troops in the Province. Based upon a similar exercise in Aden it was designed to provide legal protection for the soldier in the circumstances of his opening fire and killing someone. In its initial form, issued in September 1969, the Yellow Card's first point was general: 'Always remember that you must never use more force than is absolutely necessary to enable you to carry out your duties.' A soldier could only open fire if he were being attacked or persons whom he was under a duty to protect were being attacked 'in such a way that you or they are in danger of being killed or seriously injured and there is no other way in which you can defend yourself or them'; or if property which the soldier had been ordered to guard with firearms was being attacked, destroyed or stolen by a person or persons in such a way that they could not be restrained except by the use of firearms. If a soldier was able to repel the use of force without opening fire, 'you must do so. If you have to open fire you must fire no more rounds than absolutely necessary' and 'must NOT' fire at an assailant who had commenced to retreat and was no longer a threat to the soldier unless he had killed or seriously injured a member of the Security Forces or was a person whom the soldier was under a duty to protect, or if the assailant would not stop when called upon to do so and could not be arrested by any other means. Only aimed shots were to be fired. The soldier was told that he must always challenge before opening fire unless an attack came without warning and 'even a moment's delay could lead to death or serious injury to yourself or persons whom you are under a duty to protect'.

If forced to open fire on his own initiative, a soldier would continue to act independently until a military superior took charge. From the moment the superior took charge of the incident the solider was to act only on his orders. In issuing a challenge the soldier should say 'in a firm, distinct voice "HALT – HANDS UP"'. If the person halted the soldier was to shout 'STAND STILL AND KEEP YOUR HANDS UP'. The soldier was then to ask the person why he was there and if not satisfied to call his Commander immediately and hand the person over to him. If the person did not halt at once the soldier was to challenge him again and if the person did not halt on the second challenge the soldier was to cock his weapon, apply the safety catch and shout: 'STAND STILL, I AM READY TO FIRE' and then summon his Commander. If the person still did not halt and was not attacking the soldier or person under his protection or destroying or stealing property the soldier was to use every means in his power to stop him and detain him 'but you will NOT fire. If the person runs away, you are NOT to fire. You are to report the incident to your Commander.' Similarly, in the event of a vehicle failing to halt at a road check, 'you will NOT open fire', but instead note its description, make, registered number and the direction the vehicle was travelling. The soldier would then report the incident to his Commander. As for the safety precautions relating to a soldier's weapon, the magazine was to be loaded with live ammunition but the weapon was always to be made safe: that was, every live round was to be carried in the breach and the working parts were to be forward. The soldier was told: 'You are NOT to cock your weapon until the person has failed to halt on your second challenge, or you have to take immediate defensive action to save life.'[6] But Freeland's relaxation of the rules of engagement created a problem. As the Chief of the General Staff explained to Lord Carrington, the GOC's statement that individuals carrying firearms were liable to be shot without warning was primarily a deterrent – which did not take into account that HQNI had actually authorized the use of firearms on the basis of Freeland's instructions in June which were clearly not a deterrent. But, as Sir Geoffrey Baker pointed out, while the Yellow Card did not exclude the possibility that a soldier might have to open fire without having been fired at first – the guiding intention and principle had been that fire would be opened only in retaliation; Baker was prepared to sanction the relaxing of the rules of engagement relating to the first use of firearms by soldiers against those carrying weapons and using petrol bombs along the lines outlined by the GOC.[7] With the steady deterioration in public order, it became increasingly likely that soldiers would be involved in the use of lethal force. This was soon apparent.

At the end of July there was a series of disturbances in the New Lodge starting at about 1.20 a.m. and finishing at 7 a.m. during which crowds of up to about fifty gathered on three occasions. They were dispersed by the Army on the first two occasions after throwing stones and bottles but without more serious incident. On the third occasion, although CS was used, the crowd did not disperse and petrol bombs were thrown at the Security Forces, setting fire to two armoured trucks. After three warnings to stop were given by loudhailer, without success, troops fired three shots and one man, petrol bomb in hand according to the Army, was killed. About thirty petrol bombs in all, it was estimated, were thrown during the incident. The man killed was 19-year-old Daniel O'Hagan of Annadale Flats.[8] The disorder followed a bogus 999 call to police who on arrival were immediately attacked with stones and bottles. After a lull military reinforcements were attacked and a small number of petrol bombs, about thirty in all, thrown. The authorities believed that the disorder was deliberately contrived by the Provisionals as a reaction to earlier events. This referred to a search on 29 July of a house on the northern boundary of Belfast, occupied by a priest, during which ammunition was found. Suspicions were entertained about the use of the house and the character of the priest. The ammunition belonged to a Catholic licensee from the New Lodge Road; a raid was carried out on the licensee's bar for non-compliance with licensing laws. The licensee was influential and popular in the area. Added to this was the known policy of the Provisionals to 'contrive confrontations between security forces and civilian crowds in order to discredit government and security forces'.[9] Paddy Kennedy, the Republican Labour MP, claimed that, from his talks with local people, he was satisfied that the soldiers had given no warning of their intention to fire and that the dead youth had not been carrying a petrol bomb. He compared the riots on 3 July when three men had been shot allegedly when sniping: it was now established that all had been run over by armoured vehicles (this was wrong). The riots on 3 July had happened because the RUC, now back in Catholic areas, were 'up to their old tricks' of intimidation.[10] The comment from the British Embassy in Dublin was: 'We know Paddy Kennedy's true colours (IRA) but most people in the south will accept what he says.'[11]

The shooting of O'Hagan – a member of the Provisional IRA – was but the first in a series of disputed killings by the Security Forces. O'Hagan's father thought that his son had gone out in the early hours of the morning to look after his cousin's family in a nearby street. O'Hagan was struck by a high velocity (HV) shot on the point of his chin. It passed through his neck and struck his spinal cord. The shooting had been carried out by soldiers of The King's Own Scottish Borderers. Lieutenant 'A' had been ordered to take his platoon and clear the New Lodge Road early on the morning of 31 July. They cleared one barbed wire barricade and were approaching another barricade when they came under attack from petrol bombs being thrown by people behind the barricade.

Two of the petrol bombs struck their armoured cars and burning petrol struck the visor of a corporal. The barricade stretched from Edlingham Street across to Shandon Street. Through a loud hailer Lieutenant 'A' warned the crowd that petrol bombers would be shot. He then ordered three of his marksmen to take up position. He gave a second warning but there was no response and more petrol bombs were thrown. The Army marksmen then fired a total of three shots. In the opinion of Lieutenant 'A' this had been an ambush; but he also admitted that since he was not looking in the direction of the shot man, 'I did not personally see anything to justify the shooting before this man was shot.' Private 'B', one of the marksmen concerned, stated that he had kept an eye on a man who, he claimed, had thrown the petrol bomb which hit one of the armoured cars. He heard his Lieutenant give the warning that petrol bombers would be shot and then saw the man light the fuse of the petrol bomb he was holding in his hand. Private 'B' took aim and fired. The man fell. Private 'C' and Private 'D' gave similar accounts. However, Mrs Catherine Black, of Edlingham Street, disputed this account. She was at her bedroom window when she saw a young lad walk along Edlingham Street and then cross over the New Lodge Road. He had just reached the footpath at Shandon Street when she heard shots and the man fell. She was clear that he did not have a petrol bomb in his hand at the time and she did not see him throwing a petrol bomb. The man had his side to the Army who were to his left. She could not account, however, for the fact that he was shot on the point of the chin.[12]

That the GOC's decision to relax the rules of engagement was 'probably' lawful was confirmed when the Treasury Solicitor stated that the increasing use of firearms by the civilian population had introduced a new element into the situation which could be held to justify action going beyond the instructions contained in the Yellow Card with certain modifications.[13] The military were thus satisfied that the killing of O'Hagan, which occurred after the revised Yellow Card instructions were confirmed in July, was warranted despite the troops opening fire as the officer 'finished the second warning'.[14] The Attorney General's assessment of the incident was that no two Internal Security situations were ever exactly the same and Northern Ireland was no exception to this generality. In the past the Army had usually either been dealing with civil unrest or had been hunting down insurgents. Its doctrine for the former problem, usually applied in built-up areas, involved the control and dispersal of disorderly crowds by way of physically blocking streets, calling upon the crowd to disperse in various ways and then using the minimum force to achieve the aim. Firearms were used only as a last resort, and then only under the careful command and control of the senior officer present. Counter insurgency operations were restricted by various political and legal considerations but generally speaking they were closer to warfare and armed insurgents were often engaged on sight. As long as rioters in Northern Ireland limited their aggressive acts to throwing stones and other generally non-lethal missiles the military reaction could be based on lesser degrees of violence, that is, the crowd control doctrine. But as petrol bombs could be lethal it was therefore proper for platoons operating in the streets to be prepared to use firearms against petrol bombers if necessary. The new situation was half-way between controlling civil unrest and counter insurgency. In the circumstances the Attorney General was satisfied that the platoon commander's orders were appropriate and that the three soldiers who fired without orders acted correctly. The soldiers 'appear to have acted in good faith and to have used minimum force'.[15]

The rioting, which had led to O'Hagan's death, was part of a sustained sequence over several nights. Paddy Kennedy accused the Army of meting out beatings to people arrested by Army snatch squads: 'It appears that the whole object of the snatch parties is to seize people regardless of whether they have been involved in stone-throwing or not and then producing false and misleading evidence against them.'[16] For example, at the height of trouble in Ballymurphy, on the night of 4 August, troops smashed through the front door of a Glenalina Park house where Mrs Rose Rooney was bathing some of her nine children. Three soldiers ran into the living room and dragged out a 16-year-old boy: 'The boy hadn't been out of the house all night. He was sitting here with his father when the soldiers burst in. I think some boys ran down the side of the house just before the troops arrived.' The Rooney children were carried into a neighbour's house while Mrs Rooney received treatment for shock from a St John's Ambulance nurse.[17] Yet while Kennedy was articulating the anger of many victims of the Army's rough tactics on the ground, once again there was a diversity in Catholic responses. Kennedy was attacked by one Catholic for claiming that the violence was a reaction against unnecessary provocation by British troops: 'The fact is that the vast majority of people in this area are appalled by what has taken place' just as they were by Kennedy who, 'even though he speaks for a small minority of Catholics, can find approval for the actions of those involved. These disturbances were not a spontaneous reaction, they were organised. Proof of this was plain to be seen. There was no army provocation.' Relations between the residents and the Army were cordial; there was 'no justification for the rioting, burning and looting which took place'.[18]

Relations between the Catholic community and the Army remained flexible, oscillating between a welcoming tolerance and a resentful antagonism. On 18 August, following severe flooding in Belfast, *The Irish News* reported that: 'The British Army reached its best popularity rating in Belfast since it was welcomed with open arms by the Catholics almost a year ago. The troops' weekend flood rescue work could well pave the way for a new relationship between Belfast and the Army. People, who on Saturday swore and spat at soldiers, yesterday offered cups of tea and food and paid warm tributes to them.' Women from Hutchinson Street, which lay between the Grosvenor Road and the Lower Falls area, could not speak too highly of the unselfish manner in which The Coldstream Guards went about their work in helping the victims of the flooding. One man spoke of a soldier up to his neck in water rescuing three greyhounds from the rear of a heavily flooded house. Others spoke of the Army getting food to people.[19] As members of the Guards used dinghies, while others waded shoulder high, to rescue families and elderly people trapped in the upstairs of their Falls homes by the floods, Paddy Devlin paid tribute to their work. The St Paul's Citizen Defence Committee expressed its gratitude, particularly to Lieutenant Michael

Willoughby, the soldiers' OC, as they 'got down on their knees and cleaned the floors of flooded houses'.[20] Forty-five soldiers from The Green Howards had 'drinks on the house' in a club in west Belfast as Catholics and Protestants joined in the tributes.[21]

This was but an interlude. A sign of things to come was provided on 12 August when Constable Samuel Donaldson, aged 23, and Constable Robert Millar, aged 26, were the first two members of the RUC to be killed by the IRA in the Troubles. They were both fatally injured by an IRA booby-trap bomb hidden in a stolen car parked a mile from Crossmaglen. On 11 August the two constables were attempting to tow away a Ford Cortina car left on the Lisseraw Road off the main Crossmaglen to Dundalk road.[22] Fifteen pounds of gelignite placed under the bonnet of the stolen car had been wired to the courtesy light inside the passenger compartment. It was believed that Constable Millar had edged his way around to the locked passenger door, put his arm through the half-opened window, clicked the lock back and pulled the door slowly open. As he inched it free, the micro-switch that would have put on the interior light triggered the detonator and the bomb exploded. Bob Millar's arm remained inside the door, torn off and mangled by the heat and pressure of the gases. What was left of the shiny red car was now lying, upside down, a smoking, blackened, oily mess of twisted wreckage, barely recognizable. Over a hedge, half in and half out of a shallow ditch, were the heaving, moaning bodies of the two policemen, both horribly mangled, bleeding heavily. Millar died before dawn the next day. Sam Donaldson, who had been on the driver's side of the car, was dead just after midnight. The bomb was plant by a Provisional unit operating out of Navan.[23] There was nothing defensive about this attack or, indeed, the bombing campaign.

The remainder of the year remained relatively quiet compared to later times: but there was an underlayer of increasing violence and sniping at troops in Belfast. Indeed, by December, Ronnie Burroughs, the UK Representative, was reporting that a very different, more optimistic, atmosphere was abound in Belfast. But he cautioned: 'I need however hardly add that the situation is still fragile. An important kidnapping, the murder by the I.R.A. of two or three soldiers, or an explosion which caused a large number of casualties, would set the clock back a long way.'[24] Things began to hot up on the evening of 12 January 1971, as crowd trouble began in the Springfield Road. On the following night eighteen petrol bombs were hurled at troops after hours of intermittent pelting of troops with stones and bottles. At one stage girls linked arms and danced around in a circle, singing something like a 'ring-a-ring-o-roses' chant, taunting the soldiers. This seemed to provoke the soldiers. Complaints of Army brutality followed.[25] By the third night girls were shouting 'If you hit the British Army, clap your hands' as the troops were again pelted. Trouble also flared in Ballymurphy. On both nights the Army also tried to keep Catholic and Protestant mobs apart.[26]

On the morning of 15 January, joint Army–RUC raids took place on houses in Ballymurphy. An angry crowd, mostly of women, attacked the raiding party with stones and bin lids. When a police Land Rover arrived on the scene it was overturned and two policemen had to run for safety to a house which the military were raiding. One of the other searches, in Andersonstown, revealed a machine-gun. During sporadic skirmishes throughout the evening thirty-five petrol bombs and three acid bombs were thrown at troops. Early in the morning of 16 January a series of minor explosions in Ballymurphy followed a night of mounting tension over the house searches. Paddy Devlin, who had been in the area for most of the night, reported that soldiers had entered a further ten houses and that there had been 'bashings left, right and centre' in at least two of them. As troops were withdrawing from the area a soldier was shot and wounded in the leg by sniper fire just after 2 a.m.[27] On the fourth night troops were attacked by between 50 and 60 people with stones and petrol bombs after they moved in to remove barricades. By 12.30 a.m. forty-two petrol bombs had been hurled at troops bringing the total, since the first night, to ninety-seven. In addition, three acid bombs – milk bottles filled with dilute sulphuric acid from car batteries – were thrown. Around 600 troops were involved in containing the disturbances.[28] It appeared that several residents had been prepared for the searches: for example, when a number of police entered one house, two men raced through the back door and started beating bin lids. The clatter of the bin lids was soon taken up in several back yards throughout the estate and within seconds the 'bush telegraph' had warned residents of the search. And while this was going on the women in the house began hurling ornaments at the troops through the front downstairs windows of the house.[29] A dossier compiled by Republicans described how during one search women and children were frisked in an upstairs room by a policewoman. The roofspace was searched. Rooms were numbered and searched methodically. The furniture and clothing were knocked about and the floor covering lifted. A soldier fired a shot over the heads of a crowd outside as unrest intensified. Similar scenes were repeated in a number of other homes.[30] Gerry Fitt agreed to make representations to Lord Baniel at the MOD for the withdrawal of troops from the Springfield Road and Ballymurphy. This followed an appeal from Ballymurphy residents, most of them women, who claimed that there would be no trouble in the area if the soldiers were removed. A youth of 17 who took part in attacks on the troops said he had been angered by the obscene language which the soldiers had directed towards them and the manner in which they kept dashing about the estate with guns at the ready. Another allegation made against the troops was that they were enticing young girls in the dances in the Taggart Memorial Hall Army base and were giving them drink.[31]

For the Northern Ireland Government and the Army, however, the disturbances were far more than a simple reaction to Army brutality. Chichester-Clark believed that the main aim of those who had been fermenting and encouraging the disturbances was the withdrawal of the Security Forces from these areas. Under no circumstances, said Chichester-Clark, would troops be withdrawn from Ballymurphy in response to 'either physical force or to any form of political pressure'. Earlier, Tony Farrar-Hockley had claimed he possessed evidence that the Ballymurphy riots had been deliberately provoked and organized. The CLF told a press conference that warning systems, such as the banging of dust bin lids, led him to 'deduce from that, that there is some organisation behind it'.[32] He blamed a 'small and sinister group of men' for terrorizing citizens and putting pressure on them to follow a certain line of thought: 'People are being threatened when all they want to do is get back to normal life.' Farrar-Hockley claimed that a handful of men had gone around to houses in the New Barnsley area urging people to come out and join the fighting in Ballymurphy: 'Pressure was put to bear on these innocent people and the call came well in advance of any trouble on the streets.'[33] Paddy Devlin responded by challenging Farrar-Hockley to meet him in a public debate on the claims of military brutality in Ballymurphy during house searches.[34]

With the situation in Belfast bubbling away, Chichester-Clark postponed a trip to the United States as the Government announced another security clampdown in Belfast following overnight troubles. Restrictions on movement in certain areas were liable to be imposed at short notice. The RUC also issued a special anti-arson warning to shopkeepers, calling for premises to be searched after they were closed and for night watchmen to be put on duty[35] as five city centre shops were extensively damaged when fire bombs exploded after the stores closed.[36] In Ardoyne the Army fired at least fifteen rubber bullets after trouble flared. About fifty petrol bombs were thrown during the disturbances.[37] Early on the morning of 17 January street violence erupted in the New Lodge Road after a night of tension at several city flashpoints. Twenty arrests were made and seventeen men were remanded in custody. Rubber bullets were fired at the crowd by troops in full battle gear as the crowd pelted them with stones and bottles. A series of running street battles ended up with the Army using tear gas. Water cannon were later employed to force the rioters into the heart of the New Lodge Road where Army snatch squads went into action. At one stage three men arrested by the Army were freed by a crowd of women who attacked the soldiers holding them. Army–UDR–RUC units ringed other city flashpoints to prevent rioting spreading.[38] The following morning a Falls Road bar was damaged by an explosion. Trouble had lasted throughout the night during which a burst of machine-gun fire hit an Army Land Rover in the New Lodge Road. Rival crowds had been kept apart by the Security Forces and it was after the police presence down-scaled that eight shots were fired at the Army. A sergeant alighting from the Land Rover was saved by his cap badge. A bullet glanced off it.[39] The Provisionals claimed that the 'basic root' of the troubles in Nationalist areas of Belfast was the 'continued interference by the British Government in Irish affairs'. This interference, backed up by 'heavily armed occupation forces' was bitterly resented by 'nationally minded people' in the city. More specifically the immediate reasons for the local unrest in Ballymurphy were:

1. The British Army base in Ballymurphy, against the express wish of the people in the district, 95 per cent of whom have signed a demand calling for the evacuation of the British troops and the removal of their base from the district.

2. The action of the British troops in running dances in their base, aimed at getting the young girls into the hall to satisfy their wants ...
3. The insulting of men, women and children in Ballymurphy by British Army personnel. This is a daily occurrence ...

> Any sane, honest person who witnessed the brave resistance put up against the British Army by the people of Ballymurphy, must dismiss with contempt the allegation by the local British commander that the people of Ballymurphy are being forced against their will to fight, almost with their bare hands, against heavily armed troops.
>
> How can the British commander claim that his men are innocent? They are not conscripts. They are all volunteers. They are trained professional killers.

The Provisionals added that the British did not produce a single shred of evidence that the Republican Movement was behind the unrest. It was clear that the British Army, working under new directions and in full cooperation with the RUC, were trying to create a situation in Belfast to justify internment. The Provisionals referred to an incident in which two RUC jeeps drove onto the pavement, scattering groups of people, following which people were 'taken out of their beds... and badly beaten'; this, they claimed, led to the conflict between the people of the New Lodge Road and the British Army. As a result the Provisionals stated:

> We must now ask ourselves: Are the RUC building up an atmosphere to encourage Orange extremists to resume their campaign of house burnings and sectarian killings started in August 1969? Are they planning to put Republican leaders behind prison bars without trial or charge in order to leave Nationalist areas unprotected? We are sure people have not forgotten what happened to Bombay Street after local Republicans were put in prison... It is more important than ever that people stand four-square behind the Republican Movement. We pledge that our members will not go like lambs to internment. We urge that defence measures be strengthened immediately in all Nationalists areas.[40]

On 18 January, Chichester-Clark warned that fresh outbreaks of violence were to be tackled on a 'firm and determined basis' following an emergency meeting of the Cabinet. The Prime Minister headed to London declaring that: 'No cause whatever now exists for violent agitation in Northern Ireland directed towards the rectification of grievances.'[41] The meeting in London had been called at the Northern Ireland Government's request; once there, Chichester-Clark, Faulkner and Jack Andrews saw Maudling and Carrington. Chichester-Clark believed that when petrol bombs or even shots were directed towards police or soldiers from an area this was clear evidence that petrol bombs or arms were to be found in that area and that it should be entered and searched. He did not think it right to limit searches to individual houses about which there was specific information. Chichester-Clark also asked that a firm reaction to trouble should be made at the outset. He argued that the military action now being taken to subdue the disorders in Ballymurphy and the Ardoyne should have been taken the day they first occurred. There was a difference of approach here between those who emphasized the need to avoid provocation and his own view that trouble should be dealt with firmly at the outset. His Government could not continue if the former approach prevailed. Chichester-Clark felt the Army should act under the directive of providing aid to the civil power and that more regard should be paid to the feelings of the Northern Ireland Government. He suggested that, subject to a veto from Ministers in London, the Northern Ireland Government should be able to tell the Army what to do in given circumstances. Carrington, in particular, turned him down flat: the experience of the operation in the Falls Road did not encourage repetition.[42] On his return from London, Chichester-Clark tried to put a brave face on the talks. He warned that internment could not be ruled out in the future. Several demonstrators were there to meet him, one of them carrying a placard stating 'No Interment'; a police officer lent the protester a pen to insert the missing 'n' which had gone astray. 'We have every intention of beating the IRA,' declared a defiant Chichester-Clark.[43] At Stormont the Prime Minister came under attack from Paisley who said that it was perfectly clear to the community that the Army and police had been dealing with the disturbances with 'one hand tied behind their back'. Paisley called for a return of the B Specials.[44]

Carrington and Richard Sharples, a junior minister in the MOD, arrived in Belfast, on 28 January, to hear the concerns of the Stormont Cabinet; but first they met with the GOC, CLF and Chief of Staff NI. It was a chance for the British Ministers to get a first-hand assessment of the situation on the ground. In strategic terms Freeland emphasized to the visitors that the military commitment would be a 'long haul' and stressed that he opposed the basic idea of internment. Specifically, he agreed that the Army had been slow in its reactions at the beginning of the recent disturbances. But, as Farrar-Hockley pointed out, the temptation to go 'fly swotting' had to be avoided. Freeland stressed that by over reaction 'you can easily alienate a whole district'. As for criticisms relating to Army/RUC relations, Freeland believed that they really stemmed from old criticisms of his own position as Director of Operations. The aim had always been to get the police back in their proper role and for the Army 'to stand shoulder to shoulder' with them as one security force, but Sir Arthur Young had asked for joint Army/RUC patrols to be stopped. The GOC said that if the police wanted to go in on their own then let them. Carrington was curious to know if life went on ordinarily, whether 'the silent majority' were having a good effect, and how the public regarded the Army. Freeland replied that life went on ordinarily except in the bad areas where gangs were often hanging about. As for the silent majority, it was very disheartening that they did not take any positive action. Their attitude to the Army depended on the area in question, and the unit responsible for it. Carrington asked about the soldiers themselves. Farrar-Hockley said that, above all, they were forbearing. He would be surprised if they showed any hatred or animosity when Ministers met them. They were not brutal. They treated the locals like children. Freeland added that in the heat of battle, for instance in the snatch squads, they might rough it up a bit. Carrington agreed that the ones he had seen appeared most forbearing. As an aside Freeland warned that the Province would need 20,000 troops 'if everything went sour on us'.[45]

The next morning, Carrington and Staples met with the Northern Ireland Cabinet and listened to their concerns.[46] After the meeting, Carrington and Sharples were anxious to clear up some of the points raised, so once more they met with the military as the Army had not been directly represented. As well as again meeting the GOC and CLF they met with the Commanders of 8 (Londonderry) and 39 (Belfast) Brigades – Brigadiers Cowan and Kitson respectively. Carrington raised the problem of vigilantes. The Cabinet's criticism was: 'Why do you deal with people we don't recognise?' Sharples added: 'Why are bargains struck is the implication behind it.' By way of reply Freeland asked: 'Who do you speak to? The vigilantes are the leaders on the streets. One doesn't want to talk to them, but... In the early days, it was maybe right that deals were struck in the interests of the preservation of the peace.' Kitson added that all too often the vigilantes were the IRA but with the force levels available in Belfast it was necessary to keep some areas quiet, in case all of them went wrong simultaneously. Brigadier Cowan added that in Londonderry they called the vigilantes something else and persuaded them to attend joint meetings and go to the local police stations. Carrington asked if all Army intelligence was shared: Chichester-Clark had intimated that he felt that it was not available to him. There followed an outburst by the GOC and CLF against the RUC Head of Special Branch – David Johnston. All Army intelligence was available to him, they said, and if the Prime Minister did not get it, then it was the Chief Constable's fault.[47] Ironically, just before the Ministers attended the customary press conference, the Chief Constable brought them some disconcerting news: he had received that morning an alarming intelligence report of possible IRA action in early February.[48]

How accurate this information was became apparent when five soldiers were shot and another injured by a gelignite bomb as violence spread through Catholic areas in Belfast on 3 February. The background to these disturbances was Army intelligence that the January disturbances were the work of the Provisionals and of their 1st and 2nd Battalions of the Belfast Brigade in particular whose leaders operated from the Clonard. Towards the end of January, the Army had found evidence that the Clonard Provisionals were manufacturing locally the incendiary devices being planted in shops and offices in Belfast. An informant in this connection – J.J. Kavanagh – was murdered on 27 January. The Army thus decided to search a part of the Clonard as soon as possible, the need for speed being accentuated by the fact that the 2 Battalion The Royal Anglians, which occupied the area, was due for relief during 9/11 February. A strong force was assembled including reserves drawn from Londonderry. However, since only eight houses were on the target list plus a garage, all widely separated, a mass reaction was not anticipated. Searching began at first light on the morning of 3 February. There was no reaction until 12:15hrs by which time the only finds were training pamphlets and Sinn Féin literature. At this time, a crowd of women, girls and youths assembled and attempted to stone the troops. Children came forward to stone and to jump on to vehicles. The adults were kept under control by arrests and the baton round. The children were pushed to one side. In the evening, however, a crowd of about 150 men began stoning and bottle throwing. Others assembled in Leeson Street and shots were fired at the Army by fleeting gunmen at Flax Street Mill, Tyrone House and Albert Street Mill. Between 22:30 and 04:00 on 3/4 February, attempts were made to bring crowds out in all Catholic/Republican areas of the city. The Army noted that there was little support in Ballymurphy and none in Ballymacarrett. A small crowd formed in the New Lodge Road, of whom thirty were adults with some seventy juveniles. Crowds grew to a peak of 200 in Leeson Street. About fifty men began to throw stones into the Crumlin Road from the Ardoyne. Petrol bombs were thrown at random from all these places and there was further shooting from the Clonard and Ardoyne. Fifty-four arrests were made including thirty adults. Many of these, particularly those in Leeson Street, were found to be IRA members or associates from other districts. The maximum number who turned out in all districts concerned at any one time was 370 at the peak. None were Officials. On the evening of 3 February, intelligence from a 'reserved secret source' reported that the Provisionals were, even prior to the events in the Clonard, planning to increase hostilities. At the same time, there was a concerted effort in the Republican press to state that the Clonard had been searched without reason as the inhabitants were 'defenceless and innocent people'. To combat this 'propaganda', it was decided by the Army and RUC to identify the Clonard openly as a 'nest of Bradyites'. In order to unsettle the local IRA leadership, it was also agreed with the Chief Constable and Special Branch to name them publicly, aiming also in the long-term to discredit them by Psychological Operations (PsyOps). These identifications were made at a press briefing next day, 4 February, by the CLF.[49]

Farrar-Hockley declared that: 'Battle has been joined with the Provisional IRA. It is not war, but it is definitely battle.' The Joint Security Committee appealed to people outside Belfast not to make unnecessary visits to the city and to those living in riot areas or near them to remain indoors after dark. The JSC warned that movement controls were likely to be imposed at short notice. The UDR was also put on alert and an extra 1,400 men from it were mobilized and moved close to Belfast to assist in manning road blocks and check points. With the extra troops – composed of one battalion of The Royal Regiment of Fusiliers and an armoured car squadron of The Royal Scots Greys – Army strength in Northern Ireland rose to nearly 7,000. The armoured car squadron was under the command of the Duke of Kent, a member of the Royal Family. As house searches continued, Farrar-Hockley announced that thirty-two houses and other buildings had been searched since 16 January. This, he said, was only a fraction of the number of houses in Belfast 'and of the houses in Catholic Republican areas, call them what you will, its not always the same thing'. Farrar-Hockley commented on a statement he had seen to the effect that, because the Army was searching in such a 'repressive' way, whole areas were seething with indignation. His response was: 'This is not my point of view and it is further not my point of view that searching a few houses in the Clonard area could possibly justify the sort of behaviour that has followed in a civilised country in a time of peace. Gunmen come unto the streets, supplemented on a wide basis by not only stoning but by petrol bombing, acid and ammonia explosives.' Troops had searched the Clonard area because it was an area which harboured a number of people in the Provisional IRA: 'And if there are people who say "Well who are these mysterious IRA Provisionals", I would ask the following gentlemen whether they are members and officers of that organisation: Mr William McKee, Mr Liam Hanaway and Mr Kevin Hanaway, his son; Mr Francis Card and... Patrick Leo Martin.' Farrar-Hockley claimed that some people had been going about the Clonard area with a great show of braggadocio for some months, including a whispering campaign which had been deliberately brought to the attention of the military that the RUC and the Army dared not come into Clonard to search. The Army did not want to take up challenges but that was the information which was being passed to the troops on the ground and if they needed to go into the area they would go and search 'in order to see that law and order is maintained'. Recent events were clearly attempts by the Provisional IRA to stir up trouble in the whole of Belfast or at least in areas where they thought they would have some support. The CLF viewed the situation as the Provisionals' reaction to a movement by the Army against an area which the IRA regarded as a sanctuary of their own: 'They either had to react to the situation or be seen to be paper tigers.'[50]

On 5 February, the Army received further intelligence that the Provisionals were determined to press hostilities, their aim being to create a crisis for Catholics in the North immediately prior to and during Fianna Fáil's Ard Fheis. Thus on the night of 5/6, bombs and firearms came into use, the former on a heavy scale. In the New Lodge area, a gunman emerged twice from a crowd of bombers to kill one soldier and wound five others of 32 Heavy Regiment. An armoured 1-ton truck of 1 PARA was set on fire when a platoon entered the Ardoyne to deal with about forty men bombing vehicles, civil and military, passing on the Crumlin Road. The troops jumping from the blazing truck came under fire and further bombing. They opened fire, killing one man and hitting at least three others with a total of seven shots. In the Bone, an NCO of the 3 Battalion The Queen's Regiment killed a man he believed to have been firing a pistol from a crowd of bombers and about the same time claimed a bomber was killed by a premature explosion of his grenade. The Army believed that the total of IRA casualties was not less than one dead and five wounded.[51]

The confirmed dead were James Saunders, a 21-year-old member of the IRA; Bernard Watt, a 28-year-old Catholic civilian; and Gunner Robert Curtis, a 20-year-old soldier from the 32 Heavy Regiment, Royal Artillery. Saunders, a Staff Officer in F Company of the Provisionals' 3rd Battalion was shot by one of two Army snipers positioned in the upper windows of a house in Louisa Street. Watt was shot in the chest by soldiers near his home in Hooker Street in the Ardoyne following the incident in which an APC had been hit by nail and petrol bombs. The Army claimed they were returning fire and there were allegations that the dead man was about to throw an oblong object which was alight when soldiers shot him. There was no forensic evidence that Watt had been in contact with lead, the most common indication that someone had been handling weapons and explosives. At the same time a pathologist found that while there was no evidence that the deceased had been thrown back by a blast, there were two high velocity bullet wounds in the chest and an exit wound on the back of the left buttock which could have been consistent with a man about to throw something. Gunner Curtis was the first serving soldier to die violently in the Troubles. A trainee surveyor in the Royal Artillery, he had joined the Army eighteen months later. He was among a contingent of soldiers drafted into Northern Ireland because of the shortage of available infantry troops. After coming under attack from about 100 rioters – some of whom were throwing petrol and blast bombs – a colleague heard a burst of automatic fire and saw two soldiers fall to the ground. As Curtis fell he let out a loud scream. He was struck by a bullet from a Thompson sub-machine gun (SMG) which entered his shoulder at the edge of his flak jacket and struck him in the heart. According to some reports he shed little blood, and those who went to help him did not realise he was dead until a lighted cigarette placed in his mouth failed to glow. Gunner Curtis's wife, who was three months pregnant at the time, was placed under heavy sedation after learning of her husband's death. Joan Curtis gave birth to a daughter six months later.[52] On 15 February, Lance-Bombardier John Lawrie, aged 22, also from 32 Heavy Regiment, became the second soldier to die in the Troubles when he died from wounds. He had been hit in the head after two bombs were thrown at two Army Scout cars the previous week.[53]

On the morning of 6 February the Army learned that the named members of the Provisionals' Belfast Brigade had 'taken fright' on being identified and had been unable to contact one another on the previous night when, 'to their surprise', British troops had fired back at them. Hence, the main attack petered out as no orders were given to deploy reserves. That night, attempts were made to attack the Security Forces again but, as before, the Army found that the mass of the populace would not support them, declining to answer agents knocking on doors. Those forty to fifty in the Lower Falls attempting to throw up barricades and obtain covered fire positions were thwarted by quick action from the 1 Battalion of The Royal Regiment of Wales. Perhaps two weapons were used to fire on troops in the Ardoyne but one gunman was shot by a sniper of 32 Heavy Regiment at midnight after which all shooting stopped.[54] Although the level of the disturbances was declining, a soldier was shot in the head and another was injured by a nail bomb in an ambush on two Army Land Rovers in the Ardoyne on the night of 8 February. Rioting in the New Lodge Road at tea time saw four young Protestants – two boys aged about 14 and two girls aged about 17 and 18 – who were at the junction of North Queen Street and Garden Street shot at while the RUC were keeping sectarian crowds apart. A man emerged from the Catholic crowd and fired towards the Protestants. The rioting had been sparked off when an Army vehicle knocked down and killed Denise Doxon, a 5-year-old girl. After the little girl was killed a crowd of about 200 gathered and attacked troops.[55] Many residents were taken aback by the intensity of the rioting: reflecting on the intensity of the disturbances, Tom Conaty, chairman of the CCDC, was shocked at how quickly they had evolved. 'Like so many of these riots,' he said, 'it didn't start off so seriously. The people... opened their doors... to find a mass deployment of British Army personnel in their area... But the fact is that it escalated to this very serious and sad rioting which... really amounts to the explosion of resentment at the one sided searching which is going on.'[56] Gerry Fitt went a little further: while there were many factors in the disturbances one undoubtedly was that a section of the Republican Movement had taken advantage of the very real discontent in the Catholic areas.[57] Somewhere, in between these two statements, lay the truth. What was clear was that relations between the Catholic community and the Army were deteriorating fast.

Almost as an aside was the heightening of tensions between the Officials and the Provisionals. The Officials claimed that the Provisionals had been responsible for the shooting of one of their Volunteers, in Ballymurphy, on 5 February. The man who was shot was John MacGuinness. He was ordered by four Provisionals to surrender his weapon. When he refused he was shot in the head. The Provisionals had alleged that their units operating in Lesson Street had been warned by the Officials not to engage in action against British troops. They were told by the Officials that they would be 'dealt with' if they did so. The Officials, in turn, denied this, stressing instead that their units had been engaging the British.[58] While the Officials described the tactics of the Provisionals as morally and militarily wrong, the Provos countered that: 'We don't believe that either the people on the Falls or the Shankill road want a Marxist-Leninist State and we don't believe you could unite them on such an issue.'[59] The Provisionals believed that it was they who were the future of Republicanism: Rory Ó Brádaigh claimed that from the present movement in the North would come the forces to transform the country from top to bottom and which would bring about a democratic, socialist republic based upon the Proclamation of 1916 and the rights of the Northern people. The solution lay in the Irish people, North and South, taking possession of their country and its resources and building a state structure with a new economic system which would be national, Gaelic and Christian.[60]

The Provisionals now buried their dead. At the funeral of James Saunders, twelve men flanked the coffin wearing green battle jackets, black berets and black armbands. They also wore heavy black boots and military-style overshoes like shinguards. A volley of shots was fired at the funeral and the twelve marched to military commands given by another man. At least half of the mourners were observed to have marched rather than walked. The sight of paramilitary-style uniforms put more pressure on Chichester-Clark, who made it clear that the Government intended to be particularly hard on such displays to ensure that 'funeral processions cannot with impunity be given any of the features of provocative political displays which tend to incite or cause a breach of the public peace'. The Prime Minister found it intolerable that when the Security Forces were involved in a battle with subversive elements that such elements should be able to flaunt themselves openly on public thoroughfares. If that could not be guaranteed with the currently available forces then it had to be seen if those forces could be strengthened so that decent people would not be again affronted by such events.[61] The Prime Minister was reflecting the anger of ordinary Protestants: the funerals of Saunders and Bernard Watt had been harassed and attacked by groups of Protestants as they made their way through the city to Milltown Cemetery. The first funeral was stormed by a group of Protestants who seized a Tricolour from the hearse. Saunders's funeral had to be rerouted twice after a crowd of 2,000 Protestants blocked part of the original route which was to pass through Protestant areas. At the graveside, Joe Cahill delivered the oration:

> James Saunders died that Ireland might be free. And so that all Ireland would have the right to live in freedom and a just unity under whatever form of government the majority wished... Jim had often said that he felt that God had appointed him to sacrifice his life for the freedom of his country... He was a disciplined soldier. It is only by complete unity and discipline that we will surely achieve the aims for which he sacrificed his all. We can take consolation in the fact that he has gone to join a band of gallant martyrs.[62]

The killing, however, was not over yet. The body of Albert Bell, a 25-year-old Protestant, was found in a ditch on 7 February. He had been shot twice in the head at close range. Republicans were assumed to have killed him but no organization ever claimed responsibility. Although a Protestant, he was believed to have Republican sympathies. On 9 February, five men, three of them Protestants and two from England and Wales respectively – John Aiken (aged 52), Harry Edgar (43), William Thomas (35), George Beck (43) and Malcolm Henson (24) – were killed by an IRA bomb intended for the Security Forces. They were travelling in a BBC Land Rover, on the way to inspect a BBC transmitter. The device had been planted under boulders at the side of a track on Brougher Mountain, County Tyrone. The Land Rover ran into a tripwire set knee-high across the track. The impact of the wire pulled a plug out from between the jaws of a clothes-peg contact; contact was made and a mine exploded by the vehicle. The trap was designed to catch an Army patrol that had been patrolling up the mountain checking the damaged transmitter site. But that morning the civilian engineers arrived first on the site.[63]

Despite these deaths it seemed that, overall, the response of the Security Forces to the recent disturbances had restored some of Chichester-Clark's confidence: so much so that he appeared cautiously optimistic about the situation in Northern Ireland when he met with Heath, Maudling and Carrington at Chequers on 13 February. He saw no great change ahead. He did not expect the forthcoming UUC meeting to present any great difficulties – unless there was some unforeseen development in the meantime. He thought that Craig and West had lost a good deal of ground – 'Craig was a sick man' – and the real centre of right-wing opinion was now Paisley. But Paisley's only real platform was the line that the British Army did not protect the Protestants and did not allow them to protect themselves. Chichester-Clark did not think that Paisley had gained ground substantially; he might even have been losing ground until the recent rioting. He concurred with Maudling that it was difficult to see any scope for a new political initiative in Northern Ireland and was inclined to agree that, at any rate until the shootings began a week ago, relations between the communities had been improving, though there was a long way to go before the ground lost in the last two years was recovered. Progress with the programme of reforms, and particularly of local government reform, had helped to bring about this improvement. As for internment, Chichester-Clark identified three possible sets of circumstances in which the Northern Ireland Government might be faced with this inevitability:

(i) if the Government of the Republic started to intern;
(ii) if the IRA proceeded to a campaign of political assassination;
(iii) if it proved impossible otherwise to break the 'wall of silence'.

He was against introducing internment, and so were the police. They would have to take in about 300 to 400 people, but there would be a lot of younger people whom the police did not know and who would not be picked up. The introduction of internment would bring crowds into the streets again; all the Civil Rights demonstrators would be given a new cause, just as their old causes were disappearing; and there would be risks of kidnappings. While Chichester-Clark made it clear that it was for the Northern Ireland Government to decide whether to introduce internment he promised that they would not do so without consulting the British Government.[64]

In the days after the Chequers meeting, Heath suggested to Carrington that 'If we believed that there was a constant come-and-go of IRA terrorists between the North and the South, there might be something to be said for transferring some of the Army's effort from the cities to the border.' The main point here was that 'our strategic dispositions should be related to an up-to-date assessment of the strategic situation and objectives.'[65] Carrington agreed 'that we must vary our strategic dispositions according to the current assessment of the situation and objectives in Northern Ireland if we are to achieve our aims and use our available Security Forces to the best effect. You can be sure that we have this problem very much in mind both in the Ministry of Defence and in Headquarters Northern Ireland.' The problem was essentially one of deciding what proportions of the total available effort should be directed at any one time towards deterring and if necessary stamping out any riots or disturbances in the cities; towards isolating, seeking out and bringing to trial the extremist ringleaders, and capturing their arsenals; and towards protective and deterrent operations in the rural areas and along the Border. 'We have to be careful not to over-react to any one threat', explained Carrington. What the Security Forces therefore tried to do was to retain enough flexibility in their operations to deal with a variety of threats, as best they could, within the available force levels. Carrington conceded it was true that at present the IRA were able to take the initiative; but this stemmed not nearly so much from their use of the Border for two-way traffic as from the scope they had for operating, within Northern Ireland, from urban bases in the Catholic areas, made relatively secure by intimidation and even murder. This was not to say that the existence of a sanctuary in Éire, with an unmarked land border 300 miles long – enabling reinforcement or withdrawal by stealth at minimum risk – was not a considerable advantage to them. But the Security Forces would not be able to maintain close and continuous surveillance of the entire Border except by withdrawing to a large extent from the urban areas where Carrington believed the greater part of the danger lurked – and, even then, probably not unless their numbers were increased substantially which could only be done at the expense of the British Army of the Rhine (BAOR) – 'and this, as you know, would involve political as well as military penalties'. However, Carrington was anxious that Heath did not think that the Border was undefended. The main task of the armoured cars based in Omagh was to patrol it; and this was an important part of the UDR's *raison d'être* as well. But 'what we need most of all in Northern Ireland was continuous and accurate intelligence and this particularly applied to effective counter-action against the extremists.' With good intelligence

> we can forestall the enemy's plans, arrest their ringleaders, locate their arms dumps and hiding places and generally thwart their intentions. Without good intelligence we can do none of these things and we largely waste our resources. We are making every effort to improve the organisation and effectiveness of our intelligence network, and I believe that it is principally by an improvement in this respect that the initiative will be transferred to the Security Forces.[66]

CHICHESTER-CLARK GOES

Chichester-Clark's confidence boost proved to be only temporary as it soon became apparent that IRA violence had not been quelled. Security remained the key political issue for the Protestant community as the Northern Ireland Government pushed for more robust measures while the Army continued to reject them on the basis that they were unnecessary. On 27 February the evidence that the Provisionals were still keen to move onto the offensive was provided by the double killing of two RUC officers in north Belfast. Detective Inspector Cecil Patterson, aged 47, and Constable Robert Buckley, aged 32, were shot dead in a gun attack. Patterson was a senior officer in the Special Branch. He and other officers went to Alliance Crescent in Ardoyne in response to a radio message that rioting was going on in the area. They had just walked from Alliance Crescent to Alliance Parade when they were fired on. Patterson told a Detective Sergeant accompanying him: 'Hit the deck, Tom.' The Detective Sergeant recalled: 'We were lying on the road. Automatic gunfire was being directed continuously from the Etna Drive direction and the bullets were bouncing off the road all around us. Inspector Patterson turned around and said, "I'm hit". He became unconscious and blood was coming from his body quickly. I raised my head and shouted for help.' The Chief Constable, Graham Shillington, who had replaced Young (much to the concern of many Catholics) rang Faulkner at home to tell him he was withdrawing all unarmed patrols in Belfast and was issuing revolvers to any RUC men going out on duty. Faulkner recorded that 'this was the effective end of hopes that the RUC could operate as an unarmed "English Bobby" style police force'.[67] A further Security Force casualty occurred on 1 March when Lance-Corporal William Jolliffe, aged 18, of the RMP died after an Army Land Rover was hit by a petrol bomb and crashed into a wall in Londonderry. The soldier succumbed to the asphyxiant and anaesthetic effect of a high concentration of chemicals after he had been doused by a fire extinguisher. The vehicle had been attacked by youths during what appeared to be a planned assault.[68]

These deaths had a significant political impact. On 2 March, the UKREP, Ronnie Burroughs, despatched an urgent telegram from Belfast to be on the desks of the Private Secretaries of the MOD, Home Office and Foreign Office by 09:00 hours the next morning. Its opening line read: 'Major Chichester-Clark and his Cabinet are agreed that unless they can convince their supporters that they can promise a fortunate outcome to the present security situation during the next 48 hours they will have to abandon office... This seems to be no idle threat and it is almost universally agreed that if this were to happen the result would be unprecedently serious for Ulster.'[69] The Northern Ireland Government produced a statement of its position which contained a number of proposals to improve the security situation, including: 'a military and police presence... maintained, within the enclaves where intimidation by subversive elements is now apparent, or where there has been persistent rioting'; the use of offensive weapons to be followed at once by a 'hot pursuit' search undertaken in the general area where they have been used; and a cordon to be thrown around the immediate area to seal it off and prevent the users of offensive weapons from escaping. This should be followed up by searching as soon as possible where this was likely to be effective.[70]

In his assessment of the statement the Acting GOC – Freeland was succeeded, on 3 February, by Lieutenant-General Vernon Esrkine-Crum but the new GOC suffered a severe heart attack twelve days later and died in hospital on 17 March[71] – went through each point and effectively dismantled the Northern Ireland Government's entire argument. He argued that a permanent military presence in Catholic enclaves would lead to a fragmentation of his available forces and 'a standing invitation to defeat in detail'. It seemed to the Army that the comment relating to 'hot pursuit' illustrated that the term was not correctly understood. Hot pursuit implied immediate follow-up action to apprehend an identified assailant who was known to have fired from, or fled to, a given spot, not a general area. Cordons were expensive in the use of manpower. An effective cordon of even two streets could use up one company. Were this policy to be followed, the extremists could create widely scattered, simultaneous incidents, requiring the commitment of all available forces thus leaving troops undefended elsewhere. The Acting GOC explained that it was pointless to search an area without hard intelligence. This had been proved time and again. It was equally pointless to search an area from which fire had been directed earlier unless a cordon had been imposed to prevent the assailants from slipping away. Wild pursuit of the sort suggested would only alienate the majority and play into the hands of the extremists.[72] In general terms the Acting GOC emphasized that, as a matter of principle, it would be wrong for HMG to submit to what amounted to an ultimatum: 'If we once allow Stormont to lay down detailed instructions for military action the future freedom of action of the Security Forces will be seriously prejudiced.' Some of the measures were militarily unsound. Stormont Ministers wanted a more active search policy more for its effect on public opinion and morale than for its effectiveness in securing more arrests and arms finds. And, crucially, he repeated the key military point: there had been no serious deterioration in the military situation which would warrant any major change in policy.[73] As Burroughs put it, to pretend to announce a new and unrealistic policy based on Chichester-Clark's recommendations would in the military's view be a sham which would be exposed by events: while Chichester-Clark might temporarily be given the will to survive the present crisis to the degree that such measures were ineffective, 'he would be hoist by his own petard'. Burroughs had come to the conclusion that Chichester-Clark's position was 'barely tenable'.[74]

As London was considering its formal response more violence broke out in Belfast. According to security sources the genesis of the trouble seemed to have been the kidnapping of three Protestants by the IRA early in the morning of 5 March. These Protestants were members of a group with whom the Officials had deposited a cache of arms for safekeeping. Because of a shortness of funds they had begun to sell the deposited weapons and ammunition for their own profit. The IRA learned of this and were holding two of the kidnapped men as hostages while the third was released to inform his friends that the other two would be killed if the complete arms cache was not returned to the IRA. In an attempt to find the hostages the Security Forces searched a bar in the Falls area at 1.30 p.m. This resulted in some rioting. Subsequently the hostages were released from another part of Belfast and the arms cache, amounting to nearly 6,000 rounds of ammunition, was uncovered by the Security Forces in a house in a 'non-sectarian' northern suburb of the city. Sporadic rioting continued in the Falls throughout the afternoon and, with less intensity, into the evening. Vehicles were hijacked and used as barricades; petrol and nail bombs were thrown. These became particularly serious around midnight and, after a warning was given, soldiers of 3 PARA opened fire. Two men were hit, one of whom later died. During the same evening and night there was also trouble in the Ballymurphy, Ardoyne and New Lodge Road areas involving occasional petrol bomb and firearm attacks on the Security Forces. During this 24 hour period it was estimated that over 200 bombs of various sorts were thrown at the Security Forces and forty rounds fired. The Security Forces were satisfied: they suffered six minor casualties; killed one alleged assailant and wounded three, possibly four, others, and effected twenty-eight arrests.[75]

The young man killed by the soldiers was William Halligan, aged 21. The Terence Penny Republican Club said he did not have nail or petrol bombs but had been one of a crowd of men taunting soldiers. The Army claimed that he had thrown a nail bomb immediately before he was shot. A Lieutenant-Colonel from

The Parachute Regiment gave the order to open fire after several of his soldiers had been injured. Petrol and gelignite bombs had been thrown at his troops. He warned the crowd with a loudhailer but as he finished speaking a nail bomb landed only a short distance away. He said soldiers were ordered to open fire when they had a target: someone who had been positively identified as being in the act of throwing a missile. Eight soldiers had been organized into a sniper party and they fired fifteen shots at people who had been identified as targets. An RUC constable claimed that Halligan's clothes had a strong smell of petrol. Years later the Halligan family were awarded undisclosed damages after successfully suing the MOD.[76] But it was not just the Army and the Provisionals who were responsible for deaths on the streets. On 8 March, Charles Hughes, a 26-year-old Lieutenant in the Provisional IRA was shot dead by a member of the Official IRA. Hughes had been walking along a street in west Belfast when a gunman emerged from a house and opened fire. Another man was shot in the face at close range by one of three men as he sat in his milk van. Subsequently sources suggested that the Officials had planned to kill up to eighteen leading members of the Provisionals. The operation was, however, called off. But the Official IRA squad apparently did not receive the countermanding order. Hughes – a relative of Brendan Hughes – had a high status in the local community having almost single-handedly repelled a loyalist mob in August 1969. He was one of two Republican gunmen who opened fire from the grounds of St Comgall's Primary School in Divis Street. Herbert Roy was killed by the gunfire.[77]

These deaths were the prelude to one of the worst outrages of the Troubles – even by the standards of later outrages its brutality still stands out. And what is significant here is that Chichester-Clark's administration was tottering before the outrage: afterwards it was like a punch drunk boxer caught on the ropes unable to defend himself from his opponent's onslaught. It was only a matter of time before the towel would be thrown in. The outrage which delivered the final knockout blow to Chichester-Clark was the cold-blooded slaying of three young Scottish soldiers. The signal from HQNI which reached the Prime Minister in London stated:

> At 3.50 p.m. on the afternoon of 10th March three Fusiliers of 1st Battalion The Royal Highland Fusiliers stationed in GIRDWOOD PARK BELFAST were seen drinking in a public house in ANN STREET in the centre of the city, by two corporals from the same Company. The three Fusiliers, two brothers JOHN CRAIG and JOSEPH CRAIG and a third, Fusilier DOUGALD McCAUGHY, were in the company of five civilians. All the soldiers were officially off duty on a rest day.
>
> At between 4 p.m. and 5 p.m. an hysterical phone call was received by the ambulance service, reporting an accident in the LIGONIEL area of NORTH WEST BELFAST. The call was answered but nothing was found. This may or may not have any connexion with what occurred later.
>
> At approximately 8 p.m. the police received an anonymous 999 call to say that there were three bodies in a ditch beside a lane in the SQUIRES HILL area of NORTH WEST BELFAST. The police recovered the bodies who were

later identified by the murdered soldiers' Company Commander. All three had been shot in the head.

A good description of one of the five civilians was obtained and Special Branch investigations began immediately and continue. The next of kin of the three soldiers were informed by 1 a.m. 11th March.

Press enquiries began at 9.50 p.m. and the item was included in news broadcasts from 10 p.m. onwards. A simple press release was issued concurrently by Public Relations staffs in HQ Northern Ireland, and in London at 10.30 p.m. confirming that three soldiers had been found murdered and that next of kin were being informed.[78]

The soldiers were the first to be killed off-duty. They had been drinking with other soldiers in a bar in Cornmarket in central Belfast during the day. The Craig brothers – John was aged 20 and Joseph was aged 18 – were from Ayr; McCaughey – aged 23 – was from Glasgow. Their bodies were first found by children. One of them, a boy aged 12, said: 'We were just standing there frightened and not knowing what to do. Two men came along and one of them touched the head of a man who was lying over another. His head fell back and the man said, "They are stone dead".' The soldiers had probably been lured from the bar by someone or some people who pretended to be their friends. Beer glasses were found at the murder scene. The soldiers were probably relieving themselves when they were shot, standing beside each other. According to local rumours in north Belfast one of those involved in the killings was IRA member Patrick McAdorey. The killings had a tremendous impact on the Protestant community in particular. Twenty thousand people turned out in Belfast and Carrickfergus to express sympathy as the funerals took place in Scotland.[79] Lord Carrington decided that 'in view of the special circumstances in Northern Ireland we should not in future send Servicemen who are below the age of 18 to the Province for operational service with the Security Forces there. We shall gradually replace those under 18 who are already in Northern Ireland.'[80]

For Chichester-Clark the murder of the three soldiers was a watershed. When Maudling visited Northern Ireland on 5 March, he noticed a deterioration in Chichester-Clark's confidence. It was clear that the killings of the soldiers had made a great impact on him. Chichester-Clark believed that it had brought home to the general public the danger under which they all lay.[81] By 14 March, Burroughs was reporting to London that the 'morale of Ministers has sunk to new depths': three of them had received votes of no confidence from their constituencies and 'I must revise my guess that Major Chichester Clark might just squeak through'.[82]

While Burroughs seemed resigned to the fall of Chichester-Clark's Government, Heath desperately tried to find some formula that might preserve him in power. Chichester-Clark flew to England to meet with Heath on 16 March. Prior to meeting the Prime Minister, Chichester-Clark met with Maudling and Carrington where he explained that there had been a 'massive deterioration' in the political situation following the shooting of the three soldiers: if his Government was to survive it had to be seen to 'do something drastic' in the next few days. He saw imminent danger of a violent Protestant outburst and this worried him more than the Unionist Council meeting at the end of the month. There was a need to provoke a confrontation with the IRA to bring the present intolerable situation to a decision. But Carrington told him that there was no military need for additional troops. If they were sent as a political gesture they would not prevent incidents such as the recent murders. Any political gains would soon fade and there would be a need for another such gesture. Chichester-Clark admitted that if reinforcements were sent he could be asking for more in a few weeks on similar political grounds. The GOC, who was attending with the CGS, confirmed that he was not hampered in operations such as cordoning by lack of troops. Sir Geoffrey Baker explained that it was the intention to clamp down hard on an area immediately if a new murder took place and the GOC was willing and able to do this with his present strength. As for stationing troops in difficult areas, this could hamper movement by providing a tempting target for stone throwers; it was usually better to be stationed just outside the area so that proximity could be combined with freedom of movement. Chichester-Clark then confirmed that he remained opposed to internment. He accepted that, following the recent publicity, most of those one wanted to arrest would not be found. Moreover, the action would lead to massive retaliation and the IRA might kidnap a couple of girls from Shankill and threaten to kill them unless the internees were released. He mentioned that the head of the RUC Special Branch was marginally in favour of internment. What the Prime Minister was now pushing for was a 'third force'. He saw this arrangement as inevitable and thought that recruiting and training should start immediately. The new force should be armed. Maudling, however, regarded it as a fundamental principle that any armed force in the United Kingdom must be a United Kingdom force under United Kingdom control.[83]

When he met Heath, Chichester-Clark outlined the proposals he put to Carrington and Maudling. Heath began his reply by stating that the policy had been to try and isolate the IRA from the more moderate elements in the Catholic community. The aim had been to create the impression that such problems as remained were limited problems and that the bulk of the population could be left to pursue a normal life. As a result the Army's activities had not been made too obtrusive. But if it was thought desirable, for political reasons, for the Army to be seen to be more active, it was necessary to consider first what further action could and should be taken and, secondly, whether any changes in policy thought desirable could be implemented within the present strength of the forces in Northern Ireland. As part of such a development it would be possible to introduce cordoning and curfews in limited areas and for limited periods. But, as the CGS pointed out, there were certain obvious disadvantages in the proposal that Army units should be established within IRA areas. Moderate Catholic opinion might be antagonized and Catholics living in the areas could be provoked. The unit would be vulnerable to attack, and, if trouble arose, reinforcements would probably have to be brought in from outside. It might be difficult to extricate the unit without some loss of prestige and credibility. Heath then suggested that while the proposal to station troops within the IRA areas was being examined there might be a change to a more active policy on patrolling, cordons and curfews. But Chichester-Clark warned that time was fast running out. He feared that, within the next few days, there might be some violent reaction from the Protestants. There was bound to be some delay before the troops arrived and he therefore felt that additional troops should be provided immediately. He had in mind another four or five battalions to add to the existing ten battalions. Heath, however, thought that it was unrealistic to suppose that if the communities in Northern Ireland were really bent on civil war, this could be effectively prevented by the provision of more British troops. Chichester-Clark accepted that in purely military terms there would be little advantage from reinforcements; but his administration would be in danger unless he could produce 'something to show' in his statement in the Northern Ireland Parliament on the following Thursday (18 March). But Heath remained unclear about the aims of those in Chichester-Clark's own party who were trying to bring about the fall of the Northern Ireland Government. They ought not to suppose that by this means they could bring about a change of policy in Northern Ireland.[84]

In reality the game was up. The security situation dominated debate in Unionist circles. Faulkner recognized that the feeling within the Unionist Party against the Northern Ireland Government was virtually restricted to the law and order situation and, in expressing such feelings of misgivings 'people in our party are reflecting the feeling throughout the community right outside the ranks of political activities'.[85] Where the disagreement lay was in the implementation, on the ground, of practical law and order policies. It involved for the Government vis-à-vis the party, a question of self-confidence, of reassuring their supporters that, on a day to day basis, the most effective measures were being taken and of reassuring the party that Ulster's case was being put clearly and forcefully to Westminster and to the world at large.[86] But it was increasingly obvious that Government reassurances were worthless. On 18 March over 3,000 loyalists marched to Stormont from the centre of Belfast to protest against the Government and to lobby MPs. Outside Stormont the following resolution was passed by all the groups who took part:

We British subjects, met at Stormont to lobby the members of the Northern Ireland Parliament, and place on record:

1. Our condemnation of the policy of the Northern Ireland Government, which has left large areas of this province improperly policed and set at risk our internal security with the disbanding of the Ulster Special Constabulary and the disarming of the Royal Ulster Constabulary.
2. Our concern that the Westminster Government has not adequately grasped the situation, and, through improper interference and foolish policy decisions, has jeopardised the safety, peace and prosperity of this part of the United Kingdom.
3. Our conviction that we will not be bullied, bribed, beaten or badgered into a union with the Republic of Ireland.

4. We demand, as our legal right and just due, that leaders be appointed who will defend the Constitution of Northern Ireland and safeguard her Parliament and people from all threats, and that immediate action be taken, and be seen to be taken, to deal with the terrorist and renewed hostilities from Southern Ireland.

The marchers also handed in a petition demanding the immediate internment of known IRA leaders, the rearming of the RUC and the creation of an internal security force under the control of Stormont similar to the American National Guard which would be suitably armed.[87]

With Protestant disillusionment with the Government, attention was turning to Chichester-Clark's successor. Burroughs warned London that there could be no doubt that a General Election at the present time would result in an unacceptable administration. 'If we then abolished Stormont in the face of a popular vote a Protestant revolt would become a virtual certainty.'[88] In the UKREP's opinion Chichester-Clark was 'suffering from agonies of indecision and is a spent force'.[89] At this stage it seemed that Chichester-Clark's resignation, while inevitable, was not imminent. But, suddenly, on the morning of 19 March, Chichester-Clark's position changed. It sent London into a panic. On the 18th, Heath had left London for Sheffield at 3.30 p.m. to speak at the Cutlers Feast. When he arrived at Sheffield, at about 7.00 p.m., Robert Armstrong, Edward Heath's Principal Private Secretary, spoke to his Cabinet Office colleague Peter Gregson, who reported that Chichester-Clark had made his Parliamentary statement and that things seemed to be reasonably quiet in Northern Ireland. There appeared to be no probability of Chichester-Clark putting in his resignation before the following week. But, when Armstrong spoke to Gregson again at about 11.00 a.m. the following morning, his report was more disquieting. It was clear that Chichester-Clark's own Party were more dissatisfied with this statement than had first appeared. On Heath's instructions, Armstrong rang Gregson back to ask him to make it clear to the Home Office that the possibility of the Prime Minister going to Northern Ireland should not be dismissed out of hand as Burroughs had done in his conversation with Chichester-Clark the day before. When Heath and Armstrong arrived back in Downing Street at about 4.00 p.m. reports made it clear that Chichester-Clark was once again contemplating immediate resignation and that he was disposed publicly to base his decision on the ground that he had not obtained what he wanted when he came to London earlier in the week. He was asking to speak to the Home Secretary on the telephone. Unfortunately at that moment Maudling was in his car, which had broken down at Watford. Arrangements were made to bring him back to the Home Office in a police car and he agreed, by radio telephone from his broken-down car, that the Prime Minister should speak to Chichester-Clark. After a discussion with the Cabinet Secretary, Sir Burke Trend, Heath spoke to Chichester-Clark just before 5.00 p.m.[90]

PM [Heath] Hello.
CC   Hello.

PM	The Prime Minister.
CC	Oh, good evening Prime Minister.
PM	I am sorry that Reggie is delayed on his way back.
CC	I hear he has had a breakdown.
PM	He has, yes.
CC	I am really ringing to tell him that I feel myself that I can no longer go on in this job and I am intending to resign this evening.
PM	I am sorry I could not hear the last part of that sentence.
CC	That I was intending to resign this evening.
PM	Oh, what is the reason for this?
CC	Well, quite honestly I am afraid that I was very disappointed with the results of our discussion on Tuesday.
PM	In what way are you disappointed? We have sent you additional forces.
CC	The plain fact of the matter is that I simply do not see any way of carrying on unless we do produce some drastic change. Frankly, I don't think we're able to do it. I'm the first here to admit that the situation here is not entirely rational. I can't hold it; it's not that I'm not willing to try. I reckon that I've exhausted every possibility...
	I think one of the things that somehow or other has to be got across here is that we are not a Sovereign Parliament which nobody here at the moment believes.
PM	With great respect, what has got to be got across to Northern Ireland is that you are two communities that have got to live together. If you want to do in the IRA you don't do it by doing a series of useless gestures. You do it by understanding the situation and then taking effective action. That is really what has got to be got across to Northern Ireland. And we have lived too long now in a world of unreality and useless gestures...
CC	Well I do see that, but I mean the situation here has deteriorated again yesterday, when I made the statement in the House... and I am afraid that the situation is that it has fallen short of expectations and hopes, and this is why I didn't...
PM	Yes. Well, the decision has now been taken and the Cabinet informed, there is nothing I can do in that respect... Well, I don't think there is anything further to discuss really.
CC	Well thank you very much for ringing. Indeed may I say thank you very much for your help.
PM	Really, our help doesn't seem to have been of very great value.
CC	Well thank you very much anyway.
PM	Goodbye, Prime Minister.
CC	Goodbye.

When this conversation ended Heath had a short interval for other business, but returned to the subject of Northern Ireland speaking to the Acting GOC at 6.10

p.m.[91] Heath wanted to know whether or not the Army had looked into the possibility of more drastic cordoning as agreed. He was told that there had indeed been a cordoning operation. It was also made clear that the Army would be prepared to ask for a curfew if there was a major breach of the present peaceful situation. When Heath asked whether there had been any disturbances with which the Army had been unable to deal for lack of a curfew, he was told that there had been no such disturbances. Indeed Belfast had been very quiet. Heath then mentioned that the MOD were investigating the question of speeding up reinforcements for the Army in Belfast: Chichester-Clark had complained that the Army did not get out and kill the IRA, but had then agreed that he could quote no example of their having failed to take action when an incident occurred. He had then revived the suggestion that British troops should be stationed in some of the Catholic areas. The Army, however, still took the view that any such suggestion would 'make military nonsense'. What Northern Ireland Ministers really wanted was to provoke a confrontation with the IRA. The Army could do this by searching a number of houses in the Catholic areas indiscriminately. A crowd would then gather and the IRA would come out and start shooting. The Acting GOC knew only too well it was easy to provoke a confrontation, but he did not think that the IRA wanted to be provoked. He thought that the Army had fully met their brief. The Army had bent over backwards, within the agreement that they should use minimum force, and within the agreed rules of engagement.

With the military advice so clear there was now no chance of saving Chichester-Clark. That didn't stop people trying to do this anyway. At 6.10 p.m. Brian Cummings, Chichester-Clark's Private Secretary, rang up Robert Armstrong to announce that the 'irreversible decision' of Chichester-Clark to resign had not yet been announced and probably would not be announced for twenty-four hours, partly because of Heath's apparent willingness to help in any way possible, and partly because Chichester-Clark was anxious to ensure that his resignation statement was drafted so as to be 'as little unhelpful' as possible. Armstrong asked whether there was a specific 'X' for which the Northern Ireland Government were looking which would prevent Chichester-Clark's resignation. Cummings replied that the 'X' was the continuing presence of British troops in some Catholic areas. This did not necessarily mean 'bricks and mortar', but periodic mobile patrols were not enough. If some way could be found for a continuing military presence in some of these areas, this would probably be sufficient.[92] Plainly, given the military advice just proffered to Heath, this was out of the question. At 6.45 p.m. there was a meeting of Ministers at 10 Downing Street. It was decided that Lord Carrington, who was on his way to Yorkshire for the weekend, should be called back, and arrangements were made for him to be intercepted on his journey. He was driving up the motorway to Yorkshire in his Jensen, and the police eventually flagged him down within seven miles of his destination. Lady Carrington went on in the police car while Lord Carrington turned back. Later in the meeting it was decided that Carrington and the CGS should go to Belfast the following morning, in order to remove any misunderstandings there might be about what the British Government's policies were and how they were carried out. It was agreed that the news of this visit should be conveyed to Chichester-Clark shortly before his Cabinet meeting at 9.00 p.m. and released to the media simultaneously. It was thought desirable to try to warn Carrington of this before an announcement was made, and Armstrong therefore made arrangements for the Defence Secretary to be flagged down again by the police. By the time the police caught up with him, he had reached the Newport Pagnell area, and he preferred to come straight to London rather than spend further time speaking on the telephone.

At 8.40 p.m. Armstrong spoke to Burroughs, and asked him to convey to Chichester-Clark the news of the visit of Carrington and the CGS to Belfast the following day. Burroughs's immediate reaction was that this would make for more bitter recriminations, and he told Armstrong that Chichester-Clark had now decided to announce his resignation immediately that evening. Armstrong said that the proposal that Carrington and the CGS should go to Belfast had been on the basis that he had been informed by Chichester-Clark's Private Secretary that his resignation would not be announced until the following day. Burroughs promised to 'sit on the heads' of the Northern Ireland Cabinet. At 8.55 p.m. Armstrong again spoke to Brian Cummings and conveyed to him the decision to send Carrington and the CGS to Belfast. Cummings assured Armstrong that Chichester-Clark would not announce his resignation until after that visit; Burroughs subsequently rang to confirm that news. When Carrington arrived back at Downing Street at 9.30 p.m., he saw the Prime Minister (who had a speaking engagement that evening) at about 11.00 p.m. Carrington was concerned lest his mission should appear to be a last-minute bid to save Chichester-Clark, and it should be thought he was going to make further offers. He was, however, reassured by the tone of some of the broadcasts that evening. When Heath returned from his speaking engagement he and Carrington discussed the situation and Carrington's mission. The Prime Minister agreed that there was some risk of misinterpretation, but his reading of the situation was that Chichester-Clark wanted to resign, that a number of his closest associates were anxious to see him cast the blame on the British Government and that the extremists in the Ulster Unionist Party were trying to get him out. Carrington's visit could serve to make it clear to Chichester-Clark and his Cabinet 'not only that we could not accept that we had failed to meet any reasonable request by Major Chichester-Clark, but also that no alternative Prime Minister could expect any British Government to adopt different policies'.[93]

Carrington and Sir Geoffrey Baker arrived in Northern Ireland the next morning, 20 March. They met Chichester-Clark in his office at noon. Chichester-Clark began with a general statement in which he said that he no longer had any authority or any credibility as Prime Minister of Northern Ireland. Carrington pointed out that so long as the terrorists were active there would be discontent in Northern Ireland whatever help the United Kingdom Government gave. If Chichester-Clark were to resign, the problem would still remain – and so would the policies which Her Majesty's Government were determined to pursue. Carrington thought that many people in Northern Ireland underestimated the disgust felt in Great Britain at what was going on and that unless the politicians in Northern Ireland became more sensible British public opinion would become increasingly disenchanted with the Union. Chichester-Clark accepted that though he realized this personally it was not generally realized in Northern Ireland; one of the things he hoped from his resignation was that it would bring home some of these facts to the people and make them recognize that Stormont was not a sovereign Parliament. There was then some discussion on Army tactics; Carrington asked Chichester-Clark to recognize that the British Army had a good deal of experience as well as professional training so that deliberately to antagonize certain sections of the population would defer indefinitely a solution of the problem. Chichester-Clark answered that he did not think it mattered if some sections of the population were antagonized at the present time and added that he thought that some sort of 'rough house' in the troublesome areas essential. He admitted however that the tactics he was proposing were political rather than military. He could not challenge the professional rightness of the Army's methods but time had run out for him and he would have to go. At this point Chichester-Clark asked the Chief Constable to join the meeting. When Shillington arrived, Chichester-Clark said that the Chief Constable was in favour of the Army camping out in areas such as the Ardoyne and asked him to explain his reasons. In fact, Shillington did not either confirm or deny that this was his view but explained several times that he fully understood why the Army thought that it would be difficult. He knew that there was a good deal of covert activity by the Army in the so-called no-go areas but suggested that this should be combined with overt activity to restore confidence. When the meeting adjourned Carrington had a brief private chat with Chichester-Clark; the Prime Minister confirmed that he had reached an irrevocable decision to resign as soon as possible. He undertook, however, to defer any announcement long enough to enable Carrington to report to Heath and for both of them to have a conversation.[94] Next Carrington met the full Northern Ireland Cabinet where he had an ample opportunity to hear the raw concerns of those representing the Unionist population. He suggested that the differences between the two sides seemed to be more a matter of emphasis than of principle. There had been no major suggestions for new initiatives. The policy of the Army was not one of containment: they were determined to take action against the IRA; but for this it was essential to build up intelligence, which was necessarily a slow process. However, he accepted the need for an intensification of military activity, primarily to restore public confidence. The situation was placing a severe strain on the Army and he warned that if there were sustained criticism of the Army's actions public opinion in Britain would increasingly favour leaving the Irish to get on with settling their differences on their own.[95]

Back in England, Heath had travelled down to Chequers at 12.30 a.m. on 20 March to await the news from Belfast. The initial reports which came through of Carrington's meeting with Chichester-Clark suggested that the Prime Minister might be prepared to postpone his resignation for two or three days. After Carrington's meeting with the full Cabinet in Belfast, however, it became clear that he was not so prepared. Carrington, accompanied by the CGS, returned to Chequers at 6.00 p.m. coming straight from RAF Northolt to report to Heath the results of his mission; Maudling and Douglas-Home were also there. Carrington brought back with him a first draft of Chichester-Clark's resignation statement, the text of which had been telephoned through by Burroughs earlier on. Shortly after Carrington arrived, Burroughs telephoned with a revised text, adding that Chichester-Clark had done his utmost to avoid recriminations, that he proposed to put the statement out without gloss or comment, and he hoped that Heath would be prepared likewise to refrain from comment or recrimination. Carrington reported that he had persuaded Chichester-Clark to postpone the announcement of his resignation until he had spoken to the Prime Minister on the telephone. Heath accordingly spoke to Major Chichester-Clark. Chichester-Clark said that all but two of his colleagues thought that he was right to resign. The longer he delayed an announcement, the greater the uncertainty would be; and, if he made his statement that evening, notice of a meeting to elect a successor could be given for 23 March. If his resignation were delayed until Sunday, the election meeting could not be held until 24 March. Heath urged Chichester-Clark to delay his announcement until the following day, in order to avoid the risk of its being interpreted as an immediate reaction to Carrington's visit; but Chichester-Clark was unwilling to do this, because he wanted to minimize the period of interregnum and thought that people in Ulster would not much like his taking action on a Sunday. He agreed, however, to postpone his announcement until 10.00 p.m.[96]

Chichester-Clark resigned on the evening of 21 March. In his resignation statement he explained that he had decided to resign because he could see no other way of bringing home to all concerned the realities of the present constitutional, political and security situation. It was apparent that public and Parliamentary opinion in Northern Ireland alike looked to the Northern Ireland Government for measures which could bring the current IRA campaign swiftly to an end. He had expressed to British Ministers the full force of this opinion and had pressed upon them his view that some further initiative was required. While they had agreed to take any feasible steps open to them to intensify the effort against the IRA, it remained the professional military view – and one which he indeed often expressed himself – that it would be misleading the Northern Ireland community to suggest that 'we are faced with anything but a long haul, and that such initiatives as can be taken are unlikely to effect a radical improvement in the short term'.[97]

Notes

1. NAUK PRO DEFE 24/980 Relations Between the Army and the RUC, 29 July 1970.
2. NAUK PRO DEFE 25/273-11 Analysis of the Force Levels Required in Northern Ireland. Assessment by the GOC Northern Ireland, August 1970.
3. BSI 1208, Statement of General Sir Robert Ford.
4. Ibid.
5. BSI CD1, Statement of Major General (retired) Dalzell-Payne.
6. NAUK PRO DEFE 24/980 HQ Instruction for Opening Fire in Northern Ireland, 25 September 1969.
7. NAUK PRO DEFE 24/980 CGS to Secretary of State, July 1970.

8. NAUK PRO FCO 33/1076 Telegram No.152 to UK Rep Belfast, 31 July 1970.
9. NAUK PRO FCO 33/1076-15 Telegram No.7 Burroughs to Home Office, 31 July 1970.
10. NAUK PRO FCO 33/1076-13 Telegram No.255 Dublin Embassy to FCO, 31 July 1970.
11. NAUK PRO FCO 33/1076-12 Telegram No.256 Dublin Embassy to FCO, 31 July 1970.
12. *Belfast Telegraph*, 29 October 1970.
13. NAUK PRO DEFE 24/980 Use of Firearms in Northern Ireland, 30 June 1970.
14. NAUK PRO DEFE 24/980 Shooting of Daniel O'Hagan: 31 July 1970; 3 September 1970.
15. NAUK PRO DEFE 24/980 Shooting of Daniel O'Hagan: 31 July 1970.
16. *Irish News*, 5 August 1970.
17. Ibid., 5 August 1970.
18. Ibid., 12 August 1970, BT11 letter.
19. Ibid., 18 August 1970.
20. Ibid., 17 August 1970.
21. Ibid., 20 August 1970.
22. McKittrick, *Lost Lives*, pp.56–7.
23. Bishop and Mallie, *Provisional IRA*, p.168.
24. NAUK PRO FCO 33/1077 Burroughs to Home Office; Peck; Freeland, 8 December 1970.
25. *News Letter*, 13 January 1971.
26. Ibid., 14 January 1971.
27. *Irish News*, 15 January 1971.
28. *News Letter*, 15 January 1971.
29. Ibid.
30. *Irish News*, 15 January 1971.
31. Ibid.
32. Ibid., 16 January 1971.
33. *News Letter*, 16 January 1971.
34. *Irish News*, 16 January 1971.
35. *Belfast Telegraph*, 16 January 1971.
36. *Irish News*, 16 January 1971.
37. Ibid.
38. Ibid., 18 January 1971.
39. Ibid.
40. Ibid.
41. Ibid.
42. NAUK PRO DEFE 24/873 Note of a Meeting at the House of Commons, 18 January 1971.
43. *Irish News*, 19 January 1971.
44. *News Letter*, 20 January 1971.
45. NAUK PRO DEFE 24/873 A Summary of Questions by Ministers and Answers by the GOC, CLF and COS at the Initial Discussion on Arrival, 28 January 1971.
46. NAUK PRO DEFE 25/303 Meeting of Secretary of State for Defence and Minister of State, Home Office with the Northern Ireland Cabinet, 29 January 1971.
47. NAUK PRO DEFE 24/873 A Record of Some Points Raised at an Impromptu Meeting at Girdwood Park after Lunch on 29 January 1971.
48. NAUK PRO DEFE 24/873 Meeting Prior to the Press Conference, 29 January 1971.
49. NAUK PRO DEFE 25/303 Summary of Operations in Northern Ireland, 3–7 February 1971
50. *Irish Times*, 5 February 1971.
51. Ibid., 9 February 1971.
52. McKittrick et al., *Lost Lives*, pp.63–5.

53. Ibid., p.67.
54. NAUK PRO DEFE 25/303 Summary of Operations in Northern Ireland, 3–7 February 1971.
55. *Irish Times*, 9 February 1971.
56. Ibid., 5 February 1971.
57. Ibid., 8 February 1971.
58. Ibid.
59. Ibid., 9 February 1971.
60. Ibid., 8 February 1971.
61. Ibid., 10 February 1971.
62. Ibid.
63. McKittrick et al., *Lost Lives*, p.66.
64. NAUK PRO PREM 15/475 Note for the Record: Meeting at Chequers, 13 February 1971.
65. NAUK PRO PREM 15/475 Prime Minister's Personal Minute No.M8/71, 15 February 1971.
66. NAUK PRO PREM 15/476 Defence Secretary to Prime Minister, 19 February 1971.
67. McKitterick et al., *Lost Lives*, pp.67–8.
68. Ibid., pp.68–9.
69. NAUK PRO PREM 15/475 Telegram No.2 UK Rep Belfast to MOD/Home Office/FCO, 2 March 1971.
70. NAUK PRO DEFE 25/303 Statement by Stormont Ministers, 2 March 1971.
71. Bew and Gillespie, *Chronology*, p.32.
72. NAUK PRO DEFE 25/303 Annex A Detailed Comments, 2 March 1971.
73. NAUK PRO DEFE 25/303 Statement by Stormont Ministers Memo from DMO, 2 March 1971.
74. NAUK PRO PREM 15/475 Telegram No.2 UK Rep Belfast to MOD/Home Office/FCO, 2 March 1971.
75. NAUK PRO PREM 15/475 Report on Northern Ireland for Period from 9 a.m. 5 March to 8 a.m. 8 March 1971.
76. McKitterick et al., *Lost Lives*, p.69.
77. Ibid., p.70.
78. NAUK PRO PREM 15/475 Confidential.
79. McKitterick et al., *Lost Lives*, pp.70–1.
80. NAUK PRO PREM 15/476 A.W. Stephens to P.L. Gregson, 12 March 1971.
81. NAUK PRO PREM 15/476 Note for the Record, 24 March 1971.
82. NAUK PRO PREM 15/476 Telegram UK Rep to Home Office, 14 March 1971.
83. NAUK PRO PREM 15/476 Discussions with Major Chichester-Clark, 16 March 1971.
84. NAUK PRO PREM 15/476 Prime Minister's Meeting with the Prime Minister of Northern Ireland at 4.15 p.m., 16 March 1971.
85. *Irish Times*, 13 March 1971.
86. Ibid., 16 March 1971.
87. Ibid., 19 March 1971.
88. NAUK PRO PREM 15/476 Telegram No.6 UK Rep to Home Office, n.d.
89. NAUK PRO PREM 15/476 Telegram No.7 UK Rep to Home Office, n.d.
90. NAUK PRO PREM 15/476 Note for the Record, 25 March 1971.
91. Ibid.
92. NAUK PRO PREM 15/476 Note for the Record, 23 March 1971.
93. NAUK PRO PREM 15/476 Note for the Record, 25 March 1971.
94. NAUK PRO PREM 15/476 Note of a Meeting held in the Prime Minister's Office at Stormont Castle at Noon on 20 March 1971.
95. NAUK PRO PREM 15/476 Meeting between the Defence Secretary and the Northern Ireland Government, 20 March 1971.
96. NAUK PRO PREM 15/476 Note for the Record, 25 March 1971.
97. *Irish Times*, 22 March 1971.

3

The Road to Internment: March–August 1971

FAULKNER BECOMES PRIME MINISTER

On Sunday 21 March, Harold Wilson, the Leader of the Opposition, came to see Heath at 11 a.m. by appointment[1] where they spoke on Privy Counsellors' terms. After Heath filled him in on the political and military background to events Wilson said that he understood that it was likely that Brian Faulkner would succeed Chichester-Clark. His own impression of Faulkner was that he was a 'very tough egg' – in 1968, Faulkner had seemed to be an even tougher egg than Bill Craig. At that time Wilson had uttered, in public as well as in private, the warning that if Craig came in, some very distasteful things were bound to happen. Since that time, however, Faulkner seemed to have played it very straight. Heath agreed that Faulkner was likely to succeed Chichester-Clark; he also noted that Faulkner had been completely loyal to Chichester-Clark and that there was no question of his going back on the reform programme. Wilson presumed that the last thing which the Government wanted was Direct Rule, even though the Ulster Unionists knew that that was the last resort. Heath agreed. He had every sympathy with the Northern Irish in their problem of dealing with the IRA but Chichester-Clark had made the important point: it would be a long haul, and they wanted a short haul. The meeting concluded with Wilson assuring Heath that he would make it clear that Northern Ireland was not a matter of dispute between the political parties in Westminster.[2]

While the British seemed fairly relaxed at the prospect of a Faulkner premiership, in Dublin the prospect of him becoming Prime Minister had not exactly appealed to the Irish Government. Nor did it seem very enticing to the SDLP. The problem for constitutional Nationalists was that the new Prime Minister came with baggage. They never trusted him and were bound to see any security response to an increased IRA threat as part of a wider repressive agenda dictated by Faulkner and the Unionist right-wing. And issues of state repression were high on the agenda when the SDLP met with the British in February 1971. When Carrington and Sharples had gone to Belfast the visit had been devoted to security aspects and there had been no time to meet party deputations. So, the first opportunity for the SDLP to meet British Ministers was on 12 February when Gerry Fitt, John Hume, Austin Currie, Ivan Cooper and Paddy O'Hanlon met with Sharples and another junior Minister, Ian Gilmour. They expressed their concerns about the situation developing in Northern Ireland.

Fitt recognized the Army's difficulties, but he felt they were overreacting. They were acting on misleading information to make searches in volatile areas, and were being used deliberately by extremists to cause trouble. The main political argument which Fitt put forward was the need for participation. He and his colleagues had formed their new movement the year before, although they had been attacked on all sides. They would have welcomed a gesture from Stormont: for instance, they could and should have been consulted about the membership of the several Boards set up under the new reforms. Instead only 'castle Catholics' had been chosen, and they were not representative. There was no acceptance of the SDLP's existence by the Stormont Government. Hume reiterated that the recent outbreak of violence was deplored by most of the Irish people. But it was caused by sectarianism, and this in turn derived from the Unionist Government. Reasons existed for the pattern of violence over the years: they lay in the permanent instability of society. The framework of Government had broken down. When the British Government had put troops on the streets and pressed through reform this amounted to a public admission that the Northern Ireland Government was not capable of governing themselves. The present violence was only the logical result of that and the logical answer was a change of Government. Hume restated the plea for participation, and for a real examination of possible permanent solutions. The minority wanted to have a real stake in the institutions of their society: at the moment they had nothing. If only there could be an acceptance that the Government had failed it might be possible to discuss new possibilities for a solution.[3] What is interesting about this meeting is that the SDLP were quite clearly opposed to internment; but, only a few weeks later when Chichester-Clark was facing his political demise, Fitt – who had expressly stated his opposition – was, according to Ronnie Burroughs, at any rate, advocating the 'immediate internment of all provisional IRA men known to the police in order to rid Belfast of intimidation...He assures me that the Catholic population of the city would on the whole be vastly relieved by the removal of the IRA yoke on their necks.'[4]

While the SDLP were critical of Army tactics they were equally critical of Republicans who advocated the use of force. Paddy Devlin, for example, while stressing that violence had been created, first, as an extreme Unionist backlash in August 1969 to the reform programme, attacked the counter-backlash from a small group of armed Nationalist activists who, by exploiting every single incident, particularly in Belfast, had made the 'zealots of the UVF look like pikers in the mountain of sectarian hatred they had created, and in the viciousness of its expression in Northern society'. It was clear to Devlin that if this violence continued, hundreds of lives would be lost in a large scale religious war that was building up rapidly. No possible political solution could apply to Northern Ireland's problems while the million Protestants who lived there felt they were under attack by bigots. No new initiative could be taken up or pursued if people, through fear, 'jump back into their trenches to repel an expected attack'. Each new riot increased that volume of fear. Political change, stressed Devlin, would be brought about only because of the increasing confidence felt by Protestants when they saw evidence that their rights and opportunities were as equally secure as everyone else's would be in any future change; and they should receive ample assurance that they would not be coerced into accepting anything less: 'Under no circumstance must he [the Protestant] be made to feel that change relates to the blast of a gelignite bomb, or comes out of the menacing muzzle of a gun.'[5]

Hume developed a variation of this also. He felt that the Irish dissension was at present being paraded before the world at its ugliest. Terrible deeds had been done in Northern Ireland 'in the name of this and that noble cause'. The great danger was that everyone would be swept forward by the emotion of the moment: 'Nothing could be more foolish or irresponsible.' Never had it been so necessary to utterly reject violence and those who perpetrated it because violence had no solution to Ireland's problems. Some people claimed that violence was justified as a means of reuniting Ireland. What did that mean? Ireland was not a piece of earth – it was a lot of people: 'You cannot unite the people with the point of a gun.' People talked about divisions. To talk about divisions was not to talk about a line on the map. Hume was talking about a real division between people: a division based on sectarianism, hatred, prejudice, bigotry and fear – but nevertheless a real division. There was no instant solution. Unity could only come about through the slow progressive removal of the barriers that divided 'our people'. It had everything to do with removing these barriers and building up 'our country'. They could not proceed, he believed, to any decent future on the basis of hatred, fear and bigotry. What was fundamentally wrong in itself could never be politically right. But, in condemning the recent brutal and callous murder of the three Scottish soldiers, Hume made an important point: that there was more than one terrorist organization. There had been victims of a 'double bluff' in Northern Ireland before. Explosions, wrongly attributed by some in the media to one side, had helped get rid of O'Neill. Crucially, Hume felt that he must not omit to condemn 'other forms of violence'. An 'evil form of psychological violence' had, for a long time, been perpetrated against a section of the Northern Ireland people. It had left them in conditions that had been a breeding ground for the recent violence. It was Hume's firm conviction that the real Irish problem rested with those who perpetrated injustice because injustice and the rejection of change, coupled with violence of different kinds, had created the other kind of violence. The real Irish problem rested with the people who thought that their way of life could only be preserved by destroying the way of life of other people: 'Until the British Government confronts these people there will be no real lasting solution to our problem.' In the last analysis, there could only be a real solution when 'we solved our own problems'. In order to do that a just and proper framework was needed in which this could be achieved 'and we could look forward if there was a new framework of Government in which each section of the community could proportionately share'.[6]

Senior members of the SDLP were in no mood to compromise with the Unionist Government. Paddy Devlin rejection a suggestion from Jack Lynch that there should be a greater participation of the minority in Stormont: the SDLP had no intention of making themselves 'available, obtainable or involved' with the Unionist Government except in the role of an Opposition. Devlin rejected the idea that a member of the SDLP might become, for example, a

Parliamentary Secretary to the Minister for Community Relations or that another Opposition MP might be appointed to the Privy Council. The SDLP were not interested in these positions nor in the promotion of more 'Castle Catholics or token Taigues' to Government bodies. But the SDLP were interested in the establishment of Government Committees and seeing that every single member was appointed to them not because of a commitment to the Unionist Party but because of the unassailable qualifications, regardless of religion, that should reside in such appointments.[7] Hume also rejected the idea of a coalition Government, or even that members of the Opposition should be given Government positions. What was needed was the drafting of a completely new 'framework' which would provide minority participation. For an Opposition member to accept a job in the Government would mean they would be doing a patching up operation on a situation that had fallen apart already. Stormont was only an administration, and there was no reason why it should not be representative of the community as a whole.[8]

What this meant, particularly as developed by Hume, would become apparent later – Catholic-Nationalist participation in Northern Ireland's Government as of right. The more immediate problem for the SDLP was a Faulkner premiership. Ivan Cooper feared this would mean the setting up of a new security force: Westminster would have little choice but to cooperate with a Faulkner-led administration and concede such a force. Devlin thought that the only person who could replace Chichester-Clark was a right-winger: a compromise candidate would be vulnerable to every kind of right-wing pressure. Fitt believed that a new Prime Minister would be inevitably forced to backtrack on the reform programme. Only Hume saw a positive side to the crisis: 'I would think that we must be very close to the real crunch of the Northern Ireland problem.' As Hume saw it, for the past two years one question had been posed to the Unionist Party: 'can you as a party – and can your supporters who have survived and existed and maintained this State through injustice – can you, in fact, live with justice? The answer for quite some time had been clearly "no".' If Chichester-Clark went he went because people disagreed with policies – and for no other reason – yet his policies were the 'pure minimum' to bring Northern Ireland up to a respectful level of civil rights. Hume believed that, 'We have reached, I think, the crunch, and I've always said that the extreme forces of Unionism, the Right Wing of Unionism is the Northern Ireland problem: they have created this State, maintained it through injustice, resisted change and created violence in our society and until Westminster confronts them we will always have a problem, and I hope that confrontation is coming soon.' The situation now was that Unionism was facing the logic of its own past and 'That logic is that Unionism ... cannot ... survive without repression'.[9]

On the eve of the election of the new Unionist Party leader, Fitt rang Burroughs to say the there had been much nervousness among 'Republican politicians' who were afraid that Faulkner would 'slide out from under the reform programme'. Burroughs told him that in his view these fears were groundless and that in any case the position of the Westminster Government was quite clear in the matter. Fitt explained that some of his colleagues in the SDLP were under great pressure from their supporters to walk out of Parliament in the hope of hastening the end of Stormont rule. They had, however, now agreed to remain until such time as they could extract a statement from the next Prime Minister of a complete commitment to the reform programme. The only remaining waverer was Currie; Fitt asked Burroughs to 'stiffen him up'. Burroughs agreed to do so. If, however, the next Prime Minister did not give them the assurances they sought the SDLP would walk out and Fitt predicted that the greater part of the Catholic community would isolate themselves from the state in a passive resistance movement including the non-payment of taxes and rates.[10] Clearly, even before he was elected, the new Prime Minister of Northern Ireland would have little margin for error as far as Nationalists were concerned.

There were only two candidates for the premiership: Craig and Faulkner. Minutes after Chichester-Clark announced his resignation Craig declared that he would be prepared to lead a new administration.[11] He warned that 'We have only seen the tip of the iceberg in violence. We've a very bad time coming in front of us and we've got to stop playing politics.'[12] He believed that Faulkner could not form a Government without the Unionist right-wing, which he considered the mainstream of the Unionist Party; Faulkner was unpopular and untrusted in the constituencies. Craig said there had to be a leader who could bring unity in the country which was more important than unity in the Parliamentary Party. He felt that the constituencies were looking to him to represent their interests. If the Parliamentary Party went against the feeling in the country they would pay the penalty. He summed up that feeling as: 'Do not pick Faulkner or else – I am just warning what the constituency feeling is.' If elected Craig promised not to do anything unconstitutional, undemocratic or repressive. His first act would be to reorganize the RUC in order to make it effective against terrorism and to create a reserve force. He would, as a matter of courtesy, outline to Westminster what these policies would be: 'I would act as the Government of Northern Ireland within our Constitution. I would bring them along with our proposals but would not accept a situation where anyone would try to limit the powers of Northern Ireland.' Craig considered that: 'Direct rule is an impossibility. I don't know how anyone could seriously think about it.' It would meet massive opposition from the people who would see the British Government acting unconstitutionally; Westminster would have the real power but 'it would be unconstitutional for them to use it without our consent. We would not sit back and see unilateral action. They can in theory revoke the Government of Ireland Act but they would be embarking on a most irresponsible course. If they did attempt this it would unleash a holocaust.' The minority could become the innocent victims of a situation created by Westminster because people were getting angry in defence of their vital interests. They might not have time to stop and distinguish the innocent from the guilty. A blood bath could be easily triggered off. Craig warned that it would take very little to push a lot of people into violent reactions. If, on the other hand, there was a 'Catholic backlash' against his premiership it would have to be dealt with; but he did not believe this would happen. Catholics had as much interest as Protestants in crushing illegal organizations. If Westminster were to impose Direct Rule without the consent of the Northern Ireland Parliament, the Northern Ireland Government would have no alternative 'but to take similar steps to Carson and Craig: set up a provisional Government... We would exist as a separate State'. This would be a tragedy, he added, but they would be far better off on their own than in an Irish Republic.[13]

The favourite, however, remained Faulkner. And he knew it: when Burroughs spoke to Faulkner on 20 March he found a man confident of the nomination by the Parliamentary Party to the post of Prime Minister. He also gave an unequivocal assurance that if appointed as Prime Minister he would abide by all the principles of the 1969 Downing Street Declaration. There would be no going back on the reform programme, no re-arming of the RUC and no attempt to recreate the B Specials. He showed a 'maidenly modesty' when Burroughs asked him about the composition of any future Cabinet and said that he had not given any thought to the matter. He wished, however, to assure Burroughs that any Cabinet which might be chosen by him would only include people who would subscribe to his own policies. Faulkner had been encouraged by the recent meeting with Lord Carrington and the CGS and their robust attitude towards security problems. The touchstone was whether this attitude would be reflected by the troops on the ground. But, while recognizing his confidence, Burroughs also noted that: 'Faulkner is a realist and knows that although his chances of remaining in office for long are not very bright, he can only do so by remaining in the good graces of Westminster.'[14]

On 23 March, Faulkner trounced Craig by twenty-six votes to four in the vote of the Unionist Parliamentary Party for the leadership. Faulkner was now prepared to discuss his future Cabinet with Burroughs. He proposed to invite the rebel Harry West to join his administration as Minister of Agriculture and to offset this appointment by either Robin Baillie or Basil McIvor who were both acknowledged liberals. His object in inviting West into the Cabinet was to split the Craig/West axis and to draw the teeth of the latter's supporters. Burroughs reminded him – as had the Governor already – of the principle of collective Cabinet responsibility and suggested that he should check on West's voting record on the various reform measures to which he, as the incoming Prime Minister, had unequivocally committed himself. Burroughs was sure that the British Government and Parliament would wish to be quite clear that West was equally committed to this programme. Faulkner agreed that this was necessary. Burroughs noted that West had not been as extreme as Craig, but the abandonment by West of his previous stance would throw the right wing into serious disarray: 'I would not expect him to accept. The trap is too obvious.'[15] As it turned out he did: West, to the shock of many of his supporters, accepted Faulkner's offer. He claimed to have been persuaded that the interests of Ulster were not to be served by pursuing past disagreements to the point where they could give comfort to enemies or threaten Northern Ireland's position within the United Kingdom. He effectively conceded that he would abandon calls for the rearming of the RUC and the recall of the USC when he publicly accepted that the decisions which had been taken 'cannot be altered' and that the aim was now to ensure that the campaign against terrorism 'within the framework of accepted policy' was to be pursued with the utmost vigour and effectiveness. West was convinced that Faulkner was the man to do this and pointed to his success as Minister of Home Affairs during the border campaign.[16]

Phelim O'Neill, a noted liberal, was the man West replaced. In what was a radical departure from the norm – for a Unionist Government anyway – Faulkner appointed David Bleakley, of the Northern Ireland Labour Party, as Minister of Community Relations in place of Robert Simpson. Bleakley was not a member of the Northern Ireland Parliament but Faulkner was able to make the appointment due to powers resident in the Government of Ireland Act permitting a person who was not a member of either House of Parliament to hold ministerial office for a period of not longer than six months.[17] Faulkner explained that he had appointed Bleakley because 'at this difficult moment' for the country the needs of Northern Ireland overrode other considerations.[18] Elsewhere, Herbie Kirk stayed at Finance, William Fitzsimmons at Health and Captain Long at Education; Roy Bradford moved from Commerce to Development, with his place taken by Robin Ballie. Nat Minford gained promotion to the Cabinet as Leader of the Commons, while also retaining his job as Minister of State at the Ministry of Development. Captain John Brooke moved into the Cabinet as Minister of State at Finance and Chief Government Whip. Joe Burns was rewarded for his support of Faulkner with a junior job in a new post of Parliamentary Secretary to the Minister for Health and Social Services. At Stormont the first order of business for the new Government was the discussion of a motion of confidence tabled by the Unionist front bench. Opening the debate, Faulkner set out the issue which was to dominate his premiership: security. He said that it was a plain fact that unless the law and order situation could be dealt with more vigorously it would be difficult to advance on any other front. In the field of law and order the aims would be firmness and efficiency. The new Prime Minister also made it clear that there would be no going back on any of the radical legislation which had been enacted over the past two years: 'I was a party to them in the last administration because I believed them to be right. My change of office has in no way changed my views.'[19]

In Dublin the Irish Government remained more than a little nervous with the Faulkner succession – although it was better than the alternative: Craig. When the British Ambassador, John Peck, met with Paddy Hillery in Dublin the latter emphasized that he was waiting to see what Faulkner did as distinct from what he said. Hillery had already inquired of Hume whether: 'If the Catholic leaders in Belfast were persuaded that the Reform Programme was being fully implemented and their physical security (i.e. against pogroms etc.) assured, would they be prepared to encourage the minority to cease relying on the IRA for their protection and to stop any harbouring of gunmen?' Hume, who was expecting London to make concessions to the right wing Unionists, said that, given convincing reassurance, he thought they would. Hillery therefore thought that a new Prime Minister who felt able to initiate some form of consultation, either institutionalised or informal, with the Opposition leaders would offer the best hope of stopping the IRA gunmen.[20] From this, and other conversations and statements, Peck deduced that Lynch was clearly trying to do two things. He was pressing the Catholics in the North to play along with the authorities and desert the IRA and he was publicly taking Westminster and Stormont at their word about reform. The former Peck considered a courageous political act, as Fianna Fáil was largely suspending judgement on Lynch's peaceful approach until results were visible and the Taoiseach could scarcely have done this except in the context of publicly assuming that the Reform Programme would be fully and practically implemented. From Dublin's point of view, the best way to undermine the IRA would be for the Catholic minority to feel that their moderate leaders had regular access to the Prime Minister.[21]

Faulkner was aware of Dublin's misgivings; so, in a dramatic attempt to reassure the Irish Government, Faulkner sent a secret message to Lynch. Sir Harold Black, the Stormont Cabinet Secretary, telephoned the Irish Ambassador, Dr O'Sullivan, in his London home at about midnight on 25 March to say that his new Prime Minister had asked him to convey a message to the Taoiseach in connection with the composition of the new Government of Northern Ireland: 'The new Government should be looked on very much as a package. The inclusion in it of Mr Harry West is, by no means, to be interpreted as a lurch to the Right – in fact, it represents a devastating blow to the Craig–West axis' bringing him in on the basis of his acceptance of the Government's policies of reform, no re-arming of the RUC and no bringing back of the B Specials. Faulkner's attitude to the Irish Government was 'one of goodwill'. The Prime Minister was anxious that this message should reach the Taoiseach as soon as possible, in case he might feel called on to make any public comment on the new Government's composition. Dr O'Sullivan contacted Lynch at 12.35 in the morning to convey Faulkner's message.[22]

But Faulkner also needed reassuring that Dublin's intentions towards the North were honourable. What the British wanted from the Irish, in order to ease the security pressures on Faulkner, was some evidence of a crackdown on the IRA in the Republic. In one publicized case, in early March, Louth County Hospital, in Dundalk, had confirmed that 'some people' suffering from gunshot wounds believed to have been inflicted in Belfast, had been treated at the hospital.[23] There was a similar incident near the end of the month again. The British raised their concerns about these sorts of incidents. On 26 March the Irish responded. Hugh McCann, from the Department of External Affairs, summoned Peck to convey a number of messages from Lynch and Hillery. The first message was that the Irish Government was aware that there were some men in Irish hospitals who had been brought across the Border with gunshot wounds. Hillery had raised with the Minister for Justice the general and hypothetical question of whether a request for extradition would be likely to be upheld by Irish Courts. The answer given upon legal advice was:

(A) This is entirely a matter for the Courts
(B) Each case would be determined on its merits but
(C) In general it seemed highly improbable that the Courts would agree to extradite. In these circumstances I [Peck] was asked to convey the hope that HMG would not make the request.

Irish courts could not extradite suspects of a 'political' nature – and paramilitary violence in the North had historically come under this definition. The second message was that while Irish Ministers were startled by the appointment of West in Faulkner's Cabinet they were not going to make any public comment and would stick to the position that they would wait and judge his administration by results. They were however very worried about the reaction of Catholics in the North and the capital that the IRA would make out of it. They therefore hoped that Faulkner would very quickly publicly commit his administration collectively to full support of the policies laid down by successive British Governments.[24] Peck had a further conversation, by chance, with McCann later that night. McCann was concerned lest in oral transmission the Taoiseach's message might appear negative, whereas his whole aim was to be constructive and realistic. He made three points about possible action against the IRA; as recorded by Peck they were:

(l) Particular steps might be taken but if so they would have to be demonstrably on Irish initiative and not through pressure from us [the British]
(ll) The Taoiseach's policy was risky for himself and it was better to incur the risks by working against the IRA in the North
(lll) Overt action against the IRA in the South could be unhelpful to efforts to wean away their supporters in the North. It was a question of timing.[25]

Reassured that the Irish were onside – for the moment anyway – London's main concern shifted to the SDLP's attitude towards Faulkner's Government. When Burroughs spoke to Hume he was made aware of what this attitude was likely to be: he found that Hume's attitude 'remains intransigent. I sought to persuade him that if Faulkner were to be able to extend the hand to the minority it was important that the Opposition should not greet his appointment with embittered attacks.' Burroughs did not record a positive response to this suggestion. Personal relations between Faulkner on the one hand and Hume and Currie on the other 'are bad and that this influences their attitudes. I will, however, do my best to keep the temperature down and to persuade the Opposition to judge Faulkner by his performance.'[26] As a result of this despatch being sent to Peck in Dublin, Eamonn Gallagher, from External Affairs, contacted the Department of the Taoiseach to say that they had had another approach from the British hinting that another intervention by the Irish Government with the SDLP would be warmly welcomed. They thought it would be 'unwise' for the SDLP to demand specific answers from Faulkner to their concerns. Lynch agreed that 'It would seem better if the SDLP would lay off' although he thought it would be awkward to try and get them to do this in light of suggestions that 'certain undertakings' were given to West and other right-wing Unionists.[27]

Thus, it quickly became apparent that the burden of proof would fall on Faulkner to prove his commitment to the reform programme. He would have a short honeymoon. At Stormont, Fitt deplored and condemned the appointment to the Cabinet of people to whom 'secret assurances' on policy matters had been given by the Prime Minister and which would represent the reversal of the reform programme. Fitt said that one would have needed very good hearing to have heard the Prime Minister, in all the years since his election to the House, say that there had been a necessity for reform. So, the Prime Minister could not now say: 'look how liberal we are', because the Opposition could say 'look how reactionary you have been'. This theme was taken up by Hume who asked the new Minister for Agriculture if he accepted the Hunt Report. When West ignored the question the SDLP withdrew from the House, only to return when the Minister had completed his speech. Hume then dismissed Faulkner's hope of uniting the community and the Unionist Party as two irreconcilable hopes because uniting the Unionist Party with the concepts of justice and honesty was impossible. It was irreconcilable with the acceptance of the reform programme. West, for example, was a man opposed to all reform. Personalities, when they were in public office, were important. He regretted the departure of Phelim O'Neill who had never offended when in office 'even though he was a Unionist'.[28]

While he had a not unexpectedly frosty reception from the Stormont Opposition, Faulkner found a warmer welcome awaiting him in London. On 1 April, Faulkner held his first Prime Minister to Prime Minister meeting with Heath at Downing Street; also attending was the new Chief of the General Staff, Sir Michael Carver, and the man he had selected as GOC NI, Sir Harry Tuzo, of The Royal Artillery. Faulkner began by reassuring the British Ministers gathered there that there would be no going back on the reform programme and emphasized how he wanted to bring the minority in Northern Ireland into discussions on public affairs at all levels, and not only the political level; he wanted to involve them in the activities of public boards as well. The British were pleased to hear this and Faulkner must have been equally pleased to hear that Heath believed that the most urgent problem for discussion was the restoration of public confidence by the maintenance of order and the suppression of IRA terrorism. Faulkner agreed immediately that the most pressing problem was Internal Security. Both Faulkner and Heath agreed that, generally, relations with the Republic were good. Faulkner said that Lynch had 'so far been extremely helpful' although he did not think the time was yet ripe for any discussions between Lynch and himself, or for any Ministerial discussions; but it was soon to be announced at Stormont that Northern Ireland officials would shortly be visiting Dublin to discuss economic cooperation in the Border areas. When the meeting turned to the possibility of internment, Faulkner pledged that he would not agree to any proposal for the use of the internment powers unless he was advised by the Army and the police that it would bring IRA terrorism decisively to an end. The GOC had indicated to him that he was against internment and the Chief Constable, Sir Graham Shillington, also, although the RUC Special Branch was marginally in favour of it. Although the use of internment on both sides of the Border appeared to have been a significant factor in bringing IRA terrorism to an end in 1962, Faulkner acknowledged that the IRA campaign then was of a different character to their present operation and he himself was not in favour of internment at this juncture. There would be advantages in bringing in a number of suspects for questioning, but that too would entail the use of special powers of detention which he was anxious to avoid. He agreed nevertheless that it would be prudent to have plans ready, should internment have to be resorted to.[29]

This period represented a more aggressive policy on the part of the Army. On 24 March a new directive from the GOC made modifications to the Army's Policy for Operations to recognize the change in the circumstances governing its task. The directive set out the broad lines of the policy now to be followed by the Army:

> The first and overriding priority is to bring to justice all subversive elements.
> ... The second priority is to re-assert unequivocally the rule of law in every part of the Province.
> ... The third priority is the capture of arms, explosives and other destructive devices.

The role of intelligence was essential: good information remained the cornerstone of the Army's operations. Public cooperation could only flow from confidence that 'we do not intend to countenance anything in the nature of intimidation or gang rule. The imposition of our will in the worst areas can only be a gradual process but we must press on with firmness, impartiality and determination.' There were to be 'no "no-go" areas'. There had to be frequent foot and vehicle patrols throughout these difficult areas aimed at 'demonstrating that bad elements will operate only at grave risk and that individuals of good will can have faith in the Security Forces'. The anticipation and countering of riot situations remained essential components of the Army's second priority. Equally, the frequency and pace of military operations had to persist in country and border areas both to catch or deter terrorists and to instil confidence amongst the public in outlying districts. The need for instant reaction to identified gunfire needed no emphasis. It should always be the aim to follow this with a hot pursuit and an immediate search for gunmen in houses in the suspect area unless it was clear that they had withdrawn. This was to be distinguished from a deliberate search for arms and formed part of the immediate reaction. Block searches required his approval as did the imposition of a local curfew. The GOC encouraged Commanders of all ranks to try out new tactics and methods. In conclusion, Tuzo explained that the directive

> is intended to tilt the balance towards a somewhat more positive, obtrusive, even aggressive, attitude than we have thought it right to adopt hitherto. We remain bound by the Yellow Card and the normal tenets of sound military practice. Within these boundaries there is scope for action which could improve the standing and authority of all the security forces and which has the approval of both the Westminster and Stormont governments.[30]

By late April the Army's intelligence picture gave cause for cautious optimism, although the MOD was worried that 'it must be remembered that a solitary burst of automatic fire in the night, resulting in the deaths of soldiers, policemen or civilians (particularly Protestant civilians) would go far to dissipate the small stock of confidence built up since Mr. Faulkner's accession to power.' The situation thus remained highly unstable. An intelligence brief told Lord Carrington: 'We are at present experiencing a relative lull in the pattern of violence in the Province. There is always a temptation to imagine that a quiet period portends the start of reasonableness and calm. Unfortunately a new peak of terrorist activity invariably follows a lull. Violence in the Province is cyclical.' Apart from the tragic effects of each peak in the graph of violence, these peaks in the past were often associated with increased activity by the Security Forces. The lulls on the other hand frequently coincided with political crises, or with a threat or fears of internment, or with increases in force levels of the Army in the Province, or with a combination of these events. The capture of key Provisionals, including the Belfast Brady Brigade Commander, Billy McKee, a Belfast Battalion Commander and the Officer Commanding the Portadown unit, with his Quartermaster – all charged with illegal possession – had 'undoubtedly frightened some of the IRA'.[31]

On the surface the situation in Northern Ireland from the end of March until the end of June was relatively quiet with only a handful of fatalities. Three Republicans lost their lives during this period: one, Tony Henderson, from the Falls Road was killed by the accidental discharge of a weapon in an IRA training camp near Portlaoise in the Republic on 4 April; Billy Reid was shot in a gun battle with soldiers near the centre of Belfast on 15 May; and Martin O'Leary was fatally injured in a premature explosion on 4 July. Reid, a Staff Officer with C Company of the Provisionals' 3 Battalion Belfast Brigade, was involved in a ninety-second exchange of fire with an Army patrol who found him acting suspiciously near a car in Academy Street in the York Street area behind Belfast College of Art. Two soldiers were wounded and two other IRA men escaped, one of them injured. Reid was believed to have been the Volunteer who fired the round which killed Gunner Curtis in February; he was shot in Curtis Street.

Two soldiers died during this period as well. Corporal Robert Baniker, a 24-year-old soldier in the 1 Battalion The Royal Green Jackets, was shot dead by the Official IRA on 22 May in the Markets area of Belfast. He was in charge of a patrol which had been ordered to go to the Cormac Street area shortly after midnight because members of the RMP had been attacked. As the soldiers approached the street more than a dozen youths threw stones and bottles at their vehicle. Soldiers followed the youths to Cormac Square where they disappeared. The patrol then moved into Lagan Street where Corporal Baniker, who was operating the radio, got out. As soon as he alighted the soldiers were fired upon from the front of Lagan Street by between three and five gunmen using automatic weapons. The Corporal was hit by a .9mm round. It appeared to the Army that the youths had been part of a well laid ambush. The other soldier killed, Sergeant Michael Willets, aged 27, of the 3 Battalion The Parachute Regiment, was killed by an IRA blast bomb thrown into the reception area of Springfield Road RUC Station. A car stopped outside the station and a man emerged with a suitcase which he hurled through the front door. Several civilians were sitting inside when the device was thrown, including two children, one of whom was a 4-year-old boy. Willets, realizing what was about to happen, thrust the two children down into a corner and stood above them, shielding them as the 30lbs of explosive in the suitcase went off. He was killed instantly but the children survived. Across the road a 2-year-old being pushed in a pram by his mother was blown through a shop window. He only regained consciousness after months in hospital. As ambulances ferried the injured to hospital a crowd of youths started to jeer and scream obscenities. Sergeant Willets was posthumously awarded the George Cross for his act of heroism.[32]

FAULKNER SPRINGS A SURPRISE

This period witnessed a key personnel change in British Government circles in relation to Northern Ireland. Ronnie Burroughs was preparing to depart Northern Ireland to pastures new. He was to be replaced by Howard Smith, a former Ambassador to Czechoslovakia and a future 'C' – head of MI6. In April, as he prepared to leave Belfast, after some fourteen months, Burroughs sent Maudling his observations on events during this period, together with a description of some of the problems which he thought lay ahead. In particular he reflected on the significance of Chichester-Clark's resignation, the key point of which was that he had been destroyed by his own party. Burroughs feared that Faulkner was only enjoying a honeymoon largely by permission of the IRA and the street mobs. And Burroughs predicted forthcoming violence from the IRA.[33]

On 6 June, it was the turn of the new UKREP to submit his – first – report to Maudling. He also concentrated on Faulkner's political prospects. Smith had intended to give himself longer but the drift of affairs in Northern Ireland obliged him to do so now. He recalled that when Faulkner became Prime Minister he was seen to suffer from one serious disadvantage: as a politician he was not trusted. The Catholic minority believed that his political background made it very difficult for him to understand, let alone have sympathy for, their feelings of injustice and inequality. They feared that although he was committed to the reform programme, he was not sufficiently devoted to it to ensure that legislation would be translated into genuine reform. Many Unionists in Parliament and in the country at large attributed to ambition Faulkner's conversion to reform, feared that ambition might lead him to betray their interests, and put him down as a man of uncertain principle. Yet Faulkner also seemed to enjoy certain advantages. He was thought to be the last Prime Minister standing between Stormont and Direct Rule. Smith thought this might strengthen his authority over his own party; it was also seen by some people in Northern Ireland, and perhaps by Faulkner himself, as strengthening his position in dealing with the British Government. He was accounted to be a resourceful politician, tough and professional. He was a good speaker who could get his points across. On his own side of the House it was felt that he would be firm on security. On the other side there was just a hope that he would be up to the mark on reform if he saw that Westminster was determined upon it. Whatever pressures might have to be applied in private, the new administration had to be seen to stand on its own feet in those fields of Government which were constitutionally assigned to it. Faulkner's Government had to be credible. The question was: 'credible to whom?' Smith also thought that Faulkner's reaction to becoming Premier had been to over-emphasize the issue of security. He talked rather too much, and sometimes too optimistically, of the security effort, and distinctly too little, and with too little action to back his words, about equality of treatment for all. Nor did he satisfy his critics on the Unionist and Paisleyite sides, because the more he talked about security the more they complained that the security effort was producing inadequate results. When he was under pressure, and sometimes when he was not, Faulkner tended to forget the wise advice that he received from the Army command, which was that the security task would be a long one, with its ups and downs. But more than this, his concentration on the security issue led to the suspicion that he did not understand that if there was to be a solution to the problems of Northern Ireland it was not, at bottom, a military one.[34]

Just as these concerns were being aired, Faulkner caught observers off guard with a surprise offer to the Opposition in Stormont. He certainly caught the SDLP off guard as he offered them a form of low-level power-sharing. The idea had been drawn up by civil servants during Chichester-Clark's term of office; but it was Faulkner who got to make the headlines. On 22 June, the Prime Minster, within the context of the maintenance of majority rule, suggested to the Northern Ireland House of Commons the setting up of three functional committees at Stormont, covering the social services, the environment and industry. Without executive powers the committees would review and consider Government policy and provide a means of 'expressing legitimate parliamentary interest in the overall quality of government proposals and performance'. The committees would be composed of not more than nine members each, broadly representative of party strengths in the House of Commons. Adding the three new committees to the already existing Public Accounts Committee, the Opposition, and in particular the SDLP, would provide at least two chairmen. This would, Faulkner argued, allow the House of Commons' functions of scrutiny and control to perform more effectively; to permit genuine and constructive participation in the work of Parliament by all its members; and encourage the development of much greater specialization and expertise. As a final enticement, Faulkner hinted that other constitutional changes, such as the introduction of proportional representation, could be introduced in the future. He finished his Commons announcement by suggesting a start with the three committees: 'see how they go, learn from our experience, but above all let us trust one another.' The SDLP's response was generally favourable (some thought ecstatic so unexpected was the offer). Austin Currie praised Faulkner for speaking of 'genuine and constructive participation'; Gerry Fitt 'read his remarks with great care and we hope we shall be able to co-operate with him'. By the end of the opening Stormont debates on the proposals, the SDLP appeared to have accepted the proposals wholeheartedly.[35]

DEATH IN DERRY

But July 1971 proved a watershed in Northern Ireland and altered the parameters of political debate. There was an upsurge in Provisional IRA violence which the military described as an offensive against the Northern state. This, and Security Force killings in Derry, transformed the political atmosphere. Protestants demanded a robust security response from the authorities. Catholics regarded the security response as confirmation of a formal policy of state repression. On 25 May Faulkner told Stormont that: 'At this moment any soldier seeing any person with a weapon or seeing any person acting suspiciously may fire either to warn or may fire with effect, depending on the circumstances and without waiting for orders from anyone.'[36] This set off alarm bells among Opposition MPs. Austin Currie said that 'on the surface, it would appear to mean that a soldier can shoot to kill at a person acting suspiciously.' In a situation where many soldiers were obviously jittery, and where some members of The Royal Highland Fusiliers obviously believed that their comrades were killed earlier in the year by Catholics, the Prime Minister's statement was extremely dangerous and irresponsible.[37] Paddy Kennedy, while deploring the incident, suggested that Faulkner's statement 'may have precipitated the outrage perpetrated on the Springfield Road' – the killing of Sergeant Willets occurred later that day.[38] Dublin took the matter up with John Peck and asked for a statement which would 'neutralise' the damage done. Peck made it clear that, while it was up to Faulkner to explain away what he said, insofar as the British were concerned it was the Army instructions that mattered.[39]

Faulkner was forced to clarify his comments. He said he made the statement for two reasons: first, to reassure the law-abiding population of Northern Ireland that while guerrilla warfare favoured the terrorists, the Army would lose no opportunity at striking hard and fast; and, second, to warn not only the hard core of the IRA – 'for they are past warning' – but any 'misguided dupes' on the fringe of terrorism that they could be playing with their lives. Faulkner claimed that some people had disingenuously asked what he meant when he said that soldiers would fire on those 'acting suspiciously': it related to circumstances in which firearms or explosives might be used. The man who carried the bomb which was to bring death, injury and destruction to the Springfield Road would, had he been seen in time, 'have been the sort of target I had in mind'.[40] At Westminster, Lord Baniel reassured Parliament that it remained the case that soldiers should use no more force than was necessary for the accomplishment of his immediate task.[41] He added that 'there can be no military solution' to Northern Ireland's problems. All the Army could do was to create, in time, conditions in which an agreement could be worked out.[42] This, in turn, reassured the Taoiseach who told the Dáil that no new powers had been conferred on British forces.[43] But, for many Catholics in Northern Ireland there remained the suspicion that there had been a change in security policy. The statement was deemed significant because it appeared to supply an open political justification for any future contentious shooting involving the British Army. This was not lost on the SDLP; and Paddy Devlin warned that 'If authority is now being put into the hands of soldiers... we [the SDLP] will withdraw from parliament.'[44] The subsequent killing, in July, of two young Catholic men in Londonderry by the Security Forces was seen by many Nationalists as the manifestation of such a shift in security.

However, a survey of internal British Army thinking on the security situation in the run up to the Provisional IRA 'offensive' suggests no such intention. In fact it reveals the opposite. Londonderry was situated under 8 Brigade and commanded by Brigadier Cowan. On 2 July he issued OP Directive Number 3 of 1971 to military units which set out the Army's view of the political situation since March and 8 Brigade's specific tasks. In it Cowan outlined how, during the last six months, the principal security threat had swung away from that of street violence to an overt campaign of explosive, arson and ambush attacks against the Security Forces by the Provisional wing of the IRA. Yet, despite the political crisis of March, the period was one of the most peaceful for many months: there was no serious street violence in either Belfast or Londonderry and country areas also remained quiet, while an uneasy truce between the two factions of the IRA continued. Explosive attacks on soft targets continued, the majority of which were apparently Provisional inspired. But on 7 May the first remote-controlled ambush took place on a UDR Land Rover in the Border area to the west of Londonderry. Cowan noted that, since that first ambush, the number of incidents of ambushes, claymore mining and overt attacks upon members of the Security Forces had steadily increased, and these had included explosive attacks against RUC stations. The level of street violence had also risen with street disturbances in the New Lodge area of Belfast in May and a resurgence of hooligan activity after a long period of comparative peace on the streets of Londonderry towards the end of June. The Government under Faulkner continued on a stable and successful course with no signs of any loss of confidence, indeed with a measure of support from the Opposition, particularly as a result of a decision to ban an Orange Order march in Dungiven.

Nevertheless, it seemed clear that the Provisional IRA, in particular, were steadily increasing their attacks. On 2 July, Cowan warned units in 8 Brigade that all reports indicated that the Provisionals intended to maintain and intensify their attacks with explosives and small arms and that these would be primarily directed against the Security Forces. It was 'reliably reported' that recent street disorders in Londonderry were instigated by the Provisionals with the aim of drawing the Security Forces into the Bogside where they could be attacked with grenades, nail bombs and small arms fire. The Officials, on the other hand, continued to condemn the Provisionals' policy of violence while at the same time publicizing their own non-militant and politically orientated policy. However, there was evidence that the group were being propelled to join in with the violence on the grounds that otherwise they would lose their members to the Provisionals. This was borne out by a report that one of the attacks on an RUC patrol in Belfast was an Official IRA operation, and that should they adopt a more militant posture they could be expected to conduct ambush, assassination and kidnap attacks against members of the Security Forces. Cowan predicted that the present level of explosive attacks was likely to be continued, especially those directed against the Security Forces. As the Orange Order marching season got into full swing, the Provisionals could be expected to 'defend their Catholic areas and repel incursions and to take advantage of the parades to draw the security forces into positions from which they could be attacked'. Cowan emphasized that: 'When committed to a riot situation, military forces are to disperse crowds using the minimum of force required and are to effect as many arrests as possible.' The Directive set out precisely how troops were to deal with riot situations. Military commanders were instructed to be selective in the use of Internal Security weapons. The most appropriate weapon was to be used to ensure that the force used was the minimum necessary to achieve the objective of keeping the peace. The rules for opening fire with small arms remained those contained in the Yellow Card and 'must be observed'.[45] In a later Brigade directive Cowan recalled how, at the beginning of July, there had been a feeling of cautious optimism about the security situation in Londonderry. At that time no shooting attacks had been mounted against the Security Forces and the level of overt military activity was low. The hooligan element had been isolated from the vast majority of the community and the IRA were quiescent. There had been 'significant and perceptible' progress towards stability and normality. There were signs that the 'policy of restraint which the security forces had been following since June 1970, was at last beginning to succeed'. But within two days of the directive being signed, the

> situation changed dramatically. On 4th July the IRA mounted a campaign in the city with the short-term aim of so disrupting the life of the city that the Apprentice Boys annual celebrations on August 12th would have to be cancelled. The campaign opened with an ever-increasing number of shooting incidents on succeeding days, until the reaction by the security forces to the IRA gunmen led to the return of fire and the death of two of the rioters.

Cowan recognized that the effect of this 'first ever return of fire' in Londonderry 'instantly turned the Catholic community from benevolent support to complete alienation'.[46]

While the Provisional 'offensive' was deemed to have begun on 4 July there was a portent of what was to come a few days earlier. The annual Protestants parades on 1 July, recalling the sacrifice of the Ulster Division at the Battle of the Somme, provided an opportunity for the bombers to strike and set the pattern for the rest of the month. But, on this occasion, they were foiled in their attempts to cause explosions when the fuse to a 20lb gelignite bomb, at Donegall Pass, in Belfast, fizzled out just six inches from the charge. As Orangemen marched in Coalisland a bomb was rendered harmless twenty minutes before it was due to explode.[47] The following day, however, a young girl received burns and was taken to hospital when one of five fire-bombs exploded in the new £2.5 million Europa Hotel complex in Belfast.[48] Trouble was avoided in Belfast, on the Crumlin Road, when the Army and police rerouted 15,000 Protestant spectators, preventing them from following the parade. Orange leaders agreed to the rerouting while the Army deployed APCs and steel barriers on either side of the road allowing just enough room for the Orangemen to pass through.[49] Even without the bombers' intervention sectarian tension would be mounting as the Twelfth approached.

Soldiers and civilians had a near miss on 4 July, in Belfast, when a machine-gun attack on an Army Land Rover in Leeson Street left two soldiers, from The Royal Green Jackets, and two civilians wounded. The soldiers were wounded in the leg and in the arm respectively. One of the civilians was wounded by a gunshot wound to the head while shielding his three young children. The ambush was followed by protests from public representatives from the area, including Paddy Devlin, who accused soldiers of 'abominable' behaviour following the shooting. Devlin claimed that he had been sneered at by a sergeant-major when he attempted to get into the area to speak to his constituents. Councillor Harry Donaghy, of the NILP, complained of the troops' 'overreaction' when youths were pulled out from a Republican Club in Leeson Street and were forced to stand against the wall with their hands outstretched for half an hour. After the Army left, tensions remained high and police had to draw revolvers to prevent a Catholic crowd from attacking a nearby Protestant area. It was noticeable that it was left to the Lower Falls CCDC to condemn those responsible for ambushing and bombing in heavily populated areas and for showing a callous disregard for life and inviting possible military retaliation.[50]

At Stormont, Devlin produced a booklet which he claimed was issued to British military staff for briefing purposes and was clearly actionable under the provisions of the Incitement to Hatred Act (one of the reforms introduced since 1969). It contained an old, and fabricated, Sinn Féin 'oath' which Devlin quoted part of. He had become increasingly concerned about aspects of the Security Forces' interpretation of their role as peacekeepers in Northern Ireland and connected this to the one-sidedness in Army activities. He argued that if anyone was to examine the amount of violence that was going on in Belfast outside his constituency it would be reasonable to assume that the Security Forces would be spread out more than they were. Despite the fact that there were arms found elsewhere, there were more intensive arms searches in the 'anti-Unionist' areas because of the orientation of the military staff. It was Devlin's belief that the booklet in question had some responsibility for this bias. Part of the alleged oath contained in the booklet pledged a 'wading in the fields of the red gore of the Saxon tyrants and murderers, for the glorious cause of Irish nationality'. Devlin also used the opportunity to follow up his complaints about the Army's behaviour after the Leeson Street shooting. In reply, the Army, as John Taylor from the Unionist Government pointed out, had retorted that Devlin had been most uncooperative and throughout the whole incident had acted in an agitated and abusive manner, doing nothing to calm the situation.[51]

Back on the streets the bombing campaign continued. Four persons were rushed to hospital – one with a serious heart attack – after a large gelignite charge wrecked a service depot at the Donegall Road end of the M1 motorway on 6 July.[52] In Armagh, on 8 July, four soldiers on a routine patrol were lucky not to be killed when their Land Rover hit a road mine at Tullymore; one soldier, a 24-year-old Jamaican-born corporal, lost an eye.[53] More shots were fired at troops in Belfast and Derry on the night of 6 July and the early morning of 8 July. Automatic fire was directed at an Army observation post (OP) on Derry's walls in Bishop Street. Another five rounds were discharged in the direction of soldiers at nearby Henrietta Street. The Bishop Street district was also the scene of a confrontation between Catholics, who attacked the Protestant Fountain Street, and troops who kept the two sides apart. There were other incidents elsewhere in the city.[54] By now it was clear that these were not isolated incidents in Derry.

On the evening of 7 July rioting had once again erupted. During the disturbances Seamus Cusack, a 28-year-old Catholic, was shot dead by soldiers in disputed circumstances near Old Bogside Road. The Army claimed he had a rifle but civilian witnesses denied this. The soldier involved in the incident later said: 'I shot to kill him. He was bringing his weapon up – what do you want me to do, let him kill me?' The soldier was acquitted in a subsequent court case. An unofficial inquiry, headed by Lord Gifford QC, concluded that Cusack was not armed when he was shot. It found that Cusack and a teenager were playing a cat and mouse game with soldiers while trying to retrieve a soldier's helmet as a trophy. A soldier stepped out from the far end of a wall and fired once almost at point blank range from a crouched position. The bullet hit Cusack on the inside of the upper part of his left leg, piercing the main artery and exiting at the rear of the thigh. Instead of taking him to the nearby Altnagelvin Hospital, locals took him twenty miles to a hospital over the Border in Letterkenny. He died within minutes of his arrival there at 1.40 a.m. on 8 July. A coroner subsequently found that he probably would not have died if he had been brought to the Derry hospital.[55]

Cusack was the first of the day's two civilian fatalities from Derry's Catholic community. Desmond Beattie, aged 19, was also shot in disputed circumstances by soldiers of The Royal Anglian Regiment, at Lecky Road, after a series of explosions in the area. The soldier who shot him was in charge of a twenty-strong platoon sent to protect a Royal Green Jackets vehicle which had come under attack by a crowd of around seventy people. A Land Rover had been rammed by a coal lorry and was stoned. Nail bombs were thrown at it, injuring one of the soldiers on board. There were three loud explosions after which only a small group of rioters remained. One of the soldiers who opened fire claimed that one of the men held a dark object in one hand and a flaming object in the other. Believing that the man was about to light and throw a bomb, the soldier dropped on one knee cocking his rifle and bringing it to aim as he did so. The man was continuing to bring the two objects together and looking towards the troops in a manner which indicated that he was seeking a target to attack. To prevent him doing so the soldier, from a range of forty metres, aimed at the centre of his chest and fired one round. Immediately he heard another shot to his left from another soldier. The man stumbled and fell to the ground. The soldier later explained: 'All soldiers in Northern Ireland are taught that when lives or people whom it is our duty to protect are in serious danger from someone about to throw a bomb we may fire without warning in order to prevent this action. This is why I opened fire.' Lord Gifford's unofficial inquiry did not agree. It found that Desmond Beattie was unarmed when he was shot. At the inquiry a forensic expert said there were no traces of explosives in his pockets.[56]

While there is no evidence, apart from the soldiers' testimony, that Beattie had an explosive device, what was unusual about the incident was that he was shot almost simultaneously by two soldiers firing independently of each other, suggesting that they thought there was a threat of some kind. In the immediate aftermath of the killings there was outrage in Catholic Derry. The Army tried to set the shootings in context: during the previous few days small groups of terrorists and hooligans had been attempting to draw the Security Forces into operations in the Bogside. Despite considerable provocation, including the use of petrol bombs against troops, police and the civil community, counter-action had been restrained. However, the introduction of firearms and nail-bombs by the terrorists against the troops, with a consequent high risk, could not be tolerated. Hence, it had been necessary to return fire.[57] At a hastily summoned press conference the CO of the troops involved, Lieutenant Colonel Roy Jackson, claimed:

> Both men were armed. There is no possibility whatsoever that my soldiers could have made a mistake. I would point out that since Sunday last my men have been fired on every night, attacked with nail bombs and other missiles and that only on Wednesday did we fire back. One of these men had a nail bomb, the other man was levelling a rifle to fire at soldiers. That is why they were shot.[58]

The GOC, Harry Tuzo, accused the IRA of triggering the trouble in Derry during the marching season. There was evidence of 'ill-intentioned' people being stirred up by the IRA. Tuzo said it was time to get stern with the 'right people' but not in an indiscriminate way: 'If these people want to mix it they may come to grief.'[59] However, the eyewitness reports received by John Hume contradicted the Army's account: neither man was armed. Hume warned that the Army's action had caused widespread resentment in the community and their allegations had only added fuel to the fire.[60] He added: 'I personally publicly challenge the British Army to face an inquiry which will prove that they are telling lies about these deaths.' By now Ivan Cooper was calling the situation in Derry the 'most serious for years' and the veteran Nationalist, Eddie McAteer, said bluntly what many in the Bogside were thinking: 'Protocol be damned. Directly or indirectly Dublin must take effective action in the protection of their Northern people.'[61]

The deaths did have an impact on the diplomatic front. In the afternoon of 8 July, Jack Lynch had telephoned Hugh McCann to say that Hume had been in touch with the Leader of the Opposition, Liam Cosgrave, 'about a critical situation which was developing in Derry'. The Taoiseach was concerned lest the British troops were over-reacting and 'getting a little trigger happy'.

McCann spoke to John T. Williams, the British Charge d'Affaires, and conveyed to him the Taoiseach's concerns about Derry. Williams called to see McCann later with more information giving the Army's version of events. McCann, pointing out that there seemed to be a conflict of evidence, reminded Williams that Derry had been peaceful for a long time and that it would be tragic if any excessive use of force or overreaction on the part of British troops led to an outbreak of violence in that city.[62] The following morning, 9 July, the Ambassador in London was instructed to approach the Foreign Office stressing the conflict of evidence, the need for an inquiry and the difficult situation in which the Taoiseach was now placed. Dr O'Sullivan reported back to Dublin that he had received a 'cool reception' from the senior official he met, Sir Stewart Crawford, who said there was 'absolutely nothing to enquire about in these cases'. On the morning of 10 July, Hume was on the phone to Eamonn Gallagher. He told Hume that it was his personal opinion that, as the British Army could be seen as the 'last line of defence of current British policy in the North' there was no prospect of obtaining an independent inquiry. There were no further substantive exchanges between the SDLP and Dublin after this before the SDLP decided on its next move.[63]

And what dictated the SDLP's next move were the Provisionals. The deaths allowed Republicans to highlight to the Catholic population of Derry their interpretation of the conflict. The Official IRA described Cusack's death as a brutal murder and a clear statement of the British Army's role in the Six Counties. Here was an innocent victim who was shot at point blank range and not, as claimed by the British Army, by a marksman: the meaning of the Army's 'shoot-for-effect is now horribly clear. It is simply a licence to murder Irish civilians... [the] Murder of all our young people would be met with all the force we can muster.'[64] On Sunday 11 July the Provisionals gave their response during a meeting in Derry. Mrs Marie Drumm, who was later to get a six-month prison sentence for her speech, said that by continuing to resist the British Army the people of Derry had got up off their knees. 'For Christ's sake stay up,' she pleaded. Then she said:

> The only way you can avenge these deaths is by being organised, trained and disciplined until you can chase that cursed Army away. I would personally prefer to see all the British Army going back dead. But the people will not succeed with stones and bottles. They should come into the one organisation which will organise and train them. You should not shout 'Up the IRA'. You should join the IRA. The men must be organised and trained to fight so that they can go out and destroy the British Army for ever and ever.

Mrs Drumm's speech was followed in much the same vein by Walter Lynch, described as general secretary of Kevin Street (Provisional) Sinn Féin. He told the crowd that the only way to put Tuzo and his 'mad dogs' out of Ireland was through the IRA. Finally Rory Ó Brádaigh spoke. He told the crowd in a detailed political speech: 'We want to stand together and walk together and struggle together under leadership and discipline and please God we'll finish it this time.' He asked the crowd: 'Are we going to put up with it for another ten years or more?'; when his words were greeted with shouts of 'No, No', he added: 'I'm glad to hear you say that because we are going to finish it this time. We're on the high road to freedom and what we need to do is to rock Stormont and to keep it rocking until Stormont comes down.' A few hundred yards away John Hume and his colleagues heard the words and their message. They met in the company of Labour TD Michael O'Leary who was visiting from Dublin and when the question of withdrawing from Stormont came up O'Leary suggested that the vacuum this would create would be filled by the Provos unless the SDLP decided to try some alternative assembly idea. For the moment the idea was no more than a germ but the meeting decided to issue an ultimatum to the British Government: unless there was a full-scale public inquiry into the two deaths announced within a few days they would withdraw from Stormont. The immediate problem was that the rest of the SDLP leadership were spread around the country. Devlin had taken off for Dublin to attend the 1921 Truce celebrations in the city, Currie was at home in Coalisland, Paddy O'Hanlon in Armagh, and Gerry Fitt was at his country retreat in Cushendun. Fitt could not be contacted, but Devlin was reached by telephone about the decision; since it was only an ultimatum he agreed but insisted that if the party did withdraw they would have to broaden the basis for leaving and not just leave it because of a 'Derry thing'.[65]

Devlin was, of course, equally concerned by similar incidents in Belfast. For him, and many other Nationalists, military statements concerning controversial incidents no longer had any credibility. The sooner this fact was realized, he felt, the sooner and more realistically and more honestly would the problems caused by military 'overkill' be dealt with. Devlin complained that there was scarcely a critical glance cast in the direction of the local residents who felt the full weight of the military's heavy handed tactics. Yet every single military activity or engagement in which people were seriously or fatally wounded was followed in every paper, TV channel and radio wave length by an automatic denial of Army guilt or involvement. The killings in Derry were just the latest example. He also specifically referred to an incident in Belfast in which a soldier fired a shot through the window of a woman's bedroom after the soldier had warned her that he would shoot her head off if she did not take her head in. When he had asked the Prime Minister about the incident, Faulkner had answered that he accepted the military's statement that it had been a stray bullet from another attack which had gone through the window. This encapsulated the problem: the Prime Minister was accepting a statement from a body against whom the complaint was made. He had placed them in a position to investigate and pass judgement on their own behaviour.[66]

So, with nearly everyone on board the SDLP went public with their demands. It was announced that after receiving a report on the shootings from Hume, the SDLP Parliamentary Party was demanding an impartial inquiry and warned that if this were not forthcoming than it would withdraw from Stormont and set up an alternative assembly to deal with the minority's problems. The SDLP were questioning the role of the Army in Northern Ireland, asking, 'Is "shoot on suspicion" not the reality?' But they also identified a second, even more important, question, related to the Parliamentary Party's role as elected representatives. The SDLP pointed out that throughout the extremely turbulent and difficult period through which their community had gone they had at all times done their utmost to give responsible leadership. They had urged continuing restraint. They had opposed any attempts by their supporters to protest on the streets and they had fought doggedly in Parliament to have meaningful reform in order to create the conditions for justice and peace in their society. In spite of the ever increasing doubts in their minds, strengthened by the actions of the Northern Ireland Government and the inaction of the British Government, they had continued their struggle in a responsible Parliamentary manner even to a point where, in the eyes of those they represented, they were carrying some of the responsibility for the unjust system they had been trying to change. The SDLP regarded their demand for an inquiry as a decisive test of the sincerity and determination of the British Government. If it was not granted then as public representatives 'we will accept the logic of our position which is that there is no role that we can usefully play within the present system'. This would mean the immediate withdrawal from Stormont and the establishment of an alternative assembly to become the authoritative voice to negotiate a political solution on behalf of the people the SDLP represented.[67] As Hume explained, one consequence of the killings was that some people were being driven from feelings of moderation.[68] The SDLP withdrew from Stormont on 16 July to form an alternative institution – the Assembly of the Northern Irish People.

The upsurge in violence continued. On 10 July a large bomb, containing 50lb of gelignite, exploded in Flax Street, off the Crumlin Road in Belfast, but missed its intended target – an Army OP. The bomb was laid in a sewer too far from the Army post. It blew a crater eight feet by twenty feet in the roadway. The Army had installed obstacles and infra-red detectors near sewers to detect such attacks. Immediately afterwards troops were attacked by stones and nail bombs by a mob, which the Army thought was pre-planned.[69] This was followed by six bombs in as many minutes in the early hours of the Twelfth. Nine people were injured as city centre stores and a restaurant were wrecked, a telephone kiosk was demolished and an Army Land Rover was blown off the road by a landmine.[70] For Faulkner, who spent most of the Twelfth in a helicopter with Tuzo observing the parades from the air, these were just undisguised attempts to stir up sectarian animosity. There were another four explosions – ten in all – over the route of the Orange parade. After watching the Belfast parades and satisfying themselves that no serious trouble was likely the Prime Minister and GOC flew to Londonderry. There they also found peaceful parades but, when passing over the Bogside, Faulkner saw for the first time a hijacking actually taking place. A crowd of youths stopped a lorry and pulled the driver out before driving it off, presumably to help build some barricade, but almost immediately crashed off the road. Neither Tuzo nor Faulkner enjoyed watching helplessly while this kind of lawlessness flourished in a part of the state they were supposedly governing.[71]

Worse was to follow when Rifleman David Walker, of The Royal Green

Jackets, was killed in an IRA attack on an OP in the Lower Falls area. A sniper shot him as he stood in the OP cited on the roof of a mill of the corner of Northumberland Street and the Falls Road. The attack happened shortly after midnight.[72] The Provisionals confirmed that one of their Active Service Units (ASU) had 'executed a member of the British Army of occupation. The action was in retaliation for the Derry killings.' Further retaliatory action would be taken in due course: 'Let bullies beware,' they warned, 'This is not August 1969'.[73] The attacks continued the next day as an attempted attack on sentries in the lower Shankill failed when what appeared to be a Thompson sub-machine gun jammed. An accomplice carrying a parcel containing high explosives panicked and threw the bomb down.[74] The IRA were more successful the following day when Private Richard Barton, aged 24, of The Parachute Regiment, was shot dead. Around three gunmen opened fire with automatic weapons on his patrol just after midnight. The gunmen had waited in ambush in the garden of a house. At least thirty-five shots were fired by the gunmen. Barton, who was driving a Land Rover, accelerated towards the gunmen in an attempt to provide cover for his colleagues. Soldiers who jumped off the back of the Land Rover returned fire but the gunmen had fled. When they turned to the vehicle they found that Private Barton had been shot in the lung. Lieutenant-Colonel Geoffrey Howard, the dead soldier's CO, observed that the IRA was becoming more effective because of the training they were receiving. His soldiers had been subjected to over twenty bomb and gun attacks, some efficient, some inefficient. This was the first time anyone had been killed but Howard would not say that it marked a particular spot in the campaign. The Paras had been made aware that reprisals were likely.[75] The Provisionals claimed responsibility and described Private Barton's killing as retaliation for the 'murder of two Irish civilians' in Derry.[76]

LINKLATER

As far as Faulkner was concerned it was no longer adequate to issue bland assurances that this was a temporary difficulty which 'restraint and goodwill' on all sides would overcome. It was becoming obvious to him that 'action was needed now', and it was action which the public, by which he did not meant just the Protestant public, was demanding. After holding long discussions with the GOC, the Chief Constable and his security advisers to see if they could improve their tactics in any way, the message which was beginning to come through to Faulkner was that there was only one major unused weapon in the Government's anti-terrorist arsenal: internment. During the Chichester-Clark Government the possibility of internment had been discussed a few times in the Cabinet. Faulkner generally argued against, and recalled at least two occasions on which the Prime Minister appeared in favour and he had attempted to dissuade him, backed up by the other members of the Joint Security Committee. Faulkner had already operated internment as Minister of Home Affairs during the last three years of the previous IRA campaign, but he regarded it as a weapon only to be used in extremity by a democratic Government, and was concerned lest the 'No Go' areas of 1969–70 had undermined the RUC intelligence on which any successful internment operation would depend. Nor, realized Faulkner, was the position in 1971 similar to that in 1960, when the IRA campaign had been largely confined to the rural and border areas; the urban guerrilla now posed a more difficult problem. It was simply too easy and superficial to say 'internment solved the problem before, and it will do it again'.

In April several senior Army officers, but significantly not including the GOC, had argued for internment. A list of potential internees had been drawn up by the RUC Special Branch and Military Intelligence early in the year. Faulkner's Cabinet discussed the issue several times in April and May. West, Baillie and Bradford were the most hardline on security, while Bleakley, the Labour Minister of Community Relations, was less so. Faulkner was still hopeful that the new Army tactics, combined with effective political action, would pay off and make internment unnecessary. But, by July it was becoming obvious to Faulkner that these hopes were not being realized and the matter was again seriously considered in the Cabinet. There it was made clear that if Faulkner exercised the powers vested in him as Minister of Home Affairs under the Special Powers Act, he would have the firm backing of his Cabinet colleagues. The decision and the timing were to be left to himself and the security chiefs, but there was a general acceptance that unless the situation improved it would soon become necessary. Faulkner also claimed that pressures were also being exerted from less expected quarters for dramatic action to break the grip of the IRA on Catholic areas. Secret representations from 'responsible members' of the Catholic community prominent in politics urged him to 'lock up' those men who were making life intolerable for ordinary Catholics through intimidation and violence. His personal mailbag confirmed the intense desire for a return to some form of law and order; he received many letters from housewives in places such as Andersonstown in west Belfast, urging him to get the terrorists 'off our backs'. Thus, while recognizing the dangers of misrepresentation, Faulkner believed there would be very many Catholics willing to tolerate internment in order to break the IRA, and he hoped that these people would be given a lead by moderate politicians. A contingency decision had already been taken to build a new temporary prison for high-risk prisoners. The old prison on the Crumlin Road in Belfast was declared insecure by an investigating committee but it was clear that a top-security prison for convicted prisoners was needed even if internment was not introduced. The MOD and the Home Office undertook to design and build the temporary prison. Unfortunately, because of the speed with which the new structure at Long Kesh, a few miles outside Belfast, was erected, and because of its temporary nature, it came to look like the pictures of prisoner-of-war camps. Faulkner believed that, by the middle of July, a consensus was developing among his security advisers on the need for internment. His recollection, some years later, was that the process was such a gradual one that it was difficult to pick out a decisive point in their discussions. Faulkner claimed that he, Tuzo and Graham Shillington, the Chief Constable, were very anxious not to introduce internment, but were rapidly running out of arguments against it. They had examined all sorts of alternatives, such as special courts, but came to the conclusion that a court was no longer a court in any real sense if the accused and the accuser were not brought face to face.[77]

Here we find that there is an inconsistency with other evidence. Field Marshall Lord Carver, who in 1971 as General Sir Michael Carver was the CGS, recorded in his memoirs that he and Tuzo were in agreement that internment should not be recommended to Ministers in London. They reached a consensus on this on 11 June when Carver visited Northern Ireland. On 19 July, Tuzo and Carver had a meeting in London with Lord Carrington to consider what should be done about the forthcoming 12 August Apprentice Boys march in Londonderry. They stuck to an agreed line that, with some changes from its traditional route, it should be allowed to go ahead and that internment should not be introduced, but that 'disruptive operations' should be carried out, with the primary aim of reducing the pressure on Faulkner to take positive action against the IRA.[78] Shillington, however, supports Faulkner's account. He later recalled that by the middle of 1971 it had become very difficult to convict anyone involved in sectarian violence under the normal criminal justice system. The level of civil unrest was getting out of control and 'I believe we had reached a point where some form of action had to be taken in order to restore order. I recall discussing the possibility of bringing in internment with my Prime Minister and Harry Tuzo... The GOC gave the impression that he was in favour of bringing in internment. Like me, he believed that the time had come to adopt such a measure.'[79] If Shillington was right it would mean that Tuzo had reversed his earlier position when he had told Carrington that he was opposed to the principle of internment; he later told British Ministers that it would be ineffective. More likely the GOC was formulating the 'disruptive operations' to which Carver referred and so did not want to give a definitive opinion on internment to Faulkner and Shillington. Certainly, Tuzo was under political pressure from the Northern Ireland Government to come up with something. For example, at the beginning of the Provisionals' offensive, there was tension between the GOC and Stormont Ministers at a meeting held on 6 July. Tuzo had been invited by Faulkner to address the meeting. The GOC rejected out of hand allegations of partiality and claims that the Army was reluctant to attack law breakers; his answer was that targets could only be fired on where clearly identifiable and where there was no possible danger to innocent bystanders. In reply to a question about the Army's apparent reluctance to move in and 'mop up' militant elements in the Bogside, Tuzo recalled that, while there had been minor troubles recently, unarmed police patrols had been able to go into the area for the last year and it was debatable whether it was wise to risk a reversal of this acceptable situation through precipitate action.[80]

For Faulkner the final straw came on 17 July when Northern Ireland witnessed its most expensive explosion to date as a blast wrecked the plant and works section of the *Daily Mirror* and *Sunday Mirror* newspapers at Suffolk, about seven miles from Belfast. Damage to plant and machinery was estimated at around two million pounds. It had been just after 4.30 p.m. on a Saturday afternoon that a dozen armed and masked men drove into the courtyard of the plant and rushed into the building. They told the staff on duty – about twenty men – to get into a small toilet and to keep quiet. They warned them that a bomb would explode after about forty seconds. The intruders placed explosives at strategic positions in the building and then left in three cars. The explosions went off almost immediately. The Provisionals claimed responsibility: the *Daily Mirror*, they said, had been 'putting out British propaganda in Northern Ireland'.[81] This piled more pressure on Faulkner. The following day, John Taylor warned that if IRA activities were not brought to a prompt end over the next few months he would find it very difficult to continue in Faulkner's Government. For Nationalists the significance of Taylor's remarks revolved around his position as a member of the Joint Security Committee after having been promoted to Minister of State in the Ministry of Home Affairs when Chichester-Clark had doubled up as Prime Minister and Minister of Home Affairs (the latter practice was continued by Faulkner).

Following changes made by the Prime Minister, Taylor and Faulkner were the only politicians with day-to-day executive responsibility for security matters. In the course of a number of radio interviews, Taylor made his remarks in the context of the IRA's growing strength and organization. Prompt action was required to bring this to an end. On the shootings in Derry, Taylor warned that it might be necessary for the Security Forces to take an even firmer line with rioters. He defended 'without hesitation' the actions taken by the Army in Derry against 'subversives' when it had proved necessary to shoot to kill. Indeed, he felt that it might be necessary to shoot even more in the forthcoming months. Taylor's articulation of Unionist frustration was echoed by John Brooke. The Unionist Party's Chief Whip warned: 'People are fed up with seeing British soldiers being shot without enough action apparently being taken to stop it. But it's very difficult to see how much more can be done. But from the grassroots they are saying quite clearly to the Government that we were in a state of attempted revolution from the very start. It wasn't revolution that the people who were pushing us were involved in.'[82] Almost immediately, Austin Currie called for Taylor's resignation on the grounds that it confirmed that there were members of the Unionist Government who were thinking of 'wholesale butchery as a solution to our problems'.[83] Republicans also seized on Taylor's comments to justify their campaign. The Provisionals interpreted them as a threat to repeat the Derry shootings, meaning that British occupation forces were planning 'future murders of Irish citizens'. They pointed out that the people of the North of Ireland were no longer defenceless and if the British Army carried out Taylor's threats 'we guarantee that they will pay a heavy price for any such action against Irish people in their own country'.[84]

But, as has been stated, the real significance of city bombings of mid-July was to be that they tipped the scales for Faulkner and he took the decision to operate internment. 'No one objected,' he recalled and the mechanics of the operation were discussed on the relative merits of spreading the net wide in the initial swoop, or simply confining it to the leaders and organizers of the IRA, both Official and Provisional. The former would involve perhaps five hundred arrests, the latter around a hundred. Faulkner was also conscious of the problem of not appearing to be victimizing Catholics, as the main objective of the operation would be to destroy the operational capacity of the IRA which consisted almost entirely of 'self-styled Catholics'. On both these matters Faulkner relied on the advice of the Security Forces. The Army and the police proposed a wide sweep involving the arrest of over five hundred, in order to strike a crippling blow at the terrorist organization. Faulkner agreed to this. With hindsight, Faulkner thought that a more selective sweep as in previous RUC operations would have been more effective. The Security Forces were also adamant that there was no evidence of organized terrorism by Protestants which would justify detention of persons other than IRA members. Faulkner had no doubt that this was an accurate conclusion at that time. The idea of arresting anyone as an exercise in political cosmetics was 'repugnant to me', he later wrote.[85] But Faulkner still had to get the go-ahead from the British Government. And they were reluctant to agree to it if they could avoid it.

On 19 July, Maudling and his officials met with the GOC and the UK Representative at the Home Office to discuss the security situation and explore any alternatives. Howard Smith began by outlining his view that recent IRA activity was grounded in confidence, not desperation. The weekend incidents at the *Daily Mirror* and another at a Belfast hospital showed a disturbing element of planning and organization. The Stormont Government was worried at the attitude of business. Some, perhaps most, of the Northern Ireland Ministers favoured internment. Smith's assessment was that internment would upset the IRA but would not prevent their carrying on their activities. If internment in the North could be accompanied by internment in the Republic the political difficulties would be largely overcome and the effectiveness of the action greatly increased. Smith also favoured the banning of the Apprentice Boys' march on 12 August. The balance of argument was a difficult one but he thought the best course was to ban the march, accompanying the ban with stern action to deal with terrorism.

At this point the meeting was interrupted by a telephone call from Faulkner. He warned that the flagrant activity of the IRA over the weekend had made the situation much worse. Faulkner was worried that the business community was losing confidence. He was finding it difficult to hold the line with anybody; in his view internment was almost inevitable. When Maudling asked if he thought the time was near, he replied that he thought that the time had come unless some other new measure could be suggested; he had discussed the matter with General Tuzo but did not see any other acceptable major alternative. Faulkner described the security situation at the Border as 'lacking'. He suggested that blowing larger craters on the Border roads would be helpful. Faulkner had come to the conclusion that the failure of his political initiatives to evoke any real response justified firm action without excessive regard for the susceptibilities of those who had declined to cooperate. After Faulkner's call had finished, Tuzo joined the discussion. He offered an alternative to internment. Tuzo explained to Maudling that current difficulties could be surmounted, but a hardening of current policies was needed. His information was that the Official and Provisional factions were coalescing. He proposed more operations to disturb

IRA activity which would have many of the advantages of internment without the same disadvantages. Tuzo had in mind swooping on a number of known IRA leaders, taking them away for questioning for forty-eight hours and searching their homes. After forty-eight hours they would have to be released unless something incriminating was discovered. Hitherto the view had been taken that arrest followed by release could only make those arrested heroes, but he now took the view that this disadvantage was worth accepting in the interests of disrupting IRA activities. Intelligence suggested that repeated swoops of this kind would have a substantial effect. Of the 400 people who were on the list for internment about 100 would be arrested if action were taken that night. Tuzo emphasized that the number who would be caught varied from day to day. A maximum of 150 could be accommodated in a ship, HMS *Maidstone*, with considerable improvisation. Proper facilities were expected to be ready at the end of September. But Tuzo's view was that it would be better to try the scheme he had described before resorting to internment. He planned the first swoop operation for the following week. He had told Faulkner of the kind of operation he had in mind but had given no indication about the timing. Past experience of security among Northern Ireland Ministers led him to the view that providing more detailed information would jeopardize the exercise. He was not sure how many people he would attempt to collect in the first swoop but mentioned figures from ten to a hundred.

On hearing this, Maudling indicated his approval with a preference for a large number to be brought in so that the operation should be seen to be the start of a new phase. When asked if he thought the approaching Apprentice Boys' march should be banned, Tuzo answered that it would be easier to have a controlled march than to attempt to ban it. There was a risk that extreme Protestants would come onto the streets and perhaps use the rifles they had hidden away. Smith interjected to point out that if the activity of the Army in the proposed swoops could be presented as a major new drive against the IRA it might be possible to call upon the Protestants to give up their march without too drastic a reaction. Tuzo agreed: the question of banning could be considered again closer to the occasion. The GOC, however, was less than impressed with Faulkner's plea for the cratering of border roads: it was a waste of time. Any farmer with a bulldozer could fill in the crater and such measures had no security value to balance the ill-will they created amongst the wider population. If, however, it were thought politically desirable, blowing holes in roads was technically not a difficult operation for the Army. Smith added that although cratering might temporarily please Unionist opinion, views would change when it became apparent that cratering was ineffective and the Security Forces would be open to ridicule. In the end, Maudling decided that, although the security advantages might be meagre, this appeared to be a matter to which Faulkner attached political importance and he found it attractive for that reason.[86] When Heath was informed of Tuzo's plans for the new disruptive tactics he instructed that they should be introduced as soon as possible.[87] This became Operation LINKLATER.

Internment, however, was still on the horizon. Before Cabinet, on 21 July, Maudling asked Douglas-Home to explore the possibility of cooperation with

Dublin on internment. With Faulkner pressing for internment and Maudling reluctantly prepared to contemplate it, the Home Secretary was aware that it would be ineffectual without Irish help. The Irish Government had the requisite powers and Maudling wanted to discuss the chances of success if London pressed Dublin to make use of them. Douglas-Home agreed that there would be no harm in sounding out Lynch on the issue of internment, but doubted if the Taoiseach would be willing to cooperate.[88] Officials in the Foreign Office concurred: for Lynch to agree to internment would first require an IRA policy of violence in the South and, moreover, violence involving persons rather than just property. At the moment there were some IRA incidents aimed against foreign investment, but these seemed to be the work of the 'Gouldingites' or Officials; the 'Bradyites' or Provisionals were deemed to be less concerned with political philosophy and foreign investment. Indeed, when Lynch had threatened internment in late 1970 this had been in response to the suspected plan of Saor Éire, a small Republican splinter group, to kidnap a Dublin Minister as a hostage for one of their own men on trial for murder. The Foreign Office concluded that if internment were introduced in the North there would be the inevitable howls of protest in the South and, whatever he thought privately, Lynch would publicly have to join the chorus.[89]

Maudling did not receive any more reassuring news from Belfast regarding the probable impact of the Army's new security measures. Howard Smith telegraphed to London his opinion that it was unrealistic to expect the measures to reduce terrorism to tolerable proportions. They might, with luck, give pause to the growing pressure of public opinion on Faulkner, who also was in serious difficulties with his Cabinet. But the pressure would undoubtedly regain momentum if terrorism continued on anything like the present scale. Faulkner would give the new military measures a chance but felt that he did not have much time at his disposal. Smith concluded that internment alone would not do the trick. The estimate was that 25 per cent of the 400 on the list would be pulled in initially. Some would cross the Border while others would disperse, hoping to operate from other bases. So, in Smith's judgement, a considerable capacity for terror would remain. The authorities would probably be faced with increased unrest on the Catholic side, and if terror continued the Protestant demands for 'sterner action' would be renewed. This was, he warned, an all too familiar road, leading almost certainly to the collapse of the Stormont Government and this time with little in prospect except Direct Rule. Internment on both sides of the Border would, however, make much more sense in both military and UK political terms. While Smith was well aware of the difficulties and the slim chances of success with Lynch, this had to be set against the prospect that faced them. There was, of course, no guarantee that internment on both sides of the Border would save Stormont; but if Stormont failed and Direct Rule should come, it would be desirable that internment should already be in existence in view of the many military and political problems that confronted the British Government.[90]

The new tactics began with dawn raids on 23 July involving around 2,000 troops, backed up by the RUC. Homes were raided in Belfast, Newry, Lurgan, Portadown, Armagh, Derrymacash, Dungannon, Blackwatertown, Coalisland

and Cookstown. Most of the homes raided appear to have been those of the Official IRA: in Belfast of twenty men taken into custody only two of those identified were identified with the Provisionals. There was a storm of protest from Nationalists and Republicans. Ivan Cooper described the arrests as the actions of a fascist Government and warned of the possibility of bringing people back onto the streets in protest against what he called 'virtual internment'. Maudling, on the other hand, described the Army operation as 'marking a new phase' in the battle against the IRA. Its significance, he said, was that it laid stress on the fact that the function of the Security Forces was not merely to contain disorder and violence but to search out the men and the organizations responsible. This was to serve as further confirmation of the British Government's determination to suppress violence and terrorism and to maintain Northern Ireland's constitutional position.

The Army's second swoop began just after 4 a.m., on 27 July, involving 1,800 troops, this time on houses and other premises in Belfast's Ardoyne, Falls, Finaghy, Ballymurphy, Whiterock, Markets and Stranmillis areas, and in nine towns, including Armagh, Portadown and Lurgan. By the afternoon at least forty-eight people were being interviewed. In response, Republican organizations and Civil Rights groups began arranging protest meetings against what was regarded as 'obvious' moves towards internment. The Officials declared that all pretence that the 'normal law' was in use in the Six Counties had now been abandoned and a police state proper now existed: it was 'undeclared martial law' operated, controlled and directed at Westminster, the seat of oppression in Ireland for hundreds of years. The Provisionals claimed that as a result of the 'new offensive' the Irish nation as a whole 'stands at a crossroads'. Many of 'our people', they stated, had to date deliberately avoided a decision that now confronted all of them: to either declare that they were to determine their own future or to continue living in bondage. Now the moment of truth had arrived. Whitehall's mask was off: the 'tyrant and oppressor stands by his own primitive actions exposed for all to see'. Nothing could justify the mass breakings and enterings, the callous searching of male and female, young and old. The decision facing the people was: 'Either we, as a nation, meekly and simply accept the jackbooted oppressor, or we all together, man, woman and child, stand and state that we have had enough.'[91]

John Hume took the view that the British Government had only two courses open to it. One was outright repression. The other was a change in the system of Government, which was the root of all the unrest and troubles. The Government had chosen repression, which might work temporarily but would not solve the problems in the longer term; it might even result in a 'mammoth reaction'.[92] And it was not long before Paddy Devlin was calling the Army 'Green and Tans' as the 'density of terror' in his constituency could 'only be equalled in Irish history by their Black and Tans counter-parts of the Twenties'.[93] Devlin called on NICRA to institute a civil disobedience campaign so that the troops would be stretched 'from one end of the Statelet to the other'. Devlin alleged that many of the explosions which took place each night were being caused by Unionist extremists who were 'operating in full scale outside minority areas'. Only the previous week, he clamed, they had exploded bombs, wrecked houses and expelled Catholics from their homes while the military still closed their eyes to the breaches of the law 'committed by these bigots' and they concentrated on 'imaginary' breaches of the law by Republicans.[94] Devlin believed that there was 'clear proof' of the involvement of UVF-type organizations in bombings. The 'conspiracy going from the [Unionist] Government down' was to give the impression that all bombs and bullets were Catholic inspired and had deceived the press, the Security Forces and the British Government into believing that Catholics alone were responsible for the present troubles. The Tory Government wanted to be deceived because their simplistic policy of keeping Faulkner in power at all costs was based on the belief that the troubles came from one element alone. This meant that a situation could be built up so that when internment was introduced, Faulkner's Government was given breathing space for another week or fortnight but the Catholic side of the population was left leaderless.[95] Devlin explained that he would not have a problem with the raids if they took place across the city and guns were taken in from all sections of the community, which would give a better chance of lasting peace being brought about. Devlin listed the places he wanted raided as the Protestant districts of the Shankill Road, Sandy Row, and the Donegall Road.[96] And, of course, from a Nationalist perspective there was some plausibility in these arguments: Austin Currie said that only a fool would believe that one side of the political fence was responsible for all the recent explosions. He pointed out that when he alleged in 1969 that an extremist Protestant group was responsible for the explosions at that time, he was accused of 'irresponsible and dangerous politicking'. Subsequent events had proved him right. There was no doubt that Protestant extremists were drilling and that the Security Forces were well aware of their activities but were doing little or nothing to stop them. It was these people and their supporters in Government who were the real Northern Ireland problem and had been since 1912. Sooner or later they would have to be confronted and their bluff called. Currie saw no chance of anything approximating to normal politics in Northern Ireland until this happened.[97]

This last point was a reference to the impending Apprentice Boys march in Derry. It was, of course, the very same march which, two years before, had been the spark which ignited the flame of communal violence. Many Nationalists viewed the possibility of a repeat performance with horror. In the Dáil, Jack Lynch departed from convention and publicly intervened with an appeal to the British Government to ban it. The Taoiseach warned the Dáil of impending disaster and of the British Army being seen to take the side of the Unionist Government rather than keeping the peace. If Britain did not stop the parade he urged the people of Derry not to permit themselves to be provoked in such a way as to play further into the hands of the Stormont bigots. Surely it was recognized in London, he said, that 'responsibility goes hand in hand with trained authority'. If the responsibility were shirked and the Stormont Government were seen to depend for continuance in office on appeasing intolerant and bigoted men, then it could not survive very long the contempt of fair-minded British people.[98] In the North, Austin Currie, warning that there could be no horse-trading with fundamental freedoms, observed that an announcement that more troops were being sent to Northern Ireland appeared to confirm the impression that the Apprentice Boys were to be forced through Derry. But he also observed that impressions could be wrong. It was also still possible that the Derry march could be banned and internment could be introduced at the same time. This could be the idea of a 'certain tricky little man [Faulkner]'.[99] Nationalist fears about the attitude of the authorities were not eased by the shooting dead, on 7 August, of Harry Thornton, a 28-year-old Catholic from Crossmaglen temporarily resident in Belfast. When a van he was driving twice backfired outside Springfield Road RUC Station a soldier rushed out of the station and opened fire. A paratrooper claimed to have seen what looked like a weapon protruding from the open driver's window of the van as it passed the police station. He said he heard two retorts and saw smoke coming from the cab of the van. Another soldier, the NCO on desk duty, heard what he believed were two shots. He grabbed his rifle and went into the street. When the sentry told him shots had come from the small grey van he dropped on one knee and fired two shots at it. Thornton's companion was arrested and taken into the barracks. When the man was released some hours later his face was swollen and bandaged. By the early afternoon local Republicans were distributing leaflets headed: 'Murder murder murder'.[100]

By now Faulkner was being assailed from all sides. The military raids had satisfied no one: they further alienated Catholics while failing to reassure Protestants. It seemed that only internment could save him and Stormont.

Notes

1. NAUK PRO PREM 15/476 Note for the Record, 25 March 1971.
2. NAUK PRO PREM 15/476 Note for the Record, 24 March 1971.
3. NAUK PRO DEFE 24/873 Note for the Record, 12 February 1971.
4. NAUK PRO PREM 15/475 Telegram No.2 UK Rep Belfast to MOD/Home Office/FCO, 2 March 1971.
5. *Irish Times*, 1 March 1971.
6. Ibid., 18 March 1971.
7. Ibid., 1 March 1971.
8. Ibid., 6 March 1971.
9. Ibid., 20 March 1971.
10. NAUK PRO PREM 15/476 Telegram No.10 UK Rep to Home Office, 22 March 1971.
11. *Irish Times*, 22 March 1971.
12. Ibid.
13. Ibid.
14. NAUK PRO PREM 15/476 Telegram No.8 UK Rep to Home Office, 21 March 1971.
15. NAUK PRO PREM 15/476 Telegram No.11 UK Rep to Home Office, 23 March 1971.
16. *Irish Times*, 26 March 1971.
17. Ibid.
18. Ibid.
19. Ibid., 31 March 1971.
20. NAUK PRO PREM 15/476 Telegram No.93 Dublin Embassy to FCO, 22 March 1971.
21. NAUK PRO PREM 15/476 Telegram No.102 Dublin Embassy to FCO, 24 March 1971.
22. NAI D/T 2002/8/77 Donal O'Sullivan message, 26 March 1971.

23. *Irish Times*, 3 March 1971.
24. NAUK PRO PREM 15/476 Telegram No.105 Dublin Embassy to FCO, 26 March 1971.
25. NAUK PRO PREM 15/476 Telegram No.107 Dublin Embassy to FCO, 27 March 1971.
26. NAUK PRO PREM 15/476 Telegram No.15 UK Rep to Home Office, 29 March 1971.
27. NAI D/T 2002/8/77 Roinn an Taoisigh, 30 March 1971.
28. *Irish Times*, 31 March 1971.
29. NAUK PRO PREM 15/477 Note of a Meeting held at 10 Downing Street, 1 April 1971.
30. NAUK PRO DEFE 25/304 Policy for Operations, 24 March 1971.
31. NAUK PRO DEFE 25/304 Northern Ireland – Ministerial Meeting, 27 April 1971.
32. McKittrick et al., *Lost Lives*, pp.72–5.
33. NAUK PRO DEFE 25/304 Valedictory Despatch from Mr R.A. Burroughs, 14 April 1971.
34. NAUK PRO PREM 15/477 Smith to Maudling, 10 June 1971.
35. Ian McAllister, *The Northern Ireland Social Democratic and Labour Party: Political Opposition in a Divided Society* (London: 1977), pp.88–90.
36. Northern Ireland House of Commons Col. 468, 25 May 1971.
37. *Irish Press*, 25 May 1971.
38. Northern Ireland House of Commons Col. 481, 26 May 1971.
39. NAI D/T 2002/8/78 DFA to An Runaí Roinn an Taoisigh, 13 Iuil 1971.
40. NAI D/T 2002/8/78 Statement Issued by the Northern Ireland Information Service on Behalf of the Northern Ireland Premier, Mr Brian Faulkner, Concerning the Explosion at the Springfield Road RUC Station, 26 May 1971.
41. Northern Ireland House of Commons Col.375, 26 May 1971.
42. Ibid., Col.378.
43. Dáil Debates Col.235, 26 May 1971.
44. Kelly, *Fall of Stormont*, pp.91–2.
45. BSI G1 OP Directive Number 3 of 1971, 2 July 1971.
46. BSI. G27.196. OP Directive Number 4 of 1971, 10 November 1971.
47. *News Letter*, 2 July 1971.
48. Ibid., 3 July 1971.
49. Ibid.
50. *Irish News*, 5 July 1971.
51. Ibid., 8 July 1971.
52. Ibid., 7 July 1971.
53. Ibid., 9 July and 10 July 1971.
54. Ibid., 7 July 1971.
55. McKittrick et al., *Lost Lives*, pp.75–6.
56. Ibid., pp.76–7.
57. *Irish News*, 9 July 1971.
58. Kelly, *Fall of Stormont*, p.46.
59. *News Letter*, 14 July 1971.
60. *Irish News*, 9 July 1971.
61. Kelly, *Fall of Stormont*, p.46.
62. NAI D/T 2002/8/78 Note by Hugh McCann, 9 Iuil 1971.
63. NAI D/T 2002/8/78 The Derry Killings Memorandum by Hugh McCann, 14 July 1971.
64. *Irish News*, 9 July 1971.
65. Kelly, *Fall of Stormont*, pp.47–8.
66. *Irish News*, 10 July 1971.
67. Ibid., 12 July 1971.
68. Ibid., 13 July 1971.
69. *News Letter*, 12 July 1971.
70. Ibid., 12 July 1971; *Irish News*, 12 July 1971.
71. Brian Faulkner, *Memoirs of a Statesman* (London: 1977), p.116.

72. McKittrick et al., *Lost Lives*, p.77.
73. *News Letter*, 14 July 1971.
74. Ibid., 15 July 1971.
75. McKittrick et al., *Lost Lives*, pp.77–8.
76. *News Letter*, 15 July 1971.
77. Faulkner, *Memoirs*, pp.117–19.
78. Michael Carver, *Out of Step. Memoirs of a Field Marshall,* (London: 1989), p.407.
79. BSI JS8 Statement of Sir Graham Shillington.
80. BSI G2.
81. *Irish Times*, 19 July 1971.
82. Ibid., 19 July 1971.
83. Ibid., 20 July 1971.
84. Ibid., 19 July 1971.
85. Faulkner, *Memoirs*, p.119.
86. NAUK PRO FCO 33/1465 Discussion in the Home Secretary's Room, 19 July 1971.
87. NAUK PRO PREM 15/478 Peter Gregson to A.W. Stephens, 22 July 1971.
88. NAUK PRO FCO 33/1465 19 July 1971.
89. NAUK PRO FCO 33/1465 Republic of Ireland: Attitude to Internment.
90. NAUK PRO FCO 33/1465 Belfast Telegram No.18 of 20 July to Home Office.
91. *Irish News*, 28 July 1971.
92. Ibid., 24 July 1971.
93. Ibid., 2 August 1971.
94. *Irish Times*, 31 July 1971.
95. *Irish News*, 6 August 1971.
96. Ibid., 29 July 1971.
97. Ibid., 7 August 1971.
98. Ibid.
99. Ibid.
100. McKittrick et al., *Lost Lives*, pp.78–9.

4

Internment without Trial

INTERNMENT: THE DECISION

The question now was: how long before Faulkner requested internment? London did not have long to wait in order to find out. On 28 July, Faulkner telephoned Maudling to inform him that every one of his Cabinet colleagues now believed the time had come for internment. Faulkner had told them that he would not ask for internment until he had received advice from those professionally concerned with security. But he thought the time was coming near when internment would become necessary. Maudling replied that this might well be so but that it was right to try other initiatives short of internment such as the recent swoop operations. Faulkner agreed – provided these were pursued with the utmost vigour.[1] Crucially, Tuzo remained completely opposed to the introduction of internment. When the CGS, Sir Michael Carver and Tuzo spoke, on 2 August, the GOC stated that 'he did not recommend internment on military grounds: he considered it militarily unnecessary'. Nor did, apparently, Faulkner, to whom Tuzo had spoken that morning. At the same time Faulkner felt that if something was not seen to produce decisive results fairly rapidly 'he would be cut down'. Tuzo believed he had a number of 'possible shots' in his locker, such as, in addition to LINKLATER, recourse to block searches, curfews or greater restriction on Border traffic; but these measures, he pointed out to Carver, bore on large numbers of innocent people and the GOC did not think he could produce the sufficiently rapid military effect that was necessary for political purposes. Tuzo was still in favour of allowing the 12 August march to go ahead – 'a decision to ban it would be a victory for the IRA' – but he fully appreciated that in the event of a 'package deal' it would be necessary to intern before the ban on marches was announced – in effect to intern a few days before 12 August.[2]

Given the seeming inevitability of internment, at some point soon, London pressed ahead with preparations. The first stage was for the FCO to follow up Maudling's suggestion to sound out the Irish. On 27 July, John Peck was informed by Douglas-Home of the probability of internment. The British Government accepted that while the introduction of internment in Northern Ireland alone would bring some benefit, the expectation was that a large number of those IRA members responsible for violence would escape the net and go into hiding; the majority would cross the Border. Given a little time for regrouping, their capacity for violence and terrorism could be expected to be built up again. In this situation, Douglas-Home emphasized that it would make a material difference if internment could be introduced in parallel in the Republic. This would not only result in immobilizing a substantial number of active terrorists, but it would also remove a safe haven for those in the North. Without internment in the South, there had to be a serious danger that, after a short lull, the security situation would again deteriorate and put the whole programme of reform and Faulkner's effort to integrate the minority into Northern Ireland's system of Government and administration at risk. In this situation, the possibility of London having to resort to Direct Rule could not be excluded, despite all the disadvantages which this would bring. Direct Rule would represent a grave setback to the search on which Faulkner and Lynch had both been engaged for conditions in which the two parts of Ireland could peacefully co-exist through the building up of cooperation and confidence. So, London hoped that it could look to Lynch for his understanding of the problems and for his cooperation in seeking to avert such developments. Finally, Douglas-Home emphasized that London hoped that Lynch would be prepared to treat the present approach in the utmost confidence, whatever response he might decide to make. Should it prove necessary, however, to introduce internment in the North, it was most important that those who might be taken into custody should have no prior warning of what was proposed.[3] Therefore, the approach had to be made, in the first instance, on a hypothetical basis, mentioning no dates and leaving the final decision to be made in the future. The approach was to be made orally by Peck to Lynch using, if possible, some other subject to explain the meeting, so as to minimize the risk of leakage.[4]

In reply, Peck had two general points to make. The first was that Lynch would only introduce internment if this were judged necessary for domestic reasons; that was, if the Irish Government felt that there was no other means of maintaining public order. The second was that if he was to speak to Lynch on purely hypothetical lines, the Taoiseach's formal reply would probably be that he could not give an answer to a hypothetical question. In fact, Peck did not believe that Lynch would regard Direct Rule as a disaster, although he would regret its introduction. Nor did Peck believe that Lynch had the same view of practical co-existence as Faulkner – the former was on a converging course, the latter on a parallel: Irish views were complex. Peck pointed out that the Irish Government had decided on a tough line against both IRA factions, and even if convictions were not obtained in the courts they would harass them by administrative action. George Colley, the Minister for Finance, had repeated this to Peck only the previous week and had added that internment was not excluded. Peck warned, however, that the introduction of internment in the Republic would be an extremely contentious political issue which might involve the recalling of the Dáil. Lynch would be accused by Sinn Féin of acting in collusion with London and Peck did not see how the Taoiseach could agree to any timing which could confirm such suspicions. It might therefore be easier if internment could be introduced after, and so as a consequence of, similar action in the North. Peck could not see Lynch agreeing to synchronized action. He thought that Lynch's reply would be that he was indeed thinking about internment, that internment in the North would have obvious repercussions in the South but that he would have to wait to see what these were before taking a decision.[5]

Back in London, a brief for GEN 47, the Northern Ireland Ministerial Committee, drawn up by Kelvin White of the FCO's Western European Department, noted that there was a tendency to say that internment in the North alone was not worthwhile. This, claimed White, was questionable. Some benefits were certain and IRA men would not be able to return to the North without risking arrest. Crucially, White emphasized that 'Any decision to intern must be taken on security grounds and not [to] alleviate Unionist pressures on Faulkner.' Finally, White pointed out that if Craig or Paisley were the only alternatives to Faulkner 'direct rule must be introduced. And before they took over, not after a trial period' so that neither could argue that they were the legitimate 'Government in exile'.[6] Further assessments focused on the general belief that there would be a substantial intelligence dividend, the benefits of which could not be easily divorced from the balance sheet on the military effectiveness of internment. It was reasonable to assume that those caught in the first swoop would fall into three categories: the senior commanders, middle-ranking officers and the 'small fry'. The last category would probably not know very much that was not known already. The middle-ranking officers would know a good deal to carry out their duties and within the thirty days for interrogation which Regulation 11 of the Special Powers Act afforded it was probable that a good number of them would yield substantial intelligence. The same was true of at least some of the senior officers, though this third category was more likely to contain the 'hard cases' with the capacity to withstand sustained interrogation. A further dividend might occur in that sources amongst the minority hitherto reluctant to help the Security Forces would be encouraged to come forward once the threat of reprisals was markedly reduced by internment. Finally, the descriptions and photographs of those who escaped the net could be circulated. This could produce reports on the whereabouts of the wanted men, for example from customs officials and the Protestant community.[7]

By now Ministers were left in no doubt as to what the Irish reaction would be to internment when Peck saw Lynch at 3 p.m. on 30 July; equally, Lynch could not now be in any doubt that internment was imminent. It proved to be a long and frank discussion. Peck prefixed it by suggesting that ostensibly, if his visit was noticed, it concerned the Taoiseach's forthcoming visit to London – but actually it was to discuss a secret matter and the fact that it had been discussed would not be disclosed. The Ambassador then showed Lynch an 'agreed text' drawn up by London which the British hoped the Taoiseach would sign up to. He then spoke as instructed. Peck made two comments: first that the recurring word 'parallel' in the text did not mean simultaneous or concerted internment by the British and Irish and, secondly, that the word 'hypothetical' in the penultimate paragraph only meant that no final decision had yet been taken by London to introduce internment. Lynch studied the document carefully and handed it back. He explained to Peck that he could state categorically that he could not possibly contemplate internment at the present time – there were no immediate grounds for doing so – and if he tried to introduce it in consequence of the British doing so neither he nor his Government could survive such a measure. It was true that they had threatened it in a special internal situation the previous December, and the threat had apparently succeeded. He could introduce it as a drastic measure if there were a total breakdown of the system of justice. But neither now, nor in the visible future, did there seem to be any grounds for introducing internment. Lynch predicted that a massive influx of the IRA from the North might cause some further lawlessness in the South, but he would not expect it to be unmanageable and it offered no grounds for preventive action in advance. Lynch then urged Britain to reflect very seriously before taking the grave step of introducing internment. He feared that it would produce an explosion that it would be impossible to contain. When Peck asked him how, Lynch replied: 'If you round up 1,000 people and intern 20 because they are bad, you immediately make bad people of the other 980.' With the extreme Unionists apparently on the rampage, all the moderates would identify themselves with the internees. Peck then referred to the ultimate possibility of Direct Rule and asked Lynch how he felt about it. Lynch answered that he would prefer it to a General Election and a Paisley-led Government. Lynch instead reverted again and again to the 'unwisdom' of internment, arguing that Britain surely had enough troops, police and intelligence resources to manage without it. The Irish Government, on the other hand, had very few of each, a point which enabled Peck to touch on cooperation along the Border. Lynch's view on this was that police cooperation was functioning discreetly: there were no means of organizing any planned military cooperation, but if by chance a patrol one side of the Border passed a friendly word to one on the other side, no harm would be done. Finally, Lynch asked when a decision was likely to be taken on internment. Peck replied that it might arise at any time from now on, although Peck thought it unlikely over the coming weekend.[8]

Back in the Province the Army were putting their final preparations in place. An outline plan for internment had been prepared by HQ Northern Ireland. Planning had been carried out on a 'need-to-know' principle between the Government Security Unit of the Northern Ireland Government, HQ RUC, and HQ Northern Ireland. Its codename was DEMETRIUS. Arrest arrangements were reviewed periodically by a committee consisting of representatives from the HQ RUC, RUC Special Branch and HQNI. The Army plan assumed that internment could have already been implemented prior to the imposition of Direct Rule; conversely, internment could be ordered after the imposition of Direct Rule in which case the internment plan would require updating to allow for special circumstances that might arise. The Army estimated that a minimum of fourteen major units would be required to implement internment. This force level would allow for the arrest plan; the security of internees; the possibility of increased border activity by the IRA; and the likelihood of widespread disturbances, particularly in Belfast and Londonderry. Under Direct Rule the force level would already be at least fifteen major units as provided for in the contingency planned for this – Operation FOURSQUARE. Up to a further two major units might be required to assist in implementing internment. The construction of Phase I of the detainment facilities for internees – known as Long Kesh Camp III – accommodating 150, was due for completion by 11 September. Special security arrangements including security fencing and lighting would require an additional fourteen days construction time. This could run concurrently with Phase I if the decision to implement internment was made before September. The construction of Phase II was due for completion by 13 November and provided accommodation for up to 450 internees and staff. Phase III, the special security measures, could be completed by 30 November if required.[9]

The politicians in London were thinking of internment after 12 August. And it was with this timescale in mind that Whitehall's senior civil servant, Sir Burke Trend, the Cabinet Secretary, produced a report on 'Clandestine Action' for Heath on 2 August. He was seeking the agreement of Ministers for the planning of all Northern Ireland operations to be brought forward and up to as high a state of readiness as possible, but on the pretext that no action should be initiated until 12 August had come and gone.[10] With Parliament due to rise quite soon and the Prime Minister heading off to skipper his yacht, *Morning Cloud*, in competition the following week, Trend reminded Heath that before Ministers finally dispersed the Government ought to be clear where it stood, particularly if the Home Secretary was to meet Faulkner later in the week as had been planned some time ago. The Prime Minister also needed to obtain from the Cabinet delegated authority for himself, the Home Secretary, the Foreign Secretary, and the Defence Secretary to take whatever action might be required by developments during the next few weeks, although if there was a move to Direct Rule, the Cabinet and Parliament would presumably have to be summoned. And, if internment was introduced, the Government must be ready to move to Direct Rule at short notice thereafter. The necessary plans and arrangements for this purpose should therefore be completed.[11] A more immediate problem was Faulkner's forthcoming meeting with Maudling. Robert Armstrong minuted the Prime Minister: 'This is beginning to look unpleasantly like Major Chichester-Clark's last visit.' The timing appeared as about as bad as it could be, in relation to a forthcoming Northern Ireland debate in the House of Commons. What particularly concerned Armstrong was that:

> Mr. Faulkner will be expected to have brought something home with him. If he is to come, and Ministers are not prepared to agree to internment, there ought to be something else for him to take back, and to be seen to take back; otherwise his own position becomes very weak. If Ministers are not prepared to agree to internment, and there is nothing else, he had better not come, despite the Home Secretary's agreement that he should.

As to internment itself, the argument that seemed to Armstrong to have any great force was Lord Carrington's: 'It is a last fling. If this is right, it seems to me that it should be something which you do when you visibly have to, and not before: not as part of a deal for banning marches.'[12]

Carrington's opinions also impressed Kelvin White who recalled that the Defence Secretary was determined that any decision to intern should be properly underwritten by the politicians in Northern Ireland who 'should not be allowed to shuffle off the responsibility for so unpopular a move onto the Army'. Not that such a prospect seemed imminent: it was clear by the next morning, 3 August, when White attended the DMO's debriefing of the departing CLF, Farrar-Hockley, that there seemed no sense of impending crisis. White noted that Ministers had decided that Faulkner should not now come to London on the basis that 'if he did come he would have to take away with him some goodies, and there were no goodies to give.' London had also decided that internment was now neither necessary nor desirable and that the Apprentice Boys march would be routed so that it marched out of the city, would then return and disperse. These decisions now permitted a more academic discussion of the pros and cons of internment between White and Farrar-Hockley.

The former CLF's thesis was that in the early months of the year internment made no sense. Now it did. The LINKLATER series of operations – the pulling in of IRA members – had badly rattled them. Their organization and command structure was poor; if some of them could be got rid of – Farrar-Hockley gave a dozen or so names – substantial damage would be done. Since these operations began the IRA had been hard pushed even to place a few bombs in public lavatories. If internment took place a substantial intelligence dividend was expected, especially from middle ranking members. The effects of internment, according to the military appreciation, would be forty-eight hours or so of rioting on the streets, in which many participants would be Catholics who might privately welcome internment but would be anxious to be seen to be doing their bit – lest reprisals followed. Thereafter there would be a strong propaganda attack, led by MPs such as Paddy Devlin and Paddy Kennedy, and at the same time, though lasting only a few weeks, the residue of IRA men left with arms 'would throw their bombs and shoot wildly'. A lull would then ensue while the IRA reorganized within the Republic. Finally IRA activity would begin again, but probably in the form of flying columns operating in the Border area. There was a fair chance here of pitched battles, in which the Army would come off the best. Then activity would tail off. White particularly questioned the last point about the reappearance of flying columns, since it seemed to him odd that the IRA would adopt a solution which led to defeats whereas the urban guerrilla role offered profit. Farrar-Hockley, however, had confidence that once the IRA were eliminated from the Belfast enclaves they would not easily achieve their return. White reported the GOC's view – that internment was not now necessary on military grounds alone – back to Farrar-Hockley. He agreed: the Army were steadily cutting the IRA down, a process which would continue even without internment, but the question was ultimately political – would the politicians' will to govern erode faster? Farrar-Hockley pointed out that there would be grave criticism from the Protestants were Direct Rule to precede internment. They would say that a major weapon had been denied them.[13]

Thus, on 3 August it seemed that the political pressure to introduce internment had somewhat receded. But then Faulkner phoned Maudling the next day and said that he wished to speak to himself and the Prime Minister 'on a grave security matter'. Maudling knew immediately what Faulkner meant and the meeting was arranged for the following day, 5 August, at Downing Street.[14] Later in the day Maudling sent Faulkner the following message:

> I said I would set out the position as clearly as I can.
>
> The decision whether to proceed to internment is yours to make under the Constitution but it is our mutual understanding, particularly in view of the involvement of UK forces, that such a decision would be agreed beforehand with us. You had yourself often said, and I have supported this view, that you would be guided by the recommendations of the security authorities.
>
> As I understand it the GOC is not in present circumstances recommending internment on military grounds. This of course is the basis on which he would advise Ministers of either Government who would be responsible for the decision. It would be for them to take into account the political considerations which are numerous and complex.
>
> I understand that pressure for internment is considerable and I agree that it may well become necessary. I have stated in public that we would raise no objection to internment if we were satisfied on the advice of the security authorities and after consultation with you on the wider aspects that this would help in the campaign against the IRA. I have further stressed that no prior announcement would be possible or desirable. This remains our position.
>
> We must look at the immediate situation against the background of the Apprentice Boys march on 12 August. If internment were introduced before then it would in our view be essential to proceed simultaneously with the indefinite banning of all political processions. I understand it is the GOC's view on military grounds that he would not advise the banning of the procession. If the procession is to proceed it seems to me to be wiser to postpone any decision about internment until after it has taken place when we can review the situation again on the existing principles and wholly without prejudice to a decision either way. As so much attention has been paid to this march on 12 August its outcome one way or another will be of considerable significance for any decision about the future conduct of the campaign against the terrorists.
>
> This is the position as I see it. I should be most grateful for your comments.[15]

Heath was informed that the Home Secretary had been talking to Faulkner that afternoon and that 'Mr. Faulkner seems now to be firmly of the opinion that internment is desirable.' He had asked to come and see the Home Secretary the following day and this had been agreed. It was not intended that the visit should be announced in advance although no effort would be made to conceal it and when questions were asked it would be said that this was a regular meeting to discuss the situation.[16]

GEN 47 gathered the next day, 5 August, where Maudling explained to his colleagues that he had told Faulkner – who had by this stage arrived in London – that there appeared to be two courses open: before 12 August both to resort to internment and to prohibit all processions in Northern Ireland; or to reconsider the possible use of internment in the light of the situation prevailing thereafter. The UK Government preferred the latter course. Faulkner had, however, urged the former course, pointing out that the RUC Chief Constable now favoured the early use of internment. The political situation had deteriorated and pressure on him to adopt internment had become so strong that, unless some dramatic military success was achieved during the next few days, it might well become irresistible. Maudling added that the UK Representative in Belfast now thought that the political situation required the use of internment. The Home Secretary pointed out to the Committee that it seemed clear that internment would have to be used at some time in the near future and the arguments in favour of using it sooner rather than later were strong.[17] Maudling had already laid out in a memorandum the pros and cons relating to internment – they did not make comfortable reading. It stated:

The arguments in favour of using this power in the present situation are:

(a) it would enable Mr Faulkner to demonstrate to his supporters his determination to suppress violence;
(b) whatever unknown IRA sympathisers there may be there is reliable intelligence about a substantial number of known dangerous men whose removal from the scene could be a major contribution to lessening tension;
(c) the normal processes of investigation, detection and trial are obstructed by a wall of silence, created either by intimidation or sympathy. Information gained during the processes of detention and internment should produce information which could lead to the conviction of some of those who are at present escaping the courts.

The considerations against internment are:

(a) there is no certainty that all dangerous men could be identified;
(b others not at present active or identified would come forward from the North or from the Republic to replace the internees and recruitment to the IRA generally would be stimulated;
(c) the sympathies of the minority would rally to the IRA;
(d) it would be politically damaging, domestically and internationally.

To be fully effective it would need to be accompanied by a similar operation in the Republic but Lynch had made it clear that this was not a measure which he was at present prepared to contemplate. It was also not easy to predict how the IRA would react. Those who were not caught up in the operation would, no doubt, mount as much terrorist activity as possible but there was a 'fair chance that, deprived of active leadership, the campaign would quickly lose its effectiveness'. The reaction of the Catholic community was likely to be more marked on this occasion than on previous occasions of internment because of the more marked affinity between the activity of the IRA and the strong claims of the minority community for a larger share in the Government of Northern Ireland. Faulkner's supporters and the Protestant community at large would, no doubt, welcome internment: 'Whether their enthusiasm would survive for any length of time if in the event the operation did not have a major effect on the situation in Northern Ireland id[sic] doubtful.'[18] Carrington then explained to the Committee that 500 persons were on the list of potential internees and the GOC hoped that it would be possible to apprehend 300 of them in the first instance. Forty-eight hours would be required from the decision to use internment before the first arrests could be made. As GEN 47 proceeded to discuss the options, a number of points emerged: in deciding whether or not to agree the immediate use of internment it had to be borne in mind that it was the last action available short of Direct Rule. It could not be argued that internment would enable Faulkner to carry on his administration indefinitely. On the other hand, it seemed inevitable that internment would have to be used sooner or later. If, when Faulkner met GEN 47 that afternoon, he were to formally seek London's agreement to internment, and London were to refuse it, the fact would become known and Faulkner's political position would become impossible. Direct Rule would then almost inevitably follow, and in that event London would want to use the power of internment. Therefore, it would be better if London allowed the Northern Ireland Government to use internment earlier. Heath, however, reminded his colleagues that although a refusal to accede to Faulkner's demand for internment would seriously damage his political position, it had to be borne in mind that the British Government would be bearing the effective responsibility for the act.[19]

The meeting then moved into private session with Faulkner. He stressed the seriousness of the security situation, the decline in public confidence, the increasingly serious implications for commerce and industry and the absence of any initiative that the Security Forces could suggest to make an early impact. Accordingly he argued that there should be an early use of internment powers. The British Ministers pointed out the difficulty with this: military advice that internment was necessary had not been given and they stressed the national and international implications of so serious a step. Heath made the point that if internment was tried and did not succeed in improving matters the only further option could be Direct Rule. None of the measures taken so far had really succeeded in uniting the community. Faulkner replied that in his view Direct Rule would be a calamity; and if they could really get a grip on the security position there was a genuine hope of not merely restoring the pre-1968 position, when people had been for the most part living harmoniously together, but moving forward to something better in conditions where the changes of the past two years could take effect. Moreover, there were other initiatives, notably his Committee proposals, still 'on the table' to be taken up. At the second stage of the meeting, Carver, Tuzo and Shillington were called in. Shillington gave his view that the time for internment had now arrived. Carver and Tuzo, however, took the position that they 'could not describe it as an essential measure in purely military terms'. The IRA could be defeated by present methods, but whether the likely timescale was acceptable was essentially a political question, and thus not one for determination by them. After an interval during which the British Ministers discussed the position with their advisors, the meeting resumed with Faulkner. Heath 'gave the firm decision of the UK Government that if, as the responsible Minister, Mr Faulkner informed them that it would be his intention to proceed to early internment, they would concur and ensure the necessary Army support'. This had to be accompanied by a ban on all parades. If there was any evidence of the involvement of Protestants in any form of subversive or terrorist activity they too should be interned. Faulkner pointed out that, whatever their involvement in past acts, 'there was no intelligence indicating an existing or imminent potential Protestant threat'. It was only on these grounds that internment of Protestants 'was not envisaged at present'. There would be no hesitation to intern such elements if circumstances changed; but the present threat was from the IRA.[20]

All that was left to do was to make the final military preparations to implement DEMETRIUS. This task fell to Major General Robert Ford, who had just taken over as CLF, and was still unpacking in his house when given his instructions. He called a conference at Lisburn of his Brigade Commanders, together with the Deputy Chief Constable, the Head of Special Branch, the Army's Director of Intelligence and a number of other personnel. The Brigade Commanders brought their own area Special Branch Commanders with them. It soon became apparent to Ford that the list of suspects 'was extremely questionable'. At the conference there was 'much argument over whether X or Y should be included, or whether indeed some suspects were north of the Border or south. My Brigade Commanders and I fully realised that the list was doubtful but we also knew that we had nothing better to work on.' Ford was also concerned about the security of the operation. It seemed to him that too many people knew about it in Whitehall and Stormont. It was decided, therefore, to bring the operation forward to 9 August.[21]

There was still the delicate matter of how to inform the Irish Government that internment was to be introduced. A draft of the message to the Taoiseach had included the sentence: 'Protestants as well as Catholic and IRA extremists will be liable to internment.' This was now crossed out.[22] Dublin Telegram Number 155 from the FCO on 8 August contained Douglas Home's final instructions to Peck. The Ambassador was to deliver a personal message from Heath to Lynch announcing the implementation of internment. It was to be given to him on the morning of 9 August not earlier than 9.00 a.m. It was intended that Faulkner should make an announcement regarding internment in Belfast at 11.15 a.m. that morning. Peck was to draw particular attention to paragraph 9 expressing Heath's hope that Lynch's public response would be helpful particularly in condemning violence, making clear to the minority in the North that they should not interpret the measures taken as directed against them but only at individuals who were deliberately using violence to create disorder. What Lynch said in public might well set the tone for the response of the minority themselves. In view of the danger of IRA reprisals Peck was instructed to immediately review security arrangements for himself and his staff, as well as for other British offices in the Republic.[23] From Dublin, Peck told London to expect that, in the outcry following the announcement, Lynch was going to be heavily pressed to say whether he was consulted before the decision was taken. It was imperative that he should be able to say no.[24]

DEMETRIUS

At 1 a.m. on 9 August we were given our orders: they were to be ready at 3.30 a.m. and to go in at 4 a.m. The whole platoon would have about two blokes to pick up and about six houses to visit. We'd lift whoever was there. We would knock on the door discreetly for three seconds and then charge in. You'd get an awful lot of old blokes in dressing gowns and an awful lot of serious abuse. It was pretty desperate really.[25]

This was how Second Lieutenant James Roderick Campbell, of The Royal Green Jackets, recalled the opening of DEMETRIUS. The overriding requirement that governed the planning and execution of DEMETRIUS was that complete security should be maintained about the identity of the persons to be arrested and the date and time when the arrests were to be carried out.[26] The operation itself consisted of five phases. The first was the arrests. Parties of soldiers effected arrests according to the lists prepared by the RUC (SB). Very occasionally RUC officers acted as guides but in all cases the arresting was done by the military. Speed was the prime consideration to avoid the chance of hostile crowds gathering even at that early hour. Each arrester completed a report relating to the person he arrested. The arrests took place at 04.30, or as near to that time as possible. The arresting soldiers were governed by a general instruction requiring them never to use more force than the minimum necessary to enable them to carry out their duties. Except in one Brigade area, they had no specific orders about the use of restraints on arrested persons.

The second phase involved the transport to Regional Holding Centres (RCH). There were three RHCs, each under the overall charge of a senior officer where identification of arrested persons was confirmed and the decision taken as to whether they should be detained or released. These were Magilligan Weekend Training Centre in County Londonderry, Ballykinler Weekend Training Centre in County Down and Girdwood Park Territorial Army Centre in Belfast. In Belfast the movement of the arrested person was short in time and distance from the point of arrest to a rendezvous for preliminary identification (often at the vehicle to be used for the next stage of the journey) and thence to the RHC at Girdwood Park. In the other two regions the distances were in most cases much greater and the arrested person was usually taken from the point of arrest to a rendezvous for preliminary identification (normally at an established point like a barracks) designated a Prisoner Collection Point and thence to either the Ballykinler or Magilligan RHC. The third phase involved processing at RHCs. All arrested persons were to be interviewed by RUC Special Branch officers prior to the decision about detention. The processing at Holding Centres lasted from early 9 August to early 11 August, but arrested persons whom it was decided not to detain were released at any time during those forty-eight hours. At all the Holding Centres a uniform system of records was maintained, including entry and exit registers and a photograph of each arrested person on entry. At Ballykinler and Magilligan a medical officer was in post who carried out an examination of each arrested person on entry and recorded the result of the examination. At Girdwood a medical orderly was in attendance and a doctor was within call at 30 minutes' notice. There was no system of medical examination on entry. The fourth phase was the transportation to places of detention. Arrested persons who were to be detained – apart from those selected for special questioning – were sent by helicopter from Ballykinler and Magilligan to the prison ship *Maidstone* in Belfast harbour, and on foot from Girdwood to Crumlin Jail. Girdwood was immediately adjacent to the prison, and the arrested persons passed into the prison through a hole, made early on the 9 August, in the wall that divided the prison area from Girdwood Park. A wing of the prison was also used as an annex to the Girdwood Regional Holding Centre. The fifth phase involved those selected for interrogation in depth. On 11 August these persons were moved for that purpose from their Holding Centres to a place other than the place specified in the detention order before being lodged in detention in Crumlin Jail on 16 and 17 August. The number of persons arrested and handled by the Holding Centres was as follows:

TABLE 1[27]

	Ballykinler	Magilligan	Girdwood Park
Arrested and admitted to:			
Regional Holding Centre	89	68	185
Moved into detention	80	40	117
Released	9	28	68

In London the MOD reported that of the initial grab of 320 persons, detention orders had been issued for about 250. Half of these were from the Belfast area where important inroads had been made into the 'Brady' organization. It was assessed that about 50 per cent of the Belfast Provisional leadership had been eliminated. In terms of total numbers, up to 2,000 IRA members might still be at large, but these would include a large number of part time auxiliaries and by no means would all be gunmen. Many of these would have moved into Southern Ireland or would be preparing to do so.[28] By 11.50 a.m. on 9 August, Kelvin White delivered a situation report on those lifted to Douglas-Home. There were now 464 names on the list made up as follows:

Bradyites	283
Gouldingites	143
IRA unspecified	29
People's democracy	7
Anarchists	1
Saor Éire	1

At the last count 347 had been detained ater releases. This was, to White's mind, 'outstandingly good': even optimists before had thought 60 per cent would be good going, but the figure was nearer 74 per cent.[29] Heath, who was away racing *Morning Cloud* in the Fastnet race, did not hear the results of the first internment swoop until the next day, when Peter Gregson connected him. Further reports were to be sent to the Prime Minister at Plymouth. Gregson pointed out that the 'best news is the good "catch" (304 out of 464)'.[30]

That was the good news. Back in Belfast violence erupted in Nationalist areas with barricades erected, arson, riots, shootings and bombings. Jamie Campbell's Royal Green Jackets found that, in Belfast: 'The place went completely berserk. There were burning cars and burning tyres and barricades everywhere. The place was solid with people raining rocks and bottles down on us. We provided them with a lovely target in their angst. Our orders were to try and keep the main roads open.' At the height of the rioting, Campbell's platoon was in Albert Street, trying to keep it open to traffic, at a point near St Peter's Church next to the Divis Flats. Suddenly, in the middle of the chaos, one of his men ran up to him and asked him to train his 'binos' on the church, where he thought he'd spotted a sniper in the tower. But the sniper was elsewhere.

> I swung around and looked, and as I looked, I was hit by a shot from the Divis – and it was quite a good shot at about 200 yards. The bullet went through my right arm and then through my chest. All I knew was that I was flying through the air with the greatest of ease, completely winded – I couldn't breathe – and I landed with a great thump on the ground. I remember thinking, 'I've been shot – in the stomach, which can't be a good thing!' I can remember seeing things, like the sky, and hearing things, but nobody appeared to be doing anything: and I thought, 'Why isn't everybody helping? Perhaps they've all been shot!' And then someone appeared and there were lots of other faces and things started happening. They got my flack jacket open and tried to staunch what was obviously a very serious wound – the bullet had gone in one side and out the other. Then more anxious faces started appearing and they all had those little morphine things and I remember thinking, 'I hope they're not going to fill me full of all that stuff!' I heard what was quite obviously fire being returned and thought, 'They'll be enjoying that!' It turned out that one of my men thought I'd been shot from behind the crowd at the top of Albert Street, where the crowd was whooping and jeering anyway at seeing me hit the ground. He thought he spotted a gunman and let fly at him. Whether he hit the target history doesn't relate.

Seventeen field dressings were used on Campbell. 'There was no pain. Everything just shuts down, a complete blank. My hand was twitching uncontrollably, opening and closing... It was a nervous reaction. The bullet took out a couple of ribs.' Campbell had been shot, he and his men believed, by an IRA sniper whom they knew as 'The Rifleman'. The same day the same sniper was also thought to have shot another one of Campbell's men, Corporal Dave Fairhurst, who was fortifying a sangar (a concrete OP) with sandbags. The bullet travelled through the observation slit and hit Fairhurst in the chest, the bullet going in one side and out the other. It then ricocheted and wounded another Rifleman in the elbow. The sniper was also thought to have shot another Green Jacket through the neck as he was manning an OP on top of Albert Street mill. The soldier lived but never fully recovered from his injuries. The reaction among Campbell's troops to this was aggressive: 'They were pretty unhappy about it really and needed to be curbed in their enthusiasm. That's about as much as I would dare – or care – to say about it really. I think they needed very careful management ... Feelings were running pretty high ... They were very angry.' Jamie Campbell recovered and returned to Northern Ireland for five further tours of duty.[31]

The first deaths, in an escalating spiral of violence, soon occurred. In the midst of a riot Private Malcolm Hatton, aged 19, of The Green Howards was shot in the head as troops and the IRA exchanged fire in the Ardoyne. A short time later his alleged assailant, Provisional IRA Volunteer Patrick McAdorey, aged 24, was shot dead by troops. He was a Lieutenant in the 3 Battalion of the Belfast Brigade. He was locally reputed to have been one of the three IRA men involved in the killing of the three young Scottish soldiers in March.[32] Leo McGuigan, a 16-year-old Catholic apprentice car sprayer, was fatally wounded, and two companions injured, after troops opened fire on them in the Ardoyne. Locals disputed the soldiers' account of events. Troops claimed that they were firing on gunmen shooting from the back windows of two houses in Estoril Park. A civilian witness claimed that McGuigan was shot while at the front of the same two houses. The *Irish Times* journalist, Kevin Myers, was present at the incident. A gunman had fired at him from a house in Ardoyne and was only prevented from doing so again by a soldier who fired a single shot at the gunman. Myers fled across the street where three Catholic youths were throwing stones through a gap in the houses. They scoffed at Myers when he warned them about gunmen. In the next second they were all down. The soldier who had earlier saved Myers' life had fired again at what he thought was a sniper. His shot ricocheted off a wall, and fragments of the one bullet hit the three boys who he could not even see; one lost the fingers of one hand; another lost the back of his head but survived; the third was Leo McGuigan.[33] Again in Ardoyne, Sarah Worthington, a 50-year-old Protestant widow, was shot dead by a soldier as she stood inside her home at Velsheda Park. A heavy gun battle had been going on in the area at the time and many families were moving out of the district. Mrs Worthington's family had been helping her to remove her personal belongings in a car amid spasmodic sniper fire. The soldier who killed her told an inquest that he entered the house and shouted twice but got no reply. The soldier feared that a gunman might be hiding in the house. He saw a figure and thought it was a gunman. He fired his SLR from the hip and the figure fell. He went over to the body only to discover it was a woman. Mrs Worthington left nine children.[34]

Father Hugh Mullan, a 40-year-old Catholic priest, was shot dead, probably by soldiers positioned on the top of the loyalist Springmartin estate. A few hours before he was shot, Father Mullan had been trying to defuse sectarian tension which had been building throughout the day when a loyalist mob began stoning the back of Springfield Park estate, a mixed but predominately Catholic housing development. The first shots were fired by a man in Springfield Park as a crowd broke through from Springmartin. Several men from Springfield Park then fired warning shots, one of which hit a fellow resident as he made his way across a field. Father Mullan went to administer the Last Rites, waving a white Babygro. He discovered the man was still alive. As they were making their way back he was shot. Father Mullan moaned and motioned to wave the Babygro again but was then hit by another bullet. Another man who crawled out to help, Frank Quinn, a 19-year-old Catholic, was also shot dead. The Army claimed that they had exchanged fire with snipers in the area for several hours, but local people claimed both men had been shot by troops.[35] Joan Brigid Connelly, a 50-year-old Catholic housewife, was shot when soldiers opened fire as she was searching the streets for her children during the post-internment searches. She was shot on wasteground in front of the Henry Taggart Memorial Army base on the Springfield Road. Her death took place as an intensive three-way gun battle started around Ballymurphy. After shots were fired by soldiers from rooftops in Springmartin, their colleagues in the Henry Taggart base and Vere Foster School opened fire into the surrounding area. Loyalist gunmen fired at Springfield Park and Ballymurphy from the Springmartin estate while IRA gunmen there and in Moyard fired back. Mrs Connelly and at least two others were hit by bullets fired from the Army base.[36] She was not alone as the body of Noel Philips, a 20-year-old Catholic, was found, the next day, lying on the bank of a stream between Springhill and Ballymurphy. The stream was in the line of fire from the Henry Taggart Army base.[37] They were joined in death by Daniel Teggart, a 44-year-old Catholic, who was hit by more than a dozen high-velocity rounds fired by soldiers in the base.[38]

William Atwell, a 40-year-old Protestant security guard was killed by a nail bomb at his work, the Mackies factory on the Springfield Road. His killers were most likely Republicans. Although Mackies was in a Catholic district its workforce was predominantly Protestant and was located near Protestant streets. A crowd broke windows in the factory and tore a grille off a window. A nail bomb was lobbed through the window and exploded. William Atwell was found by his colleagues lying in a pool of blood. A nail had penetrated his head.[39] Francis McGuinness, a 17-year-old Catholic, was shot dead by soldiers at the junction of Ladybrook Park and Finaghy Road North. He was one of a group of youths behind a barricade dismantled by an APC. The Army claimed that he was throwing a petrol bomb but this was denied by a witness. The Army fired ten rubber bullets at youths. These were followed by two shots, one of which killed the teenager.[40] Desmond Healy, a 14-year-old Catholic, was shot dead, again in disputed circumstances, during rioting in west Belfast. 1 PARA claimed that a youth had been shot dead and another wounded after being warned to stop throwing petrol bombs. A witness claimed that bottles were thrown but not petrol bombs.[41] In Derry, Hugh Herron, a 31-year-old Catholic, was shot dead in Long Tower Street by a soldier after, said the Army, shots were fired at their OP in Bishop Street. The Army stated that his body was found with a revolver beside it. The Herron family and friends denied that the dead man had any connection with the IRA. The subsequent inquest was told that swabs taken from Herron's hands indicated that he had been in close contact with a weapon which had been fired. There were no paramilitary trappings at his funeral and his name did not subsequently appear on any Republican roll of honour.[42] The first serving member of the UDR killed in the Troubles was Private Winston Donnell, a 22-year-old Protestant. The shooting took place near Clady close to the Tyrone–Donegal border. Private Donnell, who was serving with 6 UDR, was part of a patrol that had mounted a vehicle checkpoint. Shortly before midnight two shots were fired at the patrol but no one was injured. Ten minutes later there were three more bursts of gunfire, with up to thirty shots from a Thompson sub-machine gun. Private Donnell was killed instantly.[43]

That was the first day. The Army's Situation Report (SITREP) of 10 August began: 'Dawn found BELFAST a sorry sight in areas like the ARDOYNE, FALLS, BALLYMACARRETT and ANDERSONSTOWN. Both the terrorists and the security forces were tired.' Barrier building had gone apace and would take time to remove but there were no 'no go areas' and the Security Forces were patrolling through the barricades. However, it would be a major operation to remove them and there was no question of achieving this in one night on current force levels. Apart from Belfast and Derry the general security situation in the Province remained relatively quiet. In Belfast the areas causing the most trouble were Andersonstown and the Falls. In Derry tension was rising and there had been a number of incidents. In Andersonstown, during the morning, a crowd of about 100 people were roaming the streets, petrol bombing the Security Forces. The 3 Battalion Queens, who were responsible for the area, fired 6 CS grenades and a number of baton rounds while removing a barricade. In Springfield Park, Protestants were leaving their homes and it was thought that they intended to burn them. Of the immediate operational priorities the first was to prevent inter-sectarian clashes later that night; the second to keep up the pressure on the IRA 'because, otherwise we will lose the immediate benefits of internment'; and, third, at first light on 11 August, using 1 PARA and any available reserve, to clear the barriers in half the Falls area. In the short term the Director of Intelligence at HQNI expected that the violent reactions that had marked the last twenty-four hours of fighting would continue on a diminishing scale on the next few nights. The Army believed that the short-term primary aim of the IRA was to exacerbate inter-sectarian clashes to keep the temperature up and hopefully divert the available effort of the Security Forces from themselves. Those IRA units which had been partially disrupted would continue to act in a more or less disorganized way as flying columns for as long as their arms and ammunition allowed; those that retained their original organization and leadership would continue the fight normally within their allotted areas. But it was also expected that Active Service Units on the Border would be augmented by IRA men on the run. It was noted that Provisionals were moving north, from Dublin, in small numbers. If they crossed over into Northern Ireland they would probably be used in rural areas with the aim of taking some of the Security Force pressure off Belfast and Londonderry. Some of these groups could be used to undertake reprisal actions against Security Forces and Government officials: such reprisals 'have long been planned'.[44]

By the early evening crowds had gathered once more and the incidence of stoning, petrol bombing and shooting approached the intensity of the previous evening. By 23.00 the crowds had started to dwindle and the battle developed into a firefight between the gunmen and the Security Forces. Several members of the Security Forces sustained gunshot wounds: one soldier was hit by a burst of automatic fire in Londonderry and died. The Security Forces attempted to clear barricades in the Falls at first light but immediately came under fire and a battle developed: 'Several bombers/gunmen are believed to have been hit by fire from S[Security]F[Forces] but only 4 dead and 10 injured can be positively accounted' recorded the SITREP. In the Falls area a bank was set on fire in Malt Street and during an incident in Eglinton Street it was reported that a gunman, Peter Donnelly, had been shot dead by Security Forces. At first light 1 PARA started clearing barriers in the Whiterock Road/Springfield Road area. They immediately came under fire and when they returned fire 'they killed at least 1 gunman and injured 2 others'. The clearing operation continued. As on the previous night, substantial firing was directed against 2 PARA's post at Henry Taggart Memorial Hall: 'Several gunmen/bombers were thought to have been hit but they were dragged away by their comrades.' In the Beechmount Street area of Ballymurphy a patrol came under heavy fire and in the ensuing battle 'at least one gunman was killed and 4 others injured'. Over 100 rounds were fired by the Security Forces at gunmen and petrol bombers in the New Lodge; although several were seen to be hit 'they were dragged away by crowds in the area'. Shortly before midnight, in Elisa Street, a bakery was occupied by several gunmen. The Security Forces were unable to dislodge them at the time but an operation was mounted at 04.00 by the Green Jackets. In the ensuing gun battle one gunman was killed and at least four wounded. Two gunmen tried to escape in a car. However, the car overturned and one man sustained a broken back while the other had to have a leg amputated. The battle was still in progress at 07.00. The Army noted that while the crowds were generally smaller than on the previous evening the gunmen were becoming more daring, 'fortunately with little success'. Several straight firefights had developed and the Security Forces seemed to have inflicted several casualties without suffering themselves. They were less hampered by 'onlookers' than on previous occasions. There had also been little Protestant reaction to the disturbances although there 'is definite evidence of Protestants intimidating other Protestants to move from "unsafe" areas'. By the early morning of 11 August, after a lull in the violence, shooting again broke out and crowds began to assemble in protest at the removal of the barricades.[45]

The soldier killed in Derry was Bombardier Paul Challenor, aged 22, of The Royal Horse Artillery. He was shot by a sniper while on observation duty at the Bligh's Lane post. The fatal round, fired from a .303 rifle, struck him on the right shoulder severing a main artery. Bombardier Challenor's mother in Leicester wrote an open letter to the people of Northern Ireland: 'You say you are all Christians. For God's sake, start acting like Christians. I wish you could see the grief that my son's death has caused in my house and in his wife's home.'[46] William Stronge, a 46-year-old Protestant from north Belfast, was killed by Republican gunmen during disturbances in the Oldpark area after he had gone to help relatives move out of their house to safety elsewhere. Residents claimed that the dead man was shot by three men while he was standing at the back door of his brother-in-law's house. This followed a day of intimidation by Catholics.[47] Norman Watson, a 53-year-old Protestant draper and shop manager, was shot by a soldier in crossfire between the Army and the IRA. Soldiers from the 2 Battalion The Light Infantry were fired at simultaneously from a moving vehicle and from a high embankment. Fire was returned at the gunmen's car which sped off. At that moment Watson's car drove into the immediate aftermath of the gun attack. When a second burst of gunfire came from the embankment, a soldier wrongly assumed that this was designed to give cover for the second car to escape. At this point he fired the fatal shot to the head which killed Norman Watson.[48] John Beattie, a 17-year-old Catholic, was shot through the heart by an Army sniper who fired on his father's van near his home at Canmore Street during a heavy gun battle. Soldiers claimed the youth was driving a van which was being used as a cover by snipers. Soldiers in an OP said they opened fire after a man who had been firing at them got into the van. The dead man's father said some people he did not know had jumped on the back of the van apparently to take cover as he drove into the street. The sniper in question had been shooting at the soldiers for a period of about three hours. At about 1.30 a.m. the van emerged into Canmore Street from the Shankill Road. It had no lights on but flashed its headlights once as it came down the street. A man on the right fired one quick shot and got into the back of the van. The soldiers then fired at the van.[49] Edward Doherty, a 28-year-old Catholic, was killed by soldiers in the Whiterock area of west Belfast. Soldiers arrived at McCrory Park, a GAA playing field just off the Whiterock Road. Locals tried to set fire to a barricade and claimed a Saladin armoured car opened fire with a Browning machine gun. They claimed that when people in the street scattered the firing stopped, but then a single shot was fired which killed Doherty. The soldiers claimed that the dead man was shot as he was throwing a petrol bomb. The soldier who fired the fatal shot was trying to break down a barricade at the time. A crowd of about 300 people forced the Army to withdraw from the area and they were unable to remove the barricade.[50] John Laverty, a 30-year-old Catholic barman and labourer was shot dead by soldiers as he tried to make his way home to Whitecliffe Parade in the Ballymurphy estate. A soldier claimed that an Army patrol moving down the Whiterock Road had come under fire at the Springfield Road junction. He saw three or four men crawling along the Whiterock Road towards his position, one firing a machine gun and the other a pistol. The soldier fired six shots and hit one of the men. The soldier found a man lying face downwards. The single round which killed Laverty had entered through his back. Another man, Joseph Corr, aged 43 and also Catholic, was fatally wounded in the same incident, dying sixteen days later. The families of both men denied they had any connection with paramilitary organizations.[51]

In Londonderry the SITREP recorded that the 'customary stoning and fire bombing' continued until around 03.00. Rosemount RUC station came under attack. Petrol bombs were thrown and shots exchanged. Two soldiers were wounded. Shortly before midnight there were five explosions, two on the Waterside and three elsewhere in the city. All premises were either Protestant or state owned. Considerable damage was caused. Nine civilians were slightly injured. Disturbances died down at around 03.00 and at first light the city was reasonably quiet. In Strabane the RUC station there was attacked and the Dunlop factory and barricades near the City Hall were set on fire. In Toome Bridge a patrol from 45 Regiment of The Royal Artillery was ambushed. One soldier sustained a thigh wound. The gunmen escaped. A crowd of about 150 roamed the streets of Newry during the night smashing windows and setting fire to cars. The Security Forces made several arrests and there were no serious casualties. Shortly after midnight there was a large explosion and several buildings in the town centre were damaged.[52] In Derry, James Christopher O'Hagan, a 16-year-old IRA Volunteer, was found fatally injured after what appeared to be an accidental shooting on land at Limavady Road. In the follow-up operation the police and soldiers found a Smith and Wesson revolver, ammunition, a spent cartridge, fuse wire and 25lb of gelignite. Two men were later jailed in connection with the discovery of the weapon and explosives.[53] Eamon McDavitt, a 28-year-old Catholic, was shot dead in Fountain Street, Strabane after soldiers pursued stone-throwing youths. He was a deaf mute and was holding a rubber bullet – possibly as a trophy – when shot.[54] In 19 Brigade, covering the Border, an ambush contact was made at 22.45. An ambush patrol of the 2 Light Infantry saw a party of ten to fifteen armed men moving up from the South in the Border area near Newry. The men were dressed in combat jackets and were wearing berets. When challenged they ran and the patrol opened fire. They fired a total of 131 rounds. No bodies were found but during a daylight search there were indications that bodies had been dragged away.[55]

This was the situation on the ground: at a diplomatic level it was no less turbulent. Within a day of internment Hillery flew into London to meet with Maudling and deliver his Government's protests personally. Hillery was angry. He told Maudling that he thought the current policies would lead to war in Ireland and not only in the North. He claimed that the IRA had been recreated as a reaction to the British Government's policies of preserving the dominance of the Orange Order which, he believed, still ran the Northern Ireland Government. Maudling replied that the policy of the United Kingdom Government was to support the lawfully and democratically elected Government in Northern Ireland. Hillery countered that, while the Army had originally gone into Northern Ireland to protect the Catholics, its role had changed and the Catholics now saw the Army as having taken the place of the B Specials. Maudling, in turn, countered that it was not that the role of the Army had changed but that circumstances had changed in that the Army found itself attacked by terrorists from Catholic areas. The soldier did not know or care about the affiliations of someone sniping at him. He emphasized that the bombing, the murder and the withdrawal of the Opposition from Stormont had all taken place *before* internment had been introduced: the IRA had deliberately intensified operations to frustrate progress which was being made. Hillery suggested that those interned were mostly talkers rather than terrorists. When Maudling asked Hillery to do all he could to help in the campaign against the IRA, who trained, organized and found refuge south of the Border, he replied that this could not be proved. When the Home Secretary referred to two incidents, in one of which a member of the UDR had been shot dead from across the Border, and stated that Brady and Goulding gloried in their activities from the sanctity of the Republic, Hillery countered that the Irish Government had no control over the IRA: 'They hate us as much as they hate you.' It would be politically impossible for the Irish Government to take action against the IRA which would appear to be for the benefit of the Unionists in Stormont.[56] The meeting then concluded.

From Dublin, Peck offered his observations: it seemed to him that the account of Hillery's conversation with Maudling brought out very clearly the essential differences between the Irish and British views of events in Northern Ireland. The Irish believed that there was widespread minority sympathy for the IRA and that the IRA could not be put down unless this sympathy was destroyed. The Irish Government's view was that the Unionists were the real obstacles to peace and progress. They claimed that there was no evidence that the Unionists were willing to see the reforms bite, especially in view of Paisleyite pressure and Faulkner's deference to it. They claimed that the only way to alienate the minority from the IRA – the only means of defeating terrorism – was for the British Government to make it clear once again that they would not see the Unionists obstructing reform; and the only real evidence on this point that the minority would accept was some indication from the British Government that they would not tolerate the continuing total denial of power to Catholics. This, so far as it went, was a consistent case which the Irish claimed was based on a proper knowledge of the North which they contrasted with an alleged ignorance on the part of the British authorities of what made Ulster tick. They believed that Faulkner knew very well what made Ulster tick and that was why he was Prime Minister and why they mistrusted him so profoundly. But what the Irish underestimated, noted Peck, was the power of the Unionists and their potential for trouble-making. Hillery would not accept that if the British were to lean hard against the Unionists, London would risk an unaccountable Protestant reaction involving not only Direct Rule, but possible armed revolt and complications at Westminster too: 'So the basic difference is that Dr Hillery and the Taoiseach are firmly and unshakeably convinced that if we call the extreme Unionists' bluff they will crumble.'[57] Some of these points were put to Heath soon after he telephoned Lynch; the following transcript captures the sense of this better than any summary could:

Greetings exchanged.
MR. LYNCH The first thing is, I take it that Maudling has reported to you on the talks he had with Paddy Hillery yesterday.
PRIME MINISTER Yes he has, he reported to me last evening.
MR. LYNCH Yes, I see, yes... I have absolutely refrained from meeting anybody in order not to do anything that might endanger the present situation. But I may yet float an idea of some suggestion of a constitutional change or some structural alteration... I feel that I have to be free at least to float that idea myself in the absence of an agreement from you... The Press are in hordes around the place here so I might just as well have a

considered statement on the general position... I just can't continue just saying nothing... Another thing is that there is a very strong feeling (we are having these refugees coming over in thousands at the moment – we are having difficulty in accommodating them in fact) that the Army up there are not being completely impartial – in other words they are taking action against one side and they are letting the Ulster Unionists roam around at will with stones and with their taunting attitudes. Again, without telling you your business I think the Army ought to be told of their true role. I think that everybody, more or less, can make one group appear arrogant and appear to be taunting the other side. Is it possible for you to get that across to the Army?

PRIME MINISTER The Home Secretary did discuss this with Dr Hillery quite rightly, and told him that the Army had got the firmest and strictest instructions, that they should be absolutely impartial to all. The situation is again, as the Home Secretary has pointed out, that when the Army is being shot at they do not know or enquire as to who the person shooting at them is. They are being shot at and their job, they have been told very firmly, is to protect the community. What religious faith those people have is not of concern to them and they do not know. When one watches television and sees the stone-throwing and the bottles and the bombs and so on... well, now, this is happening in the Catholic quarters. Alas, we all deplore it. The same thing applies to the refugees – if it were not for a lot of the pressure which is being brought by the IRA in the Catholic communities, often deliberately to get them out of Northern Ireland then your refugee camps would not be full. What we are most anxious to do (and we have been discussing it again today) is to ensure that these unfortunate people who are affected in these areas are given immediate help in Northern Ireland itself. We will be talking further with the Northern Ireland Government as to how this can be brought about.

MR. LYNCH I fear the pips came in there just at the start of that sentence.

PRIME MINISTER I said that we shall be discussing with the Northern Ireland Government further measures as to how this can be brought about – to help those who are suffering from their houses being destroyed or burned by the agitators in these areas. We are most anxious to help in this respect... I think in fairness to Mr. Faulkner, to the Northern Ireland Prime Minister, it must be accepted that he has gone a very long way towards the Opposition with his proposals for the Committees. They would have half the chairmanships and so on, and when having done this the Opposition deliberately walks out of Stormont it makes it very difficult for him, in dealing with his own party and others who are being critical of this, to say that there must be much more participation. They say: 'Why don't they use the participation which is now offered to them?'

MR. LYNCH The answer to that is according to the people who were offered it, that the participation came too late and is not enough. In any case events had overtaken the whole situation to make the whole gesture meaningless.

PRIME MINISTER Well, that is the customary political argument. When you want to try and do in your opponent, instead of trying to create a new situation, it is really no answer to say it came too late if, when you are offered it, you don't use what there is. But as far as I know there has been no suggestion as to what more participation they want. The fact is that the offer which he made to them, as he said quite rightly to me last Thursday, goes much further than we have in the British Parliament. The Opposition does not automatically get chairmanships of our committees.

MR. LYNCH... there is this difficulty, that producing... results now, in the light of the activities of the IRA in the north, could be attributed to their activities rather than to reasonable and reasoned discussion. That is a big difficulty we have here with the Opposition MPs having opted out of parliament and the IRA having taken over... There is just one other thing. Again it has been canvassed here – it was not mentioned yesterday as far as I know in the talks between Maudling and Hillery – a United Nations presence. I take it that that has not come into your reckoning at all. I know the answer to that and I know the difficulty about it, but I take it that you have not contemplated that at all in present circumstances.

PRIME MINISTER Not for a moment, no. This is part of the United Kingdom.

MR. LYNCH That is right yes and, well, anyway, I know all the arguments here. Very well, Mr. Prime Minister... My boys [the Cabinet] are meeting downstairs and I shall rejoin them... Well, we reckon that the Stormont regime has apparently been influenced if not directed by outside control, by Orangism and Unionism. We believe that in this present set-up it will never produce peace, it will never produce a stable democracy or the kind of democracy the British people would want in their territory.

PRIME MINISTER We do not of course accept that it is run by the Orange Lodges, but that is a matter which we agreed in the past to disagree.

MR. LYNCH Quite so. Well right oh. Then I take it that in the next few days I can feel free to get on to you.

PRIME MINISTER At any time.

MR. LYNCH Thanks very much for calling back...

PRIME MINISTER Now what about this afternoon's telephone conversation... Do you want it not to have taken place?

MR LYNCH No. I prefer it not to have taken place. I can say that I have had access to Mr. Heath without saying when and on what terms.

PRIME MINISTER Quite.

MR. LYNCH So this conversation need not have taken place either...

PRIME MINISTER We will do the same... Thank you.[58]

The Taoiseach, as he had warned Heath, was left with no choice but to go on the offensive. Under tremendous domestic pressure from his Opposition he also had to attempt a counter to the Provisionals' influence in the North and reassert his leadership within Nationalist Ireland. Lynch now launched the campaign to dismantle the existing Stormont system and to replace it with a new administration that would have equal representation from the two communities. For the present this would take precedence over the aim of a united Ireland, although he added that if people could live together in the North in friendship, then they could live in one Ireland. Lynch insisted that for the past two years every effort had been made by the Irish Government not merely to prevent the deterioration of the situation in the North but to obtain the implementation there of such policies as would provide and protect the civil and human rights of the non-Unionist population. But Lynch concluded: 'There exists in Northern Ireland a Government whose main concern seems to be to meet the wishes and demands of the most extreme elements within the Unionist community.'[59]

By the time Lynch had pronounced on the situation in the North there had been yet more deaths. On 11 August the body of William McKavanagh, a 21-year-old Catholic, was found in McAuley Street, in the Markets area of Belfast, shortly after he was shot by the Army. The Army claimed he was a gunman but the IRA denied that he was a member of the Republican Movement. According to a later British explanation, McKavanagh was shot after troops found four youths acting suspiciously. They were challenged to halt but failed to stop, whereupon one of them was shot. The Official IRA claimed that the dead man was shot after soldiers' jitters, following a sustained action by their Volunteers, got the better of them and led to the killing of an innocent civilian.[60] Seamus Simpson, a 21-year-old IRA Volunteer and member of E Company of the Belfast Brigade's 2 Battalion, was shot dead by soldiers in Andersonstown where the Army said that he was throwing nail bombs. This was denied by locals who claimed he was only throwing stones.[61] Other deaths were indirectly caused by the violence occurring on the streets: Paddy McCarthy, a 44-year-old Catholic youth worker and member of the Ballymurphy Tenants Association, collapsed and died from a heart attack after apparently confronting troops in the area.[62] Alphonsus Cunningham, a 13-year-old Catholic schoolboy, was knocked down and fatally injured the previous day when a mob surrounded a car at the corner of the Falls Road and Springfield Road. The driver sped off, apparently hitting the boy in the process.[63] William Ferris, a 38-year-old Protestant tyre worker, was shot and fatally injured by soldiers on 10 August; he died on 12 August. He was a back-seat passenger in a car with other men returning from work when the shooting occurred at an Army checkpoint. The car driver recalled one of the men in the back said: 'That's a soldier shouting for us to stop'; but Ferris added: 'That's all right. I think he's waving you to go on.' The driver then accelerated and a shot was fired. When he stopped the car the soldiers administered first aid to the victim. The soldier who fired the fatal shot said he had called three times for the car to halt before opening fire. A second soldier corroborated this statement, adding: 'I expected a burst of gunfire to come from the car.'[64] In Belfast, The Green Howards arrested a woman in Butler Street, in the Ardoyne, for abusive language. A crowd of about 100 gathered and Security Forces were deployed. As they were deploying, a gunman at the junction of the Crumlin and Kerrera roads fired three shots. Private Robinson of the 1 Green Howards was hit in the head by one round and died instantly. The area was searched but nothing was found. In Derry, minor rioting saw a member of the RUC, Constable Barr, who was in civilian clothes, caught and beaten up by the mob. He was given protection by a Catholic priest and taken into a school. The Security Forces surrounded the building but were told by the constable's captors that he was injured and must be taken to Letterkenny hospital in County Donegal. They would not allow him to be taken to the Londonderry hospital. The RUC asked the Army to allow a Knights of Malta ambulance through without interference. This they did and the ambulance was met at the Border by Gardai. Elsewhere a patrol of the 14/20 Hussars was ambushed in the area of the Cullaville customs post. The leading vehicle set off an explosive device and the patrol came under automatic fire. The patrol leader, Sergeant Webb, was hit in the jaw but rallied his patrol and returned fire at the gunmen who immediately fled.[65]

Northern Ireland had not witnessed an intensity of violence like it. In a three week period following the introduction of internment there were recorded 2,069 housing movements which resulted from the violence. This was deemed to be an underestimate with the true figure higher than 2,500. The concentration was in the western and north-eastern parts of Belfast, especially in the Ardoyne, where two entire streets were destroyed by fire.[66] Despite the violence, Brigadier Marston Tickell, Chief of Staff Northern Ireland, triumphantly claimed of the battle against the IRA: 'We have undoubtedly inflicted a major defeat on them.' The figure of known deaths of IRA men was fifteen, but it was felt that a more accurate figure was probably between twenty and thirty. However, he warned of a continuing battle, though perhaps it would now return to the type of hit and run attacks which had occurred in the past. Tickell assessed the arrest operation as having gone smoothly with the 'catch up to the highest expectations'. In subsequent operations the Security Forces had defeated the 'hard core' of the gunmen. They had sustained well over fifty casualties. However, isolated gunmen remained and the Army expected individual attacks to continue. The Army dismissed claims that Protestant gunmen had been engaged on a large scale. Tickell believed that remarkably few bullets had been fired by Protestants. Therefore, the Army refuted any suggestion that the Army had not been impartial.[67] Furthermore, the Army claimed that more than eighty of the 230 men detained were known officers of the IRA.[68] No Protestants had been arrested because there was no comparable organization to the IRA, the two main factions of which were said to have had a 'near monopoly of gunmen, bomb throwers and subversives'. Brigadier Tickell was not aware of a similar organization on the Protestant side and if there was any organization it was not of any such strength as on the other sectarian side; there had been incidents of Protestant shooting during the outbreaks of violence in Belfast on 9 and 10 August. In some incidents there had clearly been some 'provocation' in that fire had been directed at soldiers who had travelled on into Protestant areas. But the Army did not take the view that this conformed to shooting by Protestants. Certainly, the Army felt that any Protestant shooting there was on a very much smaller scale than from the IRA side.[69]

The Army was certainly correct to say that there was no comparable Protestant organization to either IRA faction – the UVF were incapable, at this stage, of organizing violence on the scale of Republicans. But this took no account of the psychological or political impact that the use of internment against only one section of the community would have. It was Oliver Napier, of the cross-community Alliance Party, who summed up why this was so. He described the decision to introduce internment as a 'catastrophic error of judgement'. Napier believed that the majority of Catholics were opposed to the IRA; too many, due to intimidation, were afraid to openly admit it:

> But there is one issue, and only one issue, upon which every Catholic without exception, moderate and extremist, anti-Partitionist and Pro-Partitionist, is united and that is an almost psychological revulsion and fear of internment. It is the result of history and environment. Remember that on this issue internment has never been used against Protestants and therefore they can consider it without emotion. But the terror and revulsion of Catholics towards internment is so deep-rooted that to ignore it will polarise this community as it has never been polarised before. Internment has been used before. Some say that it has worked. But that was before the reform programme. Every Northern Ireland Catholic sees the introduction of internment as the abandonment of the reform programme and the end of the principle of equal citizenship.

Napier warned that this was an issue upon which Catholics felt so strongly that utter disaster could result if this feeling was ignored. The Stormont Government had failed to understand Catholic feelings about internment. It was correct that the terrorist and gunman had to be rooted out and brought to justice; but if the weapons used to attempt this permanently and irretrievably alienated the Catholic community, the terrorist would win.[70]

As the death toll mounted the Catholic community laid the blame at the authorities' door: on 13 August, Paddy Devlin pointed out that the Army had claimed that it had killed up to thirty IRA gunmen – which was six more than the total casualties.[71] An emergency meeting of the SDLP, Nationalist and Republican Labour parties, in Dungannon, called for a withholding of all rents and rates. Also present was a representative of the NICRA executive. An agreed statement called on all those holding public positions, whether elected or appointed, to express their opposition to internment by immediately withdrawing from their positions. This was to demonstrate that the system set up by the Government of Ireland Act had failed. The parties expected 100 per cent support from the general public in the rents and rates strike. They also called on the British Government to suspend immediately the Northern Ireland system of government in view of its 'absolute failure to provide peace, justice and stability' and to commence at once talks on new political and constitutional arrangements. After an SDLP meeting, also in Dungannon, John Hume explained the strategy: he was trying to give firm leadership and directions to the frustration of the people. Everyone desperately wanted to end the violence and death that was taking place in the streets. But they all also believed that the present system of government had failed completely to control it and to put an end to it, because it was impossible within the present system to do this.[72]

Hume then joined Fitt in a flight to London for an emergency meeting with

Maudling. Hume began by formally asking the Home Secretary that all internees should be released. If this could not be done he asked for assurances about the conditions in which they were to be kept and complained that MPs had been denied access to them. According to his information most of those arrested were people publicly identified with the Republican Movement over a long time rather than those active in violence. Fitt asked that where it was established that innocent people had died as a result of the recent violence, their families should be compensated. He said that Catholics were incensed at the Army's methods of searching which involved wrecking any premises they searched. Hume then said that the main purpose of their visit was to put forward constructive proposals. He and his colleagues deplored the violence on the streets and had said so publicly. They had tried to lead their communities away from violence, even to the point of being stoned by their own supporters. The Provisional IRA was born in 1969 as a reaction to the Protestant attack on the Falls Road. As the situation had developed the opportunities for moderation had diminished and even their cautious welcome for Faulkner's initiative on Parliamentary committees had led their constituents to accuse them of selling out. They could not now go back to Stormont. Indeed they would be useless and represent no-one if they did.

The difficulty, said Hume, was that the Catholic population did not have confidence in the forces of law and order. When this confidence was lacking, repression on an increasing scale would be unsuccessful. If confidence was to be restored it had to be recognized that in Northern Ireland the British Parliamentary system did not work. It produced a permanent minority alienated from the system. A new system of government for the Province was required in which the minority shared as a right. He had in mind an assembly elected by proportional representation and an executive either appointed by the Governor or elected on a proportional basis through the assembly. The minority should be guaranteed representation in all the organs of government in proportion to population. That representation would have to be genuine, not 'Castle Catholics'. A variant of the scheme would be an appointed Commission. If this form of participation could be guaranteed as part of the Constitution, he and his colleagues would have a basis from which to lead their community away from the gunmen. Such a system could be put to the people constituency by constituency and he and his colleagues were confident that they could obtain through it the support they needed to deal with the violent men. Hume suggested that the Home Secretary might move towards the kind of scheme he had outlined by announcing, first, that while violence continued there could be no discussion of further changes but once violence ceased he would be prepared to discuss wide-ranging changes in the Constitution. He accepted that the Home Secretary should then reaffirm the traditional guarantees about the Border and was himself prepared to repeat publicly that he did not wish to impose Irish unity against the wish of the majority of the population of Northern Ireland. If the United Kingdom Government did not accept this approach the SDLP planned a campaign of passive resistance and civil disobedience including withholding of rates and rents. Maudling's reply was, as expected, non-committal: he expressed interest in Hume's ideas and undertook to think carefully about them.[73]

The campaign of civil disobedience was launched on 16 August. On 15 August, the SDLP leadership, and three Nationalists MPs, met in Belfast to declare that the campaign would continue until the last internee was released. The purpose of the campaign was to 'demonstrate clearly that a large section of this community has withdrawn its consent from the system of government. No system of government can survive if a significant section of the population is determined that it will not be governed under this system.' They reiterated that violence could not solve their problems and urged everyone who agreed with the objectives of the campaign to channel their protest through non-violent means. The evening was not without drama after the Army rushed into the area and surrounded the building. After the meeting, as the MPs were leaving, they were taken from their cars at gunpoint at a road block and searched. Their vehicles were also searched, although cars on the road outside the venue were allowed to pass through unhindered.[74] The Chief of Staff Northern Ireland, Brigadier Tickell, was forced to apologize to the MPs the next day, explaining that the Army had received information of a possible IRA press conference.[75] Earlier in the day Ivan Cooper and Paddy Devlin had addressed a Civil Rights rally in which they stressed the significance of passive resistance. Devlin estimated that the campaign would cost the Northern Ireland Government £100 million. About £10 million could be withheld through refusing to pay rents, a further £10 to £12 million through refusing to pay rates. At least 40 per cent of the £70 million gained through direct taxation could be withheld and if one added indirect taxation the figure could reach £100 million. Cooper claimed that the strike in Derry already had a 90 per cent response. Out of 850 houses in Dungiven, only two rents had been paid in the last week.[76] On the first day of the campaign itself, business was almost brought to a halt in Derry as a one day strike gained widespread support. In Coalisland, where there was also a strike, crowds were on the street and troops opened fire with CS gas and rubber bullets. Opposition MPs continued their plans to widen the protest. In Belfast, two Catholic UDR officers made arrangements for Opposition MPs to address the Catholic members of the regiment.[77]

Paddy Devlin reassured his community that no rent arrears would be paid in when the strike ended. While the rent strike was restricted only to those tenants who occupied publicly owned houses and local authority houses, the rates strike would be carried on by everyone who paid rates directly to local authorities or by tenants who paid rents to landlords which included rates, thereby paying rates indirectly to local authorities. Again there should be no arrears kept for later on. By following this course of action, explained Devlin, it was possible for every single member of the community to participate in a massive non-violent exercise against the Faulkner regime. Financial threats were dismissed. Devlin explained that payments from the Ministry of Health, whether for unemployment, sickness, maternity injury or supplementary benefits, were protected from political interference by statute or legal precedent. These threats were 'nothing more than what goes into balloons when inflated – people should pay no attention to them'.[78] Fitt argued that it was now clear that the Unionist Government clearly regarded every Catholic in the North as being a member of a subversive organization. Allied to this thinking, the so-called Unionist moderate was now unmistakeably allying himself with Paisleyism. 'Now we see Unionism in its true colours,' he declared. And the old alliance of 'Paisleyism, Orange Order B-Specials' was now attempting to take over the Unionist Government, believing that they could engage in even further repression to maintain their superiority in the North. Fitt believed that they were now entering the most decisive phase of the struggle that had been waged since the setting up of the Northern Ireland state. He was convinced that the brutal killings of the previous week, supported by internment, must have made it clear, even to Heath's Government, that the political situation in Northern Ireland could not last. The stand taken by the Civil Rights movement, supported by all non-Unionists, would be carried on until the last internee was released and a new social order was implemented: 'In 1968 when we demanded one man one vote, let us now make our clarion call "no freedom, no rent".'[79]

On 18 August, Hume and Cooper were arrested in Derry following a sit-down protest of hundreds of people. Hume and Cooper were charged under the Special Powers Act with 'failing to move on command of a member of Her Majesty's forces'. Hugh Logue, one of their colleagues, was also arrested and charged with stone throwing. This was the culmination of trouble which had begun early in the morning when 1,300 troops had moved into the Bogside, Brandywell and Creggan districts to clear barricades. Twenty-three shooting incidents were reported in two hours, between 6 a.m. and 8 a.m. The fighting was most fierce in the Brandywell and Creggan areas. Eamon Lafferty, a 19-year-old adjutant on the Provisional IRA's Derry Brigade and O/C of the Creggan unit, was shot dead by troops. Lafferty was lying on the pavement above a playground when soldiers, who had crawled to within fifty yards of his position, shot him from behind a children's roundabout. A man who ran out from flats to try and help Lafferty was shot at and slightly wounded, but managed to escape. Lafferty was then shot again through the head. Soldiers ran forward and recovered a rifle from beside the body before retreating. Later four men were arrested in a car containing the dead man's body. The MPs were arrested at 5 p.m. that day. The incidents followed two hours of negotiation on the streets between Hume and the Army. A crowd had blocked the road and in doing so had prevented the Army passing along it. Lines of young boys and girls, led by Father Denis Bradley, linked arms forming a human barrier. The crowd then sat down on the road, singing 'We Shall Overcome' and 'We shall not be moved'. A water cannon, codenamed 'Neptune', then came down the street shooting out a jet of purple coloured water. Hume, Cooper and Bradley, followed by a couple of hundred people, walked towards the water cannon. It retreated. A line of troops formed up and fired rubber bullets into the demonstrators. The soldiers then advanced up the street, firing rubber bullets and CS gas. The demonstrators were chased, whereupon the MPs were arrested. After they were released, later that evening, Hume claimed that the day's events marked a new phase of passive resistance and that the spirit of 1968 was reborn.[80] Further down the street, Father Bradley, his glasses, face and hair covered with purple dye, told the crowd to disperse. 'Go home. You have behaved magnificently well. Keep this up. Don't go back to the stone.' A man in the crowd shouted back: 'Tell Hume and Cooper to stick with us now. They led us today for the first time in two years. Let them organise us, the people on the streets, and we will win.'

The events in Derry proved a much needed focus for those Nationalists opposed to the IRA. Hume now saw the political situation developing into a 'massive' campaign of civil disobedience and passive resistance. It was his hope that the energies and anger of the people would be channelled into passive resistance. As far as Hume and the SDLP was concerned there was no Government in Northern Ireland, just a Unionist led administration, and there was no point in talking to any Unionists: 'We believe that the only people we can now talk to are the people who have the power to take decisions, and when they call us to talk we will go to talk, provided, of course, that they abandon their present policy of repression.' Hume did not see Faulkner as the Prime Minister; he saw him as the leader of the Unionist Party, or in other words, the 'leader of the political wing of the Orange Order'. What was required was the removal of the 1920 Act system of government, probably with a commission running Northern Ireland for a limited period while a permanent solution was worked out. The SDLP were completely opposed to tripartite talks between Heath, Lynch and Faulkner; instead, there should either be two groups at the talks, London and Dublin, or four groups – London, Dublin, the Unionists and the SDLP – because Faulkner was not a sovereign Prime Minister and he did not have a sovereign Government. Technically and constitutionally, Heath was Prime Minister of Northern Ireland; Faulkner was the head of a local administration while Jack Lynch was a sovereign Prime Minister. If Northern Ireland was to be involved in the discussions then both sides in Northern Ireland must be involved. Hume hoped that Westminster would quickly realize its mistakes, cut its losses, cut its repressive policy, suspend the 1920 Act and call for constitutional discussions. He dismissed the threat of a Protestant right-wing backlash. It had

> hung over Ireland since 1912 – in fact it created this State. It's the threat that has held Northern Ireland in the grip of injustice and opposed Civil Rights and created the Provisional IRA as a reaction to it. It has opposed every single reform with the same threats. It has opposed two Prime Ministers and brought them down. It is opposing a third now, and it is opposing the British Government. And it is a threat that moderate Unionists use themselves when talking to the British Government. They say 'Unless you preserve us, look at what you're going to get.' That threat has to be faced before there can be any solution to our problem, and we'll see whether the Orange card is an ace or a deuce, and I believe it's a deuce.[81]

With the campaign of passive resistance spreading throughout the Nationalist population the collapse of the UDR, which maintained a non-sectarian character, seemed imminent when twenty-four Catholic members of 7 Battalion, Belfast, announced that they had either resigned or were about to resign. Thirty-one Catholic UDR members had attended an hour-long meeting addressed by Austin Currie. The organizer of the meeting, Phil Curran, an ex-UDR sergeant, warned: 'If something is not done to change Army policy, the UDR is just going to become another sectarian force.' Currie told his audience that, because of Army actions and the British Government's policies, he was no longer prepared to say that Catholics should join the UDR. He had earlier been in favour of Catholics joining at a time when it was accepted that it took considerable political courage to advocate such a course. No longer. Curran, speaking of his resignation, explained: 'I didn't feel it was my duty to release soldiers to go and raid Catholic areas while I was out guarding key points.' Some members, however, were reluctant to resign; as one Catholic member reflected: 'I would like to see the UDR non-sectarian, but if we leave we're just recreating the B-Specials.'[82] But this was, increasingly, a minority view. In County Tyrone, four Catholic UDR members resigned from 29 Platoon, E Company, citing among their reasons that promotion was denied to Catholic members while former B-Specials rose quickly through the ranks. The men also complained that patrols were, in the majority of cases, carried out in Catholic areas. One of the men claimed to have witnessed the selective searching of vehicles by UDR patrols: Protestants were allowed to drive through check points while cars driven by Catholics were subjected to rigorous searches. The men also complained that, on an excessive number of occasions, Catholics were given the task of carrying out 'point' duty where they were isolated from the main body of the platoon. One of the men who resigned, Patrick Cullen, who had been a member since the UDR's formation, felt:

> My conscience would not allow me to put on the UDR uniform and to try and administer British justice when three men apprehended in the Coalisland area, and found to have a firearm and ammunition in their possession, were subsequently released on £100 bail. If the men before the court had been Catholic they would immediately have been arrested on leaving the court and detained under the Special Powers Act in the Crumlin Road prison or on the prison ship, *Maidstone*.

All the men agreed that incidents building up over the past few months had made their position intolerable and this, together with the selective raiding of homes and the manner in which the law was being administered, had influenced their decision.[83] Elsewhere, thirty prominent Catholic public representatives in Derry announced their immediate withdrawal from public office, on 19 August, in protest against internment, the 'reign of oppression in the city' and the 'humiliating treatment' of the two arrested MPs. The local Government figures who resigned included the chairman and two other members of the Police Liaison Committee; the Vice-Chairman of the Derry Development Corporation and three other members; eight JPs; a former Derry High Sheriff; and members of the Port and Harbour Commissioners, the Hospital Management Committee, and the city's Health, Education and Welfare committees, including its chairman.[84] On 22 August, non-Unionist councillors on twenty local authorities announced their withdrawal from their elected positions and pledged their allegiance to an alternative Six Counties assembly – the Assembly of Northern Ireland set up as a Northern Nationalist alternative to Stormont. This followed a meeting in Coalisland of Parliamentary representatives and councillors, representing the SDLP, the Nationalist Party and the Irish Labour Party. Hume, Fitt, Currie and Cooper attended for the SDLP. More than 130 councillors came from all over Northern Ireland.[85]

Notes

1. NAUK PRO CJ 4/56 Note for the Record, 28 July 1971.
2. NAUK PRO CJ 4/56 Northern Ireland – Internment, 2 August 1971.
3. NAUK PRO CAB 164/879 FCO Telegram to Dublin, 27 July 1971.
4. NAUK PRO FCO 33/1465 Dublin Telegram, 27 July 1971.
5. NAUK PRO FCO 33/1465 Telegram No.283, 28 July 1971.
6. NAUK PRO FCO 33/1465 Brief for Cabinet Ministerial Committee on Northern Ireland, 28 July 1971.
7. NAUK PRO FCO 33/1465 The Intelligence Implications.
8. NAUK PRO PREM 15/478 Dublin Telegram, 30 July 1971.
9. NAUK PRO FCO 46/736 Military Instructions for the Implementation of Internment (of DEMETRIUS), 2 August 1971.
10. NAUK PRO PREM 15/478 Gregson to Prime Minister, 4 August 1971.
11. NAUK PRO PREM 15/478 Cabinet: Northern Ireland, 2 August 1971.
12. NAUK PRO PREM 15/478 Armstrong to Prime Minister, 4 August 1971.
13. NAUK PRO FCO 33/1465, 3 August 1971.
14. Brian Faulkner, *Memoirs of a Statesman* (London: 1978), p.119.
15. NAUK PRO PREM 15/478 Message to the Prime Minister of Northern Ireland from the Home Secretary, 4 August 1971.
16. NAUK PRO PREM 15/478 Gregson to Prime Minister, 4 August 1971.
17. NAUK PRO CAB 130/522/1 GEN 47 (71) 2nd Meeting, 5 August 1971.
18. NAUK PRO CJ 4/57 Memorandum by the Secretary of State for the Home Department.
19. NAUK PRO CAB 130/522/1 GEN 47 (71) 2nd Meeting, 5 August 1971.
20. BSI KC8 Note of a Meeting at 10 Downing Street on Thursday 5 August 1971.
21. BSI B1123, Statement of General Sir Robert Ford.
22. NAUK PRO PREM 15/478 Draft Message to the Taoiseach.
23. NAUK PRO FCO 33/1465; 8 August 1971.
24. NAUK PRO FCO 33/1465 Dublin Telegram No.298, 8 August 1971.
25. Peter Taylor, *Families at War: Voices from the Troubles* (London: 1989), p.24.
26. *Report of the enquiry into allegations against the Security Forces of physical brutality in Northern Ireland arising out of events on 9th August 1971*, Cmnd 4823 (HMSO 1971) para. 46 [Herafter Compton].
27. Ibid., paras. 31–41.
28. NAUK PRO FCO 1464 Internment.
29. NAUK PRO FCO 33/1465 Internment, 9 August 1971.
30. NAUK PRO PREM 15/478 Gregson to Prime Minister, 10 August 1971.
31. Taylor, *Families*, pp.24–5.
32. McKittrick et al., *Lost Lives*, pp.79–80.
33. Ibid., p.81.
34. Ibid., pp.81–2.
35. Ibid., pp.82–3.
36. Ibid., pp.83–4.

37. Ibid., p.84.
38. Ibid.
39. Ibid., pp.84–5.
40. Ibid., p.85.
41. Ibid.
42. Ibid., p.86.
43. Ibid.
44. NAUK PRO CAB 164/879 Northern Ireland SITREP as at 101800A, August 1971.
45. NAUK PRO CAB 164/879 Northern Ireland SITREP as at 110800A, August 1971.
46. McKittrick et al., *Lost Lives*, p.88.
47. Ibid., pp.88–9.
48. Ibid., pp.86–7.
49. Ibid., p.87.
50. Ibid.
51. Ibid., pp.87–8 and p.95.
52. NAUK PRO CAB 164/879 Northern Ireland SITREP as at 110800A, August 1971.
53. McKittrick et al., *Lost Lives*, pp.91–2.
54. Ibid., p.91.
55. NAUK PRO CAB 164/879 Appendix 1.
56. NAUK PRO PREM 15/478 Northern Ireland: Dr. Hillery's discussion with the Home Secretary. Note of a meeting at the Home Office on Wednesday 11th August.
57. NAUK PRO FCO 33/1464, 12 August 1971.
58. NAUK PRO PREM 15/478 Text of a Conversation between Mr Lynch and the Prime Minister at 4.11 p.m. on Thursday 10 August 1971.
59. *Irish Times*, 13 August 1971.
60. McKittrick et al., *Lost Lives*, p.89.
61. Ibid., pp.89–90.
62. Ibid., p.90.
63. Ibid.
64. Ibid., pp.90–1.
65. NAUK PRO CAB 164/879 Appendix 1.
66. McKittrick et al., *Lost Lives*, pp.80–1.
67. *Belfast Telegraph*, 13 August 1971.
68. Ibid., 16 August 1971.
69. Ibid., 20 August 1971.
70. *Irish News*, 12 August 1971.
71. Ibid., 14 August 1971.
72. *Irish Times*, 10 August 1971.
73. NAUK CAB 164/879.
74. *Irish Times*, 16 August 1971.
75. Ibid., 17 August 1971.
76. Ibid., 16 August 1971.
77. Ibid., 17 August 1971.
78. *Irish News*, 19 August 1971.
79. Ibid.
80. *Irish Times*, 19 August 1971.
81. Ibid., 20 August 1971.
82. Ibid., 19 August 1971.
83. Ibid., 20 August 1971.
84. Ibid.
85. Ibid., 23 August 1971.

5

The Real War:
Intelligence, Interrogation and Propaganda

OPERATION CALABA: INTERROGATION IN DEPTH

Without doubt the decision to introduce internment would have been controversial in any circumstances. But what made it doubly so was the additional decision to select suspected IRA members and subject them to deep interrogation: it proved to be one of the most controversial aspects of the Troubles. Interrogation in depth had become a long – and successful – part of counter-insurgency operations. The military interrogation system in insurgency situations was the product of gradual evolution over the previous two decades. No revolutionary idea had profoundly altered it at any one time. But a gradual codification had emerged, and perhaps the two major steps in this process were the laying down of a set of principles, but not techniques, by the Joint Intelligence Committee in 1965 and the subsequent amendment of their paper in 1967 as a result of the Bowen Report on the interrogation processes in Aden. This report on interrogation in Aden might be said to constitute the watershed in the subsequent flow of interrogation techniques. From 1945 to 1956 the interrogation skills acquired during the Second World War were kept alive by a Territorial Army unit known as IS 9, which also had a wartime role for the organization of escape and evasion in battle. In 1956 the Interrogation Branch was formed at Maresfield, Sussex, on a Joint Service basis, in the Intelligence Centre. This organization had direct access to the Director of Military Intelligence (DMI) at the War Office. The task of this organization was to run Interrogation Courses for Army Officers who were linguists and for Intelligence Corps NCOs. It was also responsible for command and control of the three Services' reserve interrogation units. These courses were directed at the interrogation of prisoners of war and refugees, and lasted approximately three to four weeks. The commander of the branch was always an Army officer. In 1953, as a result of previous Colonial insurgencies and in particular because of the situation in Cyprus, courses were modified to include interrogation of suspects in anti-terrorist and counter-insurgency operations. At the same time the Interrogation Branch was absorbed into the School of Military Intelligence where it remained until April 1965, when it was renamed the Joint Services Interrogation Wing (JSIW) and became independent of the School. In 1966, as part of the Intelligence Centre, it moved to Ashford, Kent. Finally, in April 1969 it became one of the three Wings of what was now known as the School of Service Intelligence, a part of the Intelligence Centre.

In 1964, at about the time of the first Aden operation, a draft directive was drawn up by the DMI, with advice from the school, and presented in 1965 to the Joint Intelligence Committee, who subsequently published it as a Joint Directive on Military Interrogation in Internal Security Operations Overseas JIC (65) 15, dated 17 February 1965. Two years later, as a result of the allegations of brutality at the Interrogation Centre in Aden, the then Foreign Secretary, George Brown, set up an Inquiry under Mr Roderic Bowen QC. His terms of reference were: 'To examine the procedures current in Aden for the arrest, interrogation, and detention of persons suspected of terrorist activities and to advise whether there are any ways in which these procedures can be improved having in mind on the one hand the rights of the individual and on the other the duties of the authorities to safeguard the Community as a whole from lawless acts.' After detailed examination Bowen recommended, inter alia, certain medical safeguards for the suspected persons (including the keeping of medical records) and that civilian interrogations should be used exclusively in Internal Security situations in future. The former recommendation was put into effect by the amendment to JIC (65) 15; the latter had so far not been implemented with one result that the only source of instruction in interrogation had remained with the Joint Services Interrogation Wing. As far back as 1956 a Medical Intelligence Working Party reviewed the whole field of drugs techniques, grouped under the general heading of 'States of Isolation' as aids to interrogation. The Working Party concluded that the risks involved were too great and no further research was carried out. The matter was raised again in 1965, when an ad hoc Working Party was set up 'to explore the possibility of instituting research into acceptable and legitimate means of carrying out military interrogation'. No formal report was issued but in general the views of the 1956 Working Party were upheld and no new means or procedures were recommended. There were a number of techniques and these were varied according to the personality of the subject and to his state of resistance, amongst other things. The techniques all fell strictly within the principles and safeguards laid down in the JIC directive and had not come under criticism.[1]

The first intimation of a request for RUC Special Branch training was in a telephone message from Lt Colonel Brennan (NI HQ) on 17 March 1971. Subsequently at a meeting on 24 March the implications of an Interrogation Centre were discussed at the MOD with representatives of the Security Service (MI5). Thereafter the MOD despatched a member of the Joint Services Interrogation Wing to Northern Ireland to advise generally. The Head of RUC SB requested training assistance that was supported by the Director of Intelligence.[2] Following a visit to Northern Ireland by the Intelligence Coordinator, whose report emphasized the importance of interrogation and the desirability of assisting the RUC Special Branch in every way possible, a request for assistance in the setting up of an RUC Interrogation Centre was discussed on 24 March at a meeting in the Ministry of Defence with representatives of the Security Service. As MI5 was not prepared to undertake the commitment, it was agreed that assistance should be provided by the Joint Services Interrogation Wing which was recognized as the only official school for interrogation training. The Home Office was informed at official level of this agreement, and the Director General of Intelligence mentioned the matter in general terms to the Minister of State at the end of March.[3] The Service team worked closely with the RUC Special Branch and consisted of four to six officers and six to eight NCOs formed from all three Services, all being members of the Joint Service Interrogation Wing.[4] In discussion on the pros and cons of internment in early August, Lord Carrington was advised that one of the advantages would be the intelligence dividend expected to be obtained through interrogation. Following the decision to proceed to internment, the Vice-Chief of the General Staff forwarded to Carrington on 9 August a note which:

(a) summarized the safeguards provided in JIC (65)15;
(b) explained that the supporting methods designed to heighten the subject's desire to communicate with his fellow human beings included isolation, fatigue, white sound, and deprivation of sense of place and time;
(c) made clear that the interrogation would be conducted by the RUC and that JSIW had provided, and would continue to provide, advice and support from the technical intelligence aspects.

On 10 August, Carrington discussed the matter with Maudling. Neither Secretary of State indicated any dissatisfaction with the situation as explained to them. Carrington considered, therefore, that he, and Maudling, in the Prime Minister's absence, had acquiesced in the provision by the Army of advisory services for the interrogations that were expected to be authorized by the Northern Ireland Minister of Home Affairs and to produce a valuable intelligence dividend. The selection of individuals to be interrogated was, however, entirely a matter for the RUC and the Northern Ireland Government. On 11 August, Faulkner, acting as Minister of Home Affairs, and on the advice of the RUC, signed orders (in accordance with Regulation 11 (5) made under the Special Powers Acts) authorizing the removal of each of twelve persons from the place specified in his detention order to 'any place where his presence is required in the interest of justice'. This was the formula prescribed in the Special Powers Act Regulation; but Faulkner had received recommendations that these individuals should be interrogated, and he had been extensively briefed by the Director of Intelligence in Northern Ireland on the techniques of interrogation. By authorizing the removal of these persons in these circumstances, 'Mr. Faulkner must be deemed to have agreed that they should be interrogated'.[5] Although the Interrogation Centre was formally an RUC (SB) responsibility it was, by nature of the Army team's role, a joint operation in which the Army was as concerned as the RUC in extracting the maximum intelligence in the minimum time within the prescribed guidelines. It had always been held that the morale of the RUC (SB) would be badly shaken and their willingness to cooperate with the Army in future severely reduced if ever responsibility for carrying out interrogation in depth was attributed solely to them. If they did cease to collaborate effectively with the Army this in turn would make the Army's task very much more difficult. For this reason the GOC gave the Special Branch an assurance that provided they carried out interrogation in depth using only the methods which they had been told about by the JSIW team, the Army would do its best to see that they were not blamed and did not suffer if there were any repercussions from interrogation.[6] The task of the Army unit was to provide technical assistance and advice to the RUC on all aspects of interrogation and prisoner handling at 25 Communications Unit. Specific tasks were:

a. Monitoring all interrogations and advising RUC interrogators before and after each interrogation.
b. Providing all technical facilities for monitoring and maintenance of equipment.
c. Providing the intelligence support staff for the unit.
d. Advising the commander of the RUC element on all aspects of interrogation and prisoner handling.
e. Advising the commander of the RUC element on the provisions of the JIC Directive on Interrogation.

Under no circumstances were the members of the Unit to undertake interrogation or search of prisoners and all contact with interrogatees should be avoided if possible. However, if it became apparent that the RUC were not exploiting the situation the Unit Commander was to report this immediately. The Unit Commander was to ensure to the best of his ability that all interrogation carried out by the RUC was conducted as closely as possible in accordance with the JIC Directive. Should the RUC element fail to comply with the provisions of the Directive, he was to advise the commander of the RUC element to do so and inform his military superiors as well.[7] The general rules for interrogation included the following safeguards:

(a) Medical examination and record of weight of subject on admission and discharge.
(b) Subjects to be seen daily by a Medical Officer.
(c) The following are prohibited:–
  (i) Violence to life and person, in particular, mutilation, cruel treatment and torture.
  (ii) Outrages upon personal dignity, in particular humiliating and degrading treatment.
(d) Subjects are to be treated humanely but with strict discipline. (These rules follow the broad principles for the treatment of persons under arrest or detention during civil disturbances as laid down in Article 3 of the Geneva Convention relative to the Treatment of Prisoners of War (1949).)[8]

There were to be twelve members of the JSIW personnel providing technical support and advice, twenty interrogators from RUC SB, and twenty-six members of the RUC Special Patrol Group who provided all internal guarding and escort duties. The selected internees were to be exposed to five techniques of in-depth interrogation. Wall standing required detainees to stand with their arms against a wall but not in a position of stress. It was supposed to provide security for detainees and guards against physical violence during the reception and search period and whenever detainees were together outside their own rooms in a holding room awaiting interrogation. It was also to assist the interrogation process by imposing discipline. Although the security need for this technique could be reduced by an increase of staff sufficient to provide for the separate custody of each individual while in transit between his own room and the interrogation room, there would be increased risks of physical contact between detainees and guards. A hood (a black pillow-slip which the detainee was not required to wear while he was being interrogated or while he was alone in his room) was supposed to reduce to the minimum the possibility that while he was in transit or with other detainees he would be identified or would be able to identify other persons or the locations to which he was moved. It thus provided security both for the detainee and for his guards. It could also, in the case of some detainees, increase their sense of isolation and so be helpful to the interrogator thereafter. The continuous noise to which detainees might be subjected prevented their overhearing or being overheard by each other and was thus a further security measure. By masking extraneous sound and making communication more difficult it might also enhance the detainee's sense of isolation. The diet of bread and water at six-hourly intervals formed part of the atmosphere of discipline imposed upon detainees while under control for the purpose of interrogation.[9] The justification for these methods was that they were used in support of the interrogation of persons who were believed to possess information of a kind 'which it was operationally necessary to obtain as rapidly as possible in the interest of saving lives, while at the same time providing the detainees with the necessary security for their own persons and identities'.[10]

COMPTON

If there was anger in the Catholic community at the one-sidedness of DEMETRIUS this was compounded by the allegations of ill-treatment meted out to those arrested by the troops. The most controversial aspect of this concerned deep interrogation. But this came later. Right from the off allegations of ill-treatment surrounded the arrest operation: for example, one Derry man, who was quickly released from Magilligan Army Camp, alleged that he had been brutally treated by soldiers. Liam Cummins, a 30-year-old unemployed factory worker, recalled how he was picked up at about 4.30 a.m. on 9 August at his mother's home in Limavady. His hands were tied behind his back and an empty sandbag was pulled over his head. Then he was told to lie on the floor of an armoured vehicle. Extensive body bruising was caused, he claimed, by being kicked repeatedly by the soldiers in the vehicle. Two of the soldiers were jumping up and down on his back and another was tapping him on the head repeatedly with a wooden baton. 'They called me an Irish peasant and said I was the leader of the IRA in Derry,' said Cummins. The soldiers refused to take off the sandbag when he had a coughing fit caused by dirt inside it. They said they were paying him back for what had happened to the soldiers in Belfast and for what their men had suffered. However, once he was delivered to Magilligan for questioning the physical abuse ceased although soldiers kept the arrested men awake at night by beating on the huts they were kept in with batons.[11]

Pressure groups, such as the Association for Legal Justice, spoke of certain 'new and disturbing elements' in the behaviour of the Army towards detainees. These included the use of anti-Catholic obscenities which hitherto seemed peculiar to the 'Orange bigots' of Northern Ireland; the brandishing of firearms in a most dangerous manner as a form of threat to arrested people; the use of electric shocks as a form of torture in at least one case; the 'misuse of religion as indicated by the pretence of a Catholic Chaplin' in the midst of brutalities at Girdwood Barracks; and the imposition of a 'personal curfew' on released detainees which was only one degree less immoral than internment itself.[12] Statements taken by the Association from men detained and subsequently released revealed a 'ghastly story of inhumanity, torture and degradation'.[13] Cardinal Conway called for an inquiry into the allegations. He described internment as a 'terrible power to give to any political authority'. It was important that publicity should be focused not merely on the reasons put forward to justify internment but also on the manner in which it had been exercised because: 'Already there is prima facie evidence that entirely innocent men... were subjected to humiliating and brutal treatment by [the] security forces.' Conway called for this evidence to be open to rigorous and independent examination, noting that suggestions from the authorities that complaints should be forwarded to the police for examination 'must inevitably seem to those concerned in the climate of Northern Ireland at the present time as bordering on cynicism'. The Church's hope was that British and world opinion would maintain close and impartial scrutiny over this 'terrible power' of internment. To say this, emphasized Conway, was not to condone in any way the activities of those who deliberately stimulated violence and who had, therefore, to share with others the responsibility for the deaths and terrible suffering of so many thousands in recent weeks. Conway appealed to Catholics not to allow themselves to be persuaded into violent or sterile or self-destructive forms of protest. They should rather seek to follow positive 'responsible political leadership'.[14]

This, however, was nothing compared to the outrage generated by the allegations relating to deep interrogation. IRA suspects were interrogated in two distinct ways: at Police Holding Centres using conventional police questioning techniques; and at the specially set up interrogation centre where in-depth interrogation known as Operation CALABA was undertaken and was used only on the small number of men thought to possess considerable knowledge of the IRA but who were considered unlikely to respond to normal police questioning.[15] The initial eleven detainees selected (two more were selected later) for deep interrogation – James Auld, Joseph Clarke, Michael Joseph Donnelly, Kevin Hannaway, Patrick Joseph McClean, Francis McGuigan, Sean McKenna, Gerald McKerr, Patrick McNally, Patrick Joseph Shivers and Brian Turley[16] – arrived at 06.30hrs on 11 August, from a Regional Holding Centre to an interrogation centre. At 15.45hrs they departed from the centre to Crumlin

Road Jail for service of detention and removal orders, returning to the centre on the same day by 19.00 hours. From this time, on 11 August, 19.00 until 17 August 11.50hrs (in one case until 11.15hrs on 16 August) they were held at the centre. At this point they were transferred to be lodged in detention in Crumlin Road Jail.[17] The actual interrogation took place in Hut 60 on Ballykelly airfield from about 05.30 hours on Wednesday, 11 August to 11.30 hours Tuesday 17 August. There were twelve members of the JSIW personnel providing technical support and advice; twenty interrogators from RUC SB; and twenty-six members of the RUC Special Patrol Group who provided all internal guarding and escort duties. The Essential Elements of Information (EEI) to be extracted from the detainees by their RUC SB interrogators were:

(1) 1st PRIORITY – Imminent enemy operations.
(2) 2nd PRIORITY – Location of people, arms and explosives.
(3) 3rd PRIORITY – Future enemy intentions.

The above remained as EEI until 19.00 hours 13 August, when HQ RUC SB began to issue different items and priorities for interrogation.[18]

From time to time pending and between interrogations, the detainees were made to stand against a wall in a required posture (facing a wall, legs apart, leaning with hands raised up against wall) for anything between four and six hours, except for periodical lowering of the arms to restore circulation. The posture was not the same as the standard search position. This was not supposed to be a stress posture: that is, the legs were not so wide apart, the arms so stretched up, or the weight of the body put forward to the same extent as in the search position. Detainees attempting to rest or sleep by propping their heads against the wall were prevented from doing so. If a detainee collapsed on the floor, he was picked up by the armpits and placed against the wall to resume the approved posture. The men were at the wall for periods totalling as follows:—

Auld	43 hours
Clarke	40 hours
Donnelly	9 hours
Hannaway	20 hours
McClean	29 hours
McGuigan	14 hours
McKenna	30 hours
McKerr	15 hours
McNally	13 hours
Shivers	23 hours
Turley	9 hours

Thus the general policy was to deprive the men of opportunity to sleep during the early days of the operation. Bread and water was offered at 6-hourly intervals from 12.30 on the 11 August until the morning of the 15 August, when the diet began to be increased to normal rations. The records kept by the doctor for each detainee on entering and leaving the centre all showed loss of weight during the time spent there.[19]

A number of interrogatees made specific complaints of ill-treatment at the centre. James Auld claimed that, when he had been placed against the wall in the required posture, he asked to go to the toilet; he was refused, and his hooded head banged against the wall for talking. When his back arched a baton was rammed into it to straighten it. Joseph Clarke claimed that, when in the required position against the wall, his hands kept going numb. If as a result he closed his fist his hands were beaten against the wall until he opened them and replaced them in the required posture. If he rested his head against the wall it was banged and shaken. After interrogation he was beaten until he collapsed. When brought round he was beaten again, and fought back. He then suffered another severe beating. He continued to fight back, and his wrists were handcuffed behind his back. The handcuffs were pulled back as he stood with his head to the wall, causing his wrists to be chafed and cut. Michael Joseph Donnelly claimed that if he did not keep his head straight and his back rigid in the required posture at the wall, he was struck with a fist. On occasions, though not very often, he said, he was struck in the genitals with a hard object, and on other occasions a similar object was thrust into his anus. Kevin Hannaway claimed that if he relaxed from the required posture at the wall he was kicked, 'kneed' and beaten with fists. On another occasion his head was beaten against the wall. A further allegation which appeared in the *Irish Press* of 18 August was that Hannaway had a head wound requiring twenty-seven stitches. Patrick Joseph McClean claimed he was assaulted on a number of occasions in different ways. He was bounced on, and rolled along the ground, punched with fingers in the stomach, kicked in the testicles, his arms were twisted backwards and his head bumped on the floor and he suffered various other assaults of varying severity. As to toilet facilities McClean stated: 'Toilet, no. Wet where we lay. No inclination to excrete. Slept in wet.' Sean McKenna claimed that he was beaten on the legs, hands and buttocks to force him to maintain the required posture at the wall. Gerald McKerr claimed he was beaten around the kidneys when he collapsed from the required posture. He kept falling and was invariably beaten when he did so. Brian Turley claimed he was kicked and beaten in an effort to force him to adopt the required posture on the wall and after interrogation his head was rammed several times against a door.[20]

Aside from the allegations above, alarm bells began to ring back at the MOD when Sir Michael Carver arrived back from leave in Scotland. The CGS returned to snowballing controversy surrounding deep interrogation – which he had not recommended to the Secretary of State. The deep interrogation plan was approved by the Director General of Intelligence in the MOD who was not responsible to the CGS. Carver was not aware of, and had not inquired into, the details of the methods to be employed. When he did inquire more deeply into what the details of the methods had been, who had carried them out and the extent to which this had been explained to Ministers, Carver received evasive answers. With some difficulty he obtained a description of the methods. 'My immediate reaction was surprise that Ministers should have authorised these: I personally would not have done.' When he probed deeper Carver discovered that Ministers had not been given a description of the details but had been shown the rules approved by the Labour Defence Secretary, Denis Healy, in 1967 and told that the methods conformed with them, 'which they did', provided that the rule 'subjects are to be treated humanely' was given 'a fairly generous interpretation'. Carver insisted that Lord Carrington should be told the full details of what in fact had been done. As a result of this it was agreed that the responsibility for ensuring the Secretary of State was informed about intelligence matters concerning Northern Ireland was transferred, from now on, to Carver as CGS and not left, as it had been vaguely before. Carver felt that Carrington, Heath and Maudling had been misled and he blamed himself for not inquiring more deeply; he later found out that Tuzo had also been unaware of the detailed methods of interrogation.[21]

When the details of the deep interrogation techniques – and the claims of brutality that accompanied – became public, the outcry was such that the British and Northern Ireland Governments had little alternative but to set up an inquiry. On 31 August, Maudling appointed a Committee of Inquiry under the chairmanship of Sir Edmund Compton, with His Honour Edgar Fay QC, and Dr Ronald Gibson as the other members, to investigate allegations by those arrested on 9 August of physical brutality while in the custody of the Security Forces prior to either their subsequent release, the preferring of a criminal charge or their being lodged in a place specified in a detention order.[22] The Compton Committee received considerable hostility and criticism from Nationalists and Republicans who regarded it as a whitewash. The Irish Government, in particular, was sceptical from the start; even before the Inquiry had been announced, Dublin, through the Ambassador in London, had formally called for a full and impartial inquiry on 25 August. The British were also told that the Irish would have to consider action at the European Court of Human Rights in Strasbourg. The British seemed taken aback by this and asked Dublin not to make a public statement or take any action without informing them in advance. In calling for a full and impartial inquiry – 'which should have non-British membership' – the Irish Government also requested that the terms of reference of the inquiry body be sufficiently wide to cover not only the allegations of brutality by Security Forces in the North but also cases like those involving other killings by the Security Forces, including Cusack and Beattie.

The Compton Committee did not satisfy Dublin which noted that there was, throughout Nationalist Ireland, general dissatisfaction with the composition and terms of reference of the Committee: the inquiry would not be held in public; would not have full judicial powers to summon witnesses and examine records; people giving evidence would not be legally represented; and there would be no cross-examination of witnesses. Dublin also noted how the appointment of Sir Edmund Compton himself had been criticized by Northern Nationalists. As the Ombudsman in Northern Ireland – one of the key parts of the reform package – his second report had stated: 'My first years of office in Northern Ireland has not produced a single instance of culpable action in the organs of central government.' In the same report Compton went on to say:

I think it is fair to say that the quality of administrative performance in the Northern Ireland Ministries compares well with my experience of Government Departments in the United Kingdom. Indeed the individual citizen frequently gets a better service from a Northern Ireland Ministry than he would from a United Kingdom Department in similar circumstances owing to the easier access to central government.

The Irish Government felt that while this might be true 'within the very narrow terms of the Ombudsman's mandate, the minority would find it very difficult to accept such a sweeping statement'. Compton's decision, on 2 September, that the boycott of his inquiry by the detainees would not frustrate his Committee's investigation meant, for Dublin, that while the prospects of carrying out a fair investigation within the announced terms of reference had been doubtful from the start 'the likelihood of doing so now without the cooperation of the detainees is minimal and the report when it emerges will be totally rejected by the minority in general and the detainees in particular.' The Irish also noted that one member of the Inquiry – Edgar Fay QC – had participated in the inquiry into the Munich air disaster: 'It is thought in some quarters that he was chosen because of the desire of the British to ensure that blame was pinned to the German pilot. The investigating body duly reported accordingly.'[23]

The allegations of brutality made Lynch's life even more difficult in responding to internment. Sean MacBride, a former IRA Chief of Staff but now a representative of Amnesty International, pressed the Taoiseach on how the Irish Government was going to respond. He wrote to Lynch 'with some hesitation' because: 'Every suggestion I have made to you so far has been ignored; since last October you have been unable to find a convenient time to meet me.' However, in the current grave situation MacBride drew the Taoiseach's attention to the fact that the European Convention for Human Rights (ECHR), to which Ireland and the UK were parties, provided by Article 15 for 'derogation' from certain of its obligations 'in time of war or other public emergency threatening the life of the nation'. MacBride assumed that the British Government had served a Notice of Derogation in regard to the Six Counties. However, it was not possible to derogate 'under any circumstances' from the provisions of Articles 2, 3, 4(1) and 7. Article 2 prohibited the unlawful killing of anyone. Article 3 prohibited the infliction of torture, inhuman or degrading treatment or punishment. MacBride believed that these two Articles encompassed clearly a case regarding the killing and ill-treatment of several persons in Northern Ireland. No Notice of Derogation could exclude the British Government's responsibility for the action of its forces in unlawful killings or in the ill-treatment of a prisoner in their custody. By virtue of Article 24 of the Convention the Irish Government, or any of the parties, might refer to the European Commission of Human Rights 'any alleged breach' of the provisions of the Convention by another party to the Convention. By virtue of Article 44 a party had the right to bring a case before the Court of Human Rights. Accordingly, prima facie, in MacBride's view, it was open to the Irish Government to refer these cases to the ECHR.[24]

This was a drastic step which Dublin was reluctant to take despite the threat implied in their earlier comments to the British. The legal advice to the Government described MacBride's use of the term 'under any circumstances' as 'scarcely justified', as paragraph 2 of Article 15, while excluding Article 2 from derogation, expressly excepted deaths resulting from lawful acts of war. This would be an obvious British defence to a complaint from the Irish Government in respect of killings and it was by no means certain that the Commission of the European Court would reject it. Furthermore, under Article 26 the Commission might only deal with a complaint after all domestic remedies had been exhausted. This would mean that a complaint arising out of ill-treatment would be rejected unless it could be shown that all claims for compensation under domestic law had been exhausted.[25] Lynch replied to MacBride pointing this out. Having regard to these difficulties and also the fact that a complaint, if successful, would not be finally adjudicated upon for a long time, and in view of the relevant political considerations, the Government did not consider that it would be advisable to pursue the course of action MacBride suggested.[26] But MacBride was not giving up. He raised the matter of the priest shot dead in the early stages of internment. The Attorney General rejected this also and concluded that there did not appear to be clear evidence that there had been a violation under Article 2: it could not be proved that the British Army had shot him and Article 2 (2) (c) covered the fact that a riot or insurrection was in existence at the time while other deaths seemed to be precluded because Article 2 (2) (a) (b) and (c) would cover deaths caused through 'mistakes'.[27] For now Dublin kept its powder dry.

As for Compton, the detainees did, indeed, boycott the Inquiry: at the start of its proceedings Compton offered the opportunity to all those arrested on 9 August to come forward to the Committee, if they wished, to substantiate an allegation. NICRA let it be known that the inquiry was unacceptable to them because of its constitution and private procedure (which was to protect the identity of the security personnel involved). Few replied to the letters sent by the Inquiry to those released. Most of those signified refusal for the reasons given by the Association. Of the nine released men who originally indicated a wish to make a formal complaint to the Inquiry, only two pursued their intention. None of the others replied to further letters, save one, who wrote withdrawing the complaint because, he said, although he was wrongfully arrested he suffered no physical brutality.[28] As a result only one of those arrested on 9 August availed himself of the opportunity to substantiate his complaint by appearing before the Inquiry.[29] It followed from this that with two exceptions the evidence of complaints was 'hearsay'. Apart from press reports it consisted of written statements purporting to be signed by complainants and in many cases obtained by the Association for Legal Justice. Many of the newspaper reports were founded on these statements. From other sources the Inquiry obtained one similar photocopy and forty-seven transcripts of recorded statements.[30]

The Inquiry found that there was an absence of any record of significant physical damage in the medical record made for each of these men, or of any sign of such damage in the photographs taken of these men, on exit from the centre on the 16 and 17 August – except for the case of Clarke. It found there was no evidence at all of a major trauma, either from medical reports or photographs, that might have been expected to follow from some of the rough treatment complained of by individual detainees (for example, being struck in the genitals, beating hands against the wall; punched with fingers in the stomach).[31] The allegations relating to interrogation in depth found no evidence of physical *brutality*.[32] However, Compton did accept that there had been physical *ill-treatment*:

> As regarded the posture on the wall, we find that the action taken to enforce this posture constituted physical ill-treatment...As regards hooding, the general allegations are substantiated, and we consider that they constituted physical ill-treatment...As regards noise, we find that the men were subjected to continuous and monotonous noise of a volume calculated to isolate them from communication, and this we consider to be a form of physical ill-treatment...As regards deprivation of sleep we consider that this constituted physical ill-treatment...As regards deprivation of food and water, we find physical ill-treatment in the diet of 1 round of bread and 1 pint of water every 6 hours for men who were being exhausted by other measures at the same time.[33]

The outcome of the Compton Report seemed to change everything from Dublin's perspective. On 19 October, Sir John Peck was informed that the Taoiseach was satisfied, after careful examinations made from the material put at his disposal from a number of reliable sources, that breaches of the ECHR appeared to have taken place in a substantial number of cases. Humanitarian considerations now compelled the Government to consider the position. This did not, immediately, trigger action by Dublin. The Legal Section of the Attorney General's office believed that while there was clear evidence of ill-treatment the outcome would turn on whether the European body would regard this as amounting to inhuman or degrading treatment or torture. The Compton Report had sought to brand the ill-treatment as less than brutality 'and not very successfully at that'. It was important to note, however, that the Compton Committee had confined their investigation to that of a complaint that related to physical treatment and did not deal with the mental aspects. The Attorney General advised that 'we have a sustainable case'. Hillery asked Hugh McCann, from the Ministry of External Affairs, for a Departmental view on taking action before the Commission. McCann warned that a move to bring Britain before the bar of European opinion would inevitably be strongly resented by the British Government and lead to a considerable deterioration in Anglo-Irish relations: 'If Mr Heath's previous outbursts are any guide he would probably be furious – at least in the short run. One might expect that Britain would get "really dirty" in handling our affairs.' The Government's EEC Section preferred that the Accession Treaty be signed before moving in on Strasbourg. On the other hand, pointed out McCann, action in Strasbourg would inevitably make the British much more careful in their handling of detainees and interness [sic] in the North. To the extent that this would slow down their gathering of intelligence information it would make it more difficult for them to make progress in the direction of a military solution. If they succeeded in containing the situation from a military point of view there would be less incentive for them to take unpalatable political action.

It seemed clear to McCann that the Northern minority favoured action now while domestic opinion would find it difficult to understand failure to take action. But from the viewpoint of relations with Britain and Europe the balance of the argument was probably against taking action now.[34] Despite this advice, on 30 November the Cabinet instructed Hillery to refer Britain to the Commission for breaches of the ECHR.[35]

While many in Ireland considered the Compton Report a whitewash this was not how it was viewed in Downing Street. When GEN 47 – including Heath, Maudling and Carrington – received a draft of the findings it was noted that to make the detainees wear hoods continuously, and to subject them to long periods of standing in uncomfortable positions 'was unnecessarily harsh'. Against this it had to be remembered that: 'We were dealing with an enemy who had no scruples, and we should not be unduly squeamish over methods of interrogation in these circumstances.'[36] When the Prime Minister received the final report Heath could not contain his anger as his note to the Cabinet Secretary, Sir Burke Trend, made clear:

> I have now carefully considered the Compton Report. It seems to me to be one of the most unbalanced, ill-judged reports I have ever read. It is astonishing that men of such experience should have got themselves so lost in the trees, or indeed the undergrowth, that they are proved quite incapable of seeing the wood.
>
> Their remit was two-fold. First to look at the manner in which the general arrests were carried out on 9 August. In fact, when you go through the Report carefully, the number of incidents involved in the arrest of 300 odd men were small and, in the conditions of the war against the IRA, trivial. But nowhere is this stated loud and clear... Secondly, they were asked to look at the allegations about interrogation. And here they seem to have gone to endless lengths to show that anyone not given 3-star hotel facilities suffered hardship and ill-treatment. Again, nowhere is this set in the context of the war against the IRA.
>
> What, above all, I object to – and I think many others will share this view to the point of driving themselves to a lesser degree or greater degree of fury – is that the unfounded allegations made for the most part by outsiders are put on exactly the same level as tested evidence from the Army and the RUC. This I believe to be intolerable. Surely, if men are not prepared to come to substantiate their allegations, these allegations should have been dismissed. The case for doing this is well strengthened when the records show that they made no complaints at the time and that medical examination revealed no grounds for complaint.

> I believe the consequences of the publication of this report ... will be to infuriate Commanders in the Army, undermine the position of the soldiers and RUC in Northern Ireland, and produce grave international repercussions for us throughout the world.[37]

What seems to have upset many Nationalists and Republicans was the dismissal of allegations of physical brutality. There are two aspects to this. The first relates to the substance of the detainees' allegations. The key point is that physical brutality was not necessary in this interrogation process. In Aden the instructions to interrogators included the following:

Why don't we use Physical Torture?

a. It is not necessary.
b. It is forbidden by the Geneva Convention and the Joint Service Directive.
c. Under torture, a man will say anything, true or false, to achieve relief.
d. It is morally wrong.

What is our Interrogation Teaching?

a. Exploitation of the 'Shock of Arrest'.
b. Psychological attack by intensive questioning.
c. All forms of trickery.
d. Show of knowledge.
e. Stoolpigeons.
f. Monitored conversations.
g. Confrontation.
h. Rewards.

We believe that kindness and the friendly approach are more likely to get results by promoting a state of 'emotional dependence' between the subject and his interrogator.[38]

Physical abuse was deemed counter-productive. If a detainee collapsed he was allowed to get his second wind and was not put straight back to the wall because: 'In our own interests we did not want detainees to be in such a state of collapse that they could not talk to us.' In fact – extraordinary as some Republicans might find it – the authorities were concerned with the welfare of the detainees: as the Permanent Under Secretary at the MOD explained to Sir Dick White, the Intelligence Co-ordinator, since the information obtained had been of great value and saved lives, the amount of intelligence harvested made the authorities concerned lest the personal safety of the detainees be put at risk: it had to be remembered that 'we were dealing with a very dangerous enemy and there was good evidence of vengeance ...taken against those who had informed on them ...we were dealing with men's lives.' Given the amount of information the detainees were giving to their interrogators it was suggested that most of the detainees actually wanted to keep their hoods on in the cells quite voluntarily[39] for fear of reprisals.

Alongside this there was a certain level of contempt for the Republican

Movement who, it was felt, might consider themselves an army but then squealed when squeezed in a military fashion. In short they could dish it out but could not take it. A subsequent testing of the 'white noise' found that, while there were differences between the Northern Ireland environment and that at Ashford where the interrogation techniques were honed, they appeared to be roughly the same. With the equipment adjusted to give maximum output the measured level approached 100dB; when the output was adjusted, by ear, to compare with that used in Northern Ireland the measured level was 85dB average, peaking at 87dB. There was a change of 2dB between measurements taken at a loud speaker and at about 15 feet from the loudspeaker. Levels did not change with distance above floor level within the range of 5–7 feet. The black hood gave an attenuation of 2dB with the sensation of reducing the high frequencies. The sound was described:

a. accurately, like a VHF FM radio receiver when NOT tuned to a station;
b. similar to a railway train letting off steam.

The level of 85dB was sufficiently loud to prevent normal conversation. Standing side by side with slightly raised voices, brief instructions were understood without difficulty. The level was compared, with a fair degree of similarity, to a Southern Electric train travelling through a tunnel at speed. Eighty decibels was given in a text book as the sound level in a train compartment with the windows open; while the 90dB was compared with the interior of a Tube train, with windows open.[40] Farrar-Hockley, himself a POW in Korea, did not subscribe to the view that internment and deep interrogation was either wrong or a disaster:

> The IRA call themselves soldiers and say they're carrying out warfare so they must be prepared to be frightened if they're captured or interrogated ... The dozen or so people who were taken, and not by any means the most junior ranks of the IRA, were described by those who were carrying out interrogations as "singing like canaries". It's something I've seen in other operational situations across the world. People were shaken and shocked out of their environment and for one reason or another they begin talking and they can't be stopped. So in that sense a lot of very good information, though of course of relatively short-term value, was obtained.[41]

Information supplied by the Director of Army Psychiatry put it thus:

> The bulk of the Army's experience of the psychological effects of interrogation has been gained in the course of training members of our own Armed Forces in how to resist the interrogation techniques which might be practised on them if they fell into enemy hands. During training exercises of this kind soldiers who are already extremely fatigued by being on the run for 3 days beforehand are subjected to continuous pressures of one sort or another for up to 24 hours, during which continuous interrogation itself may go on for up to 8 hours. The

techniques of hooding, wall-standing and so on are all used. As a result some of these men experience confusion and anxiety at the time. But so far as is known – and these soldiers have periodical medical examinations – not one has shown any evidence of long-term medical traumatic effects, and their mental condition rapidly reverts to normal after the exercise is over...the interrogation to which troops are subjected is more rigorous and intensive than the interrogation of detainees in Northern Ireland.[42]

In other words, British soldiers could take it but IRA 'soldiers' could not.

Notes

1. NAUK PRO DEFE 23/109 Interrogations in Internal Security Situations since 1945, 21 November 1971.
2. NAUK PRO DEFE 23/108 Summary of Events Leading Up to Interrogation of August 12 and the Results of Subsequent Interrogation Operation Annex A.
3. NAUK PRO DEFE 23/117 Northern Ireland – Authority for Interrogation, 9 November 1971.
4. NAUK PRO DEFE 23/109 Interrogations in Internal Security Situations since 1945, 21 November 1971.
5. NAUK PRO DEFE 23/117 Northern Ireland – Authority for Interrogation, 9 November 1971.
6. NAUK PRO DEFE 23/117 The Role of the Army in Interrogation in Depth in Northern Ireland, 9 November 1971.
7. NAUK PRO DEFE 23/108 Draft Directive for [name removed], 6 August 1971.
8. *Report of the enquiry into allegations against the Security Forces of physical brutality in Northern Irelan arising out of events on the 9th August 1971*. Cmnd. 4823 (HMSO 1971) para. 46 [Hereafter Compton].
9. Paras. 47–51.
10. Para. 52.
11. *Irish News*, 12 August 1971.
12. Ibid., 17 August 1971.
13. Ibid., 18 August 1971.
14. Ibid., 16 August 1971.
15. NAUK PRO DEFE 23/110 Interrogation in Northern Ireland: An Assessment of Local Factors Affecting its Operation and a Record of its Value in Security Force Activities.
16. Compton, Para. 44.
17. Ibid., Para. 45.
18. NAUK PRO DEFE 23/108 Annex A.
19. Ibid., Paras. 59–68.
20. Ibid., Paras. 70–7.
21. Carver, *Out of Step*, pp.410–11.
22. Compton, Introduction paras. 1–2.
23. NAI DT/2003/17/30 British Committee of Inquiry into Allegations of Brutality.
24. NAI D/T 2002/8/484 MacBride to Lynch, 9 August 1971.
25. NAI D/T 2002/8/484 Note to Ronan, 10 August 1971.
26. NAI D/T 2002/8/484 Lynch to MacBride, 12 August 1971.
27. NAI D/T 2002/8/484 Quigley letter, 30 August 1971.
28. Compton, Paras. 5–7.
29. Ibid., Para. 9.
30. Ibid., Para. 13.
31. Ibid., Paras. 97–8.
32. Ibid., Para. 14.

33. Ibid., Paras. 92–6.
34. NAI D/T 2002/8/495 McCann Note, 18 Samhain 1971.
35. NAI D/T 2002/8/495 Cabinet Minutes, 30 November 1971.
36. NAUK NAUK PRO CAB 130/522 Minutes of a Meeting held on 18 October 1971.
37. NAUK PRO PREM 15/485 Prime Minister's Personal Minute No.M66/71, 8 November 1971.
38. NAUK PRO DEFE 23/110 Interrogation in Aden, October 1966.
39. NAUK PRO DEFE 23/108 Note of a Meeting held by PUS to Discuss Interrogation Procedures at 15.50 on 26 October 1971.
40. NAUK PRO DEFE 23/109 Sound Level Measurements, Ashford, 24 November 1971.
41. Peter Taylor, *Brits*, p.69.
42. NAUK PRO DEFE 23/119 Psychological Effects of Interrogation Techniques.

6

British Disillusionment and Reassessment: August 1971–January 1972

DOUBTS

The concerns of Nationalists did not fall on deaf ears within the Whitehall system. As early as 17 August the UKREP was expressing his concerns about the political impact of internment to the Home Office. Howard Smith noted that, while there was a reasonable hope that terrorist activity would be kept at a much lower level than it was in the weeks preceding internment, the political and social consequences of internment had been more serious than many people in Northern Ireland had anticipated. There had been an almost complete polarization between the communities. This, stated Smith, was serious. The morale of moderate Catholics was low. The Stormont Opposition were removing themselves even further from the area of negotiation. Smith feared that they were very near the point of no return. He thought it was becoming clear that they wanted Stormont dismantled. He doubted whether even the inclusion of Opposition MPs in the Northern Ireland Government would meet their point. It was unlikely that Faulkner and his colleagues would, at best, go beyond a token of participation and even to that Unionist opposition in the country would be formidable. It was doubtful whether, having gone so far, the Opposition could agree to accept the degree of political restraint which would be necessary if a coalition were to work. The Opposition might not have thought it through, or realized that the consequence or maintaining their present attitude could well be the disappearance of all politicians from places of power: that was to say they, and equally unenlightened Unionists, might be forcing the country into Direct Rule under which participation at the executive and advisory levels might be more equitable than it was now, but political participation in Government no longer existed. Lynch's position also seemed to point to Direct Rule and it afforded encouragement to the Catholic minority to pursue courses which would make Opposition participation in Parliamentary Government even more unlikely than it already was. It seemed to Smith that Direct Rule was being brought significantly closer by the present mood of the country. Could London not shake the public out of that mood? Perhaps it was time to bring home to the politicians in the North what the implications of Direct Rule would be for them. This would be a delicate operation. It would be a mistake to encourage public opinion in Northern Ireland to think too badly of Direct Rule if the British Government had, in the end, to decide on it. But if the politicians were to realize that it would mean the long suspension if not the end of their Parliamentary careers, it might serve to concentrate their minds. Smith put no great hope in this, but as things were going he thought London had to see outside chances if they were to avoid or delay a Direct Rule situation. Smith finished by warning that the public mood was deeply shaken by the way things were going and that people were hoping for some external initiative. An initiative could only come from London and he thought that a stern review of the situation could have a strong impact on public opinion, which in turn could influence the attitude of politicians. The cry was 'Why is Heath not here: why is Maudling not here?'[1]

All of Smith's concerns were incorporated, and developed, into a Ministerial brief for another British meeting with Faulkner. It gives some idea of how concerned the Whitehall machine was becoming at events in Ulster. While the internment operation had been a considerable success 'technically', internment was 'only a means to an end: and the political and social consequences have been serious – more serious than many people in Northern Ireland expected'. The impression had been widely given that the Army's role had changed and that it was now there to maintain the dominance of the Unionist majority and to concentrate its attentions on the Catholic minority. The problem, the brief continued, had been written about endlessly. But the present predicament could be stated fairly simply: Faulkner had made what he regarded as a number of heroic proposals, but felt that he could not carry his party any further, particularly if by so doing it looked as though he would be making concessions to Lynch and the irresponsible reactions of the Opposition. The Opposition had taken up such an extreme position that they would find it difficult to return to Stormont on anything like Faulkner's terms without losing credibility and were imposing requirements which it was impossible for Faulkner to meet. Lynch, by throwing the weight of his Government against the continued existence of Stormont, had stiffened the attitude of Unionist leaders. And the fact remained that, if Faulkner were to go, there was no alternative to Direct Rule in sight. Behind all this were the two underlying problems of Northern Ireland. First, 'our ordinary democratic processes do not work there. Our electoral arrangements are based on the doctrine "winner takes all". This is all right if each side wins from time to time.' In Northern Ireland, however, these arrangements invariably produced a majority for the same party, and the opposition had no prospect of ever enjoying power. Fifty years of perpetual opposition, with the prospect of this continuing indefinitely, was bound to encourage despair, and resulted in irresponsible and splintered groups of Opposition members. Secondly, there was the fact that many members of the minority did not believe in the continued separate existence of Northern Ireland. The Swiss, for example, had a constitution which guaranteed rights for different communities; but 'they all do want to remain Swiss. Nor are they divided on religious grounds.' The question, asked the brief, was 'What is to be done?' The best that might be considered was an expansion of Faulkner's committee system and the introduction of proportional representation.[2] In summary, Whitehall was short on ideas.

To discuss the aftermath of internment, Heath, Maudling and Faulkner gathered with their respective colleagues at Chequers, on 19 August. As they did so Lynch despatched a telegram to them declaring that internment and military operations had failed as solutions to Northern Ireland's problems and that, in the event of the continuation of existing policies of attempting military solutions, he intended to support the policy of passive resistance now being pursued by the non-Unionist population.[3] Heath sent a stinging reply: 'Your telegram today is unjustified in its content, unacceptable in its attempt to interfere in the affairs of the United Kingdom, and can in no way contribute to the solution of the problems of Northern Ireland.' The Prime Minister added that: 'I cannot accept that anyone outside the United Kingdom can participate in meetings designed to promote the political development of any part of the United Kingdom.'[4] Lynch hit back: he found it regrettable that Heath should have interpreted his message in the way that he did. The Taoiseach had hoped the Prime Minister would have accepted his offer to participate in discussions among all those concerned to find an amicable solution to Northern Ireland's problems. Heath's assertion that what was happening in Northern Ireland was 'no concern of mine is unacceptable. The division of Ireland has never been, and is not now, acceptable to the great majority of the Irish people who were not consulted in the matter when that division was made... No generation of Irishmen has ever willingly acquiesced in that division. Nor can this problem remain forever in its present situation.' Apart from this statement of principle a situation where the destiny, well-being and even the lives of Irish people were involved 'must involve us greatly'. Lynch remained convinced that the time had arrived for all those who could contribute to a peaceful solution to Northern Ireland's problems to come together to discuss constructively how this could be achieved.[5]

Faulkner must have been reassured by Heath telling Lynch to keep his nose out. But this would gradually change. For the moment, though, Faulkner could be content to think that he and Heath were singing from the same hymn sheet. At Chequers, he raised no objections to discussions between Heath and Lynch, so long as it was clear that Northern Ireland's position within the United Kingdom was not an issue. It was constitutionally proper for any discussions to be between the British and Irish Government; in any event, Faulkner stated he would hardly undertake discussions with Lynch in view of the latter's failure to cooperate in any measures to remove the source of terrorism, and of Dublin's support and encouragement of the SDLP's tactics. Indeed, Faulkner questioned whether the maintenance of the present Irish Government advanced London and Stormont's interests. It took no action against terrorism and its courts of justice were intimidated. A coalition Government in Dublin might well better accord with British and Northern Irish Government interests; then again, reflected Faulkner, at least they knew where they stood with a Government that was more openly hostile towards the North. As for the political situation in the Province, Faulkner found it hard to see what further political initiatives were possible. A coalition Government would not be practicable.

Maudling, however, warned Faulkner that some steps must be taken immediately to offer a hope that a solution would be found. Otherwise the pressure for a tripartite solution involving the Republic would grow. Maudling had proposed to Faulkner that he should, when the violence ended, preside at a meeting between him and members of the Northern Ireland Parliament to find a means of providing a 'permanent and guaranteed participation by the minority in government and administration'. It would be made clear that the position of Northern Ireland as part of the UK would not be brought into issue and solutions would have to be found within the 'present democratic framework' of the Northern Ireland constitution (a phrase that might be open to interpretation). Faulkner had not felt disposed to accept this suggestion then; nor did he now. Instead, Faulkner focused on the danger inherent in the type of meeting Maudling proposed: that the range of constitutional reforms discussed might be extended beyond acceptable limits and be taken, for example, to include discussion of Lynch's proposal for a nominated body to replace Stormont. Faulkner warned that he could not take part in discussions whose scope might include the suppression of the democratic principle of majority rule. If it could be made clear that this principle was not an issue he would be prepared to commend a proposal for a meeting, on the lines suggested, to his Cabinet colleagues. At this point, Heath reassured Faulkner that there was no intention to suggest that the discussion should go beyond what was involved in the principle of 'democratic majority rule'. He instructed the Home Secretary to lay out the terms for his proposed talks[6] although, technically, it would be Faulkner who invited Maudling to arrange, as soon as the security situation had sufficiently improved, talks under his chairmanship with the Northern Ireland Government, representatives of both sides of the Northern Ireland Parliament and other representatives of the majority and minority communities. The purpose of the discussions would be to see what agreed ways and means could be devised, within the constitutional and democratic framework, of giving representatives of the minority as well as the majority community in Northern Ireland 'an active, permanent and guaranteed role, in the life and public affairs of the Province'.[7]

Faulkner could take heart from his meeting with Heath; but he also realized that the Unionist Government could not sit on its laurels: back in Belfast he told his Cabinet that he considered it imperative for the Northern Ireland Government to be seen to be taking the initiative and not to be responding once again to outside pressures. His Cabinet colleagues were, however, concerned lest any early decisions be taken as further concessions in the face of 'Republican' – meaning SDLP – demands, or that the Home Secretary would be left with no bargaining counters for his proposed talks with Opposition leaders. Roy Bradford, the Minister of Development, warned that nothing short of executive power would satisfy the SDLP and that influential sections of the British press would not support any solution short of 'Community Government'. Faulkner, however, 'rejected completely the idea of a Cabinet in which some members had as their objective the overthrow of the State'. In the end the Cabinet agreed that, to test the opinion of the Opposition, the Unionist Party and the press and public generally, the Government's proposals should be ventilated in the form of a discussion Green Paper.[8]

Since the SDLP had no intention of talking to Faulkner anyway it was left to the British to try and entice them into talks. An attempt was made when Gerry Fitt was admitted to a Dublin nursing home suffering from a slipped disc that had rendered him immobile. After speaking by telephone to Maudling, Fitt expressed a desire to see the Ambassador, the recently knighted John Peck. The Ambassador sent him a message via his Information Secretary. Peck reported to London how he got the reply that Fitt would like to see him at 12.30 p.m. on 8 September: 'He then kept me waiting for a considerable period while giving a television interview. I was observed and filmed on arrival and departure and my call will probably figure in the News. We shall stick to the story that it was a courtesy call on a Westminster MP ill in Dublin, which will obviously not be believed.' When he finally got to meet Fitt, the SDLP leader told Peck that he was in touch with both Opposition parties in the Dáil and was confident that he would obtain their agreement to a policy of minority participation in Maudling's talks provided that most of the detainees were freed and the 'real bad men' charged. He seemed keen that Peck should use his influence with Hillery to get Fianna Fáil to wear this. The Ambassador was non-committal. After lunch, Fitt telephoned another Embassy official, Peter Evans, and said that he had succeeded in persuading his fellow SDLP members to agree to withdraw their pre-conditions to talks. The only pre-condition which would now be insisted upon by the SDLP would be that Faulkner should release the 'political' detainees and institute criminal proceedings against the rest, that is, the gunmen. Fitt expressed confidence that Faulkner would find this pre-condition politically feasible to fulfil given his political skill and sense of political realities. After hearing this, Peck thought that: 'Whatever Mr Fitt's capacity to persuade Mr Faulkner to do what he wants', the situation regarding the SDLP certainly seemed healthier than it did in the morning and provided some evidence that Fitt's counsels were being listened to within the SDLP. If Faulkner felt able to make any encouraging response to the SDLP, Lynch's present policy of intransigence would be dealt a severe blow since he could not credibly pose as the leader of what he referred to as the 'vast majority of the Irish people' if the SDLP were not prepared to boycott Maudling's offer.[9]

Evans saw Fitt later in the evening, again, at the latter's request. Fitt showed Evans the draft of a statement he now thought he would issue fairly quickly. The statement welcomed Maudling's offer of talks, regretted that there had been no progress over internment in the North and called for some clarification before any commitment could be made. Evans was not as optimistic as Peck regarding Fitt's powers of persuasion: he represented strongly to Fitt that it was vital for him to take his SDLP colleagues with him, while Fitt expressed concern lest his colleagues in the North, unable to reach him by telephone at his Dublin nursing home, should issue a premature and hostile statement – 'which is precisely what they have done', noted Peck later. On internment, Fitt explained that although for 'political purposes' he had to be seen to show at least disappointment in public, he felt pretty sure that Faulkner would quietly and without publicity release the 'political' detainees and frame criminal charges against the gunmen who remained in custody. Generally, reported Peck to London, he 'exuded a considerable degree of confidence about the capacity of himself, and, he hoped, his colleagues, to find ways and means of re-establishing practical collaboration with Mr Faulkner's Government and of finding a formula for participation in the talks proposed by Mr Maudling'.[10] But then, in a BBC Radio interview Fitt announced that the SDLP would not take part in talks on the future of Northern Ireland unless internment was lifted. This, it was noted by the British, 'is of course a very different line from that which he was taking with a member of our Embassy in Dublin'.[11] When Evans again saw Fitt the next day, the SDLP leader expressed confidence that his talks with his colleagues from the North over the weekend – they were due to arrive in Dublin – would enable the SDLP to go to London to see Maudling some time the following week. He realized this would mean for him a journey on a stretcher, 'but he saw the obvious publicity advantages in this'.

His object in seeing Evans was to say that he wanted, for the purposes of the talks that lay ahead, to set up a go-between between himself and Faulkner, the idea being that it should be possible to find some common tactical ground with the Prime Minister. He seemed to have no idea who the go-between might be and at one stage suggested that Evans or a member of Howard Smith's staff might fill the role. Evans pointed out that this was a non-starter, and Fitt then consulted Brendan Halligan, Secretary of the Irish Labour Party, who was also present, but no suitable names occurred to them. At this point Fitt asked Evans to convey to Faulkner, via Smith, his desire for a go-between and his willingness to agree to whomever Faulkner suggested as a suitable person. Evans put this to Smith later that night and it was agreed that Evans should tell Fitt that it would be more to the point for someone in Fitt's political confidence to make the approach to Faulkner directly. Fitt told Evans the next morning that he was sending somebody up later in the day to see Faulkner to suggest that a suitable intermediary would be Maurice Hayes, of the Northern Ireland Community Relations Commission, and a Catholic. Fitt then remarked that he would make very strong public objections to any claim by Lynch to represent the interests of the minority in the North. That representation lay with the SDLP and Nationalist parties. Peck commented in his telegram to London that their talks with Fitt in the last few days had brought out the 'curious relationship' between Fitt and the other members of the SDLP in the sense that, at least as Fitt professed to see it, 'there is a kind of struggle for their allegiance between himself and the Lynch Government'. Fitt, thought Peck, 'gives us the strong impression, since confirmed by Howard Smith, of being a cynical and devious operator. He seems to have no interest in the civil disobedience campaign and certainly no real objections to the policy of internment in the North, but is quite prepared to use either issue to his own tactical advantage.'[12]

Evans again saw Fitt on 11 September; also there was Garret FitzGerald from Fine Gael and Maurice Hayes. Fitt's earlier optimism about lining up his SDLP colleagues for Maudling was showing signs of wear. Asked point-blank by Evans when the SDLP would now be going to London, Fitt could do no more than assure him that he hoped he would be able to get a decision sometime the following week. His problem was that his colleagues had now dispersed to various destinations in the North. But it was Hayes who remarked privately to Evans that Fitt's colleagues in the SDLP were more likely to be swayed by Lynch than by Fitt. He was generally pessimistic about the chances of getting the SDLP to the conference table.[13] This appeared to be confirmed when, following the signing of more internment orders by Faulkner, the radio reported Fitt as saying that this put an end to any prospect of SDLP participation in talks.[14] With these contacts coming to nothing, Howard Smith, who had been watching events from Belfast, expressed his concerns. He told London and the Dublin Embassy that:

> My own view of Fitt... is that while he is devious and temperamentally unreliable he is not so much cynical as a Walter Mitty character. I am sure it is right that we should be careful, as officials, not to get too much involved in manoeuvrings between him and the other SDLP members (none of whom have much regard for him while some of them cordially dislike him) or between him and Faulkner;[15]

later adding:

> From some of the things Fitt said to Evans I fear he is sadly out of touch. His confidence in Paddy Devlin (who dislikes him) and Ivan Cooper (who probably dislikes everybody) is not to be relied upon. The suggestion that Hume is less opposed to violence than the others is very much open to question. The [suggested] sending of a personal message to [Cardinal] Conway asking him to bring pressure to bear on Hume to align himself with Fitt is little short of lunatic. Since I do not rate Fitt's discretion any higher than his judgment... I do not think that the assumptions on which the advice was given were sound ones, e.g. that it is a likely case that Hume would be on one side with all the rest on the other: and since if we are in the end going to make progress in this country we shall need to be able to talk with the SDLP I do not think it would help for them to discover that we are engaging, either here or in Dublin, in their internal party relationships.[16]

THE HEATH–LYNCH SUMMIT

The sense of frustration within British diplomatic circles at the outcome of internment had already been demonstrated before the failure of the Fitt contacts. Peck had set down his thoughts in a personal letter to Sir Denis Greenhill, Permanent Under-Secretary of State at the FCO, on 24 August. It was also circulated to other key officials such as Kelvin White in the Foreign Office and Sir Philip Allen at the Home Office. Peck included the views put to him by Hugh McCann, Greenhill's opposite number in Dublin, and his observations on them. Peck warned Greenhill that he would find them pretty blunt and, politically, probably unwelcome, but they were the honest views of a realistic and down to earth official's prevailing opinions. McCann pointed out that while no Irish politician could renounce the ideal of ultimate reunification, the present crisis was in fact about peace and social justice in the North. Whatever British views might be about the formal claim of the Irish Government to the Six

Counties, they could not deny that the Irish had a right to be concerned with events there and that for obvious reasons they were well informed and the best judges of likely Irish reactions to events. McCann emphasized that the Irish Government, and all Irishmen with a knowledge of Northern Ireland, were horrified when they learnt of the British intention to introduce internment – not for internal political reasons – but because they knew it would fail in its purpose, would greatly increase bloodshed, vastly strengthen the IRA and unite the Catholics behind them. Nothing had happened to alter that view. Lynch and Hillery were deeply hurt at what they regarded as the blank refusal to listen to their sincerely offered advice; they were mystified at London persisting in what they regarded as a demonstrably mistaken policy. McCann stressed that the Irish Government deplored the killings and the violence in the North. Efforts to act against the IRA in the South would continue, but the Government were hamstrung by the fact that internment, which produced a gut reaction in any Irishman, had greatly reduced any prospect of judge and jury convicting gunmen and had probably ruled out any possibility of internment in the South for an indefinite period. The Irish Government, explained McCann, would continue to denounce violence in any form anywhere, but as every IRA man interned by the British was replaced by two or three volunteers from within the North, the murders and violence would continue until the British Government made some move towards a political settlement.

According to McCann the Irish were asking themselves why the British could not see this; in fact they maintained that many of the British involved in the North did in fact see this very clearly. They concluded that this was a matter of party politics. He was blunt to Peck: under the Labour Government the British Army was brought in and welcomed as an impartial force to bring protection to the Catholics and the reform programme was introduced. Despite misgivings when the Conservative Government was elected, the Irish Government hoped for the best. The situation deteriorated steadily as Stormont whittled away the reform programme and the last straw was an internment policy which locked up political opponents of the Unionist Party without a trace of IRA connections, left all the Protestant thugs at liberty and left tens or hundreds of thousands of guns in Protestant hands. Why? Solely because the Paisleyite tail was wagging the Unionist dog and the Unionist tail was wagging the Conservative dog. McCann asked if the British preferred this to a reasonable and constructive discussion with the Irish Government about measures to retrieve the situation. The Taoiseach had interpreted Heath's offer of a 'serious and sensible discussion of the whole range of matters of common interest' as including a discussion of how to get a system of real Catholic participation in the Government of Northern Ireland and thus remove the root causes of bloodshed. If this was ruled out as 'raising constitutional questions which cannot be discussed', there was no point in the Prime Minister and the Taoiseach meeting. McCann took pains to point out how Lynch's reference to supporting a policy of passive resistance in the North was hypothetical and wholly conditional upon the British trying to rely on existing policies of attempting military solutions. The Taoiseach was under tremendous pressure from within

Fianna Fáil and from the Northern minority and was fighting to maintain some liberty of manoeuvre. In any case he would never countenance violence. 'Thus McCann,' ended Peck. It was a 'pretty neat summary of what we hear on all sides'. One point McCann did not mention was one made forcefully to Peck by an 'elder statesman'. He said he and everyone else was fed up with the refrain 'there will be no change in the status of Northern Ireland without the consent of Stormont'. First, it was dishonest, since the only purpose of the function of Stormont was to ensure the preservation of the status quo. Secondly, it was untrue, since it was conditional upon the continuing will of the British electorate as a whole, who voted to set up Stormont fifty years before and could one day equally decide to set it down again. But, emphasized Peck, 'this is not, repeat not, what Mr Lynch wants to talk about'. His concern was to join constructively with London in making sense of Northern Ireland. The guts of what McCann was trying to say was 'can't the Foreign Office do something?'[17]

Peck was clearly sympathetic to McCann and the Irish Government's concern with London's policy – which was essentially being driven by the desire to keep Faulkner in a job and prevent a British Minister from having to take his. But it was not just officials within the Foreign Office and the Home Office – earlier personified by the UKREP – who were expressing concern with the aftermath of internment: so was the Cabinet Office. And they did not come more senior than the Cabinet Secretary, Sir Burke Trend, who had direct access to the Prime Minister. In early September, he set out his thoughts to Heath. Trend thought that there seemed to be only two possible approaches to the problem of Northern Ireland: '(1) We can go on as we are. (2) We can try to devise some new political initiative.' But the Cabinet Secretary believed that, by sticking with the first option:

> If we are honest with ourselves... we must admit that this means, essentially, that we go on living from day to day and from hand to mouth, arguing first with the North and then with the South about each successive 'incident', adjusting our tactics to developments in the situation as they occur, hoping that sooner or later things will get better but always waiting on events and the reaction which they dictate.

The advantage of this course was that – so far at least – it had succeeded in preventing the pot from finally boiling over; and it might, of course, continue to do so. If so, 'we might be well-advised to stick to this policy.' Its disadvantage, however, was that it offered no permanent solution, no light at the distant end of the tunnel and, it must be admitted, no current prospect of success in the short term. On the contrary, the situation seemed to be steadily deteriorating; the relations between Ulster and Éire appeared to be becoming increasingly polarized; the IRA were adopting a daily more flagrant attitude of defiance towards all three Governments involved; civil disobedience in Ulster, encouraged by Dublin, was approaching the point when really serious social and economic damage could be inflicted on the Province (at the ultimate expense of the British taxpayer); and the Opposition at Westminster were beginning to try to snatch the political initiative from the Government's hands. If this process continued, sooner or later 'the elastic must snap'; and one of the main objections to merely 'going on as we are' was that this course offered no insurance that the breaking point would not come sooner rather than later. Another objection was that disobedience and violence were apt to be infectious; and Great Britain was uncomfortably close to Northern Ireland from this point of view. The alternative policy – that is, a radical new political initiative – would be designed to anticipate the point at which the elastic snaps and to ensure that 'we received the credit for having tried to avert calamity while there was still time to do so'. Trend, however, felt that the form of such an initiative could not be decided until:

> ... we had made up our minds whether or not the basic constitutional position of Ulster was open to negotiation. If it were not – i.e. if the Border was to remain sacrosanct and Ulster was to remain an integral part of the United Kingdom – the only form which a radical new political initiative could take would appear to be direct rule; and the only question for decision would be whether we should institute direct rule forthwith instead of waiting until it is forced on us as the (probably inescapable) conclusion of our present policy of 'going on as we are'. We have assumed hitherto that direct rule would entail such appalling consequences that it should not be considered except as a measure of absolutely last resort. To question this assumption is not to cast doubt on the consequences, which would indeed be liable to be appalling. But, if we instituted direct rule forthwith and eliminated Stormont (even if only temporarily) from the scene, Westminster would at least be left confronting Dublin direct; political power and authority would be seen to be being exercised from the centres where they really reside; and it might become possible to institute a realistic political dialogue with Dublin, directed to a new solution. It might then be feasible to think in terms of a settlement whereby, on the one hand, the restoration of some form of genuinely representative Government of Ulster would be dependent on the institution of new safeguards for the rights and interests of the Roman Catholics in the Six Counties (safeguards which the Government in Dublin would have accepted as adequate) and, on the other hand, the Dublin Government themselves would enter into a new undertaking to respect the sanctity of the Border and the integrity of Ulster and to co-operate actively with the Government of the United Kingdom in repressing any attempts to overthrow or to undermine the settlement. The fact that direct rule is what the IRA say that they want and are, indeed, trying to provoke us into instituting is not necessarily a decisive objection. It may be wiser to agree with your adversary while you are in the way with him than to wait until your respective ways have diverged irretrievably; and it might prove easier to deal with Mr Lynch's Government than with a successor regime which was more under the IRA thumb. Nor should the undoubted opposition of Stormont to direct rule be accepted as necessarily conclusive. It is certain that the Northern Ireland Government would oppose it if it were imposed unilaterally and forthwith, while they could claim that they were still capable of governing the Province. But they

might accept it less unreadily if they were assured at the outset that the new settlement to which it was only a prelude would still preserve the Border and would still leave intact the constitutional status of Ulster as an integral part of the United Kingdom.

Alternatively, Trend suggested that, if it were possible to go even further and to contemplate a negotiation in which the Border itself might be open to discussion and the concept of some form of reunification of the whole of Ireland were allowed to emerge more explicitly than hitherto, 'we should have to be prepared to "let Ulster go" to some extent'. Trend thought that to let Ulster go totally – in the sense of expelling it from the United Kingdom and leaving it to its own resources and to the mercy of its Southern neighbour – was presumably unthinkable in the current political climate. But was it less unrealistic to think in terms of an arrangement which would give Dublin not complete control over Ulster but at least a more effective say in its administration? 'At first blush the idea sounds mad,' wrote Trend. But 'some people believe that, if Faulkner could be finessed, Paisley would not be wholly averse from sitting down at the table with Lynch and trying to hammer out some new means whereby Protestants and Roman Catholics could live together in the North; and the concept of Westminster's giving Dublin some share of the responsibility of governing Ulster may not be quite as crazy as it sounds.' Trend was trying to nudge his Premier's thinking forward on such matters:

> We should be warned – by Vietnam and Rhodesia if we have forgotten our own earlier experience in dealing with recalcitrant colonies – against allowing ourselves to be drawn deeper and deeper into a situation from which there is no escape other than capitulation at the eleventh hour. Sooner or later all the parties will be driven to the negotiating table; it will be both more honourable and more economic to go there sooner rather than later. It would be best of all if the British Government could publicly take the initiative in this respect forthwith. But, if domestic political inhibitions make it difficult for them to be seen to take the first step, can they not arrange for public opinion to give them a lead which they could hardly refuse to follow?[18]

So, very soon after internment senior officials, right across Whitehall, were dismayed by the political fallout and were voicing their concerns to their political masters. But Trend's radical suggestions were too much for any politician; the Cabinet Secretary's role was to act as a lightning conductor to stimulate debate. But, under no circumstances were Heath and his colleagues prepared to grasp the nettle of Direct Rule – yet. Instead, what Heath was prepared to accept was a bringing forward of a proposed summit with Lynch and to see what might emerge from this. Both sides were eager to talk. In preparing the brief for Lynch's visit Trend could not help but tell Heath that he was 'left with a feeling of dismay about the bareness of the landscape and the absence of any realistic prospect of making progress on the basis of our present assumptions'. Trend had 'an uncomfortable feeling that sooner or later – and perhaps sooner rather than later – we shall be driven to call in question some of the political and constitutional assumptions which we have hitherto accepted'.[19] But for the moment the Government were concerned merely with the preparations for a summit between Heath and Lynch. When Peck met with McCann the Irish official was very anxious that it should be made clear that the initiative to advance the meeting came from the British side: it would be extremely difficult for Lynch if it were presented publicly as a move by him forced upon him by political pressures at home. McCann's main point was to underline the risk to the Taoiseach: if Lynch returned 'visibly empty handed he was finished'. He repeated that he was not coming to talk about reunification but about 'positive measures to restore peace and justice in the North'.[20] No promises were, however, made – as they could not – by the British. Both sides wanted to meet if only to be seen to do something. And so it was that Prime Minister and Taoiseach met, at Chequers, for a two day summit beginning on 6 September. The discussions were the first opportunity (apart from ad hoc meetings on the fringes of other events) for the two Heads of Government to face each other and thrash out, on the level of personal diplomacy, the perspectives of both sides with regard to the North.

The talks commenced at approximately 11 a.m. Heath had Trend with him, while Lynch was accompanied by Ambassador O'Sullivan. The Prime Minister began by saying that there seemed to be some genuine misunderstandings about what his Government were trying to do in relation to the North. Both countries would shortly be joining the EEC and 'we would be in an intolerable position if we had to bring this present serious problem with us'. The existence of trouble in the North would also present the current six members of the EEC with problems. Heath feared the situation could escalate more and more unless there was a breakthrough. A main purpose of the meeting, therefore, was to remove misunderstandings and to see how the situation could best be dealt with. Lynch's reply included a talk about how the two communities in the North came about. The current situation, he said, derived from partition. Partition was imposed and its existence always constituted a threat of violence because of the efforts to maintain the Unionists in power. One-third of the population of the North favoured unification of the country. The attitude of the Unionists was quite contrary. The Taoiseach wanted to say quite categorically that everybody in the Republic was dedicated to unification and the great majority wanted it by peaceful means. The approach to unity by peaceful means had come to the fore in the Taoiseach's own time. Lynch fully shared the Prime Minister's view that the situation in the North was very grave indeed. His policy had always been to seek unity through peace and as a result of the events of 1968 and 1969 he had come to symbolize this approach. The majority in the Dáil and Senate agreed with this line. If, however, the position of the Dáil were to be weakened, this could lead to a situation of near civil war. The Taoiseach passionately felt that, unless there was some political breakthrough at this meeting, the exercise would be of doubtful value. An attempt at a military solution could only increase disaffection among the minority. He did not say that Stormont must go but rather that it should be replaced by something else. Faulkner's offer to the minority of participation in committees was not enough. What had to be realized was that the SDLP, having withdrawn from Stormont, could not go back on the present basis. The IRA were a reality but acts of violence were not necessarily exclusive to the IRA. Some of these acts might have been perpetrated by others. The Taoiseach asked the British Government to reformulate its guarantee to the Northern majority. Without a new guarantee, the majority would be permanently in power and in that situation there would inevitably be a recurrence of trouble. The IRA was a by-product of the situation. If Heath could find it possible to state that the unification of Ireland would have to be the ultimate solution and gave an assurance of interest in working towards this end, this would be enormously helpful at the present time.

Heath, in his response, fully acknowledged that the Taoiseach was working for unity and peace. Indeed, all commentators had acknowledged the Taoiseach's policy of striving for unification through peaceful means. But the constitutional position had been repeated by successive British Governments. If the majority wanted to change the status of the North, the British Government would not stand in their way. Heath could not accept the Taoiseach's proposal for a change in the constitutional position; he believed the EEC would in time lead to a final solution of the Irish problem. Indeed, he had been saying it since the early 1960s and this was still strongly his belief. And he could not accept the point of view that the Unionists could remain permanently in power. If the minority had in the past accepted the Border until such time as there was majority support for unification, then they would have had the possibility of getting into power in Stormont. He admitted, however, that he could not see the minority changing their minds. Heath then argued that the life of the community in the North was being paralysed by the gunmen. There was urban guerrilla warfare and the Catholic community was being intimidated. The Army was, therefore, being wrongly accused of coming to the rescue of the Unionists. The Army was in fact doing everything possible to prevent the alienation of Catholics. He repeated that Westminster was not trying to find a military solution; they were simply trying to deal with urban guerrillas who wanted a united Ireland by force and who were a threat to the established authority. There was a democratically elected Government in Stormont and the majority had come to power as a result of a fair election. This was a powerful argument against the walk-out from Parliament by the minority's representatives. Heath recalled that, at one stage, Clement Atlee had said that a walk-out was ridiculous in a democratic system because if you walk out you have to walk back in again.

Lynch replied that it had to be realised that the North was an artificially created territory. It had always had a Unionist Government and under present circumstances would always continue to have one. It had two separate communities who were now almost irreconcilable. He greatly welcomed the reforms announced in the Downing Street Declaration of 1969 but these reforms were not working out as expected. For example, even though there was a Police Authority, there were instances where the Northern Ireland Government still continued to dictate the policy of the police. The Taoiseach continued by saying that internment was a wrong decision. It was being operated on a one-sided basis and could only polarize the two communities. Furthermore, many of those interned were known to be quite innocent. What obviously happened was that the authorities used old lists in deciding who to intern. Most of those interned clearly wanted to see an end to Stormont but it should be recognized as a legitimate ideal for them to favour the unification of their country. A meeting some time ago at Lurgan at which Faulkner and half his Cabinet had met (to explain his proposed Stormont reforms) with the Orange Order showed that the Order exercised a very strong influence over the Stormont Government. Most members of the Unionist Party were hand-picked by the Orange Order. Even the leaders were in the hands of the Order. It was well known too that constituency association work in the North took place quite independently of the Government authority. Lynch pointed out that men like John Hume were very reasonable and intelligent. However, because of his frustration as a member of the Opposition, he could not carry the IRA with him. The Taoiseach very much wanted to keep the minority representatives in a position of influence. In fact, he specifically asked them when they came to see him recently whether, in the event of their being put in a position of influence, they would be able to bring their minority followers to heel. Their reaction was positive but only in certain circumstances. Their permanent exclusion from Government clearly weakened their position. Unless there was some form of Commission they would not be able to influence the minority community. Lynch pointed out that urban guerrilla warfare could only work if there was cooperation from the people. This cooperation certainly existed because the minority were looking to the Provisionals for protection. If popular support could be diverted this would help to eliminate the bombing. It would be a great help if one could alienate support for the Provisionals. But the minority representatives said they would return to Stormont only if three conditions were met, namely:

(1) The release of all internees and the institution of prosecutions against those in respect of whom a charge can be made.
(2) The establishment of a Commission to administer the area.
(3) A quadrupartite meeting between representatives of Westminster, representatives of the Dublin government, Mr Faulkner as leader of the Unionist Party and representatives of the Parliamentary Opposition.

If there were some semblance of a political solution this would help the minority representatives to establish themselves with their followers and to eliminate support for the militants. Heath, however, was doubtful about the possibility of eliminating support for the militants but was in favour of a policy which would bring this about. A Commission which would abolish the democratic majority would not be acceptable. It would be contrary to British traditions of Government. Many Catholics would not like non-elected representatives claiming to represent them. The basic difficulty was that the proposal was undemocratic. Anyhow, a fifty-fifty participation would not be a fair division. Lynch acknowledged the undemocratic nature of a Commission for the North; but the Commission would, he argued, be no more than an interim step towards some form of democratic administration. Stormont had failed and it would not be accepted by the minority. This was Westminster's problem. A system which in practice resulted in alienation of the minority was not democratic. The minority did not accept that democracy existed in the North. When Heath asked what the Taoiseach wanted to be able to say had arisen from the meeting, Lynch answered that he would like to be able to say that the Prime Minister recognized that there must be some movement towards constitutional change and that the unification of Ireland was the only eventual solution. Heath replied that nobody was asking the Taoiseach to abandon his objective of unification by peaceful means. This was an entirely valid aspiration and represented the wish of the majority of the Irish people. However, in the meantime two things were essential, namely:

1. To put an end to violence; and
2. To find a way of guaranteeing full rights for the minority 'with participation in government' until such time as a majority favour unification.

Heath wanted to see a situation created where the minority would have a permanent guarantee of fair treatment until unification was reached. The Taoiseach then asked what type of participation Heath envisaged. Heath said that nothing was excluded. The introduction of proportional representation in local and central Government was likely. The question was in what way could the minority take part further in Government. If the minority wanted proper participation they should say how they wanted to take part. He had doubts about the possibility of a coalition Government in the North and it might be necessary to accept the democratically elected majority until the majority of the people in the North wanted a change in the constitutional position. Lynch enquired whether it would be possible to have participation in Government by people who favoured unification; Heath replied that it would be difficult to have participation on that basis. Lynch answered that if Heath's proposal for the Maudling conference was as far as he could go then he could only regard the outcome of their discussions as unsatisfactory and this would not help the minority leadership to accept the proposal. Heath warned that, if the Taoiseach were to say publicly that discussions under British leadership were not important, this would have a boomerang effect in Britain. But Lynch insisted that it would be impossible for him to go back to Dublin and say this is the only outcome of their talks. He would have to indicate that a suggestion had been made to him in which he could not acquiesce.

Heath confessed to being slightly perplexed at the Taoiseach's reaction. The Border solution was a long-term problem. The immediate task was to find means of restoring peace. Nobody was asking the Taoiseach to abandon his objective of unification. What was being attempted was an effort to find a way for the two communities to live together until the Border was removed. A British Government would do everything possible to ensure fair treatment for the minority. The Taoiseach then refocused the debate by stating that the minority in the North would not at this time agree to tripartite talks. All they would agree to, as they had clearly indicated, would be quadripartite talks, and these in certain specified circumstances. Heath intervened to say that at the moment the Taoiseach had no official status in relation to the North. However, his influence in bringing peace to the area would be greatly welcomed. Because of the great need for peace there was every reason for talks between London and Dublin. Heath added that he would welcome more contact between Dublin and Belfast because this could be one important way in which problems might be solved. His invitation to the Taoiseach to come to London was an acknowledgement of the Republic's interest in the Northern problem. But Heath repeated that the Taoiseach could have no status in relation to the Maudling proposal. The inclusion of the Taoiseach in a conference on the internal position in the North would simply not be on. A quadripartite meeting would raise a constitutional issue. If he were to say that representatives of the Republic were to take part in the proposal affecting the organization of the North, he would not get the support of the Conservative Party. Lynch, however, argued that the matter should be looked at from the point of view of the minority in the North. If Dublin were to be excluded from the exercise, this could well escalate violence. His exclusion would be interpreted as abandonment of the minority. It was important that both sides should face realities in this matter. Heath, at this point 'showing some signs of irritation', said that everybody recognized the Opposition in the North as being run by the Taoiseach or as running the Taoiseach. No British Government could accept that the Republic has a constitutional right to be involved in such talks.

When the two Premiers resumed their discussion the next morning, Heath began by saying that he was in a position to give the results of his reflections overnight. What was necessary was a political initiative to get the communities together. However, despite such an initiative the gunmen would still be there. The reform programme was a major political initiative. He was prepared for a further political initiative now. A lot of work had been done on the proposal he had mentioned and it could lead to a conference under a UK chairman. As to the possible inclusion of Dublin in this proposal, he had already pointed out the constitutional difficulty involved. His overnight consideration had not brought about any change in his attitude. There was no reason, however, why the Taoiseach and he could not continue to talk. Heath believed that he had gone further than any of his predecessors and indeed many in the North would blame him for talking at all. At this point Heath enquired whether it would be useful to have a meeting with Faulkner. Lynch replied that he had been invited to come to London to discuss the Northern situation and a proposal in relation to the North had been put to him from which he would be excluded. He doubted very much if in the circumstances the proposal would be acceptable to the minority representatives. Lynch thought that, in effect, what the Prime Minister was doing was asking him to admit that, as head of the Irish Government, he should opt out of his responsibilities in relation to a problem affecting Ireland. The Taoiseach pointed out that both he and the Prime Minister were heads of sovereign Governments; Faulkner was not. Tripartite talks would give Faulkner a status. The Taoiseach then threw out the suggestion of bilateral talks in which

Heath would have Faulkner with him and the Taoiseach would have a representative of the Northern minority.

This did not appeal to Heath, who warned that one had to take account of the facts of life in the North. What the Taoiseach was suggesting could only inflame the position. Heath added, 'with considerable force', that if it was the Taoiseach's intention to seize the minority and to seize the North, then he would meet with very strong resistance. The offer of a conference under UK chairmanship was a substantial one. Heath was not asking the Taoiseach to opt out because he was not in. Lynch had the opportunity of separate talks at the highest level. He hoped the Taoiseach could see merit in the proposal and would urge the minority to take full advantage of it and went on to say that there was never sympathy in Britain for the abolition of an established institution; therefore it would be impossible to abolish Stormont and to substitute a Commission. Lynch, however, suggested that it should not be beyond the wit of politicians to devise a more suitable administrative system. Possibilities could be suggested by the situation in Switzerland or Belgium. The 1920 Act envisaged two subsidiary Parliaments with a Council of Ireland. The position of the majority in the North was greatly helped by the 1949 Act. At this point Heath explained that the objective of Mr Attlee and of his successors was to give assurances to the majority so as to remove their fears and enable them to work peaceably with the minority. In this, he said, Labour Governments had not changed their position. It was true that there might be lessons to be learned from the Swiss position. The difference, however, was that no part of Switzerland wanted to opt out. When Heath asked if the Taoiseach thought that the Council of Ireland could have worked, Lynch replied that if there were an Economic Council first this might be of help in deciding the scope of the Council of Ireland. There was a lot of similarity between the economic problems North and South of the Border. Discussion of them could be valuable, particularly in the context of membership of the EEC. Unfortunately, the atmosphere for economic cooperation was not particularly good at this stage. When Heath asked whether it would be necessary for Britain to be involved in an Economic Council the Taoiseach said he doubted if this would be necessary.[21] This exchange represented the dying embers of the summit. At one level nothing substantial had been achieved. But, for the first time, both Premiers had a real idea of each other's position. The question was: could there be any bridge between the two sides? For the British the next stage was to try and elevate the discussion from a bilateral to a tripartite meeting so that, for the first time since 1925, the Premiers of Ireland, Northern Ireland and the United Kingdom could discuss and, perhaps, understand each other's positions better. The problem with this was trying to persuade Faulkner and Lynch that this was necessary.

THE TRIPARTITE SUMMIT

Two days later, on 9 September, Heath invited Lynch to a tripartite meeting with Faulkner.[22] But this was only half the problem – Faulkner needed to be convinced too. So, when Heath and Faulkner spoke, via telephone, on the morning of 10 September, the latter explained that 'any question of tripartite talks is a very very difficult thing for me'. His position had always been that he could not take part in any such talks until Lynch had done 'something' about the security situation. And, with every day that passed, this became more difficult: 'He released that wretched man Cahill last night,' said Faulkner. He feared a tripartite meeting meant bringing Lynch in on the internal administration in Northern Ireland; to this Heath replied: 'Well no more than it did in my talks... For us to discuss security in the South and urge him to intern is just as much a matter of dealing with his internal problems.' Faulkner accepted this; but he was finding his Cabinet colleagues 'very very difficult' about any questions at all on tripartite talks, and a message had come through to him that the Chairman and the Secretary of the Unionist Party would resign if he agreed to tripartite talks. Heath then warned: 'They will find themselves in an impossible position so far as the British public and the Forces are concerned if they are just not prepared to have three Prime Ministers discussing a crisis like this.' To allay Faulkner's concerns as to how the meetings could be 'sold', Heath pointed out that everyone knew the talks would include discussions on security since Lynch had talked about this in public and Faulkner had some responsibility for security alongside Westminster; therefore it would be quite natural for Faulkner to ask to join the talks. The bottom line was that British public opinion 'isn't going to have 17 battalions over there and just have people refusing to talk as to how to deal with the problem'.[23] Put as diplomatically as this, Faulkner had little option but to agree.

Lynch also accepted, on 11 September, 'on the basis that there are no preconditions'.[24] The British accepted that there would be no preconditions on anybody's part except that Heath had agreed with Faulkner that the constitutional issue – the status of Northern Ireland as a part of the United Kingdom and the related question of the Border – would not be for debate. But they accepted that this would not, of course, prevent Lynch from mentioning them if he wanted to.[25] Events moved fast – Heath got a message of Lynch's acceptance while visiting The Queen at Balmoral and contacted Faulkner while en route to Edinburgh. He got hold of Faulkner on an open line – 'I'm in a callbox I'm afraid' – which forced the two men to adopt a semi-confidential stance: Heath told Faulkner that 'the gentleman was accepting the invitation'. But soon Heath could not avoid being explicit in giving Faulkner the text of the official British response: 'The Taoiseach has accepted an invitation from the Prime Minister to meet him and the Prime Minister of Northern Ireland for discussions on matters of common interest.' Lynch's statement of acceptance stated that he had decided to 'accept without preconditions the invitation from the British Prime Minister to have another meeting with him soon at which Mr Brian Faulkner will also be present'. While it did not accord Faulkner recognition as the Prime Minister of Northern Ireland, Heath pointed out that the pre-condition that the Northern Opposition should be present was abandoned.[26]

Now, with all sides preparing for the summit, Sir Burke Trend reminded Heath of the stakes they were playing for: Hugh Fraser, a Tory backbencher, had come to see Trend at his own request, to give him his impressions after a visit to Northern Ireland during which he saw a good many people. Put pretty briefly, the main points which he wanted to make were that the Army were getting into an increasingly untenable position. The hostility of the Catholics was now so great that there were not merely Catholic 'no go' areas and Protestant 'no go' areas; there were also Army 'no go' areas, in which the Army were compelled to remain more or less permanently on the defensive in their own enclaves, with occasional sallies to deal with some local disturbance. Moreover, relations between the Army and the RUC were now very bad; and the RUC had practically withdrawn from the business of maintaining law and order in the worst areas. General Tuzo had been compelled to fall back on the expedient of sending troops out in police cars; this was a very ambiguous development in the role of the troops 'which we ought not to countenance'. Authority was now disintegrating rapidly at all levels and Faulkner's writ no longer really ran in a large part of the Province. On the other hand, pointed out Trend, there was no reason why Mr Faulkner should not survive politically for an indefinite time. There was no obvious means by which he could legitimately be overthrown. Hence the growth of 'rival' and unconstitutional bodies, for example the SDLP's 'Assembly of Northern Irish People' – a kind of Catholic Stormont. Hence, also, the idea of a Paisley–Catholic initiative, which Fraser urged the Government to take seriously. Like Cecil King, owner of the *Daily Mirror*, he believed Paisley to be a serious and practical politician, who would be prepared in certain circumstances to reach an accommodation with the Catholics – and even with Dublin – provided that Faulkner could be eliminated from the scene. Trend thought that 'we should keep at least an open mind about the possibility of a deal between Paisley and the Catholics; it is not impossible that, if we were faced with a situation in which we should otherwise have no alternative but to impose direct rule, a Paisley–Catholic deal might be preferable.' But, if Direct Rule did prove to be inevitable

> ... we must be ready for it. I have checked around Whitehall unofficially; and, so far as I can judge, the Departments mainly concerned are as prepared as one can be for a wholly unfamiliar and unpredictable situation. But this ought to be verified formally by the Home Secretary, whose responsibility it is. Moreover, the preparations for direct rule, as hitherto conceived, rest on an assumption that we should be able to continue to rely on the loyalty of the public services in Ulster and the RUC. But, if Paisley came out strongly with some alternative solution, this assumption might be falsified. We should then face a more difficult and even more dangerous situation; and I am not satisfied that our plans cater for this.[27]

Meanwhile, in Dublin, following his acceptance of Heath's invitation, External Affairs prepared their brief for Lynch. In sum it set out, in the clearest possible terms, the practical and ideological foundations of Dublin's Northern policy: for example, there were certain concepts that were central to the Irish understanding of the situation. These were:

...The Northern Ireland Government is not a sovereign Government.
...There is no refusal of the minority to be governed – they refuse to be governed under the present system.
...The Northern majority have a constitutional guarantee – but there are no constitutional guarantees for the minority.
...We are not in the business of protecting the unionist regime. That is neither our intention nor our interest.
...Why go on repeating a guarantee of the constitutional position of Northern Ireland? This depresses the minority, encourages the majority along a false track and makes policy...[in] the South very difficult.
...The Northern majority have a very small minority in UK terms and a 20% minority in Irish terms and cannot be allowed to dictate policy either in London or in Dublin.
...The North in fact is a dual State and should be organised accordingly.
...The British army are now seen to be shoring up the Unionist regime.
...The contact established between the Dublin Government and the Northern Parliamentary Opposition is designed to hold the moderate centers [sic] in the North. This can only be achieved if political options are opened up.
...The participation for the minority that we want is one which will tend to bring about Irish unity not one intended to maintain 'British unity'.[28]

On the ground, internment had shown the potency of the IRA. The IRA, as an active phenomenon, could not be defeated by the military forces at present in the North. It could only be beaten by anti-Unionist leaders who could separate the Catholic community from the IRA. In order to preserve and strengthen their position there must be immediate and radical changes in the North. Failure to face up to this would mean a continuation indefinitely of the IRA threat and all the consequences that might flow from that.[29] Based on evidence of '(a) lack of impartiality (b) appeasement of majority and (c) repression of minority' the mistakes which had led to the alienation on the minority could be summarized by the following:

1. Falls Road Curfew...a blunder of major proportions.
2. Semi-Promotion of John Taylor...at the sensitive Ministry of Home Affairs on resignation of Sir Robert Porter who commanded respect.
3. Premature replacement of Sir Arthur Young as head of the RUC [by the Ulster Protestant, Sir Graham Shillington]...
4. Half-hearted implementation of ban on parades against Orangemen in latter half of 1970.
5. Failure to administer the law impartially especially in cases resulting from riots...
6. Failure to carry out serious arms searches in Unionist areas.
7. Tolerating the legislation of reforms which were so watered down and distorted as to be acceptable to hardline Unionists.
8. Failure to take action in obvious cases of incitement to hatred.
9. The decision to permit the formation of gun clubs – some composed

wholly or in part of ex 'B Specials'.
10. Failure to withdraw the 102,000 licensed guns in the North...
11. Increased use of the Special Powers Acts including the making of new Orders thereunder notwithstanding the recommendations of Lord Hunt and the existence of a special committee to examine their repeal.
12. Resignation of Major Chichester-Clark and his replacement by Mr Brian Faulkner.
13. Composition of Mr Faulkner's Cabinet... and formation of New Security Unit...
14. Derry Shootings – failure to meet demands for official enquiry leading to withdrawal of Opposition from Stormont.
15. Lurgan meeting between Orange leaders and Faulkner plus half his Cabinet (It is believed that secret deal on parades was made).
16. Post-Lurgan policy on Orange parades – failure of British Government to act decisively and impartially, including failure to ban Apprentice Boys parade well in advance.
17. Large-scale secret rearming of RUC with pistols – a longstanding demand of the Unionist Right-Wing.
18. The failure of the British Government to effect a loosing of the Orange Order in the Stormont Government and Unionist Party.
19. The complete lack of consultation with Opposition MPs before the appointment of minority representatives on public bodies.
20. Brutality of British soldiers against minority.
21. Absurd terms of reference of Committee of enquiry into allegations of brutality against British Army in further alienation of the aggrieved.[30]

Given all this the centre-piece of Dublin's policy would be that the 'Unionist monopoly of power must disappear'. This implied a form of Government or administration which would enable considerable consensus to be reached across a central band of opinion from moderate Unionism to moderate non-Unionism. Secondly, the British Government 'should indicate publicly that it is in favour of Irish unity'. Thirdly, an All-Ireland Council should be set up which would work towards bringing the two parts of Ireland 'into harmony'. This Council might include an advisory role for the British Government but should, in principle, be bilateral as between Dublin and Belfast while perhaps bringing in London at the 'technical levels' when necessary.[31] As a first step, power, in regard to the administration of justice, should be transferred temporarily from Stormont to Westminster.[32] Among the options being considered was a central structure of Government for Northern Ireland that retained the present links with Britain,[33] maintained the Border but did not rule out links with Dublin. This was designed simply as a way of involving the non-Unionist population in the Government of Northern Ireland. Particular attention had been paid to constitutional structures such as the Netherlands, Belgium, Switzerland, Cyprus and Lebanon which had difficulties arising out of confessional, linguistic or ethnic divisions within the country. Taking the proposed new twenty-six district councils in the North as a useful base for the proposed structure, assuming a 60 per cent Unionist/40 per cent non-Unionist division of the population, and including a Bill of Rights, the proposals incorporated the following principles:

- the non-Unionist population must be given a fairly direct influence in the administration of sensitive services, especially police and related matters. Hence the transfer of these services to a local level;
- as many people as possible must be directly involved in conventional politics and... be able to aspire to offices of real power;
- no one body or individual should alone have a great deal of power.

In one option considered by Dublin the sharing of power among the twenty-six district councils would result in sixteen being controlled by Unionists and ten by non-Unionists. Each council would have a deliberative body and an executive arm. The deliberative body would have about fifty members elected on a PR basis. The executive arm could consist of four commissioners and would be answerable to the deliberative body. The councils would have considerable delegated power, especially in the sensitive areas such as the administration of law and order, housing, education and social services, each one in charge of a commissioner. Stormont would remain bi-cameral but each council would elect one senator so that the Senate would consist of sixteen Unionists and ten non-Unionists. The Senate would have the power to block legislation on basic issues. This would be achieved by requiring a two-thirds majority for legislation on such issues. The lower house would be directly elected but on a PR basis and with new electoral boundaries so as to ensure a fair distribution of about seventy-five seats. A Cabinet would be directly elected by MPs and Senators acting jointly and elections would be such that the Cabinet would reflect the pattern of representation prevailing in Parliament. This could be done by having each party caucus elect Cabinet members in proportion to their strength in Parliament. The constitution should lay down the allocation of posts to ensure a fair distribution and rotation of power: for example, in one Cabinet the Prime Minister might be Unionist and the Minister for Home Affairs non-Unionist; next time around the Prime Minister might be non-Unionist and the Minister for Home Affairs Unionist.[34]

A second option was 'Community Government' based upon a proposal formulated by the NILP. As a temporary measure the Northern Ireland Senate could be exchanged for fifteen appointed Government nominees some of whom would become Cabinet representatives of Unionist and non-Unionist opinion. Stormont would be prorogued for six months, and a commission would be set up to recommend the optimum size of the Parliament under the most suitable PR system. The problem with this model, for the Irish, was that it did not guarantee an effective long-term role in Government for non-Unionists and it could lead to a situation where non-Unionists would be placated with two or three minor Cabinet posts. Similarly, the reform of Stormont along the lines of Faulkner's committee proposals would 'hardly result in any significant transfer of power to non-Unionists since the Cabinet would still be Unionist and parliament would continue to have a Unionist majority'. The introduction of PR was also unlikely to lead to any change in the existing proportion of Unionist/non-Unionist representation. Even the Irish Government's current policy of calling for Stormont's suspension and replacing it with a Commission responsible to the British Government through its Northern Ireland representative was 'attractive as an immediate solution but because of its non-democratic nature, it cannot be envisaged as a long-term solution'. The problem with the integration of Northern Ireland into the United Kingdom was that it 'would probably make even more remote the prospect of reunification'. The setting up of a Condominium, under which Northern Ireland would be controlled jointly by Dublin and London, through a mixed Dublin/London commission was 'an attractive idea but is presumably total[ly] unacceptable to the British'. Its main attraction was that it would set up a powerful body to which Unionists and non-Unionists could give allegiance. Finally there could be an implementation of the principles contained in the Government of Ireland Act regarding a Council of Ireland. This envisaged a gradual transfer of power to the Council of Ireland 'and an ultimate reunification'. Presumably this option was also totally unacceptable to the British.[35]

A different approach might be to recognize the Alternative Assembly, set up by the SDLP, as the anti-Unionist representative body and the Unionist Party as the Unionist representative body. There would be two separate electoral lists, one Unionist and one non-Unionist. These lists would be based on political and not geographic divisions and when registering a person would have to opt for either the Unionist or non-Unionist list. The Assemblies would create a joint executive either with 50/50 or 60/40 representation or representation as indicated by the electoral registers. The executive might be constituted on the cantonal model. While in the short run this might tend to perpetuate the community divisions, in the long-term it might create a situation whereby, through working together, each community gradually began to respect the other. The major advantage of this proposal for the Irish Government was that it accorded with its recognition of the Alternative Assembly. If there were to be re-partition, from the Irish view, incorporating as much non-Unionist territory as possible under Dublin's control, this would confine further violence and agitation to a smaller area but, in the immediate future, would do little to improve the lot of the non-Unionists in Belfast. However, in the long run, the Unionists, being in an 80 per cent majority would have nothing to fear or lose by treating the small non-Unionist population on a fair basis. If the country were to be reunited this might be on the basis of a re-entry into the Commonwealth. The reunification might be on a federal basis and the advantage of this proposal might be to make reunification palatable to the Unionists. Alternatively, both parts of Ireland could be federated with England, Scotland and Wales and form a 'Federation of the British Isles' with Parliaments in London, Edinburgh, Belfast, Dublin and Cardiff and a central parliament in an agreed location. Finally, Dublin could 'recognise the *colonial status* of the NI Unionists' and aim at a long-term solution which would envisage their withdrawal from Northern Ireland. This 'is not in accord with our view which is aimed at persuading the Unionists to recognise the necessity of their integrating with earlier migrations'.[36]

As for the threat of a 'Protestant Backlash', this had been used for many generations; but no authority had ever challenged the theory of the backlash. It was in the interest of any Unionist Government to nurture and maintain such a threat: 'Our thesis is that whether the backlash is real or imaginery [sic] it must be confronted.' Policy must first be decided and then arrangements to take care of the backlash would be made. To begin to seek a policy on the basis of fear of the threat of a backlash 'meant that no policy can be found'.[37] Finally, the Irish believed, and had put it to the British, that the political control of the British Army seemed to reside too much in the MOD and received little, if any influence, from the FCO and Home Office. Nothing appeared to have been done about this. The Irish were aware that Tuzo had opposed internment but believed that Carrington had come down in favour of it while Maudling and Douglas-Home did not appear to have had much influence. From this 'It could even be argued that the Military officers themselves had better political intelligence than the political chiefs of the Ministry of Defence.'[38]

The scene was now set for the meeting of three Premiers from the British Isles. It was the first time that the British, Northern Irish and Irish Premiers had met together since Ramsey MacDonald, Sir James Craig and W.T. Cosgrave had done so in 1925. The venue was, once again, Chequers. At noon, on Monday 27 September 1971, after Heath had extended a warm welcome to Lynch and Faulkner, the three Prime Ministers got down to business. No punches were pulled. Lynch began by emphasizing that the IRA was no more than a by-product of the situation in the North; and it was that situation which was at the root of the trouble. The settlement which had been imposed on Ireland fifty years before had progressively polarized the two communities; and the belated reforms which were now under discussion merely showed how unfairly one of those communities had hitherto been treated. The Government in Dublin still believed that all the people of Ireland should live under one Government. The Administration in the North had clearly broken down; the two communities there were further apart than ever before; and a movement which had started as a genuine civil rights campaign had been progressively taken over by the IRA. These developments had culminated in the major error of internment. This had proved a feasible measure in the South years before; but, if the Dublin Government tried to implement it again in present circumstances, the result would be disastrous. In short, said Lynch, the whole system of Stormont must be changed; and the minority must be allowed to participate in decision-making as of right. But the representatives of the minority had now withdrawn from Stormont; and they were determined not to return until their conditions were satisfied. In these circumstances he asked: 'How could we find for them some acceptable basis for resuming contact and discussing the possibilities of constitutional change?' The great obstacle was internment, since the minority insisted on 'release or trial'. He had done his best to establish the minority spokesmen as genuine representatives of their communities; otherwise, this role would be taken over by the IRA. Military methods, even if they were effective in the short term, could not provide any longer-term solution. What was needed for that was a political solution and one which would be acceptable to the minority. Lynch himself was under some political pressure. Even by undertaking to meet Mr Faulkner he was thought to have gone too far in acquiescing in the existence of Stormont. But continuing violence created so terrible a prospect in human terms and so grave a threat to political stability that he felt that he must do anything he could to ease the tension. But for this there must be some change at Stormont. He was not the minority's spokesman. On the other hand they had told him that they were not prepared to enter constitutional discussions until the problem of internment had been cleared out of the way. This was corroborated by reports which reached him from quite independent sources.

Faulkner replied by saying that he was wholly at one with Lynch in condemning violence, in wishing to promote cooperation between the North and the South on social and economic issues and in accepting that there was a genuine need for reform at Stormont. Where he differed was, of course, on the fundamental issue of the constitutional link between Northern Ireland and Great Britain. Since the original settlement fifty years before there had been only two major outbreaks of violence – the first in the years 1956–60 which had been brought to an end when internment was introduced in the South (and the same would be true if the same action could be taken now); the second in the period starting in 1969. The fact that there had been only these two periods of disorder in fifty years showed that the minority were not in fact badly disposed towards the Stormont system. Nor was it true to say that it was internment which had provoked the Opposition's walk-out from Stormont. That had taken place earlier, on the basis of a single incident involving a complaint about the attitude of the Army; and at that point the Opposition had already extended a cautious welcome to his promise of further reforms. He had no doubt that, if only violence could be brought to an end, the minority would be willing to cooperate once again. Moreover, the scope for their cooperation would be greater than ever, since it was certain that when the next local government elections took place in the following year a good many local authorities would pass from Unionist to Nationalist control. The introduction of the points system for housing and of the two Commissioners for Complaints had been genuine and significant reforms in themselves; but it was the change in local government which would provide the really conclusive demonstration of the greater opportunities for participation which would henceforward be open to the minority. It followed that the first priority must be to restore law and order. In the light of the escalation of violence, internment had been inevitable. Moreover, it was unreasonable on the part of the minority to want to bargain an end of internment against their participation at Stormont. They could have participated before internment if they had wanted to; and did they want the gunmen loose on the streets once again? The Northern Ireland Government believed very firmly that internment had been right and that it was being effective in curbing the activities of the IRA. The first step must be to get the security situation in firm control. Only then could constitutional progress be resumed. But, if Lynch really felt unable to cooperate as regards internment, were there any other security measures which he could agree to take jointly with the British and Northern Ireland Governments?

Lynch took Faulkner's point that the minority could have participated before internment if they had wanted to. He did not contest this argument. But the fact remained that the minority were now saying that they could not break with the IRA unless internment were ended. If Faulkner was asking him to consider internment in the South, this would not be legally possible in present circumstances. The derogation under the European Convention of Human Rights permitted internment only in circumstances of war or of some grave threat to the nation's life; but neither was the case at present. Moreover, the trouble originated in the North, not in the South; and there was no case on merits for internment in the South. For the rest, the Government of the Republic had done what they could with their limited resources to reinforce security – for example, by instituting court proceedings against individuals who promoted street collections in support of the IRA or indulged in illegal arms traffic. As regarded the alleged IRA training camps, these were now on a minimal scale; and such of them as existed had no great difficulty in concealing themselves effectively. But he must come back to his main point – namely that, even if the Government of the Republic introduced internment, the violence would continue because it started in the North, not in the South. Even the skirmishes on the Border drew very little support from the South. In short there was nothing that he could really do in terms of security; his action must be confined to the political field.[39]

With regard to that political field, Lynch wanted to know whether it would be possible for a member of the SDLP to be appointed to the Cabinet. Faulkner was clear on this point: he did not see how members of the SDLP could become members of the Cabinet because they differed so fundamentally from members of the existing Government on the constitutional position. Lynch doubted if Faulkner's proposals would be of interest to the SDLP without some form of participation in the Government: they would suspect the proposals as coming from the same old Unionist Government. Faulkner reminded him that the SDLP had always said that they would not serve with the Unionist Party in a Northern Ireland Government. Lynch, however, thought that, if given a chance, they would join such a Government. But Faulkner could not see how they could join a Government of Northern Ireland if they were committed to a thirty-two-county Republic, although he thought that in taking that line they did not represent a majority of the Catholic community in Northern Ireland. Nevertheless, his proposals for enlarging the Senate should give Catholics a chance of coming into the Government, provided that they accepted the Union with Great Britain. It would, of course, remain open to a 'Republican' to become one of the Chairmen of the Parliamentary Committees. Lynch suggested that this would not satisfy the SDLP since these Committees would have only the right to make recommendations, which the Government would remain free to reject. To this Faulkner merely remarked that in the end the Government must govern. But the new Committees would be very strong bodies, with powers to propose policy changes; and it would not be a light matter for the Government to reject their proposals. Lynch, however, was clear: there ought to be minority representation in Cabinet. How else could the minority be assured of 'permanent and guaranteed participation in the life and public affairs' of Northern Ireland? To this Faulkner reminded Lynch that the minority would have 50 per cent of the Chairmen of the Parliamentary Committees, together with guaranteed places on public Boards such as the Housing Executive.

Heath, having left most of the talking to the two Irishmen, then intervened to ask whether there were any other strands of opinion in Northern Ireland, apart from Unionists and non-Unionist Republicans; Lynch thought that most of those who were not Unionists would favour a united Irish Republic. Heath probed some more: apart from the sectarian split there must surely be people who, while in principle favouring a united Ireland, would say that so long as the majority preferred to remain in the United Kingdom they were prepared to work the system. That was a different position from those who believed in a united Ireland and were not prepared to work the existing system even though a majority still favoured the Union. He did not see how people of the latter kind could participate in Government in Northern Ireland. Heath pointed out that when a National Government was formed at Westminster in 1931 it had disintegrated shortly after its component parts had been forced to disclose that they had 'agreed to disagree'. Commenting, Faulkner explained that he was prepared to have Catholics in his administration but he thought that it would be very difficult as a matter of practical politics to include anyone whose avowed objective was to do away with the system; he also recalled that in a poll taken in 1968, 75 per cent of the Catholic community had opted for remaining in the United Kingdom. But Lynch countered that his impression remained that the SDLP would not settle for less than they had said. On the basis of the discussions so far he could not hold out to them much prospect of their getting the terms which they wanted on internment. As to the reform proposals, they would see in them the perpetuation of the Unionist regime. They would not look favourably on the proposal that additional members of the Senate should be nominated by the Government; and they would want proportional representation in the Cabinet as of right. Faulkner replied that this was impossible; it would mean representation in the Cabinet for all kinds of minority groups, including the extreme right wing. Lynch, however, thought that these matters were all negotiable – provided that the SDLP could be persuaded to discuss them at all. At this point Heath said that what was important was that the outcome of the Home Secretary's discussions should be reasonable and sensible and should be seen to be so. No Opposition ever got all that it asked for. Lynch then asked whether it was not possible to devise some system whereby the main political groups would have the main portfolios and other groups a few for themselves; but Faulkner reiterated that in his view proportional representation in the Cabinet was unworkable. At this point the meeting adjourned for the evening[40] and effectively ended the in-depth tripartite discussions.

The following morning discussions began with a bilateral meeting between Heath and Lynch. The Prime Minister started with a warning that neither the British Government nor the British Parliament could accept SDLP dictation on the issues at stake; and, if the SDLP were seeking to insist that internment must be brought to an end as a prior condition of their taking part in the Home

Secretary's discussions, then this was not acceptable. The crux of the problem was to get the Opposition back to sharing in the Government of the country. It was not true that Stormont was no more than a regional administration. It was a duly constituted Government, with defined statutory powers; and the people who regarded it as no more than a county council should remember that even a county council had to have a due sense of collective responsibility. The truth was – and this was the essence of the matter – that some people thought that Northern Ireland should simply not exist as a separate country at all. But, even if Faulkner were prepared to accept people holding such views in his Government, Gerry Fitt had already said publicly that he would not enter that Government unless it were accepted that he was there as of right. But how could you have a compulsory coalition? How could you have a system in which people said that they would not accept an invitation from the Prime Minister to serve in his Government but insisted on being there as of right, regardless of their compatibility with the rest of the Government? It was enough to ask these questions to be convinced that the method of discussion which the Home Secretary had proposed offered the only real hope of progress.

Lynch replied that in that case the minority leaders simply would not come to these discussions. And this was not just a matter of the SDLP's own attitude – they had the support of the great bulk of minority opinion. There could be no progress until this stumbling block had been removed. He did not deny that it was quite reasonable for Faulkner to put forward his proposals and equally reasonable for the Home Secretary to try to promote discussion of them. But, if the terms of reference for that discussion were not acceptable, the minority would become steadily more intransigent; and, if the time came when Faulkner positively wanted to talk, he might find that he would have to talk to the IRA. As he had told the Prime Minister on an earlier occasion, his sources of intelligence about the state of affairs in Northern Ireland were usually reliable; and, although he could not claim to speak for the SDLP, he was confident that he knew their mind, particularly on the subject of internment. Somehow or other, means must be found to end the alienation of some half a million people in the North. Lynch had made no public comment at the time on the withdrawal of the SDLP from Stormont. But he had been alarmed by it and had done his best to ensure that they were not so wholly alienated as to fall under the control of the IRA. He feared that the Protestants in the North now foresaw their position of power being slowly eroded and were preparing to react accordingly. If they suspected that the minority were falling finally under the control of the IRA – as might, indeed, become inevitable if their elected representatives were seen to be helpless – the risk of a Protestant backlash would be very real. Heath answered that the great majority of people in Northern Ireland were thoroughly sick of the whole business; all they wanted was that both communities should work together in the Government. The people in Belfast had so far shown commendable restraint. But he warned that if the conditions in Belfast were repeated in, for example, Birmingham, there could be little doubt what would happen. People would look to their own protection and vigilante bands would spring up overnight. Remembering the B Specials, the British Government could not permit this sort of thing in Northern Ireland. But there was a risk that it might happen, and, if so, it would merely widen the breach still further. That was why the British Government were insisting that the Army must remain firmly in control of security measures. But it was not easy to sustain this position.[41] This exchange effectively ended the summit. Faulkner joined the discussion soon afterwards but little of substance was added. The meeting ended at about 3.30 p.m. on 28 September; Lynch left Chequers shortly thereafter.[42]

After the Taoiseach had left, Heath and Faulkner were joined by Maudling for a brief, final, exchange of views. Faulkner commented that, as he saw the situation, the SDLP were seeking to play Lynch off against his Opposition, Fine Gael. Heath felt that there must be another meeting, very soon, between British and Northern Ireland Ministers to try to get to closer grips with the whole problem. Internment was now a front-line issue at Westminster. Maudling asked whether it was clear what Lynch's terms for helping them really were; Faulkner thought the terms were quite clear – the end of internment and something which would bring the Opposition back to Stormont. But Heath wondered whether Lynch was in fact thinking in quite such specific terms or was determined to bargain quite so rigidly. He judged that Lynch was very well aware of the danger to himself if the IRA took over. Faulkner suspected that the SDLP were more basically Republican in their sympathies and objectives 'than they would like us to believe... If we met them on an end of internment, they would simply ask for something else. What they really wanted was the end of Stormont.'[43] On the last point Faulkner was right.

AFTERMATH

Heath's suggested follow-up meeting with Faulkner took place at Downing Street on 7 October. Now it was the latter's turn to feel the pressure that was Heath's negotiating style when he was frustrated. Faulkner was told by Heath that both Governments could no longer risk giving the impression of being borne along by events; the situation was now grave socially, economically and politically, and the British public was losing patience. The Westminster Government could not continue to support Stormont unless public opinion at home was behind it. Furthermore, the UK Government's policies in other fields were being jeopardized. The situation was thus one of danger for both Governments. Faulkner remained calm. He argued that confidence, both in the Province and in Great Britain, might be restored if there were clear signs that both Governments were working towards a realistic political settlement that reasonably satisfied the desire of the minority to have their interests represented. Maudling wanted to know how far was Faulkner prepared to go in broadening the base of his own Ministry to include minority representatives? Many responsible members of the minority would tend largely to dismiss proposals not accompanied by some indication of willingness to move on this central issue. But Faulkner remained emphatic that he could not contemplate leading or serving in a Government of Northern Ireland which included Republicans, whether or not they eschewed the use of violence in bringing about a unified Ireland. Nor would he serve in a Ministry composed according to proportional principles. In neither case could a workable Government be formed since its component parts would be too disparate. If the British Government had it in mind to propose the inclusion of the Republicans – that is, the SDLP – in the Government he would have to tell his colleagues forthwith and they would 'act accordingly'. For now this was Faulkner's strongest card.

On the other hand, he pointed out that there were prominent Catholics who took a 'constitutionalist view'. He hoped that discussion of his forthcoming Green Paper proposals, in the Home Secretary's talks, might give an opportunity to air a proposal for a Minority Council composed of representatives of interest groups (for example, trade Unionists, and professional and business organizations) from the Catholic community, whose Chairman might have a seat in the Cabinet. This would provide the permanent and guaranteed share in Government which he had promised the minority. There were Catholics – many of them still serving on statutory boards – who would be suitable, but none of them came from among the present elected representatives. Faulkner believed that, provided the security situation were improved, Catholic support could be obtained for a political solution on these lines. Heath did not hide his disappointment: he, and Maudling, had hoped that Faulkner would be prepared to consider broadening his Government to include Republicans who had undertaken for the period of the emergency to forswear any active political campaigning for a united Ireland – but Faulkner was unwilling to meet the emergency by seeking to form a Government which was neutral on the matter of reunification. They did, at least, attach value to Faulkner's proposed appointment of a Cabinet Minister or Ministers who would be widely regarded as representative of responsible minority opinion.[44]

This was an interesting meeting. On his return to Northern Ireland, Faulkner described the meeting as 'one of the most satisfactory meetings with the British Government that I have ever had'. There was complete unanimity of purpose on the Northern Ireland situation, he said.[45] He was wrong and had missed its significance. For the first time the Conservative Government had actually advocated a departure from simple majority rule: in every other meeting Heath had backed the established formula. Now he had partially taken on board the concerns expressed by Lynch in their summits. The logic of where this might be leading appears to have been lost on Faulkner. The basic fact was that Stormont's survival rested upon the passive alienation of the Catholic minority. When that alienation was accentuated and demonstrated in a violent manner the lack of consent from about a third of the population meant trouble for the system. Terminal trouble – although the death was a long-drawn-out affair. As long as the violence persisted the SDLP had a very strong negotiating position – although they might abhor the violence itself.

The dominant figure within the party was John Hume. And the Irish Government, as Eamonn Gallagher expressly did from within External Affairs, recognized that Hume had emerged as the 'real leader of the non-Unionists in the North'. Initially Gallagher believed that the Alternative Assembly would be a forum for the minority for formulating and publicizing their demands: the 'duality of the North would be emphasised in physical terms. The British would have to face up to the realities of their intervention in 1969. The obduracy of the Northern Protestants may have been increased in the short-term but' – and here Gallagher used a phrase to be associated with Hume in the distant future – 'the boil had to be lanced sooner or later.'[46] The 'boil', of course, was the Unionist one. An 'informal direction' was given by the Irish Government for its Inter-Departmental Unit on the North of Ireland to prepare a draft structure, standing orders and so on for the Alternative Assembly.[47] In the end the Alternative Assembly proved to be a false dawn – meeting only once in Dungannon. But it illustrated Dublin's commitment to the end of Stormont in its present form. To find out the latest thinking among the Northern Opposition, Gallagher went north on 29 October, returning on 2 November. There he met with Fitt, Devlin, Currie, Hume, Oliver Napier of the Alliance Party and James Doherty of the Nationalist Party. Gallagher found that the SDLP still would not talk until internment ended. This was not so much intransigence but 'is a considered view on their part that the effect of internment accompanied by torture and brutality, British Army behaviour etc ... is such that they would lose their influence altogether if they agreed to talks while internment lasts' – the only member of the SDLP who did think the IRA could be beaten was Devlin. Everyone believed that Faulkner would not survive beyond the end of the year. Gallagher reported: 'There seems to be a growing, but not precisely stated, feeling that the question of Irish unity is now a live issue and that no solution can be found that does not take it into account.' He also found that 'Moderate leaders have given up trying to influence anybody so far as I can judge and even the most pacific of them have now begun to say that they have a vested interest in the continuance of violence as long as Stormont exists.'[48]

Fitt and Hume met again with Gallagher on 15 November. Fitt told Gallagher that the suspension of Stormont would create a new political situation, hinting at a readiness to engage in a conference even if internment did not go in the immediate aftermath. Hume took the view that getting rid of Stormont was the main policy objective at present and that internment was an issue which could bring this about. On the whole, therefore, Gallagher had detected a gradual shift in SDLP policy towards bringing down Stormont as a preliminary to anything else.[49] But, gradually, another issue was increasingly surfacing: Irish unity. In September, Hume had urged Lynch to ask just what the objections to reunification were; he wanted to know this for the following reasons:

(1) to enable an offensive position to be adopted by ourselves [the Irish Government] and by the Northern opposition;
(2) to get the objections on the record; and
(3) to have the objections listed so that remedies could be put forward to deal with them by ourselves and by the Northern opposition.[50]

Irish unity, not reform within the United Kingdom, was now the objective: in October, Hume had disclosed to Gallagher that, at an SDLP meeting the previous week, the party agreed on their objective at a future conference: 'Quite simply it is to bring about Irish unity. I asked him [Hume] to consider his tactics on this – for example it might be preferable to let the conference continue for a time to talk about radical reform structures on the North plus a connection with Dublin, and when, as is reasonably certain, the Unionist conferees prove intransigent about this the ultimate question could be thrown in.'[51]

One of the principal aims of the Irish Government, from 1969 onwards, was to encourage emerging Northern Opposition groups to make unity one of their policy objectives. This was now coming to fruition with the SDLP. Despite what Lynch might say during talks about the primary aim being the ending of violence, whenever the prospect of unity was seen on the horizon – however far away – the Irish were intoxicated by its siren call. So, when Harold Wilson floated the possibility of a united Ireland within the Commonwealth, over a 15-year period, Gallagher was keen to exploit any openings that might push the British towards Irish unity by breaking the bi-partisan approach to the North at Westminster. Principally, he thought, this would serve notice on Unionism that a new order of things would be enforced on them sooner or later by a British Labour Government; but, whether it could force Heath's hand and change policy now was problematic. As he pointed out in a note for Lynch, Heath's reputation for loathing any Wilson proposals or 'gimmickry' was formidable and he might react by increasing military and other pressures on the minority while endorsing Faulkner's ideas on superficial reform. There was also the argument that, in the face of a return to power of a Labour Party with radically different policies, the Unionists might throw caution to the winds and prepare for the long awaited backlash. Nevertheless it was unlikely that Heath could maintain a 'do nothing' policy much longer. He was hardly likely to be so foolish as to yield to this but did not seem to realize that he was being inexorably driven into a situation where he was merely becoming Faulkner's tool. The other factor might be that Heath, Maudling and Carrington thought that they could 'take out the IRA' and 'free' the minority from IRA influences. Gallagher believed that only when Unionism was reduced to being an equal partner with the minority would it become realistic about its position. The question of Irish unity could not be evaded either. The minority's leaders 'cannot enter an administration designed to maintain the division of Ireland in perpetuity. Consequently in settling the terms of a future bi-polar administration of the North we must also open the door to Irish unity.' If a Council of Ireland were to be revived now,

> it must be done in a manner agreed essentially between the Dublin and London Governments. Its functions should be to harmonise economic, social, cultural, and all other matters between North and South that may have grown apart since 1921. These are its functions. Its objective, however – whether stated or not – must be to prepare for the transfer of sovereignty in the North from London to an all-Ireland Parliament in progressive steps.

In Gallagher's view the steps to be taken to bring this about should be as follows:

1. that Stormont should now be suspended;
2. that internment without trial should end;
3. that a new form of interim administration be created for the North principally by equal consideration between Unionist and non-Unionist leaders but with London and Dublin both involved;
4. that a Council of Ireland be created between the Irish Government and the new Stormont administration which has specific functions and an understood objective;
5. that the economic and similar disparities between North and South should be negotiated simultaneously with the working out of the Council of Ireland; and
6. that there be negotiation of Unionist demands in the context of an independent Irish state.'[52]

For constitutional Nationalists, North and South, unity was definitely back on the agenda; in contrast, the British were concerned with practicalities: for example, an option that was rapidly gaining favour – particularly among the military – was a complete takeover of security by Westminster. On 22 December, Sir Michael Carver told Lord Carrington: 'We should aim at some positive political initiative about February when he judged that the security situation would be just right for it.' There would only be a short time available for such a move before any hardening of attitudes or backlash set in. It seemed to Carver that this initiative should have three parts. First, the transfer of responsibility for law and order to Westminster 'whether we liked the idea or not'. Secondly, transferring all those areas of Governmental activity which were subject to inter-sectarian strife, for example education and housing, to public boards. Thirdly, to inquire into and reorganize representation at Stormont. Such proposals might be put forward in the context of the Home Secretary's inter-party talks. Meanwhile the Army should continue its operations aimed at reducing local support for the IRA and isolating them from the community, as had been achieved recently in the Ballymacarrett area of Belfast. Carver did not see any need to 'up rate Army activity from its current level, although it was a moot point whether, if we expected the Protestant backlash to any proposals which were put forward, we ought to reinforce the garrison before carrying them out.'[53] Eyebrows might be raised at the extent to which a Chief of the General Staff was offering opinions in matters far beyond security – but Carver was a cut above the average British general. Nevertheless it also reflected the route that British policy, in general, was heading down.

The key point here is that Irish and British policy were divergent: the British were looking for an initiative that would ease the polarization between both communities; so were the Irish – except they had another agenda as well: unity and the creation of institutions that could deliver it. As far as the British were concerned both Dublin and London had the same, more moderate, goal. And they were encouraged along this path by the contacts they had with the Irish. On 10 December, Trend suggested Heath glance through a letter that Sir Andrew Gilchrist had sent him at the end of November – 'As you probably know, he rather fell in love with Eire when he was our Ambassador in Dublin; and even though he has now retired and is promoting developments in the Highlands and Islands of Scotland, he is still faithful to his earlier passion and inflicts reflections on me from time to time.'[54] On 17 November, Gilchrist and his wife had 'refused an invitation to dine at the Irish Embassy (poor Donal O'Sullivan says he gets a very high proportion of refusals nowadays); but the dinner was cancelled and we agreed to go round for a quiet drink.' In brief, the 'deal' as suggested by O'Sullivan would be:

> (a) some (public) light at the end of the tunnel for the Republic. This would point not so much to a unified Ireland which they are scared to death of – but towards their entitlement to have some say in considering the future of the North; (b) a constitutional change in Northern Ireland by which the minority would have a fair share in the management of affairs; (c) the internment of the IRA by the Dublin Government.

Naturally Gilchrist asked whether the Irish Government was in a position to deliver (c). On this the Ambassador was 'most emphatic'. Lynch was known to be willing, and Hillery, 'who was in many ways an awkward customer', had specifically said to O'Sullivan: 'We would certainly do it – I would be for it.'

But any move could come *only* as part of a deal: no Irish Government in the present climate of opinion would dare to move significantly against the IRA without something which would really enable them to sway the Irish public in favour of a peaceful solution, and into acceptance of the measures needed to secure peace. That was the main point, and indeed O'Sullivan came back several times to the possibility of internment in the South. The Ambassador repeatedly pressed Gilchrist on whether some new political initiative by the British Government might be expected soon. 'I professed total ignorance (and very genuinely).' O'Sullivan's anxiety for an early British initiative seemed to arise from fears over the position of Lynch. He contested with 'earnest emotion' Gilchrist's suggestion that whoever succeeded Lynch would unavoidably and very speedily learn to follow – no worse than – a Lynch policy. The probable successor at present, O'Sullivan said, was Hillery – possibly a Hillery/Haughey partnership – which would be

> a reckless combination and cause us infinite trouble. An election with a victory for the Opposition would be a disaster: even if they were to be regarded as worthy, they were incompetent and could not possibly cope with the IRA the way Lynch could. (I suppose one could translate this by saying that Fianna Fáil are closer to the IRA than Fine Gael and the Irish Labour Party; which is true.)[55]

This was quite extraordinary loose talk from the Ambassador and one is left wondering what the catalyst for such opinions were: personal frustration; an unorthodox but authorized approach knowing where the comments might end up; or just an exceedingly good dinner. But it reflected the sense of anxiety in

Dublin's circles about the situation in the North and was coupled with the new suggestion that Dublin should have some say in the North's affairs. Thus, when Sir John Peck received a sudden summons to see Lynch, on 7 January 1972, the Taoiseach expressed his concern that there seemed to be no political moves concerning the North at all. He had hoped that there would be some sense of urgency in getting inter-party talks started. Against this static background Lynch was worried about the high unemployment figures in Ireland, which were going to get worse: 'The Devil found mischief for idle hands to do, the trade unions insisted on "last in, first out" and there would be a lot of idle young men on the streets for the IRA to exploit.' Lynch was also worried about stories circulating concerning the proposed internment of women – 'There were some bad ones but he was afraid that Irish traditions and attitudes being what they were we should turn the whole island against us [the British] if we interned them.'[56]

From the British perspective the key problem remained the SDLP's refusal to participate in inter-party talks unless the British Government stated that they were prepared to end internment. But, as Trend – now a lot less gloomy than in the immediate aftermath of internment – told Heath: 'This is not necessarily an unsatisfactory position for the Government, at least in the short term, since public opinion is not likely to agree that the Government should let loose a lot of gunmen and terrorists in return for no more than a promise merely to take part in inter-Party talks without any assurance that they will have a successful outcome.' And, provided internment itself was properly managed and the Army seemed to be continuing to gain the upper hand over the IRA, the Government could probably afford to rest in this position at least for the time being; but Trend also warned 'it is not a long-term policy' and sooner or later the Government would be driven to try and devise some new political initiative which offered better prospects of success than inter-party talks as presently envisaged. 'Here we confront the old dilemma – should any new initiative be based on the fundamental premises that the Border remains intact and that the Stormont system continues; or should it envisage some basic modification on these assumptions?' Trend recommended that the Government should concentrate on trying to convince Catholics that 'when the IRA are finally worsted – but not until then – reforms will be effected.' He saw merit in the proposal contained in a GEN 47 memorandum – Constitutional Devices to Protect the Minority – suggesting legislation at Westminster guaranteeing to the Catholic minority an undefined 'reasonable' share in representation not only in the Parliament but in the Government of Northern Ireland, and incorporating blocking devices to prevent its purposes being frustrated by the Protestant majority. It was possible to conceive of such legislation being further strengthened by provisions safeguarding the minority against 'administrative' discrimination, for example by prescribing that a certain number of posts on public authorities must be filled by Catholics and could not be filled by Protestants.[57] Gradually the British had moved away from their commitment to preserving majority rule at Stormont. A range of options were now discussed and on the table. Yet there was, as yet, no immediate catalyst to force the British to move. This would soon change.

Notes

1. NAUK PRO FCO 33/1464 UKREP to Home Office, 17 August 1971.
2. NAUK PRO CAB 164/879 Memorandum, n.d.
3. NAUK PRO PREM 15/479 Dublin Telegram to London, 19 August 1971.
4. NAUK PRO PREM 15/479 Prime Minister's Personal Message No.T196/71.
5. *Irish Times*, 21 August 1971.
6. NAUK PRO CAB 164/879 Note of a Meeting held at Chequers on 19 August 1971.
7. PRONI CAB/9R/238 Text of Announcement Agreed Between the UK and NI Governments.
8. PRONI CAB 4/1613/15 Cabinet Conclusions, 2 September 1971.
9. NAUK FCO 33/1608 Telegram Number 384 of 8 September to UKRep Belfast.
10. NAUK FCO 33/1608 Prime Minister from Christopher Roberts: Peck Telegram, 8 September 1971.
11. NAUK FCO 33/1608 Roberts to Armstrong, 8 September 1971.
12. NAUK FCO 33/1608 Telegram Number 393 of 9 September 1971 and to UK REP Belfast.
13. NAUK FCO 33/1608 FCO Telegram No.396 of 11 September 1971 and to UK REP Belfast.
14. NAUK FCO 33/1608 Prime Minister from Peter Gregson: UK REP Belfast Telegram No.1 of 15 September 1971 to Dublin Embassy.
15. NAUK FCO 33/1608 UK REP Belfast Telegram No.15 to FCO of 10 September 1971.
16. NAUK FCO 33/1608 Prime Minister from Peter Gregson: UK REP Belfast Telegram No.1 of 15 September 1971 to Dublin Embassy.
17. NAUK PRO FCO 33/1465 24 August 1971.
18. NAUK PRO PREM 15/486 Trend Note to Prime Minister, 3 September 1971.
19. NAUK PRO PREM 15/486 Trend to Prime Minister, Mr. Lynch's Visit, 3 September 1971.
20. NAUK PRO PREM 15/486 Telegram from Peck, 28 August 1971.
21. NAI DFA/2003/13/6 Report of discussions on 6th and 7th September 1971 at Chequers between the Taoiseach and the British Prime Minister.
22. NAUK PRO PREM 15/486 Prime Minister's personal message serial no t215/71, text of message from Mr Lynch to the Prime Minister, 11 September 1971.
23. NAUK PRO PREM 15/486 Text of a telephone conversation between Mr Faulkner and the Prime Minister at 10.05 a.m. on 10 September 1971.
24. NAUK PRO PREM 15/486 Prime Minister's personal message serial no t215/71, text of message from Mr Lynch to the Prime Minister, 11 September 1971.
25. NAUK PRO PREM 15/486 Trend to Prime Minister, 14 September 1971.
26. NAUK PRO PREM 15/486 Prime Minister's personal message serial no T214/71 telephone conversation between the Prime Minister and Mr. Faulkner on Saturday 11 September at 6.00 p.m.
27. NAUK PRO PREM 15/486 Trend to Prime Minister, Northern Ireland, 20 September 1971.
28. NAI DT/2003/17/30 Series of Concepts.
29. NAI DT/2003/17/30 The IRA in the North.
30. NAI DT/2003/17/30 Conservative Government's Policies in Northern Ireland.
31. NAI DT/2003/17/30 What the Taoiseach Should Ask For.
31. NAI DT/2003/17/30 General Notes.
33. NAI DT/2003/17/30 Some Options.
34. NAI DT/2003/17/30 An Approach to a Structure of Government for Northern Ireland.
35. NAI DT/2003/17/30 Some Options.
36. NAI DT/2003/17/30 Addendum to the List of Options.
37. NAI DT/2003/17/30 The Protestant Backlash.
38. NAI DT/2003/17/30 British Army Policy in the North.
39. NAUK PRO CAB 133/406 Record of a discussion with the Prime Ministers of the Irish

Republic and of Northern Ireland held at Chequers on Monday, 27 September, 1971 at 12 noon.
40. NAUK PRO CAB 133/406 Record of a discussion with the Prime Ministers of the Irish Republic and of Northern Ireland held at Chequers on Monday, 27 September, 1971 at 3.15 p.m.
41. NAUK PRO CAB 133/406 Record of a discussion with the Prime Ministers of the Irish Republic and of Northern Ireland held at Chequers on Monday, 27 September, 1971 at 11.15 a.m.
42. NAUK PRO CAB 133/406 Record of a discussion with the Prime Ministers of the Irish Republic and of Northern Ireland held at Chequers on Tuesday, 28 September, 1971 at 3 p.m.
43. NAUK PRO CAB 133/406 Record of a discussion with the Prime Ministers of the Irish Republic and of Northern Ireland held at Chequers on Tuesday, 28 September, 1971 at 3.45 p.m.
44. NAUK PRO PREM 15/1034 Record of a Discussion with the Prime Minister of Northern Ireland 7 October 1971.
45. *News Letter*, 8 October 1971.
46. NAI DT/2002/8/416 Aonad Idir-Rannach um an Tuaisceart/Inter-Departmental Unit on the North of Ireland: Minutes of the Fourteenth Meeting, 15 July 1971.
47. NAI DT/2002/8/416 Aonad Idir-Rannach um an Tuaisceart/Inter-Departmental Unit on the North of Ireland: Minutes of Twentieth, Twenty-First, Twenty-Second, Twenty-Third, Twenty-Fourth and Twenty-Fifth Meetings held on 25th, 26th, 27th and 31st August 1971 and 2nd and 8th September 1971.
48. NAI D/T 2002/8/483 Gallagher Note, 3 November 1971.
49. NAI D/T 2002/8/484 Gallagher Note, 15 November 1971.
50. NAI D/T 2002/8/488 CV Whelan to Ambassador, 27 September 1971.
51. NAI D/T 2002/8/484 Gallagher Note, 15 November 1971.
52. NAI D/T 2002/8/484 The Wilson Visit, November 1971.
53. BSI G44B.282.004.
54. NAUK PRO PREM 15/1000 Trend to Prime Minister, 10 December 1971.
55. NAUK PRO PREM 15/1000 Gilchrist to Trend, 24 November 1971.
56. NAUK PRO PREM 15/1000 Peck to UKREP, 7 January 1972.
57. NAUK PRO PREM 15/1000 Trend to Heath.

7

The War on the Ground: August 1971–January 1972

In 1976 the journalist, Alf McCreary, reflected on what seemed the then uniqueness of the violence in the Northern Ireland conflict: during the Second World War, and in the Korean and Vietnam wars, some 80 per cent of head wounds were caused by flying metal fragments from shells, bombs and mines. Only 15–20 per cent were caused by bullets. The wounding pattern in Northern Ireland was different: less than 10 per cent were caused by explosions by the mid-1970s: 90 per cent were caused by bullets.[1] A bullet and the weapon that discharged it are fascinating instruments of craftsmanship. Low velocity bullets – mostly commonly used by the IRA at this stage – smacked into a body and usually stayed there. They damaged bones and tissues in their path but they were relatively easy to treat provided they had not damaged any vital structures. High velocity rounds, such as those from the Army's SLR, caused enormous damage. The SLR's 7.62mm bullet had a velocity of some 2,800ft per second. When the trigger was squeezed, a firing pin was propelled forward, it made contact with a percussion cap at the end of the cartridge and the cap exploded, thus igniting the charge inside the cartridge. The combustion of the cordite created extremely high pressure and the bullet was forced out by the pressure of gases at the top of the gun-barrel. The bullet was normally about half an inch long and the diameter varied according to the size of the weapon used. The centre of the bullet was made of lead, with a hard jacket of copper and nickel to give it more punch. The inside of the gun-barrel was grooved in a corkscrew pattern and the bullet was thus turned round like a drill on its way out. This helped to give increased accuracy and hitting-power and when it left the barrel the bullet was still spinning. The top of the SLR had openings to allow the hot air to escape. The bang from the weapon occurred when the hot gases in the gun-barrel made contact with the cold air outside. The low velocity bullets from a Thompson had, roughly, half the speed of an SLR bullet. People under fire from low velocity weapons usually heard the crack and then the whiz of the bullet. With high velocity weapons they usually heard the whiz of the bullet and then the crack – one as the bullet broke the sound barrier and one as the hot gases met the cold air. At the point of departure inside the SLR gun-barrel there was a pressure of $4^1/_2$ tons per square inch. The wounds caused by HV bullets could be devastating. The nature of the wounds depended on the speed and the shape of the bullet at the point of impact, on whether it was still spinning, and on whether it hit the target sideways or head-on. HV bullets were often deflected by bones. A bullet could strike a man's collar-bone and be found later embedded in his thigh. The bullet still travelled at high speed and often created appalling damage as it ploughed through. It could pass through an area of tissue and flesh of up to 8 centimetres across although the degree of damage was relative to the distance from the target. Some bullets fractured bones though they did not hit them – it was the shock waves that caused the damage.[2] A bullet travelling at low velocity usually left a narrow track in the brain which was not much wider than the diameter of the bullet itself. The exit wound was only slightly larger than the entrance wound. In contrast a HV bullet created its damage in a different way. It normally entered the skull in a stable flight path and created a hole not much bigger than that of a low velocity bullet. But its passage through skin, skull and brain made it unstable and this resulted in the yawing or the cartwheeling of the missile. The whole process led to increased resistance and therefore created a deeper wound with a large exit area and a large cavity of damage around the track of the bullet.[3] Of course, for each bullet discharged into flesh and bone there was more than physical distortion of human anatomy. Each bullet affected an individual. It extinguished a life; it injured a person's body; it devastated the lives of others around them. Every time someone was shot there were profound human consequences.

Sean Hughes was a Catholic who worked as a clerk in the Electricity Board headquarters in Belfast. In 1970 he decided to join the RUC. He felt that there was no point in sitting back and accusing the police of being anti-Catholic: he thought that Catholics themselves had to make an effort. One night, in October 1971, his door bell rang. Sean Hughes had been entertaining guests that evening; they had left a short time previously. When he heard the door bell, he assumed that his friends had forgotten something and had returned to the house. Instead of going downstairs he went to the bedroom of his son, Ciaran, who was aged four months. He opened the window which directly overlooked the door. Sean Hughes was then hit by a burst of gunfire and lay slumped over the window sill, wounded. His wife, Patricia, heard the shots from their bedroom. She called his name but there was no reply. As she went to rush downstairs she saw her husband lying in a pool of blood. She lifted him in her arms and felt over his body. Confused and terrified, Patricia Hughes crawled on her hands and knees back to her bedroom where she phoned the police and ambulance and then crawled back. She lifted the baby and took him to another bedroom. He was screaming. His tiny nightdress was covered in blood. Patricia Hughes thought that he too had been shot but the blood had come from her own hands and clothes. She went back to her husband and kneeled over him, recited an act of contrition, talked to him, shouted at him, tried to revive him. When the police and ambulance arrived Sean Hughes was taken to the City Hospital and moved, next day, to the Royal Victoria Hospital. He had serious brain damage. He was given little hope of recovery. A priest shook his head and said: 'I'm sorry, Mrs Hughes.' But Patricia Hughes refused to accept that her husband was going to die. She talked to him, sang to him and recited poetry even though he was unconscious. Sean Hughes did not die. For almost two years he lay in hospital. He could not remember regaining consciousness. At first, while his wife talked to him, he could only grunt and make unintelligible sounds; but words and then sentences came eventually. But he could become unbearably frustrated, lashing out verbally and physically at those around him. He was angry with God also:

'If God was so good why did He not pick the fellow next door?' But, slowly, his faith increased and he found comfort and strength in prayer. His wife remained an inspiration: 'I suppose most people in my position would have done the same. I felt that Sean was too good to die, that he should not die, that he would not die. A gunman could not snuff out a life just like that. If he had died it would have been a one-day wonder, a sensation in the Press, but for me there would have been nothing left, just nothing.' Sean Hughes did not make a full recovery from his injuries. His left side was paralysed; he had restricted vision; and he had to use a wheelchair. But he had a fighting spirit: 'Medicine can only go a certain distance. Then it is up to you. I had so many people asking for me, praying for me, willing me on. The world loves a trier. If you are going to lie in a ward and feel sorry for yourself, no one wants to know you. I was always a great fighter. No matter what, I'd fight to the bitter end.'[4]

THE IMPACT OF THE IRA CAMPAIGN

Tommy McKearney, born in Moy, County Tyrone, in 1952, joined the Provisional IRA in 1971, a few months after internment:

> At the very least there would have been two main streams influencing my decision to join the Republican movement. One would be the historical background to my family, which was a Republican background in the Fenian tradition. Both my grandfathers were active IRA men; my parents were Republican sympathisers without being active members. That, plus the fact that I was from the Tyrone area, which was a Republican stronghold, combined with the circumstances of the day and propelled me towards the Republican movement.

McKearney had a clear perception 'that we were Catholic (I am using that term to define a position). I was eighteen years of age in 1971 and would have been well aware of things like housing conditions, job opportunities and general bias against Catholics.' But it was internment that was the catalyst for combining all the other factors to propel him towards the IRA:

> My first reaction to internment was one of outrage. Outrage at the arbitrariness of the decision, and at the sheer arrogance of the decision... It made it very clear that the British government was supporting the Stormont regime, and was therefore not a neutral agent in the conflict. So it confirmed my position and went a long way for me in justifying the use of the armed option. It demonstrated clearly that the state, Stormont and its sponsor, the British, were acting arbitrarily, beyond the law. They were not accountable to any peaceful political, democratic or electoral initiative. So internment had a tremendous impact in terms of intellectual analysis and the morality of the situation... one was the intellectual rationale for the resort to armed resistance, and also the practical incentive to act on the basis of that rationale.

Tommy Gorman, who had joined the Provos in 1970, just

> wanted to get involved and hit back. That was my initial motive. The state was irreformable, so the only way forward was to take it head on. I felt there had to [be] some kind of struggle, some kind of resistance. I know it was elitist in that we didn't care for politics as such. We just done operations and then watched them at home on the six o'clock news. We were more interested in surviving from day to day than in politics. Sinn Féin in the early days was for people who were not right in the head, you know, we just wanted to get out and fight.[5]

For McKearney the moral dilemmas and agonizing took place before he joined the IRA rather than after:

> I would argue that morality is not about individuals and heaven and hell, but whether the cause is justified, is it achievable, and is it worth the taking of human life? We were attacked and were responding in the first instance. We still operated within certain moral boundaries, certain operations we would not do. Non-participants should not be targeted. Of course there were discussions about whether it was right to target off-duty RUC or UDR personnel, but no-one talked about killing non-combatants because it wasn't an issue. Sometimes the Army Council would decide, but there was an element of anarchy in the early days.

Once beyond the question of individual morality and a decision that the cause was worth fighting for, the next stage was

> the strategic utility of violence. The cause may be just but is the objective achievable in any way? Through the 1970s this wasn't a major problem for me because to us it seemed that we could win the war... We felt that if we could inflict casualties on the British then the British population would become disenchanted and pressurise the government to leave.[6]

As another activist, Mickey McMullen, put it: 'We thought we could win.'[7]

Such a belief was encouraged in Belfast, as Brendan Hughes explains:

> Behind the barricades we had more or less total control, and gunmen were out in the streets in the early days. It was urban guerrilla warfare and ambushes would take place regularly. The IRA would place men at cross-sections of streets so that no matter what way the army came into the area they were attacked. Almost every time they came in they sustained casualties. Another form of attack was sandbagging a lorry with armed men in the back looking for targets... The Lower Falls was a perfect area for guerrilla warfare because the public were extremely supportive and the whole area was a warren of yard walls and back alleys... For a time we were almost in a liberated part of Ireland, and all of those people taking on the Brits were just ordinary people.[8]

One of the tactics used was commercial bombing which tied up the city centre. The IRA would

> hit the economic interests of the rulers, the capitalist class if you like. This had the effect of also drawing troops from the ghetto areas, to reduce the pressure on the people. In some cases civilians were killed but there is no doubt in some instances the Brits manipulated that situation because warnings were not passed on. They wanted to turn public opinion against the IRA. The last people that the IRA wanted to hurt or kill were civilians, but the country was occupied and the police were sectarian – we were at war.[9]

But kill civilians they did – often excusing the deaths, as Hughes did, with claims that the British did not pass on warnings. Such was the case with the Provisionals' bomb that killed Harry Beggs, aged 23, and injured thirty-five other people in August 1971, at the Electricity Board offices in Malone Road, Belfast. Most of the injured were typists and secretaries, one of whom was pregnant; another received severe eye injuries and another serious leg injuries. Among the injured was Ann Owens: she was later killed by the Provos in the Abercorn bombing of March 1972. On this occasion the alarm was raised when a female caller hung up after telling a Board telephone operator: 'There's a bomb in the building.' Harry Beggs was leaving the building and was on the ground floor near the 15lb bomb when it exploded. It had been left in a locker close to an exit where staff escaping had to pass. A stairway packed with escaping workers collapsed when the bomb exploded. Several people, including young women, were trapped under rubble. A second 15lb device had also been planted but the force of the first blast damaged its mechanism and prevented it from exploding. Beggs, from east Belfast, was engaged to be married to a 21-year-old social worker; they were described as 'very much in love' and had chosen the house where they intended to live. The bombing had a decisive impact on one of the victim's young friends, Peter Robinson; the death of his school friend prompted his career in politics.[10]

The bombing reflected a conscious intensification of the Provisionals' campaign. Up to 9 August, according to their Chief of Staff Sean MacStiofain, the sabotage offensive had been restricted to selected units in certain areas. With the introduction of internment, operational tactics were immediately changed. All units now went into a widespread bombing campaign against pre-listed economic targets. MacStiofain noted that 'Unionist-dominated industry put losses for 1971 at £400,000.' With internment, Provisional policy towards the UDR and RUC was 'also altered'. Prior to this, Provisional units had instructions that UDR personnel were not to be subjected to deliberate attack. But four thousand UDR men had been called out in support of the internment operation, freeing British troops to 'harass' the Nationalist areas. With the subsequent announcement of the expansion of the UDR to 10,000 personnel the Provisionals' sabotage campaign, designed to tie down British troops on static guard duties, was undermined as they could now be released for operations. The RUC had taken part in the internment operation and the accompanying exercise in state terror... And... had taken part in the brutal interrogation practices carried out on prisoners... From internment on, UDR and RUC personnel, like British soldiers, were treated as legitimate combatant targets at all times, whether on duty or not, armed or not, in uniform or not. This may sound a harsh ruling, but the facts of life were that IRA members were liable to be arrested or shot by any of these forces at any time. In addition the RUC and UDR were the eyes and ears of the enemy intelligence machine, particularly in the detailed knowledge of rural districts which would be so difficult for the occupation forces to obtain on their own.[11]

So, after internment, the deaths mounted up, particularly in Belfast. Clifford Loring, aged 18, of The Royal Artillery Regiment, was fatally wounded in a gun attack at Stockman's Lane in the Andersonstown area on 29 August; he died two days later. He was standing on checkpoint duty when he was hit in the head by a sniper; the bullet passed through another soldier's flak jacket, knocking him to the ground, before hitting Loring. Soldiers and police regularly mounted checkpoint duty at Stockman's Lane so as to stop and search cars turning off the slipway from the nearby motorway, the M1.[12] Angela Gallagher, an 18-month-old baby girl, died in the arms of her 7-year-old sister on 6 September after a bullet fired by the IRA ricocheted and hit her. The 7-year-old had been playing, pushing a pram close to their grandmother's house in Iveagh Street, west Belfast, when the IRA opened fire from a car on an Army patrol. Angela's sister had a lucky escape when a bullet passed through her skirt. She recalled:

> Angela had just been learning to walk. She was holding onto the pram in front of me. I saw the soldiers, then there was a big bang. Angela fell down and I couldn't get her up. She was too heavy to lift and I started to cry. I asked a big girl who was passing to pick her up and she carried her to the corner. A lady came up and took Angela. Then my mummy arrived and took her away.[13]

Private Paul Carter, 21, of The Queen's Regiment was shot by the IRA as he stood guard on other soldiers delivering medical supplies to the Royal Victoria Hospital. His father walked behind the gun carriage at the funeral in Brighton: 'I told my son a few minutes before he died that I would walk behind him all the way... It was my promise.'[14] Two days later, on 16 September, Lance-Corporal Peter Herrington, 26, was shot by an IRA sniper in Ardoyne as he and other members of his unit provided cover for a colleague who was attempting to dismantle a bomb. He was the fourth member of The Green Howards to be killed in six weeks. As the fatally wounded soldier was being put into an ambulance a crowd laughed and sneered at the remaining soldiers.[15] Private Peter Sharpe of The Green Howards became the fifth member of the 1 Battalion to be killed when he was shot while on a routine patrol in the Ardoyne. He had been married less than six months and his 18-year-old wife's brother was serving in the same Company; Mrs Sharpe was placed under heavy sedation. A family member said: 'She is heartbroken. They cannot have been more than ten days together since they were married.'[16]

In early October, an RUC Inspector was leaving Celtic Park greyhound track in his car when gunmen opened up. He was hit twice but escaped serious injury. Two weeks later Detective Sergeant Bernard McCullough and a civilian companion where shot on the Donegall Road, again near Celtic Park. Their two would-be assassins walked up behind them and shot McCullough in the back and his companion in the stomach.[17] The following night a soldier from The Scots Guards and a civilian were wounded near the Rock Bar, at the Whiterock Road–Falls Road junction, when shots were fired at the Army patrol. The Army noticed that this seemed part of a shift away from bombing.[18] Fusilier Patrick King had a double escape when his steel helmet was struck by a high velocity bullet as he stepped from an OP on top of Unity Flats. The force of the bullet knocked him over a parapet – four storeys up. Fifteen feet down he landed on a lower roof. Apart from a sore head and a few bruises he was all right.[19] A woman blew a whistle to trigger an ambush on soldiers in Ardoyne. When a patrol from the 1 Battalion The Green Howards stopped a woman on the junction of Berwick Street and Homedean Street, two other women approached and objected to the soldiers talking to the first woman. One of them blew a shrill blast on a whistle. Seconds later a hail of missiles began and the soldiers were forced to retreat down Berwick Street and took refuge in a garden in Brompton Park. By this time a crowd of more than a hundred moved in behind the troops and cut off their way to safety. Shots were fired at the soldiers. They returned fire and the crowd inched back. IRA gunmen continued to fire at the troops and a gelignite bomb was thrown as well. The Howards were pulled out when an armoured car pushed through the mob to rescue them.[20] Major Nurton, CO of the Scots Guards, said that the patrol became suspicious when the Ballymurphy estate suddenly went quiet. 'It was as though the people knew something was going to happen,' he said. Even the children stopped playing: 'It was like a herd instinct – or by a pre-arranged signal.' Guardsman George Hamilton, aged 21, was the twenty-eighth soldier killed since the beginning of the year. Earlier in the day Sergeant Graham Cox, from the Parachute Squadron RAC, had died from a head wound received in the Oldpark Road area two days before. Just before dusk a gunman had stepped out from Herbert Street and fired six or seven shots into Chief Street on the Protestant side of the Crumlin Road.[21] The weekend violence had left seven dead.

Four people – two soldiers, a policeman and a gunman – were wounded in Belfast on 25 October – the policeman was Sean Hughes. Private John Alfred Girder, of the 3 Battalion The Queen's Regiment was shot in the neck in Roden Street.[22] Six policemen and seven civilians were injured when a bomb damaged Larne RUC station. The bomb was placed at the door of the station.[23] The next day the IRA killed a police sergeant and seriously wounded a constable in an ambush near Toomebridge, County Antrim. They were lured into the ambush by a bogus call which told them of a barn fire near the town. The dead policeman was Sergeant Ron Dodd. Two soldiers were seriously injured when a Claymore mine exploded as their patrol was passing along a road between Enniskillen and Kinawley.[24] Earlier a bomb had exploded at the youth unemployment centre in Belfast. Several people were taken to hospital suffering from shock. The bomb was planted by three men and a woman who escaped in a car. It was the third attack on the building. Elsewhere, in the Oldpark area of the city, seven soldiers were injured when a bomb exploded beside a patrol. All had cut hands and legs and one suffered a fractured arm.[25] The nail bomb was apparently detonated by a trip wire. This was the latest in a series of attacks that day. The attacks began at 11.30 a.m. when twelve shots were directed at a Green Howards patrol on duty during the funeral of John Copeland shot by troops the previous week. Half an hour later a single shot was fired at a Scots Guard patrol in North Howard Street. In mid-afternoon a shot was fired at a Scots Guard sentry at the Henry Taggart Hall. In Ardoyne five shots were fired at The Green Howards in Herbert Street. At 4.30 p.m. a Royal Scots platoon were moving towards two crowds of stone throwing civilians off the Crumlin Road when twenty shots were directed at them from the area of Holy Cross Church. The soldiers returned fire.[26] A gun battle was waged between soldiers and gunmen near Belfast's city centre after one civilian had been shot dead and another critically injured. Earlier, Glenravel Street police station and a police foot patrol on the Crumlin Road came under fire. About twelve shots were fired at the station and three and the two-man foot patrol. There were five attacks on the Army. A military patrol was twice shot at – once at Carlisle Circus and fifteen minutes later at Townsend Street and Peter's Hill. Later two Claymore mines exploded at the Monagh Road roundabout in Turf Lodge near an Army Land Rover. The attacks came after a twelve hour search operation during which twenty-nine men were arrested and guns and ammunition found in a parochial hall in Oldpark.[27] The Army later sprayed purple dye on walls painted white in the Lower Falls.[28] The walls had been painted white to silhouette troops at night for IRA snipers to shoot at.

Despite issuing a number of demands in September – the immediate cessation of the British forces' 'campaign of violence against the Irish people'; the abolition of Stormont; a guarantee of non-interference with a free election to establish a new Governmental structure for the 'entire country', that is, the island of Ireland; the release of all 'political prisoners', tried or untried, in Ireland and Britain; and a guarantee of compensation for all those who had 'suffered as a result of direct or indirect British violence'[29] – there seems to have been real tensions within the Provo leadership as to the running of the campaign. At this stage the Army Council consisted of MacStiofain, Daithi Ó Conaill, Ruairi Ó Brádaigh, Joe Cahill, J.B. O'Hagan (who had been on the Army Council during the 1957–62 campaign), Dennis McInerney (another 1950s veteran), and Paddy Ryan, an explosives and training officer. The tensions related to strategy. Ó'Conaill, it was believed, had tried to oust MacStiofain as Chief of Staff and replace him with Cahill; but only Ó Brádaigh voted for the proposal.[30] Ó'Conaill believed that MacStiofain was opposed to the need for a political campaign alongside the military one. According to one observer, Maria McGuire, MacStiofain had, at first, seen no point in communicating with the British at all, feeling that to have any contact with the British was in itself a compromise, a betrayal; he seemed to think that the Movement's aims would be achieved by military means alone. For example, he agreed to attend the fortnightly meetings of the Ard Comhairle, the policy-making committee of Sinn Féin; but if he went he would demonstrate his disdain for the meeting by making an excuse to leave – for example an essential telephone call – and then not return.[31]

In military terms the main examples followed by the Provisionals in trying to kill British soldiers were the guerrilla campaigns against the British in Cyprus and Aden. One book studied closely, with comparisons and summaries of these campaigns and those of China, Cuba, Vietnam and Israel amongst others, was *The War of the Flea* – a study of guerrilla warfare theory and practice by Robert Tauber. Ó Brádaigh bought seven copies of the paperback edition and sent one to each of the members of the Army Council. The Army Council's first target was to kill thirty-six British soldiers – the same number who died in Aden. The target was reached in early November 1971. This was not enough. Ó Conaill declared: 'We've got to get eighty.' Once eighty had been killed he felt the pressure on the British to negotiate would be immense. Maria McGuire recalled: 'I remember the feeling of satisfaction we had at hearing another one had died.' A Volunteer once told McGuire that, in the Catholic ghettos, 'it was like aiming at moving ducks in a fairground shooting-gallery'. There was, she recalled, 'always admiration for fine examples of marksmanship – killing a British soldier with a single shot, or hitting one through the observation slit of a Saracen'.[32]

INTERNMENT: A MILITARY DISASTER?

There is no doubt that the intelligence aspect of DEMETRIUS was deeply flawed: to some of the soldiers on the ground it soon became apparent that all was not well with regard to the suspects being rounded up on 9 August. 'Jonathan', a young officer remembered:

> I have to say that many of the people we arrested were known but had not been active since about 1922. I remember arresting one elderly gentlemen who was well into his eighties who was rather proud to be arrested. He said "I'm delighted to think that I'm still trouble to the British Government but I have to tell you I've not been active since the Easter Rising"... The intelligence was very, very poor because the army hadn't built up its own store of intelligence by then and we acted on information we were given.[33]

The intelligence on the IRA, which was crucial to the success or failure of DEMETRIUS, had come from the RUC (SB). 'Paul', one of the Special Branch officers involved, admitted that many of the files were based on individuals from the pre-1969 IRA who had been involved in the Border Campaign. Special Branch was caught out after the 1969 IRA split:

> We knew what their structure was and who the leaders were in most areas, people like Billy McKee and Joe Cahill. We knew... what their 'battalions' were, as they were very much geographically organised. But we wouldn't have known exactly the layout of the 'company' units within each 'battalion' and we wouldn't have known the individual members of the units. At ground level, the information was patchy.

When Tony Farrar-Hockley examined the contents of Special Branch files he was not overly impressed: 'It became apparent to us that though the records had been excellent up to the 1950s, after the "triumph" of that period...there had been very little updating of information. There were some excellent people in Special Branch and there were some not so excellent people. The excellent people were working hard on getting an up-to-date record of everything and the others were doing it when it suited them.'[34]

Right from the beginning of Westminster intervention in Ulster in 1969, concern had been expressed in London with regard to the intelligence deficiencies they found in the Province. Various attempts had been made to improve intelligence gathering. In mid-1970, with assistance and advice from the Army and the Security Service, the RUC (SB) had been increased in numbers and improved in organization. A Director of Intelligence had been appointed to HQNI; and a committee system had been established to process and evaluate intelligence.[35] A number of different political and intelligence summaries, appreciations and assessments were prepared every week or fortnight but, as the MOD noted, since it received copies of all of them the total effect 'can be fairly confusing', especially as the periods covered did not exactly coincide. There were three main categories. The Home Office produced, weekly, a Political Summary (HONIP) which was prepared by the UK Representative at Belfast. The period covered was Friday – Thursday. It was 'usually readable and informative' and 'puts events into a better perspective than the others'. The Director of Intelligence at HQ Northern Ireland issued a weekly Intelligence Summary (INTSUM), covering the period Thursday – Wednesday, giving a round-up of significant developments and with annexes containing full details of recent incidents, reported activities and forthcoming events. It was usually comprehensive and quite well-marshalled but the minutiae in the Annexes 'is best left to specialists'. He also produced a fortnightly Intelligence Assessment that summed up intelligence material providing a useful complement to INTSUM. And finally Special Branch produced a Weekly Assessment for submission to the Joint Security Committee. These assessments tended, in the MOD's view, to be 'pretty turgid and not very successful at distinguishing between wood and trees; unfortunately one has to look at them briefly because the Committee's minutes – which are of course significant, if also turgid – are framed as a series of comments on the latest assessment.'[36]

Following an initiative from Heath, in early 1971, to strengthen the intelligence organization, the number of Military Intelligence Officers (MIO) assigned to Northern Ireland was doubled. By April more were earmarked but there proved to be a natural limit to the number that could usefully be employed; moreover the RUC remained the arbiters of how many could be deployed within their chain of command. At the GOC's Headquarters there was now a much larger, and more balanced, intelligence staff. This included a General Staff Officer Grade 1 (GSO1), an MOD Principal to assist in assessment work, and a specialist Signal Intelligence (SIGNIT) officer. A thorough overhaul of the Army intelligence machine had also been undertaken with the advice of Sir Dick White, the Intelligence Coordinator (the only person to have been the Director General of MI5 and 'C' or head of MI6) and the School of Service Intelligence. But the main problem remained that Special Branch regarded intelligence as their prerogative – and they were not about to surrender it. Nevertheless, by April, the MOD was reporting that the Director of Intelligence at HQNI had established a close relationship with David Johnston, the Head of Special Branch (HSB). This had resulted in the records and reports of Special Branch being made completely available to the Army's Senior MIO operating within Special Branch who had, furthermore, gained the confidence of the RUC. The Army's Director of Intelligence and the HSB, with the MIO, now worked as a triumvirate and, apart from daily informal contacts, met regularly to produce joint assessments. The quality of these assessments was therefore steadily rising. From London's point of view it could not be said that the Director had the constitutional right to direct and control Special Branch, which was what would be needed in an 'ideal' organization, but he was, in practice, achieving a large measure of control by these informal means. The MOD considered it extremely important that nothing should be done, either in Whitehall or in Ulster, to upset this hard-won relationship of the Director with the RUC. Any attempt either to introduce an 'expert Englishman' into the Special Branch hierarchy at the top level, or to give the Director formal command over the HSB would 'under current conditions' be not only doomed to failure but also a 'very unwise step that would undo all the good work of the last two months'.[37]

Despite these changes the Joint Intelligence Committee in London – the apex of the Whitehall intelligence community – made a crucial observation: the Army's contribution was probably only about 10 per cent of the total intelligence take – the balance being principally from RUC Special Branch. Thus, 'however much we improve our own arrangements, there cannot be a consequential radical improvement in the intelligence situation as a whole. For this we must look to the RUC (SB).'[38] The failures inherent in this division of intelligence meant that the chickens came home to roost on 9 August. The success of DEMETRIUS was further undermined by the fact that the Provisionals had good intelligence themselves: their Belfast Brigade had been receiving information from a sympathizer working inside the Ministry of Home Affairs. 'We knew from our source inside Stormont,' recalled Joe Cahill, 'that Heath had already given the OK for Faulkner to bring in internment. Senior IRA members were instructed in late July not to sleep at home.' The Provos interpreted the LINKLATER operation as a rehearsal for the actual internment operation. Cahill remembered that in the first week of August, 'our person at the office of the minister of home affairs told us that internment would be introduced within forty-eight hours.' Cahill and MacStiofain travelled around the North to different company areas giving the general order that no Volunteers were to sleep in their own houses.[39] MacStiofain noted that the value of internment was most striking of all in its effect on the Provisionals' personnel strength. When everybody had been accounted for only fifty-six Provos had been interned. Adding the three Volunteers killed in action, the total depletion was fifty-nine. Against this the new intake of Volunteers was so great that it caused serious difficulties in several areas. There were real problems getting this influx properly integrated into the Movement and putting the new Volunteers to work: in Derry 'there was nothing for it but to open a waiting list'. The Provisionals' strength was further increased by defections from the Officials. After the 1969 split the Strabane unit had remained loyal to the Goulding leadership but came over *en masse* to the Provos with internment.[40]

This sits uneasily with the assessment made by the British. At one level the claims made by the British appeared widely over optimistic. How could the British get it so wrong? The question is: did they? Clearly, many of the British estimates – particularly the 'kills' claimed – were wide of the mark. But on what basis should Republican estimates – which have been virtually accepted without question – be accepted? For example, one young Provisional Staff Officer suddenly found himself the Derry OC because all his superiors had been interned on 9 August.[41] Not all the intelligence was wrong, nor were all those interned innocent or retired old Republicans; furthermore, assessments of internment usually judge it on the basis of raids on 9 August alone. Internment went on. And on. By 14 August the British estimate – for internal consumption, not propaganda purposes – was that the Provisionals had lost fifty officers and 107 Volunteers. These included, in Belfast, six officers from the Brigade Staff, two Battalion Commanders, seven Company Commanders (plus one Company Commander killed) and one complete ASU. Those taken outside Belfast included the area organizer for Tyrone, Armagh and South Down. From the Officials, thirty-three officers and thirty-seven Volunteers were detained, including four out of eight Company Commanders in Belfast, three Company Adjutants, two Company Quartermasters and one Battalion Quartermaster. The assertions that an elderly man who was taken into custody could not conceivably, because of his age, be dangerously engaged was 'wrong': 'The man referred to is very probably Mulholland, who is the intelligence officer of the Brady Brigade in Belfast.' Five PD members were included: 'They have been active in organising militant disorder, which has made an important success of the IRA...they too wish to create a revolutionary situation.'[42] Even if such figures proved wrong in the longer term it was not the number of IRA members lifted that was of critical value but the quality of the information held by an individual and whether that individual talked during interrogation. In terms of intelligence, size really did not matter: it is what you do with it that counts.

And this is the significance of deep interrogation. While much of the controversy relating to internment has focused on its disastrous impact – both politically and in security terms – this is only half the picture: in intelligence terms, and the view of the Security Forces, in-depth interrogation was a spectacular success.[43] The results of these interrogations were described as 'remarkable'.[44] Initially the large-scale arrests on 9 August had the effect of disrupting not only the IRA but also Special Branch agent coverage which was at the time the main source of the relatively limited amount of intelligence then available to the Security Forces. The reason for this was that in order to maintain their cover a number of agents and their contacts had to be arrested. However, following the introduction of internment the interrogation of arrested persons became the principal source of intelligence, the volume of which rapidly increased.

The principal objective of the interrogation of suspected members of the IRA was to obtain information concerning the personnel, plans and weaponry of the IRA, with sufficient speed to permit immediate action through search and arrest operations before the value of the information was reduced by the movement of men and weapons. These operations would continue the process of attrition and disrupt IRA activities. The relationship between Police Holding Centres – where routine police questioning took place – and CALABA (deep interrogation) proved a complementary one. The detailed interrogation provided by CALABA was not necessary for all suspects, nor was it considered desirable, practical or economical to provide it for all. It took longer than PHC questioning and it was found that many suspects gave much information to an RUC questioner – particularly if it was known that detailed interrogation was available for those thought to be concealing important information. An MOD assessment of the impact of CALABA found that, generally, the introduction of internment 'brought about a profound change in the attitudes of IRA members arrested by the security forces, and the interrogators were able to establish an ascendancy over them not previously possible'. With the threat of detention and possibly internment hanging over them, 'they were far more willing to talk about the IRA and its activities than previously.' Of the twelve initially selected for detailed interrogation: 'Ten of these men provided large quantities of information of great value to the security forces.' This type of interrogation 'undoubtedly came as a complete surprise to the subject'. The Security Forces found that as soon as the arrest of an IRA member became known to his colleagues they themselves moved on and any arms caches of which they had knowledge were moved to new locations. Rapid and successful interrogation was therefore vital if the Security Forces were to obtain information on which they could act in time. As a result the MOD concluded that:

a. the IRA policy of terrorising suspected informants makes interrogation a vital and irreplaceable source of intelligence;
b. the introduction of internment and the two separate but complementary types of interrogation have made members of the IRA much more willing to talk and have as a result produced much very useful intelligence;
c. speed in interrogation is vital if successful follow-up operations are to be mounted. Experience has shown that when interrogation of the CALABA type is known to be used where necessary, IRA men are willing to talk more freely at the early PHC stage, and the abandonment of the CALABA type of operation would be likely to reduce substantially the effectiveness of PHC interrogation;
d. the bulk of successful search and arrest operations which have been carried out recently have been mounted on the basis of intelligence derived from interrogation.[45]

CALABA was eventually abandoned. But not before it had delivered a significant intelligence yield. In short, most of those selected for deep interrogation sang like the proverbial canary. In January 1972 the MOD estimated that 'something like three-quarters of the arms and explosives found since 9 August are directly or indirectly attributable to interrogation in depth'.[46] This led to the disruption of a Fianna unit of thirty-seven when twenty-five of their number were arrested in Andersonstown. Additionally, a hitherto unknown Fianna unit was considerably weakened when twenty out of thirty of their members were arrested. CALABA led, in one instance, to a considerable arms find at Ballymena on 13 November which included: twenty-eight shotguns; nineteen rifles; two revolvers; two automatic pistols; one anti-tank rifle; one Thompson sub-machine gun; one M1 Carbine; 9,840 rounds of ammunition; 1,144 shotgun cartridges; one grenade; one plunger igniter; 1,500 feet of cordtex; and 45lbs of gelignite.[47] Overall, the following intelligence was obtained from those exposed to deep interrogation: the identification of a further 700 members of both IRA factions and their positions in the organizations was made; over forty sheets giving details of the organization and structure of sub-units; details of possible IRA operations, arms caches, safe houses, communications and supply routes, including those across the Border, together with locations of wanted persons; details of morale, operational directives, propaganda techniques, relations with other organizations and future plans; and the discovery of individual responsibility for about eighty-five incidents recorded on police files which had previously remained unexplained.[48] The rate at which arms, ammunition and explosives were discovered increased markedly after 9 August as the following figures testify.

TABLE 2

	1 January to 8 August	9 August to 31 December
Machine guns	1	25
Rifles	66	178
Pistols/revolvers	86	158
Shotguns	40	52
Rockets	–	55
Ammunition	41,000 rounds	115,000 rounds
Explosives	1,194lbs	2,541lbs

(source: Parker Report para.20)

Such results have been dismissed in some quarters as insignificant: they were not. Both IRA factions were short of weapons and ammunition: future transAtlantic and Libyan arms ties were still some way off in 1971. The attrition of material was a key aim and such results were a success. But, beyond this, deep interrogation allowed the Security Forces to build up intelligence on the IRA that, hitherto, they just did not have. The key period in assessing internment, therefore, occurs in the months, not days, after 9 August; and internment now became the main weapon used by the Army in its campaign of attrition against the IRA. So, although General Tuzo had been opposed to its introduction, once it had been introduced he became a firm advocate of its continuation. IRA suspects no longer had the assistance of the normal legal system with its requirement for evidence to be put before a court; a suspect was interned solely on the basis of intelligence. Thus, on 13 September, Tuzo took the 'liberty of transgressing' into a field which was essentially Faulkner's personal concern but which, he felt, had a strong military flavour: he wrote to the Prime Minister to express his concern at the strong pressure which was appearing from all sides for the release of detainees. 'Naturally I concede that a fair number of these people should be let out,' he wrote; but he also regarded it as quite a serious matter if any man who had past or present IRA 'traces' were to reappear on the streets at this stage. The GOC was conscious of his advice on 5 August that the disadvantages of internment outweighed the advantages:

> But once the decision to intern was taken the Army threw its entire weight behind the operation and, in doing so, has brought down upon itself not only a physical retaliation but a fair amount of opprobrium. It would be wholly bad if IRA men, many of whom were known by sight to our soldiers, were to be put back in circulation after all we had endured to get them locked up; but what is far more important is the fact that detention is now the main weapon in our campaign against the bomber and the gunman. We are taking a steady flow of men, averaging about two per day, and this intake may well increase as the effects of interrogation begin to tell. Thus we are neutralising a large number of the enemy and I feel sure we should not allow any amount of pressure to reduce this effect unless and until the IRA call off their campaign.[49]

Internment became increasingly effective as 1971 drew to a close. Most studies of the impact of internment have focused on the hard statistics that show how the number of deaths prior to internment was far lower in the six months before internment and significantly higher for the following six months. Before February 1971 not a soldier had been killed. Between February 1971 and the imposition of internment on 9 August, the Army lost ten killed. Between 9 August and 9 September the losses (including UDR) were ten killed and forty-eight wounded. In August, there were 120 bomb incidents involving 1,800lbs of explosives; in September 175 incidents and 2,200lbs. However, this fails to take into account that the IRA – overwhelmingly the Provisionals – were steadily increasing the level of violence *before* internment was introduced: in January 1971 there were thirty-six bomb incidents involving 230lbs of explosives; in May, forty-five incidents and 417lbs. A Military Appreciation of the Security Situation in Northern Ireland, in October 1971, described IRA tactics: a well coordinated bombing campaign; armed attacks on police stations, usually involving automatic fire and occasionally even rockets; indiscriminate shooting at individuals of the Security Forces either from snipers or by hit and run raids from cars; and cross border raids and ambushes by Active Service Units against customs posts and police stations. This, however, was inevitable. In short, 'the IRA has the initiative and is causing disruption out of all proportion to the relatively small numbers engaged. This is not to credit the IRA with any unusual skill; it is the normal pattern of urban guerrilla activity when the guerrillas are not opposed by a ruthless and authoritarian Governmental machine.'[50]

In military terms there is no evidence that the IRA campaign had any real impact in undermining British military strategy. The fact that more British soldiers were killed by the IRA in the months after internment than before had a relatively limited military impact. The British Army regarded this as the inevitable, but regrettable, consequence of fighting an urban insurgency. And, in simple terms, IRA snipers were merely getting better at their job. It is accurate to state that the IRA campaign was accelerated by internment in the short-term; but in the long-term internment proved very effective in grinding down the IRA in Belfast. Lord Carrington was satisfied that the introduction of internment had been a major step forward in 'bringing the poison of terrorism to the surface'; the task for the Security Forces was now one of 'cleaning up', which was bound to take quite a long time but which he was sure could be completed successfully provided that the political situation remained reasonably stable. In particular, internment had increased the amount of available information about the IRA and the Army's main task was now to follow up this intelligence so that terrorists were given no respite.[51] Using intelligence derived from the initial internment swoops the Army built up a picture, in Belfast, of the IRA. Rounding them up was the next, attritional, stage.

At the beginning of November the Army detained six IRA officers. Troops detained a further twenty-four men in raids in Lurgan and Belfast. Four of the men were picked up in Lurgan, the rest in Belfast.[52] The following day about fifty men were arrested in Belfast and Derry as 1,500 troops carried out a series of dawn swoops.[53] Most of these men would be released: however, the intelligence gleaned from such swoops all contributed to building up a more complete picture of activities and movements in a given area. The Army judged the success of its campaign not only on the success of its arrests but also on the basis of how much it reduced the level of violence. Belfast was considered the key battleground. When the MOD's Northern Ireland Policy Committee met on 15 November (later it became the Northern Ireland Policy Group) – consisting of Carrington, Lord Baniel, the Chief of the Defence Staff, the Chief of the General Staff and the Permanent Under-Secretary – Sir Michael Carver reported that the previous week had been an encouraging one: the numbers of shootings, explosions and Security Forces casualties were all down, and arrests of wanted persons up on previous weeks. The arrests had included two IRA Company Commanders and a man suspected of complicity in the murder of the three young Royal Scots Fusiliers earlier in the year; there had also been a large find of explosives. As a consequence of such successes the IRA were expected to concentrate on attacking the softest targets, the families of Security Force members and those who lived away from barracks and other defended points.[54] Carver later reported that IRA activities remained at a relatively low level. There were signs that both IRA factions in Northern Ireland were under pressure and becoming disorganized. If the trend continued, the IRA had two possible courses: to put forward truce proposals or to switch their effort to a new field, for example kidnapping or assassination.[55] By 13 December, Carver was informing GEN 47 that while the number of explosions had shown a decrease, casualties had been heavier. Nevertheless, some 100 wanted men had been arrested and there had been two significant arms finds. Intelligence was continuing to come in at a 'gratifying rate'. It seemed likely that the IRA were making great efforts to show that their capacity for inflicting damage had not been significantly blunted by the successes of the Security Forces. The targets on which they now appeared to be concentrating, however, were, for the most part, away from the areas where the Security Forces mainly operated.[56]

The IRA's pre-Christmas activities continued. On 22 December there were six explosions in Belfast, four of them major: three public houses were extensively damaged, the owner of one being killed in the explosion, and a bicycle shop was destroyed. There were eight shooting incidents in Belfast. But there were also IRA setbacks. A Staff Officer in the Provisionals – Gerald McDade – was shot dead attempting to break through a cordon. The cordon was fired on by a sniper who also injured a civilian, and a RAMC sergeant was slightly injured by a ricochet from the same round. But fifteen wanted persons were arrested as well. They included three Company Commanders and one Quartermaster from the Ardoyne's Provisionals.[57] A lull during the Christmas holiday saw relatively few incidents. The emphasis tended to be outbreaks of shooting rather than explosions. In the Falls a former British soldier – O'Toole, aged 20, who was discharged half-way through a six year engagement with the Royal Irish Rangers – was snatched into a car by three men, taken round the corner and shot in both legs, leaving him seriously injured. Against this, nine persons on the wanted list were arrested.[58] Increasingly, as predicted, a shift in IRA tactics was reflected on the ground in Belfast towards softer targets. On 8 December, five young children watched as their father was shot dead in front of them in their living room in New Barnsley Crescent, Belfast. Sean Russell, a 30-year-old steel fixer, Catholic and a member of the UDR, had just arrived home from work and settled down to watch television with his children, aged between 2 and 10, while his wife, Jean, was in the kitchen preparing the evening meal. There was a knock at the door which one of the children, 8-year-old Sean, answered. A masked man, with a revolver, rushed in and asked: 'Are you Sean Russell?' As he said 'Yes', Russell rose to grapple with the gunman but the first of two shots hit him in the back of the head, the bullet emerging through his face and striking his daughter, Geraldine, on the leg. She was also hit by the second bullet. The children screamed in terror as Jean Russell rushed to her dying husband's aid.[59] Sean Russell was the first Catholic member of the UDR to be killed in the Troubles. A few days later, John Garrett, a part-time soldier in the Territorials was shot and seriously wounded at his Belfast home when he was lured to the front door of his house by the raised voices of two men who were apparently trying to sell his wife some 'Christian literature'. This seemed part of a coordinated number of attacks on persons and property in Belfast that day: a bomb damaged the home of a Unionist Association official in the Malone Road and that of a JP in Springfield Parade – his elderly wife punched and kicked gunmen before slamming the door in one of the men's faces.[60]

As 1972 arrived there was an explosion in the central shopping area of Belfast, on 4 January, which caused injuries to between fifty and sixty people. A bomb had been attached to a hijacked brewery lorry which was then parked in a fairly narrow street near to some large shops. The bomb itself was small by recent standards – estimated at around 10lbs of gelignite – and did little damage to surrounding buildings; most of the injuries were caused by flying glass. Unlike practically all previous cases of deliberate bombings in the city, no prior warning was given on this occasion – which accounted for the unusually large number of casualties. The injured were mainly women and children.[61] The next two largest explosions again occurred in Belfast. In Ballymacarrett, twenty-six people – eight soldiers and eighteen civilians – were injured by a bomb which had been left as a booby trap; this was the first significant incident in this area of east Belfast for some time 'and therefore represents a disappointing setback',[62] observed a Current Situation Report delivered to Heath. But bombs were spectaculars; they did not necessarily reflect the situation on the ground. And the attrition of the IRA continued. The first weekend of the new year a club in the Ardoyne was successfully cordoned and searched for wanted men; after seventy people had been screened, four were found to be wanted – including two Company Commanders from the Provisionals. A similar operation in the north of Belfast on the Sunday met with resistance, and some damage to property, before the screening could be carried out. Two men were finally arrested.[63]

By the time GEN 47 met, on 11 January, Carver reported that the marked increase in terrorist activity shortly before Christmas had not brought pre-Christmas shopping activity to a standstill as the Provisionals had threatened. Since Christmas, shooting and bombing incidents had been relatively limited in point of number. The attrition of the Provisionals had continued with the arrest of a further eight officers in Belfast; the Provisionals were now virtually leaderless in the Ardoyne. In the ensuing discussion it was suggested that the continuing attrition of the Provisionals might provide an opportunity for the Officials to present their less violent policy as the more productive; alternatively, the Officials might be under some temptation to resort to greater violence in order to prevent their more militant members from joining the Provisionals. The relatively low number of violent incidents since Christmas gave rise to the question as to whether the present level of violence in Belfast was as low as could be reasonably expected there short of a deliberate decision by the IRA to reduce drastically or to call off its campaign.[64] This was more a hope than anything but it reflected the pressure the Provos were under in Belfast. The Army, though, remained optimistic. On 24 January the Chief of the Defence Staff visited Northern Ireland to be briefed, at HQNI, on the security situation by Tuzo, Ford and the Director of Intelligence. Tuzo felt that the attrition operation was going well: it was 'designed to make the IRA desist and the policy is working but at the price of implacable and growing Roman Catholic hostility, not only to the Protestants but to the Army'. This hostility was tending to spread upwards through the middle class, encouraged by some Catholic priests (probably a reference to Father Denis Faul and Father Raymond

Murray who were publicizing alleged brutalities by the Security Forces) and 'behind it all stands NICRA, the active ally of the IRA'. Tuzo thought there was an 'extraordinary degree of Roman Catholic ignorance and prejudice' about the Army's role in support of the 'legally constituted Government'. The GOC considered the 'IRA propaganda machine' to be the 'main enemy', not the IRA itself. Its efforts tended to leapfrog Britain but found more acceptance abroad. As for the future, there was a continuing need to:

(1) Sustain the attrition operation.
(2) Seek reconciliation with the Catholic community at every opportunity.
(3) Seek to defeat IRA hostile propaganda and preserve the good name of the Army, which is being assailed with evil intent.

Ford noted that statistics showed some change in IRA operations with a move away from Belfast to the Border and rural areas over the past two weeks. He agreed with Tuzo about the IRA propaganda effort: it had reached such a pitch and scale that it had to be taken account of at all levels in planning and executing operations. An otherwise successful operation 'can so easily lead to a propaganda victory for the enemy by faulty handling'. Londonderry, though, remained a problem. Since 1 January up to fifteen IRA gunmen had been seen to fall in Derry. It was noted that: 'The interesting thing is that there is always an instant reaction to our patrolling but none to the casualties we inflict by our own sniper fire.' The Creggan and the Bogside were IRA strongholds. To go into the Creggan to pick up, say three wanted men, was virtually a four or five company operation. The situation in Belfast was different. There was every reason to hope that the current rate of attrition could well reduce the level of violence in Belfast even further. The month of March was likely to be the key moment 'but a wary eye must be kept on the Border and rural areas'. The decisive factor in Belfast might 'not be so much a matter of statistics as of declining IRA morale'. It was for this reason that it was most important that the current rate of attrition in Belfast was sustained over the next six weeks. The Provisionals, it was felt, appeared to have two options 'if they accept neutralisation' in Belfast:

(1) To throw in their lot with the Officials and indulge in civil disobedience and subversion, which needs high force levels to counter, or
(2) To change the emphasis of their operations to the border and rural areas, which will mean the introduction of new IRA elements against which the possible employment of SAS may pay big dividends.

Tuzo and Ford thought Catholic antagonism could possibly be countered by the transfer of law and order from Stormont to Westminster and some positive signs of a political initiative by HMG. In military terms the major problem outside 39 Brigade (where the 'tide is definitely going in our favour. Some Roman Catholic areas are virtually cleared of IRA violence'; others were half cleared, with one or two – such as Andersonstown – 'still hard core') was the lack of intelligence coverage, which was relatively poor. A new complication was the increasing part played by the Fianna: the range of action possible against those of age 16 and below was 'strictly limited'. With continuing security success HQNI was prepared to contemplate amending the current internment policy. The first step would be the segregation of internees into three classes, thus allowing the release of the least dangerous as a political gesture at the appropriate time. It would then be possible to make the initial apprehension of suspects even more selective and say so; there would, however, be security consequences: in Ford's opinion violence would escalate if this was done. The Director of Intelligence warned that 'we would lose intelligence' and the problem would be how to start it again. Tuzo emphasized that it was 'absolutely necessary' to keep internment going in as discriminating a way as possible until the IRA were seen to have reduced the level of violence. When they had clearly done so 'it would be right to make a gesture to test their reaction'. While the level of violence in Belfast might be significantly lower in six weeks' time this could be countered by an increase in the rural areas; the Director of Intelligence considered that urban guerrillas in Belfast would not be transferred to the rural areas – cross border ASU operations would, instead, be stepped up.[65]

The evidence on the ground did, indeed, reflect the optimism shown by Tuzo and his staff. The Special Branch assessment for the period up to 19 January noted that it had been one of 'continuing success for the Security Forces and a gradual scaling down in IRA activity with a decrease in both the number and size of explosive attacks and a decrease in the number of attacks with firearms on the Security Forces'. Belfast had enjoyed a marked reduction in explosive attacks with only fifteen incidents out of the total of forty-six reported occurring there. This fact, together with evidence that a number of bombs contained gelignite adulterated with fertilizer, pointed to a need on the part of the IRA to conserve explosives and/or distribution difficulties: few of the Belfast explosions were thought to have involved the use of explosives of over 10lbs. The Provisionals' Ballymacarrett and Markets Companies had been suspended shortly before Christmas due to the loss of manpower and material. Morale was reported to be low because local residents were not supporting the Republican Movement as they had been in the past. The Markets unit, however, was later reported to have been in action again on 17 January following the escape of detainees from the *Maidstone*.

As both wings of the IRA became less effective the Fianna was playing an increasingly active role. On 8 January the Army detained three youths and a 14-year-old girl in possession of 50ft knotted rope and a docker's hook at the rear of HM Prison in Crumlin Road; they were acting under orders from the local Provisional battalion. The incident coincided with a disturbance in the exercise yard of the prison. Three of the youths were known members of the Fianna's New Lodge Road unit. On 12 January a youth armed with a Walther pistol and an empty magazine was arrested in Belfast and proved to be a member of a Provisional Fianna unit.[66] This tied in with signs that attacks in Belfast were being carried out by 'unenthusiastic and unskilled terrorists'. Shooting incidents had, in general, been less effective, although one soldier was very seriously wounded by a sniper on 15 January. The Dublin leadership were reported to be insistent on continuing the present campaign indefinitely: individual units would continue to plan and conduct their own operations in the North. HQNI's assessment of the security outlook was that:

> Despite the continuing attrition of men and material, and the consequent effect on morale, both factions of the IRA must be expected to attempt to maintain at least their present level of operations. As in previous weeks, spectacular or dramatic operations, aimed at securing maximum publicity, and boosting morale, might be expected to occur. As security force search and arrest activity continues to affect the IRA's freedom to act in pursuit of these objectives, the assassination of off-duty security force personnel and selected civilians is likely to become a terrorist tactic.[67]

In addition, ASU operations from across the Border were expected to increase. On another front the anti-internment campaign had been given new momentum by the opening of the new Magilligan internment camp near Derry: 'The planned [Civil Rights] march in Londonderry on 30th January 1972 would therefore represent a serious security problem.'[68] Despite this cloud on the horizon, Carver was reporting to GEN 47, on 27 January, that, within the last week, the number of incidents in Belfast had shown a further decline, although the focus of terrorist activity had – as predicted – shifted to the country areas.[69] So, in January 1972, IRA activity had been reduced with internment grinding down many IRA units in terms of personnel and material. The prediction was that Security Force successes would continue, although violence could not be eliminated. But these successes were soon to be nullified by the events of 30 January 1972.

Notes

1. McCreary, *Survivors*, pp.93–5.
2. Ibid., pp.86–7.
3. Ibid., p.95.
4. Ibid., pp.50–1.
5. Bean and Hayes op.cit p.49.
6. Ibid., p.54.
7. Ibid., p.52.
8. Ibid., p.56.
9. Ibid.
10. McKittrick et al., *Lost Lives*, pp.94–5.
11. MacStiofain, *Revolutionary in Ireland*, pp.207–8.
12. McKittrick et al., *Lost Lives*, p.96.
13. Ibid., p.97.
14. Ibid., p.100.
15. Ibid., pp.100–1.
16. Ibid., p.103.
17. *News Letter*, 7 October 1971.
18. Ibid., 9 October 1971.
19. Ibid., 29 October 1971.
20. Ibid., 26 October 1971.

21. Ibid., 18 October 1971.
22. Ibid., 26 October 1971.
23. Ibid., 27 October 1971.
24. Ibid., 28 October 1971.
25. *Irish News*, 3 November 1971.
26. Ibid., 4 November 1971.
27. Ibid.
28. Ibid., 6 November 1971.
29. MacStiofain, *Revolutionary in Ireland*, p.209.
30. Maria McGuire, *To Take Arms: A Year in the Provisional IRA* (London: 1973), p.33.
31. Ibid., pp.32–3.
32. Ibid., pp.74–5.
33. Peter Taylor, *Provos*, p.93.
34. Peter Taylor, *Brits*, pp.63–4.
35. NAUK PRO PREM 15/100 Cabinet: Northern Ireland. Minutes of a Meeting on 22 June 1970.
36. NAUK PRO DEFE 24/980 Northern Ireland: Political & Intelligence Assessments.
37. NAUK PRO DEFE 25/304 Northern Ireland – Ministerial Meeting 27 April 1971.
38. NAUK PRO DEFE 25/304 Northern Ireland Intelligence Arrangements April 1971 JIC (A) 23.
39. Anderson, *Joe Cahill*, pp.221–2.
40. MacStiofain, *Revolutionary in Ireland*, p.193.
41. BSI APIRA 24 Statement of PIRA 24.
42. NAUK PRO CJ 4/56 UKREP Telegram No.35 of 14 August 1971 to Home Office.
43. NAUK PRO DEFE 23/110 Interrogation in Northern Ireland: An Assessment of Local Factors Affecting its Operation and a Record of its Value in Security Force Activities.
44. NAUK PRO DEFE 23/109 Interrogations in Internal Security Situations since 1945, 21 November 1971.
45. NAUK PRO DEFE 23/110 Interrogation in Northern Ireland: An Assessment of Local Factors Affecting its Operation and a Record of its Value in Security Force Activities.
46. NAUK PRO DEFE 23/160 Stephens to Moore, 21 January 1972.
47. NAUK PRO DEFE 23/119 Interrogation in Northern Ireland: An Assessment of Local Factors Affecting its Operation, and a Record of its Value in Security Force Activities.
48. Report of the Committee of Privy Counsellors appointed to consider authorised procedures for the Interrogation of persons Suspected of Terrorism Cmnd 4901 (HMSO 1972) Majority Report para. 20.
49. BSI JS8 Tuzo to Faulkner 13 September 1971.
50. NAUK PRO 163/170 A military appreciation of the security situation in Northern Ireland as at 4th October 1971.
51. Ibid.
52. *Irish News*, 4 November 1971.
53. Ibid., 5 November 1971.
54. BSI G29 A.224.001.
55. BSI G34.238.
56. BSI G38.253.
57. NAUK PRO PREM 15/1000 Northern Ireland: Current Situation Report No.41 – 22 December 1971.
58. NAUK PRO PREM 15/1000 Northern Ireland: Current Situation Report No.45 – 31 December 1971.
59. *Irish News*, 9 December 1971.
60. *News Letter*, 15 December 1971.
61. NAUK PRO PREM 15/1000 Northern Ireland: Current Situation Report No.47 – 4 January 1972.

62. NAUK PRO PREM 15/1000 Northern Ireland: Current Situation Report No.51 – 10 January 1972.
63. NAUK PRO PREM 15/1000 Northern Ireland: Current Situation Report No.46 – 3 January 1972.
64. BSI G50.307.
65. BSI CT1 Northern Ireland. Visit of CDS on 24 January 1972.
66. BSI CT1 Special Branch Assessment for the Period... 19 January 1971.
67. BSI CT1 Headquarters Northern Ireland Intelligence Summary No. 3/72 for the Period 13–19 January 1972.
68. BSI G68.430. Headquarters Northern Ireland Operational Summary for the Week Ending 07.00 hours on 21st January 1971.
69. BSI G79.486 GEN 47 27 January 1972.

8

The Road to Bloody Sunday: Derry, July 1971–January 1972

In November 1971, Mrs Emily Groves, the mother of eleven children, was blinded by a rubber bullet which was fired through the window of her Andersonstown home by a British Paratrooper from close range. She recalled how:

> We were wakened about 6 a.m. when the Army were searching houses in our area. The first soldiers who came were reasonable, and the man who searched my house was courteous. I treated him well too. Then...someone said, 'Here come the Paras'. It was about 9 a.m....and my God their attitude was not normal. They put us under house arrest and placed a soldier in every hallway ...I said to one of my children 'Put a record on the record-player and build up our morale'...She put on...'Four Green Fields'...The record was playing for two minutes until a paratrooper came out. I did not see him at all but a neighbour opposite me said later that the soldier ran out from behind a Saracen, jumped up in the air and fired a rubber bullet. The bullet ploughed across my face and took my eyes and nose away. I was taken down to the Royal Victoria Hospital and the doctors there looked after me. They fixed up my face, but I have been blind ever since I was hit by the rubber bullet. Someone told me later that the other paratrooper who was at my door was sick when he saw what had happened...The Army apologised to my parish priest, but they never came to me. I still don't know the soldier who did it. He may have been watching us miming, it was not a rousing song to aggravate anyone. Why did it have to happen to me?

The Army said later that the soldier had been disciplined. In March 1973, Mrs Groves was awarded £35,000 damages against the MOD. She said afterwards: 'I'd still rather take a fourpenny bus ride into town and see Belfast for myself.'[1] After she had been injured, Mrs Groves recalled:

> No one would tell me that I could never see again. Neither my husband nor my children could tell me. At the time, Mother Teresa from Calcutta was visiting Belfast. One of the doctors knew her and he asked her to speak to me. She broke the news. When I knew that I could never see again, I just wanted to die. After I left hospital I lay in bed all the time. I was broken-hearted... Though I am blind and I miss a lot, I think that case is nothing now after all that has happened. One day I decided that I would have to live or die with it, so I decided to live with it. One thing that does hurt is that I can sense children

are afraid of me. They won't stay on my knee, they want down all the time. One afternoon I overheard one grandchild saying to her friend 'Are you afraid of my blind granny?' That really hurt. But you have to accept it. Thank God I have never felt bitter. I don't wish any harm to the soldier who did it.

But Billy Groves, her husband, remained 'very bitter. I am very bitter against the Army and against that soldier. I often think about him. It makes me bitter to think that my wife was an innocent victim. She was blinded for no apparent reason, just to teach the people a lesson.' But Emily Groves could see the wider picture: 'No, I would not wish that the same thing would happen to the soldier. I don't think that violence is the answer to anything. This does not just apply to my own country. We have had all sorts of wars in all sorts of places and at the end, people have to sit round a table and talk. Why not sit round at the start and cut out all the violence?'[2] The soldier who had blinded Mrs Groves was from 1 PARA.

THE CONFLICT IN DERRY JULY–DECEMBER 1971

Bloody Sunday, 30 January 1972, is, arguably, the most controversial incident in the history of the Troubles – for Catholics that is; Protestants would cite other trauma. But, however one views the events of that day, the shooting dead of thirteen citizens (a fourteenth died later) within the United Kingdom, in a single incident, by the State's military forces elevates it to a seminal event. It was yet another defining moment in the Catholic community's relationship with the British State. An inquiry, conducted by Lord Widgery, the Lord Chief Justice of England, reported on Bloody Sunday in April 1972. It proved almost as controversial as the day itself. Widgery found that although none of those killed was proved to have been shot whilst handling a firearm or bomb there remained a suspicion that some of them had or were in close proximity to someone who had. Nationalists throughout Ireland have since attacked Widgery as a cover-up, whether intentional or not. Bishop Edward Daly, a key witness to the events on the day, commented: 'What really made Bloody Sunday so obscene was the fact that people afterwards at the highest level of British justice justified it and I think that is the real obscenity.' Major Hubert O'Neill, the Coroner who held the inquest on those who died, issued a statement on 21 August 1973 in which he said:

> This Sunday became known as Bloody Sunday and bloody it was. It was quite unnecessary. It strikes me that the Army ran amok that day and shot without thinking what they were doing. They were shooting innocent people. These people may have been taking part in a march that was banned but that does not justify the troops coming in and firing live rounds indiscriminately. I would say without hesitation that it was sheer, unadulterated murder. It was murder.[3]

British Irish Rights Watch concluded that the events which took place on Bloody Sunday 'amounted to the summary and arbitrary execution of unarmed civilians who were victims of soldiers acting under the military and political command of the United Kingdom Government'. In support of that submission, British Irish Rights Watch cited the fact that the plan for policing the demonstration – opposed by the local police chief – 'always encompassed the possibility of risk to the life of the demonstrators and others in the vicinity'; that the choice of the Paras to conduct the arrest operation was 'both deliberate and reckless' in that their training was 'completely inappropriate for such a task and their deployment made the risk of casualties inevitable'; that the overwhelming evidence of eyewitnesses and from press photographs was that none of the deceased or injured was armed with any weapon; that although individual soldiers may have genuinely believed themselves under fire there was no evidence that they came under sustained firing or a hail of nail/petrol and acid bombs which they claimed to have endured; and that no weapons, other than the nail bombs 'obviously planted' on one of the deceased, were recovered.[4] In 1974, in light of Widgery acknowledging that none of the deceased was proved to have been shot whilst handling a firearm or bomb, the British Government recognized that 'some of the deceased were wholly acquitted of complicity' in handling firearms and bombs and accepted that 'all of the deceased should be regarded as having been found not guilty of the allegation of having been shot whilst handling a firearm or bomb'. In 1992, a letter to John Hume from Prime Minister John Major, referred to the 1974 declaration as regarding those killed on Bloody Sunday as 'innocent of any allegation that they were shot whilst handling firearms or explosives'. The relatives of the deceased regarded the shift from 'not guilty' to 'innocent' as a limited form of progress.[5] In the late 1990s, as the Northern Ireland Peace Process evolved, a new inquiry was set up to look into the events of Bloody Sunday.

The process that led to the deployment of 1 PARA in Derry on 30 January 1972 began with the State's frustration that, by late 1971, Londonderry had virtually seceded from its authority. The Bogside and Creggan, the predominantly Catholic districts, and their population amounting to about 33,000 out of a total population of about 55,000, were the scene of continuing large scale rioting. At the beginning of July 1971 widespread violence was followed by military counter-action. At the end of August it was decided, after consultation with a group of prominent local citizens – the so-called Committee of 30 – to reduce the level of military activity in the hope that moderate opinion would prevail and the IRA gunmen be isolated from the community. From the end of August to the end of October, in a conscious effort to avoid provocation, the Army made itself less obvious. Though parts of the Bogside and Creggan were patrolled, no military initiative was taken except in response to aggression or for specific search or arrest operations. The improvement hoped for did not, however, take place. The residents of the Bogside and Creggan threw up or repaired over fifty barricades; frequent sniping and bombing attacks were made on the Security Forces; and the IRA tightened its grip on the district. The RUC had not operated in the Bogside and Creggan since June or July. Apart from one

Company location at the Blighs Lane factory in the centre of the area, all military posts were located round the edges of the district. The State's authority was not effectively enforced in the area.[6]

In Derry, 'PIRA 24' was the 28-year-old OC of the Provisional IRA. The Provos, he remembered, had come into being because the Officials 'did not want to carry out any operations and there were younger men who got tired of pushing the Officials to take action'. PIRA 24 was never in the Officials but went straight into the Provisionals a few months before Seamus Cusack and Desmond Beattie were killed. They had no weapons and had to steal them – prior to internment at least 50 per cent were stolen from the Officials. Despite this, the relationship between the Provos and the Stickies in Derry was not one of great animosity: 'Yes, there was a cat and mouse game about stealing weapons from one another, but there was no real bad feeling about that even. After all the Officials weren't going to use the weapons anyway. I did not want to fall into the same trap as Belfast where the two wings of the IRA ended up shooting each other.' It was clear to PIRA 24 that even the older men from the 1956 era, ex-Officials who had come over to the Provos, 'were not going to do anything much either. It wasn't working well. They were always walking about with suits and had no street credibility. It was said they always had their toothbrushes packed in case they were lifted!' At this time – PIRA 24 was Quartermaster – 'we got rid of the older guys and when internment happened in 1971, many of the officers who were set over me were lifted and I was left in charge. I therefore became OC of the Provisionals in Derry City in August 1971.' PIRA 24 probably escaped internment because he was not known to the Security Forces. After internment there were 'only about 8 or 9 of us. There were 3 girls and 6 fellows... We used to look out for likely recruits amongst the rioters to see whether they had the right attitude and spot those who were useful and then encourage them to join.'[7] PIRA 24's second-in-command was Martin McGuinness, the 21-year-old Adjutant. He recalled: 'Frankly I was not sure what an Adjutant did. I was only 21 at the time and found myself in a position and role that was not defined.' In practice the title was to maintain the integrity, discipline and structure of the organization. 'This was not a conventional army. A lot of the volunteers were younger than me. There were very few older men. We were inexperienced. My role was to ensure that the units met regularly, that the organisation was properly structured and that discipline was maintained.'[8]

The inner circle was the Command Staff. There was an OC, an Adjutant, a Quartermaster, an Intelligence Officer, a Training Officer, an Explosives Officer and a Finance Officer. The Command Staff was replicated in each Company and it was up to the local Company OC to appoint his own Section Leader and staff. Only locals would be appointed to look after their area on the basis that there was no point sending people from one area of the city to look after another where they did not know the people well and did not know the back streets.[9] There was a loose system for the passing around of instructions. The Command Staff gave instructions to Section Leaders who passed them on to Volunteers. As Sean Keenan remembered: 'There were different places in the Bogside we used to go for contact. We used to meet there twice a day. It is a small place and it was easy to meet up. Everybody knew everybody and everybody had been at school together. There were very few formal meetings.'[10] The organization, in PIRA 24's words, 'spread out like an umbrella. It was a volunteer force and no one was paid. It operated on trust, and a shared belief of common principles... Effectively the buck stopped with me and that was how I liked it. If any operation had been planned, it would have had to have been discussed with me and I would have to had to approve it.' By January 1972 there were about forty to fifty Volunteers in 5 Companies in the Creggan, Bogside, Brandywell, Shantallow and the Waterside. The Creggan unit was the largest with around twenty-five members; Brandywell, the Bogside and the Waterside averaged around seven Volunteers; in Shantallow there were around fifteen. Numbers were always changing. The Command Staff knew all the Volunteers in each area but the Volunteers themselves would only know those in their area. As the areas got bigger and more Volunteers joined 'it became territorial' and Volunteers did not operate outside their own areas. As OC, PIRA 24's aims were to set up no-go areas with 'the proper structures' and to organize things within them. In running the no-go areas 'we dealt with mundane matters such as domestic rows, up to and including fighting the on-going war with the security forces'. It was

> very important that the Provisionals were seen to do the right thing because otherwise the people would turn against you. In the early days, the Provisional IRA had no great support and I wanted us to gain a good name in Derry. The no-go area operated a 'doors open' policy. This meant that no one locked their doors, but were safe in the knowledge that no one would come in and steal their things from their houses.

This worked because of the 'social work' carried out by the Provos and the policing organized by the Command Staff.[11] Sean Keenan, 21-year-old Explosives Officer of the Bogside section of the Provisionals, recalled:

> It is difficult to estimate our actual support base. It was inevitably relatively small because the IRA did not become popular until after Bloody Sunday. After Bloody Sunday any young man would have joined. Tens of thousands of people wanted to help even if they did not join and people were queuing up to join as well. Before Bloody Sunday support was fragile. People would have tolerated IRA activity provided nothing went wrong.[12]

Any latent sympathy for the IRA might be extended to cooperation if there was anger with the Security Forces – particularly with lethal force incidents. Annette McGavigan, a 14-year-old Catholic schoolgirl, was shot dead – apparently by a soldier – during an exchange of fire between troops and the IRA. She was hit in Abbey Street in Derry as she attempted to get a rubber bullet to add to her collection of riot souvenirs. Annette had the dubious distinction to be the 100th civilian to die during the current phase of the Troubles.[13] William McGreanery, a 41-year-old Catholic shop assistant, was shot by a soldier in the early hours of 14 September. He died shortly after 3 a.m. The soldier claimed he fired at a man aiming a rifle at the OP in Bligh's Lane. Civilian witnesses said the victim was unarmed. Swabs taken from the deceased's hands revealed no lead traces. There were disturbances occurring at the time of the shooting. Four other people – two soldiers and two civilians – also received gunshot wounds. John Hume criticized the Army's version of events as being 'without the slightest shed of truth'. He asked:

> Can the army not in this case at least tell the full truth about what happened? He was not armed, nor had he any association with any sort of political body in this city. He was walking in the street with some friends at the time. He was shot down by an army bullet. Army statements about incidents in Derry have lost all credibility among people because they have been proved incorrect so often.[14]

The same day a soldier of 45 Medium Regiment Royal Artillery, Martin Carroll, was shot while on duty with his brother at the Bligh's Lane OP. Sergeant Carroll's brother – his half-brother, a Sergeant-Major – heard his shout '"I've been shot." I was 20 yards away. I rushed over. He lost consciousness immediately and I helped to get him into an armoured car. My brother was a popular kid with all the boys. He was a great mimic, always livening up duties.' The IRA carried out the attack in retaliation for 'brutality to young children on their way to school by the British army'. Sergeant Carroll's 23-year-old wife gave birth to a son four months after his death. She later said: 'At the time I just felt numb but I did not have feelings at all towards the Irish. I don't think you can blame a whole country for the mistakes of a minority. Martin's father's family hail from Éire. Martin was a Catholic and his brother has just married an Irish girl who is very nice. I am very proud of my husband in that he gave his life to a cause.'[15]

This was the cost in human terms. In wider, strategic terms Catholic Derry remained a law unto itself. PIRA 24 noted how:

> We used to gain a lot of intelligence from people doing ordinary day jobs who would see extra military activity such as transport or troop movements and would let us know what was going on. People gave us the intelligence which traditionally they would have given to the RUC. The people were more loyal to us than the police... intelligence came from places like the City Hotel in Derry.

It was not long before

> We got to the position where the people, themselves, were keeping the security forces out in order to protect the Provisionals. The people effectively ran the no-go area and only came to the Command Staff if there was a problem... Also we were consulted by Council staff about where they could work. I remember the local Water Board officials contacting us to see if it was okay for them to carry out repair work in a particular street. They didn't want us stealing their vehicles... we were careful not to steal a car which

someone desperately needed for their work. We were very keen not to mount operations which exposed civilians to danger...Marches were never used by us for those sorts of purposes, although it is possible that riots or their aftermath might be so used. What we used to do was to send a well known volunteer down to a riot in order to clear the rioters from the street. There were a couple of our volunteers who were so well known that you only had to see them on the streets for people to get off sides so an operation would commence.[16]

Riots and rioters were thus, as in Belfast, a suitable prelude for attacks on the Security Forces. Among the rioters were the IRA's youth wing, the Fianna. Gearoid O'hEara occupied a senior position in the Fianna. Before Bloody Sunday it was loosely organized. There was a leadership group that was, in a sense, collective. Nominally, O'hEara was leader of that 'inner circle'. The Fianna was connected to the Provisionals by a Liaison Officer appointed by the IRA. O'hEara was chosen to be the Fianna representative: 'I had no formal title, such as OC, but in a manner of speaking, the IRA liaison officer was my "line manager" above me which would confirm my status as Fianna Leader.' In early 1971, O'hEara, together with other members of the Fianna, were affiliated to the Officials. But, in about October or November 1971, they – numbering fifteen to twenty – defected to the Provisionals; only three remained loyal to the Officials. If somebody wanted to join it was a collective decision by existing members, although, since it was a loose structure, it was possible for somebody else to trail along with the other members of the Fianna. Members were not involved in car hijacking, nor did they have access to weapons or scout for military operations. Riots 'happened spontaneously. They didn't need organising. Riots involved hundreds of young people. They had a form known in the Community. If that form was to be changed, then rioters needed to be warned. Occasionally shots were fired and a shout would be heard for the streets to be cleared, but the Fianna were not sent out to organise riots as a precursor to shooting.'[17] Riots proved a suitable recruiting ground for the Provisionals. PIRA 19 was a 17-year-old Provisional IRA Volunteer who progressed from rioting to the IRA:

> I became involved in rioting and, as a result of this, I got to know a few guys who were already in the Provisional IRA. They did robberies – banks or holding up of the insurance man, bread man or milkman when they did their rounds to collect money. Me and a few of the other guys from the Waterside area acted as lookouts and kept an eye out for them. At the time I lived near Ebrington Barracks so I also kept an eye on the troop movements. We were told what to do, where to go – to gather information and pass it on to a higher level...I was not a member of any organisation. There were no regular meetings. We just hung around on street corners, starting the riots and the like. We never talked of, or talked about, the 'Fianna'. We were youngsters on the fringes of the IRA who were keen to be involved in the excitement of it all and who wanted to be closer to the movement.

PIRA 19 started going to a few meetings to see what was going on. He met with older men from outside the Waterside area. They were interested in youngsters who took a leading role in the riots. They kept them on the 'long finger' but giving them glimpses of what it was like to be a Volunteer so as to encourage them to go to meetings. These were training sessions that took place in the old shops beside the Bogside Inn. There were three shops in a row and the walls between them had been partly knocked down. There were still three separate areas: the first was a general area where the youngsters met. The second room was used for training of the 'more senior guys... I remember once they had effigies of soldiers – stolen uniforms filled with straw. These were used for kicking and punching practice. The training for full volunteers was in the second separate room. You could see the guns and you were told that you would have access to guns if you joined.'

About twenty to thirty attended these meetings which usually took place twice a week on a Tuesday and a Thursday. When PIRA 19 finally joined, just before Bloody Sunday, he found everyone 'in good spirits because there had been 2 successful hits on the RUC that day'. He was not shown the IRA's rule book – the Green Book – instead he was given sheets of paper with rules, instructions were read out. There were about four or five in each section.[18]

Despite the level of disorder created in Derry, neither IRA faction had large quantities of weapons or ammunition. The difference between the two wings was that the Provisionals took the offensive while the Officials regarded themselves as a defensive organization. At the time of Bloody Sunday, Reg Tester was a Command Quartermaster for the Official IRA. Originally from Nottinghamshire and formally in the Royal Navy, he was third in command of the local Brigade. Weapons were in short supply. On one occasion two men, who were deep sea divers, dived to an old aeroplane wreck in Lough Foyle and retrieved an old Browning gun from the plane. Members of the Official IRA cleaned up the gun; the barrel looked like new once it had been cleaned. The Officials paraded the barrel of the gun around the Bogside underneath a blanket but ensured that the barrel of the gun was peeping out to make sure that it looked as though they had a Browning gun. Then, the Officials built a sandbag post by the Bogside Inn and poked the gun out of a hole in the sandbags. Two Army jeeps came down towards the sandbag post but beat a hasty retreat once they saw the gun.[19] With weapons scarce, both IRA factions kept a strict control on their arsenals – except that although all weapons were theoretically accounted for, the Provisionals' OC had his own dump that was separate from that of the Quartermaster who did not know about it. The weapons in this dump were used for replacement purposes.[20]

The Provisionals had better weaponry than the Officials – 'We would not have been able to keep a platoon of the British Army out for more than half an hour,' noted Tester – because after the split, county arsenals had fallen into their hands. The Derry Officials used to get messages from Dublin HQ to come and collect packages but it would usually be a supply of ammunition or a weapon or two. Tester did not keep a written inventory or count things in or out; he did, however, 'know what we had, and know who would have it. If any weapon got lost, then I would know about it.' Explosives were also a problem. Gelignite used to come from quarries as a rule. It was in very short supply. Effectively it was sawdust that had been impregnated with nitro-glycerine. This seeped and drained to the bottom. On occasions it had to be destroyed because of poor storage conditions. This would be done by mixing it with axle grease: 'you would then work it in and then put a match to it'. Alternatively it would be disposed of in deep water: it would not blow up unless there was a detonator involved. Tester did not personally make nail bombs but those who did broke down the sticks of gelignite and would put them in a tin. Effectively they were 'a poor man's hand grenade, lit with a short length of safety fuse which would be lit with a match.' Tester did not like the attitude of the Provos:

> I can remember on one occasion a Provo volunteer just firing a pistol generally up the fields through a gap in the walls in the Creggan estate. He was simply wasting ammunition and then running away. My view was simple. We were at war with the British Army. If the British Army and the security forces left us alone, we left them alone... we were very much a defence force... our rule of thumb was that we did not shoot at someone just because they wore an army or RUC uniform.

The Officials did not want civilian casualties. A low key incursion would be tolerated. If anyone came into the area then the 'duck patrols' would come into operation. These were kids who ran behind anyone who was coming in making duck noises so that the Officials and others would be alerted to the fact that someone was in the area. 'If push came to shove and we were forced to defend an area, then we would step in and do so. Otherwise we would let anybody who came into the area go away.'[21] The Provisionals, on the other hand, wanted to take the war to the British. But they, too, had problems with weapons and ammunition: thus, attacks would often involve the use of nail bombs against the Security Forces as much as sniping attacks. Nail bombs were devices that were only made up when they were needed. Tins were abandoned because the explosive tended to sink to the bottom so that when the bomb went off the nails didn't go anywhere. They were also too heavy.[22] Sean Keenan, as Bogside Section Explosives Officer, recalled:

> You make a nail bomb by using full or half sticks of gelignite depending on how powerful you want it to be. You tape the sticks together and then tape nails onto the sticks of gelignite. Alternatively you wrap the gelignite in rough cardboard and tape the nails to that. Then you use a pencil to push a hole into the gelignite into which you put the detonator and the fuse. All that is necessary then is to light the fuse... I did not use a can to hold the bomb together. I used tape to bind it all together. Sometime matches were taped to the fuse or you lit the fuse with a match... A nail bomb was crude but effective against people. Once the fuse had been lit you could not stop it except by cutting the fuse below where it had burned to, or by pulling the detonator out with the fuse attached. Fuses were generally waterproof and it

would not matter if they were dropped in water because they would still keep on burning down. If you drop one it is practically 100% certain that it will go off anyway.[23]

Explosive attacks could be very effective. Two soldiers died when the IRA lobbed a bomb into their OP in Londonderry on 27 October. The men, members of the 45th Medium Regiment Royal Artillery, were killed instantly when the 20lb bomb was thrown over a ten-foot wall from the bowling green in Brooke Park in the Rosemount area of the city. Three men were seen to run away after the explosion. The OP was a twelve-foot high barricade of sandbags and corrugated sheeting which stretched across the narrow Warke's Lane. The post was about eighty yards inside the lane, bounded on one side by the park wall and on the other by small terraced houses, many of them abandoned. A narrow gap was left between the wall and the edge of the sandbagging and it appeared that the bombers had accurately pinpointed the point at which to lob the bomb over the wall. It landed either on the parapet or inside the OP itself. The OP was a defensive point for the Rosemount RUC station which had been the target of many attacks. The Provisionals claimed that the attack was in revenge for the killing of two Republican sisters the previous weekend in Belfast.[24] The soldiers killed were Lance Bombardier David Tilbury, aged 28, and Gunner Angus Stevens, aged 18.[25]

At the end of October, 8 Infantry Brigade, within whose area of command the City of Londonderry lay, was given instructions progressively to regain the initiative from the terrorists and reimpose the rule of law on the Creggan and Bogside. Hooligan activity was to be vigorously countered and arrest operations were to be mounted.[26] This task fell to Brigadier Andrew MacLellan who, on 27 October (the day Tilbury and Stevens were killed), arrived at Ebrington Barracks to take up the command of 8 Infantry Brigade, responsible for Derry, from Brigadier Cowan. Brigadier MacLellan was described by Field Marshall Lord Carver as 'a quiet man, in some ways unassuming'. He was very different to his counterpart at 39 Brigade, Frank Kitson: 'probably the sort of man to take the safe course. He provided a steady reliable safe pair of hands.'[27] As he departed, Cowan left handover remarks for MacLellan. He warned: 'RCs [Roman Catholics] will resent invasion of their homeland, we are going to thump the majority not, as in Belfast, the minority. Must expect active hostility from 25,000 plus gunmen and professional hooligans. Small bodies of troops if they show restraint will be surrounded and eaten up by large hostile crowds, or be forced to use the full range of IS weapons at very early stage which will further aggravate situation.'[28] Derry, explained Cowan, was therefore different from the situation that prevailed in Belfast: there Catholics were the minority; here they were the majority.

> So long as it appears to the majority of Catholics that the British Army is a threat to their community by acting as an 'instrument of Stormont' and is believed by many as being an obstacle to their political aspirations, they can be expected to believe most of [the] IRA statements; and, so long as they

believe, they repeat. The indigenous Irish, once convinced that their cause is just, possess a breathtaking ability to lie with absolute conviction, not just in support of something they will believe to be true.

His Brigade tactics had been based on the attrition of IRA strength, by searches, arrests and internment, with the infliction of casualties in gun battles as an important bonus, leading to a collapse of IRA morale and capability. Cowan did point out, however, that there was no direct correlation between the attrition of IRA numbers and the IRA's ability to shoot and bomb:

> During the critical period that we and the IRA now face it is obvious that they will go to all lengths to intensify their attacks and, as their real power lessens so their attacks may become more savage and indiscriminate even when the number of terrorists is quite small, as the Angry Brigade have shown, incidents can still be arranged. Nevertheless, it is attrition that will finally break the IRA, and hopefully destroy their morale at some point along the path to total elimination, and the public in Britain has a duty to be at least as patient as the Northern Ireland population, who are suffering the direct effects of the IRA's campaign.[29]

MacLellan subsequently conducted a series of operations in the Bogside and Creggan at battalion strength with the object of clearing barricades, making arrests and searching premises about which intelligence reports had been received.[30] On 10 November 1971, as a result of a Directive issued on 26 October by the CLF, MacLellan issued OP Directive number 4 of 1971:

> We believe that the present rate of attrition is beginning to affect the morale of the IRA and to weaken their operational ability. Furthermore there is evidence that a proportion of the community of the Bogside and Creggan are fed up with the disruption of their lives, with the disorder and with the gunmen in their midst. Taken in concert these features indicate that if the security forces can continue to operate at a high level of intensity and can re-establish control and stability, the IRA will be defeated.

But he also noted how the 'hooligans in Londonderry are particularly youthful, agile, cunning and fleet of foot and any arrest manoeuvre which smacks of ponderousness will not catch them, they must be dispersed by the minimum use of force, and arrested by the use of imaginative tactics.' Commanders were to ensure that the personal standards of conduct of their soldiers 'do not deteriorate whatever the provocation. At all costs the soldier must be, and must be seen to be, impartial, humane and courteous. Similarly his professional standards must remain high, particularly in the field of fire, discipline, weapon training and alertness.' MacLellan acknowledged that there must, at times,

> inevitably be a tendency for our soldiers to become frustrated and angry and even to regard the entire community of the Bogside and Creggan as supporters

if not actual members of the IRA. Of course this is not true. It does not automatically follow that because most of them are against the Stormont Government that they actively support the IRA. Nevertheless in their desire to see the fall of the Stormont Government, they share, to some extent, a common aim with the gunmen and are very susceptible to anti-security forces propaganda. Our successes against the IRA cannot therefore be seen in isolation and must be balanced against our success in convincing moderate opinion that the defeat of the IRA is in the best interests of the community as a whole... Our enemies' propaganda machine is both efficient and unscrupulous and is quick to exploit any weakness in our position. It is therefore imperative that we act honourably and in our relentless pursuit of the IRA do everything we can to avoid alienating the decent people who are at present being cowed and intimidated by the gunmen and thugs. We shall defeat the IRA, but if we do not also win the battle on the public information front we shall have gained a pyrrhic victory. It is vital, therefore, that not only should the behaviour of troops be impeccable, but also that commanders should exploit every opportunity to gain favourable publicity for our activities.

The current programme of arrest operations was to be continued at the highest possible intensity. The aim was to conduct a never-ending series of small arrest operations and to harass the IRA to such an extent that 'they do not know where to turn to next for a safe bed for the night'. Units were to carry out frequent irregular patrolling by day and night 'throughout their areas of responsibility'. The aim of these patrols would be to re-establish law and order in the Bogside and Creggan areas of the city.[31]

In fact these operations hardened the attitude of the community against the Army, with the result that the troops were operating in an entirely hostile environment and as time went on were opposed by all elements of the community when they entered the Bogside and Creggan. The Army's static positions and observation posts were fired on and a large number of youths, many of them unemployed, gathered daily at the points of entry into the areas which were guarded by troops in order to attack them with stones and other missiles. Many nail and petrol bombs were thrown during these attacks. Gunmen made full use of the cover offered to them by the gangs of youths, which made it more and more difficult to engage the youths at close quarters and make arrests. The Creggan became almost a fortress. Whenever troops appeared near there at night search-lights were switched on and car horns blazed. The terrorists were still in control.[32]

On 13 December, Sir Michael Carver, the CGS, briefed Heath on how, during the last week, there had been an increase both in the shooting incidents and in nail and petrol bomb incidents.[33] The extent and strength of reaction to the Army's operations was such that it was decided to review the whole military situation in Londonderry.[34] On 14 December, General Ford produced a paper for Tuzo's consideration. It was entitled 'Future Military Policy for Londonderry'. The CLF reported that none of the expectations of the meeting with the Committee of 30 had materialized. In fact the situation seemed to be getting progressively worse:

neither the RUC nor the military had control of the Bogside and Creggan areas; law and order were not being effectively maintained; and the Security Forces now faced an entirely hostile Catholic community numbering 33,000 in these two areas alone. Between 4 July and 13 December, the Security Forces had suffered twenty-two casualties from gunmen, seven of which were fatal; there had been 380 confirmed shooting incidents; 1,932 rounds had been fired with 364 rounds being fired in reply; 1,741 pounds of explosives had been used; and there had been 211 explosions (not counting about 180 nail bombs). There were at present twenty-nine barricades up, sixteen of which were impassable to one ton armoured vehicles. Military action was therefore required to establish control and stability and enable the political situation to evolve. There were three options now open to the Security Forces:

(a): Course 1. To revert to the previous policy of containment of the Creggan and Bogside from their periphery, but adopt a much more offensive attitude than in previous months.
(b): Course 2. To continue the present policy of undertaking major operations within the Creggan and Bogside but without providing a permanent presence in these areas.
(c): Course 3. To establish, on a permanent basis, a full-scale military presence in the Creggan and Bogside.

Ford concluded that, since moderates had failed to assert their influence and the Bogside and Creggan areas were completely dominated by the extremists, the pause for political activity was now over and some new initiative was clearly necessary if the present stalemate was to be broken. The only way to restore law and order in the Bogside

> is to adopt course 3 and there is no doubt that this is the best military solution. The difficulty of course is that the problem is not an entirely military one; indeed it can be argued that there is really no military necessity to enter the area at all, since it could be contained from the outside until such time as a solution is reached elsewhere in the Province. The political disadvantages of course 3 are considerable. It will be represented as repressive against one section of the community and will generate an emotive reaction which could become politically counter-productive.

Taking into account the history of Londonderry; the fact that it was almost universally recognized as something different from the rest of the Province; its proximity to the Border; the Republican reaction; and the fact that the IRA might well call off their campaign if defeated in Belfast, Ford came to the conclusion that the decision whether or not to adopt course 3 at the present time was entirely a political one. There seemed to be little military value in continuing the present policy – course 2 – of major operations in the Creggan and Bogside but without providing a permanent presence – compared with the antagonism that it was arousing in the community: 'It is true that gunmen may be shot, some intelligence may be gained and our ability to enter the area is demonstrated, albeit only in battalion strength and with copious use of CS gas.' However, the basic fault of this policy remained its temporary nature and its very harmful effect on those who might otherwise be prepared to forsake the IRA cause. 'It can be argued that all that it achieves is to drive the community further into the arms of the IRA and to increase the danger of a massive reaction. The wisdom of continuing with course 2 is therefore in doubt unless the introduction of course 3 was imminent.' The best that Ford could say of course 1 was that 'it does not stir the pot unduly in Creggan and the Bogside, but it must be recognised that the price to be paid is the fact that a community of some 33,000 citizens of the UK will be allowed to remain in a state of anarchy and revolt.' In the end Ford recommended a reversion to course 1 – or rather a 'course 1 and a half' so as to avoid comparison with the previous course 1 which was adopted up to mid-November and was 'too defensive and defeatist in concept'.[35] In London, Lord Carrington agreed that the Bogside and Creggan 'should only be entered by troops on specific information and for a minimum of routine patrolling'.[36] This was exactly the advice that Tuzo gave to Maudling when the latter visited Northern Ireland on the day Ford produced his memorandum. Maudling agreed with the GOC's advice: he had no doubt that the military judgement was right and that it would be wrong to provoke a major confrontation at this stage.[37] Carver visited Northern Ireland between 15 and 17 December. When he returned to England, he gave a report on his visit to Carrington:

> It is clear that the only policy we can sensibly pursue in Londonderry is to maintain a level of military activity which maintains the morale of the Protestants and of our own soldiers, without provoking the Catholic population to an extent which causes us severe casualties, further antagonises them and brings no dividends. Our recent increased activity has tended in this direction and I recommend, as does the GOC and the Brigade Commander, that we adopt a policy of rather less provocative activity than of recent weeks.[38]

What all this tells us is that there is no evidence of a strategy to 'teach' the Catholic citizens of Derry a lesson – at least until December 1971. A clear pattern emerges in British military thinking towards Derry: the combined recommendations of the CLF, GOC and the CGS (as well as the Brigade Commander) – all the senior military personnel concerned with Northern Ireland in general and specifically with the problems of Derry – were for a relatively low level military response to the violence in Derry. That advice was accepted and approved by the Secretary of State for Defence and the Home Secretary. Did it, however, change in January 1972?

PRELUDE

On 7 January 1972, Ford visited Londonderry and saw representatives of the Strand Traders Association – local, predominately Protestant, businessmen. The CLF visited with the RUC's Assistant Chief Constable of Operations and held discussions with the Commander of 8 Brigade, Brigadier MacLellan and the Police Divisional Commander, Chief Superintendent Frank Lagan. Ford produced a memorandum for the GOC describing what he had found. In it Ford came close to admitting that the Army had lost control of the situation in Derry – or at least were virtually powerless to end the constant violence. He was disturbed by the attitude of the Brigade Commander, the Battalion Commander and the Police Divisional Commander. Essentially the rioters from the Bogside and the Creggan were advancing incrementally towards the city centre. All the Security Force commanders in Derry admitted that 'the front' was gradually moving northwards and in their view, 'not only would Great James Street go up in time, but also Clarendon Street... This admission meant that this major shopping centre would, in their opinion, become extinct during the next few months.' In the last two weeks there had been the 'usual daily yobbo activity' in the William Street area and this had been combined with bombers making sorties into Great James Street and the Waterloo Place area. Neither foot nor mounted patrols now operated beyond the bend in William Street to the west of Waterloo Place. The soldiers and Lagan told Ford that all foot patrols were put at risk from snipers from the Rossville Flats area (the ground all around there dominating the William Street area) and that if mounted patrols moved in Pigs [APCs], the Pigs were surrounded by yobbos and this meant that dismounted men had to go with them with the consequential sniper reaction. The bombers were mostly teenagers carrying small five to ten pound devices who operated in the thickness of the shopping crowds and could not be detected by the considerable number of three-man infantry patrols. Because of the number of ruined buildings and back alleys which led into the general area from the Bogside, it was impossible to either confine public movement or control it. In addition the vast majority of people in the shopping area 'not only give no help to our patrols but, if they saw a youth with a very small bag which might contain a bomb, they would be likely to shield the youth's movements from the view of our patrols. We now have 52 men patrolling in this very small area constantly – a very large number of patrols, as I saw myself.'

The situation was further complicated by one additional ingredient. This was

> the Derry Young Hooligans (DYH). Gangs of tough, teenaged youths permanently unemployed, have developed sophisticated tactics of brick and stone throwing, destruction and arson. Under cover of snipers in nearby buildings, they operate just beyond the hard core areas and extend the radius of anarchy by degrees into additional streets and areas. Against the DYH – described by the People's Democracy as 'brave fighters in the Republican cause' – the Army in Londonderry is for the moment virtually incapable. This incapacity undermines our ability to deal with the gunmen and bombers and threatens what is left of law and order on the west bank of the River Foyle.

The weapons at the Army's disposal – CS gas and baton rounds – were ineffective. This was because the DYH operated mainly in open areas where they could avoid the gas (some had respirators, many others makeshift wet rag masks) and in open order beyond the accurate range of baton rounds. Alternatively they operated in built-up areas, where, because of their tactics and the personal protection they had, CS gas had to be used in vast quantities and to such an extent that it seeped into nearby buildings and affected innocent people, often women and children. Attempts to close with the DYH brought the troops into the killing zones of the snipers. As Ford understood it, the commander of a body of troops called out to restore law and order had a duty to use minimal force; but he also had a duty to restore law and order:

> We have fulfilled the first duty but are failing in the second. I am coming to the conclusion that the minimum force necessary to achieve a restoration of law and order is to shoot selective ring leaders amongst the DYH, after clear warnings have been issued. I believe we would be justified in using 7.62 millimetre [bullets] but in view of the devastating effects of this weapon and the danger of rounds killing more than the person aimed at, I believe we must consider using rifles adapted to fire H[igh]V[elocity] .22 inch ammunition to sufficient members of the unit dealing with this problem, to enable ring leaders to be engaged with this less lethal ammunition. 30 of these weapons have been sent to 8th Brigade this weekend for zeroing and familiarisation training. They of course will not be used operationally without authorisation.
>
> If this cause is implemented, as I believe it may have to be, we would have to accept the possibility that .22 rounds may be lethal. In other words, we would be reverting to the methods of IS found successful on many occasions overseas, but would merely be trying to minimise the lethal effects by using the .22 round. I am convinced that our duty to restore law and order requires us to consider this step.

Ford then turned his attention to the possibility of a proposed NICRA anti-internment march from the Creggan to the Guildhall Square at 14.00 hours on Sunday, 16 January – this was later postponed and became the march of 30 January. Ford instructed the Commander of 8 Brigade to prepare a plan over the weekend, based on the assumption that the march was to be stopped as near to its starting point as was practical 'and taking into account the likelihood of some form of battle (therefore he must choose a place of tactical advantage) and also the fact that the minimum damage must be done to the shopping centre'. Ford asked the Director of Intelligence to get the best intelligence of the possible strengths of the march and its real intentions. It was the opinion of the senior commanders in Londonderry that if the march took place, 'however good the intentions of NICRA may be, the DYH, backed up by the gunmen, will undoubtedly take over control at an early stage.'[39]

The significance of Ford's memorandum to the events of Bloody Sunday is clear: the suggestion that selective leaders of the DYH might be identified and shot – a tried and tested approach in IS situations encountered in colonial operations – could be interpreted as evidence of a clear intention to execute this on Bloody Sunday. In this regard the Ford memorandum could be described as a 'smoking gun' document. In fact, it is nothing of the sort. The memorandum was a proposal from Ford to Tuzo to stimulate some debate on a clearly deteriorating situation in Derry. Furthermore, the memorandum is in two parts: Ford presents his proposal for the consideration of the shooting of selected individuals *before turning his attention* to the possible NICRA march on 16 January which became the Bloody Sunday march. They are two different issues – the first for future consideration, the second the immediate problem; there was no suggestion of the more aggressive response being employed with regard to the forthcoming march. As he later explained, Ford considered that the situation with the DYH had reached such an impasse in January 1972,

> that I felt that I had to explore something new...I was exploring the possibility of converting 7.62 millimetre SLR weapons to use .22 inch ammunition. I did not know whether this was a practical proposition, but I wished to initiate some thoughts as to how we could break the impasse in which we found ourselves. .22 weapons have a limited range and the amount of damage that they cause is far less. The SLR was never designed for the sort of role that the British Army at that time was undertaking in Northern Ireland, it was intended for use in war conditions in Europe. But, like it or not, that was the weapon that was standard issue at that time.

Ford, therefore, thought that it was worth exploring the use of rifles that would fire .22 ammunition, with appropriate modifications to the Yellow Card:

> If someone was shot with a 7.62 round, it would be lethal if it hit the target in a vital part. It was also quite possible with such a round for the bullet to pass through one body and kill or injure someone else behind the original target. The .22 round was a much lower velocity bullet and could only be fired accurately at reasonably short ranges. A rioter would be far less likely to be killed, but would certainly be incapacitated... The suggestion therefore made to shoot a few leaders was not a suggestion to kill them; 'shoot' and 'kill' are obviously different words... It was usually possible to identify the ring leaders amongst the DYH, the people who were orchestrating events. Clear warnings would be given by a loud hailer and/or a banner with words such as 'disperse or we fire' would be displayed before opening fire.

The memorandum was sent to Tuzo, and not copied elsewhere, and

> was therefore me looking into new dimensions to see what alternatives there were to sort out the problem of the DYH. My memorandum stated that the weapons would not be used operationally without authorisation. There was no question of implementing any such policy without proper authorisation. By 'proper authorisation', I mean the Ministry of Defence and ultimately the Cabinet.

The details of any changes needed to accommodate new tactics would have involved many other parties, including the Government's legal advisors. That never happened in this case.[40]

That the memo's suggestions did not become official policy was confirmed by Michael Carver: he never saw this memo and was not aware of it. As .22 rifles were never used and as the possibility of their use was never referred to him, he assumed that Tuzo did not approve the suggestion. Carver recalled that, as the situation in Londonderry deteriorated, information was 'passed down from Faulkner to Tuzo through Heath to me', that the security situation must be improved. The problem was how to achieve this. The Army were dependent upon the RUC for all intelligence.

> Apart from standing still at road blocks to stop marches, having missiles, et cetera thrown and firing back the water cannons, CS gas and rubber bullets, what could we do? It was not a situation like Cyprus, Malaya or Kenya where there were prohibited areas in which the Army could shoot people. Even in these areas, it was no longer appropriate to read the Riot Act, hold up banners and then shout through loud hailers to hold fire or they would be shot dead. It was certainly not appropriate in Northern Ireland. Consequently, the Army was effectively occupying areas between the Catholics and the Protestants in both Belfast and Londonderry and patrolling the countryside in order to try and stop intersectarian clashes. There was never any question of shooting the ring leaders of a riot in Northern Ireland. It would have been totally inappropriate; we did not want to create martyrs. It has always been a principle of Army training in anti-riot drill that if soldiers were forced to open fire, they would shoot to kill and not wound.[41]

Brigadier MacLellan, at 8 Brigade, did not see the memorandum either[42] while Graham Shillington, the Chief Constable, 'would have been horrified if this had been suggested in any meeting I attended'.[43] As General Sir Mike Jackson, a future CGS himself but in 1972 Captain Jackson, the Adjutant of 1 PARA on Bloody Sunday, explained:

> People should be careful not to make a ridiculous jump from a memorandum like that to an allegation that there was a deliberate policy to shoot people. Of course, I can only surmise, but I do know how the Army works. Doubtless there was many a conversation between the two of them [Tuzo and Ford] wondering about how they were going to deal with the situation. I expect Tuzo would have asked Ford to jot his thoughts down and give him a note. In the Army we call this an 'estimate process'. We analyse factors and courses of action. To do nothing is a decision in itself. This would have been an entirely internal process along the lines of, 'What the hell do we do about Derry?' There would have been absolutely nothing of substance until an order had been issued from headquarters. Trying to make a policy leap from such an internal memorandum to an order to kill is absolutely miles away. If the course of action was to do some killing then a written order would have reflected it. 'Killing' in the blanket sense would also be completely outside the rules of engagement, the Yellow Card.[44]

At the top of the command structure, meaning political control, Lord Carrington is also clear:

> All I can say is that we were 'Yellow Carding' for all we were worth. I was involved in drafting the amendments to the Yellow Card and we would never have agreed to any course of action which involved the deliberate loss of civilian life. I cannot believe General Ford meant this by his memorandum. He probably simply meant to indicate that given the situation, fatalities were inevitable. There can be no suggestion that he was actually seeking them. I am sure that no such plan was in existence and even if it had been, the MoD, the Government and Michael Carver would have had no part in it... I can state quite categorically that it was never policy to shoot unless a target had been identified as a threat. It is ridiculous to suggest there was a plot. People always find plots in everything. I suspect the Army was frustrated at the time with the situation in Northern Ireland at the time, but to suggest that there was a deliberate policy to shoot civilians is ludicrous and something that no politician would ever agree to.[45]

Revisions to the Yellow Card, in January 1971, authorized a soldier to fire at a person carrying a firearm and thought to be about to use it and refusing to halt; at a person throwing a petrol bomb; and in certain other circumstances. In each of the circumstances listed it was specified that a warning must be given before fire was opened. The card went on to specify certain occasions when a firearm could still be used without prior warning. The Yellow Card was further revised in November 1971 in particular to give guidance to soldiers as to how to deal with armed terrorists in vehicles. The main changes were: to allow soldiers, when so authorized by Company Commanders or officers of higher rank, to have their weapons loaded, cocked and with a bullet in the breech and with the safety catch on; to allow the use of automatic fire against identified targets when that was considered by the Commander on the spot to be the minimum force necessary; and to allow fire to be opened at terrorists in vehicles.[46] Quite clearly, then, the official policy was to operate within the Yellow Card rules. There is no evidence of an instruction to operate outside these perimeters; however, what was official policy and what actually happened on the ground could be different – as the following Army radio transmission of an incident in Derry, on Friday 28 January 1972, illustrates:

Soldier: I can see the nailbomber, do you want me to shoot him, over, he has nothing in his hands at the moment?
Officer: Say again, over.
S: 1.9, wrong 6.1 [his call sign] this is, I can see the nailbomber but he does not appear to have anything in his hands, over.
O: 1.9 Roger, out.
S: 1.9 Roger out.
O: 6.1, this is 1.9, are you absolutely certain the person you can see is the nailbomber, over?

S: 6.1 positive, over.
O: 1.9, shoot him dead, over.
S: 1.9, this is 6.1, missed him by about two inches, over.
O: 1.9, bad shooting, out.[47]

In this incident the alleged nailbomber was no longer an immediate danger to any troops when the soldier opened fire; yet he was given permission to shoot at the target by an officer. This was outside the rules of engagement contained in the Yellow Card. What it illustrates is the reality of individual actions taken by troops on the ground contrary to what they were instructed to do by their senior political and military masters.

In London, when GEN 47 met on 11 January 1972, Carver reported that a military operation to reimpose law and order in Londonderry would require seven battalions and would probably involve the commitment for a long time of four battalions to the city. This would be a major operation, necessarily involving numerous civilian casualties and thereby hardening even further the attitude of the Catholic population. Heath, summing-up the discussion, said that the relative quietness of the security situation in Belfast underlined the importance of the search for a political initiative which the meeting would discuss as the next item on its agenda: 'A military operation to reimpose law and order in Londonderry might in time become inevitable, but should not be undertaken while there still remained some prospect of a successful political initiative.'[48] Overall, then, the security situation in Belfast was going well – so the last thing needed was to stir up a hornet's nest in Derry – and, indeed, the Cabinet Committee specifically ruled out any such option for the present.

Two days later the Joint Security Committee met at Stormont and renewed the marching ban for another year. The importance of enforcement was emphasized.[49] The other significant news was that the projected NICRA march from the Creggan had now been rescheduled for Sunday 30 January. It was noted that the march from the Creggan to the Guildhall had been planned in direct defiance of the ban on marches.[50] In fact there was some debate in the SDLP as to whether or not the NICRA march of 30 January should be supported. The march was discussed at formal party level by their six MPs. There were three MPs in favour of the march: Ivan Cooper, Paddy Devlin and Paddy O'Hanlon. John Hume and Gerry Fitt were opposed to the march while Austin Currie assumed a neutral role. Hume made it quite clear that he was not happy at the thought of a march taking place. In retrospect, Cooper acknowledged that Hume's fears about a violent confrontation with the Army were correct. There was concern expressed by all of them as to the manner in which the march should be controlled. Cooper had played a large part in the organization, by the Derry Citizens' Action Committee, of previous marches; but, by January 1972, street marches generally were becoming less favoured. There was a realization that street violence had to be avoided, which led to debate and discussion as to how the march should be controlled and the stewarding of the march.[51] Nevertheless, the majority of the MPs voiced their support for the march; by now feelings were running high in Catholic Derry: the opening of a camp at

Magilligan as a second internment centre had produced the threat of marches and demonstrations there. Cooper declared that 'There is no change in the initial mood of angry determination to cause the greatest possible trouble for the British Army at Magilligan. I can tell you that the Civil Rights Association in north Derry, with my full backing, have plans to cause them plenty of trouble and make them sorry they ever opened a second camp.'[52]

Back in Belfast the JSC were informed, on 20 January, by Special Branch that the rioting and hooliganism in Londonderry was sponsored jointly by both IRA groups.[53] As the JSC considered this report, Tuzo explained to the meeting that the Army were dealing with the problem as best they could, employing a variety of tactics within the constraints of the law. Their operations in the city against the IRA had been very successful of late – fifty gunmen killed or injured during the last two and a half months – and they would aim to maintain this rate of attrition.[54] Despite the problems in Derry it was also true that the Special Branch assessment for the period ending 19 January, referring to the forthcoming NICRA march, stated: 'No trouble anticipated'.[55] This brings us to the events of Saturday, 22 January. On that date an anti-internment march was organized by the North Derry Civil Rights Association and took place close to the Magilligan/Strand 14 Internment Centre, which had begun to receive internees the previous Monday. The marchers clashed with troops from 1 PARA's Composite (C) Company, operating under the command of the 2 Battalion of The Royal Green Jackets. The clash occurred when the marchers attempted to bypass the wire surrounding the internment camp, which only extended to the high water mark by going round the wire, the tide being out, and were prevented from doing so. Rubber bullets and CS gas were fired. Allegations of brutality and violence were made and television cameras recorded the event.

The rally had begun at 14.00 hours five miles from the camp where approximately 400 people had assembled. They set off across country after being addressed by Ivan Cooper. The military warned them of prohibitions. They marched across private land and by the time they reached the wire enclosing the prohibited area they totalled about 1,500. The wire was trampled and the military used baton rounds to drive the crowd back. The crowd withdrew to their original rendezvous. They were not permitted to form any sort of a marching procession. The wire was clear by 16.55 hours. Two fires were started along the protestors' route. One was quickly put out, the other destroyed the Golden Slipper dance hall.[55] The reaction of the troops guarding the internment camp, and particularly those of 1 PARA's C Company, proved controversial. The following account by Daniel McGuiness, is typical:

> As I had been working abroad in the oil industry for a few years, I had only been able to keep in touch with what was happening at home in Northern Ireland by way of newspapers, television and radio. I had been back home in July and August 1969, when there were major riots in Derry at Waterloo Place on 12th August, 1969. I remember the British Army coming into Northern Ireland at that time. I then went back to work abroad and kept up with some

of the news... From the news coverage I was receiving, I could not understand why people back home were still complaining when I considered that a solution to the problem had been in process. I thought that the nationalists were being unreasonable in resorting to confrontation, in view of the fact that a solution to the problem appeared to be underway.

That was why, when I returned home again on leave at the end of 1971, Dr McClean [a prominent civil rights campaigner in Derry] asked me to go on the march at the beach at Magilligan with him. He said that my thinking was coming from the news coverage and said that if I went with him to Magilligan I would see the reality of what was happening... When I actually saw the paratroopers in action at Magilligan, my opinion of what was happening in Northern Ireland changed dramatically. I saw the paratroopers shooting rubber bullets into the crowd and using their batons to beat civilians. One incident in particular shocked me. I saw a young man throw all caution to the wind and leap on to the back of a paratrooper to prevent him batoning another marcher. I saw the paratrooper turn around and lift his rubber bullet gun and discharge it. I saw the discharge of the shot coming out under the flap of the young man's jacket. If the discharge had gone off in the young man's stomach, he would surely have killed him at such close range. Immediately afterwards, I saw that soldier's superior give him a blistering reprimand and striking him with a baton.

Seeing the paratroopers deployed for such vigorous crowd control did not to me reflect the actions of a civilised regime. I began to question the way that London was handling the Irish situation. I now realised that the news coverage I had heard did not give a full story of what was going on. I began to think that there was some justice in the course of action taken by the nationalists.[57]

This was the first time that Ivan Cooper became conscious of the role of the Paras,

who seemed to me to be a different breed of soldier, a different species, to that which I was used to seeing in Northern Ireland. The Paras struck me as very 'soldierly' men who took a pride in their fitness and their belligerence. The Paras at Magilligan were very belligerent, and the impression I had gained was that this Regiment had been brought in to 'clean up' the civil unrest in Northern Ireland and that the Paras saw themselves in this role. The Paras at Magilligan engaged themselves in confrontations with the marchers, readily using batons to thrash the marchers with impunity. The Paras had none of the reservations which other regiments of the military had had in the past. The march at Magilligan gave me a taste of the nature of a paratrooper.[58]

Magilligan had a profound effect on John Hume who was on the march too. He had insisted that the march proceed along a beach specifically to avoid any violence and any rioting. There were no stones on the beach and Hume felt that by marching there 'we had in effect removed the risk of trouble. It was therefore much to my astonishment' to find that the Army had set themselves up on the beach behind barbed wire where they 'behaved very aggressively towards the peaceful protesters' using rubber bullets. To Hume it was of no particular significance that The Parachute Regiment was involved at Magilligan or deployed in Derry the flowing week. They were simply the British Army 'and what was frightening was the level of aggression that was displayed to the marchers in Magilligan that day'. It was as a direct result of the Magilligan march and the whole demeanour and attitude of the British Army that Hume consciously decided not to support the Civil Rights march the following weekend: 'If a peaceful march proceeding in a non built up area on a beach with no stones resulted in a violent confrontation, I shuddered to think what would happen in the streets of Derry.' During the week, at a meeting held at the Ardown Hotel, in Derry, Hume expressed the view that he thought it would be dangerous, in the light of the attitude of the British Army manifested at Magilligan, for this march to proceed and he actively sought to persuade people not to have a march and not to attend it. Though some of the clergy supported Hume, such was the strength of feeling at the meeting that the march organizers decided to go ahead.[59] Indeed, for some the blood was up: young Gerard Doherty, who was on the march on 30 January but not at Magilligan beach the week before, recalled: 'We had all heard what had happened there and we had seen the media coverage of what the Paras had done. Their reputation was as the guys who had beaten women on the beach and everyone felt angry with them. The word was about that the Paras were going to be at the march on Bloody Sunday. My friends and I had a lot of bravado and we wanted to sort them out.'[60] It seems that only limited action was taken by 1 PARA's senior officers: their CO, Derek Wilford, denied that C Company had fired rubber bullets at point blank range; but he ordered an inquiry into the behaviour of the Company at Magilligan. The inquiry confirmed that a soldier had in fact kicked a man on the ground, 'but the circumstances were such that he might easily and justifiably have lost his temper'. The soldier was called to appear before Wilford.[61]

It is from this point that some Catholics have since recalled a sense of foreboding with regard to the forthcoming march on 30 January. Roisin Stewart, who was 16 at the time of Bloody Sunday, remembered that, when speaking to Willie Meenan he told her about a conversation he had had with a soldier, one week before Bloody Sunday, when he was at the demonstration at Magilligan: 'Willie told me he said to the soldier: "You may have stopped us here, but you will not stop us next week" (Willie was referring to the civil rights march on 30th January 1972). The soldier replied: "Next week we are going to sort you out. We are going to shoot you".'[62] Shaun Anthony Doherty, who was 27 years old on Bloody Sunday, was told by a soldier at Magilligan something like: 'we had a good time today, see you next week.' After the events of Bloody Sunday 'I remember looking back and realising that what he said had been quite sinister.'[63] Joseph McKinney, a brother of Willie McKinney who was shot dead on Bloody Sunday, recalled the Paras at Magilligan shouting at the crowd: 'When we get to Creggan we will sort you out.'[64] Father Carolan 'had a funny feeling about the march that I could not put my finger on'.[65] Charles McDaid, who was 32 at the time of Bloody Sunday and had sat on the Derry City Council as a Nationalist Party councillor, was told by his wife that a lady, who did not leave her name, had called him on the telephone and left a message. The message was this: 'Tell Junior [McDaid's nickname] not to go to the march because the Paras are coming in and coming in shooting and others have been informed.'[66] Superintendent Lagan heard before Bloody Sunday that there was information that some local women who had boyfriends in the Army were told by their boyfriends to stay away from the march because it was going to be 'a rough day'.[67] Against this it has to be said that no decision to deploy 1 PARA had in fact been taken at this stage.

But concern regarding the Paras was beginning to manifest itself in other quarters as well. On 25 August there appeared an article in *The Guardian*, from Simon Hoggart in Belfast, to this effect:

> At least two British Army units in Belfast have made informal requests to Brigade headquarters for the Parachute Regiment to be kept out of their areas. Senior officers in these units regard the paratroops tactics as too rough and on occasions brutal. One officer whose Commanding Officer has made a request to headquarters said: 'The paratroops undid in ten minutes the community relations which it had taken us four weeks to build up'. The news of the requests which are to say the least extraordinary within the British Army, came after the Parachute Regiment had completed its own investigation of events at Magilligan internment camp at the weekend when reporters saw paratroops club demonstrators and fire rubber bullets at point blank range.

A senior officer based in Lisburn was reported as saying: 'Some areas are in a very delicate state at the moment and we would prefer it if the tough boys did not go in there now.' A captain in one regiment was alleged to have said: 'They are frankly disliked by many officers here, who regard some of their men as little better than thugs. I have seen them arrive on the scene, thump up a few people who might be doing nothing more than shouting and jeering and roar off again. They seem to think that they can get away with whatever they like.' Hoggart reported that the kind of incident

> which is disturbing many officers here was one which happened two months before, and in which a woman in Andersonstown was blinded by a rubber bullet fired by a paratrooper following a relatively peaceful search of the area. The woman's family admitted that she was playing Republican songs on her gramophone with the window open, while soldiers guarded the street. When she put her head out of the window, the paratrooper fired, and the bullet crashed into her upper cheek, across her nose and into both eyes. A senior officer of the Northern Ireland Headquarters said after the incident that whatever the woman had been doing, she had got much more than she could have deserved.

On the same occasion, local residents alleged paratroopers had fired rubber bullets into a peaceful crowd of young children, who a few minutes earlier had been playing and joking with men of The Royal Artillery. 'One problem for the paratroops is that they are instantly recognizable. To the civilian eye many regiments are almost indistinguishable in their green caps, but the Paras with their distinctive maroon berets are usually rather older than other units. Paras reckon to make one arrest per man when a party sent in to break up a hostile group, and they accept 10 per cent casualties to their own men as normal.'[68]

The Army were angered by the article, which they attributed to Hoggart and Simon Winchester, whom they regarded as no friend of the military. Hoggart had not checked back to say he was using the story or to request official comment. The Army alleged that Winchester 'tacitly disowned the article and agreed that Hoggart's conduct had been somewhat unethical'. The Army put this down to a 'tactic... agreed between the two Simons' with Hoggart 'the fall guy in this incident'.[69] Although the Army did not have specific examples of Winchester questioning officers about their views on the Paras, a Colonel on the General Staff wrote how it 'is known that Winchester and Hoggart have been going to units over the last three weeks and asking questions. The questions have been carefully disguised and posed amidst general conversation and where possible have been off the record.' The units were allegedly asked:

A: Do you find the community in your area more hostile after 1st Para have been there to support you in an operation?
B: Does it make your task more difficult?
C: Do you regard the Paras as the 'heavy mob' who are called in when you have a knotty problem?

I think the lawyers would regard those questions as leading... Acting Colonel GS information policy believes that we have not got enough concrete evidence to launch attacks on Winchester who has covered his tracks very carefully. However Hoggart is professionally vulnerable as a result of his unethical conduct.[70]

Why is this important in the context of Bloody Sunday? The answer lies in the continuing propaganda war that was almost as important as the war on the ground. Colonel Tugwell at Information Policy, and by implication the Army hierarchy, saw this as part of a campaign to discredit 1 PARA in particular. He identified a propaganda campaign against The Parachute Regiment as being launched through Nationalist newspapers and other media in September 1971. Tugwell classified such campaigns as 'survival propaganda' because they were aimed at people, units or methods that were effective in the anti-terrorist cause and therefore posed a threat to the Provisionals and other violent organizations. Scottish battalions, Brigadier Kitson and internment were similar targets from the 1970–71 period. This was the context of the Army view of *The Guardian* article.[71] What it meant in practical terms was that the Army brass were always inclined to see attacks on 1 PARA and other 'successful' regiments as merely part of the ongoing Republican propaganda campaign against these units.

At this point we need to ask the question: was the decision to halt the NICRA march of 30 January and conduct a subsequent arrest operation the right one? At

8 Brigade HQ it had fallen to the Brigade Major, Lieutenant-Colonel Steele, to prepare a plan, on 10 January, for dealing with the NICRA march – initially on 16 January. Steele took it as read that whilst NICRA may state that it would be a non-violent protest, 'they will have no control over the hooligan element, who will be a major part in the event. Violence at some stage of the demonstration will inevitably occur.' The key principle was that 'the march is to be stopped. There is a point before which it can be stopped and this must be accepted whatever the propaganda penalties. No matter which of the traditional routes is selected by the organisers, we must be prepared to stop it anywhere along our chosen lines.' The Army had to be prepared for 'aggro' anywhere along the line, not only during the march, but especially during the dispersal phase at the end. Hooligan action before the march started was possible but unlikely. But whichever way this event was to be handled, the following assumptions could be made:

(a) the march will have to be halted at some stage, on ground of our own choosing.
(b) hooligan violence is inevitable, probably during the event itself and definitely during the withdrawal phase after the meeting.
(c) bombing attacks and shooting incidents may intensify during the event.[72]

The reason, of course, the march had to be halted was because it was deemed illegal following the earlier JSC decision to renew the ban on marches. There was, however, a dissenting voice. Before he received any orders from General Ford in relation to the march that was now to take place on the 30th, Brigadier MacLellan discussed the situation with Chief Superintendent Frank Lagan, who, as the Divisional Commander of N Division, in which Londonderry lay, was the senior police officer in the city. That discussion took place on Monday 24 January. Superintendent Lagan's view was that if the Security Forces stopped the march, intense violence or at least intense confrontation would ensue then and subsequently.[73] Lagan and MacLellan discussed the whole range of eventualities that might arise: should the march be stopped at its origin or should it be stopped en route; should it be stopped at a place of their choice; or should it be allowed to proceed? They quickly eliminated the first two as situations which they could not implement. It became then a question of 'did we allow them through' – the march organizers wanted to proceed to the Guildhall in the city centre – 'or did we stop them?' Lagan's view was that 'if we stopped them, there would be confrontations on the day and subsequently.' Referring back to experiences of earlier marches in Derry, when a ban was imposed, Lagan was aware how factory workers, and other groups of people, 'on the drop of a hat', had decided to have a march through part of the city and the forces then available could not control them: 'For this situation to arise after the 30th, to me was bringing the law into disrepute.' It would cause people to have informal marches in the succeeding day.

Lagan believed that the marchers should be allowed to proceed to the Guildhall. He was under the impression that MacLellan agreed with him and indicated to the Brigadier that he was sending a paper through to the Chief Constable giving his views and his recommendation; MacLellan indicated he would do likewise to his authorities.[74] Lagan was worried that any smaller marches elsewhere in the city would be the ones which would cause the Security Forces the biggest headache with people marching through areas where there would be confrontations between the two religious factions. This, Lagan feared, would be much more serious than the confrontation in the Bogside. It was, according to Lagan, the first occasion he was at variance with the military in Derry over such matters.[75] Superintendent Lagan accordingly recommended that the wisest course might be to allow the marchers to continue to the Guildhall Square, to identify them by taking photographs of them and to prosecute them later. He believed that if this happened, then after the march got to the Guildhall and the speeches were over, the majority would have gone home and there would have been only limited stone throwing by hooligans.[76] Lagan left the meeting with MacLellan convinced the Brigadier was in agreement with him as to the best course to take. He described the discussion with the Brigadier as

> ...a long one. We both did the devil's advocate about what should take place. At the end of the meeting the consensus of opinion was that in the interests of the city the parade should be allowed to go through to its meeting in the Guildhall, where, I admit, this was in breach of the spirit of the ban, but the law could still be enforced as it had been previously, by prosecuting in Londonderry the people who had breached the ban.[77]

Although he did not remember MacLellan expressly saying that he thought that this was a good idea, 'he did not object or suggest another course of action. There certainly was not any argument about it.' Since a united decision by the RUC and the Army was required, Lagan informed his Chief Constable of this decision. MacLellan told Lagan that he would report back to General Ford. Lagan understood that MacLellan's report would be along the same lines as his: 'That is, that we would put forward our advice that the march ought to be allowed to proceed and that that would be presented as a view that had been reached jointly by us ("our joint advice").'[78] In fact what happened was that MacLellan reported Lagan's views to Ford by a signal despatched on that evening:

At meeting with Chief SUP N Division and his deputy today, Lagan made following points...
(a) he estimates 8,000 to 12,000 will take part, using several assembly areas and routes;
(b) he believes massive confrontation with SF [Security Forces]. We will shatter such peace as is left in city... Create intense violence and remove last vestige of moderate goodwill etc;
(c) he forecasts increased violence and smaller marches, e.g., factory workers... etc will continue for days until [ban] is clearly seen to be impossible to impose effectively as SF cannot seal Bogside permanently without bringing the city to a halt;

(d) he urges identifications and photographs followed by normal court procedures, rather than direct confrontation and is representing this line to his superiors.

I agree that consequences of stopping march will be very serious and reckon that my present permanent force levels almost certainly inadequate if we are to face situation Lagan envisages.[79]

But MacLellan, in fact, did not concur with Lagan's recommendation in the signal – he merely acknowledged the serious results of halting the march. Subsequently, MacLellan emphasized to Ford that it was 'untrue' that he had explicitly supported Lagan's recommendation. He disagreed with Lagan on the basis that the subsequent arrest of people living in the Bogside and Creggan would be virtually impossible; that the main aim of the march was to demonstrate that it was impossible for Stormont to impose the ban in Londonderry; that after a similar NICRA march in Belfast on 2 January, when the ban was seen to be broken, the Northern Ireland Government were bound to decide that the march should be stopped and that the Joint Security Committee would share this view; and that the Loyalist Workers Association had let it be known that if the NICRA march was not stopped it would organize a vast march in Belfast on the following Saturday. Given all of this, the question of whether the march should or should not be stopped was 'academic'. MacLellan was well aware that 'Lagan's sympathies, and those of his deputy, McCullough, who was also present at our meeting, lie entirely with the Catholic community [Lagan was a Catholic]. His proposal that the march should be allowed to proceed was patently a gesture or "umbrella", to maintain his position with his own people.' MacLellan did not propose then, or subsequently, that the march should be allowed to proceed, 'and I regard Lagan's evidence on this point as thoroughly misleading'.[80] Nor, it seems would Lagan have received much support from his superiors either. Shillington, the Chief Constable, disagreed with Lagan's analysis. He believed that the opposite was true and that if this march were allowed to happen, then it would encourage other marches to be organized in its wake. The fact that it had been allowed would bring the law into disrepute and it would not guarantee that the march passed off peacefully.[81] Apart from Lagan, then, there was no division among the security principals as to the necessity of halting the march before it reached the commercial area bordering the Bogside. Politically, the march had to be halted otherwise the law would be shown to be worthless.

MacLellan had discussed the question with General Ford by telephone on Tuesday 25 January; but it seems that the decision had already been taken at HQNI to prevent the march reaching the Guildhall. Colonel Derek Wilford, who took command of 1 PARA on 21 July 1971, had already been told, on Monday, 24th, that 1 PARA would be needed for operations on 30 January. 1 PARA was the reserve to 39 Infantry Brigade. After receiving MacLellan's signal – stating that he had inadequate forces at his disposal – Ford alerted his Province Reserve, 1 Battalion The King's Own Border Regiment, which had become operational on 13 January but had not yet taken part in any operations. On the

24th he also telephoned Brigadier Kitson, Commander of 39 Brigade, to inform him that he would require his Brigade Reserve as the only uncommitted battalion for the forthcoming operation in Londonderry. This was 1 PARA. The CLF warned Kitson that the battalion might be away for up to four days; Kitson agreed that for this period of time he could – just – spare them. This was called a 'warning order', which was a standing operational procedure: if a commander thought it likely, for example, that a subordinate would need reinforcements to carry out a plan, then it was good policy to give that person maximum time to prepare, hence the warning order. Ford explained: 'The type of thing that it would have said would have been that the battalion should be ready to move to Londonderry on Day X for an operation and might be deployed for Y days. This then enables the Brigade HQ to adjust its plans and for the battalion commander to start thinking of the logistics of making his men available, such as provision of vehicles, petrol, rations and so on.'[82] Although some people recalled that paratroopers whom they encountered at Magilligan Strand said words to the effect of 'See you next week',[83] in fact it was not until Monday 24 January that 1 PARA was committed to the NICRA march.

If the march had to be prevented from reaching the Guildhall then the next aspect to consider is whether or not an arrest operation should have been authorized. This was Ford's decision: it was the view of the senior commanders on the spot, and Ford supported this view, that it was inevitable that at an early stage the IRA and the hooligans would take over control of the march, no matter what the NICRA organizers wished, because of the tactics which they had employed on other occasions. Ford was concerned that the 'emotional speeches' would incite a proportion of the crowd. Furthermore, having been informed that the size of the march might be anything from 20,000 to 25,000 people, 'I had every reason to believe that these emotional speeches would persuade a proportion of the people supporting the march to join the hooligans and, after the speeches were over, that they would indeed pour down, possibly on to the Waterloo Place and general commercial area around there with the aim of carrying out further rioting.' Ford foresaw their activities continuing and, therefore, it seemed to him that if a suitable opportunity occurred to the Brigade Commander, he should arrest as many of the hooligans as was practicable. On 'normal days' it was difficult to arrest the hooligans because the number of troops which Ford had in Londonderry at any given time was comparatively small, and they were fully engaged on their normal tasks of maintaining law and order. When they turned out in the 'normal days, the soldiers can be at risk if we try to pursue them forward into the Bogside. They are very fleet of foot and it is very difficult for a small number of troops on the ground to manage an arrest.' A small number of soldiers going in to try and arrest hooligans would be putting themselves at considerable risk. Surprise was essential. Ford's intention throughout was to do everything to reduce the risk 'to the absolute minimum to the non-violent marchers and, to this end, I certainly was not prepared to launch the arrest operation unless there was serious disorder and rioting and, indeed, we had gone up the scale and, furthermore, I would only then do it if the rioters and the non-violent demonstrators were widely separated.'[84]

On Wednesday, 26 January, at a meeting of the military's Director of Operations Committee, the decision as to how the march should be dealt with was effectively taken. The Director of Intelligence reported that NICRA planned two marches, one from the Creggan to the Guildhall and the other from Shantallow – which in the end did not take place – to the Guildhall. Three courses open to the Security Forces for the main march were then considered. These were:

A: To stop the march at its start point inside the Creggan.
B: To stop the march leaving the Bogside/Creggan area.
C: To stop the march short of the Guildhall.

After discussing the implications of each course it was agreed that the second course would be adopted – to stop the march leaving the Bogside/Creggan area – and that barriers would be placed up to 200 yards inside these areas. The second march from Shantallow would be stopped near its start point. It was agreed that the Army would control the main march with RUC assistance, and that the RUC would deal with the second march, with military support if needed.[85] A conference was held in the afternoon of Wednesday 26th at HQNI attended by Ford, MacLellan, and the Brigade Major, Lieutenant Colonel Steele, who drafted the order. The codename for the operation was FORECAST. 8 Infantry Brigade's mission was to prevent any illegal march taking place from the Creggan and to contain it together with any accompanying rioting within the Bogside and Creggan areas of the city. Unlike Steele's contemplated arrangements for the march of 16 January, where the RUC were to have a more forward role, the containment of the Creggan march was to be a military operation, with the RUC in support. Under the heading 'dispersal of the marches' it was decided that:

> Initially we intend to deal with any illegal marches in as low a key as possible and for as long as possible. Generally speaking the front men will be moderate and non-violent – the second rank will be those to start any violence that may erupt. The security forces are to take no action against the marches until either:
> (a) an attempt is made to breach the blocking point;
> (b) violence against the security forces, in the form of stone, bottle and nail bombing, takes place.
> ... If the Creggan march takes place entirely within the containment area of the Bogside and Creggan, it will be permitted to continue unchallenged.

Although NICRA claimed that this march was a non-violent protest, 'the organisers will have no control over the hooligans who will ensure that violence is inevitable.' The task attributed to 1 PARA was to maintain a Brigade arrest force and to conduct a 'scoop-up' operation of as many hooligans and rioters as possible. This 'operation will only be launched, either in whole or in part, on the orders of the Brigade commander.' 1 PARA was to be deployed initially to the

Foyle College car park, where it would be held at immediate notice throughout the event. The scoop-up operation 'is likely to be launched on two axis, one directed towards hooligan activity in the area of William Street/Little Diamond, and one towards the area of William Street/Little James Street' – effectively known as 'Aggro Corner'. It was expected that the arrest operation would be conducted on foot. A secondary role of this force was to act as the second Brigade mobile reserve.[86] The aim of the scoop-up operation, explained Ford, was that 'someone would be able to get behind the hooligans. Otherwise there was no object in launching it.' There was no discussion of the details of the scoop-up. This was a matter for the Brigade Commander. The scoop-up was only to commence if there was a favourable opportunity to launch the operation. This meant the separation of the marchers from the hooligans.[87] As far as MacLelland was concerned 'it was to be just another march to be contained within certain boundaries.'[88]

At the GEN 47 meeting, on 27 January, the containment plan was rubber-stamped. The Cabinet Committee agreed that in Londonderry the marchers must be prevented from coming out of the Bogside and Creggan areas; criticism of the Security Forces for not entering those areas must be countered by pointing out that it was a matter of military judgement to choose the best place for achieving the aim of preventing the march from reaching its destination. Maximum publicity should also be secured for arrests and court proceedings following the marches.[89] Heath recalled the tenor of the discussion as expecting a comparatively peaceful march; but IRA or hooligan attempts to infiltrate and exploit the march for their own purposes could never be ruled out and had to be prepared for in contingency planning. The operation was seen as very much one of containment, with no intention of actively seeking to use this march as an opportunity to retrieve any part of the 'no go' areas. Heath 'was not aware of any specific proposal to mount an arrest operation during the march'.[90] Carver recalled that while the reserve force would conduct an arrest operation on foot, they were not to enter into a direct conflict with the civilians: 'We made it clear in the order that nothing was to be done to spark a confrontation.'[91]

Back in Northern Ireland military preparations for dealing with the march proceeded apace. On Friday 28 January there was a Brigade Order Group Conference whose purpose was to constitute a conference to discuss the Brigade Order of the previous day. It was held by MacLellan at Ebrington Barracks and attended by a number of senior officers including Lieutenant-Colonel Steele; the Colonel of the 1 Battalion The Royal Anglian Regiment; Lieutenant-Colonel Welsh, the Commanding Officer of the 2 Battalion The Royal Green Jackets; the Commanding Officer of the 22 Light Air Defence Regiment; the Commanding Officer of the 1 Battalion The Coldstream Guards; and Lieutenant-Colonel Wilford of 1 PARA whose task it was to draw up the details of the arrest operation. Also attending was the Brigade Intelligence Officer (GOS3INT) – it was he who drove Colonel Wilford around the area of William Street, Great James Street and the nearby Presbyterian church (which would feature prominently in the final arrest plan) to familiarize him with the area. Superintendent Lagan also attended. MacLellan 'stressed that the whole thing was to be played in as low a key as possible'.⁹² According to MacLellan, Wilford did not discuss his plan for the arrest operation in detail 'because we did not know (a) whether there would be any hooligans on the day for sure, or rioters, or (b) where they would be. We could merely make an outline plan.'⁹³ Wilford, later, in a television documentary, said: 'I asked the question which in fact for a long time has worried me. I said "What happens if there is shooting?", to which I got really a very sparse reply to the effect that "Oh, well, we will deal with that when it comes." It is my greatest regret that I did not actually pursue that question and say "Right, you know what, what do you want us to do if we are shot at?"'⁹⁴

The Commanding Officer of the Royal Anglians, INQ 1347, however, did not remember this: 'I cannot recall Lieutenant-Colonel Wilford asking Brigadier MacLellan any questions... [about]... what would happen if 1 PARA was shot at. I cannot remember Lieutenant-Colonel Wilford asking that of Brigadier MacLelland in my presence. I would remember if it had been said, because it would have stuck in my mind as an odd question to ask from an experienced Belfast commander.' Either way, INQ 1347 was not happy with what had transpired at the meeting on 28 January and raises the question as to whether or not 1 PARA were suitable candidates for deployment in Derry:

> I had assumed, as I was the longest serving Commanding Officer in Londonderry at the time, that if anything unusual was planned for Londonderry, I would at least, have been consulted beforehand... I was surprised that 1 PARA had been nominated to be 'in reserve and enable for a scoop-up operation to be carried out on foot'. 1 PARA did not know the area and had not operated in the Bogside before. Also, everyone was aware that the Paras had a reputation for tough action and the citizens and hooligans of Londonderry would be greatly surprised if Belfast procedures were carried out on them. I just wondered who had thought out this deployment: it reflected a change of policy and emphasis on future operations in Londonderry.

INQ 1347 could hardly wait to speak with MacLellan privately after the meeting: 'I asked Brigadier MacLellan if I could speak with him in his office. There was no one else present and the meeting lasted a few minutes. I told him that 1 PARA should not be used in Londonderry, that they did not know the area and would go in blind. I said that I should be given the role of 1 PARA.' MacLelland told him that the decision to deploy 1 PARA had been made 'at the highest level' and he was not in a position to change anything. He said: 'It was not for me to fight the case.' INQ 1347 believed that MacLelland was obviously in a no-win situation. With his short experience of operational practice in Londonderry he had

> ...in my opinion, been sat upon by those also with little knowledge of Londonderry. I asked that my views should be relayed immediately to HQ Northern Ireland. I do not know if this was ever done... I was so unhappy with the situation after the coordinating meeting that I contemplated contacting HQ Northern Ireland myself and considered what further action I

could take; but if Brigadier MacLelland was in a no-win situation, who would listen to me. I was clearly responsible for my Battalion and I had to prepare instructions for them on the Sunday. I therefore wrote the instructions for my Battalion and those additional regiments under my command soon after leaving the meeting.[95]

INQ 1347 was not alone in his concerns about the use of 1 PARA. Sir David Ramsbotham (thirty years later Her Majesty's Chief Inspector of Prisons, but in 1972, the military assistant to the CGS, General Carver, with the rank of Lieutenant-Colonel in The Royal Green Jackets) spoke to Peter Welsh, the Commanding Officer of the 2 Battalion The Royal Green Jackets in the run up to Bloody Sunday. He telephoned to describe what had happened at Magilligan, where some soldiers from The Parachute Regiment had to be told by his adjutant that soldiers had to behave differently in Londonderry to Belfast. Ramsbotham considered that while 1 PARA had been used as shock troops in Belfast they 'were the wrong people to bring into this particular operation. My concern was not, solely, because it was 1 PARA; it was because it was reserve troops who were to be used, who were from outside the area and therefore not familiar with the ground.' Ramsbotham appreciated that General Ford might not have had anyone else to assist the situation in Londonderry but:

> In my view, it would not have been a satisfactory alternative to have the reserve troops manning the barriers, with the local troops actually carrying out any snatch squad operations, because even the soldiers at the barriers would need to know what the local tactics were in dealing with any particular situation. To my mind troops, if at all possible, should not be put into an area they do not know, particularly in Londonderry which is so small.
> When I later commanded Belfast, one of my principles was to ensure that troops from outside Belfast were not called in to assist because they did not know the territory. This was partly as a result of what may have happened on Bloody Sunday and from my own experiences in Borneo, where my first mission had been to operate in someone else's area with someone else's troops, which was incredibly difficult to do.[96]

In the opinion of INQ 1347, FORECAST should have been an operation to contain the NICRA march. Just that. If 'someone' had wanted to sort out the hooligan element, 'let it be done later in the day when the reasonable people of Londonderry had returned to their homes.' Any Londonderry-based battalion could be rough and tough, if required, 'but for two years we had our hands tied behind our backs' by HQNI whilst the Belfast battalions seemed to have had free range on operations. 'In my opinion it was wrong to nominate a Belfast Battalion for a scoop operation in Londonderry, but I do not say that the results would have been any different.' But those responsible for planning FORECAST forgot the differences between Belfast and Londonderry: their histories, the geography and topography, the sectarian mix, the traditional confrontation areas, the effect of the recent internment operation, Londonderry Development

Corporation's successful house building programme, the military's community relations successes, and the different roles of the Belfast and Londonderry Brigades from December 1969 to December 1971. 'We, in Londonderry, wanted the civilian populations to turn against both the IRA and the hooligan element (both increased in size since internment in August 1971) by building on our previous successes. What arrogance at all levels not to even consult those with rather more local experience for their views.'[97]

Given these reasonable concerns, why then were 1 PARA selected for this operation? According to Ford, in a note written after Bloody Sunday, it was because the deterrent effect in Londonderry was 'almost nil' and the baton round 'is treated with disdain by the DYH' with 'only by the massive use of CS gas that has prevented our troops from being overwhelmed on numerous occasions' that 'we included in the plan for 8th Brigade a quick snatch operation... to pick up a high proportion of the hooligans and in this way prevent major hooligan activity after the meeting.' 1 PARA were moved across for this specific purpose because of their expertise and their training in this very role. They were also unlikely to be panicked by gunmen should they intervene.[98] In one sense 1 PARA was the natural choice: they were the Brigade reserve for 39 Brigade; but as reserve they had no defined geographical area to cover and were available to operate wherever and whenever the need arose. The resident battalions already had their respective tasks and areas and responsibilities. If extra resources were needed for out of the ordinary events, why not the battalion reserve, asked Ford? The decision to give 1 PARA to 8 Brigade was Ford's. He selected 1 PARA for this part of the operation for the following reasons:

(i) the units in 8 Brigade were already committed in areas which they knew around the perimeter of the city;
(ii) the city battalion (that is the one covering the William Street area etc) was 22nd Light Air Defence Regiment of the Royal Artillery. This was not an Infantry Battalion but an artillery Regiment temporarily being used in an Infantry role and was not suited for a major arrest operation;
(iii) the Province Reserve (1KOB) were my reserve. They only became operational on 13th January 1972 and had no experience of arrest operations, major or minor. A major arrest operation would certainly have been beyond their capability until at least the middle of February or so;
(iv) as the reserve battalion of 39th Brigade in Belfast, 1 Para were not committed to permanently holding any particular area. The third Brigade in Northern Ireland had no reserve Battalion;
(v) 1 Para had been in the Province for well over a year. They had much experience, more than any other Battalion in Northern Ireland, both in carrying out arrest operations and in coming under and countering terrorist fire;
(vi) they could be spared for three or four days by commander 39th Brigade.

Ford selected 1 PARA because they were the only experienced uncommitted battalion he had in Northern Ireland. He needed extra troops in Londonderry and would not have used the Paras if he had alternatives because 1 PARA were the reserve brigade in Belfast and Ford was denying the Brigade Commander the use of his reserve for that day. It was a calculated risk.[99] As Ford pointed out, it was not unusual for units to be required to operate in areas which they did not know well. They obviously had maps available to them, and the opportunity to carry out such reconnaissances as they thought necessary. Such matters of detailed planning would be for their Commanding Officer, not the CLF. In addition, the area within which it was anticipated they would carry out the arrest operation was relatively small. Each of the battalions in 8 Brigade had an area of responsibility, and they each knew their area well. To be responsible for a particular area involved not only knowing the geography but also knowing the history of operations for that area, the intelligence of that area, the relationship with the RUC, and so on. Using, for example, The Royal Anglians or The Green Jackets for the arrest operation would have meant replacing them with 1 PARA and 1 PARA then having to take over responsibility for their area. In military terms, such a short-term situation made no sense to Ford. He did accept, however, that whatever role 1 PARA or another reserve battalion would have had on the day, they would have been at a slight disadvantage, but any such disadvantage would have been far greater had they undertaken duties other than as an arrest battalion held in reserve.[100] Ford was certainly not made aware of any formal or informal requests that 1 PARA should not be used as intended on 30 January. 1 PARA had been particularly successful in Belfast. Like any other successful unit or individual,

> they automatically became the focus of IRA/Sinn Féin propaganda. This is usual in a counter insurgency campaign, 'the other side' would always try and make the maximum of any incident, whether real or reported, in the hope that in turn this propaganda will reduce operational capabilities. I certainly knew that 1 PARA was the focus of such propaganda at the time. I had confidence in Brigadier Kitson and 1 PARA, I knew Brigadier Kitson very well and had seen 1 PARA operating on earlier occasions. I knew Kitson's view of that particular Battalion, he thought they were very good and he depended on them.[101]

At this point it is appropriate to consider another accusation relating to the Army's actions on Bloody Sunday: that the arrest operation was designed to teach the IRA in Derry a lesson. In fact this was not the first time that an arrest operation had been contemplated for Derry. An operation, known as HAILSTONE, was set for July 1971. The mission was to 'capture as many, Provisionals auxiliaries and hooligans as possible' on17/18 July.[102] Captain Mike Jackson was present when 1 PARA was deployed for this arrest operation. But it did not take place: 'We sat up there for a couple of hours before being told to "knock it on the head".'[103] In the aftermath of Bloody Sunday, Jackson was anonymously quoted by *The Sunday Times*:

> The bloody July operation never got off the ground, an officer recalled. We were sitting up behind the reservoirs and they kept putting it back 30 minutes

and another 30 minutes until it was dark. We could not get the yobbos out. They had been throwing stones for weeks, but as soon as we turned up our luck goes. According to the Para officer his men tried very hard last July to provoke a confrontation. We tried a bit of Aggro Corner searches and things to bring them out. But they were not falling for it.[104]

Jackson recalls this differently:

There was no attempt to provoke a confrontation in the July 1971 operation. It was simply an abortive arrest operation. If such things were said by me then I suspect they were the bravado of a young officer... All I can say is that in general terms, there was a feeling that Londonderry was getting out of control. This was not only a feeling of 1 PARA, but a feeling in political, media and military circles generally. I cannot recall saying anything like this.[105]

Nor, in January 1972, would such a plan make military sense. Ford explained there was no plan to provoke a confrontation with the IRA because to have done so would have meant that the troops involved in the arrest operation would inevitably have been at a tactical disadvantage, being in ground dominated by buildings and rising ground.

This was why we planned a swift arrest operation (in and out as quickly as possible) and required 'massive numbers of snipers in the counter sniper role' to cover them and to deter the anticipated IRA reaction. Firing was not specifically dealt with in the operation order as the Yellow Card governed that issue. Nor was it intended, to make an example of the Bogside community and show them who was in charge. This suggestion is nonsense. All the indicators show we hoped for a peaceful (but diverted) illegal march and also the plan was clearly and intentionally to arrest the maximum number of DYH, not members of the general Bogside community. Finally, such an operation (flushing out IRA members or giving the Bogsiders a rough handling) would have been contrary to all I had concluded in my... 'Future Military Policy for Londonderry'... It is certainly not the case, (if it be suggested), that the march on 30th January was used, or was intended to be used, as an opportunity to put into effect the discussion points I had put to the GOC in my memorandum of 7th January 1972. Such suggestions are all the more ridiculous when one considers the presence of the media in numbers, and the stress we laid on the maximum co-operation with them. This was intended to highlight the purpose of the operation, as well as to deter the IRA from taking any part. The aim of the plan was to stop the illegal march from leaving the Bogside and thus to prevent damage by rioters and bombers to the commercial centre of the city.[106]

Likewise, Jackson described claims that the arrest operation was an opportunity to 'teach the IRA a lesson' as

absurd... there was absolutely nothing more sinister in 1 PARA's involvement. It would be absurd to suggest that there was a secret oral instruction that would in some way take precedence over written orders. For such a complex operation written orders would have been needed. The mission was to conduct an arrest operation pure and simple. If the IRA sought to open fire then we would obviously react to them but we did not seek this reaction. I have heard it said that the events that day occurred as a result of a huge conspiracy. Two cabinets, two prime ministers and two generals, Ford and Tuzo would have to know of any such 'concealed plan' as would Brigadier MacLellan, Lieutenant-Colonel Wilford and indeed the entire Battalion. Such an operation could not have been planned orally and there would have been a piece of paper somewhere. It is ridiculous to suggest that there was a plan of that nature but that nothing ever came out. It could not and did not happen. The idea is totally absurd.[107]

As we have seen, of critical importance in the military's preparation for 30 January was that not only was DYH violence expected but IRA activity as well. The events of Bloody Sunday did not occur in a vacuum. In the week immediately preceding the march there had been a marked increase in the number of attacks on members of the Security Forces in Londonderry and in other areas also. The IRA stepped up its personal attacks on members of the Security Forces and these resulted in the deaths of three policemen and two soldiers and injuries to four policemen, seven soldiers and two UDR members.[108] In the first four days of the week there was an increase in shooting attacks, and during this period alone there were thirty-six confirmed incidents. This compared with a weekly average over the last four weeks of twenty-three incidents, and it was a higher figure than in any week since 14 December. A soldier at Bligh's Lane was shot in the foot on 27 January and two civilians were shot by the Army on 29 January; a further two may also have been hit.[109] The Historical Report of the 22nd Light Air Defence Regiment Royal Artillery recorded intense exchanges between the Army and the IRA on the day before the march which was the Saturday. The Brandywell post came under fire several times in the early hours of the morning. Fire was returned at flashes of shots. Shots were also fired at OP Charlie. There was the normal pattern of activity in William Street in the afternoon, but two rounds were fired at a man seen throwing a nail bomb. Both shots were claimed to have hit and a man was seen being carried into a car at the back of the old tyre factory. In the late afternoon some groups of hooligans transferred their operations to the Hamilton Street area and a transformer house was broken into and damaged. The Brandywell OP was attacked by a crowd of over 100. Blast bombs were thrown and several shots were fired. A number of strikes on the buildings in the post were noted. The 15th Battery beat off the rioters and fired several rounds at gunmen and bombers when they could be identified as such.[110] On the Thursday before the march two RUC officers, Sergeant Gilpin and Constable Montgomery, the first a Catholic and the second a Protestant, had been ambushed and killed in the Creggan Road as their car approached Rosemount Police Station. They were the first policemen to be killed in the city during the Troubles. Given this it was not surprising to find that 'Intelligence reports indicate that the IRA are determined to produce a major confrontation by one means or another during the march.'[111]

And a key factor in shaping the Army's view of what they were about to encounter was the intelligence they were receiving from various sources. The Security Service, MI5, ran its own agents in Northern Ireland. One of those provided intelligence in the run up to Bloody Sunday. This agent had been an informant since 1970 when he was introduced to an Army Intelligence Officer, referred to as IO1. After becoming acquainted with IO1, the agent began to assist him with what information he could provide. Within a few days of meeting IO1 he introduced him to another Army Intelligence Officer referred to as IO2. He also began to assist IO2 with information. For the first few weeks he passed on information to IO1 and IO2 that he thought might be useful. Then IO1 introduced him to a man called JAMES. The agent recalled how JAMES said, 'I am taking you over, you will not have any more to do with the Army, pass all your information on to me.' JAMES wanted to tell him his full name and details, 'but I told him that I did not want to know. He also wanted to put me on the payroll and again I refused. I did, however, later receive payments from IO2 to cover my travelling expenses.' A little later on he was introduced to another man known as JULIAN. Both men were from the Security Service. Although he spoke to JAMES and JULIAN from time to time his main contacts as far as he was concerned remained IO1 and IO2. On 25 January, the Tuesday before the march, the agent was in Londonderry and was in the area of the Rossville Flats where he saw a group of about forty men between the ages of 18 and 30 dressed in civilian clothing. One of the men, aged about 28, with a pale complexion and dark hair, began to issue orders to others. The men then lined up in three rows in front of this man and he shouted to them 'attention!' and then 'at ease!'. These words were shouted in Irish. At the time the agent assumed that he was witnessing the drilling of IRA auxiliaries. He had witnessed auxiliaries before who were affiliated to the IRA but were not full members. The auxiliaries tended to be made up of men who wanted to contribute to IRA operations but were not considered to be suitable material for the IRA's ASUs.

After a short while, the agent observed the men march across Rossville Street and then enter the Rossville Flats through the main entrance located between Blocks 1 and 2. A few minutes later he saw 'X'.

> I said to him 'What is going on?' He replied 'You have noticed them.' I said 'I have noticed them, I have seen them practising. What do you think they are up to?' X replied 'They are practising for Sunday. They were here yesterday at the same time.' I said 'The best thing for you to do is to keep your head down and get on with what you are doing.' X replied that that was exactly what he would do.

The Security Service agent saw that the men had split up and that they were now spread out along the three landings of Block 2. He watched as the men appeared to be practising something. At first they stood on the inside edge of the balconies close to and with their backs to the doors of the flats. On command they moved forward to the outside edge of the balconies, keeping just to the left of each of the columns that were located on the outside edge at intervals. The MI5 agent thought that they stood near the columns in the way that they did so that they would be obscured from the sight of anyone looking towards the flats from the observation post on the city walls. A little later he saw X again.

> I said to him 'What on earth do you think they were practising for?' X and I then discussed the possibility that the Fianna were planning to attack the Army to draw them into the area and then fall back, leaving the soldiers vulnerable to sniper fire. I had seen this tactic employed before on a couple of occasions but concluded that given the amount of people likely to be present on the march, they would not do such a thing. X said words to the effect that he would not rule anything out... I telephoned IO1 that evening, describing what I had seen and informing him that I thought there was going to be serious trouble at the march on Sunday... I think that the expression that I used was 'I think you have got a problem on Sunday.' IO1 replied 'We are going to have to think on this one, ring me again in the morning.' The next morning I telephoned him again. I repeated what I had seen and he asked me 'Do you think that they will do it every day?' I took this to mean practise every day. I said that I did not know.

On Thursday 27 January he saw the men drilling in a similar fashion to that which he had seen on Tuesday. He also bumped into X. 'I said to him "They are still at it" and he replied "Every day this week". I telephoned IO1 telling him what I had just witnessed. He said he was looking into it. He seemed very excited by this information.'[112]

Both wings of the IRA subsequently denied this version of events. Reg Tester, the Official IRA Quartermaster, claimed there were no IRA volunteers or auxiliaries drilling in the area of the Rossville Flats.[113] Martin McGuinness described auxiliaries in Derry as people who were of assistance to the IRA: they were not active service volunteers for the purposes of fighting the British Army. Auxiliaries were regarded as helpers. 'Under no circumstances would any of them have been given a gun by the IRA. They were not people in a position to be physically in charge of a weapon or in charge of operations attacking the British military forces.'[114] Both the Officials and the Provisionals claimed they did not plan any offensive action for the day of the march. On Thursday 27 January, McGuinness was told that an approach had been made to his OC by people representing the Civil Rights Movement proposing that the IRA accept that Derry should be peaceful in order to facilitate what was expected to be a huge, peaceful demonstration against internment. The following day, Friday, McGuinness was asked by the OC for his opinion on this request. By this stage McGuinness was aware of the ongoing reports of a substantial military build-up in the city. Taking everything into account he expressed a view in favour of the suggestion. In McGuinness's opinion a march consisting of approximately 20–30,000 people protesting against the Unionist administration and its military forces, as well as internment, would be a very powerful expression of the people's rejection of the Unionist regime and of the repressive methods the British Government were employing.[115]

PIRA 24 recalled that the consensus was that 'we would do nothing on the Sunday, but that we would think on it, and decide what to do the following day. On the Friday there was a further meeting in the evening. I decided there should be no action. Everybody present agreed.' McGuinness, the Training Officer and the soon to be appointed IO who was Section Leader in the Brandywell for the day, were all present. 'Ultimately, they left it to me to make the final decision and, on the Friday night, I decided that we would not be taking action on the Sunday, the arms were to be taken out of the Bog, and there would be a car in each of the Brandywell and Creggan on normal patrol duty.' Nobody disagreed: 'If you were told to do something you disagreed with, you did it. No one disagreed however. No order was ever written down. We never kept notes. You kept the information in your head.'[116]

On Saturday morning, McGuinness again met the OC. At this meeting he was instructed to issue orders to all Volunteers that the IRA would not engage militarily with British forces to ensure that the Civil Rights march passed off peacefully. Following the meeting McGuinness spoke with the Command Staff and all active service Volunteers. He replayed the decision taken by the OC: 'Without exception everyone I spoke to accepted that our approach to the march was sensible.' Some concern, however, was expressed that against the backdrop of such a large demonstration which would see a large number of people from the Creggan and Brandywell areas marching to the city centre, the British Army might attempt incursions into these two areas. Instructions were issued that a small number of Volunteers, in the form of two units totalling about eight people, should remain armed and vigilant as a contingency in these two areas. The two ASUs would be the only armed PIRA units in the Free Derry area on 30 January. No IRA weapons were stored at or near Rossville Flats and there was no movement of weapons in the Bogside area for any purpose prior to or during the course of the march taking place. All PIRA weapons, except those in the possession of the two ASUs, were placed in a closed dump for the duration of the march. McGuinness spent the early hours of 30 January with an ASU patrolling the general Free Derry area. Their task was to oppose any attempt by the British Army to launch raids into the area under cover of darkness. As dawn broke and the likelihood of an Army incursion receded, McGuinness and his comrades went to safe houses for a few hours' sleep. McGuinness went to a house in the Creggan where he stayed until about 9 a.m. He then had breakfast and went to Mass. After joining the march he remained with it until the end.[117] According to Reg Tester, the Official IRA also had orders not to engage the British Army.[118]

On Friday 28th, two days prior to the demonstration, a meeting of stewards was held at the Creggan Centre where they received final instructions from members of the NICRA Executive and were fully briefed on the plans and tactics. Special emphasis was to be placed on the necessity for a peaceful incident-free day on Sunday. Civil Rights organizer Kevin McCorry pointed out that Faulkner and John Taylor were counting on an outbreak of violence to justify any British Army violence used on Sunday. Sunday would be 'make or break day' for the cause of Civil Rights and the release of internees: 'Any riot, any trouble, any incident must be confined to members of the British Army. They disgraced themselves at Magilligan on Saturday last with their unprovoked savagery. Do not let them disgrace you, the City of Derry and the whole democratic cause', said McCorry. On Saturday, January 29th, the eve of the Derry demonstration, a call for a massive turnout was made by the Executive of the Civil Rights Association. Making the call, the Executive pointed out that the British Government were now full tilt on repression and coercion and that a massive peaceful demonstration was vital if world opinion was to be impressed by the cause.[119]

The Army also continued their build-up. That morning, at 10.30, there was a Battalion Order Group of 1 PARA where Colonel Wilford discussed with the company commanders present the Brigade Order. Wilford explained that if the march took place and the confrontation became hostile, the battalion 'will deploy forward to break up the rioters and make the maximum number of arrests. At this stage I cannot give a detailed tactical plan. I will give the company deployment in our FUP [forming-up places] and then give my consent of how I think the battle can go.'[120] Major Loden, the Commanding Officer of 1 PARA's Support Company, recalled that the possibility of the Paras coming under fire if they were to go down Rossville Street was not actually mentioned; but the Rossville Flats were mentioned as a place where sniper fire might come from. Loden's appreciation was – based on his experience in Belfast – that when a large body of troops appeared in armoured vehicles, any gunmen who might have been thinking of having a go would in fact not. 'So' he remembered, 'I was surprised when the shooting started I must say.'[121] It was left to Loden's discretion as to how he would conduct the scoop-up operation which he was ordered to perform: 'although it was thought that the march would take place on a route, we did not know where the march would go... it was true to say that it would be left to my discretion, but I was not particularly told that I would go down Rossville Street. That is the way it happened.'[122]

On 29 January, at about 17.00 or 18.00 in the evening, there were Company Order Groups which were attended by the Platoon Commanders and the Company Sergeant Major and the Colour Sergeant and others in which the orders were relayed by the Company Commanders to the individual Platoon commanders.[123] At about 21.00 there were Platoon Order Groups, three of which were attended by Major Loden as CO of Support Company where the commanders of the platoons relayed the orders to the members of their platoons. S Company was to deploy into an assault position in Queen Street, and to gain access to William Street over a six foot wall in the east of the Presbyterian church there. The Mortar Platoon was to cut the wire which surrounded this wall to a height of approximately twelve feet. The Anti-Tank Platoon was instructed to take up anti-sniper positions on the rooftops of houses on the south side of Great James Street. Orders for opening fire were as given in the Yellow Card.[124] Private S, who was a member of the Mortar Platoon, was told by his Platoon Commander that 'if we were ordered forward we would have to break through a wall between the Presbyterian church and the GPO sorting office. Move forward to William Street and carry out an arrest operation in William Street in front of the area marked Tanners Row. I can remember that he told us to use minimum force when effecting arrests. We were told that the orders for shooting were in accordance with the Yellow Card.'[125] Sergeant O was in charge of a half-Platoon in a Humber APC.

> Our task originally was to go with our S Company through the wall by the GPO sorting office, and break from there into William Street. From there we were to go along to the William Street/Little James Street area and cut off and detain any rioters in that area which is known as Aggro Corner. We were warned to anticipate rifle fire, in particular from the direction of the Rossville Flats. We did in fact expect trouble of this kind, because while we were waiting at the fence by the sorting office one HV shot was fired which struck the Presbyterian church.[126]

In contrast to Major Loden, Captain Jackson believed there would be a reaction out of the IRA because the Paras would be 'invading their turf' when going in for the arrest operation. 'We therefore had an expectation of IRA activity.' There was a large 'no go' area and

> I can recall seeing maps with the so-called containment line marked on them. Beyond those lines the Security Forces simply did not go. It was known that fire fights were common in Londonderry as they were in Belfast... We could never rule out the fact that we might be shot at – any time, any place. The IRA were good at ambushes. These could take place anywhere at any time and it would be foolhardy in the extreme to assume that you would not be shot at. It would have been foolish militarily to accept any IRA assurances that they would not be on the march, if any such assurances were given. They would say anything for their cause. It would have been foolish to have been lulled into a false sense of security. It was a fundamental principle that we had to be prepared to be attacked at any time.[127]

Finally, the Brigade Commander's plan required the erection of barriers sealing off each of the streets through which the marchers might cross the containment line. Though there were twenty-six barriers in all, the most relevant to the events of Bloody Sunday were only three: No.12 in Little James Street, No.13 in Sackville Street and No.14 in William Street. The barriers, which were to consist of wooden knife rests reinforced with barbed wire and concrete slabs, were put in place early on 30 January. At some of them, notably at Barrier 14, an armoured personnel carrier was placed on either side of the street close behind and almost parallel with the barrier to reinforce it and to give the troops some cover from stone throwing. Each barrier was manned by the Army in platoon strength with representative RUC officers in support. The troops at the barriers were to be provided by units normally under command of 8 Infantry Brigade. 1 PARA waited in reserve for the arrest operation if ordered in.[128] The arrest operation was *only* to be launched if violence was used against the Security Forces, or there was an attempt to break the barricades and then *only* on the orders of the Brigade Commander if the rioters were separated from the main body of marchers. This did not happen.

Notes

1. McCreary, *Survivors*, pp.228–30.
2. Ibid., pp.260–1.
3. Bloody Sunday: British Irish Rights Watch Submission to the United Nations, paras. 10.4–10.5.
4. Ibid., para. 10.2.
5. Ibid., paras. 6.15–6.16.
6. Widgery, paras.10–12.
7. BSI APIRA 24, Statement of PIRA 24.
8. BSI KM3 Supplemental Statement of Martin McGuinness.
9. BSI APIRA 24, Statement of PIRA 24.
10. BSI AK46, Sean Keenan Statement.
11. BSI APIRA 24, Statement of PIRA 24.
12. BSI AK46, Sean Keenan Statement.
13. McKittrick et al., *Lost Lives*, pp.97–8.
14. Ibid., pp.98–9.
15. Ibid., p.99.
16. BSI APIRA 24, Statement of PIRA 24.
17. BSI AO79, Gearoid O'hEara Statement.
18. BSI APIRA19, PIRA 19 Statement.
19. BSI AT6, First Statement of Reg Tester.
20. BSI APIRA 24, Statement of PIRA 24.
21. BSI AT6, Second Statement of Reg Tester.
22. BSI APIRA 24, Statement of PIRA 24.
23. BSI AK46, Sean Keenan Statement.
24. *News Letter*, 28 October 1971.
25. *Irish News*, 28 October 1971.
26. Widgery, paras. 10–12.
27. BSI KC8 Statement of Field Marshall Lord Carver.
28. BSI G22(a).
29. G137.
30. Widgery, Para. 12.
31. BSI G27.
32. Widgery, Para. 12.
33. BSI G38 GEN 47 13 December 1971.
34. BSI G116 5 February 1972.
35. BSI G41 Future Military Policy for Londonderry, an Appreciation of the Situation by CLF 14 December 1971.
36. BSI G46 Official Committee on Northern Ireland.
37. BSI G40.259 14 December 1971.
38. BSI G44.282 20 December 1971.
39. BSI CD1 The Situation in Londonderry as at 7th January 1972.
40. BSI 1208, Statement of General Sir Robert Ford.
41. BSI KC8, Statement of Field Marshall Lord Carver.
42. BSI 10.5.
43. BSI JS8.14, Statement of Sir Graham Shillington.
44. BSI 12.8, Statement of General Jackson.
45. BSI Statement of Lord Carrington.

46. BSI KH4, Statement of Sir Edward Heath.
47. BSI Transcript of Mr Porter's tapes of Army radio transmissions on or about 28th January 1972.
48. BSI G50.307.
49. BSI 52.315 Joint Security Committee Conclusions, 13 January 1972.
50. BSI G61.368. Intelligence Summary Number 100.
51. BSI KC12.15, Statement of Ivan Cooper,
52. BSI G61.368. Intelligence Summary Number 100.
53. BSI G64.380 Special Branch assessment for the period ending 19th January 1972.
54. BSI G63.377 Joint Security Committee Conclusions, 20 January 1972.
55. BSI G66.411.
56. BSI G69A436.001 SitRep, from 08.00 on 22nd January to 08.00 on 23rd January 1972.
57. BSI AM277.1. Daniel (Dan) McGuiness.
58. BSI KC12.15, Statement of Ivan Cooper.
59. BSI KH8, Statement of John Hume.
60. BSI AD65.1, Statement of Gerard Doherty.
61. BSI Day 11, page 58.
62. BSI AS 34, Statement of Roisin Stewart.
63. BSI D177.5, Statement of Shaun Anthony Doherty.
64. BSI AM 304.1, Statement of Joseph McKinney.
65. BSI H3.1, Statement of Father Carolan.
66. BSI AM 161.1, Statement of Charles McDaid.
67. BSI JL 1.8, Statement of Frank Lagan.
68. BSI *The Guardian*, 25 January 1972, L.007.
69. BSI G75A. 462.002.
70. BSI G75A. 462.001.
71. BSI B1316 Statement of Colonel Maurice Tugwell.
72. BSI G49.302. 10th January 1972.
73. BSI Transcripts.
74. Widgery Transcripts Day 17 at page 18.
75. Ibid., Page 33.
76. BSI JL1, Statement of Frank Lagan.
77. Widgery Transcripts Page 34.
78. BSI JL1, Statement of Frank Lagan.
79. BSI G70A441.01.
80. BSI G128.849, MacLelland to Ford 15 March 1972.
81. BSI JS8, Statement of Sir Graham Shillington.
82. BSI 1208, Statement of General Sir Robert Ford.
83. BSI Transcripts.
84. Widgery Transcripts Day 10, page 5.
85. BSI G075.459. Record of D OPS meeting held at HQ Northern Ireland at 10.00 hours on Wednesday, 26th January 1972.
86. BSI G95.564. Operational Order 2/72 (OP FORECAST) 27 January 1972.
87. Widgery Transcripts Day 10, page 48.
88. BSI B1279.003.012, Hamill interview with MacLelland.
89. BSI G79.486 GEN 47, 27 January 1972.
90. BSI KH4.6, Statement of Sir Edward Heath.
91. BSI KC8.3.
92. Widgery Transcripts, Day 11 page 11.
93. Ibid., Day 11, page 35.
94. BSI B944.
95. BSI Statement of INQ 1347.
96. BSI 16.1, Statement of Sir David Ramsbotham.
97. BSI S15.14 of Inquiry 1347.
98. BSI G121.804, Note written by General Ford.

99. BSI Day 10, page 51.
100. BSI Day 14, page 13.
101. BSI 14.14, Statement of General Sir Robert Ford.
102. BSI G3.24 Operational Order for Operation HAILSTONE.
103. BSI Statement of General Jackson.
104. BSI S7. *The Sunday Times*, 4th February, 17.26. Jacobson.
105. BSI Statement of General Jackson.
106. BSI Statement of General Sir Robert Ford.
107. BSI Statement of General Jackson.
108. BSI G11 2.697 Special Branch Assessment for the period ending 3rd February 1972.
109. BSI G108.653 8th Brigade Intelligence Summary 102 for 2nd February 1972.
110. BSI G133.880. The Historical Report of the 22nd Light Air Defence Regiment Royal Artillery. This document covers 'Operations in Northern Ireland November 1971–March 1972'.
111. BSI G83.522 Headquarters Northern Ireland Operational Summary for the week ending Friday, 28th January 1972.
112. BSI S2 Temporary Statement.
113. BSI AT6 Second Statement of Reg Tester.
114. BSI KM3, Supplemental Statement of Martin McGuinness.
115. BSI KM3, Draft Statement of Martin McGuinness.
116. BSI APIRA 24 Statement of PIRA 24.
117. BSI KM3, Draft Statement of Martin McGuinness.
118. BSI AT6, First Statement of Reg Tester.
119. BSI G92, Massacre at Derry.
120. BSI G94.562, Battalion Order Group, 29 January 1972.
121. Widgery Day 12, page 35.
122. Ibid., Page 35 Letter C.
123. Ibid., Day 12, page 61.
124. BSI ED49, Statement of Major Loden.
125. BSI B.706, Statement of Private S.
126. BSI B466.
127. 12.3, Statement of General Jackson.
128. Widgery, Para 18.

9

Operation FORECAST – Bloody Sunday, 30 January 1972

THE MARCH AND RIOT

On 30 January 1972 anti-internment marchers assembled on the Creggan estate 'on a fine sunny afternoon and in carnival mood'. The total may have been something between 3,000 and 5,000 people. At their head was a lorry carrying a Civil Rights Association banner and travelling upon the lorry were some of the leaders of the march. When they appeared at the west end of William Street their direct route to the Guildhall Square lay along William Street where the march came face to face with the Army at barrier 14 in that street. When the leaders of the march reached the junction of William Street and Rossville Street the lorry turned to its right to go along Rossville Street and the stewards made strenuous efforts to persuade the marchers to follow the lorry. A substantial number, not all of them youths, continued into the cul-de-sac created by the William Street barrier manned by men of The Royal Green Jackets. Some of the crowd started stone-throwing. Other objects such as fire grates and metal rods used as lances were thrown at the troops. The troops responded with controlled volleys of rubber bullets but this was countered by the rioters bringing forward an improvised shield of corrugated iron behind which they could shelter from the bullets.[1] One of those rioting was John Dunleavey:

> I went towards barrier 14 with a crowd of a couple of hundred or so. There were quite a few people ahead of me but I was near the front. We were all young lads. I remember someone with a loud hailer asking us to disperse. He said illegal demonstration – disperse peacefully. I could hear the man with the loudhailer but I could not see him. We looked for stones, bottles, slates and drain pipes and anything we could to throw at the soldiers behind the barrier. I remember getting behind some corrugated sheeting at one time, I would say that the rioting was heavier than usual... Some of the lads started pulling at the wire on the barrier.[2]

A water cannon was brought up behind the barrier and proceeded to drench the crowd with water coloured with a purple dye. A canister of CS gas thrown by a member of the crowd exploded underneath the water cannon incommoding the crew who were not wearing their gas masks. The water cannon was withdrawn for a few minutes and rubber bullets were fired again with little more effect than on the previous occasion. When the gas had cleared from the water cannon it was brought forward a second time and used upon the crowd to some effect.[3] At 15.47

hours the CO 2 Royal Green Jackets (RGJ), airborne in a Sioux helicopter, indicated that the separation of the hooligan element from the bulk of the marchers was beginning to take place. At 15.52 hours he reported that the marchers were moving down Rossville Street towards the Flats and two minutes later that they were dispersing towards Rossville Flats. At about 15.55 C Company of 1 PARA were standing by mounted in their armoured 1 ton vehicles on the junction of William Street/Waterloo Street. The water cannon was withdrawn to allow access for them should it be decided that they should be sent in. Lieutenant-Colonel Wilford requested permission to deploy C Company through barrier 14 to arrest hooligans in the waste ground in the area of William Street/Little James Street. However, at Brigade HQ Brigadier MacLellan was anxious to confirm that there was absolute separation of the hooligans from the main bulk of the marchers as this was a pre-requisite of the arrest plan. He did not give permission at this stage. At 15.59 the CO 2 RGJ reported from his helicopter that there was a general move of the crowd from the Rossville Flats into Lecky Road and two minutes later MacLellan received the first report that a crowd was being addressed at Foxes Corner.[4] So, by 16.00 hours the pressure on barrier 14 had relaxed. There were still 100 to 200 rioters in the William Street area but most of the non-violent marchers had either turned for home or were making their way down Rossville Street to attend a meeting at Free Derry Corner where about 500 were already assembled. On the waste ground between the Rossville Flats and William Street there was a mixed crowd of perhaps 200 which included some rioters together with marchers, local residents, newspapermen and sightseers who were moving aimlessly about or chatting in groups.[5] But, crucially, 'at 16.04 hours the number of hooligans at the junction William Street/Rossville Street was reported as 150 and the separation of the hooligans was complete – 150 were in William Street, while the Northern Ireland Civil Rights Association meeting was 300 metres away, from Foxes Corner.'[6] However, as the subsequent inquiry by Lord Widgery recognized, 'this separation never really happened.'[7] The arrest operation should not have been launched.

Since the tactics of the arrest operation were to be determined by the location and strength of the rioters at the time it was launched, the Brigade Order left them to be decided by Lieutenant Colonel Wilford. He had three Companies available for the arrest operation: Administrative Company, C Company and Support Company, the latter being reinforced by a Composite Platoon from A Company. (A fourth Company had been detached and put under command of 22 Light Air Defence Regiment for duties elsewhere in Londonderry.) In the event these three Companies moved forward at the same time. A Company operated in the region of the Little Diamond. C Company went forward on foot through barrier 14 and along Chamberlain Street, while Support Company drove in vehicles through barrier 12 into Rossville Street to encircle rioters on the waste ground or pursued by C Company along Chamberlain Street. According to the Commander 8 Brigade and Lieutenant Colonel Steele the operation was authorized by the Brigadier personally, as was envisaged in the Brigade Order. The order for 1 PARA to go in and make arrests was passed by the Brigade Major to the Commanding Officer 1 PARA on a secure wireless link, that is one which was not open to eavesdropping. This link was used because the arrest operation depended on surprise for its success and it was known that normal military wireless traffic was not secure. Wilford confirmed that he received the order and all three officers agreed that the order was in terms which left the Commanding Officer free to employ all three Companies.[8] It has been contended that the Brigadier did not authorize the arrest operation and that it was carried out by Wilford in defiance of orders or without orders and on his own initiative. The suspicion that Wilford acted without authority derived from the absence of any relevant order in the verbatim record of wireless traffic on the ordinary Brigade net. This omission was due to the use of the secure wireless link for this one vital order. The Brigade Log stated:

> Serial 147, 15.55 hours from 1 Para. Would like to deploy sub-unit through barricade 14 to pick up yobbos in William Street/Little James Street.
> Serial 159, 16.09 hours from Brigade Major. Orders given to 1 Para at 16.07 hours for one sub-unit of 1 Para to do scoop-up op through barrier 14. Not to conduct running battle down Rossville Street.

It has been contended that the Brigade log shows *prima facie* that the only action which 1 PARA was authorized to carry out was the limited one for which permission had been sought in the message recorded in Serial 147. This view was supported by the evidence of Chief Superintendent Lagan, who was in the Brigadier's office at the relevant time and who formed the impression that 1 PARA had acted without authority from the Brigadier.[9] Lagan recalled that at about 4 p.m. the Brigadier came into his office and said: 'The Paras want to go in.' To that Lagan replied: 'For Heaven's sake hold them until we are satisfied that the marchers and rioters are separated.' MacLellan made no reply but left the office. After a short interval he returned and said: 'I am sorry the Paras have gone in'. Lagan interpreted the words and the tone used in saying them to mean that the Brigadier was not personally responsible for the Paras going in. In fact the order was said to have come from 'BM' – or Brigade Major – Lieutenant-Colonel Steele. The record of it took this form in the Brigade Log because the actual order was given on the secure link. Steele, having given the order on that link, went into the Operations Room and had the order entered into the Brigade Log.[10] At 16.07 hours, when 1 PARA was ordered forward, a substantial crowd remained on the waste ground between the bulk of the rioters who were in William Street and the bulk of the marchers who had either reached Free Derry Corner or gone home. The Brigade Commander, who could not see the area at all, had relied mainly upon information from the officer in a helicopter. MacLellan had considered the possibility that if a shooting match developed there would be risk to innocent people but he described this risk as 'very bare'. On the whole he considered that the arrest operation was essential in the interests of security and gave the order accordingly.[11] At 16.12 hours A Company 1 PARA passed through barrier 11, advanced into Lower Road and turned into William Street to assist S Company in their task of arresting rioters at the William Street/Rossville Street junction. The Company's movement caused the rioters to run in front of it in the direction of S Company where some of them were arrested. No arrests were made by A Company and they stopped in the area of the William Street/Creggan Street junction. No live rounds were fired by this Company. At 16.10 hours C Company 1 PARA passed through barrier 14 and arrested 'rioters' in the east end of William Street. They made a total of twenty-two arrests. No live rounds were fired by C Company.

The only live rounds fired that day were by Support Company. At 15.16 hours S Company had moved forward to an assault position in Queen Street and at 15.40 its Machine Gun (MG) Platoon moved forward to a derelict building on the north edge of William Street. The officers of 1 PARA had previously been engaged in the morning on reconnaissance of various routes that could be used if the battalion were called upon to move forward and make arrests in the area of Rossville Street and William Street. The battalion could move the barriers and go through them; but at one time it was thought that they might wish to enter William Street somewhat to the west of Little James Street in order to outflank the vacant land at Aggro Corner (the corner of William Street and Rossville Street). The Company Commander of the Support Company, Major Loden, found a route over a wall by the side of a Presbyterian church which he considered might be useful for this purpose, but which was obstructed by wire. Accordingly he sent a wire-cutting party to make this route usable if required. Loden had sent a number of men forward to cover the wire-cutting party. Some of these men established themselves on the two lower floors of a three storey derelict building on William Street, just to the west of some open land near the Presbyterian church. They had not been there very long before their presence was noticed by some of the youths who were throwing stones in Little James Street, a substantial party of whom shifted their attention to the soldiers in the derelict building. A hail of missiles was thrown at these soldiers.[12] At the same time S Company's Mortar Platoon were cutting some wire on top of a wall. At 15.50 hours rioters were throwing stones at the MG Platoon and the Mortar Platoon wire cutting party. It was claimed by the Army that two nail bombs were thrown and exploded very close to the MG Platoon.[13] Whilst some soldiers from the Mortar Platoon were cutting the wire, a single high velocity round was fired and struck a rainwater pipe on the side of the Presbyterian church just above their heads.

Soldier A, a Corporal, was covering the wire cutting party from the middle floor of a derelict building on William Street. From the window he saw some young men, who were hanging around after the main body of the march had passed, start throwing stones and bottles at the soldiers on the ground floor, some of whom replied with rubber bullets. He then saw two smoking objects, about the size of a bean can, go sailing past the window, and heard two explosions, louder than the explosion of the rubber bullet guns. As the two smoking objects went past the window he shouted 'Nail bombs' as a warning to the men on the ground floor. His Platoon Sergeant called back an order that he was to shoot any nail bombers. He then saw, about fifty yards away on the other side of the road, a man look round the corner and dart back again. The man reappeared carrying an object in his right hand and made the actions of striking a fuse match against the wall with his left hand. When he brought his two hands together Soldier A, assuming that he was about to light a nail bomb, took aim and fired at him. His first shot missed, so Soldier A fired again immediately and this time saw the man fall. Other people at once came out from the side of the building and dragged the man away. Soldier B's description of the incident was in similar terms. He noticed one man come out from the waste ground across William Street carrying in his right hand a black cylindrical object which looked like a nail bomb. With his left hand he struck the wall with a match. Thinking that the man was about to light the nail bomb, and that there was no time to wait for orders from his Platoon Sergeant, Soldier B took aim and fired. As the first shot had no effect, he fired two more shots, whereupon the man fell back and was dragged away by two of his comrades.[14] In this area two people are known to have been wounded: Damien Donaghy (aged 15) and John Johnston (aged 52). Both were wounded at a piece of waste ground south of William Street which faced the GPO Sorting Office. The principal evidence before Widgery, apart from the evidence of A and B and of Johnston himself, was that of Father McIvor and Charles McDaid. Neither McIvor nor McDaid saw or heard the throwing of nail bombs.[15] Johnston later died from his injuries.

What is particularly significant is that the HV shot fired at the soldiers in the Presbyterian church confirms the presence of gunmen active before 1 PARA began their arrest operation. The shooters were from the Official IRA. Why had they fired when, prior to Bloody Sunday, Reg Tester, the Officials' QM, had received an order from the OC Derry to ensure all weapons were collected from the Bogside and taken to the Creggan? The aim was not to leave the Creegan undefended. But, on the morning of the march, there were two weapons missing: the pistol which was carried by the OC at all times and a Sporting (cut down) .303 rifle. After retrieving all weapons they were kept in the boots of two cars.[16] It was the retrieving of the .303 rifle that led to the confrontation with the Army. OIRA1 and OIRA2 were tasked with retrieving the rifle. OIRA2 was a volunteer member on the Command Staff of the Officials. On the Saturday night before the march, OIRA2 went down to the Columbcille Court flats to recover the .303 rifle which was stored in a static dump. They could not get to the dump as there had been a shooting in the area. OIRA2 and his companion decided to come back the next day. They came from the rear of the Columbcille flats where OIRA2 caught glimpses of the march through the gaps between houses. OIRA2 heard people shouting at the pair from below and became aware from what they were saying that two people had been shot by the Army:

> I could see an Army sniper in the Presbyterian Church area, I believed that he had probably been the person who had fired the shots... The army sniper raised his head a couple of times and took aim along his rifle at the general march area. To me he appeared to be looking for a target, and having heard the commotion below us I believed that he was going to shoot again. The other volunteer who was with me lifted the rifle we had just recovered, aimed one shot at the sniper and fired. The sniper ducked down immediately and my initial thought was that he had in fact been hit.

OIRA2 did not regard this action as a breach of his orders: it was not a deliberate attempt to incite any confrontation with the British Army 'and no offensive action was taken'. OIRA2 and his companion went to the Glenfada Park area and placed the rifle in the boot of the car. The car had been put in the Glenfada area specifically for the purpose of transferring the weapon back to the Bogside. It was after this that the Paras arrived in Rossville Street.[17] This admission that the Officials had opened fire on the Army took decades to emerge. Reg Tester admitted that the OIRA 'has been economical with the truth' in relation to the firing of a shot by one of its Volunteers. This was because the Army Council decided at the time that there were to be no admissions that any shots had been fired.[18] This is, in fact, the only admitted shot fired by any members of either IRA faction prior to 1 PARA beginning their arrest operation. However, the HV round that struck the Presbyterian church was timed at 15.55 and as occurring at about that moment by Soldier 236 and appeared in his Diary of Operations of 30.1.72. It also appears that it was very shortly thereafter that Donaghy and Johnston were shot.[19] Major Loden, CO of S Company, recorded in his Diary of Operations the HV shot at 15.55 and a 'few moments after this' A and B observing a nail bomber.[20]

Either both parties were incorrect about the timing of the shot and the sequence of events, or there was another shooter. But either way, there is also evidence that, after Donaghy and Johnston were shot, there were a number of further shots that were not fired by the Army that day: a shot, which hit a wall in Kells Walk, close to Cyril Cave, a BBC cameraman; a revolver shot from 'just below the entrance to the block of flats' that is, Columbcille Court, fired, as Mr Capper, a BBC reporter thought, from the crowd there towards soldiers on a roof; or, as Ciaran Donnelly, of *The Irish Times*, thought, from the crowd throwing stones at a derelict house in William Street near Tanner's Row; and another HV round coming from the direction of Little Diamond heard at the City Cabs' office in William Street by Simon Winchester of *The Guardian* and Nigel Wade of *The Daily Telegraph* and timed by Winchester as being fired at about 16.05 – again before 1 PARA went in. This may, or may not, have been the same shot as that described by Mr Porter – who was monitoring Security Force radio traffic at the time – who, after seeing a camera crew outside Columbcille Court filming a handkerchief covered in blood, heard the twang of a bullet strike 'to my right and high up in Columbcille Court and then I heard the sharp cutting sound of a high velocity bullet travel from a direction between Stevenson's Bakery and Little James Street'. Finally there was a shot referred to by the Intelligence Officer of 1 PARA as a shot coming from the direction of Rossville Street at about 16.08 and fired towards Barrier 12.[21] Even discounting the final account of 1 PARA's IO the civilian evidence is revealing: six individuals recall firing before 1 PARA began their arrest operation. Its importance is this: it reveals active gunmen in Derry before 1 PARA go in. The identity of the firers – apart from not being Army – remains unknown. But it does cast doubt on the notion that all IRA guns have been accounted for. And these are not the only unaccounted civilian shots either. Even so the first shot, directed at the Presbyterian church, was a key event; as Sergeant O, holed up behind the church wall, recalled:

This shot... had a significant effect on the operation. Up to that point, all we thought we would be doing was going in to arrest people. We would have gone in to make the arrests with most of the men just carrying batons, a few having rubber bullet guns, and one or two having SLRs as protection. As we now knew there were gunmen operating in the area, most of the men carried SLRs and one or two carried rubber bullet guns... a baton is no use when someone is shooting at you.[22]

1 PARA GO IN

At 1616 hours Support Company advanced through barrier 12 and down Rossville Street in a convoy of ten vehicles. In the lead was the Mortar Platoon commanded by Lieutenant N, comprising eighteen all ranks and travelling in two armoured personnel carriers. Next came the Command APC of the Company Commander (Major Loden) with a Ferret scout car in attendance. Following Company Headquarters came two empty APCs belonging to the Machine Gun Platoon. The men of this Platoon had been detached earlier and did not rejoin the Company in time to take part in the arrests. The two empty APCs were followed by two soft-skinned 4-ton lorries carrying the thirty-six all ranks of the Composite Platoon, commanded by Captain SA8. The rear was brought up by two further APCs carrying the Anti-Tank Platoon, which consisted of Lieutenant 119 in command and seventeen other ranks. According to Loden his orders were simply to go through barrier 12 and arrest as many rioters as possible. As the crowd retreated down Rossville Street he went after them. The leading APC (Lieutenant N) turned left off Rossville Street and halted on the waste ground near to where Eden Place used to be. The second APC (Sergeant O) went somewhat further and halted in the courtyard of the Rossville Flats near the north end of the Western (or No 1) Block. The Platoon immediately dismounted. Soldier P and one or two others from Sergeant O's vehicle moved towards Rossville Street but the remainder of the Platoon started to make arrests near to their vehicles.[23] As the troops debussed 'they fired baton rounds at the rioters, because this is part of their arrest technique'.[24] Of course not all the 'rioters' were rioters.

At the same time the soldiers claimed they came under fire from gunmen. In particular a burst of about fifteen rounds of low velocity automatic fire was directed at the Company Commander's radio operators which hit the ground in front of them. Two gelignite bombs were said to have landed about twenty metres in front of the leading soldiers of the Mortar Platoon. Initially the troops ignored the hostile fire while they arrested those close to their vehicles.[25] Soldier 033 claimed that he was moving south across the waste ground when he heard a Thompson machine gun fire. It was a long burst, of about fifteen to twenty rounds, as if the magazine was let off in one go. He saw the strike of bullets on the ground to the front and left of him about eight to ten feet away. The gunfire caused Soldier 033 to stop: 'I can only describe it as being like something you might see in a film. I was conscious that I was more of a target because I was carrying a radio – in a conflict it is usually the signallers who are shot first by the other side as then the communications system is brought down.' Soldier 033 ran for cover towards the north garble of Block 1 of the Rossville Flats. 'This firing came out of the blue. We were carrying out an arrest operation for rioting and then, all of a sudden, there was Thompson fire.' From the direction the dust kicked up, Soldier 033 thought the fire was coming from the far side – the east or south-east side – of the Flats car park. 'It was very unusual to see a strike. Normally fire directed at us went over our heads when it missed, but I could see the shots hitting the ground. To me, it suggested that the fire was coming down from a height towards me.' As he took cover he was aware of SLR shots being fired around him. The OC was close by. It was 033's job to remain close to him.[26]

Derek Wilford was following up the rear of his troops. He heard several high velocity shots at about this time and several rubber bullet guns went off as he and his signaller left the OP to move in behind the leading companies. They ran down Great James and Little James Street, through barrier 12 and paused briefly at the Rossville Street/William Street junction. Wilford could see that several arrests had already been made. He then moved round the corner hugging close to the wall and ran forward towards the end of Rossville Flats. About half way across the ground two or three shots 'cracked uncomfortably close' so he changed direction and ran to the right where he took cover behind a low wall and just to the rear of some of his paratroopers. One paratrooper fired to his left front as Wilford arrived. He asked him what he was firing at. He said a gunman lying behind some rubble. Wilford warned them all to keep their heads down and to fire only at identifiable targets. He asked where the Company Commander was and he was pointed out as being across near the Rossville Flats. Major Loden told Wilford that there had been considerable shooting from the Flats and also from the Glenfada Flats further down and to the right.[27] According to Loden his command vehicle had come under fire forcing him to move it with his scout car in attendance to the north end of No.1 Block of the Flats to obtain cover. The soft-skinned vehicles of the Composite Platoon halted under cover of buildings at the south-east corner of the junction of William Street and Rossville Street, where the troops dismounted. The Anti-Tank Platoon's vehicles halted behind the 4-ton lorries and the men of that Platoon dismounted and moved to Kells Walk. Some of these men were to appear later in Glenfada Park. The Composite Platoon Commander deployed half of his men to the east in support of the Mortar Platoon, the other half to the west in support of the Anti-Tank Platoon. Thereafter Support Company operated in three areas: the courtyard of the Rossville Flats; Rossville Street from Kells Walk to the improvised barricade; and lastly the area of Glenfada Park and Abbey Park.[28]

A number of soldiers – Privates S, T, and U, Sergeant O, Lieutenant 119, and Major Loden – claimed there was a substantial burst of shots from the area of the Rossville Flats at an early stage. Soldiers also claimed that there was rifle fire from the alleyway between Blocks 1 and 2 (Soldiers V and S); rifle fire from the catwalk between Blocks 2 and 3 (O) and pistol fire from the alleyway between these blocks (R); fire from a man with a pistol behind a Cortina in the south-east corner (O and 038); at least one petrol bomb (V); nail bombs thrown or attempted to be thrown from in front of Block 1, east side (R), from between Blocks 2 and 3 (Q) and from behind the corner of 36 Chamberlain Street (N); and stones, bottles and acid bombs from Block 1 and in the forecourt. There were also claims of miscellaneous explosions (V – two explosions before debussing; R – explosion just after debussing; and Colonel Wilford – two 'crumps'). In addition, Soldier U heard a long burst of automatic fire from behind the Glenfada Park area as he went along Rossville Street.[29] Sergeant O had heard about twenty to thirty rounds fired in bursts from what appeared to be four or five weapons dotted around the Flats. The firing was not controlled, not the usual type of deliberately aimed sniper fire. His impression was that it was inexperienced people in the Flats who had control of these weapons and that was why the Paras did not sustain any serious casualties: 'Those that did have the weapons were not particularly good at using them.' Sergeant O claimed to have fired at a gunman with a pistol in the car park; a man with an M1 Carbine on the first floor balcony of Block 3 of the Flats; and another gunman who was, possibly, using the same M1 Carbine. He also saw an acid bomb thrown from Block 1: Private T told him that he and Private R had had their legs splashed with acid. Sergeant O knew, from Belfast, how dangerous acid bombs could be: 'They could seriously wound you and I had seen them burn through metal before. Usually, they were in a screw top bottle and were a creamy/light yellow colour, normally a mixture of acid, which burns the skin, and paint, which sticks to it.' He told Private T to open fire if he saw another bomber.[30]

Soldier 033 tells a similar tale: he got in close to the building and found other soldiers there, including Soldier T at the northern end of Block 1. He was down on the ground with his back against the wall and was complaining loudly of having acid thrown at him. 033 saw that his trousers were damaged. Water was poured over his legs. 033 gave his water bottle for the task.[31] T had noticed a person throwing acid bombs about three storeys up in the Flats; he fired two rounds at the acid bomb thrower. He thought that he did not score a hit.[32] Soldier 033 saw part of an arm and a handgun emerge from Block 1 at a ground level window or doorway. 'Seeing the gun was a surprise. It was very unusual to actually be able to see a gunman shooting a weapon, because they were usually concealed. I did not shoot because the arm and weapon did not provide enough of a target to shoot at from that range.' Soldier 033 could see that the gun was being fired by the recoil of the weapon. The shots appeared to be aimed at the troops in the area of Rossville Street by Glenfada Park North. The gunman then appeared to be engaged by troops. When he looked back south towards the barricade 033 saw one or two strikes of bullets close to a man on the ground who was waving. He assumed these were from the gunman behind the barricades. Soldier 033 found this confusing as it seemed as if the gunman was shooting at one of his own people.[33] In the opinion of Sergeant O:

> When the IRA planned sniping incidents in 1972, the weapon would be brought in from elsewhere, the sniper would be set up with clear sights and he would pick off his target. He would not generally miss. On this day, however, we were not faced with a sniping incident. My Pig arrived in the courtyard of

the Rossville Flats as a total surprise to the local people and I think that they took the view that they were being invaded by the army. I became aware that the IRA had agreed to stay out of the area well after the event when speaking with a television journalist, Peter Taylor. I think that it is probably true that the IRA had kept their hard men out of the area, up in the Creggan estate, and I believe that 'dicks' or second rate men got hold of low quality weapons which were in the Rossville Flats ready for use and disobeyed the IRA and opened fire on us. If experienced IRA snipers had been firing the weapons, there is no doubt that the paras would have lost a number of men.[34]

A number of soldiers other than those of 1 PARA gave evidence about the opening of fire. Captain 028, a Royal Artillery officer attached to 1 PARA as a Press Officer, saw the leading vehicle struck by a round before it came to a halt and saw a man open fire with a sub-machine gun from the barricade as the soldiers jumped out of their vehicles. A few minutes later, during the gun battle, he saw a man armed with a pistol come out from the south end of Block 1 of the Rossville Flats, and another man with a rifle at a window in the Flats. Lieutenant 227 of The Royal Artillery, who was in command of an observation post on the City Walls, heard two bursts of automatic fire from the Glenfada Park area after the arrest operation had begun and before he had heard any other sort of ball ammunition. He subsequently heard three or four pistol shots from the Rossville Flats area. Gunner 030, who was in a slightly different position on the City Walls, saw a youth fire five or six shots with a pistol from the south-east corner of the Rossville Flats courtyard in the direction of Rossville Street. This was before 030 heard any fire from the Paras. Later on he heard a burst of automatic fire and saw a man with a machine gun running in Glenfada Park.[35] The first gunfire which Police Sergeant Falkingham heard, while on duty at barrier 14, came from a Thompson sub-machine gun: 'The sound is a particularly regular bop, bop, bop.' He thought that at least two weapons were being used.[36] Another police officer, Robert Milton, stationed at the junction between Magazine Street and Butcher Street, opposite Butcher Gate, 'heard a bang or boom, which sounded to me like a couple of nail or blast bombs going off...I would have known the sound of a nail or blast bomb at the time and I have no doubt at all that that is what I heard.'[37] When the Paras pursued the rioters up Chamberlain Street, Constable Raymond Kirk saw automatic fire directed at the troops: 'I saw them dive in all directions for cover. I heard these bursts of automatic fire for at least 45 seconds and it appeared to me that there was more than one gunman firing on the Military.'[38]

RUC Sergeant Laird, who was on the walls near the Walker Memorial, heard four types of relevant noise: the sharp 'cracks' of rifles which he put down to the Army; lower velocity shots from different guns which came from a different direction to the Army's; the 'crump' of nail bombs; and the 'thud' of baton rounds. He described automatic fire as a burst or 'brrrrrr' of a fire from a gun that fires at will when the trigger is depressed. The SLR made a more controlled 'crack, crack, crack' sound. Laird described the fire as not heavy. There was no prolonged or sustained fire, more short snipes between opposing sides.[39] John

McVicker was a 20-year-old police officer drafted in to Derry from Dunmurry for the march. He, like other groups of policemen, were organized in groups of a sergeant and about six constables. His group's duties were to cover the area of the City Walls. Stationed below the Walls at Magazine Street Upper, McVicker recalled: 'I was amazed... I think that day was the first time I was ever involved in gunfire. It was very frightening just being there... I put my head down and my biggest worry was that bullets would come through the holes in the City Walls and hit me. That was probably in my imagination.' At just 20-years-old he could not tell the difference between different types of live ammunition, only between it and rubber bullets. After the gunfire stopped he went back up on to the walls:

> If there had been firing from the Walls, I would have seen evidence of it, for example spent cases, but there was nothing. In my own mind, I am 100 per cent certain there was no firing from up there. I think from where we stood beneath the City Walls, we would have been able to look up on to the walls and see the soldiers' entire bodies. We could also have seen what they were doing.[40]

There was also a significant body of civilian evidence about the presence of gunmen in the Bogside that afternoon, including some to the effect that they were the first to open fire. Mr Beggin, a BBC cameraman, who went through the William Street barrier with soldiers of C Company and watched the soldiers of Support Company crossing the open ground in front of the Rossville Flats, heard a number of shots fired apparently from the Flats before the soldiers themselves opened fire. Phillips, Seymour, Wilkinson and Hammond, members of an Independent Television News team, who also went through the William Street barrier behind the Paras, all heard machine gun fire as the soldiers went across the open space. They also heard single shots but were not unanimous as to whether or not the automatic fire came first. The troops did not use automatic weapons. After the initial firing at the Rossville Street barricade, Mr Mailey, a freelance photographer, heard three shots of a much lower calibre than that of the Army's weapons. Simon Winchester of *The Guardian,* who had heard a single rifle shot from the direction of the Little Diamond some time before the Paras came through the barriers, saw, a few minutes later and still before the Paras appeared, youths clearing people away from an entrance to Columbcille Court in a manner which suggested to him that they were clearing a field of fire for a sniper. After he had reached the south side of the Rossville Flats he heard some low calibre fire in answer to the Army's fire and also some automatic fire from the general direction of the Flats. Leslie Bedell, a Londoner who was on holiday in Northern Ireland, was present at the meeting at Free Derry Corner. From there he saw the armoured vehicles arrive in Rossville Street and heard firing. Some minutes later he saw several cars drive down from the Creggan. About two dozen men armed with rifles and automatic weapons got out, dispersed amongst the flats on the north side of Westland Street and fired about fifty rounds at the soldiers. When the gunmen withdrew, Bedell saw a crowd of about fifty civilians surround and give cover to one of the gunmen who had been separated from the main body, so that he was able to rejoin the others in safety. Finally, Noruki Kunioka, a Japanese student at the London Film School, saw a man armed with a rifle in Westland Street.[41]

But this is not the end of the evidence relating to active gunmen on Bloody Sunday. INQ 3, a Major in the Special Investigation Branch (SIB) of the Corps of the Royal Military Police from September 1971 until October 1973, was later surprised that when the Widgery Tribunal was published, it had ignored various incidents that had taken place elsewhere in Londonderry 'virtually simultaneously' with those involving 1 PARA, 'thereby indicating a concerted attack on the British Army that day'. One was of an Army patrol fired upon from a cemetery in the north of the city and the second of another patrol being fired on from a gas works. In the latter, the sergeant in charge shot at, and claimed to have hit, two men who had fired on his patrol.[42] This evidence was omitted because Widgery confined himself to an examination of the events involving 1 PARA. Among the control points in the Bogside controlled by 1 Royal Anglian was barrier 20 at Barrack Street. At about 16.15 hours a shot was fired at soldiers from the area of the Gasworks. As a result a number of soldiers moved forward towards Charlotte Place. Soldiers AA and AB were together and as they went they were confronted by a man who came around the corner from St Columba's Walk and Foyle Street. This man was carrying a rifle which he aimed in the direction of the soldiers. The man fired at the soldiers who each fired one round at the same time. No one was hit. AA then moved forward to locate the man. He was then fired at from a bricked up building in Lower Tower Street. He saw the figure of a man behind the muzzle flashes and fired three rounds, hitting the man.[43] This may have or may not have been the Official IRA Volunteer to whom *The Observer* journalist, Mary Holland, talked in February 1972; this Volunteer was in an empty house – the location given was on the corner of Cooke Street and Joyce Street with orders to cover Bishop Street – and was wounded by a soldier returning fire from a house opposite.[44] *The Sunday Times* archive named him as Micky Doherty.[45] Dr McDermott treated a Richard Doherty for wounds similar to this IRA Volunteer.[46] The suggestion is that this wounding took place after 1 PARA had ceased firing during the arrest operation. But the beginning of the incident at barrier 20 began as the arrest operation was still in progress. What it suggests is that there may have been access to weapons beyond those accounted for by the Officials: the recovered rifle, the pistol, and the guns in cars. Furthermore, both IRA factions claimed not to have sustained any casualties on the day. Yet one thing is sure: someone was shooting at the Army while, according to both IRA groups, all their weapons were accounted for.

THE KILLING FIELDS

As soon as military vehicles appeared in William Street the crowd on the waste ground had begun to run away to the south and was augmented by many other people driven out of Chamberlain Street by C Company. Some of the crowd ran along Rossville Street on the west side of Block 1 of the Flats, whilst the remainder ran into the courtyard on the north side of the Flats themselves. The crowd ran not because they thought the soldiers would open fire upon them but because they feared arrest. The APCs of Mortar Platoon penetrated more deeply than was expected by the crowd, which caused some panic. The only means of escape from the courtyard was the alleyway between Blocks 1 and 2 and that between Blocks 2 and 3, both of which rapidly became very congested. As soon as the vehicles halted the soldiers of Mortar Platoon began to make arrests. But within a minute or two firing broke out and within the next ten minutes the soldiers of Mortar Platoon had fired forty-two rounds of 7.62 mm ammunition and one casualty lay dead in the courtyard.[47] Jack Duddy, aged 17, was the first fatal casualty and fell in the courtyard of Rossville Flats. According to a witness, Mary Bonnor, he was shot in the back. In fact the bullet entered his right shoulder and travelled through his body from right to left. As he ran he turned from time to time to watch the soldiers. No shot described by a soldier precisely fitted Duddy's case. The nearest was one described by Soldier V who spoke of firing at a man in a white shirt in the act of throwing a petrol bomb; but Duddy was wearing a red shirt and there was no evidence of his having a bomb. Widgery concluded that the probable explanation of his death 'is that he was hit by a bullet intended for someone else'.[48]

With Duddy when he was killed was Father Edward Daly. In 1972, Daly was serving as a curate in St Eugene's Cathedral. He had responsibility for the pastoral care of people living in the Bogside. He had been serving there since 1962. On that 30 January, Daly celebrated Mass in St Eugene's and afterwards had lunch with the other priests and left the parochial house to accompany a funeral from Abbey Street to the City Cemetery. By the time he got back to the parochial house, sometime between 3 and 3.30 p.m., the march was proceeding down Creggan Street from Lone Moor Road, past the Cathedral, on its way to William Street. It was the custom of Daly to go down to Rossville Street and William Street when there were disturbances occurring and when disturbances threatened because there were large numbers of elderly people resident in that area, especially in Kells Walk, Glenfada Park and Columbcille Court. They were often frightened and they were particularly discomforted and alarmed when CS gas was used or when there were explosions or gunfire. On many occasions Daly assisted with the evacuation of such people if they felt it necessary to get out of the area. It was while he was in the area of Kells Walk and Glenfada Park that Daly heard two or three shots ring out. He knew the shots were not rubber bullets. There was a moment of panic. Someone came rushing up to him and told him that two men had been shot. After returning to Rossville Street, Daly's attention was attracted by the revving up of engines. He looked across towards Little James Street and noticed three or four Saracens moving along at increasing speed followed by soldiers on foot in the general direction of Rossville Street. Daly observed them for a few moments. Simultaneously everyone in the area began to run in the opposite direction – away from William Street and across Rossville Street towards Free Derry Corner. Daly ran with the others but veered to his left towards the courtyard of Rossville Flats:

I was running and, like most of the crowd, looking back every few moments, to see if the armoured cars and soldiers were still coming. They kept coming. Around this time, I remember seeing someone thrown in the air by a Saracen armoured car... As I was entering the courtyard, I noticed this young boy running beside me. I was running and he was running and, like me, looking back from time to time. I remember him smiling or laughing. He seemed about 16 or 17. I did not see anything in his hands. I didn't know his name. I now know his name to be John (Jackie) Duddy. When we reached the centre of the courtyard, I heard a shot and simultaneously this young boy gasped or groaned loudly. This was the first shot that I had heard since the two or three shots I had heard some time earlier in the afternoon. I looked around and this boy just fell on his face.

Daly's first impression was that he had been shot by a rubber bullet. He could not imagine that the boy had been hit by a live round. Daly ran on, still looking back. Some or all of the APCs were still progressing towards the Rossville Flats. He looked at the passageway between Blocks 1 and 2 of the Flats, the exit he had intended and hoped to use to escape from the courtyard. It was jammed by a mass of panic-stricken and frightened people. 'I remember a woman screaming. The air was filled with the sound of yells and screams of fear. Then there was a burst of gunfire which caused terror.' Daly knew they were live bullets. He sought cover behind a little low wall. There were about twenty to thirty people taking cover there. Daly threw himself on the ground at the edge of the wall. During a lull in the firing, Daly looked over from where he was lying and saw the young boy whom he had passed lying out in the middle of the car park where he had fallen. He was lying at this time on his back with his head towards Daly. This puzzled Daly. He distinctly remembered him falling on his face. It transpired that another man, William Barber, who had been running behind Daly, had turned him over. Daly could see blood on him. He decided to make his way out to him. 'I took a handkerchief from my pocket and waved it for a little time and then I got up in a crouched position and I went to the boy. I knelt beside him. There was a substantial amount of blood oozing from his shirt... I put my handkerchief inside the shirt to try and staunch the bleeding.' A young member of the Knights of Malta, Charles Glenn, suddenly appeared on the other side of the boy. Daly decided to administer the Last Rites to the boy. Gunfire started again. Both men got as close to the ground as they could. Two other men joined them, one of whom was William Barber. Daly saw a young man with long fair hair dash past him. He was Michael Bridge.[49] As they treated Duddy, Glenn 'started to weep and said, "father are we going to be killed?" I remember actually I wept too with him. We both wept, together for quite some time and we were very frightened.'[50]

Just as Daly, Glenn and two other men were about to move Duddy, the priest saw a man move along the gable wall of the last house in Chamberlain Street. The house backed on to waste ground. The man suddenly appeared at the corner of this house and moved along the gable. He produced a gun from his jacket. It was a small gun. He fired two or three shots around the corner at the soldiers. Daly and compatriots screamed at the gunman to go away because they were frightened the soldiers might think that the fire was coming from where they were located. The gunman looked at them and then just drifted away across or into the mouth of Chamberlain Street. The other men in the group said that if Daly was prepared to go before them with a handkerchief, they were prepared to carry the young man somewhere where he could receive medical attention. They decided to make a dash for it. They got up on their knees. Daly waved the handkerchief. There was a burst of gunfire. They lay down again. Eventually they got up. Daly went in front and the men behind him carried Duddy. They made their way into Chamberlain Street and then into Harvey Street. They were challenged at this point by soldiers. Eventually they arrived at the corner of Waterloo Street and Harvey Street. Barber took off his coat, laid it on the ground and laid Duddy on it. He appeared to be dead. When Daly finally got back to the parochial house he was frustrated and upset. He decided to call Superintendent Patrick McCullagh. Both men had been contemporaries at school. Daly rang him and asked what on earth had happened. McCullagh was under the impression that it was only a minor disturbance: his latest reports were that only two people had been injured and several arrested. Daly told him that he had seen a number of dead bodies and that many had been seriously injured. McCullagh expressed disbelief but said that he would check it out. He rang back to tell Daly that the latest report was that eleven bodies had been admitted to Altnagelvin Hospital.[51]

The man whom Daly had seen fire at the soldiers was OIRA 4. He was a member of the Derry Command Staff. OIRA 4 had a .32 pistol which he kept for defensive, not offensive, purposes. He was allowed to keep it in accordance with the orders issued by the OC. So long as everybody knew the weapon was in his possession and wasn't needed anywhere else it was acceptable for him to keep it and look after it. OIRA 4 had joined the march in the Creggan. After the rioting started, OIRA 4 started down Chamberlain Street. At some point he found himself running with everyone else from the snatch squad. It was as he was running down Chamberlain Street that he heard shooting for the first time that day. As far as OIRA 4 was concerned it could have been rubber bullets. He had run a few yards into the car park of the Rossville Flats when he saw a body. It was Jack Duddy's and was being attended to by Father Daly. At the northeastern corner of Block 1 of the Rossville Flats, OIRA 4 could see an Army APC sticking out. He could also see a bunch of Paras standing around it shooting in Duddy's direction: 'I just lost my temper. The Brits were gunning down innocent civilians.'[52] At this point:

> I had moved along this wall and took out my pistol as I came along the wall. I had not drawn my weapon at any time before I started to move along the gable wall. I came around the corner and fired two shots towards the APCs which were in the area. When I think back now I do not know what I hoped to achieve. The intention would have been to dissuade the Paratroopers from advancing any further but even then I realized very quickly that one man with a pistol against that number of armed soldiers was a futile gesture. My memory is that none of the soldiers even appeared to realize they were being fired upon and none actually turned to return fire in my direction.[53]

The minute he fired, OIRA 4 was confronted by people shouting at him to stop. 'I was still mad as hell' but these people brought him to his senses and 'I put my gun away in my coat pocket. It never left the pocket after that.' Just after he fired the shots a man appeared in the car park with his hands up. He had nothing in his hands. He was then shot, although not badly wounded. The man was Micky Bridge. OIRA 4 was certain 'that Jack Duddy was already shot by the time I fired and I'm sure when I think about it logically that my shooting made no difference whatsoever to what those paras were doing.'[54]

Other IRA Volunteers were enraged too – but, crucially, claimed they did not open fire on the soldiers. When Reg Tester was told about what was happening, 'I wanted to hit back. It was the only time that I can remember that I had lost my cool.' He took a gun out of one of the Official IRA cars carrying weapons. He was cheered by surrounding civilians. Tester made his way up to the balcony of a flat at the junction of Westland Street and Lecky Road. He then aimed his M1 Carbine at a soldier and tried to fire but the weapon jammed: 'I was glad that it had actually jammed because I then calmed down and realised better what I was doing.'[55]

As he was walking along Chamberlain Street, Martin McGuinness heard people running behind him. After walking through the back of Rossville Flats towards Blocks 1 and 2 he saw a woman being carried by a group of men across the car park. McGuinness had not heard any shots by this stage. Shortly after passing through the opening of the Flats he heard shooting which he believed to be rifle fire:

> I could... see people crouching, others falling or throwing themselves to the ground. Like everyone around me I was confused about what the British Army were doing and trying to work out what was happening. The shooting continued to intensify and it was high velocity. At this stage I still didn't realise that people were being shot. I didn't know what to think. Were the soldiers firing over people's heads? Were the rioters being arrested?

After being told that the soldiers were shooting people in Glenfada Park, 'I thought, "They've come to teach the people of Derry a lesson."... I wanted to get a rifle, find other Volunteers and do something.' McGuinness suggested to another Volunteer who'd been on the march that they should gather Volunteers and arm themselves as it looked likely that the soldiers were making a serious incursion. After meeting with the OC and other Volunteers it was found that the British were not moving into the Creggan and Brandywell areas. McGuinness was surprised: 'We then formed the view that what was happening in Rossville Street was an attempt to draw the IRA into a fight. This I believe is what the British Army were hoping would happen.' The Volunteers 'were angry and emotional. A critical and difficult decision had to be made.' It was concluded that any military engagement with the British Army 'would see us fall into a trap and that it would be a serious mistake to take weapons to the scene of the shootings... we should let the world see what we know to be fact: that the British Army had shot innocent civilians.'[56]

In the area of the Rossville Flats car park there was one dead there – Jack Duddy – and several wounded: Michael Bradley (aged 22) who had a small entrance and exit wound on the left forearm and an entrance and exit wound on the front of the chest; Michael Bridge (25) who had a wound to the left thigh; Peggy Deery (37) who had a gunshot wound on the front of the left thigh with a large exit wound on the back; Patrick McDaid (24) who had what was described as a glancing wound along the back of the left shoulder; in addition Alana Burke was hit by an APC. The only soldiers that it is known fired in the car park were N, O, Q, R, S, T and V. Lieutenant N fired three shots in the air and one at a man with a smoking object in his hand who came out from behind the corner of the end house in Chamberlain Street and was hit in the right thigh. Sergeant O fired two sets of shots (three at a man behind a Cortina and three at the catwalk between Blocks 2 and 3). Private Q said that he fired one shot which hit a man between Blocks 2 and 3. Private R's first shot was at a man who ran out from Block 1, making to throw a smoking object, whom he hit on the right shoulder. One of his three shots was at a man with a pistol at the corner of Blocks 2 and 3. Private S, who was in a Pig, fired twelve shots in the direction of Blocks 1 and 2. Private T's shots were upwards at a man firing from Block 1. Lance Corporal V shot from just south of the wire fence at a man with a petrol bomb in the car park. His shot seems the most likely candidate to have shot Duddy, not least because he described the body of the man he hit as being approached by men with handkerchiefs, one of whom was a priest. But V's description of where he hit the man and the appearance of the man does not tally with Duddy's actual injuries and appearance. None of the civilian evidence supports this. The evidence of Michael Bridge, F.P. Dunne and Derek Tucker suggests that Bridge was shot when, having seen a dead body in the Rossville Flats car park, he lost control, waved his arms around and shouted something like 'Shoot me' or 'Don't shoot Father Daly, shoot me.' The evidence of Derek Tucker was that he saw a man shot behind the low wall at the back of the car park. That man turned with his back to the Saracens, faced the flats and shouted 'Go away from the windows, they are firing.' Then he turned around to start to move to the right hand side of the car, clasped his hands to his stomach and fell. This may have been Bradley. Peggy Deery, shot in the thigh, said that she was shot by a soldier in front of her who appeared to be taking aim at her after she had attempted to get up from the ground to which she had slipped and fallen.[57]

After the vehicle convoy halted in Rossville Street the Anti-Tank Platoon and one half of the Composite Platoon had deployed to their right in the vicinity of the Flats known as Kells Walk. From this point it was possible to look due south down Rossville Street to the rubble barricade in that street and beyond it to Free Derry Corner. The distance from Kells Walk to Free Derry Corner was of the order of 300 yards. A considerable number of rounds were fired by soldiers from Kells Walk in the direction of the barricade, at which at least four of the fatal casualties occurred. The barricade in Rossville Street running across from Glenfada Park to Block 1 of the Rossville Flats had fallen into disrepair and was only about three feet high. There was a gap to allow a single line of traffic to go through but there were also reinforcements of barbed wire on wooden knife rests. James Chapman was a civil servant who had previously been a regular soldier in the British Army and a resident of Londonderry for thirty-six years, thirty of them in the Bogside itself. He lived at No.6 Glenfada Park, so that his sitting room window directly overlooked the Rossville Street barricade. When the APCs appeared and the rest of the crowd began to run, some 50 to 100 soldiers deployed from their vehicles and, according to Chapman, immediately opened fire into the crowd trying to flee over the barricade. He maintained that the Army fired indiscriminately upon the backs of people who were scrambling over the barricade in an effort to escape and that no firearms or bombs were being used against the soldiers at that time.[58] Robert Campbell, the Assistant Chief Constable of the Renfrew and Bute Constabulary, who was observing the scene from the City Wall, gave a very different account of events at the barricade. He could not see the entry of the vehicles but he had a clear view of part of the barricade in Rossville Street and of the whole of the area to the south of it down to Free Derry Corner. He described how people streamed through the barricade on their way to the meeting at Free Derry Corner, but he also observed a group of demonstrators who detached themselves from the main crowd and remained close to the barricade from which they threw stones and other missiles in the direction of the Army vehicles. Campbell described their stone throwing as very active. After a time he heard automatic fire from the direction of the Rossville Flats. As this did not deter the stone-throwers he assumed that the rounds did not go near them. The automatic fire was followed by a single high velocity shot which caused them to take cover. Within two or three minutes, however, the militants were throwing stones again. Then came a cluster of ten or twelve high velocity rounds which finally scattered them, leaving three or four bodies lying at the barricade.[59]

Four young men were killed in the Rossville Street area. Michael Kelly, aged 17, was shot while standing at the Rossville Street barricade. The bullet entered his abdomen from the front; he was shot by Soldier F, who described having fired one shot from the Kells Walk area at a man at the barricade who was attempting to throw what appeared to be a nail bomb.[60] Kelly was the first to be killed here. The other three fatalities occurred within a very short time frame: perhaps three to four minutes. Nobody saw any of the dead carrying, using or throwing weapons.[61] Kevin McElhinney, aged 17, was shot whilst crawling southwards along the pavement on the west side of No 1 Block of Rossville Flats at a point between the barricade and the entrance to the Flats. The bullet entered his buttock so that it is clear that he was shot from behind by a soldier in the area of Kells Walk. It seems probable that the firer was Sergeant K, a senior NCO and a qualified marksman whose rifle was fitted with a telescopic sight. He fired only one round in the course of the afternoon. Soldier K described two men crawling from the barricade in the direction of the door of the Flats and said that the rear man was carrying a rifle. He fired one aimed shot but could not say whether it hit.[62] Michael McDaid, aged 20, was shot at the Rossville Street barricade. The bullet struck him in the front in the left cheek.[63] Hugh Pius Gilmore, aged 17, died near the telephone box which stood south of

Rossville Flats and near the alleyway separating Blocks 1 and 2. He was one of a crowd of thirty to fifty people who ran away down Rossville Street when the soldiers appeared. Gilmore was shot by one of the soldiers who fired from Kells Walk at the men at the barricade.[64] William Nash, aged 19, was close to McDaid at the Rossville Street barricade and the three men were shot almost simultaneously. The bullet entered his chest from the front. Soldier P spoke of seeing a man firing a pistol from the barricade and said that he fired four shots at this man, one of which hit him in the chest. He thought that the pistol was removed by other civilians. Alexander Nash, William's father, was wounded at the barricade. From a position of cover he saw that his son had been hit and went to help him. As he did so he himself was hit in the left arm. The medical opinion was that the bullet came from a low velocity weapon and Soldier U described seeing Nash senior hit by a revolver shot fired from the entrance to the Rossville Flats. The soldier saw no more than the weapon and the hand holding it.[65]

The evidence given by the Army indicated that the troops were fired upon from various directions and sources including pistol fire, Thompson machine gun fire, rifle fire (all from the barricade); there was also similar fire from the Flats. Ciaran Donnelly of *The Irish Times* said that, when taking a picture, he heard what he thought to be a long burst of automatic fire which seemed to come 'from the position the Army were coming into' and 'from the opposite side of the Glenfada Flats...in Rossville Flats in fact somewhere'. He also heard single shots. However, his evidence was to the effect that no one behind the barricade was shooting. Father O'Garda saw a young man appear from the Cathedral side of Kells Walk – after the Army had begun firing from the wall at Kells Walk – who drew a pistol from his pocket, lent over the wall at the end of Kells Wall and fired three quick shots. Father Mulvey, from a position somewhere towards Little Diamond, heard about a dozen single shots and then what he assumed to be a burst of automatic fire – repeated sustained firing for two to three seconds.[66]

Helen Johnston was 31 on Bloody Sunday. Born and bred in Derry she worked in a bakery as a dispatch worker and packer. After witnessing the rioting Johnston and her sister, Margaret, decided to go home. As the APCs arrived on the waste ground the women ran down to the rubble barricade that was across Rossville Street. Watching from an alleyway, Helen Johnston saw three younger men and an older man waving a white hanky. She could hear shooting. Chippings began flying off the wall above her head. She did not realize that the men had been shot. The next thing she saw were two boys at the bottom of Block 1 of the Flats. They were on the far side of the road from where she was. They were on their stomachs, scrambling to get away from the Army:

> They were just crawling, not looking behind them but just trying to get to the door of the flats...The young lads were scrambling with their hands out in front of them. I do not believe there was any possibility of them having a weapon. I certainly saw none. Someone must have been a good shot that day. I do not know how you shoot someone on the ground so effectively. I saw the body of the second boy jerk. The fellow in front of him had already got to the door and this second lad almost made it, but then I saw his body jerk again.

I saw the second young fellow dragged into the flats. Hands came out of the door to the flats, presumably from others who were sheltering in there and dragged him in. Two hands pulled him in by his own outstretched hands. I think he must have been dead by then. It would have been better if he had played dead earlier.

I could not see any rifle or weapon with or the two boys who crawled towards the door to the flats, or on the boys in the barricade. I had a clear view of the second lad who was crawling.[67]

Margaret called to Helen to get down behind the wall. She noticed a small boy sitting against the wall. He had blood all over him. She asked if he was alright. He said:

'They shot me mate beside me.' He seemed to be in a dazed condition. Then when I looked to the other side of me in the courtyard four men were lying face down. They appeared to have been shot while running away from the army. As I said to Margaret to look at the four fellows, a...soldier came around the corner. He said 'Fucking bastards, move.' We immediately moved. One of the soldiers reached for Fr. Bradley and Margaret yelled at them that he was a priest. Then the soldiers started kicking us. One made a lunge at me again. Margaret got between the soldier and me again, the soldier behind yelled, 'This way'.[68]

Four people were shot dead either in Glenfada Park or Abbey Park. James Joseph Wray, Gerald McKinney, Gerald Donaghy and William McKinney were all shot somewhere near the south-west corner of the more northerly of the two courtyards of the flats at Glenfada Park. Their respective ages were 22, 35, 17 and 26. The two McKinneys were not related. Four soldiers, all from the Anti-Tank Platoon, fired in this area, namely Soldiers E, F, G and H. Initially the Platoon deployed in the Kells Walk area and was involved in the firing at the Rossville Street barricade. Corporal E described how he saw civilians firing from the barricade and then noticed some people move towards the courtyard of Glenfada Park. He said that on his own initiative he accordingly led a small group of soldiers into the courtyard from the north-east corner to cut these people off. The recollection of the Platoon Commander (Lieutenant 119) was somewhat different; he said that he sent Soldiers E and F into the courtyard of Glenfada Park to cut off a particular gunman who had been firing from the barricade. The result in any event was that Soldiers E and F advanced into the courtyard and Soldiers G and H followed shortly afterwards. In the next few minutes there was a very confused scene in which according to civilian evidence some of the people who had been sheltering near the gable end of Glenfada Park sought to escape by running through the courtyard in the direction of Abbey Park; the soldiers fired upon them, killing the four men. From the forensic evidence of a bullet recovered from the body it was clear that Soldier G shot Donaghy. The other three were shot by Soldiers E, F, G or H.[69] Donaghy was struck by only one bullet and that bullet struck his abdomen approximately 'side on', most probably with the nose of the bullet pointing downwards and the base upwards. The 'side on' contact, the lack of penetration of the body and the damage to the bullet all indicated that the bullet had struck another object or person before striking him.[70] William O'Reilly said that Donaghy ran up the steps to 9-11 Abbey Park and that he was followed by Gerald McKinney who got between a soldier and Donaghy. Donaghy had his hands in the air. The soldier fired two shots and both men fell. John Carr witnessed what he believed was the death of Gerald McKinney in Abbey Park and saw James Wray lying with his body half on and half off the kerb in Glenfada Park. A soldier came towards Wray, put his foot on him and pushed him off the pavement. Everyone scattered save one man who turned and looked at the soldier and put his hands above his head. The soldier put the gun to his shoulder and shot that man, who put his hands together, joined his hands and blessed himself. He later learnt this was Gerald McKinney. Then another man ran towards Gerald McKinney and, as that man bent over him, he was shot. That man – he said – was William McKinney.[71] Joseph Friel, Danny Gillespie, Joseph Mahon, Patrick O'Donnell and Michael Quinn were all wounded in Glenfada Park.[72]

The accounts of the soldiers do not tally with the evidence of and about the wounded and the dead. Soldier G said he fired three shots, when kneeling at the right hand of a car parked in the north-east corner of Glenfada Park, at one of two men, each of whom was holding a rifle of the M1 type. He hit one and could have hit both. F said he and G, as they came through the entry to Glenfada Park, saw three men, who had come to the barricade directly in front of them in the south-west corner. The one on the extreme left was attempting to throw what seemed to be a nail bomb. F took two aimed shots, firing on one knee. The first hit the man in the right arm. The second hit him in the chest and he fell. Meanwhile G was firing at the other two. F saw that one of the other two was carrying a rifle. F then heard pistol shots from the direction of the Rossville Flats and, covered by G, went to the south-east corner of Glenfada Park where he got down on one knee and saw a man with a pistol at the back of Block 2 at the far end by the wall. He fired two aimed shots and the man fell to the ground. The man was in a crawling position, half turned to F's right. In was only in F's third statement to Widgery that he remembered shooting the man with a pistol and he only did so when an aerial photograph reminded him of the position. H fired, from the bonnet of a car, two shots at a youth who was in a throwing position with a similar type of object as that which had previously been thrown at him – brown and about the size of a coca-cola tin. The first shot missed and the second hit. Then a youth with blue denim jeans, jacket and trousers ran over to the body and picked up the nail bomb in his right hand. H fired an aimed shot, which hit him, either in the arm or shoulder, and the youth staggered back to the way from which he had come. H then claimed that he fired, from the alleyway leading to Glenfada Park, on nineteen separate occasions at a silhouette behind a frosted window out of the open top pane of which a muzzle stuck out.[73] Mrs Margaret McCartney who lived at 57 Glenfada Park – the middle of the larger properties into which H claimed he had discharged his nineteen shots – claimed that only one shot was fired into her house. None of the known dead or wounded constituted a potential victim of H's nineteen shots. No one else witnessed the firing of them.[74] E called on a man with a nail bomb to drop it – the man had just thrown a petrol bomb – but refused. E fired two shots. One missed, the second hit. The bomb exploded. Soldier 030 of the 22 LAD Regiment at the OP on the Walls gave evidence of seeing a gunman with what looked like a Thompson SMG in the alleyway leading to Abbey Park. One of the soldiers claimed to have come under SMG fire in this area.[75]

The last moments of Patrick Joseph Doherty, aged 31, were depicted in a series of harrowing photographs that showed him with a handkerchief over the lower part of his face crawling with others near the alleyway which separated No.2 Block from No.3. He was hit from behind whilst crawling or crouching because the bullet entered his buttock and proceeded through his body almost parallel to the spine. His body was found in the area at the rear of No 2 Block of Rossville Flats between that Block and Joseph Place. The probability is that he was shot by Soldier F, who spoke of hearing pistol shots and seeing a crouching man firing a pistol from the position where Doherty's body was found. Soldier F said that he fired as the man turned away, which would account for an entry wound in the buttock.[76] The photographs were taken by Gilles Peress. He spoke of a soldier firing from the north of Block 1 and another at the back of 36 Chamberlain Street at the moment when Doherty may have been killed in the car park of the Flats.[77] Bernard McGuigan, aged 41, was shot within a short distance of Hugh Gilmore, on the south side of No.2 Block of the Rossville Flats.[78] According to Geraldine Richmond, McGuigan and another man took her away from Gilmore who died at the gable end of Block 1. They took her towards a telephone kiosk. McGuigan heard a man crying out that he did not want to die alone. He went out to that man waving a white handkerchief. After taking about four paces he was shot.[79]

All the civilian eyewitness evidence referred to the indiscriminate shooting of the Paras. Joseph Friel, 20, saw five soldiers run around a corner at the Flats 'firing from the hip. I was hit in the chest by one of three shots I heard. I was just standing, I thought I was safe...I don't know why they shot me.' Alex Nash, 52, recalled: 'I saw my son Willie...shot down with two other lads at the Rossville Street barricade. I knew he was dead but I ran forward and raised my arm to stop the soldiers shooting any more. They shot me in the arm. I fell down and they fired at least six more rounds at me. I thought "Oh Christ, if I get up they'll shoot me again."' Michael Bridge tried to get the crowd back from the barricade when he was hit in the foot with a rubber bullet: 'I ran away as fast as I could and nearly fell over a young boy lying dead. I lost my head and ran towards the Saracen shouting "You murdering bastards" and waving my arms. A solider standing next to the Saracen shot me in the thigh. I ran a few steps on my nerves and fell down.' Michael Bradley was throwing stones at the soldiers – 'my blood was up, you know.' He had just finished throwing a stone 'when I saw a soldier aiming at me from about 20 yards away and I was hit in the arm and chest'. Paddy O'Donnell, 40, could hear shooting. He tried to push an old woman to the ground when he was hit from behind. Soldiers came running up shouting 'put your hands up.' O'Donnell said he was hit and they said 'come on, get it up, you'll get it up.' He called to a priest and tried to speak to him but was hit with a soldier's baton. He was left with a six inch scalp wound. When Patrick McDaid, 17, saw an APC coming he ran in front of Rossville Flats: 'They were shooting everyone. I felt a pain in my shoulder and a man told me I was hit. I had just sort of pulled my head down or I think I would have been killed.' Gilles Peress, 25, the French photographer, saw a soldier; he held his camera over his head, shouted 'Press' and waved his cameras. He then walked slowly on. The soldier fired a single shot at him. Having subsequently seen the bullet hole he estimated that the bullet passed a few centimetres from his head: 'I do not say that the soldier was trying to kill me, but I do say that he took the risk of killing me.' Peress ran up Chamberlain Street and saw a priest waving a bloodstained white handkerchief as he stood next to a body lying on the ground. This was Duddy. He photographed the scene. In the parking lot outside the Flats he saw two soldiers kneeling and firing slowly and methodically. It seemed as if they were carrying out a drill. Unable to photograph there he went through a passage under the Flats and on the other side saw a dead or dying man and another crawling towards him to help. He photographed this. Going along the wall of the Flats he saw and photographed a man who had been shot in the eye and a young man shot in the stomach.[80]

As the carnage unfolded John Hume was at home with his wife Pat. He sat in the house and watched the march go by. The whole town had turned out, even the clergy who had spoken out against the march: 'I can remember the despair of thinking that no-one was listening to me anymore and that this would be the end of me, in political terms.'[81] Hume was sitting in his front room with a journalist, David Terehchak, when they heard a lot of shooting but didn't know what it was. Then people started to come up to the house. They were in a state of panic. The first woman was Cathy Donaghy; she said: 'They're going mad. They're murdering people down there.' Then relatives started to arrive, wanting news of what happened. Ivan Cooper arrived also. He had a story about shots and a lot of people being dead. He said six were dead. By this stage there were lots on enquiries coming through on the telephone as to who was dead. So Hume drove over to the hospital but was stopped by soldiers on the bridge who refused to let him pass. He finally argued his way through. At the hospital, the first person Hume met was Mrs McGuigan. This was doubly shocking for Hume because they had grown up in adjacent streets and so he knew her very well. She was in a hysterical state. Hume went straight to the hospital authorities – in this case Dr Harvey who was in charge of casualty – to find out who was dead. He gave Hume the names at once. One of them was Mrs McGuigan's husband. Hume also met Gerry McKinney's brother-in-law – his sister was in a 'terrible state'. Hume and Ivan Cooper drove back home; to the people there he read out the list of names of the dead. There were twelve names on the list. Which left the thirteenth man unidentified. Hume had been told by Harvey when he got the list: 'There's one more, but we[']re still trying to identify him.' By now the McDaid family had been sitting in the house for a couple of hours. When Hume read out the list he said, 'There's one more', turned to the McDaid's and said: 'It won't be yours. Its very unlikely.' They got their coats on and went home.

Just then the phone rang. It was Dr Harvey. 'We've got the 13th name', he said. 'Its Michael McDaid.' Hume went to tell the family.

Hume knew McDaid vaguely – he had worked in a local bar which was owned by the Bradley family whom he knew: 'I had always known him as a decent lad.' The only other person killed whom Hume knew was Gerry McKinney. They had once been neighbours and, before that, classmates in school: 'He was not remotely interested in politics and was a very quiet man who never had anything to do with violence whatsoever. Violent republicanism was often handed down by tradition from grandfather, to father, to son. I was not aware of any of the wounded or deceased coming from families with such a tradition.'[82] Meanwhile, John McDaid had gone to the morgue because his brother Michael had not come home. The police told him his name was not on the list but 'when I got home a priest came to the front door. When I went back to the morgue, I saw my brother. There was a triangular wound on his cheek, and the back of [the] head was matted with blood. I have been round to Rossville flats to talk to people who saw him shot. They said he was shot from five yards away with his hands in the air.'[83] The situation was made more tense by the fact that everyone knew there were a lot of people arrested – so everyone was hoping that it was arrest and not death that accounted for the missing relative. The arrests, recalled Hume, were 'laughable'. They arrested Hume's next door neighbour, Otto. He was a chemist who was putting a tourniquet on Mrs Derry's leg in Chamberlain Street when troops raided the house and arrested everyone in it just as the ambulance arrived. Hume heard rumours that there were two more bodies – either secreted away or who fell in out of the way places. This was a persistent rumour but he had no idea if it were true.[84]

After Gerald Donaghy fell he was taken into the house of Raymond Rogan. He had been shot in the abdomen. He was wearing a blue denim shirt and trousers with pockets of the kind that opened to the front rather than to the side. The evidence was that some, at least, of his pockets were examined for evidence of his identity and that his body was examined by Dr Kevin Swords, who normally worked in a hospital in Lincoln. Dr Swords' opinion was that Donaghy was alive but should go to hospital immediately. Rogan volunteered to drive him there in his car. Leo Young went with him to help. The car was stopped at a military check-point in Barrack Street, where Rogan and Young were made to get out. The car was then driven by a soldier to the Regimental Aid Post of 1 Battalion Royal Anglian Regiment, where Donaghy was examined by the Medical Officer (Soldier 138) who pronounced him dead. The Medical Officer made a more detailed examination shortly afterwards but on neither occasion did he notice anything unusual in Donaghy's pockets.[85] It was Eugene McTaggart, a Detective Sergeant, based at Victoria Station on the Strand Road, who made the controversial discovery. He and Detective Constable Neilly were stationed at an Army checkpoint on the Derry side of the lower deck of the Craigavon Bridge. A detention centre had been set up next to the checkpoint to deal with people arrested during the day. DS McTaggart and DC Neilly were there to deal with any serious offences such as the possession of firearms. If offences were minor they would then be handed over to uniformed officers. Some time after 4 p.m. a military policeman came over to their portakabin and told the detectives that there were three cars outside in the car park with injured people in them. McTaggart and Neilly rushed out to find three Cortina cars, one of which was white with red flashes, one which was light blue and one which was silver. The military policeman said the cars had been stopped as they were en route to Altnagelvin Hospital. McTaggart did not see the cars arrive in the car park. They were already there when he came out of the portakabin with the RMP. The white Cortina had a man lying in the back seat. The Army MO had already examined him and pronounced him 'life extinct'. As McTaggart stooped inside the car to check over the body he noticed an object sticking out of the right hand trouser pocket of the body. It was a creamy coloured object. He quickly realised it was a nail bomb:

> I know it has been suggested that the nail bombs were planted on the body after the army took position of the white Cortina with red flashes. For me, this is very hard to believe as I do not know how soldiers in a strange place in Derry would have been able to get access to such nail bombs. I would have not known where to go for explosives, let alone an army private. I would say that if the nail bombs had been planted on the body by the army, it would have to have been with the complicity of someone higher up in the army ranks than a mere private, and that a senior army person would have had to have the assistance of his men to comply in such a dirty trick.
>
> When I first spotted the nail bomb, I was being watched closely by the civilians who were standing just outside the car. I have certainly never seen, still less been involved with, any planting of evidence. I would not have served in the police force if such things had been going on with my knowledge. I do not know how the nail bomb came to be in the pocket of the body, but I know that I saw it there.[86]

The events of that day left a lasting impression on DS McTaggart:

> The scene at the morgue was horrific. By the time I arrived, seven or eight bodies were already there, and I remember bodies being brought in while I was there... I remember the shock at realising that 10–12 people had died during the afternoon in the Bogside. The relatives were shouting and crying and it was a horrible time. I had dealt with many bad things in my time as an RUC officer, but this was the most shocking scene I had ever witnessed. It had such an effect on me subsequently I decided to resign from the RUC despite the fact that I loved the job. In the end, I transferred to an instructor's job and remained with the force that way.

McTaggart's colleague, Constable McCormac, was also at the morgue. He was in charge of identifying the bodies and dealing with their personal effects. He went to sympathize with one of the groups of relatives and was thumped in the face by a girl. 'I thought this was awful', recalled McTaggart, 'but Constable

McCormac said that he understood and said to me "What if it was your brother lying on that table?".' The memories McTaggart retained of his time in Derry were very unhappy ones. Later, Constable McCormac was shot dead as he walked in to church with his son. McTaggart 'was very pleased when I left Derry for good'.[87]

THE WIDGERY TRIBUNAL

The British Government appointed an inquiry to investigate what happened in Derry. The subsequent inquiry into the events of Bloody Sunday were denounced by the families of the deceased, and the wider Catholic community in the North, as a whitewash or cover-up. Was this true? On the evening of 31 January, the Lord Chief Justice of England, Lord Widgery, accepted the Government's invitation to conduct a Tribunal of Inquiry into the events of Bloody Sunday. Accompanied by the Lord Chancellor, he met with Edward Heath that evening. Heath made the point to Widgery that: 'It had to be remembered that we were in Northern Ireland fighting not only a military war but a propaganda war.'[88] There are two ways to interpret this statement: a clear example of political interference in the affairs of a supposedly independent judicial inquiry; or this can be interpreted as the Prime Minister merely pointing out the basic political facts governing the conditions Widgery was about to find himself in in Northern Ireland and the potential distortions employed by enemies of the State; however, given the anger that Heath felt after reading the Compton Report, what was probably at the heart of the matter may have been the blind spot of a simple faith in the reputation and professionalism of the British Army. Heath, like Widgery, was an ex-soldier himself; ultimately the Lord Chief Justice pronounced himself impressed with the evidence provided by the soldiers who opened fire on Bloody Sunday. An exception to this was the evidence of Soldier H who fired a total of twenty-two shots. Soldier H spoke of seeing a rifleman firing from a window of a flat on the south side of the Glenfada Park courtyard. Soldier H said that he fired an aimed shot at the man, who withdrew but returned a few moments later, whereupon Soldier H fired again. This process was repeated until Soldier H had fired nineteen shots, with a break for a change of magazine. Widgery concluded that: 'It is highly improbable that this cycle of events should repeat itself 19 times; and indeed it did not. I accepted evidence subsequently given, supported by photographs, which showed that no shot at all had been fired through the window in question. So 19 of the 22 shots fired by Soldier H were wholly unaccounted for.'[89]

Despite this extraordinary account, Widgery accepted that the soldiers 'were telling the truth as they remembered it'. He acknowledged there were infringements of the rules of the Yellow Card. Lieutenant N fired three rounds over the heads of a threatening crowd – which was not permitted – and dispersed it. Corporal P did likewise. Soldier T, on the authority of Sergeant O, fired at a person whom he believed to be throwing acid bombs and Soldier V said he fired on a petrol bomber. Although these actions were not authorized by the Yellow Card, Widgery concluded: 'They do not seem to point to a breakdown in discipline or to require censure. Indeed in three of the four cases it could be held that the person firing was, as the senior officer or NCO on the spot, the person entitled to give orders for such firing.' But Widgery acknowledged that the grounds put forward for identifying gunmen at windows were sometimes flimsy. Thus Soldier F fired three rounds at a window in Rossville Flats after having been told by another soldier that there was a gunman there. He did not seem to have verified the information except by his observation of 'a movement' at the window. Whether or not it was fired by Soldier H, a round went through the window of a house in Glenfada Park into an empty room. The only people in the house were an old couple who were sitting in another room. In all, seventeen rounds were fired at the windows of flats and houses, not counting Soldier H's nineteen rounds.

The identification of supposed nail bombers was equally nebulous – 'perhaps necessarily so. A nail bomb looks very much like half a brick and often the only means of distinguishing between a stone-thrower and a nail-bomber is that a light enough stone may be thrown with a flexed elbow whereas a nail bomb is usually thrown with a straight arm as in a bowling action.' But even assuming a legitimate target, the number of rounds fired was 'sometimes excessive. Soldier S's firing of twelve rounds into the alleyway between Blocks 1 and 2 of the Rossville Flats seems to me to have been unjustifiably dangerous for people round about.' Nevertheless, Widgery concluded that, in the majority of cases the soldier gave an explanation which, if true, justified his action:

> There is no question of the soldiers firing in panic to protect their own skins. They were far too steady for that. But where soldiers are required to engage gunmen who are in close proximity to innocent civilians they are set an impossible task. Either they must go all out for the gunmen, in which case the innocent suffer; or they must put the safety of the innocent first, in which case many gunmen will escape and the risk to themselves will be increased... In 1 Para the soldiers are trained to go for the gunmen and make their decisions quickly. In these circumstances it is not remarkable that mistakes were made and some innocent civilians hit.

In general the accounts given by the soldiers of the circumstances in which they fired and the reasons why they did so were, 'in my opinion, truthful'.[90] Not everyone agreed with Widgery's description of controlled target assessment. INQ 444, a Corporal in 7 Platoon of C Company, just after he had seen a bucket of liquid being thrown at a soldier, saw another soldier shooting from the hip:

> Almost as soon as this occurred, a soldier, who seemed to appear from nowhere as far as I can recall, began shooting... I do not know what the target he found was as he was shooting out of my line of sight, but I heard rapid firing and I had never seen that before... I remember that the soldier was standing up and he was holding his rifle under his arm at a position between

his soldier and his waist. I could not see the butt of his rifle. He was firing at an angle of 30 to 40 degrees... I personally thought that he was being stupid firing as he did. I think he fired more than 10 less than 20. Our brief was always to fire aimed shots with minimum force. We always carried out disciplined fire. It is my opinion that he was fazed out by the situation, was frightened and he had 'lost the plot'.[91]

The Army case was that each of these shots was an aimed shot fired at a civilian holding or using a bomb or firearm. On the other side it was argued that none of the deceased was using a bomb or firearm and that the soldiers fired without justification and either deliberately or recklessly.[92] Yet that does not necessarily mean that there were not civilians who may have used weapons. Danny Craig was 25 at the time of Bloody Sunday. He was with Michael Kelly when he was shot. He heard Michael cry: '"Danny, I'm shot." I'll never forget him falling back saying my name.' Craig looked at him and he seemed to have nothing but a pinhole in his gut. Michael's face had changed colour and his eyes had rolled up. 'He was dying right in front of me... I had never seen a man die before.' Terrified, Craig ran away. When he was at a fence in Glenfada Park North, Craig saw a 'kid of about 10'. He was carrying a tray made of a biscuit tin with what looked like petrol or nail bombs, although he was not certain as he had never seen a nail bomb and so did not actually know what one looked like: 'They looked like fireworks.' The boy was crying 'his eyes out and said to me "Mister, what do I do with these?"' Craig saw the Paras coming across Glenfada Park and knew if they were caught with the bombs 'we would have been shot dead. I was crying at this stage' and kicked the tray out of the boy's hands shouting 'Get your arse out of here!' That particular tray 'never got used that day'.[93]

Alongside the evidence that there were petrol and nail bombs in the vicinity is the possibility that, in a confined and alien environment, some soldiers were making lethal errors. Soldier N reflected, over the years, as to whether a man he shot on Bloody Sunday really was the threat to his life he once thought:

I only saw him for a split second, but my immediate reaction was that he had a nail bomb and was about to lob it... From a standing position, I brought my rifle to my shoulder and fired an aimed shot at the man's chest. That was the target we were trained to aim at. The shot was fired before the man completed the bowling action... I recall that he clutched his right thigh with his left hand ... the incident has bothered me for years... learning that the forensic evidence was flawed. However... at the time I fired I believed that the youth was about to throw (in a bowling action) a nail bomb... there must have been something in the demeanour of the youth which made me think he was about to throw a nail bomb and made me react in the way I did. Sometimes people react without thinking. It is like driving on a motorway and suddenly you put your foot on the brakes. You might not immediately appreciate why you reacted, then you realise you did so in reaction to the brake lights in the car in front. I reacted when I saw the man about to throw something. Unpicking the incident over the years, I expressed my self doubt... that I was not sure he had a nail bomb... Whatever doubts I have had over the years about shooting that man... I am now and always have been convinced that at the moment I fired I thought he was in the act of throwing a nail bomb.[94]

Some thirty years later, at the Saville Inquiry, Soldier S admitted to errors in his 1972 statement: the RMP, he suggested, might have taken elements from other soldiers' accounts and woven them into his account which he then accepted: 'These people are quite intimidating to an 18 year old soldier who has just been trained and joined the battalion.' As a 'mature man' he could now reflect on the inaccuracies and regret them.[95] Nevertheless, on the crucial incident of having fired at an identifiable gunman Soldier S reflected:

> I regret the whole incident... even the man I identified as a gunman, who was obviously posing a threat to us... if I did hit him and kill him, it is still a tragedy, is it not; it is still – somebody grieved for him. Although I had a duty to do that, it is still a tragedy to his family; is it not?... I am trying to say I am not without compassion on this issue; I am a Christian person... I have Christian beliefs, I live by a Christian standard myself. This is a tragedy, it is a tragedy for everybody, I realise that and I am sorry that innocent people got killed on that day, I am very, very sorry for that, but for my action on the day, my particular action, I believe I was justified in what I did.[96]

Soldier S's references to the role he claims was played by the RMP in compiling statements suggest not necessarily a cover up but, rather, a structural flaw in the role the Special Investigation Branch of the RMP was expected to play in the compiling of evidence following the shooting of civilians by the Army. INQ 3, as the senior SIB officer (his role was later expanded to the title of Deputy Assistant Provost Marshal [Legal Affairs]) covering investigations of complaints and litigation directed against the Army – involving close cooperation with the Chief Crown Solicitors and the Director of Public Prosecutions – recalled how, in 1970, a decision was reached between the GOC and the Chief Constable whereby the RMP would tend to military witnesses and the RUC to civilian witnesses in the investigation of offences and incidents. With 'both RMP and RUC sympathetic towards the soldier, who after all was doing an incredibly difficult job, he was highly unlikely to make a statement incriminating himself, for the RMP investigator was out for information for managerial, not criminal, purposes, and using their powers of discretion, it was unlikely that the RUC would prefer charges against soldiers except in the most extreme of circumstances.' Only in March 1972, following the imposition of Direct Rule, was a Director of Public Prosecutions appointed for Northern Ireland and he soon made it clear that the existing standards were far from satisfactory. In November 1972 he revoked the RUC's discretionary powers in these matters, ordering all allegations made against the Security Forces to be passed to him for examination: 'The honeymoon period was over.' The pressure from the DPP's office aroused 'considerable alarm' among soldiers, recalled INQ 3. 'Who the hell were SIB working for anyway? Whose side were they on?' DPP investigators in Belfast 'who hitherto had been regarded as the soldiers' friends, suddenly began to encounter all sorts of difficulties with the units on the ground.'

Another factor may have been that the Army was inclined to believe the accounts provided by the soldiers involved in such incidents set against what were perceived as Republican propaganda. There was a proven track record of this. For example, in October 1971 a company of the 2 Battalion The Light Infantry, stationed in Newry, received a tip-off that there would be a raid on one of the banks in Hill Street on a certain night. The Company Commander made a discreet reconne and decided that there were no means of concealing his men at street level and that the only possible position would be on top of the flat-roofed Woolworths building where he placed four men. Two men at a time stood watch while the other two rested. Just before midnight one of the sentries saw a suspicious movement outside the bank and called his companion. In fact three men were attacking two others attempting to put money into the night safe. The soldiers challenged 'Halt or I will fire' and the three assailants ran away in the direction of Marcus Street. The soldiers challenged again, by which time the other two soldiers were on their feet. The fleeing civilians did not stop, so all four soldiers opened fire and the three men were killed. Fortunately for the Army it was later discovered that the tip-off had come from a double agent and that the IRA had their own ambush parties in the street to gun down the soldiers had they attempted to intervene; but, instead, the IRA had been completely taken by surprise by the military ambush and had discreetly withdrawn from the scene. At the inquest local witnesses claimed that the soldiers had fired without warning and that the attack on the men at the night safe was a harmless bit of play by the deceased. However, two Protestants passing through in a car had stopped, thinking the shouting was at them.[97]

Perhaps the most controversial aspect of Widgery's findings was that some of the deceased had fired, or been in close proximity to someone who had fired, weapons that day. It remains the firm belief of most Catholics, and indeed many outside observers, that those killed on Bloody Sunday were innocent victims. Crucial to Widgery's conclusions was the forensic evidence. In the case of each of the deceased a hand swab was taken. A piece of clean cotton damped with 1 per cent hydrochloric acid was wrapped around a pea-sized piece of cotton wool. Swabs were taken from the back, the web and the palm of the hand. In the laboratory the swab was sprayed with sodium rhodizinate which brought up lead as purple spots each about 1/150th the size of a pinhead. Dr Martin, a Principal Scientific Officer of the Department of Industrial & Forensic Science of Northern Ireland, gave evidence at Widgery that a positive result indicated that the person had: been firing a weapon; or handling one which had recently been fired; or been in close proximity to someone firing a weapon. The phrase that Dr Martin accepted was that a positive result created 'a strong suspicion' of involvement with or proximity to firearms. He explained his reasoning thus:

> When a firearm is discharged, the discharged gases that are produced force the bullet up the barrel and out, these gases issue from the breech of the weapon,

particularly in semi-automatic weapons and in revolvers, around the cylinder. They also issue from the muzzle of the gun behind the bullet. These gases contain minute particles of lead among other metals. The lead derives from the composition of the bullet itself and also from the primer composition in the cartridge case.

But he indicated that it was possible that a fragmenting bullet could cause a spray of fine particles of lead to be thrown into the air which could give results similar to those firing from a gun, though Martin also said: 'If lead contamination originates from a fragmenting bullet I would expect a gradation in size of the particle. I would not expect them to be minute or all to be large.' Martin did not find any gradation in size with any of the cases – except with McElhinney. Any gradation that there was was 'all within the range that one normally expects from the fire from discharge gases rather than from a fragmenting bullet'.

In addition, the outer garments of all the deceased were tested for lead. The clothing was pressed with filter paper damped with hydrochloric acid and the result on the filter paper was viewed. In the case of a number of the deceased Dr Martin found positive results and reached the conclusion that in the cases of at least six of the deceased: 'The nature and distribution of lead particles on the (relevant location) is similar to that produced by exposure to discharge gases from firearms. These gases, containing minute particles of lead, issue from openings of the breach and also from the muzzle.' In cross-examination Dr Martin explained that the tests were designed to cover the situation where a person fired a gun. Tests had ascertained that the SLR could on occasion throw lead up to thirty feet away from the muzzle; that it consistently did so up to twelve feet; and that between twelve and thirty feet the lead particles were subject to drift and air currents. Outside the thirty foot range the likelihood of contamination from muzzle blast was negligible; within the twelve foot range the amounts deposited were very high and could not be confused with anything else; between twelve and thirty foot the sort of level that he saw might be produced by muzzle discharge: but that was very unlikely. In cases where the amount of lead particles on the hands was above a single spot the amount would indicate that the hands were closer to the source of the lead than the clothing. In the case of Kelly and McDaid, the one spot was large, that is, on the high side of the range for discharge gases. It could have come from a fragmenting bullet, although the probability was not very high: Dr Martin described it as hardly more than a possibility.

Martin, however, accepted that if bodies were handled by soldiers who had, themselves, been firing SLRs one would expect to find traces transferred to the people they handled; and if bodies were dumped by paratroopers, one on top of another on the floor of a Saracen (as were many of them), there could be transfer from the paratroopers to the bodies and from one body to the other. In general, traces of lead found in people such as plumbers and painters were so great that there was no chance of confusion between such particles and the particles associated with the discharge from firearms; but whether this was so would depend on the period which had elapsed since the person in question was last exposed to lead and the degree of washing and the substance used to wash the relevant parts of the body since then. Martin virtually ruled out lead particles from bullet holes in clothing as a possible source of contamination but accepted the possibility of contamination of the deceased arising from those who had handled or touched the clothing of people who had, themselves, been struck by fragmenting bullets, if the velocity of the fragmenting bullet was low enough that the particles did not penetrate the clothing cleanly. Professor Simpson, who was, at the time, the Pathologist to the Home Office and, inter alia, the Professor of Forensic Medicine at the University of London and the current editor of *Taylor on Principles of Forensic Medicine*, described the standard of medical and scientific work carried out by Martin's department as very high. In his view:

> I think that the significant feature is that these are not widely scattered residues. Where a residue is more closely collected or involves solely the back of the thumb or the web or the finger it is an almost classical pattern of a hand that has been holding a firearm recently discharged. Where it is in the palm of the hand it is so much more... likely to be a consequence of handling such a weapon or handling ammunition.[98]

In the absence of other evidence Lord Widgery placed great reliance on the forensic evidence. He acknowledged that while a number of soldiers spoke of actually seeing firearms or bombs in the hands of civilians none was recovered by the Army. None of the many photographs showed a civilian holding an object that could with certainty be identified as a firearm or bomb. No casualties were suffered by the soldiers from firearms or gelignite bombs. In relation to every one of the deceased there were eye witnesses who said that they saw no bomb or firearm in his hands. The clothing of eleven of the deceased when examined for explosive residues showed no trace of gelignite. The two others were Gerald McKinney, whose clothing had been washed at the hospital and could not be tested, and Donaghy, in the pockets of whose clothing nail bombs were found. But Widgery relied heavily on the only other relevant forensic test applied to the deceased, carried out by Dr Martin, which he erroneously referred to as a 'paraffin test'.[99] As a consequence Widgery concluded that the lead particle density on Michael Kelly's right cuff was above normal and was consistent with his having been close to someone using a firearm. This lent further support to the view that someone was firing at the soldiers from the barricade, 'but I do not think that this was Kelly nor am I satisfied that he was throwing a bomb at the time when he was shot.'[100] The tests on the hand swabs and clothing of Gerald McKinney and William McKinney were negative. Dr Martin did not regard the result of the tests on Donaghy as positive but Professor Simpson did. The two experts agreed that the results of the tests on Wray were consistent with his having used a firearm.[101] Widgery concluded that, on Nash, the particles of lead detected on the web, back and palm of his left hand had a distribution consistent with his having used a firearm.[102] For McDaid the test disclosed abnormal lead particle density on his jacket and one large particle of lead on the back of the right hand. Any of the soldiers considered in connection with the death of Young might equally well have shot McDaid. Dr Martin thought that the lead density was consistent with McDaid having handled a firearm, 'but I think it more consistent with his having been in close proximity to someone firing'.[103] Martin observed, in cross-examination, that if McDaid was lying in an area near where guns were discharged, or being discharged, or where there were ricocheting bullets, it would be expected that the lead particle density on his jacket would be higher than normal. The level of contamination on Young's left hand was too high to be consistent with exposure (for example, from guns being discharged or bullets fragmenting) which covered the clothing as well. If his left hand had been caught by one or more paratroopers whose hands were contaminated that could possibly explain the contamination on his left hand.[104] The test disclosed lead particles on the web, back and palm of the left hand which were consistent with exposure to discharge gases from firearms. The body of Young, together with those of McDaid and Nash, was recovered from the barricade by soldiers of 1 PARA and taken to hospital in an APC. It was contended in evidence that the lead particles on Young's left hand might have been transferred from the hands of the soldiers who carried him or from the interior of the APC itself. Although these possibilities could not be wholly excluded, Widgery concluded that 'the distribution of the particles seems to me to be more consistent with Young having discharged a firearm.'[105]

Although eye witnesses all denied that McGuigan had a weapon, the 'paraffin test' disclosed lead deposits on the right palm and the web, back and palm of his left hand. The deposit on the right hand was in the form of a smear while those on the left hand were similar to the deposits produced by a firearm. The earlier photographs of McGuigan's body show his head uncovered but in a later one it is covered with a scarf. The scarf showed a heavy deposit of lead, the distribution and density of which was consistent with the scarf having been used to wrap a revolver which had been fired several times. His widow was called to say that the scarf did not belong to him. Widgery commented: 'I accept her evidence in concluding it is not possible to say that McGuigan was using or carrying a weapon at the time when he was shot. The paraffin test, however, constitutes ground for suspicion that he had been in close proximity to someone who had fired.'[106] Gilmore's reaction to the test was negative: 'There is no evidence that he used a weapon.'[107] Doherty's reaction to the test was also negative. In the light of all the evidence, 'I conclude that he was not carrying a weapon. If Soldier F shot Doherty in the belief that he had a pistol that belief was mistaken.'[108] As for the controversial question of the nail-bombs found in Donaghy's pockets, the Lord Chief Justice concluded:

> I think that on a balance of probabilities the bombs were in Donaghy's pockets throughout. His jacket and trousers were not removed but were merely opened as he lay on his back in the car. It seems likely that these relatively bulky objects would have been noticed when Donaghy's body was examined; but it is conceivable that they were not and the alternative explanation of a plant is mere speculation. No evidence was offered as to where the bombs might have

come from, who might have placed them or why Donaghy should have been singled out for this treatment.[109]

On the forensic evidence offered to Widgery it might be possible to conclude that some of the deceased had fired weapons or been close to someone who had fired a weapon. From this it was a small leap – given the personal history and sociological influences shaping the Lord Chief Justice's world view – to accept the evidence of the soldiers as, on the whole, truthful and their actions justified in opening fire since there would appear to have been considerable fire directed at them. Hence the high number of casualties.

However, the forensic evidence has since attracted considerable criticism. Professor Dash, in a commentary on Widgery's report, raised the possibility that pistols could have been fired from the dead hands of some of the deceased, that is, that the particles were effectively 'planted' on them. But just as importantly Dash stated: 'The paraffin test, which Lord Widgery confused with the test Dr Martin used has been discredited. Today, reliable crime laboratories do not test for lead, alone, to determine whether a weapon has been fired.' This was because of the inherent dangers of contamination, which prevented the forensic scientist from distinguishing between lead residue from a firearm and lead residue from a myriad of other sources. Instead, forensic scientists test for barium, antimony and lead. This can be done by wet chemical testing to produce characteristic colours of these elements or by detecting accurate quantitative amounts of these elements through techniques such as atomic absorption spectrometry or neutron activation analysis. There were other areas that Dash was concerned with: Martin claimed to have obtained a purple colour, identified by him as indicating lead, by exposing the swabs to sodium rhodizinate, when the paper he relied on for reaching his conclusions, written by George Price, and all of the other literature dealing with this form of lead testing, indicated that the colour produced by sodium rhodizinate and lead is pink or reddish. A blue colour is obtained when 5 per cent hydrochloric acid is added. Dash argued that Martin's finding of a purple colour is not explained when every authority speaks of blue. Further, Martin claimed he was able to see a concentration of tiny purple dots under the microscope about 1/50th of the size of a pin head. Neither in Price's paper nor in any of the other literature were there any references to the detection of lead particles under magnification. Rather the literature indicated the test should show a blue smear if lead is present. Dash believed this significant as Price referred to the test as only a screening test while Martin claims to have used it for a specific identification of lead particles. Dash quoted Dr S.S. Krishman's note on Martin's examination which stated that it was sound in principle but referred to the fact that a great number of possibilities of contamination existed. For this reason the results 'would be of limited use only in this situation'.[110]

More than thirty years after Widgery, expert analysis, for the Saville Inquiry, by J.B.F. Lloyd, pointed out that, apart from firearms-associated materials, there were many sources of lead: plumbing, cable sheathing, car batteries and their terminals, paintwork, solder, bearing metals, type metals, glazing, roofing, lead foil (over bottle caps and corks, at the time), fishing tackles and so on. He concluded that, on any interpretation of who was shooting on Bloody Sunday and of the effectiveness of laboratory procedures it would be unrealistic to suppose that at least some of the swabs and clothing connected from the deceased could not to some degree have become contaminated with lead particles originating from other sources: 'That it could be ever accepted that the presence on the hands of a single microscopic particle – virtually dust-sized – of a common substance such as lead was significant evidence of firearms residue, and accepted as a positive finding if more than three particles were present was "extraordinary".'[111] Whether or not any of the deceased may have discharged a firearm was not determinable either on the results that previously have been cited as evidence of the event or on any other results recorded on the laboratory notes or samples. 'In my view, as evidence of the event, the results are worthless.'[112] Lloyd also pointed out that traces of explosives were detected in the right lower pocket of Donaghy's jacket. The traces were of the type that would have been left by the explosive in the nail bomb recovered from the pocket. A bullet had passed through the jacket's left lower pocket, from which the nail bomb was recovered. The bomb could have been at least damaged if not exploded by the bullet if the bomb was present in the pocket at the time. On the evidence available the bomb was undamaged: 'There is no evidence on which it may be supposed that any other of the deceased was associated with explosives substances.'[113]

POSTSCRIPT

Sean Collins was aged 10 on Bloody Sunday. As a 10-year-old boy he took a lot of interest in the different regiments in Derry:

> So I remember it clearly when the soldiers came: our parents told us they were there to protect us and they were our friends. The first ones I ever saw were standing around in the street, and women were going up to them and talking to them and giving them sups of tea. To us wains they soon became sort of like hero figures: they gave us sweets, asked us our names, talked to us about the different places in the world they'd been. The biggest thrill of all would be if one specially liked you and would let you touch his rifle, and hold it while you have a look along its sights. To me the soldiers were fascinating, I thought they were wonderful. None of us feared them at all in any way: grown ups as well, we were all pleased and glad they were there.

What Collins clearly remembered from Bloody Sunday was the feeling of surprise. It was a surprise that these men – the soldiers 'who I'd liked so much and admired' – suddenly weren't good people or heroes like he thought: 'They were cruel and heartless causing death and panic, putting terror into the hearts of the ordinary people of the community I lived in. It's difficult to judge the effect of it afterwards, but I'd say for me it was like the smashing of a dream:

sort of the end to my innocence somehow, the innocence of a child who till then had thought there was something noble and romantic about soldiers.' Collins never looked at the world of adults in the same way again and got more and more sceptical and cynical about the powers that be:[114] 'Bloody Sunday changed a lot of things for me. Up to that day I believed that the British Army were the good guys. All my innocence in that regard was lost. I had no illusions about what the Brits were like and I had no sympathy when I heard subsequently about British soldiers being shot.'[115] This was Bloody Sunday's lasting legacy. It was the Provisional IRA's greatest recruiting sergeant. And, for Catholics, its aftermath seemed to add insult to injury.

Notes

1. Widgery, paras. 24–5.
2. BSI AD167, Statement of John Dunleavey.
3. Widgery, para. 25.
4. BSI CO1 A Summary of Events in Londonderry on Sunday 30 January 1972.
5. Widgery, para. 31.
6. BSI CO1 A Summary of Events in Londonderry on Sunday 30 January 1972.
7. Widgery, para. 34.
8. Ibid., paras. 26–7.
9. Ibid., paras. 28–30.
10. BSI Report No.1 from Counsel to the Tribunal by Charles Clarke QC, 4 December 1998.
11. Widgery, para. 34.
12. Ibid., para. 35.
13. BSI CO1 A Summary of Events in Londonderry on Sunday 30 January 1972.
14. Widgery, paras. 35–8.
15. BSI Report No.1 from Counsel to the Tribunal by Charles Clarke QC, 4 December 1998.
16. BSI AT6, First Statement of Reg Tester.
17. BSI AOIRA2, First Statement of OIRA2.
18. BSI AT6, Second Statement of Reg Tester.
19. BSI Report No.1 from Counsel to the Tribunal by Charles Clarke QC, 4 December 1998.
20. BSI Report No.3 from Counsel to the Tribunal para. A1.18.
21. BSI Report No.1 from Counsel to the Tribunal by Charles Clarke QC, 4 December 1998.
22. BSI 575, Statement of Sergeant O.
23. Widgery, paras. 41–3.
24. BSI CO1 A Summary of Events in Londonderry on Sunday 30 January 1972.
25. Ibid.
26. BSI B1617, Statement of Soldier 033.
27. BSI B944, Statement by Lieutenant Colonel D. Wilford Concerning the Events in Londonderry January 30th 1972.
28. Widgery, paras. 44–5.
29. BSI Report No.1 from Counsel to the Tribunal by Charles Clarke QC, 4 December 1998.
30. BSI 575, Statement of Sergeant O.
31. BSI B1617, Statement of Soldier 033.
32. Widgery, Para. 51.
33. Widgery, B1617, Statement of Soldier 033.

34. BSI B657, Statement of Sergeant O.
35. Widgery, Para. 52.
36. Widgery, JF1, Statement of Albert Neil Falkingham.
37. Widgery, W9, Statement of Robert Milton Whyte.
38. Widgery, JK 7, RUC Statement of Constable Raymond Kirk, 7 February 1972.
39. Widgery, JL2, Statement of CJ Laird.
40. BSI JM 43, Statement of Detective Chief Superintendent McVicker.
41. Widgery, para. 53.
42. BSI C3, Statement of INQ 3.
43. BSI CO1 A Summary of Events in Londonderry on Sunday 30 January 1972.
44. BSI, Statement of Mary Holland.
45. BSI AD89, *The Sunday Times* Archive.
46. BSI AM5, Statement of Dr McDermott.
47. Widgery, Paras. 46–7.
48. Ibid., Para 69.
49. BSI H5, Statement of Bishop Edward Daly.
50. BSI H5, Draft of Daly Statement for Widgery.
51. BSI H5, Statement of Bishop Edward Daly.
52. BSI AOIRA4, Second Statement of OIRA 4.
53. BSI AOIRA4, First Statement of OIRA 4.
54. BSI AOIRA4, Second Statement of OIRA 4.
55. BSI AT6 Second Statement of Reg Tester.
56. BSI KM3, Draft Statement of Martin McGuinness.
57. BSI Report No.1 from Counsel to the Tribunal by Charles Clarke QC, 4 December 1998.
58. Widgery, Paras. 55–7.
59. Ibid., Para. 58.
60. Ibid., Para. 80.
61. BSI Report No.1 from Counsel to the Tribunal by Charles Clarke QC, 4 December 1998 para. 15.16.
62. Widgery, Para. 82.
63. Ibid., Para. 77.
64. Ibid., Para. 71.
65. Ibid., Paras. 78–9.
66. BSI Report No.1 from Counsel to the Tribunal by Charles Clarke QC, 4 December 1998 paras. 15.8–15.9.
67. BSI AJ 11, Statement of Helen Johnston.
68. BSI AJ 11, Statement of Helen and Margaret Johnston.
69. Widgery, Paras. 83–4.
70. BSI Dr R.T. Shepherd and Kevin O'Callaghan Report on the Pathology and Ballistic Evidence Following the Bloody Sunday Shootings para. 7.1.3.
71. BSI Report No.1 from Counsel to the Tribunal by Charles Clarke QC, 4 December 1998 para. 16.4.
72. Ibid., para. 16.1.
73. BSI Report No.1 from Counsel to the Tribunal by Charles Clarke QC, 4 December 1998 para.18.1.
74. Ibid., para.18.3.
75. Ibid., para.18.1.
76. Widgery, Para. 70.
77. BSI Report No.1 from Counsel to the Tribunal by Charles Clarke QC, 4 December 1998 para.19.4.
78. Widgery, Para. 73.
79. BSI Report No.1 from Counsel to the Tribunal by Charles Clarke QC, 4 December 1998 para.19.5.
80. BSI Newspaper reports.

81. BSI KH8, Statement of John Hume.
82. Ibid.
83. BSI M41, *Guardian*, 1 February 1972.
84. BSI KH8, Statement of John Hume.
85. Widgery, Para. 87.
86. BSI JM41, Statement of Eugene McTaggart.
87. Ibid.
88. BSI KH9, Minute 1 February 1972.
89. Widgery, Para. 85.
90. Ibid., Paras. 97–104.
91. BSI C444.
92. Widgery, Para. 62.
93. BSI AC111, Statement of Danny Craig.
94. BSI 438, Statement of Soldier N.
95. BSI Saville, 15 May 2003, p.13.
96. BSI Saville, 15 May 2000, p.12.
97. BSI C3 RMP and the Legal Consequences of the Army's Involvement in Northern Ireland. Lecture by DAPM (Legal Affairs) for IM (Army's) Study Period, 8th November 1973.
98. BSI Report No.1 from Counsel to the Tribunal by Charles Clarke QC, 4 December 1998, Appendix C Counsel's Note on the Expert Evidence Given to Lord Widgery paras. 7.1–8.
99. Widgery, Paras. 65–6.
100. Ibid., Para. 81.
101. Ibid., Para. 85.
102. Widgery, Para. 78.
103. Ibid., Para. 77.
104. BSI Report No.1 from Counsel to the Tribunal by Charles Clarke QC 4 December 1998 Appendix C Counsel's Note on the Expert Evidence Given to Lord Widgery para. 6.
105. Widgery, Para. 76.
106. Ibid., Para. 74.
107. Ibid., Para. 71.
108. Ibid., Para. 70.
109. Ibid., Para. 88.
110. BSI Report No.1 from Counsel to the Tribunal by Charles Clarke QC, 4 December 1998 Appendix C Counsel's Note on the Expert Evidence Given to Lord Widgery paras. 7.1–8.
111. BSI J.B.F. Lloyd Bloody Sunday Inquiry Initial Report: Firearms & Explosives Residues 22 June 1999, paras. 6.2–6.3.
112. Widgery, Para. 9.
113. Ibid., Para. 11.
114. BSI AC74, Sean Collins Interview.
115. BSI AC74, Statement of Sean Collins.

10

Judgement Day – The End of Stormont

On 4 December 1971 the Ulster Volunteer Force exploded a bomb in McGurk's Bar, a Catholic-owned pub in Belfast city centre. The owner, Patrick McGurk, lived above the bar with his family:

> I saw a flash, and a very short time after that, the bar went up in the air. It just collapsed around me and I was buried underneath amidst the rubble and glassware. I just said, 'What have I done to suffer this?' I was stranded there. Then I heard some people talking in the snug behind me and a person answered them saying, 'You're all right, we'll get you out.' A short time after – and I don't know how long I was actually underneath there – this person who was trying to help people out spoke again. And so I shouted up and said, 'I'm down here.' And he said, 'We'll get you out all right.' Then somebody eventually pulled me out. I don't know who he was.[1]

Survivors recalled how, at the time of the explosion, Mr McGurk, who had facial injuries, thought his wife was not on the premises. He told rescuers: 'Thank God she wasn't here.' But Mrs McGurk had returned home and was killed in the blast.[2] It was only when he was lying in the Royal Victoria that he learnt that both his wife, Philomena, and his 14-year-old daughter, Marie, had been killed in the blast. He knew they had gone over to church but was unaware that they had returned. Marie had been due to go to an away hockey match but it had been cancelled because of the rain. Nearly thirty years later, Patrick McGurk reflected: 'It's one of those things that just hits you like a ton of bricks. It was a very difficult thing to get over. You just have to get resigned to it. It's your opportunity for praying more than you prayed before.' Was he still bitter after all this time? 'It does come into your mind periodically... But of course then you have to control it because it's no use keeping it in your mind because you'll only start getting vindictive then and that'll not serve any useful purpose.'[3] His 10-year-old son, John, was also pulled from the rubble. He had been sitting playing a board game with his older brother and two school friends, sometime between 8–8.30 p.m.:

> It really wasn't a case of the lights going off, it was like something out of a really bad horror film. I remember tumbling in air and space amid this massive rush of wind and noise. It must have been a matter of seconds. I couldn't remember anything else because I must have been unconscious for a while but I don't know how long it was... I woke up... and... my first

instinct was of complete and utter survival wondering how I would get out of this. The worst thing about it was that I'm nearly sure that I heard my sister crying for help, because there wouldn't have been any other young female stuck there. It's possible that it was my imagination. It's possible that she was already dead, but that's what I remember.

Years later the man who saved him – John Patrick O'Hanlon – was picked up by a Loyalist gang and killed. In total, fifteen people – all Catholic – were killed that day; along with Philomena and Maria McGurk, the dead were: Edward and Sarah Keenan (aged 69 and 58 respectively), a married couple; James Cromie (13); John Colton (55), Patrick McGurk's brother-in-law, Thomas McLoughlin (55); David Milligan (52); James Smyth (55); Francis Bradley (61); Thomas Kane (45); Philip Garry (73); Kathleen Irvine (45); Edward Laurence Kane (25) and Robert Charles Spotswood (38).[4] It was the shape of things to come.

SHOCKWAVES

Bloody Sunday was the event that ensured that the Provisional IRA would have the manpower to replenish those lost to the attrition of internment. It sent shockwaves throughout nationalist Ireland in a manner that internment could not. Here, for nationalists, was the massacre of the innocents. At this moment, more than any other, the concept of the Irish nation in terms of a union of the Catholics of the South with the Catholics of the North had a manifestation of reality not seen since partition. Subterranean forces were unleashed. They were, in fact, momentary; but they revealed the forces that nationalism – in the generic sense – can unleash. The sense of outrage directed at Britain affected all sections of Catholic Ireland. On the evening of 30 January, Jack Lynch contacted John Hume to ascertain the facts. His response was: 'I am appalled and stunned that British soldiers should shoot indiscriminately into a crowd of civilians who were peacefully demonstrating...this act by British troops was unbelievably and savagely inhuman.'[5] The next day Lynch announced that his Government was 'satisfied that British troops fired on unarmed civilians in Derry yesterday and that any denial of this continues and increases the provocation offered by present British policies both to the minority in Northern Ireland and us here'. He recalled Dublin's Ambassador in London to demonstrate their concern at those policies and called for the immediate withdrawal of British troops from Derry and Catholic ghettos elsewhere and the 'cessation of the harassment of the minority population in the North'.[6] With anti-British feeling running at a fever pitch amongst many people in the Republic a national day of mourning was declared. It was unprecedented in the State's history. Businesses and factories closed; transport services were stopped; and communication with Britain by telephone or telegraph was difficult if not impossible. This was the background for an event that shocked the Irish political establishment as they realized just what the Troubles could, conceivably, unleash in the Republic: the burning of the British Embassy in Dublin. The attack on the Embassy started after a massive parade of trade Unionists, Republicans, students and schoolchildren passed through the centre of the city. The crowd carried thirteen coffins and hundreds of placards proclaimed opposition to British rule in the North. 'British out, North and South', the crowd chanted. 'Take these murderers in uniform home' was typical of the placards. It took an hour for the parade to cross O'Connell Bridge in an afternoon of driving rain and bitter winds. When the parade reached the Embassy at Merrion Square the coffins were handed over the heads of the demonstrators to the entrance of the building already blackened and smashed by a gelignite bomb that had been thrown at it the night before. After about an hour – following the burning of a Union Jack and an effigy of a pig – stone-throwing started and was encouraged by the crowd; then the petrol bombing began. Each flash was acknowledged by the crowd who shouted: 'More, more, more.' The Gardai stood impassively about thirty yards from the entrance and watched[7] as the Embassy began to burn.

As London protested at this extraordinary act – the destruction of their Embassy in a friendly country – there were fears in Britain and Ireland that Derry would be repeated a week later as Catholics in the North prepared for another anti-internment march, this time in Newry. The Army were expecting many thousands to march into Newry 'and an attempt by the IRA to exploit the situation is anticipated'. It was becoming clear that, in the aftermath of Bloody Sunday, neither side was going to back down. The Army had intelligence that the IRA was going to intervene as, they believed, had happened in Derry. Everyone held their breath. The Security Forces mounted Vehicle Check Points on the roads into Newry with an inner ring of barriers surrounding the central area towards which marches from several directions apparently wanted to converge. By 8 a.m. on Sunday the military deployments were completed, comprising seventeen Vehicle Check Points around the perimeter of the town preventing access to the town centre. At 1.15 p.m. these barriers were closed and the RUC were asked to take charge. A crowd gradually formed on the Derrybeg estate, reaching about 6,000 by 3 p.m.. It then set off in groups towards the town centre but swung around when within 300 metres of the nearest barriers and headed back in much the same direction as its original starting point, heading for the Meadow estate. There it grew into a crowd estimated at between 10 and 12,000 which congregated in an open space and embarked on a meeting at 5.20 p.m. An hour later it began to disperse and there was no trouble as pedestrians and vehicles returned to their homes. To the relief of everyone there were no incidents, although it was striking at the extent to which the Security Forces and the authorities were prepared to go. The MOD reflected that: 'It is not of course known for certain why the IRA decided not to intervene in Newry... but it seems likely that both the advance publicity about their possible intentions, and the intensive searches of vehicles approaching the town during the previous 48 hours helped to deter them.' To the inevitable claims that the demonstrators 'out-witted' the Army by defying the ban on marches it could be said in reply that the meeting itself was not illegal while the demonstrators were obviously prevented from protesting wherever they wished and the Security Forces at all times had the situation in hand.[8] The measures taken at Newry became the template for future anti-internment marches such as that in Enniskillen on 13 February.[9]

Attention now focused on whether or not there would be any political moves in London as a response to Derry. In fact, as we have seen, long before Bloody Sunday the British had been considering whether or nor to bring forth a new political initiative. What Bloody Sunday did was bring this forward – it ended any more erring on the side of caution. On 3 February the Cabinet in London considered its options. Before any decisions could be taken on specifics Heath and the principals concerned with Ulster would have to carry their Cabinet colleagues with them – and the principals still hadn't decided what they were going to do in any case. In the ensuing discussion there was general agreement on the importance of maintaining a broad base of support in Great Britain for the Government's policy. A growing section of public opinion wished to see British troops withdrawn from Northern Ireland: but the key point emphasized in the Cabinet was that it was sometimes forgotten by the public that the Army was the Army of the United Kingdom and was not operating in a foreign or colonial territory. Moreover, to threaten withdrawal might create an expectation that the Government's resolution was weakening, while to carry out withdrawal could only result in extensive bloodshed in Northern Ireland, in which the Catholic element of the population might well be the main sufferers. Before the Army garrison could be reduced to a significantly lower level an acceptable state of law and order would have to be restored and a satisfactory political settlement would need to be achieved. Nevertheless, in order to retain a broad measure of public support for the maintenance of large military forces in Northern Ireland, the Cabinet thought it desirable that movement towards some political solution of the conflict should be seen to be in prospect. It was also probable that there would be increasing international pressure in favour of a political initiative. But, although any political initiative, in order to have any prospect of success, would have to command a broad measure of support from all political parties at Westminster, it had also to be acceptable to substantial numbers of both Protestants and Catholics in Ireland. Otherwise the bulk of the Protestant population would be antagonized and possibly provoked to violent reaction, while the Catholics would remain no less alienated than at present. The acceptance by Catholics of any political settlement, however, depended in large measure on its endorsement by the Irish Government. The long-term solution might therefore have to involve some kind of constitutional association between the two parts of Ireland, while permitting the Six Counties of Northern Ireland to continue to form part of the United Kingdom. Similarly, the Government of the Republic would not be able to mobilize public support against the IRA unless they could convincingly endorse whatever solution was found in Northern Ireland. The uncertainty of Lynch's political position might be relevant to this point but the importance of action by the Irish Government against the IRA was underlined by the military impossibility of completely sealing the Border.

So, in order to promote a political settlement it might be necessary to take major political risks, which might involve a substantial modification of earlier policies and even the possibility of considerable bloodshed. Nevertheless, it might be possible to reach an acceptable solution on the basis of ensuring the minority community an active, permanent and guaranteed role in Government while simultaneously giving assurances about the position of Northern Ireland in relation to the rest of the United Kingdom. If it was made clear that this latter question would be made the subject of a plebiscite, albeit not for a number of years, this might remove the emotive subject of the Border from the centre of Northern Ireland politics. Nor was it necessarily impossible to secure the continuance of the Parliamentary system of Government established by the Government of Ireland Act 1920 within a generally acceptable political solution. It had been found to be possible elsewhere, for example in the Lebanon, to devise an acceptable method of allocating Governmental responsibilities between representatives of different religious groupings. Whatever the form of any political initiative, however, it would have to take account of the problems created by internment. Heath, summing up the discussion, remarked that a major obstacle to any rational solution was likely to be the absence of any incentive to the IRA to desist from violence at any point short of the establishment of a revolutionary all-Ireland Republic. The immediate question was whether the 'tragic events' of the previous weekend in Londonderry had provided an opportunity for a political initiative or whether, on the contrary, they had made such an initiative impracticable for the time being. When Heath had met Lynch (in Brussels at the signing of the Treaties of Accession to the European Economic Community) the Taoiseach had suggested, even though in rather indefinite terms, that the moment for a political initiative might arrive when the influence of the IRA in Belfast had been perceptibly weakened but the Protestant community were still sufficiently apprehensive of violence to be prepared to offer a measure of compromise. But, even if this had been Lynch's view a few weeks earlier, Heath considered that it must probably be assumed that it would no longer be so; and, even if this analysis had been correct at the time, it could hardly be regarded as valid in present circumstances.[10] Quite clearly, as far as London was concerned the Irish Government was now a key player in the unfolding initiative. Peck was instructed, on 18 February, to speak to Lynch before the forthcoming Fianna Fáil Ard Fheis and to tell him that press speculation about a 'Northern Ireland solution reflects an underlying truth: and that therefore it would in our view be desirable if when addressing his party conference Mr Lynch could avoid specific proposals or comments or ideas that are being publicly canvassed, lest otherwise good ideas be damned in the eyes of Protestants in Northern Ireland'.[11] Lynch obliged and the resulting Ard Fheis was remarkable for its moderation which, given the anger in the Republic over Bloody Sunday, was not an easy thing to achieve;[12] but now Lynch had an indication that political changes in the North were on the way.

By this stage Faulkner had, at one level, made quite a dramatic gesture: he brought G.B. Newe, the prominent lay Catholic, into the Cabinet. Newe was not a member of the Unionist Party – but then neither was David Bleakley, the Labour MP, who had briefly been the Minister of Community Relations, having been appointed by Faulkner, before resigning in protest at internment. Unfortunately, for Nationalists, Newe was the 'wrong' sort of Catholic and this radical departure – he was the first Catholic to hold Ministerial rank since the foundation of the state – was lost in the deteriorating political and security situation. On 4 February, Faulkner went to London for further talks with Heath. In the middle of the week there had been interparty talks at Westminster between Whitelaw, the Conservative Leader of the Commons and Lord President of the Council, and Harold Wilson. And the evening before the inter-Governmental meeting there had been a meeting of the Conservative Backbench Committee – the 1922 Committee – at which Northern Ireland had been the central topic. Maudling was reported to have told the meeting that an 'initiative' as meant by most people who were pressing for one would be a surrender. Faulkner was hopeful that his meeting would show that the British Government was holding firm. It was a 'testing and probing' meeting for Faulkner. Discussions ranged widely over the spectrum of fundamental political issues, and the questions came at him thick and fast. There was 'no hint of hostility or criticism, but clearly they were casting around for a new line, for a means of diverting the storm of criticism which had followed the events of 30 January', he recorded. Heath was quite candid about the situation. He referred to the march planned by NICRA for Newry the next day. 'I am afraid there will be great pressure, especially if things go wrong at Newry tomorrow, for a change of course,' he said. Douglas-Home expressed his agreement, and Maudling added that the 1922 Committee felt the party could not continue indefinitely on its present course. Carrington elaborated: 'It is a question of being able to show that we are doing something positive about the situation.' To Faulkner it

> sounded a bit like a rehearsed chorus and I could see I would have to convince them that our present course was the right one. I laid stress on the calm and restraint of the majority of the population. 'They are relatively calm and restrained because they still have confidence that our two Governments will not let them down or submit to the IRA. If they ever come to believe, or even suspect, that this is not so, that restraint could quickly crumble.' 'What about Craig's suggestion of ceding Republican areas on the border to the Republic,' asked Heath. 'Is there any support for that?' 'No, it has not been taken very seriously in Ulster,' I replied. 'And it would do nothing about the core of the problem, the 200,000 Catholics in Belfast.'

Faulkner added that he could not see the Catholic section of the community being prepared to move, or to accept the lower living standards of the Republic. 'Would a referendum to test opinion on the constitutional position of Northern Ireland within the United Kingdom not be a good idea?,' asked Heath. 'Could Lynch not accept that?' Faulkner replied this was extremely unlikely since it would be seen as a device to tie the Catholic population to the existing constitutional position. But Heath pressed it further, asking if Unionists would not welcome such a referendum. Faulkner replied again that Unionists saw the present constitutional position as settled, and to raise the matter in a referendum might be seen as re-opening it and going back on the 1949 Act, which placed the responsibility for expressing views about the Union on the Stormont Parliament. 'And so the meeting progressed, with the four men raising targets for me to shoot at,' recalled Faulkner. Home wanted to know the effect of removing troops from Catholic areas; Faulkner answered that it would mean surrendering the people of those areas into the control of the IRA. Heath wondered if some initiative in the security field might not be necessary to end violence. Maudling added that time was running against them. Faulkner referred to Tuzo's view, repeatedly expressed over the past two months, that the IRA in Belfast would be under control by the end of March, and said the facts bore out this prediction. 'We could then, but only then, consider a de-escalation of internment and other security measures.' Carrington did not seem to accept Tuzo's view, and said that the Army always had a tendency to be overoptimistic. A general discussion on the means of involving Catholics in the Government of Northern Ireland ensued.

Faulkner argued that to attempt some constitutional innovation of a major nature while IRA violence continued would be seen as setting democracy aside to appease the IRA. 'What would be the reaction to Catholic participation in the Cabinet if there was a constitutional referendum say every twenty years?' asked Maudling. Faulkner replied that 'if we could get violence ended I would be in a strong position to urge magnanimity upon the majority, for example, in looking beyond party confines for members of the Government.' When Wilson's proposition for the transfer of all law and order powers to London was raised, Faulkner made his opposition very clear: it was a central power of Stormont under the Government of Ireland Act, and its removal now 'would reduce our Government to a mere sham'. As the meeting neared its end some indications of Westminster thinking were given to Faulkner. The idea of a referendum arose yet again, and the view was expressed that, held at twenty-year intervals, it could help take the Border out of politics. Heath said that whatever initiative was taken should be agreed between the two Governments. Direct Rule was not being contemplated, he said, and only would be if there was a complete breakdown. 'In any case, why should Unionists worry about closer integration into the United Kingdom?' Faulkner explained that Unionists saw the existence of Stormont as the only effective political obstacle to a unification of Ireland against their wishes.

> As I walked to the door with Heath I said to him, 'I have been completely frank with you about our ideas. Are you absolutely sure there is nothing else on your mind?' He said very firmly that there was not. I flew back to Belfast pondering our talks. It seemed to me that they had been setting up Aunt Sallys for me to knock down, and that the crucial remarks were those concerning an agreed initiative which we would meet again to discuss before anything was made public. We would have to put on our thinking caps yet again at Stormont and produce something which could act as a basis for new political talks in Ulster. This would, I thought, involve amendment of existing institutions and finding ways of broadening involvement in them. But there it would end.[13]

Next Sunday, much to Faulkner's annoyance, the first of a series of inspired press leaks appeared in *The Observer*. After some fairly accurate speculation about his discussions with Heath, Nova Beloff reported that 'Mr Heath himself is particularly aware of the international repercussions ... He was astonished and disconcerted by the virulence of the Irish reactions to Derry and in his gloomier moments envisages Ireland as our local Cuba.' Faulkner knew the reference to international pressures was accurate, though he was less convinced that Heath was 'disconcerted'. Speculation and leaks in London multiplied over the next few weeks, and their direction was profoundly disturbing to Unionists. On 12 February, Vanguard was launched by Craig and he announced plans for rallies across the Province to express determination to resist any capitulation to the terrorists. The rallies went ahead immediately, culminating in a massive display of strength in Belfast's Ormeau Park on 18 March by some fifty thousand supporters. The style of the rallies soon began to trouble Faulkner. Craig was arriving with motor-cycle escorts, or swooping down in a light private plane; and inspecting hundreds of men drawn up in military formation. On one occasion those present were asked to raise their hands in the air and indicate their assent to the objects of Vanguard by shouting 'I do' three times. 'Comparisons with Nazi rallies could scarcely be avoided', noted the Prime Minister:

> The Protestant backlash, so often derided by nationalists as a myth invented by Unionist politicians to frighten the British, was beginning. I attacked these 'demonstrations with an alien and unconvincing flavour' adding that there was among Unionists a 'determination not to be coerced on basic matters which is a far more formidable thing than these comic opera parades can convey'. But I was concerned about the obvious attractions of such activities for those who had been saying for months, 'Can we not do something to show that we mean what we say?'[14]

Immediately after the London meeting, Faulkner had begun a major reassessment of the political situation at Stormont.

> We had to decide what would be necessary in order to get the SDLP back to the conference table in spite of all the hooks they had got themselves caught on, how far the London Government would press us to go as a result of the new pressures it was coming under, and how far we could afford to go ourselves without sacrificing some fundamental principle and without losing our political base in the community.

On 16 February, after a Cabinet meeting at Stormont the previous day, Faulkner sent a letter to Heath outlining the basis of Stormont's approach. He assured him that they fully appreciated the need to produce, as a matter of urgency and in agreement with his Government, the means of achieving the 'active, permanent and guaranteed role' to which both Governments were publicly committed for the minority in Northern Ireland. Faulkner reminded Heath of what he had said to him at a previous meeting; that the two Governments must stick together and on no account allow a wedge to be driven between them:

Ever since, I have been concerned to conduct our relationship on a basis of complete frankness and I know that this has also been your objective ... it is our understanding that any new, albeit provisional, conclusions reached by the UK Government will be put to our Cabinet for our consideration and comment before any concrete action is taken or any public disclosure made. In this context, we regard some recent press comment, which I realise is of a speculative nature, as distinctly unhelpful.

The Northern Ireland Government had since then reviewed the whole basis of executive government and had concluded that they should not create by statutory means an entrenched position in the Cabinet for members of the Catholic community as such, since this would strengthen sectarian divisions and eliminate attempts to create non-sectarian political alignments. Nor was it possible to provide statutorily entrenched positions for the anti-partitionist (as distinct from the religious) minority, as this would lead inevitably to PR government, which they regarded as intrinsically unworkable and which would sterilize any real debate in Parliament. It was Stormont's firm view that a transfer of 'law and order' powers would leave no credible basis of viable government, and that any transfer to the Republic of parts of Northern Ireland would create more problems than it would solve. Faulkner also stressed that the Security Forces were at a crucial stage in the campaign against the terrorists, who must not, under any circumstances, be given a breathing space or have their standing and morale boosted.[15]

In a letter to Heath, Faulkner declared that he was completely opposed to any relaxation in the policy of internment. He argued that in spite of the continued bombings and shootings there was ample evidence that the effectiveness of the IRA, especially in the Belfast area, had been very seriously reduced. The removal from circulation of 700–800 members of the two main organizations was creating problems for them in terms both of morale and losses of key personnel. These losses had to some extent been made good, but the officers of some IRA companies had to be replaced two or three times over and Volunteers were now reluctant to come forward. Some units in Belfast had ceased to exist and others had been amalgamated. Several areas had been completely cleared of IRA and increasing pressure was being brought to bear on areas where groups were still active. Faulkner had two answers to the claim that internment had not worked. The first was the fact, already noted, that the IRA presence had been removed from certain areas and that this was continuing; the second was due in no small measure to the fact that there were many people outside the IRA who did not want internment to work. They included those who while ostensibly deploring the methods of the IRA had little desire to see the IRA put out of action until some at least of the organization's aims had been achieved. There was also little evidence that internment had led to a substantial increase in IRA recruitment. On the contrary, recent arrests indicated that most of those taking part in terrorist attacks were recruited in the period leading up to August 1971. So far as those already interned were concerned, the campaign to end internment and the belief that it would succeed kept their morale higher than was generally the case with men still at large. In spite of successes against the IRA it might still be claimed that the present strategy of attrition offered steadily diminishing returns in terms of opportunities for a political settlement. It might indeed appear to some that efforts to secure a settlement could not await the prior defeat of the IRA, or even the scaling down of violence to an acceptable level, and that there were greater chances of terminating violence by putting internment into reverse than by pursuing it to the bitter end. In pursuit of this argument it might be argued that internees should now be released at the rate of, say, fifty per month and the rate might be increased as the situation improved; conversely that it should be cut back if there were no improvement, and that all releases should stop if a further deterioration occurred. Alternatively there might be a programme of releases geared to the progress of talks with the Northern Ireland Opposition. Despite all these arguments Faulkner rejected them out of hand and offered the following objections to the phasing out of internment:

(1) All internees are, on the evidence available, either members of the IRA or otherwise involved in terrorism, and there is no pool of mere political activists from which releases can be made. There is, therefore, the likelihood that internees released as a political gesture would return to their previous activities and so repair the substantial damage which has been inflicted on both factions of the IRA since 9 August 1971.
(2) If internees were released prematurely, i.e. before the IRA were defeated, the prime targets for retaliatory action would undoubtedly be the members of the Special Branch of the RUC: these are for the most part known to those internees whom they have arrested or interrogated.
(3) The IRA would regard any programme of release for political reasons as an important success. It would also be so regarded by members of the Security Forces and the general public. The IRA could, therefore, dictate future terms.
(4) Any decision to make no further arrests would be regarded by the IRA as a still greater achievement; they could be expected to take the opportunity to recoup their losses and to equip themselves to intensify operations at a date of their own choosing. Those on the run would be encouraged to return to their units.
(5) The process of internment has provided, and continues to provide, a flow of intelligence on the membership, resources and plans of the IRA. If this flow were interrupted the IRA could re-group with impunity.
(6) The Joint Security Committee have noted these conclusions and have accepted that security grounds rule out any releases other than through the machinery of the Advisory Committee. Any other course would it is felt carry with it a serious risk of the prolongation of the terrorist campaign.
(7) It is difficult to visualize any solid advantages which might outweigh these security objections. It may well be that internment continues to be the main cause of Catholic alienation and that it has attracted to the IRA the sympathy of sections of the Catholic population which would

otherwise have no use for terrorism. But it can hardly be supposed that the confidence of the minority is to be won back by letting the gunmen loose to reimpose their will in areas from which they have been expelled.

(8) Nor is it easy to see how the ending of internment before the IRA are defeated can in any way assist towards a political solution. The opposition have no control over the IRA and therefore no means of bringing terrorism itself under control. And even if a total or partial ending of internment enabled political talks to start, a fully armed terrorist organization in the background with its ranks re-filled would inevitably dominate the course of any negotiations.

(9) If it is accepted that there is no painless way of ending internment it will be necessary to say so publicly and to face the unfavourable reactions which will inevitably follow.[16]

These arguments were increasingly at odds with the direction in which British policy was pulling. On 21 February, Maudling told Heath that he had become increasingly convinced that the time for a political initiative in Northern Ireland had come. The views of Faulkner 'showed that Ulster Unionists wanted to have it both ways: they wanted Northern Ireland to continue to be part of the United Kingdom, but on their terms'. Maudling was inclined to the view that Unionists, and Protestants in general, would accept the sort of arrangement Ministers had in mind, provided that they were given firm guarantees about the Border. Both Heath and Maudling realized that this would involve a referendum on the Border. If it came to Direct Rule, Maudling envisaged that the executive functions of government would be carried out by a sort of executive Council of Northern Ireland Permanent Secretaries reporting to a Secretary of State. Legislative changes would be effected by Orders-in-Council made by the Secretary of State after consultation with an advisory commission. Heath decided that the Cabinet Office should press ahead with a detailed analysis of the plans with the utmost urgency. At some point, in the not too distant future, the Prime Minister thought it would be necessary to ask Faulkner to 'come over again; but not until after Ministers were neared the point of final decision'.[17]

THE FINAL COUNTDOWN

Two weeks after writing his first letter Faulkner wrote to Heath again, outlining the broad conclusions which his Cabinet had reached after much discussion. The objective, he believed, must be to find a means of achieving for the institutions of Northern Ireland a general consensus, binding all sections of its population other than unreasonable and irreconcilable elements committed to the use of force. Such a consensus would be much easier to achieve with the cooperation and assistance of the Government of the Irish Republic. If the constitutional framework and governmental institutions were accepted as fair and reasonable throughout Ireland it would make possible, on an all-Ireland basis, determined action against terrorist organizations. Faulkner urged that, as a major contribution to peace, an attempt should be made to reach with the Republic a solemn and binding agreement on the constitutional status of Northern Ireland. This agreement would have to recognize the validity of efforts either to maintain or change that position by lawful, constitutional means and provide for an acceptable mechanism through which the people of Northern Ireland could decide in the future whether they wished to retain the existing position or change it. Faulkner now accepted that a referendum should provide this mechanism, treating Northern Ireland as a single constituency, the first to be held as soon as practically possible, and thereafter only when at least 40 per cent of MPs at Stormont presented an address to the Governor asking that one should be held. No question of a change in the constitutional position should arise unless more than 50 per cent of those entitled to vote registered a vote for a change. If the Republic's Government accepted this as a proper mechanism, both Irish Governments would be able to adopt a common policy for the suppression of terrorism, dealing with fugitive offenders who were hiding behind the pretence of 'political' murder and thereby evading extradition, and a joint Inter-Governmental Council could be set up with equal members from the Dublin and Belfast Governments to discuss economic and social matters. Faulkner repeated his view that PR government in Northern Ireland would be unworkable. An active role for the minority could be achieved in various ways, involving mainly an elaboration of the proposals in a Green Paper: the Stormont Commons should be enlarged, the Senate reconstituted to provide more representation for bodies such as trade unions, industrial interests and local authorities, and the functional committee system should be expanded to include policy proposals. Faulkner also proposed that Offices of the House, such as Speaker and Chairman of Ways and Means, should be shared between Government and Opposition, and that all Ministers should, before making appointments such as for Chairman of Public Bodies, consult the Minister of Community Relations to ensure that more members of the nationalist community were given responsibility. Faulkner asked Heath to let him know his reaction to them before the further meeting with him and his colleagues which would obviously be necessary soon.[18] Heath did not get back to Faulkner. Instead, Maudling prepared his own response – to be put to his Cabinet colleagues in London first. It was put to them on 7 March and signalled that the time for indecision was almost passed. Maudling stressed how:

> All possible courses of action or inaction are fraught with danger. There are good grounds for arguing that the problem of Northern Ireland is insoluble and that a violent confrontation between Loyalist and Republican is unavoidable. Sometimes it seems almost as if the people of Northern Ireland, or at any rate that political leaders (which in realistic terms includes the Irish Republican Army [IRA]) are possessed of a death wish. Yet the time had come when we must choose between the dangers of action and inaction. The alternative was inaction, or rather pursuing the present course of meeting IRA violence with force and supporting the reforms so far advanced by Faulkner. There were strong arguments for doing this in terms of military successes.

Any departure from the Unionist point of view would appear to be a concession to Catholics and therefore inevitably to the IRA unless, of course, they spurned it. The Protestants would argue with great vehemence that they had played fairly, that they had proposed sweeping changes and that it was wrong to penalise them for violence that they had not perpetrated.

But, concluded Maudling, the truth was that, right or wrong as they might have been in the recent past or the past fifty years, Protestants, like Catholics, had a fundamental interest in restoring the chance of peace to their country. The present system was one of total alienation between the two communities. Though Faulkner might be right in arguing that many Catholics did not really want a united Ireland, 'things have gone beyond that stage. I do not believe that there is any possibility of persuading Catholics to go back to the old system.' The Army's progress had been considerable, particularly in Belfast; but the facts were:

i The situation outside Belfast and in Londonderry is still very serious.
ii The condition of today's success is half the Army in Ulster and a growing number of detainees.
iii In the nature of modern urban society you cannot entirely eliminate the bombings and shootings, however effective Army action may be.
iv Political alienation between the two communities is now complete.
v Any temporary lull caused by the pressure of the Army on the IRA would not last long.
vi Our whole position in the world is being seriously affected by Northern Ireland, and however hard we try we will not get other countries to understand the reality of the situation.

Maudling had come to the conclusion that the dangers of continuing with the present policy were now greater than the dangers of trying to make a new start: 'I believe that if we make such an attempt and fail to get agreement we shall at least in the long run draw the benefit for having proposed a solution that is just and equitable between the differing factions. We should not underestimate the importance of this.' Protestants cared most about the Border while Catholics cared about ending the situation 'in which for decades now they have without doubt been treated as second-class citizens'. The Unionists were on strong ground when they refused to be excluded from the UK against their will:

But I think they try and have it both ways demanding the right to remain in the United Kingdom and to remain on their own terms i.e. on the basis of a regional autonomy far greater than that accorded to other parts of the United Kingdom. I think we are entitled to say to them 'we support you to the hilt in your desire to remain in the United Kingdom, but if you do so you must conform as closely as possible to the pattern of the United Kingdom and above all you must accept, as much as anyone else, the ultimate authority of the United Kingdom Government and the United Kingdom Parliament'.

This led Maudling to the question of responsibility for law and order. Faulkner thought that without this power the Northern Ireland Government would be demoted to the status of a county council. 'This a bad argument.' Neither Scotland nor Wales had a Government or Parliament of their own responsible for law and order. Maudling pointed out that:

i   At present, and for years to come, the maintenance of law and order will be the responsibility of the Army, which is answerable to the Westminster Government. It does not seem rational in those circumstances for responsibility for law and order to rest with the Northern Ireland Government, who have no control over the main instrument for maintaining it.
ii I do not believe there is any chance now of getting the minority community, or incidentally the Opposition at Westminster, to accept that the administration of law and order by Stormont as at present constituted will be impartial.
iii The recent conduct of the Northern Ireland Government leads one to doubt whether an essentially provincial organisation has the resources to handle efficiently matters of this size and complexity.

Maudling therefore proposed that the power to legislate on matters relating to law and order be transferred to Westminster and that control over the RUC, for the period of the current emergency, rest with the Army. The next decision would be how to provide a proper place for the minority community in the public life of Northern Ireland. There were two elements here:

i   The avoidance of discrimination between individuals.
ii Ending the exclusion of minority representatives from the direction of public affairs.

Of discrimination that remained after the reform programme the most serious was job discrimination: 'which is virtually beyond the power of Government. I do not think much more needs doing in this field, but the idea of a Bill of Rights is an interesting one and could be of great value.' As for the second issue, Maudling identified the alternatives: a Cabinet with minority representation chosen by the minority; a Cabinet that continued to be totally dominated by Unionists 'which I believe is no longer acceptable to the minority; or no Cabinet at all'. To devise an acceptable formula might take up to two years. In the meantime it might be necessary to govern by Commission Government under a Secretary of State. Whatever the problems, Maudling concluded that:

i   The time has come to take the initiative. Though this would be attended by great dangers, the dangers of not doing so now are now even greater.
ii Our basic principle should be that as long as...a majority wishes to remain in the United Kingdom this will be respected, but it must be on the understanding that they accept the over-riding authority of the United

Kingdom Government and Parliament, as do all other parts of the United Kingdom.
iii Responsibility for law and order should be transferred from Stormont to Westminster.
iv The protection of Protestants against a united Ireland should be buttressed by the device of periodic plebiscites.
v Proper provision must be made, after consultation, for the participation of the minority community in the life and public affairs of the Province by adapting administration, legislature and Government.
vi In the interim period, while the necessary adjustments are being made, the discussions held and legislation enacted, the powers of Stormont should be temporarily transferred to a Secretary of State.
vii We should make such changes as we can in the internment system, beginning by releasing some of the least dangerous internees and making it clear that our purpose is the total end of internment when security considerations and the state of public order enable us to do this.[19]

In the Cabinet discussion that followed Maudling recognized that Faulkner would probably find his proposals unacceptable and that he would be unlikely to keep his Administration in being until a reformed constitution took effect. In any event Maudling thought it must be doubtful whether it would be possible to move to a new structure of Government in Northern Ireland without a clean break with the past or to establish constructive consultations with all political elements in Northern Ireland so long as Faulkner remained Prime Minister. He had therefore concluded that the least dangerous course would be to proceed initially to a temporary period of Direct Rule, which might be of something approaching two years' duration. Lord Carrington agreed with Maudling that terrorism could not be extirpated by military measures alone. In Belfast the Army had almost completely disrupted the battle order of the Provisionals; and the numbers of shooting incidents and explosions would probably soon fall to as low a level as it was possible to achieve. But it was not possible to prevent a continuation of spasmodic outrages, some of which were liable to be major in scale and highly destructive of life and property. Moreover, the Army's success in Belfast had led to an intensification of IRA activity in Border areas, where terrorists could find a ready refuge within the Republic; while in Londonderry, by deliberate policy, no military operations of any size had been undertaken, with the result that the Bogside and Creggan districts had become areas where the authority of the Government had virtually ceased to be enforceable. There could thus be no purely military solution; but a political initiative might have some effect upon the intensity of the terrorist campaign; and, if it could contain elements capable of winning a measure of support among moderate Catholics, the IRA might forfeit much of the benevolent neutrality which they enjoyed at the hands of individuals who sympathized with their political aims even while abhorring their methods.

The rest of the Cabinet still took some convincing: it was suggested that a comprehensive initiative of the kind proposed by the Home Secretary would entail serious risks both in Northern Ireland and at Westminster. In Northern Ireland it might merely alienate the Protestant community without gaining any support from the Catholics; while at Westminster it might erode support for the Government both among the Ulster Unionist Members and more widely among the Conservative Party as a whole. It had long been the avowed strategy of the IRA, first, to render Northern Ireland ungovernable, then to compel the British Government to resort to Direct Rule and, finally, to achieve the severance of Northern Ireland from the United Kingdom followed by its absorption within a United Ireland. The majority of Protestants in Northern Ireland would be liable to see the proposed initiative as marking an advance from the first to the second of these stages and as bringing that final stage even nearer. Moreover, a sense of direct confrontation with the British Government might inspire the IRA to intensify their campaign of terrorism and possibly to extend it to Great Britain on a wider scale than the recent bomb outrage at Aldershot. There must also be some doubt whether the RUC, the Northern Ireland Civil Service and even, perhaps, the judiciary would be prepared to cooperate with an imposed system of Direct Rule. Nor would a plebiscite on the Border necessarily count for much as a counter weight. Its result was so easily predictable that it could not be significant as a concession to Protestant feeling. On the other hand the declaration of a single plebiscite for the whole of the Province might well provoke demands for local plebiscites in specific areas; but the Border communities were so intermingled that the problem of adjustment was insoluble, as had been shown in 1925.

Other elements of the proposed initiative were equally open to criticism. 'Community Government' could not be reconciled with the democratic concept of responsibility to a Parliamentary majority. In those countries where ministerial offices had been distributed by statute or by convention among opposing political parties there had at least been general agreement upon the broad objective of preserving the integrity of the State. In Northern Ireland this basic prerequisite was lacking. But if, for this reason, Community Government proved unworkable in practice, the British Government might find itself committed in perpetuity to the system of Direct Rule which it had envisaged as only a temporary expedient; and in earlier discussions Ministers had frequently agreed that Direct Rule represented a policy of last resort. Moreover, a modification of the internment policy would not necessarily lead to any significant reduction in the level of violence; it was the excessive level of violence which had compelled the Government to acquiesce in the introduction of internment. These objections would not only be liable to be strongly urged by the Government's supporters at Westminster; they would also be voiced by a considerable body of anti-Irish opinion in the country as a whole, which would find it very difficult to understand why the Government appeared to be conceding some of the objectives of the IRA when it might seem more appropriate to declare the IRA illegal in Great Britain (it was still a legal organization there) and to deprive citizens of the Republic of some of the privileges which they enjoyed in the United Kingdom. Reactions of this kind could seriously jeopardize the Government's political position as a whole, not least as regards their prospect of retaining adequate Parliamentary support for the legislation necessary to confirm the accession to the European Communities – which was proving controversial at the time. It was also questionable whether the proposed initiative would in fact secure the support from the Republic which was a necessary element in any ultimate solution. Most citizens of the Republic looked to the objective of a United Ireland; it must be doubtful whether they could be brought to support any system of Government of a separate Northern Ireland. Nor was it clear how the imposition of United Kingdom rule could assist Lynch in taking stronger action against the IRA within the Republic.

From this it was clear that there was little enthusiasm for where any initiative might lead: Direct Rule. But there was some support around the Cabinet table for an initiative: it was pointed out that while the Government's supporters in the House of Commons might see difficulty in endorsing the suggested initiative, public opinion in Great Britain generally was demanding that some move should be made. Recent examples of terrorism had created a sense of revulsion in the Catholic community which made the present a particularly propitious time at which to act. The object had to be to satisfy some at least of the legitimate aspirations of each community. The majority of Catholics probably had no real desire for Northern Ireland to be absorbed immediately into the Republic. They were content to remain in the United Kingdom; many of them, indeed, had served in the Armed Forces of the Crown. But it was accepted that they regarded the Army in Northern Ireland as being merely the tool of the Northern Ireland Government and saw no future for the peace and prosperity of the Province if Stormont were perpetuated in its present form. The only hope of loosening the grip of the IRA on the minority community was to adopt an initiative on the lines proposed by the Home Secretary. Any other course would simply enable the IRA to gain even firmer control. It was suggested that it might not be necessary to give immediate effect to all the proposals in order to achieve the stability required for political discussions leading to reforms in the constitution. It might be wiser to appoint a Secretary of State with specific responsibility for Northern Ireland and to invite him, initially, to concentrate on the main points of disaffection. Thus, there were strong arguments in favour of a referendum on the Border, which would reassure the Unionists about the constitutional integrity of Northern Ireland as part of the United Kingdom. There was also a good case for transferring responsibility for law and order to Westminster and combining this change with a substantial modification of the internment policy. These measures were regarded by Lynch as a fundamental necessity and were felt by a considerable body of opinion in Great Britain to be highly desirable. It was inherently unsatisfactory that, although the Army was constitutionally under the control of the United Kingdom Government, Ministers at Westminster had no responsibility for law and order in the Province which the Army played the principal part in maintaining. Moreover, they had publicly to defend the policy of internment while having neither the power to influence the detention orders which were made in particular instances nor proper access to the information upon which these decisions were made. There had to be room for some doubt whether all the internees were active and dangerous terrorists; and a policy of gradually releasing the less dangerous on suitable conditions should be pursued. Although Faulkner had said both publicly and privately that he could not continue to lead a Government which surrendered the responsibility for law and order he might not adhere to this position when confronted with the alternative. If he did, however, it would probably be unrealistic to hope that an acceptable alternative Government could be formed at Stormont. No Unionist politician could hope to lead an administration from a more moderate position than that held by Faulkner; and, although Paisley had in recent months seemed to adopt a more reasonable posture (and had, indeed, stated that he would support Government by commission), he did not command the majority in Parliament which was necessary to enable the Governor to invite him to form an administration. The most probable consequence of Faulkner's resignation on the issue of law and order, therefore, would be a disintegration of the political structure in the Province, which would make it necessary for London to impose Direct Rule whether 'we wished to or not'. Summing up the discussion, Heath acknowledged that the Cabinet were not yet ready to reach a decision about the course to be adopted in the current situation.[20] Basically the Cabinet was being softened up for the inevitable need for an initiative. But the concerns expressed within Cabinet ran deep: one of those with the gravest doubts was the Foreign Secretary himself, one of the Big Four who called the shots on Ulster policy. Douglas-Home wrote to Heath expressing his misgivings: 'I really dislike Direct Rule for Northern Ireland because I do not believe that they are like the Scots or the Welsh and doubt if they ever will be. The real British interest would I think be served best by pushing them closer towards a United Ireland rather than tying them closer to the United Kingdom. Our own parliamentary history is one long story of trouble with the Irish.' While sure that the Home Secretary was right to say that they could not go on as they were, Douglas-Home feared that the timescale in which London had been thinking for political consultations to take place would mean that once the pattern of a Secretary of State in command of security had lasted for two years or so 'we shall not get away from direct rule'.[21]

On 9 March, when the Cabinet reconvened to discuss Northern Ireland once more, Heath decided to lay on the table exactly what they were potentially facing. He pointed out that if Faulkner refused to accept the Government's proposals it was difficult to envisage either that an alternative Prime Minister could emerge capable of commanding a majority in the Northern Ireland Parliament or that a General Election could be held in the present circumstances. The consequence, therefore, of a decision to transfer law and order might therefore 'whether we wished it or not, be the imposition, at least for a time, of direct United Kingdom rule'. There was still Cabinet resistance: this time it was argued that, since a new initiative might deprive the Government of support from a number of those upon whose votes they relied on at Westminster for the implementation of the Government's European policy, it could be argued that Britain's accession to the EEC was a matter of even more fundamental importance than the solution of Northern Ireland's problems. It might be wiser, therefore, to think of an initial step going no further than the transfer to Westminster of responsibility for all aspects of internment policy, leaving other questions on law and order with Stormont. Heath ended this discussion by suggesting that the next step should be a discussion with Faulkner designed to establish his intentions and to test his probable reaction to the initiative.[22] This, however, did not happen. The gameplan that emerged was for a general agreement to be secured within the Cabinet before Faulkner was to be invited over for a chat. On 14 March, Heath told the Cabinet that it had become clear that the refusal of the SDLP to participate in any conference eliminated the hope that an acceptable settlement might emerge from current discussions. It was necessary to take the initiative. The Home Secretary's proposals, he argued, were in no sense a surrender to the IRA whose objective was the immediate reunification of Ireland by force. Heath stressed that a relaxation of internment was perhaps the most important element in undermining terrorism. But at present internment was controlled by the Northern Ireland Government 'and, in order to be sure of achieving our purpose, we should have to assume responsibility not only for internment but probably also for the maintenance of law and order'. If Faulkner were to refuse to agree to these measures and were to decide that he could not continue his administration, the question would arise as to whether the Cabinet were prepared to accept a temporary period of Direct Rule. The Cabinet finally agreed that Heath should hold discussions with Faulkner but should not give him any indication of the consequences of a refusal of cooperation on his part; instead Heath would report back to the Cabinet which would then have to reach final decisions on the measures to be taken.[23]

Faulkner was invited to meet Heath at Downing Street on 22 March. The day before his departure Faulkner met with his Cabinet. The Prime Minister explained to his colleagues that their case rested on the letters he sent Heath. In the course of a telephone conversation with Heath a few days previously, Faulkner had suggested that some indication of the likely topics for discussion would be of help; but Heath had not committed himself, saying that none of the ideas was firm enough for reduction to paper. Faulkner thought that indicated that consultation rather than the announcement of decisions was what was in Heath's mind – indeed he thought that it would be unrealistic after weeks of independent study for him to be expected to accept any new ideas on the strength of a one-day meeting. He took the view that the Government of Northern Ireland's carefully-evolved recommendations deserved firm decisions and that it would be wrong to look to interim measures aimed at getting the SDLP to the conference table but keeping the public in a state of suspense for months longer. The most Faulkner thought might be put to him was the question of a United Kingdom Minister responsible for Northern Ireland affairs; Faulkner distinguished between the appointment of a Secretary of State for Northern Ireland, which could be of advantage to Northern Ireland, and a Resident Minister which could only be interpreted as an expression of no confidence in the Government of Northern Ireland and indeed tantamount to Direct Rule. Faulkner imagined Heath would bring in suggestions over and above those already proposed by the Government of Northern Ireland but that he would not force them unduly.[24]

JUDGEMENT DAY – THE END OF STORMONT

Not all of Faulkner's Ministers were so sanguine. Roy Bradford, a member of Faulkner's Cabinet, suspected something drastic was being considered by London. He knew Ned Dunnett, the brother of the senior Whitehall civil servant Sir James Dunnett:

> I knew him very well simply because we used to play golf in Rye when I lived in London so we kept in touch – and we used to meet regularly and exchange views. I remember vividly that, just three or four weeks before the imposition of Direct Rule and I was over and it was my turn to give him lunch, we met in the Reform Club. He was uneasy, and then he said, in effect – I could sense there was something going on – he said that we could not go on meeting like this. I asked if it was anything I had said, and he said no and asked me to leave it because he could not explain. It was quite clear to me that there was something very revolutionary in the offing at that time. He did not give any indication of what that change was going to be, but I remember him saying that he would rather I did not get in touch. It was quite clear then; that was three to four weeks before. That was another reason for my being convinced that Direct Rule was in the offing, because we had talked about that sort of thing before as a possibility.[25]

The Stormont party assembled at Stormont Castle on the morning of Wednesday 22 March. Jack Andrews, Deputy Prime Minister, was accompanying Faulkner. The Prime Minister recalled:

> As usual for important London meetings we were keyed up to acquit ourselves well and put our case, and we were anxious to know what proposals the Heath Government would put to us. But it was one of many important meetings, we felt no sense of foreboding, and the usual cheerful good humour prevailed. A helicopter arrived to take us to Aldergrove, coming in over the trees and landing on the smooth lawns in front of the Castle where such noisy manoeuvres were becoming increasingly common. We piled in, and in fifteen minutes were on the ground at Aldergrove walking towards the RAF Andover which was to take us to London. Soon we were soaring over Belfast Lough, looking down on the crowded industrial city where only a few hours later another bomb was to injure sixty people going about their work. Stormont Castle was never going to seem quite the same again after that morning.

Heath greeted them in the hallway at Downing Street at 11 a.m. with 'his usual brisk good humour. Upstairs in his study were the usual triumvirate, accompanied for the first time by Whitelaw. We wasted no time before getting down to business.'[26]

In his opening statement Heath said he was grateful for the opportunity of a full discussion with Faulkner and Andrews. He proposed that this should be as frank as their previous discussions had been and it should of course be kept on a completely confidential basis until the outcome had been agreed. A lot of Press speculation had taken place lately and he suggested that the contradictory nature of press comment was indeed proof of its speculative character. Heath and his colleagues had been completely over the whole ground and their only purpose was to retain Northern Ireland as part of the United Kingdom in terms of the 1949 Act; it was fully recognized that until the majority decided otherwise Northern Ireland would remain an integral part of the Kingdom. It was their aim and hope that peace should be restored as soon as possible: in Belfast considerable progress had been made in curbing and disrupting the IRA; the Border remained difficult; and Londonderry would require a major military operation if it was to be cleared. The casualties that had occurred on 30 January would be minute compared with what would happen if there were to be an attempt at a military pacification. At present there were seventeen battalions in Northern Ireland; the Army presence had existed there for two and a half years and it was now becoming apparent that while the Army could deal with the IRA up to a point they would not be able to deal with the individual bomber; nor was it practicable to consider closing the Border. The firm conclusion they had reached was that there could be no purely military solution. The drain on United Kingdom resources was very considerable and there had been a massive interference with the British Government's international commitments. On the political front, Heath pointed out that despite all attempts to bring the two communities together the gap had widened and there had been a noticeable hardening on both sides of the sectarian divide. Internment and the problems it had given rise to were a major factor in the division; internment could not be considered a purely Northern Ireland matter because it affected the United Kingdom and had bad repercussions on its international relationships. It was true that at the time of United Kingdom agreement to internment the British Government had fully accepted that there would be serious consequences. At Westminster very considerable difficulties were arising for the Government out of the continuous debate and consideration of Northern Ireland matters. The United Kingdom Government had a situation where they had the responsibility and the blame for what happened as regarded internment and on the security front but were without real power; this was a very unsatisfactory situation which was accentuated by the growing financial dependence of Northern Ireland. The United Kingdom Government had been willing to help and had done so in many ways but the burden was becoming extremely heavy. Heath and his colleagues had gone over all these factors and had reached the conclusion that they must make a fresh attempt to break through the deadlock. The Home Secretary's attempt to bring the parties round the table had failed, despite all efforts. It was desirable, if possible, to maintain the bi-partisan approach at Westminster and it would be difficult to do so unless one could achieve a definite breakthrough in the present deadlock. The United Kingdom Government had studied the Northern Ireland proposals very carefully and would want to put forward certain suggestions of their own.[27]

Heath admired the spirit of the Northern Ireland people. But it was clear that a military solution would mean an escalation of force, whereas what was needed, in the view of his Government, was a de-escalation; the latter was needed to swing the Catholic community away from those who were using force and if this could be achieved there would be benefits in the South as well. It had been necessary accordingly to consider political moves. His Government certainly agreed that the guarantee in the 1949 Act should stand. A periodical referendum, as proposed by the Northern Ireland Government, would be a further guarantee; they were prepared to accept this proposal though they would have views on how it should be applied, for example the whole principle of a referendum was that one was seeking a majority view, that is a majority of those who actually vote. While a referendum was alien to United Kingdom practice, it was quite realized that Northern Ireland with its special problems was perhaps in a different situation and that the use of a referendum could be justified there. This was a matter the detail of which could be discussed later. It was also necessary to consider how the Roman Catholics could be brought back into community life. It was not sufficient just to go on dealing with violence. Heath realized that the Northern Ireland Government had put forward proposals. He would try to get Westminster's acceptance of such of these as were agreed. But his Government had decided that these were not sufficient to give the necessary permanent, active and guaranteed role to the minority. The problem remained of how to bring this about. If one was going to escape from violence and also enable the Republic to escape from it too – and there were some indications that the Government there were anxious to do this – further action would be necessary in Northern Ireland. This brought up the question of internment. There were obvious risks in phasing it out; it would be important to take the advice of the security authorities on this and then to weigh the disadvantages against the political advantage of deflecting the Catholic community from their passive or active support for the men of violence. The United Kingdom would have to take this responsibility; they had decided they must start unwinding the internment process. The 'hard men' would still be lifted and put away but a scale-down of the process was imperative. It was the United Kingdom view that the way to do this would be for Westminster to take over responsibility for law and order. This was defined as embracing the transfer of criminal law and prosecutions, including the organization of and appointments to the Courts; public order; prison and penal institutions; police; the creation of all new criminal offences with power to delegate to Northern Ireland on fringe matters like food and drugs. Prosecutions would be taken over by the English Attorney-General and the Northern Ireland Director of Public Prosecutions would serve under him. The control and operation of special powers would also become a matter for United Kingdom authorities (including internment). Stormont would remain with the double guarantee of the 1949 Act and a referendum. The United Kingdom Government would then seek to move in the direction of talks on how the minority could be given their active, permanent and guaranteed role. They would propose a Secretary of State with responsibility for Northern Ireland affairs in the same way as there were Secretaries of State for Scotland and Wales. Additional Ministers would also be appointed.[28]

This came as a shock to the Stormont team. 'We were puzzled more than angry,' recorded Faulkner. 'It was not a very impressive or cohesive package, its content in terms of how Northern Ireland should be governed was remarkably vague, and it did not seem like a thorough or finalized response to the comprehensive proposals we had forwarded. We had understood that this meeting would involve an exchange of ideas and provide room for compromise. So we decided that Heath was bluffing, and started to shoot down his target.' It was not long before the penny dropped for Faulkner and his colleagues: it was becoming clear to the Stormont team that Heath had 'not been making an opening bid to soften us up' but had made up his mind before he met them 'and was presenting what amounted to an ultimatum. When we adjourned for lunch at noon the Northern Ireland party was beginning to feel the effects of the blow Heath had dealt us. I was shaken and horrified, and felt completely betrayed.' But 'in spite of the natural urge to give vent to these feelings', Faulkner was determined to exhaust every conceivable avenue of agreement, and to carry the talks through to whatever conclusion:

> We had a politely friendly lunch, during which we all tried to behave normally. One of my civil servants told me later that during the lunch Reggie Maudling, who was sitting near to him, pushed his glasses up to the top of his head, leaned back in his chair, stared at the ceiling, and said in a pensive voice, 'I wonder if Brian is bluffing.' We never quite decided if this was a ploy intended for the ears of my aides, or a genuine problem which Reggie was trying to solve.[29]

Faulkner tried desperately to stave off the inevitable. He agreed that a plebiscite might help to conciliate minority opinion; but he felt the majority would regard it as adding nothing to the safeguards already inherent in the Ireland Act of 1949. More fundamentally, however, he indicated that he and his supporters could not agree to the transfer of security on the grounds that a change of this kind would imply that the UK Government no longer had confidence in the Northern Ireland Government; that the responsibilities which would remain with the Northern Ireland Government would not be sufficient to maintain its political credibility; and that the reduction in its status would be claimed by the IRA as a victory. Faulkner made it clear that he would regard the transfer of security as even less realistic and acceptable politically than Direct Rule. He offered, instead, the phased elimination of internment by agreement between the two Governments: Faulkner suggested, from amongst those of the internees whose release had not been recommended by the Advisory Committee, those who were recognized by the Security Forces as constituting a lesser degree of risk should forthwith be released; and that he and the Home Secretary should, at regular intervals, consider when and in what numbers further releases of internees might take place. In general the Stormont system would remain: but there would be provision for joint chairmanship of the Joint Security Committee by the Minister of Home Affairs and a UK Minister (each with a right of veto); the replacement of the Special Powers Acts by fresh legislation at Stormont designed (after the end of the current emergency) to assimilate the emergency powers available to the Northern Ireland authorities to those available in the rest of the UK; a Bill of Rights to be enacted at Westminster; a referendum to be held on the status of Northern Ireland as part of the UK, repeated at intervals of fifteen years; and further constitutional changes on the lines of Faulkner's letters. Faulkner admitted that his Government had not given any formal consideration to the hypothetical contingency that the assumption of Direct Rule might become inevitable; but he reassured the British Ministers that the Northern Ireland Government would not contemplate any unilateral declaration of independence. They would do all they could to moderate the political temperature in Northern Ireland if the UK Government decided they had no choice but to assume responsibility for direct Government of the Province. But Faulkner made it clear that in the event of Direct Rule, London must be prepared to deal with industrial action by Protestants and, perhaps, with acts of violence against the minority. The conference then broke up.[30]

The talks had lasted for over nine hours. Heath, Maudling, Home, Andrews and Faulkner were in the sitting-room 'talking and drinking lime juice and soda till it was almost coming out of our ears', recalled Faulkner. Maudling was arguing that

> we could accept their proposals and carry on, but – as he himself made clear to me later – they realized we could never survive politically if we did so, and that resignation was inevitable. Heath admitted, when pressed by us, that he saw government at Stormont as eventually something along the lines of a county council or the Greater London Council. To us that was insulting and completely unacceptable. There was clearly no negotiable exit from the cul-de-sac into which we had been led, and no attempt was made to disguise this.

Jack Andrews issued a forceful warning that if they persisted in this course the Conservative Party and British Governments would never again be trusted by the people of Northern Ireland. When Heath escorted the Stormont team down to the door of No.10 at 9 p.m. he said to Faulkner quietly: 'You may assume that the Cabinet will reaffirm this decision tomorrow. They have made up their minds and there is no going back.' Faulkner knew then without any doubt that his Government must resign, and that Direct Rule had arrived. But before returning to Belfast the 'condemned men' ate a hearty meal of Aberdeen Angus rib of beef and baked Alaska at the Carlton Tower Hotel. There was much gallows humour, though Faulkner was preoccupied, thinking about the effects of that day's discussions: 'Our conversation was not bitter, but I do recall several references to the Downing Street caucus as "clots". We felt they simply did not understand what they had done. Shortly after midnight we arrived back in Belfast quite shattered by the long meeting and the bad news we brought.' Next morning the Stormont and Westminster Cabinets met almost simultaneously to consider the discussion of the previous day and make their final decisions.[31]

In Downing Street, Heath observed to his colleagues that, as regarded the longer term, Faulkner did not seem to realize the nature of the problem either of persuading the representatives of the minority to resume active participation in the political life of the Province or of re-establishing law and order in Londonderry. This attitude, on his part, coupled with the fact that his counter-proposals for immediate action would merely increase the responsibility of the UK Government without giving them any significantly greater control over public order and security in the Province, confronted the Cabinet with the need to make the final decision. Douglas-Home added that it was important to take account of the probable reactions of Lynch: he would almost certainly regard as unacceptable changes which did no more than give the UK Government some degree of joint control over security. He would welcome the transfer of responsibility for law and order; but he would endorse, above all, the imposition of a period of British rule. The mood of the Cabinet had changed in the face of Faulkner's perceived 'intransigence'. Around the table it was argued that there seemed to be no prospect of bringing violence to an end and re-establishing public order in Northern Ireland unless the IRA could be deprived of its base in the minority community and Lynch could be induced to institute sterner action against it in the Republic. It was therefore necessary to adopt whatever measures seemed best calculated to achieve these purposes and to create a fresh climate in which constructive discussions might be initiated. Moreover, the limited nature of Faulkner's counter-proposals suggested that he now had little freedom of political manoeuvre in relation to his own supporters who were reluctant to recognize the importance to British public opinion of a fresh start. The joint control of security policy would place the UK Government in an impossible position, while an arrangement which would give London little more than a say in decisions on the release of internees could not be expected to have sufficient impact to precipitate the radical change in political attitudes which was essential. The Cabinet now agreed, unanimously, that if Faulkner, after reference to his Cabinet, could not advance beyond his counter-proposals, he should be informed that these were not regarded as adequate by the United Kingdom Government, who accordingly felt obliged to proceed to implement their own intentions, including the transfer to Westminster of the responsibility for law and order. If Faulkner indicated that he could not remain in office, 'he should be told that the United Kingdom Government would have no alternative but to legislate for the introduction of direct United Kingdom rule in Northern Ireland and that this would entail the prorogation of the Northern Ireland Parliament and the assumption by a Secretary of State for Northern Ireland of the powers of the Northern Ireland Government.'[32]

At Stormont all the members of Faulkner's Cabinet, including John Taylor, who had been recovering in hospital, turned up in the Cabinet room that morning. Faulkner admitted to them frankly that 'I had been wrong about the intentions of the London Government; those who had said "There is no smoke without fire" had been proved right. I explained the proposals which had been put to us and our reaction to them.' The terms were impossible, agreed Bradford; 'we would be reduced to a bunch of marionettes.' The Attorney-General, Basil Kelly, said it was an almost universal practice in democracies for devolved Governments to have law and order powers. 'We must resign', said Herbie Kirk, and the other Ministers expressed assent. One Minister suggested Westminster should be made to throw them out of office, conducting a sort of protest sit-in in the Cabinet room, but Faulkner argued that would be an unworthy end to a Northern Ireland Government, and the idea was dropped. It was unanimously agreed that the Government would refuse to accept the terms.[33] As Bradford put it many years later:

> the thesis was, and one which I must say I accepted at the time, that the only distinction you can make between a county council and a government is that a government has control of law and order... You must remember that, in those days, we were dealing with a situation where nobody's mind had been prepared for this kind of fundamental change. Given the Unionist ethos at that time, it was just not conceivable that one would go on masquerading as a government when, in fact, powers of law and order had been removed.[34]

Faulkner rang Heath and told him of the meeting. The conversation was curt and to the point:[35]

PM	Hullo
Mr Faulkner	Hullo
PM	Brian?... Hullo. Its Ted. We're on an open line I think.
Mr Faulkner	Yes I can press the [scramble] button if you can.
PM	I don't think I can here. It may be more dangerous. Well, we had our meeting this morning which reaffirmed the position and I didn't know what happened at yours.
Mr Faulkner	We had our meeting and they were taking absolutely unanimously the view that I told you yesterday they would take.
PM	Well then the question is how we work out the next stage I think and obviously the sooner the better. Would you be able to come over?
Mr Faulkner	Yes.
PM	I think its difficult to do it on the phone.
Mr Faulkner	What form does the next stage take, in fact?
PM	That's really what I'd like to work out with you. Because I think in this situation it's very important we should get as far as we can together.
Mr Faulkner	Yes. Well when would you want me to come over?
PM	Well really as soon as you can if you can fly over as soon as you can get away now.
Mr Faulkner	Yes. I'll see what I can organise right away. I would want to bring Jack Andrews with me again.
PM	Yes do.
Mr Faulkner	We'll see what we can organise now and then come back to you and confirm.
PM	All right. That's splendid.
Mr Faulkner	All right.
PM	Thank you so much.[36]

At 4.15 p.m. Faulkner and his Ministers held another hastily summoned Cabinet meeting to agree on and sign a letter of resignation to Heath. G.B. Newe summed up his feelings by saying, 'I am very sad to see a Government of Irishmen being ended, but some day it will return again.' Faulkner and Andrews then flew to London, arriving at Downing Street at 7.45 p.m. The discussions did not take long. Faulkner agreed to stay in office until the necessary legislation instituting Direct Rule could be passed at Westminster, so that Northern Ireland should not, even for a few days, be without a lawful Government. He handed over his Cabinet's letter of resignation to take effect at that time. A 'farewell dinner' had been laid on for Faulkner and Andrews at Downing Street. It was for Faulkner 'a bit of a strain, but the normal chat about world and British affairs carried on around the table. I remember Ted Heath saying to Armstrong at one stage: "Get the Prime Minister another cup of coffee." I knew it was probably the last time he would ever refer to me by such a title. It was late when we took our leave and made our way back to Belfast, where the news of our impending resignation had already broken.' The next day, after Faulkner had returned to Northern Ireland, Heath made a detailed statement in the House of Commons at Westminster. Stormont was to be suspended for one year, plebiscites would be held on the Border question at 'intervals of a substantial period of years', and a start would be made to the phasing out of internment. William Whitelaw was to be the first Secretary of State for Northern Ireland, and when Jeremy Thorpe wished him well in his new task Whitelaw was seen to shed tears. In Northern Ireland, Craig and Vanguard called for a two-day Province-wide strike in protest against the suspension of Stormont and an estimated 200,000 workers responded on Monday and Tuesday 27 and 28 March, bringing the industrial life of the Province to a halt. In Dublin, Lynch welcomed the initiative and sent the Irish Ambassador back to London. The SDLP also welcomed the latest developments, and issued a statement urging a cessation of the terrorist campaign. On 27 March Faulkner addressed a meeting of the Ulster Unionist Council in Belfast, telling them that he had lost confidence in the Heath administration and denouncing the proposal for an 'Advisory Commission' of Ulster-men who would assist Whitelaw in governing Ulster. 'Northern Ireland is not a coconut colony; and no coconut commission will be able to muster any vestige of credibility or standing,' he said. It would be an 'undemocratic sham'. Faulkner urged people to rely on the strength of their numbers, the Unionist 'veto', and not to be led into any violent activity. It was an angry meeting. The next morning, 28 March, the commercial life of the Province remained at a standstill and a massive crowd, estimated at 100,000, gathered outside Stormont, many of them carrying Ulster flags alongside Union Jacks. It was the final day of self rule. Faulkner described the last hours of the Government and Parliament of Northern Ireland:

> Just before lunch we were holding our last meeting as a Northern Ireland Cabinet, and as news came in about the huge crowd which was gathering we decided that we must all go out on to the balcony of the building and speak to them and give them a lead. The doors on to the balcony led off the Members'

JUDGEMENT DAY – THE END OF STORMONT

dining-room on the first floor where most MPs were eating lunch. Bill Craig, who was scheduled to address the crowd immediately after lunch, was there with some friends. I had a quiet word with him and we agreed that we should both address the crowd separately. At 1.15 p.m. I led my Cabinet out on to the balcony from where we could see the huge crowd stretching away down the long sweep of Stormont's one-mile long lawns and driveway almost to the gates at Newtownards Road. A cheer went up, and I began to speak through the loudspeaker:

'People of Ulster, I am speaking to you still as Prime Minister of Northern Ireland. I want to say, not just on my own behalf, but on behalf of everyone of my colleagues in the Government and the Parliamentary Party here at Stormont, that we understand absolutely the feelings which have persuaded you to come out to Parliament Buildings today... we share the resentment that you feel... We have tremendous power. Our power is the power of our numbers; our power is the justice of our cause; our power is the responsibility of our conduct... Let us never play the game of the murderers of the IRA. Let us show the world that, so far as we are concerned, violence and intimidation are out... British we are, and British we remain!'

I had scarcely started to address the crowd before I became aware that Bill Craig had come out on to the balcony and was standing beside me. It was an awkward moment, because Craig's record of right-wing politics was not one with which I or most of my colleagues wished to be identified, and I knew that liberal Unionists such as Bailie and Bradford would be angry at finding themselves on a joint platform with him. It transpired later that some of Craig's associates, together with Herbie Kirk, the Minister of Finance, had pushed Craig out on to the balcony, believing that a show of solidarity against the suspension of Stormont would be useful. Craig, never a personally vindictive man, did his best to ease my situation. He spoke to the crowd, supporting what I had said, and adding that, whatever differences we had in the past, I had done my best and had been shamefully treated. 'We will all stand together to win back Stormont for Ulster', he said. Then he called for 'three cheers for the Prime Minister', and the crowd cheered loudly as Craig and I shook hands... The Stormont Parliament met for the last time that afternoon, while at Westminster a Second Reading was given to the Northern Ireland Temporary Provisions Bill by 483 votes to 18. We all went down from the Stormont balcony to the Commons as the crowd began to disperse peacefully, confident that their point had been made forcefully and effectively and that Westminster would have to pay attention. Procedure went ahead as usual, and there were no dramatic scenes as over fifty years of history came to an end. John Brooke, the acting Leader of the House, quoted in winding up the famous loyalist poem of Rudyard Kipling, 'Ulster 1912'. There was a general air of sadness, and an absence of the boisterous squabbling which had characterized some debates over the past few months. The adjournment of the House was moved for the Easter Recess as usual. I spoke briefly on the motion, paying tribute to the security forces, to the civil servants at Stormont who had served successive governments loyally and skilfully, and to my colleagues in the Cabinet:

'I conclude with this final word, as the Government of Ulster is about to pass, temporarily at least, into other hands. I have always been proud to lead the present team in Government but never so proud as last week. We stood firm and we stood together. When we faced a hard and unpalatable decision no hint of any other interest than the interest of the whole country was heard at the Cabinet Table. We did what we believed to be right, for that is the spirit in which Ulster should always be served.

Could I express the hope and, since I believe in its power, the prayer, that we will see peace and that it will be peace with justice in our native land.'[37]

The shock within the Unionist community as to what was happening was summed up by Sir Kenneth Bloomfield:

It was the British Parliament which had endowed us with all the panoply and apparatus that people called 'Prime Minister', 'Speaker of the House of Commons', 'Minister of Home Affairs'. Not surprising, then, that people in Northern Ireland had come to believe that that was their government. I find it striking that in those days, if you gathered together, for instance, all the Unionist politicians, the members of Westminster were very much the second position. The real focus of activity in the province was the Stormont ministers; they were top dogs.[38]

No longer. Faulkner recorded:

At 4.15 p.m. the House divided on the motion for the adjournment, four MPs registering a token protest against the situation in which we found ourselves, and twenty voting for the motion. At 5.15 p.m. the House stood adjourned, theoretically until after Easter, but in effect for at least one year. It was never to meet again.[39]

Notes

1. Taylor, *Brits*, p.88.
2. *Irish News*, 6 December 1971.
3. Taylor, *Brits*, pp.88–9.
4. McKittrick *et al.*, *Lost Lives*, pp.124–5.
5. NAI D/T 2003/16/461 Irish Government Statement, 30 January 1972.
6. NAI D/T 2003/16/461 Irish Government Statement, 31 January 1972.
7. *Irish Times*, 3 February 1972.
8. NAUK NAUK PRO PREM 15/1002 Northern Ireland: Current Situation Report No.71 – 7 February 1972.
9. NAUK PRO PREM 15/1002 Northern Ireland: Current Situation Report No.75 – 11 February 1972.
10. NAUK PRO CAB 128/48 CM (72) 5th Conclusions Minute 3; 3 February 1972.
11. NAUK PRO PREM 15/1002 Douglas-Home to Peck, 18 February 1972.
12. *Irish Times*, 21 February 1972.
13. Faulkner, *Memoirs*, pp.142–4.
14. Ibid., pp.145–6.
15. Ibid. pp.146–7.

16. PRONI CAB 4/1639/5 Memorandum by the Prime Minister as Minister of Home Affairs on Internment 18 February 1972
17. NAUK PRO PREM 15/1002 Heath-Maudling Meeting, 22 February 1972.
18. Faulkner, *Memoirs*, pp.147–9.
19. NAUK PRO CAB 129/168 CP(72) 26 Northern Ireland: Memorandum by the Secretary of State for the Home Department, 3 March 1972.
20. NAUK PRO CAB 128/48 CM (72) 13th Conclusions, 7 March 1972.
21. NAUK PRO PREM 15/1004 Douglas-Home to the Prime Minister, 13 March 1972.
22. NAUK PRO CAB 129/48 CM(72) 14th Conclusions Minute 5; 9 March 1972.
23. NAUK PRO CAB 128/48 CM(72) 15th Conclusions Minute 1; 14 March 1972.
24. PRONI CAB 4/1646/16 Proposals for a Political Settlement. Supplementary Notes of Cabinet Discussion, 21 March 1972.
25. CCBH British Policy in Northern Ireland 1970–1974.
26. Faulkner, *Memoirs*, p.151.
27. PRONI CAB 4/1646/17 Main Points made by Mr Heath at the Downing Street Meeting on 22 March 1972 about the Northern Ireland Situation.
28. PRONI CAB/4/1648/18 Later Statement by Mr Heath in the Discussion in which he defined the United Kingdom Government's Ideas.
29. Faulkner, *Memoirs*, p.152.
30. NAUK PRO CAB 128/48 CM(72) 18th Conclusions Minute 3; 23 March 1972.
31. Faulkner, *Memoirs*, pp.152–3.
32. NAUK PRO CAB 128/48 CM(72) 18th Conclusions Minute 3; 23 March 1972.
33. Faulkner, *Memoirs*, pp.153–4.
34. CCBH British Policy in Northern Ireland 1970–1974.
35. Faulkner, *Memoirs of a Statesman*, pp.153–4.
36. NAUK PRO PREM 15/1034 Record of a Telephone Conversation Between the Prime Minister and the Prime Minister of Northern Ireland, Thursday 23 March 1972.
37. Faulkner, *Memoirs*, pp.157–9.
38. CCBH British Policy in Northern Ireland 1964–1970 Witness Seminars 14 January 1992.
39. Faulkner, *Memoirs*, pp.157–9.

Conclusion

Between the beginning of 1970 and early 1972, the evolution of the Troubles was that from a communal conflict into an insurgency. The principal agents in the latter were the Provisional IRA and the British state; caught in between were the Catholic and Protestant communities. It is the contention of this author that the 'real' Troubles are the conflict between Protestants and Catholics within Northern Ireland and the conflict between Nationalism and Unionism on the island of Ireland generally. The presence of the British state in Ireland distorts this core division somewhat, but it is an unavoidable one. Whatever the sins of colonialism, by the 1970s the British state was locked into a political commitment to uphold the Union as long as the majority of those in Northern Ireland wanted it.

The internal contradiction of the Northern Irish state – a discriminated, alienated and substantial minority dominated by a majority expressing a bipolar complex of ascendancy and insecurity – always had the potential for implosion. The Provisional IRA was born out of the events of August 1969. But it was the Provos' decision – by traditionalists wedded to forcing the British out of Ireland – that turned the 'natural' communal antagonism borne of history into another conflict, almost a conflict within a conflict, that obscured the original fault lines for nearly three decades. Before British security responses became more aggressive – repression in the eyes of many within the Catholic population – the Provisionals had initiated an insurgency against the British occupation of the North. British troops on the streets provided a historic opportunity for the Provisionals to engage the physical manifestation of the British state – responsible, in their view, for the artificial partition of Ireland and the denial of Irish national self-determination. Many of those drawn into the IRA at this stage had a connection – family, previous service – with the Movement already. The Provisionals were less a new army than a spin-off from traditional militant Republicanism. The world trend seemed to be against imperialism. The Provisional leadership took heart from the retreat of the British from their empire, often after counter-insurgency campaigns. But the lessons they took from these were poor ones. Apart from Aden, British counter-insurgency campaigns were remarkably successful: the fact of decolonization following a counter-insurgency campaign did not mean the British had been defeated. Decolonization occurred for a variety of reasons. But Northern Ireland was a part of the United Kingdom. This made a fundamental difference. The colonial origins of English-British involvement in Ireland might be accurate but the North had been part of the UK since before the Battles of Trafalgar and Waterloo.

The Provisionals could not have flourished without the continuing disorder on the streets. Partly, this emanated from a collapse in the respect for authority, a hangover from the riots of August 1969; partly from continuing sectarian tensions; but also, partly, from attempts to ensure confrontation between the British Army and the Catholic community – particularly in Belfast. Yet it is clear the Catholic community in Belfast was not a monolithic entity alienated by state repression. There was anger and frustration from within that community at deliberate attempts to create conflict with the Army. Catholic opinion was fluid: alienation – some of it permanent – occurred after incidents such as the Falls Road Curfew; but equally Catholic–Army relations could improve dramatically – as happened with the floods that engulfed Belfast later in the year. Much of course depended upon which regiment was doing its tour of duty at the time. But the IRA had one great advantage over the Security Forces that all insurgents have – a military force cannot stand idly by during an insurgency. Passivity would not halt the bombing campaign and the increasing use of firearms against the Security Forces.

The Falls Road Curfew may have alienated many within the Catholic community but there is ample evidence that it checked the aggression of both IRA factions – for a while at least as they regrouped. Raids for arms by the British Army were inevitable. The ending of house searches would not have meant no IRA violence: Republicans were committed to armed struggle. It was inevitable that there would be Catholic anger over these raids; but not to conduct them would have allowed the IRA to prepare for offensive operations with impunity. After the events of late June 1970, when the Army almost lost control of Belfast, the military had to respond. The popularly perceived defensive actions by the IRA in June obscures the fact that over a hundred Protestants and British soldiers were wounded by, mainly, Republicans. When one includes Republican actions during the Curfew, IRA tactics appear more like an early offensive against the British. This does not excuse the unacceptable behaviour of some soldiers during the Curfew: it merely illustrates the point that paramilitary force is met with military force. It is the nature of low intensity war that civilians are caught in the middle, although Freeland's tactics, on this occasion, were an illustration on how not to conduct urban counter-insurgency in terms of winning hearts and minds.

The belief that the change in security policy was brought about by the election of the new Conservative Government of Edward Heath is a myth – an understandable one on the part of the Catholic population but a myth nonetheless. What changed was the nature of the violence: for the first time firearms and explosives, in June and July 1970, had been directed at the Security Forces. The nature of the Republican threat had changed. The Catholic community was to be caught, increasingly, in the middle. The only group to gain by this were the Provisionals. As Cardinal Conway pointed out: an army is a 'blunt instrument'. The British Army was trained for global war against Warsaw Pact forces on the Continent. It had, it's true, much experience in Internal Security operations. But this was what the soldiers disliked most. They were not trained, primarily, to be a police force. Yet this is what the military found themselves engaged as. But, unlike in previous counter-insurgency operations, the British Army now found itself in an evolving urban guerrilla war. The security situation ended the valiant attempt by Sir Arthur Young to turn the RUC from a paramilitary police force into a civilian police service. This created no end of tension between Young and his military counterpart Sir Ian Freeland who wanted the police to take an increasing role in riot control. The attempt to create a civilian, unarmed police service, on the British model, was a sincere attempt by Young, his senior officers and the Labour and Tory Governments in London. But it was doomed to failure.

There was no security solution to the problems in Northern Ireland. This was recognized, quite early on, by the military and the politicians in London. A key problem that London faced was the continuing disunity within the Ulster Unionist Party. As the dominant loyalist organization in Protestant politics, by an Irish mile, it contained all forms of Unionist opinion. For so long masters in their own house, the level of violence leading up to internment was unprecedented. Critics of the Northern Ireland Government, such as Paisley and Craig, offered simple solutions for complex problems. The only way to defeat an insurgency is a combination of coercion to contain the level of violence while at the same time seeking a political solution. Chichester-Clark made a valiant attempt to hold the liberal line within the party; but, like O'Neill before him, he was driven from office. The issue was not reform but security. The Prime Minister was helpless as he tried to bring home to his supporters the reality of the Belfast–London relationship. Both Craig and Paisley gave the impression that the solution was simply the resurrection of the 'B' men. It should be noted here that, although both men articulated grassroots Unionist disaffection, both men remained on the periphery. The only agency that could have brought home the reality of the London–Belfast relationship was London. This would have meant Direct Rule.

In retrospect it is easy to see that Faulkner's premiership was doomed from the outset. He lacked the confidence of the SDLP with his 'tricky Dickie' image associated with his Damascus-like conversion to liberal Unionism. There seems little reason to doubt his commitment to reform; the problem was the limited nature of reform that any Unionist politician could contemplate in the circumstances. Faulkner could not concede any form of executive power-sharing to Nationalists and hope to survive in office. The UUP would never have allowed it even if the Prime Minister had desired it. And he did not. Faulkner never moved beyond having non-Republican Catholics in Cabinet. For him 'Republican' meant all Nationalists committed to a united Ireland including the SDLP. And this was the crux of the matter: the absence of this sort of Catholic, not only in the Cabinet, but also in the appointments to state bodies.

On the streets, the British Army could not defeat the IRA. But it could contain it. Progress in the political sphere depended on the actions of the British Government. The crucial difference between the Labour and Conservative Governments was that James Callaghan claimed, had Labour been returned to power in 1970, that he would have been prepared to enact Direct Rule. Callaghan claimed this from the Opposition benches and it is easy to be wise after the event. But there is evidence to back up his assertions: in 1969 he was prepared to introduce Direct Rule if necessary and he had hoped that a coalition Government of Unionists and Nationalists could be formed. But, in 1971, Callaghan was not Home Secretary. Reginald Maudling was. Maudling was no Callaghan when it came to Northern Ireland. And Heath began his premiership with a commitment to greater autonomy for the Stormont Government. The most interesting aspect of British policy is that, even in March 1972, during the Heath–Faulkner discussions in London, the UK Prime Minister was still prepared to allow a majority-rule Government at Stormont to continue – minus security powers (a policy Faulkner rejected, seemingly unaware that Chichester-Clark had mooted the possibility in 1969 without feeling the need to resign). Even after Bloody Sunday, and with much internal discussion suggesting Direct Rule as the first step towards greater participation for the Catholic minority in Government, Heath and Maudling would not take this step if it could be avoided.

Heath's greatest error was acceding to Faulkner's request to introduce internment in August 1971. This was the point at which Direct Rule should have been introduced. It is hard to imagine the previous administration introducing internment before Direct Rule. The decision to implement was a political one: Carver and Tuzo opposed it. Heath, Maudling, Home and Carrington – the senior UK Ministers responsible – made the decision to avoid Direct Rule. The extraordinary element of this decision was that the Ministers concerned took it with little hope of success and with resignation that it would fail to quell the violence.

Internment was a political disaster. It was not a military disaster. The intelligence provided by RUC Special Branch was, overall, poor in identifying Provisional IRA suspects. A minority of internees were Provisionals – but not all small fry. CALABA – deep interrogation – proved a success in giving the Security Forces the Provisional order of battle. The quality of the information was what was crucial here. For the first time the Security Forces knew who was who and had the identifiable targets that Special Branch had been unable to supply. Without having the cumbersome normal legal framework to operate in, the Security Forces could just 'lift' suspects. And they did. Attrition of both IRA factions was the primary military policy: while the Army was hopelessly wrong in compiling the number of IRA Volunteers it shot, detention was a much more accurate benchmark. And by January 1972, attrition was showing results. The short-term increase in the level of violence, most notably in shootings and deaths, together with the number of explosions rather than the nature of those explosions, has distorted the reality of violence. One explosion, however small, should not be confused with the fact that the quantity of explosive yield fell considerably by the beginning of 1972. Likewise the IRA were switching targets, including 'softer' options by attacking off-duty members of the Security Forces. Higher casualties were inevitable. The idea that, militarily, internment was working – in reducing but never able to eliminate violence – is a conclusion that many will find hard to accept; however, it is time for a reassessment.

But internment only increased Catholic alienation within an already alienated community. The SDLP appeared unclear on what to do apart from oppose most of what the ruling Protestant party proposed. This was hardly surprising considering how, since the statelet's inception, the minority had been excluded from power. And they remained excluded. Faulkner's offer of representation on Parliamentary committees (the idea for which originated in Chichester-Clark's term) was welcome but it did not alter the fundamental problem: the undemocratic nature of the statelet. Normal, British, notions of democracy – involving the ability of more than one party to hold power – did not exist in Northern Ireland. The equalling of party allegiance with sectarian division made instability inevitable. The only agency capable of resolving this was the British Government. The only factor that could move the British Government was continuing unrest. It made sense, from London's point of view, to avoid Direct Rule in 1969. It did not in 1971. And here is the crucial *political* difference between the Labour and Conservative administrations. The only other actor capable of acting as ballast to London was Dublin.

Following the Arms Crisis of 1970, Jack Lynch was master in his own house and had become a Taoiseach of some substance. Both Lynch, and John Hume, in the North, argued that some sort of power-sharing mechanism had to replace the unjust nature of majority rule. The minority community had to have a stake in the running of Northern Ireland. This analysis went straight to the heart of the problem of the communal divide in the North; both saw that this could not be achieved without the end of Stormont in its current form. Yet this could not be achieved without continuing IRA violence. Without it there would be no incentive for London to intervene.

But it should also be noted that, despite Dublin and the SDLP emphasizing to London that their primary aim was to end Catholic alienation within Northern Ireland by giving the minority a role in executive Government, it was also the case that Dublin, and Hume, consciously decided that the political situation provided the opportunity to push for structures that would lead to a united Ireland. From now on Dublin and the SDLP's policy would not be limited to reforming Northern Ireland but also creating the conditions for absorbing it into a united Ireland. All of this fell into a common Nationalist interpretation of Unionism as based upon ascendancy and privilege – not a sense of British national consciousness. With the removal of Stormont the way was open to put unity back on the agenda. It was at this point – 1970–71 – that partition re-emerged as a live issue, not during the Civil Rights era. Unity was back on the agenda for Dublin and the SDLP.

It was back on the agenda because, with the Tories in power in London, and Faulkner in power at Stormont, Nationalists had lost all faith they had in the impartiality of either. Faulkner's statement, in May 1971, that seemed to indicate a relaxation of the Army's rules of engagement was a political, not a policy, statement. The audience was the 'law-abiding' members of the population. But it created the impression that there had been a change in policy. When the two young men were shot dead by the Army in Derry it appeared to Catholics that the new policy was being implemented. The deaths were an unfortunate coincidence. The change had come not with new British Army tactics but with the launch of a new IRA offensive. The military's policy up to and during the offensive remained that of minimum force. But the reality of this was lost: one policy that continually upset Catholics of all persuasions was the persistent refusal of the British to hold any independent inquiry into lethal force killings by state forces. Whether it was the Army themselves or the RUC, there was an institutional sympathy for the plight of the soldiers.

To contain and to pursue a policy of attrition against the IRA the Catholic community, in Belfast in particular, were the meat in the sandwich. The British Army could not be passive in the face of a growing insurgency. The suspension of arms raids, for example, would have merely left the field to the IRA. Despite Nationalist claims to the contrary there was no alternative. As long as the IRA were fixed on a growing insurgency some degree of Catholic communal alienation was inevitable. But Unionist claims that the Security Forces were soft on violence were equally wide of the mark. Internment increased Catholic alienation to unprecedented levels but could not eliminate violence. The fact, unpalatable for Nationalists and Unionists alike, is that the British Army's response prior to internment was at the correct level to meet the threat. Unionists could not grasp that this was a different form of insurgency to what they had faced in 1956–62: the genesis of urban guerrilla war. And, unlike the Border Campaign that failed because of a lack of Northern Catholic support, Belfast and Derry had been radicalized by August 1969. Calls from Craig and Paisley for the Army to be let off the leash took no account of this; the call for the RUC to take a more proactive lead in quelling disturbances (something the Army wanted also) took no account of the fact that the police were a demoralised force that would take a long time to rebuild – either as an acceptable force to Catholics or as an effective security agency. Maudling's comment that a certain level of violence had to be accepted was not a consul of despair: it was a statement of realpolitik. Some situations had to be endured, however unpleasant.

By late 1971 and early 1972 the Provisional IRA, in Belfast, was under severe pressure with mounting losses of men and material. This had necessitated a shift in tactics including the opening of another 'front' on the Border. 'Spectacular' bombing attacks, such as the carnage caused by several city centre explosions – combined with small devices timed to make the main news bulletin – illustrate how the conflict was as much about propaganda as anything else. Belfast, though, remained the primary theatre of British Army operations. Derry was of secondary importance – although doing nothing there was not an option as part of the city had virtually ceded from the authority of the British state. This was, of course, quite an achievement from a Catholic point of view and demonstrated the protracted nature of the Northern Ireland problem. But this was unacceptable from the state's point of view: one of the two principal functions of a state is to maintain internal order (the other being to repel external aggression).

Up to January 1972, a relatively gentle touch had been applied to Derry yet had yielded no tangible results – beyond further encroachment towards the perceived destruction of the city centre. The NICRA march of January 1972 presented the military with an opportunity to mount an arrest operation against the, up to now, immune rioters. There was no question of deliberately shooting rioters – not in the United Kingdom anyway. But it is also apparent that individual soldiers acted in breach of Yellow Card rules of engagement – sometimes condoned by their officers. In these circumstances the issue is whether or not 1 PARA were the correct unit to be deployed in Derry to conduct the arrest operation. For Major General Robert Ford the decision was simple: they were the most effective anti-riot unit in Belfast, proven time and again. They were also the only fully operational Province reserve force. But there were genuine concerns over the aggression shown by 1 PARA. It could be said that this aggression is what made them so feared on the streets of Belfast. But in Derry they would not be operating on what had, in the capital, become their own turf.

At this point there are certain things that can be said of the background to Bloody Sunday: there was no conspiracy to teach the Catholic population of Derry a lesson – as Martin McGuiness suggested; there was no conspiracy by the Army to kill civilians or draw the IRA into a fire-fight; and there certainly was no Government conspiracy to do either of these things. In fact the arrest operation, on the day, should never have been launched. The trigger for the operation – the separation of rioters and peaceful marchers – never occurred. But 1 PARA were ordered in anyway. Very soon after they began arresting marchers the soldiers of 1 PARA claimed they came under fire. Under their rules of engagement they were permitted to return fire. But did they come under fire? The balance of probabilities is that they did: civilian gunmen were active in the lead up to the launching of the arrest operation. This is undeniable given the variety of civilian, never mind security force, witnesses. It follows from this that one, or both, IRA factions lied when they claimed that *all* of their weapons were accounted for. Clearly they were not and members of one or both IRA factions engaged the British Army on Bloody Sunday – for certain prior, and in parallel, to the arrest operation.

Even if the troops come under fire, did this justify 1 PARA's response? It can not. The number of gunshot wounds inflicted by the soldiers appears out of all proportion to the threat level. 1 PARA was one of the toughest and most experienced battalions in the British Army. It seems hard to believe that such an experienced unit could panic and lose control. Yet there seems to have been a breakdown in discipline. The best that can be said is that, in an alien environment the paratroopers who opened fire saw threats from all quarters once they had been fired upon: rocks became nail bombs; rifles were seen peering out from barricades when in fact there were none. The alternative was that this was murder. Somewhere between the two is probably the truth.

But was there a cover up on the part of the Widgery Tribunal? On the balance of the evidence I have seen I would conclude that there was not. What there was, on the other hand, was an institutional bias in favour of the agents of the state: Widgery, together with the Prime Minister, Heath, and many of the Cabinet, had served their country in the great crusade against Nazism. Their view of the British Army had, to some degree, been shaped by this experience. Heath's interview with Widgery, at Downing Street, before the latter had begun his journey to Derry should be seen less as interference in due legal process and more in the context of his reaction to the Compton Report. Heath instinctively *knew* that the professionalism of the British Army was second to none and that it was up against an effective IRA propaganda machine. The problem with Heath reminding Widgery of the nature of the IRA propaganda machine is that it exposes the inherent problem with British inquiries of this type: they were British inquiries. It is not surprising that there was an institutional sympathy for the military. This was compounded by the nature in which evidence was collected by the military police: it favoured the soldiers. Add the flawed forensics – Widgery had no reason to doubt their validity – and his conclusions are easier to understand: wrong though they were. The flaw in the inquiry was that it could not be wholly impartial. It would be a long time before a British Government could contemplate an inquiry including non-British elements to counter any potential institutional bias.

Bloody Sunday did not lead to Direct Rule. Debate about the future of Stormont had begun well before this. But when Direct Rule came it left the Unionist community in a state of shock. After fifty years of ruling the roost they were without power in their own land. Although Nationalists had urged action against Protestant paramilitaries, the Security Forces were agreed that a coherent loyalist terrorist threat was just not there. But, very soon after internment, evidence of a threat from that source became apparent – not least in the form of mass murder by the UVF (reconstituting itself after the setback of losing its essence in the arrests of 1966) – in December 1971. Already many Protestant vigilantes had formed themselves into an umbrella organization: the Ulster Defence Association in September 1971. Protestant frustration at the loss of their precious B-Specials; the apparent inability of reforms to placate Catholics; the inability of the Security Forces to quell insurrection; and now the loss of their Parliament and the control of their own destiny meant that elements within that community could hold back no longer as they were, seemingly, slipping towards a united Ireland. Despite the dismissal of it by some, a Protestant backlash had already begun, and would accelerate in 1972, exacting a terrible price on, mainly, the innocent. But there would be one more opportunity to settle the Irish Question.

Select Bibliography

PRIMARY SOURCES

National Archives of the United Kingdom: Public Record Office (NAUK PRO)
CAB   Cabinet Office
PREM   Prime Minister's Office
DEFE   Ministry of Defence
FCO   Foreign and Commonwealth Office

Public Record Office of Northern Ireland (PRONI).
CAB   Cabinet Records

National Archives of Ireland (NAI)
Department of the Taoiseach (D/T)
Department of Foreign Affairs (DFA)

Bloody Sunday Inquiry (BSI)
Witness Statements
Expert Witness Statements

Periodicals & Newspapers
An Phoblacht
Belfast Telegraph
News Letter
Irish News
Irish Times

Memoirs and Autobiographies
Bloomfield, Ken, *Stormont in Crisis: A Memoir* (Belfast: 1994).
Brady, Seamus, *Arms and the Men* (Wicklow: 1971).
Callaghan, James, *A House Divided. The Dilemma of Northern Ireland* (London: 1973).
Campbell, T.J., *Fifty Years of Ulster: 1890–1940* (Belfast: 1941).
Currie, Austin, *All Hell Will Break Loose* (Dublin: 2004).
Devlin, Bernadette, *The Price of My Soul* (London: 1969).
Devlin, Paddy, *The Fall of the NI Executive* (Belfast: 1975).
Devlin, Paddy, *Straight Left: An Autobiography* (Belfast: 1993).
Doherty, Paddy, *Paddy Bogside* (Cork: 2001).

Faulkner, Brian, *Memoirs of a Statesman* (London: 1978).
FitzGerald, Garret, *All in a Life* (Dublin: 1991).
McCann, Eamon, *War in an Irish Town* (London: 1980).
MacStiofain, Sean, *Revolutionary in Ireland* (Farnborough: 1974).
O'Neill, Terence, *The Autobiography of Terence O'Neill* (London: 1972).
Shea, Patrick, *Voices and the Sound of Drums: An Irish Autobiography* (Belfast: 1981).
Wilson, Harold *The Labour Government 1964–1970. A Personal Record* (London: 1971).

Books, Articles and Chapters

Adams, Gerry, *The Politics of Irish Freedom* (Dublin: 1986).
Adams, Gerry, *Free Ireland: Towards a Lasting Peace* (Dublin: 1995).
Adamson, Ian, *The Identity of Ulster* (Belfast: 1982).
Anderson, Don, *14 May Days: The Inside Story of the Loyalist Strike of 1974* (Dublin: 1994).
Arthur, Paul, *The People's Democracy 1968–73* (Belfast: 1974).
Arthur, Paul, *Government and Politics of Northern Ireland* (Essex: 1980).
Arthur, Paul and Keith Jeffrey, *Northern Ireland since 1968* (Oxford: 1988).
Aughey, Arthur, *Under Siege: Ulster Unionism and the Anglo-Irish Agreement* (Belfast: 1989).
Aughey, Arthur, 'Unionism and Self-Determination', in Patrick J. Roche and Brian Barton (eds), *The Northern Ireland Question: Myth and Reality* (Aldershot: 1991).
Bardon, Jonathan, *A History of Ulster* (Belfast: 1992).
Barritt, D.P. and Charles F. Carter, *The Northern Ireland Problem: A Study in Group Relations* (Oxford: 1962).
Barton, Brian, *Brookeborough: The Making of a Prime Minister* (Belfast: 1988).
Barton, Brian, *Northern Ireland in the Second World War* (Belfast: 1995).
Barzilay, David, *The British Army in Ulster Volume 1* (Belfast: 1973).
Bell, Desmond, *Acts of Union: Youth Culture and Sectarianism in Northern Ireland* (London: 1990).
Bell, J. Bowyer, *The Secret Army: The IRA 1916–1979* (Dublin: 1979).
Bell, J. Bowyer, *The Irish Troubles: A Generation of Violence 1967–1992* (Dublin: 1993).
Beresford, David, *Ten Men Dead: The Story of the 1981 Irish Hunger Strike* (London: 1987).
Bew, Paul, *Conflict and Conciliation in Ireland 1890–1910: Parnellites and Radical Agrarians* (Oxford: 1987).
Bew, Paul and Gordon Gillespie, *Northern Ireland: A Chronology of the Troubles 1968–1993* (Dublin: 1993).
Bew, Paul and Gordon Gillespie, *The Northern Ireland Peace Process 1993–1996: A Chronology* (London: 1996).
Bew, Paul, Kenneth Darwin and Gordon Gillespie, *Passion and Prejudice: Nationalist–Unionist Conflict in Ulster in the 1930s and the Foundation of the Irish Association* (Belfast: 1993).

Bew, Paul, Peter Gibbon and Henry Patterson, *Northern Ireland: Political Forces and Social Classes 1921–1994* (London: 1995).
Bew, Paul, Henry Patterson and Paul Teague, *Northern Ireland: Between War and Peace. The Political Future of Northern Ireland* (London: 1997).
Birrell, Derek and Alan Murie, *Policy and Government in Northern Ireland: Lessons of Devolution* (Dublin: 1980).
Bishop, Patrick and Eamon Mallie, *The Provisional IRA* (London: 1987).
Bowman, John, *De Valera and the Ulster Question 1917–1973* (Oxford: 1982).
Boyce, D.G., 'British Conservative Opinion, The Ulster Question and the Partition of Ireland, 1912–1921', *Irish Historical Studies*, 65, XVII (1970).
Boyce, D.G., 'British Opinion, Ireland and the War', *Historical Journal*, 3, 17 (1974).
Boyce, D.G., *Nationalism in Ireland* (London: 1982).
Boyce, D.G., *The Irish Question and British Politics 1868–1986* (London: 1988).
Boyce, D.G. (ed.), *The Revolution in Ireland 1879–1923* (London: 1988).
Boyce, D.G., 'Edward Carson and Irish Unionism', in Ciaran Brady (ed.), *Worsted in the Game: Losers in Irish History* (Dublin: 1989).
Boyce, D.G., *Nineteenth-Century Ireland: The Search for Stability* (Dublin: 1991).
Boyce, D.G. and John Stubbs, 'F.S. Oliver, Lord Shelbourne and Federalism', *Journal of Imperial and Commonwealth History*, 5 (1976).
Boyce, D.G., R. Eccleshall and V. Geoghegan (eds), *Political Thought in Ireland Since the Seventeenth Century* (London: 1993).
Boyd, Andrew, *Brian Faulkner and the Crisis of Ulster Unionism* (Kerry: 1972).
Boyle, Kevin and Tom Hadden, *Ireland: A Positive Proposal* (Harmondsworth: 1985).
Boyle, Kevin and Tom Hadden, *Northern Ireland: the Choice* (London: 1994).
Brewer, John D., with Kathleen Magee, *Inside the RUC: Routine Policing in a Divided Society* (Oxford: 1991).
Brooke, Peter, *Ulster Presbyterianism: The Historical Perspective 1610–1970* (Dublin: 1987).
Bruce, Steve, *God Save Ulster! The Religion and Politics of Paisleyism* (Oxford: 1986).
Bruce, Steve, *The Red Hand: Protestant Paramilitaries in Northern Ireland* (Oxford: 1992).
Bruce, Steve, 'Loyalists in Northern Ireland: Further Thoughts on "Pro-State Terror"', *Terrorism and Political Violence*, 5, 4 (Winter 1993), pp.262–3.
Bruce, Steve, *The Edge of the Union: The Ulster Loyalist Political Vision* (Oxford: 1994).
Bruce, Steve and Fiona Alderdice, 'Religious Belief and Behaviour', in Peter Stringer and Gillian Robinson (eds), *Social Attitudes in Northern Ireland: The Third Report 1992–1993* (Belfast: 1993).
Bryson, Lucy and Clem McCartney, *Clashing Symbols? A Report on the use of Flags, Anthems and other National Symbols in Northern Ireland* (Belfast: 1994).

SELECT BIBLIOGRAPHY

Buckland, Patrick, *Irish Unionism 1: The Anglo-Irish and the New Ireland 1885–1922* (Dublin: 1972).
Buckland, Patrick, *Irish Unionism 2: Ulster Unionism and the Origins of Northern Ireland 1886–1922* (Dublin: 1973).
Buckland, Patrick, *Irish Unionism 1885–1923: A Documentary History* (Belfast: 1973).
Buckland, Patrick, *The Factory of Grievances: Devolved Government in Northern Ireland 1921–39* (Dublin: 1979).
Buckland, Patrick, *James Craig, Lord Craigavon* (Dublin: 1980).
Buckland, Patrick, *A History of Northern Ireland* (Dublin: 1981).
Budge, Ian and Cornelius O'Leary, *Belfast: Approach to Crisis: A Study of Belfast Politics 1613–1970* (London: 1973).
Burton, Frank, *The Politics of Legitimacy: Struggles in a Belfast Community* (London: 1978).
Campbell, Brian, Laurence McKeown and Felim O'Hagan (eds), *Nor Meekly Serve My Time: The H-Block Struggle 1976–1981* (Belfast: 1994).
Campbell, Colm, *Emergency Law in Ireland 1918–1925* (Oxford: 1994).
Carver, Michael, *Out of Step. Memoirs of a Field Marshall* (London: 1989).
Cash, John D., *Identity, Ideology and Conflict: the Structuration of Politics in Northern Ireland* (Cambridge: 1996).
Cathcart, Rex, *The Most Contrary Region: The BBC in Northern Ireland 1924–1984* (Belfast: 1984).
Coldrey, B.M., *Faith and Fatherland: The Christian Brothers and the Development of Irish Nationalism 1838–1921* (Dublin: 1988).
Connolly, Michael, *Politics and Policy Making in Northern Ireland* (London: 1990).
Connolly, Michael and Andrew Erridge, 'Central Government in Northern Ireland', in M.E.H. Connolly and S. Loughlin (eds), *Public Policy in Northern Ireland: Adoption or Adaption?* (Belfast and Coleraine: 1990).
Coogan, Tim Pat, *The IRA* (London: 1970).
Coogan, Tim Pat, *Michael Collins: A Biography* (London: 1990).
Coogan, Tim Pat, *De Valera: Long Fellow, Long Shadow* (London: 1993).
Coogan, Tim Pat, *The Troubles: Ireland's Ordeal 1966–1995 and the Search for Peace* (London: 1995).
Cormack, R.J. and R.D. Osborne (eds), *Religion, Education and Employment: Aspects of Equal Opportunity in Northern Ireland* (Belfast: 1983).
Cormack, R.J. and R.D. Osborne (eds), *Discrimination and Public Policy in Northern Ireland* (Oxford: 1991).
Cormack, R.J. and R.D. Osborne, 'The Evolution of a Catholic Middle Class', in Adrian Guelke (ed.), *New Perspectives on the Northern Ireland Conflict* (Aldershot: 1994), pp. 67–76.
Cormack, R.J. and Robert Osborne, 'Education in Northern Ireland: The Struggle for Equality', in Patrick Clancy, Sheelagh Drudy, Kathleen Lynch and Liam O'Dowd (eds), *Irish Society: Sociological Perspectives* (Dublin: 1995).
Coulter, Colin, 'The Character of Unionism', *Irish Political Studies*, 9 (1994) pp.1–24.

Crawford, Colin, *Inside the UDA. Volunteers and Violence* (London: 2003).
Crawford, Robert G., *Loyal to King Billy: A Portrait of the Ulster Protestants* (Dublin: 1987).
Crozier, Maurna (ed.), *Cultural Traditions in Northern Ireland: Varieties of Irishness* (Belfast: 1989).
Crozier, Maurna (ed.), *Cultural Traditions in Northern Ireland: Varieties of Britishness* (Belfast: 1990).
Crozier, Maurna (ed.), *Cultural Traditions in Northern Ireland: All Europeans Now?* (Belfast: 1991).
Cunningham, Michael J., *British Government Policy in Northern Ireland 1969–89: Its Nature and Execution* (Manchester: 1991).
Curran, Frank, *Derry: Countdown to Disaster* (Dublin: 1986).
Cusack, Jim and Max Taylor, 'The Resurgence of a Terrorist Organization – Part 1 the UDA, A Case Study', *Terrorism and Political Violence*, 5, 3 (Autumn 1993).
Daly, Cathal, *The Price of Peace* (Belfast: 1991).
Darby, John, *Northern Ireland: the Background to the Conflict* (Belfast: 1983).
Darby, John, *Intimidation and the Control of Conflict* (Dublin: 1986).
Darby, John, 'Legitimate Targets: a Control on Violence?', in Adrian Guelke (ed.), *New Perspectives on the Northern Ireland Conflict* (Aldershot: 1994).
Davis, Richard, *Arthur Griffith and Non-Violent Sinn Féin* (Tralee: 1974).
de Baroid, Ciaran, *Ballymurphy and the Irish War* (Dublin: 1989).
Duggan, John P., *A History of the Irish Army* (Dublin: 1991).
Dunlop, John, *A Precarious Belonging: Presbyterians and the Conflict in Ireland* (Belfast: 1995).
Dunn, Seamus and Thomas Hennessey, 'Ireland', in T.G. Fraser and Seamus Dunn (eds), *Europe and Ethnicity: World War One and Contemporary Ethnic Conflict* (London: 1996).
Dunn, Seamus and Valerie Morgan, *Protestant Alienation in Northern Ireland: A Preliminary Survey* (Coleraine: 1994).
Dwyer, T. Ryle, *Eamon de Valera* (Dublin: 1980).
Eames, Robin, *Chains to be Broken: A Personal Reflection on Northern Ireland and its People* (London: 1992).
Edwards, Ruth Dudley, *Patrick Pearse: The Triumph of Failure* (Dublin: 1977).
English, Richard, *Armed Struggle. A History of the IRA* (London: 2003).
English, Richard and Graham Walker, *Unionism in Modern Ireland: New Perspectives on Politics and Culture* (Dublin: 1996).
Ervine, St John, *Craigavon, Ulsterman* (London: 1949).
Eversley, David, *Religion and Employment in Northern Ireland* (London: 1989).
Farrell, Brian, *The Founding of Dáil Éireann: Parliament and Nation-Building* (Dublin: 1971).
Farrell, Michael, *Northern Ireland: The Orange State* (London: 1976).
Farrell, Michael, *Arming the Protestants: The Formation of the Ulster Special Constabulary and the Royal Ulster Constabulary 1920–27* (London: 1983).
Fisk, Robert, *In Time of War: Ireland, Ulster and the Price of Neutrality* (London: 1985).

Flackes, W.D. and Sydney Elliott, *Northern Ireland: A Political Directory 1968–88* (Belfast: 1989).
Follis, Brian, *A State Under Siege: The Establishment of Northern Ireland 1920–1925* (Oxford: 1995).
Forester, Margaret, *Michael Collins: The Lost Leader* (London: 1971).
Forum for Peace and Reconciliation, *Paths to a Political Settlement in Ireland: Policy Papers Submitted to the Forum for Peace and Reconciliation* (Belfast: 1995).
Foster, R.F., *Modern Ireland 1600–1972* (London: 1988).
Fulton, John, *The Tragedy of Belief Politics and Religion in Northern Ireland* (Oxford: 1991).
Gailey, Andrew (ed.), *Crying in the Wilderness. Jack Sayers: A Liberal Editor in Ulster 1939–69* (Belfast: 1995).
Gallagher, Anthony M., 'The Approach of Government: Community Relations and Equity', in Seamus Dunn (ed.), *Facets of the Conflict in Northern Ireland* (London: 1995).
Gallagher, Eric and Stanley Worrall, *Christians in Ulster 1968–1980* (Oxford: 1982).
Gallagher, Frank, *The Indivisible Island* (London: 1957).
Gallagher, John F. and Jerry L. de Gregory, *Violence in Northern Ireland: Understanding Protestant Perspectives* (Dublin: 1985).
Garland, Roy, *Gusty Spence* (Belfast: 2001).
Garvin, Tom, *The Evolution of Irish Nationalist Politics* (Dublin: 1981).
Garvin, Tom, *Nationalist Revolutionaries in Ireland 1858–1928* (Oxford: 1987).
Gearty, Conor, *Terror* (London: 1991).
Gibbon, Peter, *The Origins of Ulster Unionism: The Formation of Popular Protestant Politics and Ideology in Nineteenth-Century Ireland* (Manchester: 1975).
Gordon, David, *The O'Neill Years: Unionist Politics 1963–1969* (Belfast: 1989).
Guelke, Adrian, *Northern Ireland: The International Perspective* (Dublin: 1988).
Guelke, Adrian, 'Paramilitaries, Republicans and Loyalists', in Seamus Dunn (ed.), *Facets of the Conflict in Northern Ireland* (London: 1995).
Hadfield, Brigid, *The Constitution of Northern Ireland* (Belfast: 1989).
Hadfield, Brigid, 'Legislating for Northern Ireland at Westminster', in M.E.H. Connolly and S. Loughlin (eds), *Public Policy in Northern Ireland: Adoption or Adaption?* (Belfast and Coleraine: 1990).
Hadfield, Brigid, *Northern Ireland: Politics and the Constitution* (Milton Keynes: 1992).
Hadfield, Brigid, 'The Belfast Agreement, Sovereignty and the State of the Union', *Public Law* (Winter 1998).
Hamill, Desmond, *Pig in the Middle: The Army in Northern Ireland 1969–1985* (London: 1985).
Hamilton, Andrew and Linda Moore, 'Policing a Divided Society', in Seamus Dunn (ed.), *Facets of the Conflict in Northern Ireland* (London: 1995).

Hand, Geoffrey J., *Report of the Irish Boundary Commission 1925* (Dublin: 1969).
Harbinson, John E., *The Ulster Unionist Party 1882–1973: Its Development and Organisation* (Belfast: 1973).
Harkness, David, *Northern Ireland since 1920* (Dublin: 1983).
Harris, Mary, *The Catholic Church and the Foundation of the Northern Irish State* (Cork: 1993).
Harris, Rosemary, *Prejudice and Tolerance in Ulster: A Study of Neighbours and Strangers in a Border Community* (Manchester: 1972).
Harrison, Richard T, 'Industrial Development in Northern Ireland – The Industrial Development Board', in M.E.H. Connolly and S. Loughlin (eds), *Public Policy in Northern Ireland: Adoption or Adaption?* (Belfast and Coleraine: 1990).
Hempton, David and Myrtle Hill, *Evangelical Protestantism in Ulster Society 1740–1890* (London: 1992).
Hennessey, Peter, *Whitehall* (New York: 1989).
Hennessey, Thomas, 'Ulster Unionist Territorial and National Identities 1886–1893: Province, Island, Kingdom and Empire', *Irish Political Studies*, 8 (1993).
Hennessey, Thomas, *A History of Northern Ireland 1920–1996* (Dublin: 1997).
Hennessey, Thomas, *Dividing Ireland: World War One and Partition* (London: 1998).
Hennessey, Thomas, *The Northern Ireland Peace Process. Ending the Troubles?* (Dublin: 2000).
Heskin, Ken, *Northern Ireland: A Psychological Analysis* (Dublin: 1980).
Hickey, John, *Religion and the Northern Ireland Problem* (Dublin: 1984).
Hogan, Gerald and Clive Walker, *Political Violence and the Law in Ireland* (Manchester: 1989).
Holland, Jack and Henry McDonald, *INLA: Deadly Divisions* (Dublin: 1994).
Holt, E., *Protest in Arms: The Irish Troubles 1916–1923* (London: 1963).
Howell, David, *A Lost Left: Three Studies in Socialism and Nationalism* (Manchester: 1986).
Hume, John, *Personal Views: Politics, Peace and Reconciliation in Ireland* (Dublin: 1996).
Hutchinson, John, *The Dynamics of Cultural Nationalism: the Gaelic Revival and the Creation of the Irish Nation State* (London: 1987).
Hyde, H. Montgomery, *Carson; the Life of Lord Carson of Duncairn* (London: 1953).
Jackson, Alvin, *The Ulster Party: Irish Unionists in the House of Commons, 1884–1911* (Oxford: 1989).
Jackson, Alvin, 'Unionist Myths 1912–1985', *Past and Present*, 136 (August 1992), pp.164–85.
Jackson, Alvin, *Sir Edward Carson* (Dundalk: 1993).
Jackson, Alvin, 'Irish Unionism, 1905–21', in Peter Collins (ed.), *Nationalism and Unionism: Conflict in Ireland 1885–1921* (Belfast: 1994).
Jackson, Alvin, *Ireland 1798–1998* (Oxford: 1999).

Jackson, Alvin, *Home Rule. An Irish History 1800–2000* (London: 2003).
Jalland, Patricia, *The Liberals and Ireland: The Ulster Question in British Politics to 1914* (Brighton: 1980).
Kee, Robert, *The Green Flag* (London: 1972).
Keena, Colm, *A Biography of Gerry Adams* (Dublin: 1990).
Kelly, Henry, *How Stormont Fell* (Dublin: 1972).
Kendle, John, *Ireland and the Federal Solution: the Debate over the United Kingdom Constitution 1870–1921* (Kingston: 1989).
Kennedy, Dennis, *The Widening Gulf: Northern Attitudes to the Independent Irish State 1919–1949* (Belfast: 1988).
Kennedy, Michael, *Division and Consensus. The Politics of Cross-Border Relations in Ireland 1925–1969* (Dublin: 2000).
Kennedy-Pipe, Caroline, *The Origins of the Present Troubles in Northern Ireland* (Essex: 1997).
Keogh, Dermot, *Twentieth-Century Ireland: Nation and State* (Dublin: 1994).
Knox, Colin, 'Local Government in Northern Ireland – Adoption or Adaption?', in M.E.H. Connolly and S. Loughlin (eds), *Public Policy in Northern Ireland: Adoption or Adaption* (Belfast and Coleraine: 1990), pp.35–8.
Laffan, Michael, *The Partition of Ireland 1911–1925* (Dundalk: 1983).
Lawlor, Sheila, *Britain and Ireland 1914–23* (Dublin: 1983).
Lawrence, R.J., *The Government of Northern Ireland* (Oxford: 1965).
Lee, J.J., *Ireland 1912–1985: Politics and Society* (Cambridge: 1989).
Longford, Lord and Anne McHardy, *Ulster* (London: 1981).
Longley, Edna, 'The Rising, the Somme and Irish Memory', in Mairin Ni Dhonnchadha and Theo Dorgan (eds), *Revising the Rising* (Derry: 1991).
Loughlin, James, *Gladstone, Home Rule and the Ulster Question 1882–93* (Dublin: 1986).
Loughlin, James, *Ulster Unionism and British National Identity since 1885* (London: 1995).
Lyons, F.S.L., *Ireland since the Famine* (London: 1973).
McAllister, Ian, *The Northern Ireland Social Democratic and Labour Party: Political Opposition in a Divided Society* (London: 1977).
McAuley, James W., *The Politics of Identity: A Loyalist Community in Belfast* (Aldershot: 1994).
McCabe, Ian, *A Diplomatic History of Ireland 1948–49: The Republic, the Commonwealth and NATO* (Dublin: 1991).
McElroy, Gerald, *The Catholic Church and the Northern Ireland Crisis 1969–86* (Dublin: 1991).
McGarry, John and Brendan O'Leary (eds), *The Future of Northern Ireland* (Oxford: 1990).
McGarry, John and Brendan O'Leary, *Explaining Northern Ireland: Broken Images* (Oxford: 1995).
McGuire, Maria, *To Take Arms: A Year in the Provisional IRA* (London: 1973).
McIntyre, Anthony, 'Modern Irish Republicanism: The Product of British State Strategies', *Irish Political Studies*, 10 (1995).
McKeown, Ciaran, *The Passion of Peace* (Belfast: 1984).

McMahon, Deirdre, *Republicans and Imperialists: Anglo-Irish Relations in the 1930s* (Yale: 1984).
Mallie, Eamon and David McKittrick, *The Fight for Peace: The Secret Story Behind the Irish Peace Process* (London: 1996).
Mansergh, Nicholas, *The Unresolved Question: the Anglo-Irish Settlement and its Undoing 1912–72* (Yale: 1991).
Marjoribanks, Edward and Ian Colvin, *The Life of Lord Carson,* 3 Volumes (London: 1932–4).
Miller, David, *Queen's Rebels: Ulster Loyalism in Historical Perspective* (Dublin: 1978).
Mitchell, George J., *Making Peace* (London: 1999).
Moloney, Ed and Andy Pollock, *Paisley* (Dublin: 1986).
Moxon-Browne, Edward, *Nation, Class and Creed in Northern Ireland* (Aldershot: 1983).
Mulholland, Marc, *Northern Ireland at the Crossroads. Ulster Unionism in the O'Neill Years 1960–9* (Basingstoke 2000).
Murphy, Brian P., *Patrick Pearse and the Lost Republican Ideal* (Dublin: 1991).
Murphy, Richard, 'Faction in the Conservative Party and the Home Rule Crisis 1912–14', *History*, 232, 71 (1986).
Murray, Dominic, *Worlds Apart: Segregated Schools in Northern Ireland* (Belfast: 1985).
Murray, Raymond, *The SAS in Ireland* (Dublin: 1990).
Nelson, Sarah, *Ulster's Uncertain Defenders: Loyalists and the Northern Ireland Conflict* (Belfast: 1984).
O'Brien, Brendan, *The Long War: The IRA and Sinn Féin 1985 to Today* (Dublin: 1993).
O'Brien, Justin, *The Arms Trial* (Dublin: 2000).
O'Connor, Fionnuala, *In Search of a State: Catholics in Northern Ireland* (Belfast: 1993).
O Dochartaigh, Niall, *From Civil Rights to Armalites. Derry and the Birth of the Irish Troubles* (Cork: 1997).
O'Dowd, Liam, Bill Rolston and Mike Tomlinson, *Northern Ireland: Between Civil Rights and Civil War* (London: 1980).
O'Dowd, Liam, 'Development or Dependency? State, Economy and Society in Northern Ireland', in Patrick Clancy, Sheelagh Drudy, Kathleen Lynch and Liam O'Dowd (eds), *Irish Society: Sociological Perspectives* (Dublin: 1995).
O'Halloran, Clare, *Partition and the Limits of Irish Nationalism* (Dublin: 1987).
O'Leary, Brendan and John McGarry, *The Politics of Antagonism: Understanding Northern Ireland* (London: 1993).
O'Malley, Padraig, *The Uncivil Wars: Ireland Today* (Belfast: 1983).
O'Malley, Padraig, *Biting at the Grave: The Irish Hunger Strikes and the Politics of Despair* (Belfast: 1990).
O'Malley, Padraig, *Northern Ireland: Questions of Nuance* (Belfast: 1990).
O'Neill, Terence, *Ulster at the Crossroads* (London: 1969).
Patterson, Henry, *Class Conflict and Sectarianism: The Protestant Working*

Class and the Belfast Labour Movement 1868–1920 (Belfast: 1980).
Patterson, Henry, *The Politics of Illusion: Republicanism and Socialism in Modern Ireland* (London: 1989).
Patterson, Henry, *Ireland since 1939* (Oxford: 2002).
Phoenix, Eamon, *Northern Nationalism: Nationalist Politics, Partition and the Catholic Minority in Northern Ireland 1890–1940* (Belfast: 1994).
Phoenix, Eamon, 'Northern Nationalists, Ulster Unionists and the Development of Partition 1900–1921', in Peter Collins (ed.), *Nationalism and Unionism: Conflict in Ireland 1885–1921* (Belfast: 1994).
Pollack, Andy (ed.), *A Citizens' Inquiry: The Opsahl Report on Northern Ireland* (Dublin: 1993).
Purdy, Ann, *Molyneaux: The Long View* (Belfast: 1989).
Purdy, Bob, *Politics in the Streets: The Origins of the Civil Rights Movement in Northern Ireland* (Belfast: 1990).
Quinn, Raymond, *A Rebel Voice. A History of Belfast Republicanism 1925–1972* (Belfast: 1999).
Ramsden, John (ed.), *The Oxford Companion to Twentieth-Century British Politics* (Oxford: 2002).
Rea, Desmond (ed.), *Political Co-operation in Divided Societies: A Series of Papers Relevant to the Conflict in Northern Ireland* (Dublin: 1982).
Rolston, Bill (ed.), *The Media and Northern Ireland: Covering the Troubles* (London: 1991).
Rose, Peter, *How the Troubles Came to Northern Ireland* (Basingstoke: 1997).
Rose, Richard, *Governing Without Consensus: An Irish Perspective* (London: 1971).
Rowan, Brian, *Behind the Lines: The Story of the IRA and Loyalist Ceasefires* (Belfast: 1995).
Rowthorn, Bob and Naomi Wayne, *Northern Ireland: The Political Economy of Conflict* (Cambridge: 1988).
Ruane, Joseph and Jennifer Todd, *The Dynamics of Conflict in Northern Ireland: Power, Conflict and Emancipation* (Cambridge: 1996).
Ryder, Chris, *The RUC: A Force Under Fire* (London: 1989).
Ryder, Chris, *The Ulster Defence Regiment: An Instrument of Peace?* (London: 1991).
Ryder, Chris, *The Fateful Split. Catholics and the Royal Ulster Constabulary* (London: 2004).
Scoular, Clive, *James Chichester-Clark, Prime Minister of Northern Ireland* (Killyleagh: 2000).
Smith, Alan, 'Education and the Conflict in Northern Ireland', in Seamus Dunn (ed.), *Facets of the Conflict in Northern Ireland* (London: 1995).
Smith, Alan and Alan Robinson, *Education for Mutual Understanding: The Initial Statutory Years* (Coleraine: 1996).
Smith, David and Gerald Chambers, *Inequality in Northern Ireland* (Oxford: 1991).
Smith, M.L.R., *Fighting for Ireland: The Military Strategy of the Irish Republican Movement* (London: 1995).

Smyth, Clifford, *Ian Paisley: Voice of Protestant Ulster* (Edinburgh: 1987).
Stewart, A.T.Q., *The Ulster Crisis: Resistance to Home Rule 1912–14* (London: 1967).
Stewart, A.T.Q., *The Narrow Ground: the Roots of Conflict in Ulster* (London: 1977).
Stewart, A.T.Q., *Edward Carson* (Dublin: 1981).
Stringer, Peter and Gillian Robinson (eds), *Social Attitudes in Northern Ireland* (Belfast: 1991).
Stringer, Peter and Gillian Robinson (eds), *Social Attitudes in Northern Ireland: The Second Report* (Belfast: 1992).
Stringer, Peter and Gillian Robinson (eds), *Social Attitudes in Northern Ireland: The Third Report* (Belfast: 1993).
Taylor, Peter, *Families at War* (London: 1989).
Taylor, Peter, *States of Terror. Democracy and Political Violence* (London: 1993).
Taylor, Peter, *Provos. The IRA and Sinn Féin* (London: 1997).
Taylor, Peter, *Loyalists* (London: 1999).
Taylor, Peter, *Brits. The War Against the IRA* (London: 2001).
Tools, Kevin, *Rebel Hearts: Journeys within the IRA's Soul* (London: 1995).
Townshend, Charles, *Political Violence in Ireland: Government and Resistance since 1848* (Oxford: 1983).
Townshend, Charles (ed.), *Consensus in Ireland* (Oxford: 1983).
Travers, Pauric, *Settlements and Divisions: Ireland 1870–1922* (Dublin: 1988).
Urban, Mark, *Big Boys' Rules: The Secret Struggle Against the IRA* (London: 1992).
Walker, B.M., *Ulster Politics: The Formative Years 1868–86* (Belfast: 1989).
Walker, Graham, *The Politics of Frustration: Harry Midgley and the Failure of Labour in Northern Ireland* (Manchester: 1985).
Walker, Graham, *A History of the Ulster Unionist Party: Protest, Pragmatism and Pessimism* (Manchester: Manchester University Press, 2004).
Walsh, Pat, *From Civil Rights to National War: Northern Ireland Catholic Politics 1964–74* (Belfast: 1989).
Walsh, Pat, *Irish Republicanism and Socialism: the Politics of the Movement 1905 to 1994* (Belfast: 1994).
Ward, Margaret, *Unmanageable Revolutionaries: Women and Irish Nationalism* (London: 1983).
Warner, Geoffrey, 'The Falls Road Curfew Revisited', *Irish Studies Review*, 14, 3, pp.325–42.
White, Barry, *John Hume: Statesman of the Troubles* (Belfast: 1984).
Whyte, J.H., *Church and State in Modern Ireland 1923–1979* (Dublin: 1979).
Whyte, J.H., 'How much discrimination was there under the Unionist regime 1921–1968?', in Tom Gallagher and James O'Connell (eds), *Contemporary Irish Studies* (Manchester: 1983).
Whyte, John, *Interpreting Northern Ireland* (Oxford: 1990).
Wichert, Sabine, *Northern Ireland Since 1945* (Essex: 1991).

Wilson, Derick and Jerry Tyrrell, 'Institutions for Conciliation and Mediation', in Seamus Dunn (ed.), *Facets of the Conflict in Northern Ireland* (London: 1995).
Wilson, Tom, *Ulster: Conflict and Consent* (Oxford: 1989).
Winchester, Simon, *In Holy Terror* (London: 1974).
Wright, Frank, *Northern Ireland: A Comparative Analysis* (Dublin: 1987).

Index

A
Abercorn Restaurant bomb (4 March 1972), 1–4, 210
acid bombs, 59, 65, 231, 282
Aden, 53, 152, 153, 165, 214, 342
Aiken, John, 68
Aldershot bombing (22 February 1972), 327
Allen, Sir Philip, 175
Alliance Party, 144, 199
Amnesty International, 161
Andersonstown, 7, 10, 59, 109, 135, 142, 211, 219, 224, 229–30, 252
Andrews, Jack, 61, 331, 335, 337, 338
Antrim, Co., vii, 18–19, 20, 21, 212
Apprentice Boys Parades, viii, 47, 101, 110, 112, 113, 116–17, 120, 125, 126, 189
Arbuckle, Victor, viii
Ardoyne area, 12–13, 18, 33, 46, 81, 135, 211, 212
   army action in, 60, 62, 64–6, 72–3, 133, 142–3, 213
   army searches of, 12, 36, 115, 223
   RUC and, 70–1
Armagh, vii, 18, 102–3, 106, 114, 115, 217
   Westminster seat, 19, 20
Armoured Personnel Carriers (APCs), 38, 41, 65, 102, 134, 243
   Bloody Sunday and, 270, 280, 282–3, 286–8, 290–2, 296, 306
Armstrong, Robert, 77, 79, 80, 124, 338
army, British, viii, ix
   arms searches, 39, 55, 59, 61, 63–5, 95, 145, 188, 343
   see also Falls Road Curfew
   Belfast disturbances (May 1970), 11, 12
   Belfast flooding and, 57–8, 343
   bias allegations, 44, 102, 140, 143
   brutality allegations, 41, 42–3, 44, 57, 58, 59, 60, 117, 189, 224, 249, 343
   casualtiessee British army and the IRA
   Catholic areas and, 75–6, 79, 81
   Catholic casualties and, 229–30
   Catholic fatalities and see fatalities, Catholic: British army and
   Catholics' attitude tosee Catholic-army relations
   command structure, 53
   Compton Inquiry and, 160–1, 162–5, 189, 299
   cordoning tactics, 41, 71–2, 75–6, 79, 222, 223
   counter-insurgency and, 56, 57, 152, 221, 263, 343–4
   curfew tactics, 38–47, 52–3, 75–6, 79, 95, 120, 343
   Falls Road Curfew (July 1970), 38–47, 52–3, 343
   'hot pursuit' tactics, 71–2, 95
   Internal Security role, 16, 18, 56, 101, 197, 343
   internment and, 123–4, 129, 220, 345–6
   interrogation in depth and, 152–6, 157–67, 211, 217–20, 345
   IRA andsee attrition operation, army; British army and the IRA
   Londonderry and see Londonderry, British army and
   New Lodge violence and, 55–7, 60, 61
   Northern Ireland Government and, xi, 62, 70, 99–100, 347–8
   Operation DEMETRIUS, 123–4, 129, 130–2, 156, 214–15, 216
   Operation FORECAST see Bloody Sunday (30 January 1972)
   Operation FOURSQUARE, 123–4
   Operation HAILSTONE (July 1971), 263–4
   Operation LINKLATER and, 112–17, 120, 125, 216
   Orange parades and, 36
   'overreaction' allegations, 102, 104–5
   political control of, 192, 247
   preparations for NICRA march (30 January 1972), 254–67, 269–71
   reinforcements, 31–3, 36, 38, 53, 63, 64, 75, 76, 78, 79, 117
   RUC and, 13, 16–18, 62, 187, 216, 246, 325, 344
   rules of engagementsee rules of engagement, army
   sexual impropriety allegations, 59, 61
   snatch squads, 57, 60, 62, 261, 262, 288
   Special Branch and, 216, 246
   strategy of, 95, 201, 240–2, 243–8
   see also attrition operation, army
   tactics of, 71–2, 75–6, 79, 81, 95, 239
   violence of August 1971-January 1972 and, 207–14, 220–5
   weaponry, 206–7, 244, 245, 246, 283, 304
   see also Freeland, Sir Ian (GOC NI)
Assembly of the Northern Irish People, 106, 107, 150, 187, 191, 198–9
Association for Legal Justice, 157, 162
Atlee, Clement, 181, 185
attrition operation, army, 239–40, 249, 321, 323, 326, 332, 344, 345–6, 347
   internment and, 218, 219, 223, 223–6, 239, 313, 345
Atwell, William, 134
Auld, James, 157–8, 159

B
B Specials, v, viii, 23, 24, 138, 149, 189, 196, 344
   disbandment of, vi, ix, 19
   Unionism and, 19–20, 62, 76, 90, 92, 147, 349
Baillie, Robin, 18, 90, 91, 109, 339
Baker, Sir Geoffrey (CGS), 16, 17, 32, 54–5, 75, 79–82, 90
Ballie, Jim, 20, 21
Ballymacarratt area (Short Strand), 8, 18, 33–5, 135, 223
Ballymurphy, ix, 11, 12, 57, 64, 72–3, 115
   IRA and, 7, 10, 67, 212
   riots (August 1971), 134, 136, 137, 142
   riots (January 1971), 58–62
   riots (June 1970), 18, 36
Baniel, Lord, 59, 99, 221
Baniker, Corporal Robert, 96
Barber, William, 287–8
Barton, Private Richard, 108
baton charges, vii, 18, 39, 52, 64, 262
Beattie, Desmond, xi, 103–6, 160, 232, 347
Beattie, John, 137
Beattie, William, 20
Beck, George, 68
Bedell, Leslie, 284–5
Beggin, Peter, 284
Beggs, Harry, 210
Belfast, 20, 35, 36, 37
   Clonard, vi, 7, 33, 34, 41, 63–5
   flooding, 57–8, 343
   Short Strand, 8, 18, 33–5, 135, 223
   see also Andersonstown; Ardoyne area; Ballymurphy; Falls Road; New Lodge Road area; Shankill area; Springfield Road; violence, sectarian: Belfast
Belgium, 185, 189
Bell, Albert, 68
Beloff, Nora, 319
Bereen family, 2–3
Bew, Paul, x
birth-rate, Catholic, 23
Black, Harold, 92
Black Watch, The, 42–3
Blaney, Neil, ix, 11
Bleakley, David, 91, 109, 316
Bloody Sunday (30 January 1972), 230–1, 308–9
   army decision to halt march, 253–7
   arrest operation, 275–7, 280–2, 285–6, 348
   arrest operation, preparations for, 257, 259, 260, 263–5, 271
   bombs, army claims of, 277–9, 281–3, 286, 290, 291, 294–5, 299–302
   bombs, police evidence of, 283, 298

bombs and, 280, 282, 291, 305, 306–7
British Government and, 315–19
Catholic reaction, 313
civilian casualties, 278, 289, 290, 292–3, 294, 295–6, 298
civilian fatalities, 278, 286, 287, 290, 291–8, 301, 303–8
Ford memorandum and, 243–6, 247
gunfire, army, 277–9, 281, 286–8, 290, 291–6, 299–301, 348
gunfire, IRA, 277, 278–80, 287, 288–9, 348
gunfire, unknown, 279, 280–5, 292, 348
NICRA march, 274, 275, 276, 286, 296
NICRA meeting (Free Derry Corner), 275, 276, 284, 291
rioting and, 274–5, 276–8, 280, 281, 291
rubber bullets and, 274, 277, 280, 283, 295
Saville Inquiry, 231, 302, 307–8
Widgery Inquiry, 230, 231, 275, 278, 285, 286, 294, 299–308, 348–9
Yellow Card and, 299–300
Bloomfield, Sir Kenneth, 340
Bogside, Battle of the, viii, 33
bombing campaign, Provisional IRA, 10–12, 100, 101, 102–3, 107, 212–13, 238, 347
Abercorn Restaurant (4 March 1972), 1–4, 210
booby-traps and mines, 58, 68, 103, 212, 223
commercial targets, 37, 60, 63, 101, 107, 110–12, 137–8, 210, 222, 223
internment and, 220, 222, 225
telephone warnings, 210, 223
border, Irish, viii, 94, 123, 194, 315, 317, 332
British army and, 69–70, 95, 138–9
cratering proposals, 112, 113
IRA and, 52, 69–70, 92, 100, 123, 125, 138–9, 219, 224
IRA Border campaign (1956-62), v, 94, 108, 109, 214, 347
IRA cross border ASU operations, 135, 220, 225, 226, 326, 347
see also reunification issues
Bowen Report, 152, 153
Bradford, Roy, 91, 109, 172, 331, 336, 337, 339
Bradley, Michael, 290, 295
Bradley, Revd. Denis, 147–8, 293
Brady, Rory (Rory Ó Brádaigh), 67, 105–6, 139
'Bradyite' IRA see Irish Republican Army, Provisional
Bridge, Michael, 287, 289, 290, 295
British army and the IRA, xii, 8, 9, 52, 55–7, 60–1, 63–6, 111, 326, 342
arms searches, 39, 55, 59, 61, 63–5, 95, 145, 188, 343
see also Falls Road Curfew
army casualties, 143, 343
army casualties (Belfast), 36, 37, 59, 63, 65, 66, 72, 102, 132–3, 212, 213, 225
army casualties (Falls Road Curfew), 40, 41, 343
army casualties (Londonderry), 36, 103, 137, 234, 241, 265
army fatalities, 214, 220
army fatalities (Belfast), 65–6, 96–7, 107–8, 133, 142, 211, 212
army fatalities (Belfast, 10 March 1971), 73–4, 99, 221
army fatalities (Londonderry), 71, 136, 234, 238, 241, 265
IRA casualties, 34–5, 136, 249
IRA fatalities, 138, 143, 144, 216
IRA fatalities (Belfast), 55–6, 65–6, 72–3, 96, 133, 136, 142
IRA fatalities from own bombs, 10, 96
IRA fatalities (Londonderry), 147, 224, 249
British Irish Rights Watch, 230–1
Brooke, Captain John, 22–3, 43, 91, 111, 339
Brougher Mountain (Co. Tyrone), 68
Brown, George, 153
Buckley, Constable Robert, 70
bullets, high velocity, 206–7
Bunting, Ronald, vii, 20
Burns, Joe, 91
Burns, William, 41
Burroughs, Ronnie (UKREP), 11, 37, 46, 48, 58, 90, 93, 97

Chichester-Clark and, 80, 82, 97
Gerry Fitt and, 86, 88–9
Stormont and, 71, 72, 74, 77
business community, Northern Irish, 112, 146, 198

C
Cahill, Joe, ix, 9, 68, 213, 216
Caldwell, Tom, 20
Callaghan, James, 14, 20, 26, 28, 33, 344–5
Stormont and, vi, viii, 16, 30–1
Campbell, Robert, 291
Campbell, Second Lieutenant James, 130, 132–3
Capper, David, 279
Card, Frank, 8, 65
Carlin, Thomas, 10
Carolan, Father, 251
Carrington, Lord Peter, 28, 29, 32, 54, 68, 74, 96, 164, 201, 326
Belfast visits (1971), 62–3, 79–82, 85
Brian Faulkner and, 90, 317–18
Chichester-Clark and, 61, 62, 74–5
internment and, 110, 124–5, 128, 192, 221, 345
interrogation in depth and, 154, 160
Londonderry and, 242, 247
security policy and, 69–70
Carroll, Sergeant Martin, 234
Carter, Private Paul, 211
Carver, Sir Michael (CGS), 53, 94, 159–60, 201, 226
internment and, 110, 120, 128–9, 221–2, 345
Londonderry and, 240, 242, 246, 247, 248
'Castle Catholics', 86, 88, 145
Catholic Church, 12–13, 40
Catholic-army relations, 62–3, 328, 343
Belfast flooding and, 57–8, 343
deterioration of, 11, 13, 67
Falls Road Curfew and, 44, 46–7, 343
hostility, 187, 223–4, 240
initial welcome, 6–7, 9
in Londonderry, 104, 240–2, 308–9
Catholics, 25, 115, 140, 149–50, 342
'Castle Catholics', 86, 88, 145
casualties, 1–4, 37, 210, 229–30
see also Bloody Sunday (30 January 1972); fatalities, Catholic
discrimination against, v, vi, 24, 27, 203, 325, 342
Falls Road Curfew and, xii, 38–47, 52–3, 188, 343
political participation see political participation, Catholic
see also Catholic-army relations
Cave, Cyril, 279
Central Citizen's Defence Committee (CCDC), 38–9, 41, 66–7, 102
Central Housing Authority, viii, 20, 195
Challenor, Bombadier Paul, 136
Chichester-Clark, James, vii, viii, xi, 22, 40, 47, 75, 85, 111, 189, 345
ban on marches (July 1970), 48
British army and, 62, 76, 79, 81
British Government attempts to save, 74–6, 77–81
Edward Heath and, 30, 68, 75–6, 77–8, 80–2
General Election (18 June 1970), 18–19
Ian Paisley and, 20–1, 62, 68
identity and, 27–8
Internal Security and, 16, 61–2, 71, 72
internment and, 69, 75, 108
January 1971 violence and, 59, 60
JSC and, 35–6
Lord Carrington and, 61, 62, 74–5
military intelligence and, 63
paramilitary funerals and, 67–8
Parliamentary statement (18 March 1971), 76, 77, 78
reform programme and, 23
Reginald Maudling and, 30, 37–8, 61, 68–9, 74–5, 77
resignation of, 80–2, 97, 344
Unionist Party opposition to, 76–7, 80
Chief of the General Staff (CGS), 16, 53
see also Baker, Sir Geoffrey (CGS); Carver, Sir Michael (CGS)
Citizen's Defence Committees (CDCs), 11, 34, 57–8
civil disobedience campaign, Nationalist, 145, 146–50, 174,

INDEX

177
Civil Rights Movement, vii, 21, 22, 24–5, 69
  internment and, 146, 147, 226, 268–9
  marches and protests, vi, 115, 146, 226, 251, 267, 268–9, 274, 275
  see also Bloody Sunday (30 January 1972)
  North Derry Civil Rights Association, 249–51, 269, 274
  see also Northern Ireland Civil Rights Association (NICRA)
Civil Service, Northern Ireland, xi, 98, 327, 339
Clark, Henry, 19–20
Clarke, Joseph, 157–8, 159, 163
Clonard (Belfast), vi, 7, 33, 34, 41, 63–5
Coalisland, vi, 101, 106, 114, 146, 149, 150
Coldstream Guards, 57–8, 259
Colley, George, 121
Collins, Sean, 308–9
Commander Land Forces Northern Ireland (CLF NI), 53
  see also Farrar-Hockley, Major General Anthony (CLF NI); Ford, Major General Robert (CLF NI)
commercial premises, IRA bombings of see bombing campaign, Provisional IRA
'Community Government' proposals, 172, 190, 327
Compton Inquiry, 160–1, 162–5, 189, 299
Conaty, Tom, 66–7
Connelly, Mrs. Joan Brigid, 134
Conservative Government (1970-4), xi, 28–33
  Bloody Sunday and, 299, 315–19
  Brian Faulkner and, 61, 170, 316–23, 330–8
  Compton Inquiry and, 164–5, 299, 349
  constitutional referenda and, 317, 318, 322, 326, 327, 328, 333, 338
  Direct Rule and, 30, 31, 122, 128, 139, 179, 318, 322–38, 345, 346
  internment and, 112, 126–9, 327, 328–9, 330, 333, 345
  IRA and, 200, 327–8
  minority participation and, 198, 203
  Orange Order and, 44
  reform proposals (February/March 1972), 322, 323–30, 331–6
  Republic of Ireland and, 139–42, 176, 200, 201–3
  see also Lynch, Jack: Edward Heath and
  SDLP and, 85–6, 88–9, 172–3, 195–6, 330
  security policy, 31–3, 52, 69–70, 71–2, 78–9, 197, 201, 343
  see also Carrington, Lord Peter; Heath, Edward; Home, Sir Alec Douglas-; Maudling, Reginald
Conservative Party, 184, 186–7, 317, 327
Conway, Cardinal, 13, 157, 175, 343
Coogan, Tim Pat, x–xi
Cooper, Ivan, 22–3, 24, 85, 88, 104, 115, 146, 150, 175, 249
  arrest of (18 August 1971), 147
  Bloody Sunday and, 248, 296
  Magilligan march (22 January 1972), 250
  reunification issue and, 24–5
Copeland, John, 213
Corr, Joseph, 137
Cosgrave, Liam, 104
Council of Europe, 27
Council of Ireland, 185, 191, 200, 201
Cowan, Brigadier, 63, 100–1, 238–9
Coyle, Joseph, 10
Craig, Bill, vi, 19, 68, 85, 90, 122, 317, 339, 344, 347
  general strike (27-28 March 1972), 338–40
  Unionist leadership candidate, 89–90
  Vanguard and, 319, 338
Craig, Danny, 301
Crossroads election (1969), vii, 19
Crumlin Jail, 109, 131, 149, 158, 225
Crumlin Road, 18, 33, 35, 36, 64, 65, 101, 107, 212, 213
CS gas, 11, 12, 36, 39, 40–1, 55, 135, 146
  in Londonderry, viii, 33, 36, 147, 242, 243–4, 246, 249, 262, 274, 286
Cullen, Patrick, 149
Cummings, Brian, 79, 80
Cummins, Liam, 156–7
Cunningham, Alphonsus, 142
Cunningham, Sir Knox, 19
Curran, Phil, 149

Currie, Austin, vi, 21, 24, 85, 89, 98, 106, 111, 149, 150
  attacks on home of, 10
  Brian Faulkner and, 93, 99
  NICRA Derry march (of 30 January 1972) and, 248
  on Protestant extremism, 116–17
  Republic of Ireland and, 199
  reunification issue and, 25
Curtis, Gunner Robert, 65, 66, 96
Cusack, Seamus, xi, 103–6, 160, 232, 347
Cyprus, 152, 189, 214, 246

D
Daily Mirror, The, 110–11, 112, 187
Daily Telegraph, 279
Daly, Father Edward, 230, 286–8, 290
Dalzell-Payne, Colonel, 53
Dash, Professor, 307
Deery, Peggy, 290, 297
Derry Citizens' Action Committee (DCAC), 248
Derry Young Hooligans (DYH), 238, 239, 243–4, 245
  NICRA march (30 January 1972) and, 257, 258, 259, 262, 264, 265
Devenny, Samuel, vii
Devlin, Bernadette, 33
Devlin, Paddy, 24, 86–7, 106, 115, 125, 146, 175, 199, 248
  British army and, 57, 59, 60, 100, 102, 106, 144
  Falls Road Curfew and, 40, 41, 42, 43, 44, 45
  on Protestant extremism, 115–16
  Unionist Government and, 87–8
Dickson, Anne, 18
Direct Rule, 27, 123–4, 169–70, 338–40, 349
  Brian Faulkner and, 318, 322–40
  Conservative Government and, 30, 31, 122, 128, 139, 179, 318, 322–38, 345, 346
  internment and, 114, 120, 125
  IRA and, 178, 327
  Jack Lynch and, 121, 123, 169, 338
  Labour Government and, 344–5, 346
  Sir Burke Trend and, 178–9, 187
  Unionist Party and, 89–90, 178–9, 318, 322–40
Director General of Intelligence, MOD, 154, 159
discrimination against Catholics, v, vi, 24, 27, 203, 325, 342
Dodd, Sergeant Ron, 212
Doherty, Edward, 137
Doherty, Gerard, 251
Doherty, James, 199
Doherty, Patrick Joseph, 295, 306
Doherty, Richard, 285
Donaghy, Cathy, 296
Donaghy, Damien, 278, 279
Donaghy, Gerald, 293–4, 297, 298, 305, 306–7
Donaghy, Harry, 102
Donaghy, John, 22
Donaldson, Constable Samuel, 58
Donnell, Private Winston, 135
Donnelly, Ciaran, 279, 292
Donnelly, Michael Joseph, 157–8, 159
Donnelly, Peter, 136
Downing Street Declaration (1969), 90, 181
Doxon, Denise, 66
Drumm, Mrs Marie, 105
Duddy, Jack, 286, 287–8, 289, 290, 296
Dungiven, 100
Dunleavey, John, 274
Dunnett, Sir James, 331

E
Easter Rising commemorations (1966), vi
Edgar, Harry, 68
Electricity Department bombing, 3, 10, 210
Elliman, Patrick, 42
English, Richard, xi–xii
Enniskillen anti-internment march (13 February 1972), 315
Erskine-Crum, Lietenant General Vernon, 71
Europa Hotel (Belfast), 101
European Convention on Human Rights, 27, 163–4, 194
European Court of Human Rights (ECHR), 160, 161–2
European Economic Community (EEC), 28, 163, 180, 181, 185, 316, 328, 329–30

Evans, Peter, 173, 174

F
Fairhurst, Corporal Dave, 132
Falls Road, 47, 48, 57, 62, 115
 IRA and, 1, 7, 9, 34, 35, 40, 52, 66, 145, 209–10, 213
 violence, 14, 60, 66–7, 72–3, 102, 107–8, 135, 136, 142, 212
Falls Road Curfew (July 1970), xii, 38–47, 52–3, 188, 343
Farrar-Hockley, Major General Anthony (CLF NI), 53, 59–60, 62, 63, 64–5
 internment and, 125, 166, 215
Farrell, Mairead, 44, 46
fatalities, Catholic, 37, 142
 British army and, 138, 303
 British army and (Belfast), 38, 41–2, 65–6, 117, 133–4, 137, 142, 213
 British army and (Londonderry), 99, 100, 101, 103–7, 111, 160, 189, 233–4, 347
 see also Bloody Sunday (30 January 1972)
 IRA bombs, 1–4, 210
 RUC and, vii, vii–viii
 UVF and, vi, 312–13
 see also Bloody Sunday (30 January 1972)
Faul, Father Denis, 223
Faulkner, Brian, vi, vii, 38, 76, 85, 97–8, 187
 becomes Prime Minister (23 March 1971), 90–1
 border cratering proposals, 112, 113
 British army and, xi, 99–100, 106, 347–8
 Chichester-Clark and, 85
 committee proposals (22 June 1971), 98, 140–1, 170, 180–1, 190, 192, 194–5, 196, 346
 Conservative Government and, 61, 170, 316–23, 330–8
 constitutional referenda and, 317, 318, 323, 333, 335
 Direct Rule and, 318, 322–40
 Edward Heath and, xi, 85, 94, 170–2, 197–8, 216, 316–23, 330–8, 345
 Gerry Fitt and, 173, 174, 175
 Green Paper (October 1971), xi, 172, 198
 internment and, 94–5, 108–14, 120, 126–9, 154, 175, 193–4, 320–2, 345
 Jack Lynch and, 92, 93, 94, 170, 180–1, 184
 'law and order' powers and, 318, 320, 325, 329
 minority participation and, 193–6, 197–8
 NICRA march (30 January 1972) and, 268–9
 non-Unionist cabinet members, 91, 109, 316–17, 344
 Operation LINKLATER and, 114, 117, 120
 Orange Order and, 182, 189
 Paisleyite critics, 98
 reform programme and, 85, 90, 91, 93–4, 97, 121, 344
 reform proposals (March 1972), 322–3, 330, 332, 333, 334–5, 336
 refusal of British terms (23 March 1972), 336–7
 Reginald Maudling and, 124, 125–6, 170–2, 197–8, 317–18, 326, 334, 335
 Republic of Ireland and, 85, 91, 99, 139, 189, 323
 resignation of (23 March 1972), 338
 SDLP and, xi, 85, 93, 98, 100, 148, 172, 173, 194, 197–8, 344
 security issues and, 71, 91, 94, 97, 98, 193
 tripartite summit (1971), x, 184–7, 192–7
 Tuzo and, 108, 110, 246, 249
 Unionist leadership candidate, 89, 90
Fay, Edgar (QC), 160, 161
Ferris, William, 142
Fianna Éireann (IRA youth movement), 7, 219, 225, 235–6, 267
Fianna Fáil, 65, 92, 173, 177, 202, 316
Fine Gael, 174, 197, 202
Fitt, Gerry, 24, 25, 67, 86, 150, 174, 175, 199, 248
 British Government and, 59, 85–6, 88–9, 144–5, 172–4
 Falls Road Curfew and, 42–4
 internment and, 86, 173–4, 175
 SDLP and, 24, 106, 174–5
 Unionist Government and, 23, 88, 89, 93–4, 98, 146–7, 173–5, 196
FitzGerald, Garret, 174
Fitzsimmons, William, 91
flooding in Belfast, 57–8, 343

Ford, Major General Robert (CLF NI), 53, 129, 223, 224, 225, 240–5, 264
 Bloody Sunday and, 255, 256–7, 258, 259, 261, 262–3, 265, 348
 memorandum to Tuzo, 243–6, 247
Fraser, Hugh, 186–7
Freeland, Sir Ian (GOC NI), 13, 15–16, 17, 36, 47, 48, 62, 63, 344
 army reinforcements and, 32, 38, 63
 Conservative Government and, 38, 62–3
 Falls Road Curfew and, 40, 41
 IRA and, 52–3
 rules of engagement and, 36, 54–5, 56
Friel, Joseph, 294, 295
funerals, paramilitary, 67–8

G
Gallagher, Angela, 211
Gallagher, Eamonn, 198–201
Garrett, John, 222
 gelignite bombs, 10, 58, 63, 73, 101, 102, 107, 212, 223, 225, 280
 Bloody Sunday and, 280, 305, 314
GEN 47 (Northern Ireland Ministerial Committee), x–xi, 122, 126–8, 203, 222, 226, 248, 259
General Election, UK (18 June 1970), 18–19, 28, 30, 44, 343
General Officer Commanding Northern Ireland (GOC NI), viii, 13, 31, 53, 71–2, 75, 78–9, 215
 see also Freeland, Sir Ian (GOC NI); Tuzo, Sir Harry (GOC NI)
general strike (27-28 March 1972), 338–40
George, Jimmy, 8
Gibson, Dr. Ronald, 160
Gifford, Lord, 103, 104
Gilchrist, Sir Andrew, 201–2
Gilmore, Hugh Pius, 291–2, 295, 306
Gilmour, Ian, 85
Gilpin, Sergeant, 265
Girder, Private John Alfred, 212
Gloucestershire Regiment, 6
Gogarty, Frank, 22
Gorman, Tommy, 209
Gould, Alexander, 35
Goulding, Cathal, ix, 22, 138, 217
'Gouldingite' IRA see Irish Republican Army, Official
Government of Ireland Act (1920), v, 26–7, 89, 91, 144, 148, 185, 191, 316, 318
Green Book, IRA, 236
Green Howards, The, 58, 133, 142, 211, 212, 213
Green Paper (October 1971), xi, 172, 198
Greenhill, Sir Denis, 175
Gregson, Peter, 77, 132
Groves, Mrs. Emily, 229–30, 252
Guardian, The, 38, 44, 252, 253, 279, 284
gunsee weaponry

H
Hailsham, Lord (Quintin Hogg), 29, 30, 32
Halligan, Brendan, 174
Halligan, William, 72–3
Hamilton, Guardsman George, 212
Hanna, Revd. Hugh, statue of, 10
Hannaway, Kevin, 65, 157–8, 159
Harvey, Dr., 296, 297
Hatton, Private Malcolm, 133
Haughhey, Charles, ix, 202
Hayes, Maurice, 174
Head Quarters Northern Ireland (HQNI), 36, 41, 73–4, 223, 225, 226, 256
 Director of Intelligence, 215, 216, 223, 225, 244
 internment and, 123, 135
Healy, Denis, 28, 160
Healy, Desmond, 134
Heath, Edward
 army reinforcements and, 31, 32
 background, 28, 299, 349
 Bloody Sunday and, 299, 315–19
 Brian Faulkner and, xi, 85, 94, 170–2, 197–8, 216,

316–23, 330–8, 345
    Chichester-Clark and, 30, 68, 75–6, 77–8, 80–2
    Compton Inquiry and, 164–5, 299, 349
    EEC and, 28, 316
    GOC and, 78–9
    internment and, 124, 126, 128–9, 131–2, 160, 216, 345
    Jack Lynch, 29–30, 129, 139–41, 170–1, 176, 195–7, 316
    Jack Lynch, summit with (6-7 September 1971), 179–85
    Londonderry and, 246, 248
    NICRA march (30 January 1972) and, 259
    Operation LINKLATER and, 113
    reunification issue and, 183
    security policy and, 69, 70
    tripartite summit (1971), x, 184–7, 192–7
    Widgery Inquiry, 299, 348–9
Henderson, Tony, 96
Henson, Malcolm, 68
Herrington, Corporal Peter, 211
Herron, Hugh, 134
Hillery, Patrick, 45, 45–6, 91, 92, 163, 173, 176, 202
    Reginald Maudling and, 138–9, 140
Hogg, Quintin (Lord Hailsham), 29, 30, 32
Hoggart, Simon, 252, 253
Holland, Mary, 285
Home, Sir Alec Douglas-, 28, 29, 32, 45, 46, 82, 317–18, 335
    Direct Rule and, 329, 336
    internment and, 113–14, 120, 129, 131, 192, 345
'hot pursuit' tactics, 71–2, 95
housing, violence and, 143
Housing Executive, viii, 20, 195
Howard, Lieutenant-Colonel Geoffrey, 108
Hughes, Brendan, 8–9, 40, 209–10
Hughes, Charlie, 40, 73
Hughes, Sean, 207–8, 212
Hume, John
    arrest of (18 August 1971), 147
    Bloody Sunday and, 231, 296–7, 313
    British army and, 104, 115, 234
    British Government and, 85, 115, 144–5
    constitutional issues and, 25–8
    Dublin and, 91, 104, 105
    internment and, 144–5
    Jack Lynch and, 182, 313
    Magilligan march (22 January 1972), 250–1
    NICRA Derry march (of 30 January 1972) and, 248, 251
    political participation and, 86, 88, 145, 346
    Republic of Ireland and, 104, 182, 198–200, 313
    reunification issue and, 25–8, 199–200
    RUC and, 48
    SDLP and, 24, 198–9
    Unionist Party and, 22, 23, 27–8, 88, 93, 94, 148
    on violence, 87
Hunt Committee, viii, 14, 19–20, 23, 94, 189

I
incitement to religious hatred legislation, 23–4, 102, 188
Infantry Brigades, 137, 138, 238, 256, 258, 262, 270, 303
Information Service, Government, 22–3
intelligence, military, 31, 37, 52–3, 65, 70, 95–6, 109, 113, 215–16
    internment and, 122, 125, 154, 217–19, 221, 222, 225, 345
    NICRA march (30 January 1972) and, 266–7
    sharing of, 63
    see also Special Branch, RUC: intelligence and Intelligence Centre, 152
Internal Security (IS)
    British army role, 16–18, 56, 101, 197, 343
    law and order, 201, 224, 318, 320, 325, 326, 328–30, 333, 336, 345
    RUC role, 16–18, 52, 71, 347
    see also army, British; Royal Ulster Constabulary (RUC); security policy
internment, xi, 77, 197
    Brian Faulkner and, 94–5, 108–14, 120, 126–9, 175, 193, 216, 320–2, 345

British army and, 62, 123–4, 129, 220, 345–6
    brutality allegations, 156–67
    Catholics' attitude to, 109, 144, 347
    Chichester-Clark and, 69, 75, 108
    civil disobedience campaign and, 145, 146–50, 174, 177
    Conservative Government and, 112, 126–9, 327, 328–9, 330, 333, 345
    Edward Heath and, 124, 126, 128–9, 131–2, 160, 216, 345
    effects on violence, 219–26
    Howard Smith and, 169–70
    intelligence and, 214–15, 216, 222, 225
    intelligence dividend, 122, 125, 154, 217–19, 221, 345
    interrogation in depth and, 157–67, 217–20
    introduction of (9 August 1971), 130–2
    IRA and, 61, 120, 125, 128, 129, 131, 208–11, 216–23, 232, 320–2
    Jack Lynch and, 114, 120–3, 127, 129, 161–4, 170, 181–2, 192, 194, 203
    marches against, 249–51, 252, 261, 314–15, 317
    see also Bloody Sunday (30 January 1972)
    preparations for, 120–5, 126–9
    Republic of Ireland and, 112–14, 120–3, 138–9, 161–4, 175–6, 188, 201, 202
    SDLP and, 86, 144–5, 173–4, 175, 195, 196, 199
    violent reaction to, 132–8
interrogation in depth, 152–6, 159–67, 217–20
    IRA and, 165–7, 211, 345
Ireland Act (1949), 185, 317, 332, 333
Irish Labour Party, 150, 174
Irish News, The, 57
Irish Press, The, 159
Irish Republican Army (IRA), v, 136–7, 177, 199, 200, 201, 316
    border, cross-, ASU operations, 135, 220, 225, 226, 326, 347
    border and, 52, 69–70, 92, 100, 123, 125, 138–9, 219, 224
    Border campaign (1956-62), v, 94, 108, 109, 214, 347
    British army and see attrition operation, army; British army and the IRA
    Conservative Government and, 200, 327–8
    Direct Rule and, 178, 327
    internment and, 61, 120, 125, 128, 129, 131, 208–11, 216–23, 232, 320–2
    interrogation in depth and, 157–9, 165–7, 211
    Jack Lynch and, 182, 192, 196, 197, 202, 203, 328, 336
    Londonderry and see Londonderry, IRA and
    members of, 208–10
    NICRA march (30 January 1972) and, 257, 259, 263–8, 270
    Operation LINKLATER and, 125
    propaganda, 64, 224, 240, 263, 349
    Republic of Ireland and see Republic of Ireland: IRA
    RUC and, 58, 70, 209, 210–11, 212, 265
    tactics of, 209–10, 212, 220, 222, 224, 237, 347
    UDR and, 135, 139, 210–11, 222, 265
    violent internment response, 132–4, 136–8, 142–3
    weaponry, 9, 33, 34–5, 206, 218, 219, 232, 236–7, 278, 289
    see also violence, sectarian
Irish Republican Army, Official, ix, 12
    Bloody Sunday and, 278–80, 283, 285, 287, 288–9, 348
    Falls Road Curfew and, 39–40, 52–3
    kidnappings, 72
    NICRA march (30 January 1972) and, 267, 268
    Operation LINKLATER and, 115
    Provisional IRA and, 67, 73, 100, 112–13, 217, 223, 224, 237
    Short Strand violence and, 35
    violence and, 100–1
    see also Irish Republican Army (IRA)
Irish Republican Army, Provisional, ix, 7–11, 28, 145, 208–9, 225, 342–3
    Belfast disturbances (May 1970), 11–13
    Bloody Sunday and, 285, 313, 348
    bombing campaign see bombing campaign, Provisional IRA
    British army and see British army and the IRA

capture of key members, 96
Clonard and, 7, 33, 34, 63–5
commercial targets see bombing campaign, Provisional IRA
Falls Road Curfew and, 39–40, 44, 46, 52–3, 343
intelligence, 216, 234
killings of Protestants, 33, 35, 37, 68, 135, 136–7, 265
leadership divisions, 213–14
Londonderry (July 1971), 100, 101, 104, 105–6
New Lodge violence (July 1970), 55–7
NICRA march (30 January 1972) and, 267–8
'offensive' (July 1971), 99, 100, 101–4, 107–8
Official IRA and, 67, 73, 100, 112–13, 217, 223, 224, 237
Operation LINKLATER and, 115
Orange parades and, 33–4, 37
paramilitary funerals, 67–8
politics of, xii, 67
Richard English and, xi–xii
Short Strand violence and, 34–5
strategy of, 213–14
structure of, 7, 232–3
see also Irish Republican Army (IRA)
Irish Times, The, 133, 279, 292

J
Jackson, Alvin, xi
Jackson, Captain Mike, 246, 263–5, 270
Jackson, Lieutenant Colonel Roy, 104
Jamaica Street explosives factory, 12
Johnston, David, 63, 216
Johnston, Helen, 292–3
Johnston, John, 278, 279
Joint Directive on Military Interrogation in Internal Security Operations Overseas (JIC [65] 16), 153, 154, 155
Joint Intelligence Committee, 152, 153, 216
Joint Security Committee (JSC), 16, 35–6, 64, 108, 111, 215, 248, 249, 254, 321
Joint Services Interrogation Wing (JSIW), 152, 153, 153–4, 154, 155, 158
Jolliffe, Lance-Corporal William, 71
judiciary, Northern Ireland, 327

K
Kane, Michael, 10
Kavanagh, J.J., 63
Keenan, Seán, 232, 237
Kelly, Basil, 336
Kelly, Bill, 34
Kelly, Henry, x
Kelly, Michael, 291, 301, 304, 305
Kennedy, Paddy, 23, 24, 34, 40–1, 55, 57, 99, 125
Kent, Duke of, 64
kidnapping, 58, 69, 72, 75, 101, 114, 221
Kincaid, William, 35
King, Cecil, 187
King, Fusilier Patrick, 212
King's Own Scottish Borderers, 12, 55–7
Kirk, Herbie, 91, 336
Kitson, Brigadier Frank, 63, 238, 253, 257, 263
Knights of Malta, 35, 43, 143, 287
Krishman, Dr. S.S., 307
Kunioka, Noruki, 285

L
Labour Government (1966-70), 11, 16, 18, 344–5
Harold Wilson and, vi, 18, 28, 29, 85, 200, 317, 318
see also Callaghan, James
Lafferty, Eamon, 147
Lagan, Chief Superintendent Frank, 243, 252, 254–6, 259, 276
Larne RUC Station, 212
Laverty, John, 137
law and order, responsibility for, 201, 224, 318, 320, 325, 326, 328–30, 333, 336, 345
see also Internal Security (IS); security policy
Lawrie, Lance-Bombadier John, 66
Lebanon, 189, 316
Lemass, Seán, v, vi

Light Air Defence Regiment, 259, 262, 265, 275, 295
Light Infantry Regiment, 137, 138, 303
Lisburn, 129, 252
Lloyd, J.B.F., 307–8
local government, Northern Irish, v, vi, vii, viii, ix, 20, 27, 69, 149, 189–90, 193
Loden, Major, 269, 277, 279, 280, 281
Logue, Hugh, 147
Londonderry
British army and see Londonderry, British army and
Catholic fatalities in, 99, 100, 101, 103–6, 107, 108, 111, 134, 189, 233–4, 347
Catholic resignations from office, 149–50
civil disobedience campaign, 146, 147–8
Operation HAILSTONE (July 1971), 263–4
Orange Order marches, 32, 47, 189
see also Apprentice Boys Parades
RUC and, vii, viii, 47–8, 142–3
violence in (August 1971), 134, 135, 136, 137–8, 142–3, 147
violence in (July 1971), 99, 100, 101, 103, 108, 231
Westminster seat, 20
see also Bloody Sunday (30 January 1972); violence, sectarian: Londonderry
Londonderry, British army and, 137–8, 224, 231, 238–49, 254–71, 326, 332, 347–8
army casualties, 36, 103, 137, 234, 241, 265
army fatalities, 71, 136, 234, 238, 241, 265
Brigadier Cowan, 63, 100–1, 238–9
Cusack and Beattie shootings, xi, 103–6, 160, 232, 347
Orange parades, 32, 101
see also Bloody Sunday (30 January 1972)
Londonderry, IRA and, 100–1, 137–8, 224, 231–42, 249, 265
army fatalities, 71, 136, 234, 238, 241, 265
Cusack and Beattie shootings and, 104–6
fatalities, 147, 224, 249
see also Bloody Sunday (30 January 1972)
Long, Captain, 91
Long Kesh, 109, 123–4
Loring, Clifford, 211
Loughlins, Daniel, 35
Loyalist Workers Association, 256
Lynch, Jack, vi, viii
Bloody Sunday and, 313
Brian Faulkner and, 92, 93, 94, 170, 180–1, 184
British army and, 99, 104–5
Direct Rule and, 121, 123, 169, 338
ECHR and, 161–2, 163–4
Edward Heath and, 29–30, 129, 139–41, 170–1, 176, 195–7, 316
Edward Heath, summit with (6-7 September 1971), 179–85
Falls Road Curfew and, 45, 46
internment and, 114, 120–3, 127, 129, 161–4, 170, 181–2, 192, 194, 203
IRA and, 182, 192, 196, 197, 202, 203, 328, 336
John Hume and, 182, 313
Northern Irish Catholics and, 91–2, 176–7, 184
Orange Order and, 116, 141, 182
passive resistance and, 171, 176
reunification issue and, 180, 181, 182, 183, 186, 192
SDLP and, 87–8, 93, 148, 174–5, 181, 184–5, 194–5, 196
Stormont replacement campaign, 141–2, 170, 172, 180–1, 182–3
tripartite summit (1971), x, 184–7, 192–7
Lynch, Walter, 105

M
MacAirt, Proinsias, 8, 34
MacBride, Sean, 161–2
MacGuinness, John, 67
MacLellan, Brigadier Andrew, 238, 239–40, 243, 246
Bloody Sunday and, 254–5, 256, 258, 265, 275, 276
MacStiofain, Séan, ix, 8, 210, 213–14, 216
Magilligan internment centre, 226, 249–51, 252, 261
Maginnis, Jack, 19
Maidstone prison ship, 113, 131, 149, 225
Mailey, Liam, 284

INDEX

Major, John, 231
marches and processions
  Apprentice Boys Parades, viii, 47, 101, 110, 112, 113, 116–17, 120, 125, 126, 189
  bans on, blanket, 48, 188, 189, 230, 248, 254, 255, 256, 314
  bans on, consideration of, 32, 112, 113, 116, 120, 126–7, 129
  bans on specific marches, vi, 100
  Catholic, vi, 32
  Civil Rights Movement, vi, 115, 146, 226, 251, 267, 268–9, 274, 275
  see also Bloody Sunday (30 January 1972)
  Orange Order, 31, 32, 33–8, 46, 47, 101–2, 107, 125, 126, 188
Martin, Dr., 303–7
Martin, Leo, 7, 65
Maudling, Reginald, 28, 29, 32, 33, 38, 42, 82, 97, 164, 317, 345
  Brian Faulkner and, 124, 125–6, 170–2, 197–8, 317–18, 326, 334, 335
  Chichester-Clark and, 30, 37–8, 61, 68–9, 74–5, 77
  internment and, 112, 113–14, 120, 126–7, 192, 345
  interrogation in depth and, 154, 160
  James Callaghan on, 30, 31
  Operation LINKLATER and, 114, 115
  political initiative (February/March 1972), 322, 323–30
  political style, 31
  SDLP and, 145, 172–3
  talks proposals, 171–2, 173–5, 183, 184, 185, 195–6, 198, 201, 332
  violence levels and, 344, 347
  visits to Northern Ireland, 37–8, 74, 242
McAdorey, Patrick, 74, 133
McAteer, Eddie, 104
McCaig, John, 73–4
McCaig, Joseph, 73–4
McCann, Hugh, 93, 104–5, 163–4, 175–7, 180
McCarthy, Paddy, 142
McCaughy, Dougald, 73–4
McClean, Dr., 250
McClean, Patrick Joseph, 157–8, 159
McCloskey, Francis, vii–viii
McCluskey, Conn, 22
McCool, Thomas, 10
McCormac, Constable, 298–9
McCorry, Kevin, 268–9
McCreary, Alf, 206
McCullagh, Superintendent Patrick, 288
McCullough, Detective Sergeant Bernard, 212
McCurrie, James, 35
McDade, Gerald, 222
McDaid, Charles, 251–2, 278
McDaid, Michael, 291, 297, 304, 305–6
McDaid, Patrick, 290, 296
McDavitt, Eamonn, 138
McElhinney, Kevin, 291, 304
McGarry, John, xi
McGavigan, Annette, 233
McGreanery, William, 233–4
McGuigan, Bernard, 295, 296, 306
McGuigan, Francis, 157–8
McGuigan, Leo, 133
McGuinness, Daniel, 249–50
McGuinness, Francis, 134
McGuinness, Martin, 232, 267–8, 289, 348
McGuire, Maria, 213, 214
McGurk's Bar bombing (4 December 1971), 312–13, 349
McIlhone, Henry, 34–5
McInerney, Dennis, 213
McIvor, Basil, 18, 90
McKavanagh, William, 142
McKearney, Tommy, 208, 209
McKee, Billy, 7, 8, 34–5, 39–40, 65, 96
McKenna, Sean, 157–8, 159
McKerr, Gerald, 157–8, 159
McKinney, Gerald, 293, 294, 296, 297, 305
McKinney, Willie, 251, 293, 294, 305
McManus, Frank, 43

McNally, Patrick, 157–8
McNern, Jennifer, 1, 3, 4
McNern, Rosaleen, 1, 3, 4
McTaggart, Detective Sergeant Eugene, 297–9
Meehan, Martin, 8, 33
MI5 (security service), 216, 266–7
Military Operations Branch 4 (MO4), 53
Millar, Constable Robert, 58
Mills, Stratton, 20
Minford, Nat, 91
Ministry of Defence, xi, 53, 59, 79, 95–6, 192, 245, 247, 314
  intelligence and, 153, 165, 215, 216, 218
  internment and, 131, 218, 221
  interrogation in depth and, 153, 159, 165, 218–19
  see also Carrington, Lord Peter
Molyneaux, James, 19, 20
Montgomery, Constable, 265
Morgan, William, vii
Mullan, Father Hugh, 133–4
Murray, Father Raymond, 224
Myers, Kevin, 133

N

nail bombs, 65, 66, 72, 103, 134, 142, 213, 231, 247–8, 265
  Bloody Sunday and, 277, 279, 281–3, 294–5, 298, 300–2, 305–7
  making of, 237–8
Napier, Oliver, 144, 199
Nash, Alexander, 292, 295
Nash, William, 292, 295, 305, 306
National Democratic Party, 24
Nationalist Party, Irish, 21, 24, 144, 146, 150, 199
Neill, Robert, 35
New Lodge Road area, 7, 11, 12, 55–7, 100, 136, 225
  violence (January-March 1971), 60, 61, 65, 66–7, 72–3
Newe, G.B., xi, 316–17, 338
Newry, 19, 138, 303, 314–15, 317
North Antrim Westminster seat, 20, 21
North Derry Civil Rights Association, 249–51, 269, 274
Northern Ireland Civil Rights Association (NICRA), vi, vii, 21–2, 115, 224
  Derry march (planned for 16 January 1972), 244, 245
  Derry march (rescheduled for 30 January 1972), 248, 251, 253–71, 348
  see also Bloody Sunday (30 January 1972)
  Magilligan march (22 January 1972), 249–51, 252, 261
Newry march (6 February 1972), 314–15, 317
Northern Ireland Labour Party (NILP), 21, 24, 91, 102, 109, 190
Northern Ireland Ministerial Committee (GEN 47), x–xi, 48, 122, 126–7, 203, 222, 226, 248, 259
Northern Ireland Temporary Provisions Bill (28 March 1972), 339

O

Ó Brádaigh, Rory, ix, 67, 105–6, 139, 213, 214
Ó Conhaill, Daithi, ix, 213, 214
Observer, The, 285, 318–19
O'Donnell, Father (Rector of Holy Cross), 12, 40
O'Donnell, Patrick, 294, 295–6
O'Donnell, Tom, 8, 33, 34
O'Hagan, Daniel, 55–6, 57
O'Hagan, James Christopher, 138
O'Hagan, J.B., 213
O'Hanlon, John Patrick, 313
O'Hanlon, Paddy, 24, 85, 106, 248
O'hEara, Gearoid, 235
O'Leary, Brendan, xi
O'Leary, Martin, 96
O'Leary, Michael, 106
Ombudsman, Northern Ireland, ix, 160–1
O'Neill, Captain Terence, v, vi, vii, 87, 344
O'Neill, Charles, 41
O'Neill, Major Hubert, 230
O'Neill, Phelim, 91, 94
Operation CALABA, 157, 218–19, 345
Operation DEMETRIUS, 123–4, 129, 130–2, 156, 214–15, 216
Operation FORECAST, 258, 261–2

see *also* Bloody Sunday (30 January 1972)
Operation FOURSQUARE, 123–4
Operation HAILSTONE (July 1971), 263–4
Operation LINKLATER, 112–17, 120, 125, 216
Opposition, Stormont, 22–8, 93, 98, 100, 169, 182, 338
  quadripartite talks demand, 182, 183–4
  reunification issue and, 24–8, 201
  withdrawal of, xi, 106–7, 138, 140, 141, 170, 181, 189, 193, 196
  see *also* Social Democratic and Labour Party (SDLP)
Opposition, Westminster, 177–8, 200, 325, 345
Orange Order, 20, 23, 44, 116, 141, 182
  processions, 31, 32, 33–8, 46, 47, 188, 189
  processions (1971), 101–2, 104, 107, 110, 112, 113, 116–17, 120, 125, 126
  processions, bans on, 100, 112, 113, 188
  processions, violence at, 33–7, 101–2, 107
  Unionist Party and, 147, 148, 182, 189
Orr, Captain, 20
O'Sullivan, Dr. Donal (Irish Ambassador in London), 92, 105, 180, 202
Owens, Ann, 2–3, 210

P
Paisley, Ian, vi, vii, 122, 123, 187, 329, 344, 347
  Chichester-Clark and, 20–1, 62, 68
  General Election (18 June 1970), 19, 20–1, 344
Paisleyites, 98, 139, 147, 176
Parachute Regiment, 6–7, 65, 72–3, 96, 134–6, 229–30, 252–3
  Bloody Sunday and, 231, 275–83, 285–6, 290–6, 299–302, 306, 348–9
  Magilligan march (22 January 1972), 249–52, 261
  NICRA march (30 January 1972) and, 256–7, 258–9, 260–5, 269–71, 348
partition, Irish*see* reunification issues
passive resistance movement, Nationalist, 89, 146–50, 171, 176
Patterson, Detective Inspector Cecil, 70
Patterson, Henry, x, xi
Peck, John, 11, 45–6, 91–2, 93, 99, 139, 163, 177, 203
  Gerry Fitt and, 173–4
  Hugh McCann and, 175–7, 180
  internment and, 120, 121, 122–3, 129, 175–6
People's Democracy, vi, vii, 21–2, 131
Peress, Gilles, 295, 296
petrol bombs, rules of engagement and, 36, 55–7, 104
Philips, Noel, 134
Police Authority, ix, 181
Police Holding Centres (PHCs), 157, 218
police stations, 23, 24, 63, 117, 265
  attacks on, 11, 52, 96–7, 100, 137, 138, 212, 213, 220, 238
political participation, Catholic, 176, 189–96, 200, 201, 316
  Brian Faulkner and, 193–6, 197–8, 323
  Conservative Government and, 172, 183, 198, 203, 325–6, 327, 333, 345
  John Hume and, 86, 88, 145, 346
  see *also* Opposition, Stormont
Porter, Robert, 23, 35, 38, 188
Price, George, 307
processions and marches*see* marches and processions
proportional representation, 98, 145, 170, 190, 195, 320, 323
Protestant Telegraph, 19
Protestant Unionists (Paisley faction), 19, 20–1, 176, 344
Protestants, 25, 35, 72, 77, 86–7, 342
  1969 violence, 37, 73, 145, 342, 343
  'backlash' and, 148, 192, 196–7, 201, 319, 349
  casualties, 37, 343
  extremism, vii, viii, 10, 115–16, 312–13
  see *also* Ulster Volunteer Force (UVF)
  fatalities, 33, 35, 37, 68, 133, 134, 135, 136–7, 142, 265
  identity and, 25, 27–8
  loyalist gunmen, 134, 143
  loyalist march to Stormont (18 March 1971), 76–7
  in Republic of Ireland, xi
  weaponry and, 24, 45, 113, 176, 188–9
  see *also* Orange Order; Unionist Party

Pym, Francis, 164

Q
Queen's Regiment, 39, 65, 135, 211, 212
Quinn, Frank, 134

R
Radio Telefís Éireann (RTE), 45
Ramsbotham, Lieutenant-Colonel David, 261
referenda, constitutional, proposals for, 317, 318, 322, 323, 326, 327, 328, 333, 335, 338
reform programme (1969), vi, 30, 33, 86, 144, 160, 181, 184, 193
  Brian Faulkner and, 85, 88, 90, 91, 92, 93–4, 97, 121, 344
  Chichester-Clark and, 23, 47
  Gerry Fitt and, 88, 89, 94
  Unionist Party and, 19, 20, 94, 97, 176
Regional Holding Centres (RHCs), 130–1, 157
Reid, Billy, 96
Reid, John, 35
rents and rates strike, 144, 145, 146
Republic of Ireland
  Arms Crisis (1970), ix, 11, 346
  Bloody Sunday and, 313–14
  Brian Faulkner and, 85, 91, 99, 139, 189, 323
  British Embassy, 11, 45, 55, 173–5, 313–14
  see *also* Peck, John
  British Government and, 139–42, 176, 200, 201–3
  see *also* Heath, Edward; Jack Lynch and
  Compton Inquiry and, 160–1
  EEC and, 163, 180, 181, 185, 316
  extradition issues, 92–3, 323
  Falls Road Curfew and, 45–6
  internment and, 112–14, 120–3, 138–9, 161–4, 175–6, 188, 201, 202
  IRA and, 114, 176, 181, 188, 194, 315, 328
  IRA ASU cross-border operations, 135, 220, 225, 226, 326, 347
  IRA cross-border activity, 69–70, 92–3, 120–1, 135, 138–9
  John Hume and, 104, 182, 198–200, 313
  Northern Ireland policy, 187–92, 200
  Northern Irish Catholics and, 91–2, 176–7, 178, 199
  power-sharing proposals, 189–91, 346
  Protestantism in, xi
  reunification issue and, 175–6, 179, 180, 181, 191, 199–200, 201, 328, 346
  SDLP and, 93, 104–5, 106, 171, 173, 198–9
  Stormont reform proposals, 141–2, 170, 172, 180–1, 182–3, 189–91, 199, 201
  visit by Northern Ireland officials, 94
  see *also* Hillery, Patrick; Lynch, Jack; McCann, Hugh
Republican Labour Party, 23, 24, 144
Republican News, 8
reunification issues, 179, 181, 183, 198, 330
  Jack Lynch and, 180, 181, 182, 183, 186, 192
  Republic of Ireland and, 175–6, 179, 180, 181, 191, 199–200, 201, 328, 346
  SDLP and, 24–8, 199–200, 201, 346
Rhodesia, 28, 179
Robinson, Peter, 210
Robinson, Private, 142
Rodgers, Brid, 22
Roy, Herbert, 73
Royal Anglian Regiment, 63–4, 103, 260–1, 263, 285, 297
Royal Artillery, 65, 66, 138, 211, 234, 238, 253, 262, 283
Royal Green Jackets, 96, 102, 103, 107–8, 132–3, 136, 249, 259, 261, 263
  Bloody Sunday and, 274, 275
Royal Highland Fusiliers, 73–4, 99
Royal Military Police (RMP), 47, 71, 96, 285, 298, 302–3
Royal Regiment of Fusiliers, 64
Royal Scots Regiment, 11, 38
Royal Ulster Constabulary (RUC), v, vi, viii, 18, 23, 38, 59, 60, 213, 327
  arming of, viii, 19, 24, 52, 71, 76, 77, 90, 92, 189
  Belfast disturbances (May 1970), 11, 12
  Bloody Sunday and, 283–4, 288, 297–9, 302

INDEX

British army and, 13, 16–18, 62, 187, 216, 325, 344
brutality allegations, 61
casualties, 37, 142–3, 212
Catholic fatalities and, vii–viii, vii
Catholic members, 207–8
Chief Constables see Shillington, Graham (RUC Chief Constable); Young, Sir Arthur (RUC Chief Constable)
Compton Inquiry and, 164–5
fatalities, viii, 58, 70, 212, 265
intelligence see Special Branch, RUC: intelligence and Internal Security role, 16–18, 52, 71, 347
internment and, 123, 130, 210–11
Londonderry and, vii, viii, 47–8, 231–2, 241, 242–3
NICRA march (30 January 1972) and, 254–6, 258, 270
Official IRA attacks on, 100–1
Operation LINKLATER and, 114–15
Provisional IRA and, 64, 65, 100, 209, 210–11
Sir Arthur Young and, 13–15
Special Branch see Special Branch, RUC
Special Patrol Group, 16, 18, 155, 158
rubber bullets, 38, 60, 134, 146, 147, 229, 233, 243–4, 246
Bloody Sunday and, 274, 277, 280, 283, 295
Magilligan march (22 January 1972), 249, 250, 251, 252–3
rules of engagement, army, 36–7, 53–6, 79, 95, 101, 245–8
Bloody Sunday and, 264, 269, 270, 299–300
Brian Faulkner and, 99–100, 346–7
petrol bombs and, 36, 55–7, 104
Sir Ian Freeland and, 36, 54–5, 56
Russell, Sean, 222
Ryan, Paddy, 213

S
Saor Éire, 131
Saunders, James, 65, 67–8
Saville Inquiry, 231, 302, 307–8
Scarman Tribunal, 37
School of Service Intelligence, 152, 216
Scots Guards, 212, 213
Scullion, John, vi
Secretary of State for Northern Ireland, 333, 338
security policy, xi, 16, 336
Conservative, 31–3, 52, 69–70, 78–9, 99, 343
law and order, 201, 224, 318, 320, 325, 326, 328–30, 333, 336, 345
Stormont and, 60, 71–2, 91, 94, 97, 98, 193, 336
see also army, British; Internal Security (IS); Royal Ulster Constabulary (RUC)
Security Unit, 123, 189
Senate, 194, 195, 323
Shankill area, 1, 18, 22, 33, 41, 46, 67, 75, 108, 116, 137
shootings of Catholics in, vi, viii
Sharpe, Private Peter, 211
Sharples, Richard, 62, 63, 85
Shillington, Graham (RUC Chief Constable), 70–1, 81, 108, 188, 246, 256
internment and, 94, 109–10, 127, 128–9
shipyards, Belfast, 37
Shivers, Patrick Joseph, 157–8
Short Strand (Ballymacarratt), 8, 18, 33–5, 135, 223
Simpson, Professor, 305
Simpson, Robert, 23–4, 91
Simpson, Seamus, 142
Sinn Féin, ix, 63, 102, 105, 121, 209, 213–14, 263
Smith, Howard (UKREP), 97–8, 113, 114, 169–70, 174, 175
internment and, 112, 127
snatch squads, army, 57, 60
Social Democratic and Labour Party (SDLP)
Assembly of the Northern Irish People, 106–7, 150, 187, 191, 198–9
Brian Faulkner and, xi, 85, 93, 98, 100, 148, 172, 173, 194, 197–8, 344
British Government and, 85–6, 88–9, 145, 172–3, 195–6, 330
civil disobedience campaign, 145, 146–50, 174, 177
Direct Rule and, 169, 338

internment and, 86, 144–5, 173–4, 175, 195–6, 196, 199
Jack Lynch and, 87–8, 93, 148, 174–5, 181, 184–5, 194–5, 196
NICRA Derry march (of 30 January 1972) and, 248
origins of, 21–8
rents and rates strike, 144, 145, 146
Republic of Ireland and, 93, 104–5, 106, 171, 173, 198–9
reunification issue and, 24–8, 199–200, 201, 346
Unionist Government and, 85–9
withdrawal from Stormont, xi, 106–7, 138, 140, 141, 170, 181, 189, 193, 196
see also Cooper, Ivan; Currie, Austin; Devlin, Paddy; Fitt, Gerry; Hume, John
socialism, 21–2
South Antrim Westminster seat, 18–19, 20
South Down Westminster seat, 20
Special Air Service (SAS), 224
Special Branch, RUC, 64, 70, 74, 246
intelligence and, 63, 214–15, 216, 217, 225, 246, 249, 345
internment and, 75, 94, 109, 123, 129, 130, 214–15, 217, 321
interrogation in depth and, 153–6, 158
Special Patrol Group, RUC, 16, 18, 155, 158
Special Powers Act, v, vi, 109, 122, 147, 149, 154, 189, 334–5
Springfield Park, 133–4, 135
Springfield Road, 33, 35, 44, 58, 59, 99, 134, 136, 137, 142
RUC station, 11, 96–7, 117
Taggart Memorial Hall, 59, 134, 136, 213
Steele, Jimmy, 7–8
Steele, Lieutenant-Colonel, 254, 258, 259, 275, 276
Stevens, Gunner Angus, 238
Stewart, Jimmy, 1, 2, 3, 4
Stewart, Michael, 11
Stormont
election (1969), vii, 19
loyalist march to (18 March 1971), 76–7
Opposition see Opposition, Stormont; Social Democratic and Labour Party (SDLP)
Republic of Ireland and, 141–2, 170, 172, 180–1, 182–3, 189–91, 199, 201
security policy and, 60, 71–2, 91, 94, 97, 98, 193, 336
suspension of (28 March 1972), 338–40, 349
Unionist demonstration (28 March 1972), 338–40
see also Chichester-Clark, James; Faulkner, Brian; Unionist Party
Strabane, 18, 138, 217
Stronge, William, 136–7
Sunday Times, 263–4, 285
Switzerland, 170, 185, 189

T
Taggart Memorial Hall, 59, 134, 136, 213
Taylor, John, 24, 102, 111, 188, 268–9
Taylor, Peter, x, 35, 283
Taylor on Principles of Forensic Medicine (journal), 305
Teggart, Daniel, 134
Terehchak, David, 296
Tester, Reg, 236–7, 267, 268, 278, 279, 289
Thomas, William, 68
Thornton, Harry, 117
Thorpe, Jeremy, 338
Tickell, Brigadier Marston, 143, 146
Tilbury, Lance Bombardier David, 238
Trend, Sir Burke, 31–2, 77, 124, 177–80, 186–7, 201–3
tripartite summit (1971), x, 184–7, 192–7
Troubles, these see violence, sectarian
Tugwell, Colonel, 253
Turley, Brian, 157–8, 159
Tuzo, Sir Harry (GOC NI), 94, 95, 160, 187, 223–4, 265
Brian Faulkner and, 108, 110, 246, 318
internment and, 94, 109, 110, 112–13, 120, 125, 126, 128–9, 192, 220, 225, 345
IRA and, 104, 105, 224, 318
Londonderry and, 240–1, 242, 246, 249
memorandum from Ford, 243–6, 247
Twomey, Seamus, 7

U
Uglik, Zbigniew, 42
Ulster Defence Association, 349
Ulster Defence Regiment (UDR), viii, ix, 60, 64, 70, 100, 209, 210–11
    Catholic members, 146, 148–9, 222
    fatalities, 134–5, 138–9, 222, 265
Ulster Protestant Volunteers (UPV), vi, vii
Ulster Special Constabulary (USC, B Specials) see B Specials
Ulster Volunteer Force (UVF), vi, vii, 20, 86, 143–4
    McGurk's Bar bombing (4 December 1971), 312–13, 349
Unionist Party, v, xi, 27–8, 38, 181, 188, 344
    Direct Rule and, 89–90, 178–9, 318, 322–40
    General Election (18 June 1970), 18–21
    Orange Order and, 147, 148, 182, 189
    Protestant Unionists (Paisley faction), 19, 20–1, 176, 344
    at Westminster, 19, 21, 327, 340
    see also Chichester-Clark, James; Craig, Bill; Faulkner, Brian
United Nations (UN), 141

V
Vanguard, 319, 338–40
Vietnam war, 179, 206, 214
vigilantes, 36, 63, 196, 349
violence, sectarian, vi, vii, viii, 10
    1971 increase, 220, 345
    August 1971-January 1972:, 207–14, 220–5
    Belfast (August 1971), 132–4, 135, 136–7, 142
    Belfast (February 1971), 63–8
    Belfast (January 1971), 58–62
    Belfast (July 1970), 38–45, 55–7
    Belfast (July 1971), 100, 101–2, 103, 107–8
    Belfast (June 1970), 18, 33–4, 36, 343
    Belfast (March 1971), 72–3
    Belfast (May 1970), 11–13
    Belfast (May 1971), 100
    cyclical nature of, 96
    housing movements and, 143
    internment and, 132–8, 142–3, 219–26
    Londonderry (August 1971), 134, 135, 136, 147
    Londonderry (January 1972), 243–5, 247–8, 249
    Londonderry (July 1971), 99, 100, 101, 103, 137–8
    Londonderry (June 1970), 33
    Londonderry (May 1971), 100
    Londonderry (September–December 1971), 233–41
    SDLP and, 86–7
    see also bombing campaign, Provisional IRA; Irish Republican Army (IRA); Ulster Volunteer Force (UVF)

W
Wade, Nigel, 279
Walker, Graham, xi, xii
Walker, Rifleman David, 107–8
War of the Flea, The (Robert Tauber), 214
Ward, Peter, vi
Warner, Geoffrey, xii
water cannon, viii, 60, 147, 246, 274, 275
Watson, Norman, 137
Watt, Bernard, 65–6, 68
weaponry
    acid bombs, 59, 65, 231, 282
    British army, 206–7, 244, 245, 246, 283, 304
    see also CS gas; rubber bullets
    civilians and, 56
    IRA, 9, 33, 34–5, 206, 218, 219, 232, 236–7, 278, 289
    petrol bombs, rules of engagement, 36, 55–7, 104
    Protestant ownership, 24, 45, 113, 176, 188–9
    see also gelignite bombs; nail bombs
Webb, Sergeant, 143
Welsh, Lieutenant-Colonel, 259
West, Harry, 19, 68, 90–1, 92, 93, 94, 109
White, Kelvin, 122, 124–5, 131, 175
White, Sir Dick, 165, 215–16
Whitelaw, William, 164, 317, 331, 338
Widgery Inquiry, 230, 231, 275, 278, 285, 286, 294, 299–308, 348–9
    forensic evidence, 303–8, 349
Wilford, Lieutenant-Colonel Derek, 251
    Bloody Sunday and, 256, 259–60, 265, 269, 275–6, 281, 282
Willets, Sergeant Michael, 96–7, 99
Williams, John T., 105
Willoughby, Lieutenant Michael, 58
Wilson, Harold, vi, 18, 28, 29, 85, 200, 317, 318
Wilson, Paddy, 24
Winchester, Simon, 38, 44, 253, 279, 284
Worthington, Mrs Sarah, 133
Wray, James Joseph, 293, 294
Wright, Oliver, viii, 58

Y
Yellow Card, the, 53–6, 95, 101, 245, 246, 247–8, 264
    Bloody Sunday and, 269, 270, 299–300, 348
    see also rules of engagement, army
Young, John, 306
Young, Sir Arthur (RUC Chief Constable), viii, 13–15, 23, 52, 63, 70, 188, 344
    baton charges and, 18, 52
    British army and, 16–17, 62, 344